BLINDING AS A SOLUTION TO BIAS

BLINDING AS A SOLUTION TO BIAS

STRENGTHENING BIOMEDICAL SCIENCE, FORENSIC SCIENCE, AND LAW

CHRISTOPHER T. ROBERTSON

AARON S. KESSELHEIM

ELSEVIER

AMSTERDAM • BOSTON • HEIDELBERG • LONDON
NEW YORK • OXFORD • PARIS • SAN DIEGO
SAN FRANCISCO • SINGAPORE • SYDNEY • TOKYO

Academic Press is an imprint of Elsevier

Academic Press is an imprint of Elsevier
125 London Wall, London EC2Y 5AS, UK
525 B Street, Suite 1800, San Diego, CA 92101-4495, USA
50 Hampshire Street, Cambridge, MA 02139, USA
The Boulevard, Langford Lane, Kidlington, Oxford OX5 1GB, UK

ISBN: 978-0-12-802460-7

British Library Cataloguing-in-Publication Data
A catalogue record for this book is available from the British Library

Library of Congress Cataloging-in-Publication Data
A catalog record for this book is available from the Library of Congress

Publisher: Sara Tenney
Acquisitions Editor: Elizabeth Brown
Editorial Project Manager: Joslyn Paguio-Chaiprasert
Production Project Manager: Lisa Jones
Designer: Matthew Limbert

Contents

III

BIOMEDICAL SCIENCE

10. Minimizing and Leveraging Bias in Forensic Science

ROGER KOPPL AND DAN KRANE

11. What Do Statisticians Really Need to Know, and When Do They Need to Know It?

D. JAMES GREINER

12. Using Blind Reviews to Address Biases in Medical Malpractice

JEFFREY D. ROBINSON

13. Mock Juror and Jury Assessment of Blinded Expert Witnesses

MEGAN S. WRIGHT, CHRISTOPHER T. ROBERTSON, AND DAVID V. YOKUM

14. Disclosure Discretion and Selection Bias in Blinding of Experts

CHRISTOPHER T. ROBERTSON

V
BLINDING IN LEGAL INSTITUTIONS

Legal Applications of the Disclose-or-Blindfold Question
SAUL LEVMORE

15. Why Eyes? Cautionary Tales from Law's Blindfolded Justice
JUDITH RESNIK AND DENNIS CURTIS

16. A Theory of Anonymity
JEFFREY M. SKOPEK

17. The Cases for and against Blindfolding the Jury
SHARI SEIDMAN DIAMOND

18. The Compliance Equation: Creating a More Ethical and Equitable Campaign Financing System by Blinding Contributions to Federal Candidates
BERTRAM J. LEVINE AND MICHAEL JOHNSTON

List of Contributors

Gregory Curfman Harvard Health Publications, Harvard Medical School, Boston, MA, USA

Dennis Curtis Yale Law School, New Haven, CT, USA

Karie Davis-Nozemack Georgia Institute of Technology, Scheller College of Business, Atlanta, GA, USA

Shari Seidman Diamond Northwestern University School of Law, Chicago, IL, USA; American Bar Foundation, Chicago, IL, USA

Itiel E. Dror University College London, London, UK

Yuval Feldman Faculty of Law, Bar Ilan University, Ramat-Gan, Israel

Brandon L. Garrett University of Virginia School of Law, Charlottesville, VA, USA

D. James Greiner Harvard Law School, Cambridge, MA, USA

Asbjørn Hróbjartsson The Nordic Cochrane Centre, Rigshospitalet, Copenhagen, Denmark; Center for Evidence Based Medicine, Odense University Hospital & University of Southern Denmark, Denmark

Michael Johnston Department of Political Science, Colgate University, Hamilton, NY, USA

David S. Jones Department of Global Health and Social Medicine, Harvard Medical School, Boston, MA, USA; Department of the History of Science, Harvard University, Cambridge, MA, USA

Ted J. Kaptchuk Beth Israel Deaconess Medical Center, Harvard Medical School, Boston, MA, USA

Aaron S. Kesselheim Program on Regulation, Therapeutics, and Law, Division of Pharmacoepidemiology and Pharmacoeconomics, Department of Medicine, Brigham and Women's Hospital and Harvard Medical School, Boston, MA, USA

Roger Koppl Whitman School of Management, Syracuse University, Syracuse, NY, USA

Dan Krane Wright State University, Dayton, OH, USA

Emily A. Largent Program in Health Policy, Harvard University, Cambridge, MA, USA

Lawrence Lessig Harvard Law School, Cambridge, MA, USA

Bertram J. Levine Department of Political Science, Rutgers University, New Brunswick, NJ, USA

Saul Levmore University of Chicago Law School, Chicago, IL, USA

Shahar Lifshitz Faculty of Law, Bar Ilan University, Ramat-Gan, Israel

Carla L. MacLean Psychology Department, Kwantlen Polytechnic University, Surrey, BC, Canada

Franklin G. Miller Medical Ethics in Medicine, Weill Cornell Medical College, New York, NY, USA

Scott H. Podolsky Department of Global Health and Social Medicine, Harvard Medical School, Boston, MA, USA

Sergio Puig The University of Arizona, Tucson, AZ, USA

Judith Resnik Yale Law School, New Haven, CT, USA

Christopher T. Robertson James E. Rogers College of Law, The University of Arizona, Tucson, AZ, USA

Jeffrey D. Robinson Department of Radiology, University of Washington, Seattle, WA, USA; Cleareview, Inc., Seattle, WA, USA

Marc A. Rodwin Suffolk University Law School, Boston, MA, USA

Tania Simoncelli White House Office of Science and Technology Policy, Washington, DC, USA

Jeffrey M. Skopek Faculty of Law, University of Cambridge, Cambridge, UK

Richard T. Snodgrass Department of Computer Science, The University of Arizona, Tucson, AZ, USA

William C. Thompson Department of Criminology, Law & Society, University of California, Irvine, CA, USA

Paul Wicks PatientsLikeMe, Cambridge, MA, USA

Megan S. Wright Yale Law School, New Haven, CT, USA

David V. Yokum Department of Psychology, College of Science, The University of Arizona, Tucson, AZ, USA

Foreword

Lawrence Lessig
Harvard Law School, Cambridge, MA, USA

Truth has a problem with trust. However strong the truth, however validated, its value is discounted by however much the truth is trusted. And how much it is trusted depends upon how relationships within a society are understood.

Those understandings are certainly contingent. It is possible to imagine a society where my recommendation of my brother as the "best qualified person for the job" is unaffected by the fact that he is my brother. That is not our society. And it is possible to imagine a society where the fact that a scientist depends exclusively upon a drug company for his/her income has no effect on the confidence people have in his/her views about a drug produced by that company. That is not our society either. In our society, the relationships of family and financial dependence weaken the confidence we have in claims made by people with those relationships. It is not that we necessarily think they are lying, or that they are fooling themselves, or that their claim is necessarily false. It is instead that we have a cultural understanding of the effect of such relationships generally, and, fairly or not, we apply that understanding to the particular case.

What should follow from this fact is a recognition that we need a strategy for discovering and reporting truth that avoids this trust discount. I am not the best recommender of my brother, not because I do not know him well, but because my words would be discounted. What follows is that he needs a strategy to avoid this discount—either asking someone else to recommend him, or finding a way to neutralize the fact that he is my brother in my recommendation.

Most of the conflict of interest literature focuses on the first solution: How do we establish relationships that minimize or avoid any potential conflict of interest, such that there is no reason to believe that improper motives have colored anyone's judgment. If the concern is that money from drug companies compromises a researcher, then we should demand that researcher do their work without any money from drug companies. Separation assures the independence. Once separated, no one needs to worry about the influence.

But in the years that I have been studying this question, I have become increasingly convinced that a general strategy of separation is not practical. It is wonderful to fantasize about $300 billion budgets for the U.S. National Institutes of Health (NIH), giving researchers adequate and independent support to investigate whatever scientific question they want. But in a world where the NIH's actual budget of $30 billion is under constant threat, we need to think about other strategies to avoid the trust discount: Ones that do not rely exclusively on the altruism of researchers, or the endless supply of disinterested resources.

"Blinding" is a compelling alternative. If we cannot achieve separation, is there a way to assure that the mix of interests does not compromise the research?

Blinding says there is. If we can remove the information necessary to enable the compromise, we have no reason to mistrust the result. If you are skeptical that the best violinists are only men, then conduct the auditions behind a screen. If you are worried that the vote of employees against a union was affected by their fear of retaliation by the employer, make the ballot secret. In these, and a million other contexts, we can easily imagine correcting the trust discount by blocking certain information from the mix. And once we recognize the utility of this strategy, we have a reason to study it, systematically.

Chris Robertson is blinding's most effective and prolific advocate, and with Aaron Kesselheim, one of the leading health policy scholars worldwide, they bring a wealth of expertise to this multidisciplinary project. With the work they have drawn together for this volume, they make a powerful case for the urgent need to experiment with blinding solutions to the trust problem in many different contexts. Most importantly, the work here demonstrates how, often, the blinding solution is not zero-sum. It is better for patients and drug companies, both if there were a way to fund drug research that produced results that doctors had confidence in.

More generally, this work underlines the important work done elsewhere about the limits to transparency. We live in a time with many examples of obscurity used for corrupting purposes — such as the so-called "dark money" in political campaigns. Those purposes lead many to believe that the solution to corruption is unconditional transparency. But blinding shows the limits in that inference. Transparency is a tool. Sometimes it works to advance a social end (such as identifying the large contributions to a candidate's campaign); sometimes it inhibits a social end (such as identifying the vote of employee in a union election). What is needed is not a simple rule, but a more rigorous approach to the question of how information within an economy of influence advances the identified objectives of an institution.

This book is a powerful contribution to that more general need. It is a rich addition to the particular debates that these separate chapters address as well. No fair reader will be unaffected by the insights of this volume. And I know that no more important contribution to the general problem of trust in society can be than the insights offered here, and the research this work will inspire as well.

SECTION I

INTRODUCTION AND OVERVIEW

Introduction

Aaron S. Kesselheim[1], *Christopher T. Robertson*[2]

[1]Program on Regulation, Therapeutics, and Law, Division of Pharmacoepidemiology and Pharmacoeconomics, Department of Medicine, Brigham and Women's Hospital and Harvard Medical School, Boston, MA, USA; [2]James E. Rogers College of Law, The University of Arizona, Tucson, AZ, USA

OVERVIEW

The conflicts of interests held by physicians, lawyers, and politicians in the US society have inspired many news reports and books. Disclosure and transparency are the well-worn responses to the potential for biased decision making among these professionals. However, these remedies do not directly solve the underlying problem of bias, and prior research has shown that they may have unintended consequences.

The classic icon of Lady Justice wearing a blindfold symbolizes the paradoxical insight that less information can sometimes produce better decisions. Should we encourage more opportunities for professionals to be blinded to potentially biasing influences?

The history of blinding goes back to Benjamin Franklin. In his own home, Franklin performed the first blindfolded experiment known to history to test, and debunk, a charlatan's popular theory about a mysterious healing power.

In the three centuries since then, blinding has become a fundamental tool to reduce bias in conducting clinical trials, whether it is blinding of patients, of physicians, or of the investigators who assign participants to each condition (a blind draw or randomization). Indeed, blinding is a primary criterion for quality: open any medical journal and find reports of trials in which the authors proclaim that their investigations were blinded, often in the first lines of the abstracts. Editors and reviewers, of course, consider blinding in their decisions about whether to support publication of a research study. Likewise, physicians and guideline writers consider blinding when they calibrate their reliance in making prescribing decisions and recommendations. We even blind journal peer reviewers to the identities of authors, and vice versa.

Thus, over the last 70 years, blinding has become integral to collecting high-quality scientific evidence, especially in testing the efficacy of new therapeutics. Blinding also features heavily in other areas of society. In American courtrooms, jurors are initially selected through blind draws, and once chosen, the judge carefully constructs a trial experience that blinds the jurors to evidence thought to be irrelevant or prejudicial.

More recently, blinding has started infiltrating other corners of society. Some symphonies conduct auditions with the performers behind screens, so the judges will not be distracted by race, gender, or the performer's theatrics. Similarly, businesses are now offering technology companies blind auditions of programmers, who can demonstrate their skills without managers being distracted by gender or educational pedigree. Blinding may be a key mechanism for achieving meritocracy.

Yet blinding remains underutilized. For example, even today, forensic scientists are exposed to extraneous biasing information, and a growing consensus is recognizing that this is a primary cause of wrongful convictions. Many biomedical research trials are performed without effective blinding of patients, which thereby allows spurious findings of efficacy. Unblinded statisticians are often able to message data until they support a preferred conclusion.

Now is the time to develop a new science of blinding by exploring the advantages and limitations of blinding, quantifying the biases in unblinded research, identifying vectors of bias, developing new ways to blind decision makers, clarifying the ethical problems with denying information to decision makers, and finding new applications of blinding in the design of institutions. Fundamentally, these sorts of questions—about who needs to know what—open new doors of inquiry for the design of scientific research studies, regulatory institutions, and courts.

Although many are concerned with problems of bias and institutional corruption, this book provides a focus on a particular sort of solution, which has applicability in many domains. This book should appeal to scholars, policy makers, and advocates in the fields of biomedical science, forensic science, and institutional design, and especially to those concerned with conflicts of interests and cognitive biases.

BOOK ORGANIZATION

The volume consists of some introductory material on blinding and bias, and then three focal sections describing the use and complexities of blinding in three main fields: biomedical science and medicine, the forensic sciences, and finally legal institutions. We begin each section with a foreword by experts in biomedical sciences (Greg Curfman), forensic sciences (Tania Simoncelli), and the legal institutions (Saul Levmore).

Introduction

The first background section provides a primer on the psychology of bias and explains the role that blinding can play. The first chapter, by Carla Lindsay MacLean and Itiel Dror, describes how humans' limited capacity for information processing introduces systematic errors into decision making. Psychological research has consistently demonstrated how our perceptions and judgments are affected by factors extraneous to the content of the information, including context, motivation, expectation, and experience. In addition, the often-subconscious cognitive shortcuts people take when processing information can cause bias. Both of these cognitive vulnerabilities bedevil experts in all fields.

Solutions like blinding that limit exposure to biasing contextual information are therefore needed to minimize bias and optimize decision making. The second chapter, by Christopher Robertson, provides more detail on why we blind and how blinding works. Blinding seeks to avoid bias and is motivated by a recognition that alternative solutions—such as proscribing biasing relationships, insisting on professionalism, and the provision of mandatory disclosures—may not be sufficient. Blinding functions by allowing disaggregation of interests that may create biases in outcomes. If a decision maker is never introduced to a potentially biasing effect, then she or he will be unable to favor that source in rendering a decision, promoting unbiased (and trusted) outcomes. This can be an improvement over asking a biased professional to try to "debias" himself or herself, or asking a recipient of biased advice to somehow discount for the bias. But blinding has its own practical limitations: some biasing functions cannot be disaggregated from the subsidy, and even if blinding works to eliminate bias, it may fail to rescue a dependent institution from perceptions of illegitimacy. The remainder of the book examines the tensions between the positive outcomes of blinding and its limitations in three specific fields: biomedical science, forensics sciences, and legal institutions.

Biomedical Sciences

The section on biomedical sciences starts with a history of the use of blinding in research. Scott Podolsky, David Jones, and Ted Kaptchuk recount how those evaluating medical interventions have utilized blinding for centuries as a means of reducing bias. Blinds have been applied to both patients and researchers to reduce the impact of suggestibility in patients and of the personal investment of individual researchers in the outcome of their work. By the 1950s, both forms of blinding were considered necessary for the ideal clinical study, resulting in the elevation of the "double-blind" study to the status it retains today.

Asbjørn Hróbjartsson of the Nordic Cochrane Centre and Odense University Hospital & University of Southern Denmark then takes the story to the present day, providing an overview of the scope and practice of blinding in biomedical research and various clinical trial study designs, focusing on terminology and reporting, bias mechanisms, risk of unblinding, and the main empirical studies of bias. He describes the ways that blinding of patients, health-care providers, and outcome assessors are handled and provides data showing how investigator ("assessor") blinding can overcome observer predispositions, which is therefore critical in scenarios with a high risk of bias, such as when outcomes are subjective.

With a similar approach in another domain, Emily Largent and Richard Snodgrass review current blinding practices engaged by academic medical journals, which remains the primary means through which scientific investigations are disseminated to patients, physicians, and policy makers. Blind peer review of scientific papers has been a mainstay of publication for decades; but more journals are now experimenting with other approaches, including revealing peer reviewer names to authors and blinding the authors of the paper to the reviewers (double-blind peer review). Largent and Snodgrass review the burgeoning literature on editorial blinding and describe the implications of these additional blinding mechanisms on knowledge translation.

The next two chapters review two complications of modern-day blinding practices. First, Paul Wicks of PatientsLikeMe dives deep into the risk of unblinding. PatientsLikeMe is a health information sharing Web site that connects patients with each other and allows diffusion of knowledge about advances in medical science. Wicks describes how modern technologies permit a wide range of opportunities for patients to unblind themselves. Using advocacy around new treatments for amyotrophic lateral sclerosis as an example, Wicks describes how patients collaborating online can share telltale side effects that may provide insight into whether they had been randomized to an active agents or placebo and track their own outcomes independently of researchers. Wicks suggests that blinding may not be enough in the twenty-first century—we may need to consider steps beyond blinding, such as a new social contract between patients and trialists that ensures that patients are respected as thoughtful and intelligent research partners.

Next, medical ethicist Franklin Miller describes normative problems that can arise when blinding in biomedical sciences. Miller focuses on the occasional use of placebo- or sham-controlled trials for evaluating invasive medical interventions, such as implantable medical devices or surgical procedures. For example, a patient entering a clinical trial for a surgical procedure could be randomized to a treatment arm in which they are exposed to the trappings of the surgery—and even given small surgical scars in the appropriate place—but without actually undergoing any internal manipulation. Miller uses the landmark sham-controlled trials of internal mammary artery ligation to evaluate whether it can be justified to expose subjects to the risks of sham invasive procedures for the purpose of generating clinically relevant scientific knowledge and whether the active deception involved in blinding patient-subjects is compatible with informed consent.

The final chapter in this section describes a further expansion of the use of blinding in biomedical sciences intended to address the concern that double-blinding may not solve all potentially biasing influences. When commercial interests select and fund the investigators, the overall design, conduct, and reporting of scientific research may still be biased. Toward suggesting that the products being tested are safer and more efficacious than they really are. Robertson and law professor Marc Rodwin consider whether it is possible to have companies fund the research on their products, but have an intermediary select independent investigators to design and conduct the research—a solution they term a "money blind." They review some of the histories around the concept of having biomedical research conducted independently of industry and explore the potential benefits and limitations of money blinding.

Forensic Sciences

The problems of bias are not limited to biomedical sciences. They also infect science that is used in criminal and civil litigation.

Our review of blinding in the forensic sciences begins with a chapter by psychologist William C. Thompson in which he reviews rules of relevance for experts in court, that is, the standards for determining whether a given piece of information is one that an expert should consider. He establishes some of the limitations of the role of the expert using Bayesian models. Thompson argues that even if an expert's exposure to certain facts increases the accuracy of her or his opinion, it can paradoxically undermine the diagnostic value of the expert's opinion to the fact-finder. Such an exposed expert is less helpful than if the expert had been blind to those facts. In doing so, Thompson establishes an analytical framework for understanding the problem of contextual bias for experts in court that blinding is intended to solve.

This and other biasing factors in forensic science are reviewed in the following chapter by economist Roger Koppl and biologist Dan Krane, including ways of minimizing negative outcomes from bias. Koppl and Krane posit that information hiding is essential to minimizing bias, but addressing bias in forensic science must entail more than temporarily hiding information from a bench examiner. They review how blinding functions in this field and argue that blinding measures should be embedded in a right mix of complementary measures to undercut remaining biases. They also consider economic and administrative barriers to blinding.

Harvard Law School professor and statistician D. James Greiner reviews the use of blinding in making causal determinations from statistical information, which is often a key function played by expert witnesses in court. Greiner demonstrates that quantitative analysts can and should blind themselves to the outcomes of interest when selecting their statistical models, which define which units are comparable. In short, analysts precommit to a particular analysis before knowing what the analysis will show.

Radiologist Jeffrey Robinson discusses the use of blinding in medical malpractice cases. Using radiology reviews of medical imaging in a series of case examples, Robinson describes how lack of blinding can lead to selection, undersampling, and compensation biases, and ultimately faulty expert witness testimony. Robinson reviews several methods of blinding expert witnesses, with an analysis of the advantages and disadvantages of each. He concludes that expert witness bias is difficult to eliminate, but blinding is one step that mitigates its effects on medical expert testimony in malpractice litigation.

Sociologist and lawyer Megan S. Wright offers a chapter, with Christopher T. Robertson and David V. Yokum, exploring the potential for using blinded experts in jury trials, and specifically how jurors will respond to blinded experts. They provide results from mock jury studies that manipulate whether an expert is blinded or not, in randomized design, allowing the researchers to observe civil mock jury deliberations and criminal mock juror verdicts. They find that blinding of experts caused the experts to be viewed as more credible in jury deliberations. They also show some impact on the outcomes, as the use of blinded experts increased the likelihood of a not guilty verdict for the defense in a criminal trial, but did not have a similar effect for the prosecution. These data suggest that litigants may have incentives to use blinded experts.

Finally, Christopher Robertson describes how such blinding can be practically implemented, exploring the tension between creating a blinding procedure that is robust enough to eliminate bias while nonetheless being institutionally feasible. If a blinding protocol is so strict that it prevents litigants from having any discretion over whether to disclose unfavorable expert opinions, then blinding may not be actually implemented in an adversarial system. Robertson argues that, as long as the experts are themselves blinded to which party has commissioned their opinion, and the litigants are unable to commission multiple blinded opinions while disclosing only one, then discretion over whether to disclose that one opinion is not problematic. The chapter—and forensic science section—concludes with the contention that adversarial use of blinded experts, even with disclosure discretion, can produce much more reliable opinions than the use of a single expert without disclosure discretion, as in court appointment.

Legal Institutions

The final section embraces blinding more broadly, to explore how legal institutions can and do utilize blinding mechanisms to improve decision making. The section begins with a history of blinding iconography and its use in crafting the social construct of legal institutions. Yale Law School professors Judith Resnik and Dennis Curtis show how throughout history, sight was valorized, and obscured vision was equated with disability, vice, and caprice. However, over time, political, technological, and social movements have contributed to a change in iconography, as blindfolds became emblematic of impartial judging, freed from bias.

After Resnik and Curtis provide some of the backdrops for the question of blinding in the law, University of Cambridge law professor Jeffrey M. Skopek delves into the philosophical justification for blinding in this arena. Skopek reviews contract, copyright, criminal, and constitutional law to show how anonymity has been applied in largely unrecognized ways. He argues that these diverse domains and the various anonymity rules within them may appear to lack theoretical coherence, but they may all be reconciled as part of a movement of legal interventions intended to regulate relationships of influence and dependence in the creation, evaluation, and allocation of a wide set of social goods.

The first context in which these principles are discussed is the jury system. Northwestern University law and psychology professor Shari Seidman Diamond reviews blinding juries, a common technique used to protect juror decision making. In this context, blinding involves denying access to potentially biasing evidence in court. Blindfolding is typically justified on several grounds, including reducing or avoiding the bias that might be introduced by the undisclosed information; the possibility that some facts are so complicated that they might confuse rather than inform the jury; and the common exclusion of "irrelevant" evidence that by definition lacks probative value and will at best waste the jury's time and at worse improperly bias its decision. Diamond also describes how blindfolding may be ineffective or have unanticipated negative effects and cautions against unwarranted blinding in legal decision making.

Next, political scientists Bertram J. Levine and Michael Johnston evaluate the role of blinding in the electoral process. Critics charged that the current federal campaign finance system contributes to excessive campaign costs and strongly favors incumbents. Indeed, it has been central to the "institutional corruption" narrative. Levin and Johnston contend that the ability of candidates to know the sources of contributions to their campaigns and/or expenditures made on their behalf—and the same for all other candidates—is largely responsible for its weaknesses. Ironically, disclosure requirements that were intended to be a cleansing mechanism are now used to support allegations of systemic corruption. To address this issue, they propose a system of campaign contributions and independent expenditures that relies on anonymity for the specific sources along with reasonable limitations on donation amounts, building on a concept previously developed by Ian Ayres and Jeremy Bulow. Applying a measure of blinding to the system may be more effective than the sunlight currently being employed.

University of Virginia law professor Brandon Garrett next addresses the role of blinding in a central aspect of the criminal justice system: eyewitness identifications. "Lineups," as they are widely known, are used to test the memory of a person who saw a crime occur; however, there are many notable cases of false convictions due to incorrect identifications. One problem is that the lineup administrator can influence the witness implicitly. Ensuring that the administrator does not know who the suspect is or that the administrator cannot see which images the eyewitness is looking at during the procedure can help ensure the greatest reliability and accuracy in these procedures. Garrett chronicles the 40-year history of blinding in this domain, beginning with widespread dismissal of the idea as infeasible, through leading jurisdictions beginning to implement it, and culminating with a National Academy of Sciences report calling for universal adoption.

University of Arizona law professor Sergio Puig takes a more empirical approach to assessing the role of blinding in arbitration tribunals, three-person panels that involve one arbitrator appointed by each party and a third, who acts as the chair, appointed by an independent authority. Historically, the power of parties to appoint at least some of the arbitrators has been important to maintain the perceived legitimacy of the ultimate decisions reached by those panels, so that the decisions would bind the parties. However, party-appointed arbitrators often lean in favor of the nominating party, though it is difficult to determine whether this effect is due to selection or affiliation biases. Using data from the World Bank's investor-state arbitration proceedings to demonstrate affiliation bias, Puig finds that blinding appointments is a promising intervention that can reduce bias while maintaining parties' ability to play a role in a tribunal's formation.

David Yokum, a Fellow on the White House Social and Behavioral Sciences Team, as well as Director of the General Services Administration's Office of Evaluation Sciences, returns with his own chapter. This one evaluates the role of blinding in judicial decisions about whether a judge should be disqualified from overseeing a proceeding in which she or he may have a conflict. While such events are supposed to occur when a judge's "impartiality might be reasonably questioned," determining when this criterion is reached is a difficult cognitive task and fraught with error. Yokum argues for two procedural reforms that shift the task of applying the disqualification standard to a third party, including one in which a third-party judge assesses disqualification motions under a blinding mechanism, such that the reviewed judge does not know which other judge was the reviewer. Yokum argues that such a blind, which recalls the blinding of medical journal peer reviewers, should increase the candor of the reviewer and the apparent fairness of the procedure.

Business professor Karie Davis-Nozemack then applies blinding theory to controversies related to the Internal Revenue Service (IRS). As with the electoral process, the fallback position at the IRS has been the use of transparency to improve its functionality, including combating discrimination, bias, and corruption. Davis-Nozemack argues instead that strategic ignorance has certain utilities in facilitating tax enforcement. She contemplates how the IRS tax whistleblower program could be improved using blinding strategies from the biomedical sciences to eliminate bias against the use of whistleblowers in tax enforcement.

The final chapter comes from Bar Ilan University law professors Yuval Feldman and Shahar Lifshitz. They conclude the section with a broader discussion of the importance of uncertainty in the law itself. Scholars normally assume that clear laws and predictable adjudication are good things. Feldman and Lifshitz challenge readers to consider whether a "veil of uncertainty" can lead to potential benefits for lawmakers, by reducing the ability of people to game the rules.

ACKNOWLEDGMENTS

This book grew out of an academic conference we organized on November 1, 2013 at the Edmond J. Safra Center for Ethics at Harvard University, titled "When Less Information is Better: Blinding as a Solution to Institutional Corruption." This event was cosponsored by the Petrie-Flom Center for Health Law Policy, Biotechnology, and Bioethics. During that day, 15 talks were given by scholars from across the country, including established leaders and emerging scholars, and a wide range of scholarly disciplines—law, medicine, philosophy, statistics, forensic science, organizational behavior, sociology, psychology, history of science, and economics—as well as by leaders from the National Institutes of Health and the White House Office of Science and Technology Policy. Using this interdisciplinarity, we were able elucidate blinding as a fundamental tool for addressing corruption rather than as merely a domain-specific solution. Following the conference, we pulled together many of the papers into this book, supplementing them with others to help increase the depth and breadth of discussion. We thank Larry Lessig and the staff of the Edmond J. Safra Center, including Stephanie Dant, Mark Somos, Katy Evans Pritchard, Heidi Carrell, and others, for supporting the conference organization both financially and logistically.

In preparing the book, we depended very heavily on Kathi E. Hanna, our developmental editor, for her professionalism and hard work in keeping the project on track, reviewing the chapters, and ensuring that the writing was consistent and relatable. The faculty support staff at The University of Arizona James E. Rogers College of Law, particularly Bert Skye, provided extensive help with formatting and citations, for which we are appreciative. Librarian Maureen Garmon provided excellent support as well. We would also like to thank our contacts at Elsevier, Joslyn Chaiprasert-Paguio and Lisa Jones, for helping us navigate the publishing process. In addition, Dr Kesselheim would like to thank Jerry Avorn for his mentorship and unflagging support and the Division of Pharmacoepidemiology for providing such a welcoming and collaborative environment, as well as the Greenwall Foundation's Faculty Scholar in Bioethics program, which supports innovative empirical research in bioethics. Dr Robertson thanks Dean Marc Miller for mentorship, encouragement, and funding for the project, through summer research grants. Finally, we would like to thank our families for their love, which, in the words of Alicia Keys, is blind.

SECTION II

BLINDING AND BIAS

CHAPTER

1

A Primer on the Psychology of Cognitive Bias

Carla L. MacLean[1], Itiel E. Dror[2]

[1]Psychology Department, Kwantlen Polytechnic University, Surrey, BC, Canada;
[2]University College London, London, UK

OUTLINE

A PRIMER ON THE PSYCHOLOGY OF COGNITIVE BIAS

Psychological research has demonstrated how people's perceptions and cognitions are affected by context, motivation, expectation, and experience (e.g., Gilovich et al., 2002; Koehler and Harvey, 2004). Factors extraneous to the content of the information being considered have been shown to shape people's perceptions and judgments. This chapter reviews the nature of human cognition, and how people's limited capacity for information processing is remarkably efficient, but also introduces systematic errors into decision making. The cognitive shortcuts people take and the assumptions they make when processing information largely occur outside of conscious awareness and thus go undetected by decision makers. Experts are not immune to these cognitive vulnerabilities and hence often exhibit bias in their conclusions, but might be unaware of it. It is precisely because of people's "bias blind spot"

Blinding as a Solution to Bias
http://dx.doi.org/10.1016/B978-0-12-802460-7.00001-2

(Pronin et al., 2002) that interventions akin to blinding—that is, limiting people's access to potentially biasing information—are a necessary procedural constraint when seeking ways to optimize decision making (Dror, 2013; Dror et al., 2015).

THEORETICAL FRAMEWORK OF HUMAN COGNITION

The role of contextual effects on raw sensory information is a basic tenet of human cognitive theory, that is, top-down processing (Rumelhart and McClelland, 1986). It is naïve to believe that people perceive the world objectively or that we encode and interpret the nature of a stimulus based only on the properties of the object i.e., bottom-up processing. Scores of research studies demonstrate the overwhelming power of top-down, conceptually driven processing (Kahneman, 2011). People unconsciously and seamlessly weave their knowledge of the world into their understanding of it. It is a cornerstone of human intelligence that people do not process information passively; rather, they interact and actively make sense of the world.

In the complex worlds of expert decision making, which can include medical, forensic, and legal information, top-down processing is critical. Expertise involves using past experience and knowledge in considering data and making decisions. Such top-down processing may draw on factors such as hopes, expectations, context, motivations, or states of mind—anything but the actual data being considered. These factors not only direct our attention to specific things (and ignore others), but also guide our interpretation and understanding of incoming information.

The human cognitive system has a limited capacity to process all of the information presented to it, and therefore people have to be selective in what receives attention (Simons and Chabris, 1999). As efficient consumers of information, people selectively attend to what they assume is worthy of consideration and process it in ways that fit with any preexisting knowledge or state. This information processing is largely automatic and beyond conscious awareness. While such automaticity and efficiency is the bedrock of expertise, paradoxically, it has also been found to be the source of much bias (Dror, 2011a). For instance (1) literature on the escalation of commitment has demonstrated that people at times continue to invest resources in failing or questionable strategies (Kahneman and Tversky, 1979), (2) hindsight bias has shown that once an outcome is known, people tend to believe the outcome was more predictable for the decision maker than it truly was at the time of the decision (Roese and Vohs, 2012), (3) correspondence bias has illustrated that people are inclined to infer dispositional qualities about actors from observing those actors' behaviors rather than concluding that there were situational constraints (Gilbert and Malone, 1995), (4) belief perseverance has shown that people tend to maintain their initial beliefs in the face of contradicting information (Nisbett and Ross, 1980), and (5) confirmation bias has demonstrated that people tend to seek and interpret information in a way that is consistent with their initial beliefs (Nickerson, 1998). All of these examples illustrate that the cognitive system has very effective ways to deal with information processing, especially given its limited resources; however, such effective shortcut mechanisms can also bring about vulnerability to bias and error.

CONTEXT EFFECTS

Context effects are environmental factors, such as the attributes of the stimulus, the features of the situation, or the information recipient's expectations (Edmond et al., 2014). Stemming from established theoretical roots (Tversky and Kahneman, 1974), research on context's influence on expert decision making has gained momentum in the past decade. The literature from forensic science (Dror and Rosenthal, 2008; Found, 2014), investigation—both industrial (MacLean et al., 2013) and forensic (Meissner and Kassin, 2002)—judicial process (Jones, 2013), and medical judgments (Bornstein and Emler, 2001) has consistently demonstrated that environment is a powerful influence on how people construct their initial impressions, seek and interpret information, and render their final judgments (Edmond et al., 2014; Saks et al., 2003). This literature also presents conclusive evidence that honest, hardworking decision makers can reach inaccurate conclusions not because of nefarious intent but because of the nature and limitations of human cognition (Dror, 2011a).

Initial Impressions

Judgments about events such as the likelihood of a suspect's guilt, whether a factor is causal in an event, or whether a patient has a particular ailment, are often uncertain because the decision makers may not have quick and reliable access to the ground truth. Classic work by Tversky and Kahneman (1974) suggested that when developing an initial impression about uncertain events, people often rely on how effortlessly the material is brought to mind (i.e., availability) or how well the current situation matches scenarios they have previously experienced (i.e., representativeness). These cognitive rules-of-thumb, or heuristics, are largely efficient strategies that result in many good decisions. However, there are times when such simple metrics of cognition may bias decision making. Errors emerge when features of context support quick access to some information relative to other information, or encourage viewing a scenario as more stereotypical than what would be appropriate given a truly rational weighing of the information (Kahneman, 2011).

Research has demonstrated that the presentation of information can make it overly persuasive if it is salient or distinctive (Taylor, 1982; Taylor and Fiske, 1975), encountered early rather than late in fact finding (Tetlock, 1983; but also see Price and Dahl, 2014 for the effect of recency in judgment), easy to read or understand (Reber and Schwarz, 1999), accompanied by an image (Newman et al., 2012), familiar (Bornstein, 1989), or delivered by a person who is professional looking (Furnham et al., 2013) or generally attractive (Dion et al., 1972; Eagly et al., 1991). Time of presentation can also affect early impressions. Danziger et al. (2011) found that prisoners' chances of being paroled were significantly greater if their hearings were early in the day or after the judge had taken a break for food.

Priming demonstrates how aspects of the information that may be irrelevant to the decision-making task, such as knowledge of a person's race, can guide judgments (Herring et al., 2013). In one study, Bean and colleagues showed that priming nursing and medical students with images of Hispanics activated negative stereotypes regarding these patients' compliance with treatment recommendations (Bean et al., 2013). The basic association that medical practitioners demonstrated between race and compliance is relevant because these types of implicit biases can subtly guide treatment choices (Sabin and Greenwald, 2012). Racial knowledge can also affect juror decision making because congruency between a suspect's race and a crime (e.g., as with a black man accused of auto theft) tends to result in higher ratings of suspect culpability than if the race and crime were incongruent (Jones and Kaplan, 2003).

The literature on framing demonstrates that the structure of the problem—how the problem is presented—can affect people's choices (Kahneman and Tversky, 1979). Presenting the same medical research statistics as a gain or a loss to medical students affected their selections of treatment options (Marteau, 1989). In the adversarial forum of the judicial system, forensic experts who believed that they were working for the defense rated the risk level of offenders as lower than experts who believed they were working for the prosecution rating the same offenders (Murrie et al., 2013). These experts did not willfully bias their assessments. Rather, their judgments were affected by their affiliations and the goals imposed by the side that retained them.

Judgments

Context that is consistent with a correct situational assessment will facilitate the formation of an accurate hunch or hypothesis. However, confirmation bias demonstrates that an inaccurate initial understanding of the situation can be a significantly compromising first step for experts attempting to reach correct decisions (Kassin et al., 2013; Nickerson, 1998). Once initial impressions are formed, individuals tend to seek and interpret additional information that matches their expectations (Findley and Scott, 2006). People tend to give greater weight to information consistent with their expectations. They also tend to ignore, discredit, or weigh very low information that is inconsistent and interpret ambiguous information as consistent with their working theory (see Ask et al., 2008 for a discussion of the elasticity of evidence).

An erroneous initial impression does not ensure that the decision maker will pursue a biased investigative trajectory; however, research does endorse that the initial impression can be a central predecessor to distorted final judgments (O'Brien, 2009). Once in motion, the momentum of confirmation bias can build quickly for the decision maker because people generally require less hypothesis-consistent evidence to convince themselves that their initial theories are accurate than hypothesis-inconsistent evidence to reject their theories. Contributing to such momentum are motivational factors such as personal goals, organizational norms, and the cognitive effort required for the decision. For instance, people were shown to increase their scrutiny of information in a simulated investigation not only because the information conflicted with their initial hypotheses, but also because the information conflicted with their goal of solving the case (Marksteiner et al., 2011). Research that asked participants to assume the norm of "efficiency"—versus "thoroughness"—in a simulated investigation found that efficient participants were less rigorous in processing the evidence and less open to information presented later in the investigation (Ask et al., 2011).

In a study with physicians, Redelmeier and Shafir (1995) found that 53% of participants who had decided on a treatment option and who were then informed that one more medication could be tried with the patient prior to surgery opted to stay with their original plan of just the referral. By contrast, 72% of physicians who were informed that there were two medications that could be tested with the patient chose to proceed with just the referral. In essence, the effort involved with deciding between two medications versus one medication resulted in a higher percentage of physicians defaulting to their original referral plans.

Types of Decision-Making Activities

The varied effects of context on specific decision-making activities can be illustrated by the breadth of affected judgments. For example, one of the least-complex judgments required of a decision maker is of visual matching. In one study, participants were asked to rate the facial resemblance of child–adult pairs who in reality were genetically unrelated. However, participants who were told that that the pair were related rated the dyad as significantly more similar compared to those who were told the child–adult pairs were not related or who were given no information (Bressan and Dal Martello, 2002). A study in forensic anthropology found that given contextual information that a skeleton was male (when in fact it was female) biased most examiners to conclude that the skeletal was male. This is in stark contrast to zero participants judging the skeleton to be male when given female contextual information (Nakhaeizadeh et al., 2014). In another study, fingerprint experts who had determined years earlier that certain sets of prints were a match or an exclusion for a particular suspect was given new contextual information that stated that either the suspect had confessed in questioning or that the suspect was in custody at the time of the offense. After receiving the new information, approximately 17% of the experts subsequently changed at least one of their decisions on the prints from match to exclusion or exclusion to match (Dror and Charlton, 2006).

Motivation contributes to the misinterpretation of visual stimuli as well (Dunning and Balcetis, 2013). Participants, who had a vested interest in seeing an ambiguous figure as either a letter or a number, because they would receive either a reward or punishment based on their perception, were more likely to authentically interpret the figure in a way that was consistent with their desired outcomes (Balcetis and Dunning, 2006).

The social judgments literature is where we can gain a fuller appreciation of the implications of context, because expectations have been shown to extend beyond people's private opinions and affect the behavior of others. In a famous study, Rosenthal and Jacobson (1966), provided teachers at the outset of the school year with information that some of their students had greater academic potential than others. An important feature of the experiment was that the students in the group labeled "promising" were selected at random from the class and did not differ in their academic aptitude than those in the rest of the class. At the end of the year, external evaluators who were not privy to the study details evaluated students' academic progress, and pupils who were preidentified as promising scored significantly higher than their classmates. Hence, expectation became reality as teachers' beliefs established patterns of interacting with the students that ultimately resulted in changes in the students' behaviors.

Contemporary literature on expectancy effects demonstrates the breadth of laboratory and real-world circumstances in which these results are replicated. Significant relationships have been demonstrated between the expectations of judges regarding suspects' guilt and the decisions of their juries (Blanck et al., 1985); case managers regarding schizophrenics' abilities and the duration that the affected persons maintained employment (O'Connell and Stein, 2011); dog handlers regarding where the dogs should alert to scents and dogs' performances (Lit et al., 2011); and mock investigators and their questioning styles with witnesses and then subsequent third-party evaluations of witnesses' credibility (MacLean et al., 2011).

The Bias Snowball Effect

It is clear that context can affect a range of decision making. This finding underpins a particularly perilous decision-making phenomenon termed the "bias snowball effect" (Dror, 2012). This effect occurs when information that is perceived to be independent and corroborating may in fact have been contaminated by similar sources of contextual information. Imagine that a witness erroneously identifies the suspect from a target-absent line-up and this information is shared with, and biases, the judgment of the forensic fingerprint expert making the print assessment. The investigating officer shares the positive identification decision and the fingerprint match with the suspect during questioning, which helps to elicit a false confession from the suspect. These three pieces of evidence are not orthogonal, yet when presented at trial, they will be offered as three independent sources of corroborating evidence. Importantly, the information being shared at times may not be relevant to the people it is being shared with (e.g., fingerprint examiner knowing about the identification decision), but it may have real effects on their processing and collection of information (Edmond et al., 2014; Kassin et al., 2013). Hence, rigor should be employed when deciding what information is required and when that information should be shared with those who are either providing information or fact finding.

It is important to note that contextual biasing information may be derived from many different sources.

FIGURE 1 Different levels which may contain irrelevant information that can bias decision makers.

1. The actual data, if they contain irrelevant information. For example, judging handwriting in forensic science may include biasing contextual information within the text.
2. Biasing context within the reference materials that may direct the interpretation of the actual data being evaluated. For example, a suspect's license plate number or fingerprint may direct the evaluator's interpretation of an image of a license plate or partial print obtained from a crime scene. Thus, the evaluator will be working from the suspect to the evidence rather than from the evidence to the suspect.
3. The surrounding context of the case. For example, knowing that suspects confessed or that there is additional evidence against them, such as eyewitnesses.
4. Base-rate expectation of what is typical or expected based on past experience, so there is an expectation of outcome before the actual evidence has even been seen.
5. The wider organizational and cultural factors, such as working for "a side" in the adversarial system or being part of the police team.

Figure 1, which presents the five-level taxonomy for the different sources of irrelevant and potentially biasing information, is based on four-level taxonomy suggested by Stoel et al. (2015).

MITIGATING THE EFFECT OF CONTEXT

Mitigating biasing effects is a challenge. One of the difficulties in mitigating bias is the lack of cognitive control, so when the biases are revealed and observers are aware of it, the

FIGURE 2 What do you see in this image?

observers may still be unable to adjust their cognitions and counter the effects of the biases. Therefore actual measures must be taken (Dror, 2013 ; Dror et al. 2015). To illustrate this issue, please examine Figure 2 from the previous page. Can you guess what image is presented in it? Please remember what you see. Your current interpretation of the image (or your inability to make sense of it) has been formed without any context.

Now that you have had a good look at Figure 2, please view Figure 3 (below). Now that you have seen Figure 3, you are more likely to decipher Figure 2 as consistent with the image in Figure 3. This is the effect of contextual knowledge. Furthermore, once people are exposed to the context, then it is very difficult (if not impossible) for people to turn back the clock to before the context was presented and to see the original image/evidence without the influence of the context. The experience of viewing Figures 2 and 3 shows that there is no "going back" or "blocking" context: once exposed, people are affected and biased without their control or despite their willpower. Hence, an effective frontline strategy to mitigate bias is in the first place to blind decision makers to irrelevant information that can bias their objective interpretations of the facts. Of particular importance is the need to blind information through context management. One method for managing context is Linear Sequential Unmasking (LSU), whereby some information is totally masked, while other is sequentially unmasked and presented when needed (see Dror et al., 2015 for details).

To understand the necessity of limiting people's exposure to biasing information we turn to the literature concerned with de-biasing. To control for biases, competent researchers have drawn on cognitive theory. A great deal of the literature concerned with reducing bias has

FIGURE 3 Can you also see this image in Figure 2?

focused on increasing people's cognitive investment in information processing. Awareness-based approaches have employed incentives, either through rewards or accountability, and these interventions have yielded mixed results (Samuels and Whitecotton, 2011; Stone and Ziebart, 1995; Tetlock, 1983; Vieider, 2011). These strategies employ the rationale that people generally hold the skills, knowledge, and resources to identify their errors and adjust their judgments accordingly. This approach has limited benefit because much bias is outside of awareness (Arkes, 1991). Thus, decision makers must rely on their intuitive theories of how they have been biased in their attempts to control or correct for biases (Wegener and Petty, 1995), resulting in possible under- or overcorrections to their judgments (Wilson and Brekke, 1994). An additional challenge to awareness-based approaches is that research demonstrates that people are less willing to see their own decisions as biased than those of other people (Pronin et al., 2002) and expertise breads overconfidence (Baumann et al., 1991). To find a current example of the limits of the incentives approach one needs to look no further than the evolution of the medical system's approach to error in the United States. Despite a consistent ratcheting up of fines and penalties for medical professionals who make diagnostic or surgical errors, the US health-care system has not experienced a significant decrease in mishaps (Dror, 2011b).

Researchers have also attempted to encourage deeper processing of information at a procedural level by (1) asking participants to consider alternatives (or the opposite) of their primary working hypothesis (Hirt and Markman, 1995; O'Brien, 2009), (2) introducing features designed to disrupt the fluency of participants' cognitive processes such as difficult-to-read text (Gervais and Norenzayan, 2012; Hernandez and Preston, 2013), and (3) incorporating explicit and implicit priming targeted at enhancing engagement with the material (Gervais and Norenzayan, 2012). These strategies vary in their success and also have real limitations. For example, because it can be challenging to generate multiple alternative hypotheses, participants who have been asked to consider too many alternatives may demonstrate the same level of bias as those only considering their primary hypothesis (O'Brien, 2009). The above literature, as well as our understanding of human cognition, makes a clear case that the simplest and most reliable approach to mitigating bias is to limit the cognitive contamination of the person processing the information. There are many practical ways for achieving and implementing such antibias measures (Dror, 2013) as well as the LSU method (Dror et al., 2015).

CONCLUSION

In this chapter, we have demonstrated that motivations, expectations, and context influence perception and interpretation of basic and complex stimuli, as well as information synthesis and decision making. The processes of information collection, interpretation, and deliberation underpin judgment and decision making. In developing solutions to mitigate cognitive contamination, it is imperative that we rely on the science of cognition and adopt informed approaches to become as objective as possible in our consideration of the facts. The issue of bias is applicable to all human endeavors, including experts' decision making in the medical, legal, and forensic domains. All of these domains require blinding as a cognitively informed approach to reduce contamination and bias, and use it as a powerful ally in the quest to enhance objectivity in decision making.

References

Arkes, H.R., 1991. Costs and benefits of judgment errors: implications for debiasing. Psychological Bulletin 110 (3), 486–498.

Ask, K., Granhag, P.A., Rebelius, A., 2011. Investigators under influence: how social norms activate goal-directed processing of criminal evidence. Applied Cognitive Psychology 25 (4), 548–553.

Ask, K., Rebelius, A., Granhag, P.A., 2008. The 'elasticity' of criminal evidence: a moderator of investigator bias. Applied Cognitive Psychology 22 (9), 1245–1259.

Balcetis, E., Dunning, D., 2006. See what you want to see: motivational influences on visual perception. Journal of Personality and Social Psychology 91 (4), 612–625.

Baumann, A.O., Deber, R.B., Thompson, G.G., 1991. Overconfidence among physicians and nurses: the 'micro-certainty, macro-uncertainty' phenomenon. Social Science and Medicine 32 (2), 167–174.

Bean, M.G., Stone, J., Moskowitz, G.B., Badger, T.A., Focella, E.S., 2013. Evidence of nonconscious stereotyping of Hispanic patients by nursing and medical students. Nursing Research 62 (5), 362–367.

Blanck, E.D., Rosenthal, R., Cordell, L.H., 1985. The appearance of justice: judges' verbal and nonverbal behavior in criminal jury trials. Stanford Law Review 38, 89–164.

Bornstein, B.H., Emler, A.C., 2001. Rationality in medical decision making: a review of the literature on doctors' decision-making biases. Journal of Evaluation in Clinical Practice 7 (2), 97–107.

Bornstein, R.F., 1989. Exposure and affect: overview and meta-analysis of research, 1968–1987. Psychological Bulletin 106 (2), 265–289.

Bressan, P., Dal Martello, M.F., 2002. *Talis Pater, Talis Filius*: perceived resemblance and the belief in genetic relatedness. Psychological Science 13 (3), 213–218.

Danziger, S., Levav, J., Avnaim-Pessoa, L., 2011. Extraneous factors in judicial decisions. PNAS Proceedings of the National Academy of Sciences of the United States of America 108 (17), 6889–6892.

Dion, K., Berscheid, E., Walser, E., 1972. What is beautiful is good. Journal of Personality and Social Psychology 24, 285–290.

Dror, I.E., 2011a. The paradox of human expertise: why experts can get it wrong. In: Kapur, N., Pascual-Leone, A., Ramachandran, V.S. (Eds.), The Paradoxical Brain. Cambridge University Press, Cambridge, UK, pp. 177–188.

Dror, I.E., 2011b. A novel approach to minimize error in the medical domain: cognitive neuroscientific insights into training. Medical Teacher 33 (1), 34–38.

Dror, I.E., 2012. Cognitive Bias in Forensic Science. Science and Technology Yearbook. McGraw-Hill, Charlottesville, Virginia, pp. 43–45.

Dror, I.E., 2013. Practical solutions to cognitive and human factor challenges in forensic science. Forensic Science Policy and Management 4, 105–113.

Dror, I.E., Charlton, D., 2006. Why experts make errors. Journal of Forensic Identification 56 (4), 600–616.

Dror, I.E., Rosenthal, R., 2008. Meta-analytically quantifying the reliability and biasability of forensic experts. Journal of Forensic Sciences 53 (4), 900–903.

Dror, I.E., Thompson, W.C., Meissner, C.A., Kornfield, I., Krane, D., Saks, M., & Risinger, M. 2015. Context Management Toolbox: A Linear Sequential Unmasking (LSU) Approach for Minimizing Cognitive Bias in Forensic Decision Making. Journal of Forensic Sciences, 60 (4), 1111–1112.

Dunning, D., Balcetis, E., 2013. Wishful seeing: how preferences shape visual perception. Current Directions in Psychological Science 22 (1), 33–37.

Eagly, A.H., Ashmore, R.D., Makhijani, M.G., Longo, L.C., 1991. What is beautiful is good, but…: a meta-analytic review of research on the physical attractiveness stereotype. Psychological Bulletin 110 (1), 109–128.

Edmond, G., Tangen, J.M., Searston, R.A., Dror, I.E., 2014. Contextual bias and cross-contamination in the forensic sciences: the corrosive implications for investigations, plea bargains, trials and appeals. Law, Probably and Risk Advance Access 0, 1–25.

Findley, K.A., Scott, M.S., 2006. The multiple dimensions of tunnel vision in criminal cases. Wisconsin Law Review 2, 291–397.

Found, B., 2014. Deciphering the human condition: the rise of cognitive forensics. Australian Journal of Forensic Sciences. http://dx.doi.org/10.1080/00450618.2014.965204. Advance online publication.

Furnham, A., Chan, P.S., Wilson, E., 2013. What to wear? The influence of attire on the perceived professionalism of dentists and lawyers. Journal of Applied Social Psychology 43 (9), 1838–1850.

Gervais, W.M., Norenzayan, A., 2012. Analytic thinking promotes religious disbelief. Science 336 (6080), 493–496.

Gilbert, D.T., Malone, P.S., 1995. The correspondence bias. Psychological Bulletin 117 (1), 21–38.

Gilovich, T., Griffin, D., Kahneman, D., 2002. Heuristics and Biases: The Psychology of Intuitive Judgment. Cambridge University Press, New York, NY.

Hernandez, I., Preston, J.L., 2013. Disfluency disrupts the confirmation bias. Journal of Experimental Social Psychology 49 (1), 178–182.

Herring, D.R., White, K.R., Jabeen, L.N., Hinojos, M., Terrazas, G., Reyes, S.M., Taylor, J.H., Crites, S.J., 2013. On the automatic activation of attitudes: a quarter century of evaluative priming research. Psychological Bulletin 139 (5), 1062–1089.

Hirt, E., Markman, K., 1995. Multiple explanation: a consider-an-alternative strategy for debiasing judgments. Journal of Personality and Social Psychology 69, 1069–1086.

Jones, C.E., 2013. The troubleshooting science of legal persuasion: heuristics and biases in judicial decision making. The Advocates' Quarterly 41, 49–122.

Jones, C.S., Kaplan, M.F., 2003. The effects of racially stereotypical crimes on juror decision-making and information-processing strategies. Basic and Applied Social Psychology 25 (1), 1–13.

Kahneman, D., 2011. Thinking, Fast and Slow. Random House, Toronto, Canada.

Kahneman, D., Tversky, A., 1979. Prospect theory: an analysis of decision under risk. Econometrica 47 (2), 263–291.

Kassin, S.M., Dror, I.E., Kukucka, J., 2013. The forensic confirmation bias: problems, perspectives, and proposed solutions. Journal of Applied Research in Memory and Cognition 2 (1), 42–52.

Koehler, D.J., Harvey, N., 2004. Blackwell Handbook of Judgment and Decision Making. Blackwell Publishing, Boston, Massachusetts.

Lit, L., Schweitzer, J.B., Oberbauer, A.M., 2011. Handler beliefs affect scent detection dog outcomes. Animal Cognition 14 (3), 387–394.

MacLean, C.L., Brimacombe, C.A.E., Alison, M., Dahl, L.C., Kadlec, H., 2011. Post-identification feedback effects: investigators and evaluators. Journal of Applied Cognitive Psychology 25 (5), 739–752.

MacLean, C.L., Brimacombe, C.A.E., Lindsay, D.S., 2013. The role of a priori knowledge and tunnel vision education. Law and Human Behavior 37 (6), 441–453.

Marksteiner, T., Ask, K., Reinhard, M., Granhag, P.A., 2011. Asymmetrical scepticism towards criminal evidence: the role of goal- and belief-consistency. Applied Cognitive Psychology 25 (4), 541–547.

Marteau, T.M., 1989. Framing of information: its influence upon decisions of doctors and patients. British Journal of Social Psychology 28 (1), 89–94.

Meissner, C.A., Kassin, S.M., 2002. 'He's guilty!': investigator bias in judgments of truth and deception. Law and Human Behavior 26 (5), 469–480.

Murrie, D.C., Boccaccini, M.T., Guarnera, L.A., Rufino, K.A., 2013. Are forensic experts biased by the side that retained them? Psychological Science 24 (10), 1889–1897.

Nakhaeizadeh, S., Dror, I.E., Morgan, R.M., 2014. Cognitive bias in forensic anthropology: visual assessment of skeletal remains is susceptible to confirmation bias. Science and Justice 54 (3), 208–214.

Newman, E.J., Garry, M., Bernstein, D.M., Kantner, J., Lindsay, D.S., 2012. Nonprobative photographs (or words) inflate truthiness. Psychonomic Bulletin and Review 19 (5), 969–974.

Nickerson, R.S., 1998. Confirmation bias: a ubiquitous phenomenon in many guises. Review of General Psychology 2 (2), 175–220.

Nisbett, R.E., Ross, L., 1980. Human Inference: Strategies and Shortcomings of Social Judgment. Prentice-Hall, Englewood Cliffs, New Jersey.

O'Brien, B., 2009. Prime suspect: an examination of factors that aggravate and counteract confirmation bias in criminal investigations. Psychology, Public Policy, and Law 15 (4), 315–334.

O'Connell, M.J., Stein, C.H., 2011. The relationship between case manager expectations and outcomes of persons diagnosed with schizophrenia. Community Mental Health Journal 47 (4), 424–435.

Price, L.H., Dahl, L.C., 2014. Order and strength matter for evaluation of alibi and eyewitness evidence. Applied Cognitive Psychology 28 (2), 143–150.

Pronin, E., Lin, D.Y., Ross, L., 2002. The bias blind spot: perceptions of bias in self versus others. Personality and Social Psychology Bulletin 28 (3), 369–381.

Reber, R., Schwarz, N., 1999. Effects of perceptual fluency on judgments of truth. Consciousness and Cognition: An International Journal 8 (3), 338–342.

Redelmeier, D.A., Shafir, E., 1995. Medical decision making in situations that offer multiple alternatives. Journal of the American Medical Association 273 (4), 302–305.

Roese, N.J., Vohs, K.D., 2012. Hindsight bias. Perspectives on Psychological Science 7 (5), 411–426.

Rosenthal, R., Jacobson, L., 1966. Teachers' expectancies: determinants of pupils' IQ gains. Psychological Reports 19 (1), 115–118.
Rumelhart, D.E., McClelland, J.L., 1986. Parallel Distributed Processing: Explorations in the Microstructure of Cognition. MIT Press, Cambridge, MA.
Sabin, J.A., Greenwald, A.G., 2012. The influence of implicit bias on treatment recommendations for 4 common pediatric conditions: pain, urinary tract infection, attention deficit hyperactivity disorder, and asthma. American Journal of Public Health 102 (5), 988–995.
Saks, M.J., Risinger, D.M., Rosenthal, R., Thompson, W.C., 2003. Context effects in forensic science: a review and application of the science of science to crime laboratory practice in the United States. Science and Justice 43 (2), 77–90.
Samuels, J.A., Whitecotton, S.M., 2011. An effort based analysis of the paradoxical effects of incentives on decision-aided performance. Journal of Behavioral Decision Making 24 (4), 345–360.
Simons, D.J., Chabris, C.F., 1999. Gorillas in our midst: sustained inattentional blindness for dynamic events. Perception 28 (9), 1058–1074.
Stoel, R.D., Berger, C.E., Kerkhoff, W., Mattijssen, E., Dror, I., 2015. Minimizing contextual bias in forensic casework. In: Strom, K., Hickman, M.J. (Eds.), Forensic Science and the Administration of Justice. Sage, New York, NY.
Stone, D.N., Ziebart, D.A., 1995. A model of financial incentive effects in decision making. Organizational Behavior and Human Decision Processes 61 (3), 250–261.
Taylor, S.E., 1982. The availability bias in social perception and interaction. In: Kahneman, D., Slovic, P., Tversky, A. (Eds.), Judgment under Uncertainly: Heuristics and Biases. Cambridge University Press, Cambridge, UK, pp. 190–200.
Taylor, S.E., Fiske, S.T., 1975. Point of view and perception so causality. Journal of Personality and Social Psychology 32 (3), 439–445.
Tetlock, P.E., 1983. Accountability and perseverance of first impressions. Social Psychology Quarterly 46 (4), 285–292.
Tversky, A., Kahneman, D., 1974. Judgment under uncertainty: heuristics and biases. Science 185 (4157), 1124–1131.
Vieider, F.M., 2011. Separating real incentives and accountability. Experimental Economics 14 (4), 507–518.
Wegener, D.T., Petty, R.E., 1995. Flexible correction processes in social judgement: the role of naïve theories in correction for perceived bias. Journal of Personality and Social Psychology 68, 36–51.
Wilson, T., Brekke, N., 1994. Mental contamination and mental correction: unwanted influences on judgments and evaluations. Psychological Bulletin 116, 117–142.

CHAPTER

2

Why Blinding? How Blinding? A Theory of Blinding and Its Application to Institutional Corruption

Christopher T. Robertson

James E. Rogers College of Law, The University of Arizona, Tucson, AZ, USA

OUTLINE

BLINDING AS DISAGGREGATION

Benjamin Franklin was apparently the first to conduct a blindfolded experiment, and did so in his own home, leading a royal scientific commission appointed by Louis XVI to test a "healing fluid" that Franz Anton Mesmer claimed to have "discovered" (Kaptchuk, 1998). Mesmerists claimed that highly trained specialists could perform certain procedures to evoke the fluid for ailing patients, who could then experience its healing properties. Mesmer performed high-profile demonstrations of the phenomenon, with seemingly

Blinding as a Solution to Bias
http://dx.doi.org/10.1016/B978-0-12-802460-7.00002-4

impressive results for patients. Importantly, Mesmer claimed not to be a voodoo doctor with mystical powers. Instead, he claimed that his elaborate procedures actually evoked something real in the world, not unlike gravity or other natural phenomena.

Franklin worried that the subjects may actually respond to the mesmerist's ritual, rather than responding to the natural substance that the ritual supposedly produced. In scientific terms, this mixed situation is called a "confound," since it prevents a clean test of whether a healing fluid actually exists. Alternatively, one may conceive of the effect of the ritual as a bias, since it may improperly influence the respondents' perceptions of whether they were healed and inflate the analyst's overall estimate of the effects of the healing fluid, if any.

To solve this problem, Franklin realized that a mere strip of fabric, a blindfold, could disambiguate these two potential causes, preventing the subject from perceiving the ritual but allowing the ritual to produce any healing substance, if it worked as Mesmer claimed. This procedure involved a disaggregation of roles. Franklin would watch whether the ritual was being performed, coding the independent variable. The patients merely had to report whether they were healed, coding the dependent variable.

In fact, once the blindfolds were applied, Mesmer's elaborate rituals failed to reliably produce any healing experiences. Even worse, the blindfolded patients sometimes leaped up, claiming to be healed, even when Mesmer had not yet performed the ritual. Without the visual cues, the relationship between the ritual and the healing was broken. Franklin's conclusions were clear: "this fluid has no existence." Instead, any effects were due to "imagination" (Kaptchuk, 1998 and Chapter 3, in this volume).

Let us pause for a moment to consider alternatives that Franklin could have employed, other than blinding (Robertson, 2011). First, to ensure that Mesmer's ritual did not affect the patients, Franklin could have barred Mesmer from performing his ritual at all and then assessed whether the healing fluid affected the patients. This sort of intervention would have missed the point of Mesmer's claim to efficacy. Like a surgeon who offers a procedure or a pharmacist who offers a drug, Mesmer claimed that his careful and precise efforts were necessary to invoke the healing fluid. They were inseparable. A test without the ritual would not be a test of Mesmer's claims; Franklin and Mesmer would be like ships passing in the night.

Instead, suppose that Franklin had given stern instructions to the human subjects, telling them not to be distracted by the elaborate rituals, and to be sure that they only report healing when it is real. It is, of course, an empirical question whether such mental fortitude can successfully resist bias. However, we now know from the psychological sciences that many thought processes happen implicitly, outside of our awareness and conscious control (Nisbett and Wilson, 1977). Wilson and Brekke (1994) outline at least four separate actions a person must consciously undertake to de-bias mental contamination: a person must (1) be aware that mental contamination exists, (2) be motivated to correct the bias, (3) be aware of the direction and magnitude of the bias, and (4) be able to adjust his or her response. This is a difficult mental gantlet for any person to run, and it is unclear how a third party, like Franklin, could assess whether the subject has succeeded or succumbed to bias. This solution thus engenders no trust.

Finally, suppose that Franklin had allowed Mesmer to perform his rituals in view of the patients, and then assessed whether they were healed, but appended to his final report, a disclaimer, explaining that the findings should be taken with a grain of salt, since the patients could have been biased by the ritual rather than healed by the fluid. This strategy would be altogether unsatisfactory, since it undermines the entire experiment. Although the addendum is perhaps helpful to make sure that nobody misinterprets the experiment (supposing that it produces knowledge when it does not; a false positive), the disclaimer itself does not help produce knowledge. The experiment remains irreparably confounded.

In the context of Franklin's experiment, these three alternative approaches are obviously ineffective solutions to the problem of bias. They are worth reviewing here, nonetheless, because these alternative solutions are still routinely invoked as a solution for bias in other contexts discussed below.

THE BREADTH OF BLINDING

In the centuries since Franklin's experiment, but mostly in the last 60 years, the double-blind randomized, placebo-controlled trial has become the gold standard for scientific inquiry (Schulz and Grimes, 2002). In addition to blinding of patients, whoever assigns subjects to treatment and control conditions should be blinded, to ensure that the treatment group does not disproportionately receive patients with the best or worst prognoses. Randomization is thus a form of blind assignment and is itself a key tool for producing scientific knowledge. In addition, the physicians, nurses, or others who take measurements can be biased by their hopes and expectations that an intervention will be safe and effective. This problem is most worrisome when the rater is making subjective judgments (Wood et al., 2008). As one leading methodologist concludes, "any process using a human as a perceptor, rater, or interpreter should be 'as blind as possible for as long as possible'" (Rosenthal, 1978, p. 1007). Meta-analyses have shown that blinding reduces the chance that an experiment will yield a false positive (Psaty and Prentice, 2010).

Editors of scholarly journals now routinely use blinding to allow them to assess the scientific merits of an article, rather than deciding based on the author's prestige, or worse, gender (Chapter 8, in this volume). Likewise, to avoid possible favoritism for particular students, law professors routinely use blinds when grading papers (Carrington, 1992).

Similarly, in thought experiments, philosophers have used the concept of blinding to try to distinguish proper objects of evaluation from what they claimed were distractions. David Hume defined good and evil in terms of a feeling or sentiment "considered in general, without reference to our particular interest" (Hume, 1985, p. 524). Similarly, Adam Smith's moral theory depended on the judgments of an "impartial spectator" (Smith, 1984). More recently, the economist John Harsanyi argued for a paramount ethical requirement of "impersonality" in which a person's preferences are those he would choose if he did not know his personal position (Harsanyi, 1955). Most famously, John Rawls conceived of deliberations on justice as occurring behind a "veil of ignorance," a thought experiment in which each citizen, deprived of the knowledge of "certain things that are irrelevant from the standpoint of justice," deliberates with all other citizens about the basic rules of society (1971, pp. 18–19). Rawls closed his magnum opus with this notion: "Purity of heart, if one could attain it, would be to see clearly and to act with grace and self-command from this point of view" (1971, p. 587).

Rawls himself emphasized that his veil was a "purely hypothetical" thought experiment (Rawls, 1971, p. 587). Nonetheless, Adrian Vermeule has argued that the American

Constitution actually includes "veil of ignorance" rules that cause decision makers to make generalized, prospective decisions, without knowing how they may impact particular constituencies or benefactors (Vermeule, 2001). Such decisions may have greater generalizability than decisions that are instead responsive to narrow, private interests.

In this same vein, consider the American jury, which benefits from several blinding mechanisms, although the mechanisms are not typically described in those terms. The Rules of Evidence exclude irrelevant, unreliable, and prejudicial information, on the assumption that jurors can actually make better decisions with less information (Fed. R. Evid. 401 and 403). The concern is that a jury may seek to convict a defendant based on information that he or she is a distasteful person or has done something else, which is not strictly criminal. In application, these rules depend on having a judge act as an intermediary to filter the information that reaches the ultimate decision makers (Hans, 2007).

Moreover, like patients assigned to treatment and control conditions, jurors are randomly selected from the community. The jury therefore "represents" the public from which it is drawn in a statistical sense. It is useful to distinguish this sense of representation from the political process of electoral representation used for legislatures (and many state court judges), which can introduce biases toward those with access to wealth (Fishkin et al., 2000).

Concededly, litigants enjoy a limited number of peremptory challenges and can remove other jurors for cause. This deselection function may undermine the representativeness that randomization allows. By contrast, such challenges can be used to ensure that the jurors do not have extraneous information (e.g., exposure to pretrial publicity), which would defeat the evidentiary blind.

Like Franklin's use of blinding to disambiguate the effects of the ritual from any effects due to a healing fluid, this part has shown how blinding has been used more broadly to disambiguate factors that may affect a person's assessment, whether that person is a patient, a rater, an assignor, a hypothetical deliberator, an actual public official, or a juror. The balance of this chapter approaches blinding as a generative concept, applicable to other domains, showing how it may be advantageous compared to other solutions for bias.

INSTITUTIONAL CORRUPTION AND THE FAILURE OF COMMON SOLUTIONS

It is useful to sketch the problem of institutional corruption to illustrate how blinding may work as a solution. Concerned about how Congress can be corrupted by money even if no individual member ever accepts a bribe, Dennis Thompson (1995) defined institutional corruption as a broader notion to capture systematic ways in which money can bend an institution and undermine its legitimate procedures. A campaign contribution benefits the institution, since it helps candidates communicate with the public, but it can also give the donor undue influence with the recipients. Lawrence Lessig (2011) expanded on the concept of institutional corruption, suggesting that in many other domains—from the legislature and the judiciary to biomedical science and the financial sector—there are economies of influence that weaken institutions and undermine public trust in those institutions.

A schematic may help show the problem and the potential for blinding as a solution. Figure 1 highlights the concept of "bias" as the primary problem. In this model of institutional

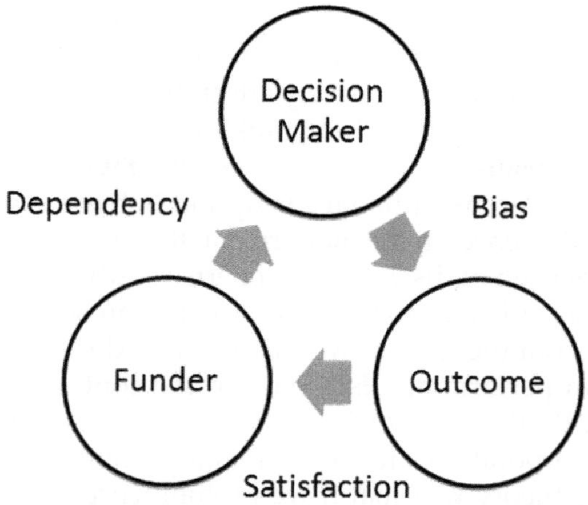

FIGURE 1 Schematic model of institutional corruption.

corruption, a funder creates a dependency, which then causes a decision maker to alter his or her behavior in a way that biases an outcome. That change in outcomes is what motivated the funder in the first place, providing satisfaction thereto. This notion of "bias" presumes that we can specify a counterfactual situation—a normative conception of the uncorrupted institution that achieves a proper set of outcomes (Lessig, 2011; Light, 2013). At a level of generality, this uncorrupted state can be conceived of as one where the institutions serve the public interests, rather than the narrow private interests of the funders.

This notion would have been familiar to the American founding fathers, who wrote of the problem of "faction" in Federalist Paper #10 (Hamilton et al., 2003). The concern was not that members of Congress would be bribed. Rather, "as long as the reason of man continues fallible, and he is at liberty to exercise it, different opinions will be formed. As long as the connection subsists between his reason and his self-love, his opinions and his passions will have a reciprocal influence on each other; and the former will be objects to which the latter will attach themselves" (Hamilton et al., 2003, p. 41). This sort of alignment between one's interests and one's ability to reason about what is best for the public interest is a confound, or a bias, not unlike the one faced by Franklin.

In addition to Congress, consider the possibility of institutional corruption in two other domains, which are explored elsewhere in this book. In civil litigation, expert witnesses may be biased by their dependency on litigants, who handpick them, affiliate them as teammates, and compensate them, contingent on them providing a favorable opinion (Robertson, 2010; Robertson and Yokum, 2012; Chapters 13 and 14, in this volume). Such "hired guns" provide biased guidance to jurors, who are trying to discern whether to impose liability, and thereby degrade the accuracy of those outcomes. Second, in biomedical science, researchers are dependent on the pharmaceutical and medical device manufacturers who select them and fund their experiments, which biases researchers in the many discretionary decisions about how to design, conduct, and report those experiments (Chapter 7, in this volume). Accordingly, systematic reviews have shown that industry-funded research more often favors company products, making them appear safer and more effective than they appear in independently funded research. If most biomedical science is funded by industry and biased in this way, it may ultimately change the opinions of physicians on whether and how to use these products, and thus negatively affect the health of patients.

Recall the three alternative solutions that Franklin could have tried to solve the problem of bias in his test of Mesmerism. They may have seemed obviously futile in that context, but they are the go-to solutions for institutional corruption in these contexts of Congress, expert witnesses, and biomedical science. In the modern era, they might be called proscription, professionalism, and the provision of disclosures (Robertson, 2011).

The first solution to bias or institutional corruption is a proscription, or ban, on the dependency. (This mode strikes out the left arrow in Figure 1, and is analogous to Franklin simply prohibiting Mesmer from performing his ritual.) In the context of Congress, this principle is exemplified by the Bi-Partisan Campaign Finance Reform Act of 2002, which provided, "it is unlawful for any corporation…to make a contribution in connection with any election" (2 USC §441b). The theory was that if we prohibit corporations from supporting candidates for Congress, then members of Congress will no longer be dependent on and biased toward them. The Supreme Court has, however, interpreted the First Amendment to forbid Congress from regulating political spending in this way (Citizens United v. Federal Election Commission, 2010). This holding expresses a sense that such a regulation, which silences speech, misses the point of American politics, by preventing corporations, and their individual members so organized, from expressing political preferences and communicating political information to others. Of course, this Supreme Court decision remains controversial. But, barring a constitutional amendment or change in the Supreme Court's interpretation of the First Amendment, it remains the law of the land.

Similarly, in the domain of litigation, it would be possible for courts to forbid litigants from selecting and paying experts. Of course, somebody has to pay for and select experts. Judges could instead appoint experts free of any such dependency, an idea that has been advocated for more than a century (Hand, 1901). Such a proscription on litigants producing expert evidence for court would be a radical change to the adversarial structure of the American judicial system, requiring new roles and conceptions for both attorneys and the judge. The reform might even undermine the role of the jury to independently determine the facts, if they instead defer to the judge's expert witness, who has not been subject to the crucible of adversarial testing. Notably, judges have explicitly had the power to appoint their own experts for four decades, but they almost never actually do so (Fed. R. Evid. 706; Cecil and Willging, 1993). Here too, there is a sense that proscription is too crude as a solution to bias; it throws out the baby with the bathwater.

One final scenario: we could forbid industry from funding biomedical science. This proscription may be most plausible. Biomedical science, of course, must still be paid for, but its costs will ultimately be born either by taxpayers or in the prices of products. For decades, reformers have suggested that government itself should fund biomedical science research, and not just the basic and translational science currently funded by the National Institutes of Health (Rodwin, 2012). Nonetheless, an outright ban would likely be an unconstitutional infringement on scientific speech, and it seems unlikely that Congress would enact such a ban, which would be met by resistance from the strong political influence of the drug and device industries.

The second regulatory solution for institutional corruption is for a policy maker to allow a dependency to persist, but ask the decision maker to exercise professionalism to resist being influenced by that dependency. (This mode strikes out the right arrow in Figure 1, and is analogous to Franklin simply asking the patients to try not to allow themselves to be affected by Mesmer's ritual.) In the context of Congress, the federal bribery statute allows officials to accept money but not "in return for…being influenced in the performance of any official act" (18 USC §201). Officials are allowed to take money, but must exercise a mental power that prevents them from being biased by those financial relationships. It is hard for the law to observe whether an official actually succeeds in this task, but can at least proscribe them from making promises to a donor that they will be so influenced.

Similarly, there is a professionalism intervention for expert witnesses. The American Medical Association's (AMA's) Code of Ethics acknowledges that physicians can enter into financial relationships with litigants, but says, "physician testimony must not be *influenced* by financial compensation" (AMA, n.d.). How, exactly, physicians are supposed to avoid that influence is left unclear. Even worse, this aspiration toward professionalism does not help jurors determine whether the particular testifying witness has or has not actually been influenced by financial compensation.

In the case of biomedical science, we expect scientists to maintain professional discretion to design rigorous studies, regardless of funding source (Rothman, 1993). The aggregate data, showing bias in industry-funded research, suggest that they may fail (Lundh et al., 2012). Mere exhortations about professionalism do not give physicians confidence that they can in fact rely on industry-funded research to inform their clinical decisions (Kesselheim et al., 2012).

So, as a solution to institutional corruption, professionalism has important limitations. Most fundamentally, it presumes a psychological ability: that an individual who is exposed to a potentially biasing factor can successfully suppress any resulting bias, and behave just as she would have behaved if she had not been so exposed. Just as Franklin's exhortations to his patients would have been futile, the scientific literature suggests that professionals are rarely so immune (Dana and Loewenstein, 2003; Fiedler, 2012; Korn and Ehringhaus, 2007; Kouchaki, 2013; Robertson et al., 2012; Sah and Loewenstein, 2015). Humans find it difficult to recognize their own biases (Pronin et al., 2002). It is even more difficult to properly correct for a bias, once recognized (Wilson and Brekke, 1994).

The third solution is the provision of disclosures. This approach allows a dependency (unlike a ban) and allows that the decision maker may succumb to it (unlike professionalism), but discloses the fact of dependency. The analogy would be to Franklin allowing his patients to be exposed to Mesmer's ritual, but then including a hand-wringing discussion of the problem in his report to the king.

Campaign finance laws have long required that candidates disclose the names of all major donors. In litigation, Federal Rule of Civil Procedure 26(a) requires expert witnesses to disclose how much litigants pay for their services. Journals require that authors disclose the funding sources in small print at the end of their articles.

Figure 1 is unhelpful for depicting the disclosure strategy, and this lacuna reflects the lack of theoretical explanations for how it is supposed to work. Aside from hackneyed analogies (for example, sunlight being a disinfectant), the causal story for how disclosure is supposed to solve institutional corruption is complicated and dependent on the particular situation in which the device is employed. In some situations, the "decision maker" shown in Figure 1 is actually an advisor (such as an expert witness), for a second decision maker (such as a juror), who is supposed to use the disclosure in deciding how to weigh the information provided by the advisor, so as to modulate its own decision in a way that neutralizes the advisor's biases in producing a final outcome (Chapter 7, in this volume). The recipient of information must discern whether the conflicting interest actually biased the advisor, and if so how much, and adjust accordingly. However, that dynamic just reduces reliance on the advice; it does not somehow make the advice better or make alternative clean advice appear in its place. When all the advisors have conflicting interests, a disclosure just breeds cynicism, without actually improving outcomes. Further, a disclosure mandate may actually make the advisor more biased, if it functions as a "moral license" (Cain et al., 2011). Or, it may have the counter-intuitive effect of causing recipients of disclosures to trust their advisors even more (Sah et al., 2013).

Thus, the three primary solutions to institutional corruption have important limitations. Blinding provides another alternative.

BLINDING AS A SOLUTION TO INSTITUTIONAL CORRUPTION

As in science, blinding can solve institutional corruption by disaggregating a dependency. Typically, a dependency is complex, consisting of several functions as shown in Figure 2. Blinding attempts to disaggregate and filter, such that the biasing factors are caught, while allowing other functions to proceed. In this way, a dependency can exist without causing a bias.

	Subsidy	Selection	Identification
Definition	Funder provides financial support for decision maker	Funder chooses which potential decision maker receives subsidy	Funder has special opportunities to influence decisions
Potential Biasing Mechanism	Goods and services are produced that might otherwise not be	Decision makers disproportionately reflect funder's preferences	Decision maker internalizes preferences of funder as funder
How to Eliminate	Create alternative source of funding, or lose subsidized goods and services	Intermediary performs alternative selection (random or intelligent)	Decision maker is unable to distinguish funders from non-funders
Risks and Cost of Elimination	Subsidy may be necessary for production of institutional outcomes; alternative funding source may be unreliable or create new biases; participatory funding may be important to institutional values	Funder may lack incentive to contribute blindly; funder may have more expertise in selecting decision maker with fitness for function; intermediary may itself be corrupted by funder (sham)	Information about source of funding may be inextricable from necessary information for decision; identification may be important to institutional values

FIGURE 2 Disaggregating three functions of a dependency.

This mechanism will typically require some sort of intermediary to perform the filtration function. Saul Levmore has noted a range of contexts where such intermediation may be useful (Levmore, 1996). Voting is generally anonymous, but depends on poll workers to confirm that an individual has the right to vote, and only does so once (Levmore, 1996). Similarly, when someone offers a reward for lost property, a thief may worry that returning the property will implicate himself, notwithstanding a promise that there will be "no questions asked" (Levmore, 1996). A credible intermediary can allow the property to be returned anonymously, and the reward secured, without passing along the incriminating information. Similarly, the publisher of a book can serve as an intermediary for the public reliably signaling that the book is authored by the same person who used the pseudonym previously, without forcing the author to disclose his or her real identity (Levmore, 1996).

In the model of institutional corruption, a dependency relationship typically involves a transfer of wealth, which performs three functions, which can be disaggregated: (a) a subsidy from the funder to the decision maker, (b) a selection by the funder of who will receive the subsidy, and (c) an identification between the funder and the decision maker, which aligns their interests at least partially. These are shown in Figure 2.

The subsidy function is obvious. The company pays for advertisements that the politician needs to get elected, the litigant pays for the expert witness to render an opinion, and the drug maker pays to recruit patients for the research. Without such payments, the ads might not run, the opinions might not be rendered, and the research may not be performed.

The subsidy itself may not be biasing. Because money is fungible, the institution's outcomes may be indifferent to the source of funds. The production of these goods and services may have an impact on outcomes that is not contrary to our normative conception of the institution—we may suppose that politics works better with the advertising that informs voters, that litigation requires experts to be paid for their services, and that science requires willing scientists and human subjects that cannot simply be coerced. Depending on how we specify the counterfactual world of a non-corrupted institution, it may turn out that such expenditures would be necessary even in an ideal world in which the institution was achieving its proper function. If so, then the source of funds may be irrelevant, and blinding is a feasible solution to institutional corruption.

The selection function is that the funder typically gets to decide who will receive his or her largesse. This selection function exploits a natural heterogeneity in potential decision makers. The funder naturally prefers to use its money in ways that maximize its chances of achieving satisfaction, and some potential decision makers are more likely to provide that satisfaction. Thus, the funders will tend to prefer potential decision makers who are inherently biased toward the funder's preferred outcomes (perhaps because they are ideologically committed to a certain sort of decision), and the funders will tend to prefer those potential decision makers who will be most responsive to whomever provides funding, because they lack any ideological commitments at all.

This selection function creates a demand-effect in a world of scarcity, such that potential recipients of funding rationally try to appear attractive in these ways to potential funders. This dynamic becomes especially strong in a world of iterative interactions, in which a decision maker can signal its behavior in the first round of funding to increase the odds of receiving more in subsequent rounds.

The identification function arises because a funder typically gets special access to the decision maker, which gives the funder an increased likelihood of biasing the outcomes. Beyond merely getting a hearing for requests and information in a noisy world, the funder seeks to build a more substantial relationship, and even an identification, between its interests and that of the decision maker. The decision maker begins to internalize the values and preferences of funder, becoming part of a common team. When the decision maker begins to satisfy the funder for non instrumental reasons, a more profound conversion has been achieved (Marks, 2013; Silverstein and Williams, 2013).

As a regulatory solution to institutional corruption, blinding seeks to preserve the subsidy function while blocking the selection and/or identification functions. To block the selection function, the regulator must substitute the funder's selection with some other mode of selection, whether a randomized selection or an independent-but-intelligent selection. Random selections are the most extreme form of "blinding," like drawing a lottery ball from a hopper without looking. But, random selection often unnecessarily blinds too much information about the relative qualities of the candidates, throwing babies out with the bathwater. Instead, an intelligent chooser can weigh those appropriate factors, while being blinded from the interests of the funder. Hybrid schemes are possible, in which an intelligent chooser screens potential decision makers based on minimal criteria, and then a random selection is made from the screened list.

Usually, the blinding of selection is partial, allowing the funder to retain discretion about whether to give. The funder may also be allowed to specify coarse criteria for the recipients of its funds, a level of discretion that is appropriate to reflect bona fide preferences, without unduly biasing outcomes. These design decisions will often depend on the regulator's normative conception of the institution, and sometimes the necessity of maintaining proper economic incentives to maintain the subsidy function.

To block the identification function, blinding would prevent the decision maker from knowing the source of funding. If such a blind is robust, it thus prevents the decision maker from preferentially affiliating with the funder. To be sure: a blind is not a ban on certain forms of interaction, but rather only a filter on certain information. The blinding of identification is partial. The decision maker may still receive information and requests from the funder, and perhaps even build an affiliation, relationship, and ultimately an identity with the funder. However, these interactions are not with the funder as funder, since that predicate fact is unknown to the decision maker. In most institutions, we must tolerate lobbying along with friendships and other personal affinities, as long as these are bona fide rather than purchased.

When paired with the causal model of institutional corruption (see Figure 1), a provocative point can here be made. If identification of the funder as funder does actually change the decision maker's behavior, compared to his behavior when blinded to the identity of the funder, then unblinded interactions are likely illegal already. A violation of the federal gratuity statute (18 USC § 201(c)) is a lesser crime than bribery, because it does not require the corrupt state of mind—the intentional quid pro quo. The gratuity crime proscribes the giving of anything of value "because of" any official act by any public official, or the giving of anything of value "because of" testimony by a witness in court. The gratuity conception is causal, not intentional, merely requiring a "link" between the gift and official action (United States v. Sun-Diamond Growers of California, 1999). It is one thing if a Congressman meets with a constituent. It is another if he meets with a constituent "because of" knowledge that the constituent is a major donor. The gratuity crime recognizes this sense in which the institution can be corrupted, even while the individual official does not have a corrupt intent. Of course, the statute is not enforced in this way, perhaps because of a conception that the First Amendment prohibits such enforcement (Lowenstein, 2004).

BLINDING APPLIED TO LITIGATION, SCIENCE, AND POLITICS

Our three examples are useful to illustrate these blinding dynamics. As it happens, blinding is likely to work better in some contexts than others, and these examples highlight some of the key considerations for its applicability.

The clearest example is likely in the domain of litigation expert witnesses, since the interactions are already highly structured by a defined set of rules and practices. To disaggregate the functions of funding an expert, from the selection and identification of the expert, some sort of intermediary would be required, whether a company, the court, or a nonprofit organization (Robertson, 2010; Chapter 13, in this volume). Once selected by the intermediary, the expert would then render an opinion on the case, without knowing which side requested the opinion, eliminating identification. The expert could receive information from one or both sides, without knowing whether it was the plaintiff or the defendant requesting that exam. The litigant would pay for the expert's opinion in advance, and the intermediary would transfer the funds to the expert, regardless of whether the opinion is favorable to the litigant. Similar solutions have been proposed to combat expert bias in the criminal context (Risinger et al., 2002; Chapters 10 and 13, in this volume).

Rational litigants could have self-interested reasons for using blinding, if it makes the ultimate expert testimony more persuasive to a fact-finder than a hired-gun expert witness, whose testimony is infected by known sources of bias. Indeed, laboratory experiments with mock jurors confirm that hypothesis: a blinded expert doubles the odds of winning, for whichever side chooses to use a blinded expert rather than a hired gun (Robertson and Yokum, 2012; Chapter 13, in this volume). This finding demonstrates one way that blinding can come about through incentives internal to the institution, here building on the adversarial norms and incentives that are built into American litigation.

The blinding of litigation experts will only be as robust as its intermediary is independent, just as Franklin's blindfolds would have failed if they were not opaque. If the intermediary selects from a skewed pool of experts, or fails to adequately blind the information provided to those experts, then the blinding procedure may descend to a sham.

Similarly, I have argued for blinding as a solution to the institutional corruption of biomedical science (Chapters 7 and 14, in this volume). A drug maker or device- maker would provide the funds to test the safety and efficacy of its own products to an intermediary, perhaps the National Institutes of Health. The drug maker could specify a particular hypothesis that it wants tested, and perhaps objective criteria for the researchers and research design, but would not be allowed to hand-pick the researchers, to favor those most likely to produce positive results for the product being tested. Instead, the intermediary would select the researchers, based on scientific merit. They would work independently, knowing that their future research funding does not depend on them producing results favorable to industry. With Marc Rodwin, I develop this concept further in Chapter 7, in this volume.

For the institutional corruption of Congress, the blinding story is not so optimistic. Ian Ayres and Jeremy Bulow have suggested a blinding solution, which inverts the normal regulatory impetus for disclosure of campaign finances, and instead borrows the anonymity norm of the voting booth (Ayres, 2001; Ayres and Bulow, 1998). Bertram Levine and Michael Johnston are now the champions for this provocative idea (Chapter 18, in this volume). Under the Ayres–Bulow proposal, donors would still be able to select the recipients or beneficiaries of campaign money (as the First Amendment arguably requires), but the recipient would be blinded from knowing the source of the largesse (identification). Thus, a selection bias will remain, compared to a world in which all individuals somehow had equal abilities to spend political money to influence their fellow citizens' votes. (Whether this is in fact a "bias" depends on a substantive theory of political justice, which could specify a plausible counterfactual institution, in which all individuals had such equalized capacities for persuasion.)

The blinding solution is complicated by the First Amendment in another way, since it would presumably not allow a regulator to prohibit a funder from disclosing the fact of his donation to the decision maker. Such speech would be protected, as a value internal to the institution of American politics. Instead of banning that speech directly, Ayres and Bulow (1998) suggest a "cheap talk" regime in which individuals would be free to claim they made such donations, but would be unable to prove such claims. An intermediary institution would disburse the money to the candidate at random intervals, eliminating timing as a meaningful signal of identity. Nonetheless, some individuals (for example, the richer people) will be able to make such claims that they have given lavishly more plausibly than other individuals can (Karlan, 2003). Thus, the identification function would seem to be weakly blinded.

CONCLUSION

This chapter has shown how blinding works by disaggregating different functions, so that one function does not bias another function. Whether it is Benjamin Franklin's literal use of blindfolds, or the rules of evidence in court, or perhaps as a solution to institutional corruption, blinding can be a feasible solution, one that works even when proscriptions, professionalism, or disclosure fail.

References

American Medical Association, n.d. Code of Medical Ethics. Retrieved from: http://www.ama-assn.org/ama/pub/physician-resources/medical-ethics/code-medical-ethics.page?.

Ayres, I., 2001. Should campaign donors be identified? Regulation 24, 12–17.

Ayres, I., Bulow, J., 1998. The donation booth: mandating donor anonymity to disrupt the market for political influence. Stanford Law Review, 1259, 837–891.

Cain, D.M., Loewenstein, G., Moore, D.A., 2011. When sunlight fails to disinfect: understanding the perverse effects of disclosing conflicts of interest. Journal of Consumer Research 37, 836–857.

Carrington, P.D., 1992. One law: the role of legal education in the opening of the legal profession since 1776. Florida Law Review 44, 501.

Cecil, J.S., Willging, T.E., 1993. Court-Appointed Experts: Defining the Role of Experts Appointed under Federal Rule of Evidence 706. Federal Judicial Center, Washington, DC.

Citizens United v. Federal Election Commission. 2010. (p. 310): (U.S. Supreme Court).

Dana, J., Loewenstein, G., 2003. A social science perspective on gifts to physicians from industry. Journal of the American Medical Association 290, 252–255.

Fiedler, S., 2012. Bad apples and dirty barrels: outliers and systematic institutional failures. Lab Dispatches, Combined 1 & 2, 144.

Fishkin, J.S., Luskin, R.C., Jowell, R., 2000. Deliberative polling and public consultation. Parliamentary Affairs 53, 657–666.

Hamilton, A., Madison, J., Jay, J., 2003. In: Ball, T. (Ed.), The Federalist. New American Library, New York, NY.

Hand, L., 1901. Historical and practical considerations regarding expert testimony. Harvard Law Review 12, 40–58.

Hans, V.P., 2007. Judges, juries, and scientific evidence. Journal of Law and Policy 16, 19.

Harsanyi, J.C., 1955. Cardinal welfare, individualistic ethics, and interpersonal comparisons of utility. Journal of Political Economy 63, 316.

Hume, D., 1985. In: Mossner, E. (Ed.), A Treatise of Human Nature. Penguin, New York, NY.

Kaptchuk, T.J., 1998. Intentional ignorance: a history of blind assessment and placebo controls in medicine. Bulletin of the History of Medicine 72, 389–433.

Karlan, P.S., 2003. Elections and change under voting with dollars. California Law Review 91, 705–722.

Kesselheim, A.S., Robertson, C.T., Myers, J.A., Rose, S.L., Gillet, V., Ross, K.M., et al., 2012. A randomized study of how physicians interpret research funding disclosures. New England Journal of Medicine 367, 1119–1127.

Korn, D., Ehringhaus, S., 2007. In: The Scientific Basis of Influence and Reciprocity: A Symposium. Association of American Medical Colleges, Washington, DC.

Kouchaki, M., 2013. Professionalism and moral behavior: does a professional self-conception make one more unethical? In: Edmond J. Safra Working Papers. Retrieved from: http://papers.ssrn.com/sol3/papers.cfm?abstract_id=2243811.

Lessig, L., 2011. Republic, Lost: How Money Corrupts Congress—and a Plan to Stop it. Twelve.

Levmore, S., 1996. The anonymity tool. University of Pennsylvania Law Review 144, 2191–2236.

Light, D.W., 2013. Strengthening the theory of institutional corruptions: broadening, clarifying, and measuring. In: Edmond J. Safra Working Papers. Retrieved from: http://papers.ssrn.com/sol3/papers.cfm?abstract_id=2236391.

Lowenstein, D.H., 2004. When is a campaign contribution a bribe? In: Heffernan, W.C., Kleinig, J. (Eds.), Private and Public Corruption. Rowman & Littlefield Publishers, Inc., Lanham, MD, pp. 127–171.

Lundh, A., Sismondo, S., Lexchin, J., Busuioc, O.A., Bero, L., 2012. Industry sponsorship and research outcome. Cochrane Database of Systematic Reviews 12.

Marks, J.H., 2013. The Perils of Public-Private Partnerships. Edmond J. Safra Research Lab Blog: Edmond J. Safra Center for Ethics.

Nisbett, R.E., Wilson, T.D., 1977. Telling more than we can know—verbal reports on mental processes. Psychological Review 84, 231–259.

Pronin, E., Lin, D.Y., Ross, L., 2002. The bias blind spot: perceptions of bias in self versus others. Personality and Social Psychology Bulletin 28, 369–381.

Psaty, B.M., Prentice, R.L., 2010. Minimizing bias in randomized trials: the importance of blinding. Journal of the American Medical Association 304, 793–794.

Rawls, J., 1971. A Theory of Justice. Belknap Press of Harvard University Press, Cambridge, MA.

Risinger, D.M., Saks, M.J., Thompson, W.C., Rosenthal, R., 2002. The Daubert/Kumho implications of observer effects in forensic science: hidden problems of expectation and suggestion. California Law Review 1–56.

Robertson, C., 2010. Blind expertise. New York University Law Review 85, 174–257.

Robertson, C., 2011. Biased advice. Emory Law Journal 60, 653.

Robertson, C., Rose, S., Kesselheim, A.S., 2012. Effect of financial relationships on the behaviors of health care professionals: a review of the evidence. The Journal of Law, Medicine and Ethics 40, 452–466.

Robertson, C., Yokum, D.V., 2012. The effect of blinded experts on juror verdicts. Journal of Empirical Legal Studies 9, 765–794.

Rodwin, M.A., 2012. Conflicts of interest, institutional corruption, and pharma: an agenda for reform. Journal of Law Medicine and Ethics 40, 511–522.

Rosenthal, R., 1978. How often are our numbers wrong? American Psychologist 33, 1005–1008.

Rothman, K.J., 1993. Conflict-of-interest—the new McCarthyism in science. Journal of the American Medical Association 269, 2782–2784.

Sah, S., Loewenstein, G., 2015. Conflicted advice and second opinions: benefits, but unintended consequences. Organizational Behavior and Human Decision Processes 130, 89–107.

Sah, S., Loewenstein, G., Cain, D.M., 2013. The burden of disclosure: increased compliance with distrusted advice. Journal of Personality and Social Psychology 104 (2), 289–304.

Schulz, K.F., Grimes, D.A., 2002. Blinding in randomised trials: hiding who got what. The Lancet 359, 696–700.

Silverstein, K., Williams, B., 2013. Membership Has Its Privileges: Donor Perks and the Atlantic Council. Edmond J. Safra Research Lab Blog. Retrieved from: http://ethics.harvard.edu/blog/membership-has-its-privileges.

Smith, A., 1984. The Theory of Moral Sentiments. Liberty Fund, Indianapolis.

Thompson, D.F., 1995. Ethics in Congress: From Individual to Institutional Corruption. Brookings Institution, Washington, DC.

United States v Sun-Diamond Growers of California. 1999. U.S. (p. 398): (U.S. Supreme Court).

Vermeule, A., 2001. Veil of ignorance rules in constitutional law. Yale Law Journal, 111, 399–433.

Wilson, T.D., Brekke, N., 1994. Mental contamination and mental correction: unwanted influences on judgments and evaluations. Psychological Bulletin 116, 117.

Wood, L., Egger, M., Gluud, L.L., Schulz, K.F., Jüni, P., Altman, D.G., et al., 2008. Empirical evidence of bias in treatment effect estimates in controlled trials with different interventions and outcomes: meta-epidemiological study. British Medical Journal 336, 601–605.

SECTION III

BIOMEDICAL SCIENCE

Rigor in Biomedical Science

Gregory Curfman

Harvard Health Publications, Harvard Medical School, Boston, MA, USA

Vertebral fractures are the most common complication of osteoporosis. Of the estimated 1.5 million osteoporotic fractures that occur each year in the United States, about 700,000 are vertebral fractures, predominantly of the lumbar and thoracic spine (Ensrud and Schousboe, 2011). In some cases, they are asymptomatic and revealed only with imaging procedures of the spine, but in other cases they can be quite painful and debilitating. It is not surprising, therefore, that when a new treatment called vertebroplasty was developed, its utilization in patients with painful vertebral fractures took off like a rocket. The procedure, which takes only about an hour, involves injecting acrylic bone cement, polymethylmethacrylate, into the fractured vertebra, in order to stabilize it.

In a randomized clinical trial in patients with painful vertebral fractures, vertebroplasty and conservative therapy were compared in an open-label manner (with no sham control) (Klazen et al., 2010). The investigators observed that pain relief with vertebroplasty was immediate and sustained for a year. However, in striking contrast to the open-label trial, in two randomized, double-blind trials with sham controls, evidence of efficacy disappeared (Buchbinder et al., 2009; Kallmes et al., 2009). The sham control, which was designed to blind the patients to their treatment assignments, involved placement of the injection stylet into the vertebra, tapping on the stylet, and opening a bottle of polymethylmethacrylate in the procedure room to allow the distinctive smell of the cement to permeate the room.

Given the distinctly positive result in the open-label setting but the negative results in two independent studies performed in blinded settings, we are left to conclude that the apparent benefit of vertebroplasty in patients with painful vertebral fractures is attributable largely, if not exclusively, to a placebo effect. Double-blind trials that included carefully implemented sham control procedures were essential to a rigorous assessment of this commonly performed procedure, which raises serious questions about its efficacy.

Still, even now, Medicare covers as many as 100,000 vertebroplasties a year, with an associated cost of $1 billion (Redberg, 2011).

Another example of the importance of blinding to the clinical trial process is the recent series of three trials of the SYMPLICITY radiofrequency renal denervation device in the management of resistant hypertension. Hypertension not adequately controlled even with multiple antihypertensive medications poses risks of cardiovascular, cerebrovascular, and renal disease, all of which may be life-threatening. Thus, the development of a radiofrequency renal denervation device, which offered promise in the management of resistant hypertension, was met with much optimism. In the wake of an encouraging uncontrolled study, a controlled open-label trial compared radiofrequency denervation with standard medical therapy (SYMPLICITY HTN-2) and found significant reductions in systolic and diastolic pressures in the active treatment group, but not in the control group (Esler et al., 2010). However, 4 years later, SYMPLICITY HTN-3 was published: a randomized, double-blind, sham-controlled trial (Bhatt et al., 2014). It showed no significant difference in blood pressure measurements between the two randomized groups. Thus, in a study in which both the patients and investigators were blinded to treatment assignment, and in which a sham control was employed, evidence of efficacy of the denervation device from earlier nonblinded studies disappeared. In a third open-label, randomized trial of renal denervation therapy (DENERHTN), the assessors (but not the investigators or patients) were blinded to treatment group (Azizi et al., 2015). The primary endpoint, reduction in ambulatory blood pressure, was slightly greater in the denervation group than in the medically treated controls, but the pretreatment blood pressure was higher in the denervation group than in the controls, and the secondary endpoints, office and home blood pressure, were not different between the two groups. This study, in which the assessors were blinded, largely confirms the findings of SYMPLICITY HTN-3, in which all parties were blinded.

The strikingly different results in blinded and nonblinded trials of renal denervation are remarkably similar to the clinical trial experience with vertebroplasty. These examples demonstrate two fundamental points: Blinding is essential to the rigorous conduct of clinical trials; and in trials of procedures employing medical devices, a sham control may be crucial, because the application of a medical device may be associated with a significant placebo effect. Redberg (2014) has made the important point that percutaneous coronary intervention (PCI), a commonly performed procedure in patients with coronary artery disease, has never been subjected to a blinded, sham-controlled clinical trial. This raises the provocative, and yet unanswered, question of whether the relief of cardiovascular symptoms observed in open-label trials would be confirmed if PCI were subjected to a blinded, sham-controlled trial.

The impact of blinded, as compared with nonblinded, assessment of the same binary outcome variables in clinical trials was systematically investigated by Hróbjartsson and collaborators (Hróbjartsson et al., 2012). They found that on average, nonblinded assessors of binary outcomes generated substantially biased effect estimates in randomized clinical trials, exaggerating odds ratios by 36%. These data further underscore the importance of blinded assessment in clinical trials, and this may have special significance for subjective endpoints, such as pain relief with vertebroplasty or PCI.

Tools are available to assess the degree of success (or failure) of blinding procedures in clinical trials. One strategy is to ask the blinded participants to guess their treatment assignment, and then test statistically whether the guesses diverge from the expected result if blinding were perfect (sometimes referred to as a "blinding index") (Bang et al., 2004; James et al., 1996; University of North Carolina School of Medicine, n.d.). However, merely asking patients or assessors such a question may only provide insight into patients' perceptions without demonstrating that the results of the study were actually biased. A better choice, therefore, may be to employ strategies to minimize blinding failures, such as testing patients for use of off-protocol therapies or the use of active placebos and standard-of-care treatments as comparators with side-effect profiles similar to the investigational treatments (Bang et al., 2004).

Yet techniques to assess the success of blinding or to minimize blinding failures are not often reported in clinical trials. It is noteworthy that in SYMPLICITY HTN-3, the trial of renal denervation therapy in resistant hypertension discussed previously, the blinding assessment tool of James et al. (1996) was used to confirm the blinding procedures used in the trial, and this information was provided in a supplementary appendix to the main article. But this does not always happen. In a review of randomized clinical trials published in general medical and psychiatric journals, one study reported that only 8% provided evidence as to the success of the blinding procedure (Fergusson et al., 2004). This low rate is an indication that journal editors and reviewers need to do a better job of ensuring that the success or failure of blinding procedures was assessed in the study and also reported in the manuscript.

In Chapters 3 through 9 of this volume, the need for careful attention to blinding in randomized clinical trials is examined in detail and from multiple perspectives. Although important biomedical information can be obtained from observational studies, the randomized clinical trial will remain the gold standard for the evaluation of new drugs and medical devices. The examples discussed herein and by the authors of Chapters 3 through 9 underscore the importance of blinding in clinical trials in order to achieve the highest standard of rigor in biomedical research. The chapters will also address, among other topics, the limits of blinding, blinding failures, ethical issues in blinding, nocebos, and blinding of peer review in biomedical journals.

Caregivers today aim to deliver health care that is based on evidence, and the highest quality evidence is a prerequisite to guide clinical decision-making and achieve optimal health outcomes for our patients. Blinded clinical trials are, and will remain, central to this mission.

References

Azizi, M., Sapoval, M., Gosse, P., Monge, M., Bobrie, G., Delsart, P., Midulla, M., Mounier-Véhier, C., Courand, P.-Y., Lantelme, P., Denolle, T., Dourmap-Collas, C., Trillaud, H., Pereira, H., Plouin, P.-F., Chatellier, G., Renal Denervation Hypertension (DENERHTN) investigators, 2015. Optimum and stepped care standardised antihypertensive treatment with or without renal denervation for resistant hypertension (DENERHTN): a multicentre, open-label, randomised controlled trial. Lancet 388 (9981), 1957–1965. http://dx.doi.org/10.1016/S0140-6736(14)61942-5. Epub 2015 January 26.

Bang, H., Ni, L., Davis, C.E., 2004. Assessment of blinding in clinical trials. Controlled Clinical Trials 25, 143–146.

Bhatt, D.L., Kandzari, D.E., O'Neill, W.W., D'Agostino, R., Flack, J.M., Katzen, B.T., Leon, M.B., Liu, M., Mauri, L., Negoita, M., Cohen, S.A., Oparil, S., Rocha-Singh, K., Townsend, R.R., Bakris, G.L., 2014. A controlled trial of renal denervation for resistant hypertension. New England Journal of Medicine 370, 1393–1401.

Buchbinder, R., Osborne, R.H., Ebeling, P.R., Wark, J.D., Mitchell, P., Wriedt, C., Graves, S.D., Staple, M.P., Murphy, B., 2009. A randomized trial of vertebroplasty for painful osteoporotic vertebral fractures. New England Journal of Medicine 361, 557–568.

Ensrud, K.E., Schousboe, J.T., 2011. Clinical practice: vertebral fractures. New England Journal of Medicine 364, 1634–1642.

Esler, M.D., Krum, H., Sobotka, P.A., Schlaich, M.P., Schmieder, R.E., Bohm, M., 2010. Renal sympathetic denervation in patients with treatment-resistant hypertension (the SYMPLICITY HTN-2 Trial): a randomised controlled trial. Lancet 376, 1903–1909.

Fergusson, D., Glass, K.C., Waring, D., Shapiro, S., 2004. Turning a blind eye: the success of blinding reported in a random sample of randomised, placebo controlled trials. British Medical Journal 328 (7437), 432.

Hróbjartsson, A., Thomsen, A.S., Emanuelsson, F., Tendal, B., Hilden, J., Boutron, I., Ravaud, P., Brorson, S., 2012. Observer bias in randomized clinical trials with binary outcomes: systematic review of trials with both blinded and non-blinded assessors. British Medical Journal 344, e1119. http://dx.doi.org/10.1136/bmj.e1119.

James, K.E., Bloch, D.A., Lee, K.K., Kraemer, H.C., Fuller, R.K., 1996. An index for assessing blindness in a multi-centre clinical trial: disulfiram for alcohol cessation—a VA cooperative study. Statistics in Medicine 15 (13), 1421–1434.

Kallmes, D.F., Comstock, B.A., Heagerty, P.J., 2009. A randomized trial of vertebroplasty for osteoporotic spinal fractures. New England Journal of Medicine 361, 569–579.

Klazen, C.A., Lohle, P.N., de Vries, J., Jansen, F.H., Tielbeek, A.V., Blonk, M.C., Venmans, A., van Rooij, W.J., Schoemaker, M.C., Juttmann, J.R., Lo, T.H., Verhaar, H.J., van der Graaf, Y., van Everdingen, K.J., Muller, A.F., Elgersma, O.E., Halkema, D.R., Fransen, H., Janssens, X., Buskens, E., Mali, W.P.Th. M., 2010. Vertebroplasty versus conservative treatment in acute osteoporotic vertebral compression fractures (Vertos II): an open-label randomised trial. Lancet 376, 1085–1092. http://dx.doi.org/10.1016/S0140-6736(10)60954-3.

Redberg, R.F., May 25, 2011. Squandering Medicare's money. The New York Times. Retrieved from: http://www.nytimes.com/2011/05/26/opinion/26redberg.html.

Redberg, R.F., 2014. Sham controls in medical device trials. New England Journal of Medicine 371, 892–893.

University of North Carolina School of Medicine, n.d. BlindingIndex.org: A Web-based Repository of Blinding Data from Controlled Trials. Retrieved from: http://www.BlindingIndex.org.

CHAPTER

3

From Trials to Trials: Blinding, Medicine, and Honest Adjudication

Scott H. Podolsky[1], David S. Jones[1,2], Ted J. Kaptchuk[3]

[1]Department of Global Health and Social Medicine, Harvard Medical School, Boston, MA, USA; [2]Department of the History of Science, Harvard University, Cambridge, MA, USA; [3]Beth Israel Deaconess Medical Center, Harvard Medical School, Boston, MA, USA

OUTLINE

> The whole history of therapeutics, especially that having to do with the action of drugs on subjective symptoms, demonstrates that the verdict of one study is frequently reversed by another unless one takes measures to rule out the psychic effect of a medication on the patient and the unconscious bias of the doctor. The double-blind insures this. (***Gold, 1954, p. 724***)

INTRODUCTION

Medicine has long concerned itself with evaluative judgments, especially regarding therapeutic efficacy. Indeed, the very term "trial" is endemic within its literature. In the first volume of the *New England Journal of Medicine*, from 1812, in an article on the treatment of burns, we find Jacob Bigelow remarking:

> Different and opposite modes of treatment have been adopted, whose apparent success or failure at different times has occasioned considerable disputes respecting their comparative efficacy. After a variety of trials has been made, and a multiplicity of cases detailed, the practice still remains undecided; and methods of treatment diametrically opposite at the present day, enlist nearly an equal number of advocates. (***Bigelow, 1812, pp. 52–53***)

http://dx.doi.org/10.1016/B978-0-12-802460-7.00003-6

Blinding, in medicine, has represented a methodological attempt to eliminate *bias* in such evaluations. This bias can interfere with the response of subjects (usually patients) to such interventions, through their knowledge of and expectations around receiving an intervention—something that has variably been called suggestion or the placebo response (Kaptchuk, 1998a). And it can influence the evaluative judgments of the researchers themselves, through what has been considered subconscious or conscious enthusiasm. The origins of blinding in medicine have important applicability as we consider how blinding is applied to other disciplines. Patients have seemingly needed to be blinded to protect them from themselves and from their hopes and enthusiasms that inspire false reports of therapeutic efficacy. Medical researchers, like expert witnesses or judges in the courtroom, likewise have interests and perspectives that may bias them; clinical investigators have again tried to root this out through blinding. Both patient and researcher blinding stem from similarly skeptical sources and provide information regarding the concern for obtaining unbiased evaluations in medicine. Ultimately, as will be seen, medical writers have long appreciated the role of bias in other domains, including (and especially) in the courtroom.

BLINDING OF PATIENTS

The use of blinding in medicine perhaps has its earliest recorded origins and best-known examples with respect to the blinding of patients (or research subjects), and thus we discuss it first. Such blinding and the related use of sham treatments have their origins in skepticism and outright distrust, and especially in the attempt to assess the efficacy of what were perceived as irregular practices. To our knowledge, their origins date back at least to what were termed the "trick trials" of the late sixteenth century, in the context of well-publicized religious battles between believers and doubters in exorcism within the Catholic (and to a lesser extent the Protestant) world. These heated disputes led to the adoption of bogus holy water and sham relics of the holy cross being used in exorcism trials to determine whether overenthusiasm, autosuggestion, or deceit—as opposed to the devil—was the cause of the behavior of those afflicted (Kaptchuk et al., 2009, pp. 1234–1235).[1] These trials and the impact of autosuggestion became well known to such Renaissance humanists as Michel de Montaigne.

Blinding rose to prominence in the late eighteenth century in response to the challenge posed by mesmerism, the use of "animal magnetism" to heal patients. Mesmerism was sweeping across France, with patients swooning, fainting, and experiencing dramatic sensations during the potentially therapeutic mesmeric process (Darnton, 1968; Kaptchuk, 1998b, pp. 393–398). In response, avid readers of Montaigne such as Benjamin Franklin and Antoine Lavoisier (who undoubtedly knew of the earlier exorcism trials) undertook what we may consider a placebo-controlled trial in 1789 in an attempt to evaluate the merits of (and ultimately debunk) Mesmer's

[1] Note that both sides performed exorcism with controls. The most famous example apparently debunked the role of the devil, but there were also interventions that seemed to prove that the devil was the cause of the behavior being evaluated.

intervention.[2] Patients were exposed to sham mesmerism, or were supposedly mesmerized without knowing it. Each approach (including the literal "blinding" of some patients through the use of blindfolds) convinced Franklin, Lavoisier, and the Royal Commission with which they were associated that any effect of mesmerism derived from the belief that mesmerism was occurring and from the "imagination" of the subjects (Franklin et al., 1785).[3]

By the nineteenth century, homeopathy, predicated on treatment with infinitesimal doses of remedies that would otherwise cause symptoms in unaffected patients, had risen to prominence in both Europe and the United States (Haller, 2005; Kaufman, 1988). In this context, mistrust and the need for patient blinding went hand in hand in the struggle between orthodox medicine and homeopathy. As Oliver Wendell Holmes stated in 1842, in his "Homoeopathy and its Kindred Delusions":

> Of course a large number of apparent cures were due solely to nature; which is true under every form of treatment, orthodox or empirical. Of course many persons experienced at least temporary relief from the strong impression made upon their minds by this novel and marvelous method of treatment. (***Holmes, 1842, p. 37***)

Implicitly suggesting a test of such efficacy, he continued:

> Suppose, then, a physician who has a 100 patients prescribes to each of them pills made of some entirely inert substance, as starch, for instance. Ninety of them get well, or if he chooses to use such language, he cures ninety of them. ... Suppose that instead of pills of starch he employs microscopic sugar-plums, with the 5 million billion trillionth part of a suspicion of aconite or pulsatilla, and then publishes his successful cases, ... does that make the impression a less erroneous one? (***Holmes, 1842, pp. 75–76***)

Over a decade earlier, in St. Petersburg, a homeopathic physician had in fact compared hospital wards treated with either homeopathic or conventional remedies against each other and against a control ward treated with "white breadcrumbs or cocoa, lactose powder or salep infusions," finding that patients on the control ward recovered better than those on either of the treatment wards (Dean, 2006, pp. 375–376). And several years later in France (while Holmes was a medical student in Paris, one might note), Armond Trousseau further tested the effects of homeopathic remedies through the sham use of bread pills, concluding that homeopathy was not "more active than the most inert substances" (Trousseau and Gourard, 1834, p. 241; Kaptchuk, 1998b, pp. 399–402).[4]

The battle between orthodox physicians and homeopaths sometimes focused on individual "provings" designed to demonstrate what symptoms a particular homeopathic remedy caused in a healthy person. Then, according to the homeopathic law of *similia similibus curantur* ("like

[2] We use the term "placebo-controlled" anachronistically yet intentionally here. While the term "placebo" has been used in its therapeutic sense since at least the eighteenth century, the earliest prominent use of the term in a trial methodological sense appears to date back only to the 1930s (Gold et al., 1937; Shapiro and Shapiro, 1997, pp. 137–141). We otherwise use the term "sham" in this paper to refer to a priori ineffectual interventions or remedies used in the control arm of a therapeutic trial and devised so as to otherwise mimic the interventions or remedies used in the active arm of the trial.

[3] On the similar disproof of the healing effect of "Perkins tractors" (metal rods), through the use of sham tractors, see Haygarth (1801) and Kaptchuk (1998b, pp. 399–400).

[4] Of note, Trousseau did not have a homeopathic treatment arm in his trial.

cures like"), the same remedy could be used (in a lower dosage) to treat a person with similar symptoms. Blinded provings were used by homeopaths to validate their system, while orthodox physicians used them to attempt to debunk the theory altogether. For example, in Nuremberg in 1835, more than 100 citizens met in a tavern to watch the preparation of homeopathic versus sham (control) remedies, placed in 100 identically appearing vials; a list of the vials' contents was sealed, and the vials were distributed to more than 50 participants to see whether they elicited a subjective response (Stolberg, 2006). When the homeopathic remedies produced the same reactions as did the sham remedies, the homeopaths received quite a blow to their reputation. But when a similar study was repeated in the United States as a cooperative venture between orthodox and homeopathic physicians and sponsored by the Milwaukee Academy of Medicine in 1879–1880, no definite refutation of homeopathy took place (Kaptchuk, 2004; Potter and Storke, 1880).[5]

By the final decades of the nineteenth century and the first decades of the twentieth century, however, orthodox medicine itself was beginning to undergo a therapeutic revolution. Physiology, bacteriology, and an expanding pharmaceutical industry (to say nothing of surgery, itself revolutionized in the latter half of the nineteenth century through first anesthesia, and later antiseptic and then aseptic technique) were transforming the practice of medical therapeutics (Greene et al., 2016; Podolsky, 2006; Rosenberg, 1979; Warner, 1986). But psychologists, psychiatrists, and neurologists had during the same period become ever more attuned to the influence of (and sophisticated in studying) the role of suggestion on subjective outcomes—even using it therapeutically, in the case of hypnotism, whereby mesmerism was essentially sanitized within conventional medicine (Kaptchuk, 1998b, pp. 407–414).

Just as homeopathy had prompted skeptics to submit its regimens to blinded provings, the rapid proliferation of new treatments within conventional medicine also prompted skeptical mainstream researchers to begin blinding patients and administering sham treatments in the evaluation of *conventional* pharmaceutical treatments. As early as 1889, scientists were willing to administer sham testicular extract to a handful of patients (serving in some instances as self-controls over time) in the assessment of Charles-Édouard Brown-Séquard's fortifying regimen, seemingly finding it to be effective (Brown-Séquard, 1889; Kaptchuk, 1998b, pp. 414–416). And as new treatments appeared in the early twentieth century and as trials became larger, skeptics continued to attempt to discern which ones were truly active, with a smattering of researchers beginning to incorporate sham treatments into their trials of concurrently treated and untreated patients (Kaptchuk, 1998b, pp. 419–422).[6]

Even pharmaceutical-company-sponsored trials—most notably, the famous assessment of sanocrysin (itself made from gold) for the treatment of tuberculosis in the 1920s—could entail sham treatment arms. In this case, the justification for the sham by Parke–Davis and its academic collaborators went beyond the subjective response of patients. Concerned that the very receipt of medicine could lead to a "psychic influence" that could impact healing, the investigators administered a sham treatment (intravenously administered distilled water) to the control group, ultimately failing to find sanocrysin any more effective than the sham treatment (Amberson et al., 1931; Gabriel, 2014).

[5] In one component of the admittedly limited trial, it seemed that the active vial could not be detected, while in another component it seemed that it could.

[6] The most extensive appears to have been Adolf Bingel's use of a sham control arm in his study of more than 900 patients being treated with antitoxin for diphtheria (Kaptchuk, 1998b, pp. 420–421; Tröhler, 2011).

From the 1930s to the 1950s, though, as the new discipline of clinical pharmacology took shape under the leadership of such investigators as Cornell's Harry Gold and Harvard's Henry Beecher, it was the ever-increasing appreciation of the placebo effect in subjective outcomes that informed declarations regarding the necessity of sham treatment arms in controlled trials. Angina—the sensation of intense chest pain ascribable to blockages of the coronary arteries (as understood by the 1930s)—became a test case. Harry Gold used lactose tablets in his assessment of the impact of the vasodilating xanthines in the 1930s (Gold et al., 1937; Shapiro and Shapiro, 1997, pp. 141–145). Beecher took things a bit further. Having studied and famously written about the "powerful placebo" in the 1950s, Beecher insisted on the need for sham treatment groups in surgical interventions, including (and especially for) cardiac surgical interventions for angina (Beecher, 1955, 1961; Podolsky, 2007). No open-heart surgeon took him up on his offer at the time; but today, as attention to the impact of the placebo effect continues to intensify, sham treatment arms are not only entailed in most pharmaceutical clinical trials (having been encoded in Food and Drug Administration regulations since 1970), but have increasingly crept into surgical evaluations as well, when deemed appropriate (Buchbinder et al., 2009; Edwards, 1970; Freeman et al., 1999; Moseley et al., 2002; Redberg, 2014).

From demoniac possession to the placebo effect, we have thus moved the image of—and defense against—patient suggestibility to the very center of orthodox medicine. Placebo studies have become a dramatically expanding field of study across wide domains of medicine, as we attempt to dissect out the multiple components—and the mechanisms, meanings, and morals—of therapeutic interventions (Finniss et al., 2010).

BLINDING OF RESEARCHERS

With respect to *observers* and those conducting clinical trials, the evolution of blinding in medical research has taken a slightly different course. In many ways, the controlled clinical trial was developed as a means to eliminate the role of personal bias—and even judgment itself—in the interpretation of clinical data and the detection of difference in therapeutic evaluation. There is no direct parallel in the legal trial machinery to the controlled clinical trial, no evidence-sifting machine; but the blinding of researchers, whether eliciting, recording, or interpreting data, has obvious legal parallels, whether with respect to the role of counsel in directly influencing subjects, or, as will be seen in the final section, with respect to the general behavior of expert witnesses themselves.[7]

Mistrust and concern about observer bias again entered the medical domain early, as skeptics feared that clinicians, eager to achieve success, could see benefit where none actually existed. This was certainly the case with the evaluation of such unorthodox practices as homeopathy. The Nuremberg and Milwaukee studies noted above entailed efforts—placing active versus sham treatments in identical bottles, with only a neutral person knowledgeable about the contents of each bottle—to make it impossible, in the choice of administering one of two matched remedies (and in the words of the Milwaukee study organizers), "for any

[7] Clinical investigators, when not blinded, can influence outcomes in their behavior toward their patients, in addition to recording outcomes in biased fashion (Schulz and Grimes, 2002).

experimenter to detect in any way the reasons for choosing one number rather than another" (Kaptchuk, 1998b, p. 403; Potter and Storke, 1880, p. 281; Stolberg, 2006).[8]

But in the nineteenth century, observer bias was noted to occur across all scientific disciplines, conventional or unconventional. Most notably, astronomers had described the impact of the "personal equation" in the recording of seemingly objective data. While variability could be ascribed to the differences in the perceptual apparatuses of different observers, as much as preconceived notions, a great deal of effort went into attempts to remove individual subjectivity or variability from such astronomical observations (Canales, 2007; Schaffer, 1988). At the same time, as Lorraine Daston and Peter Galison describe with respect to the production of nineteenth-century atlases of all kinds, practice moved from the permission of subjectivity in the attempt to record idealized truths, and toward "mechanical objectivity" and the recording of unfiltered data (Daston and Gallison, 2007). A moral as well as an epistemological ideal of the neutral recorder thus became established.

Discussions of the "personal equation" suffused the medical literature from the 1850s onward—to a degree largely forgotten in accounts of the history of medical observer blinding—as educators and researchers became increasingly attuned to the impact of observer bias in medical evaluations of all kinds and similarly sought to render observations unbiased (see, e.g., Cotton, 1899). Analogizing from astronomy was often explicit, as when Boston gynecologist Horatio Storer, describing the widely varying rates of spontaneous abortion reported by varying clinicians, surmised:

> Allowance must be made, as in all other researches of the kind, for what in astronomical language would be termed the personal equation of the observers; that is to say, for their general accuracy, their weight as authority, and the purpose, more, especially, for which the observations were made. (***Storer, 1863, p. 19; see also Bacon, 1858***)

Discussions of the personal equation could entail grand and general discussions of the role of a priori theoretical bias in the intake of novel information, as when a *JAMA* editorialist observed:

> The theory of medicine, as of all other sciences, has often been affected by the personal equation—that constant error to which each individual is subject to a greater or lesser degree. Each observer, though he may be able to see facts clearly and even to trace the relation of cause and effect among them to some extent, is liable to error in the interpretation of these facts in proportion to the degree of his fixed personal bias, whether that personal bias be in favor of a widespread belief or merely of a little private theory of his own. (***Anon, 1909, p. 1825***)

But the term "personal equation"—while used heterogeneously in the medical literature[9]—often was used humbly and self-critically to refer to bias in the specific recording of data, especially in the context of therapeutic evaluation. As Philadelphia's James Wilson, favorably evaluating his management of enteric fever (what we would today regard as typhoid fever), concluded in 1883:

> I make this statement with due regard to the personal equation, and with no willingness to permit the observed fact to differ from the actual fact, for I desire any who may make trial of this plan to be more favorably impressed with the results of it than they have been impressed with my account of it. (***Wilson, 1883, p. 101***)

[8] These were thus what would later be termed "double-blind" tests.

[9] Indeed, the "personal equation" of patients—and its impact on their subjective responses to remedies—was likewise noted alongside the personal equation of observers (Knight, 1905; Pemberton, 1925).

These were not isolated concerns. Boston's Vincent Bowditch qualified his own enthusiasm for his treatment of tuberculosis in 1900: "I have endeavored as far as possible to avoid the much dreaded and much quoted 'personal equation' in giving results which have been corroborated by others" (Bowditch, 1900, p. 129; Bowditch, 1894).

For those contemplating broader methodological attempts to differentiate effective from ineffective remedies, the personal equation held critical implications. As the American Medical Association attempted, through its Council on Pharmacy and Chemistry, to inculcate a rational therapeutics in the first decades of the twentieth century, one of its members, Michigan's A.W. Hewlett, noted specifically with respect to therapeutic trials:

> The personal equations of different observers, the tendency to bias, differences in the modes of administration, in the doses employed, and in the cases selected for treatment, all tend to obscure the significance of reported results. In order to obtain trustworthy data, it is necessary that a considerable number of observations on patients should be made under conditions which eliminate personal bias and reduce to a minimum the errors inherent in statistics. ***(Hewlett, 1913, p. 319)***

Hewlett himself, in a Council-sponsored investigation of natural versus synthetic sodium salicylate for the treatment of a number of ailments (e.g., fever, pain, delirium) in 1913, supplied the remedies in coded boxes to 82 investigators (27 of whom sent back reports), keeping them in the dark regarding which remedy each box contained, and ultimately finding the two remedies equivalent (no placebo remedies were administered). Across the Atlantic around the same time, in discussing the utility of vaccine therapy for the treatment of infectious diseases, John Freeman admitted: "If we judge a system of treatment case by case we are obliged to fall back on 'The Clinical Instinct,' that refuge of the puzzled practitioner, to decide between results and chance" (Freeman, 1910, p. 99). The controlled clinical trial was the supposed corrective to such a situation. But in describing his own tendencies in conducting clinical trials and their need for correction via "remaining in ignorance," he reported:

> After the children had been inoculated [for the treatment of whooping-cough] in the way I have described, I constructed statistics from the reports of the parents to see what effect, if any, had been produced by the vaccination. For this purpose the rambling remarks of the parents were reduced to one of five following simple statements: "Much better," "better," "no change," "worse," and "much worse." In doing this I quickly found I could not rely on my own impartiality. For instance, if the mother reported to the effect that the fits of coughing were more severe but not so frequent, I found that this statement tended to appear as 'better' in the case of the vaccinated, and 'worse' in the case of the controls! I adopted the obvious remedy of remaining in ignorance as to whether [the] child was a treated or control case until I had got the result safely classified in my note-book. I am convinced that without these precautions the investigator will usually find merely what he expects to find. ***(Freeman, 1910, p. 99)***

Efforts to reduce the impact of the evaluative personal equation could take many forms in the late nineteenth and early twentieth centuries. Harry Marks has described the advent of large-scale "cooperative studies," in which the input from a multitude of investigators could be used to dilute or balance out the tendencies of individual observers (Holt et al., 1896; Marks, 2006). But we also see, from the 1910s through the 1930s, the scattered uptake of observer blinding, whether in surgical, immunotherapeutic, pharmacological, or anesthetic interventions (see respectively, e.g., Plass, 1916; Von Sholly et al., 1917; Diehl, 1933; Hediger and Gold,

1935). For example, in a 1917 trial of pertussis vaccine for the treatment of whooping cough, in which influenza bacillus was used as the "control" vaccine in alternated patients, the investigators took pains to note:

> In recording the remarks on the charts, the investigators were not biased by a knowledge of the vaccines employed, as they did not know until the study was finished which was which. This secret was safeguarded by the maker of the vaccines. (***Von Sholly et al., 1917, p. 1453***)

We even see observer blinding in the conduct of observational studies, as in the 1897 interpretation of the role of nutritional variables in the development of beriberi by the Dutch investigator Adolphe Vorderman, in which he correlated the incidence of beriberi in prisons with the types of rice being consumed, taking extensive care to avoid the confounding of information being delivered and interpreted (Vandenbroucke, 2013).

As we head in this narrative toward the most iconic case of observer blinding—the British Medical Research Council's (MRC's) 1948 report of the impact of streptomycin on tuberculosis, entailing the randomization of patients and as judged by radiological findings—it is useful to take two quick detours as a gauge of increasing contemporary attention given to the impact of researcher bias on the conduct of clinical trials. First, another component of trial methodology, alternate allocation—the assignment of every other patient (or patients seen every other day, etc.) to a studied remedy—became increasingly advocated from the late 1890s onward as a means of ensuring the fair assessment of clinical interventions through preventing the biased assignment of patients to the study groups (Chalmers et al., 2012). However, by the 1940s, it had become clear to those conducting and analyzing trials that such allocation could be subverted by researchers, who either consciously or subconsciously steered their sicker patients toward or against the intervention (Finland, 1941; Podolsky, 2006, pp. 119–124). The randomization of patients in the MRC streptomycin trial, as Iain Chalmers has demonstrated, thus derived not from sophisticated statistical reasoning borrowed from R.A. Fisher's agricultural experiments, but rather from an attempt to eliminate the allocation bias of (usually) well-meaning researchers (Chalmers, 2005, 2011).

Second, and closer to the point at hand, the 1948 trial did not entail the blinding of patients, but rather the blinding of the radiologists interpreting the chest X-rays (Medical Research Council, 1948). In 1947, a study conducted by the U.S. Veterans Administration (aided by the U.S. Public Health Service) analyzed the interpretation of chest films in tuberculosis, finding not only a remarkable degree of interobserver variation, but also remarkable intraobserver variation on repeated readings of the same film (Birkelo et al., 1947). As an editorialist at the time remarked, continuing to invoke nineteenth-century tropes:

> Error resulting from the 'personal equation' exists in all fields of knowledge. ... There has been a tendency to assume that roentgenology [radiology] is an exact science and that the objectivity of the medium defied error. Complacency has been a consequence of such assumption. (***Anon, 1947, p. 399***).[10]

[10] This would be the last use of the term "personal equation" in this vein to appear in *JAMA*. The term would last be used as such in *Lancet* (by esteemed statistician Major Greenwood) in 1948, and in *NEJM* in 1952, before generally disappearing, it seems, from the medical literature (see Greenwood, 1948; Lewison and Chambers, 1952).

While Austin Bradford Hill and the MRC began planning their streptomycin study before such results became public, the role of the "personal equation" in the interpretation of the chest film in tuberculosis appears to have been intuitively obvious to them, and could only have been further illustrated by the Veterans Administration results.

By 1950, Harry Gold and his colleagues could for the first time officially label studies in which both patients and physicians (or subjects and researchers) were blinded as "double-blind" tests (Greiner et al., 1950; Shapiro and Shapiro, 1997, pp. 151–154).[11] And as Gold summarized at a 1954 Cornell Conference on Therapy, on "How to Evaluate a New Drug":

> The whole history of therapeutics, especially that having to do with the action of drugs on subjective symptoms, demonstrates that the verdict of one study is frequently reversed by another unless one takes measures to rule out the psychic effect of a medication on the patient and the unconscious bias of the doctor. The double-blind insures this. (***Gold, 1954, p. 724***)

Later in the conference, Gold referred to this unconscious bias as "honest subjectivity" (Gold, 1954, p. 725).[12]

BLINDING IN MEDICINE MOVES TO THE COURTROOM

But research evaluations were not the only judgments physicians were rendering; and in a final coda concerning the personal equation, we should note that the American medical profession in particular has long been aware of a situation in which physicians *do* have a conscious, biased interest (including economic) in an outcome: namely, when serving as expert witnesses.

As historian James Mohr has described, by the 1870s, in the context of the increasing use and increasingly challenged testimony of medical expert witnesses, a "crisis" concerning expert witnesses became apparent to both the legal and medical professions (Mohr, 1993, pp. 197–212). As an editorialist in the *Albany Law Journal* complained in 1872, in terms not unfamiliar to twenty-first-century observers: "The calling of experts has now come to be regarded as the signal for a display of forensic pyrotechnics, beneath whose smoke and lurid glare law, common sense, and unalloyed justice are swept away in a whirlwind of muddy metaphysics" (Anon, 1874, p. 122).

Such critiques were not just voiced by the legal profession, as physicians interested in medical jurisprudence rendered similar characterizations, predicated on the bias inherent in an adversarial system in which expert witnesses knew the source of their payment in advance. As Harvard's Frank W. Draper reported to the Boston Society for Medical Improvement in 1880:

> We know well what manner of man we may find in the typical American medical expert of modern times. He has been evolved out of the necessities of advocates and clients; he is the creature of his environment. ... In the first place, it goes without saying that he is partial; his partisanship is deliberate and inevitable. Without

[11] The term "triple-blind" is at times used to discriminate between the administering/recording and the assessing aspects of the study. In a "triple-blind" study, investigators and assessors are separate people, and are both blinded (Schulz et al., 2002).

[12] The term was first enunciated at the conference by Paul Reznikoff.

> this controlling bias, he would be of little use in fulfilling the purposes to which he is employed. … Sympathy, not less than selfish interest and professional pride, leads him to color his statements on the witness-stand according to the needs of his client; the points of evidence which are useful to his side are put prominently forward; other matters are faithfully omitted, misrepresented, or obscured. (***Draper, 1880, p. 443***)

While later physicians would emphasize the degree to which the personal equation—"a disturbing element in the mind of both physician and patient, of a variability defying the power of differential calculus" (Herrick, 1895, p. 444)—rendered the inexact science of medicine prone to multiple interpretations, Draper placed the preponderance of blame in the courtroom on the adversarial system itself:

> I want to emphasize the fact that [the behavior of the medical expert witness] is the legitimate fruit of the conditions under which the modern practice of law is pursued. The physician in the sick-room does not exhibit the disposition here depicted; but place him under the novel and subtle influences of the court-room and he becomes another creature. (***Draper, 1880, p. 444***)

The solution, for Draper, was "the complete removal of the medical witness from the influences and temptations of partiality; he must be lifted far above the plane of bias" (Draper, 1880, p. 445).[13]

Like-minded physicians made repeated attempts in the last decades of the nineteenth century to reform the expert witness system, often calling for commissions of independent, neutral experts assigned and paid for by the state (Mohr, 1993, pp. 197–212).[14] But such attempts were repeatedly rebuffed, as neutrality itself could be considered an unattainable ideal (Irish, 1899). Instead, the adversarial system could itself be portrayed as part of the *solution* to such inherent bias, balancing and rendering evident the personal equations of competing witnesses. Related one physician to the Massachusetts Medico-Legal Society, nearly two decades after Draper's report:

> Physicians are … very prone to form all sorts of theories, and when once formed, they adhere to them with a pertinacity that would even do credit to members of the clerical profession. Hence, when we descend to the practical arena of the court room, these pet theories of ours are sure to come out and stand forth in clashing inconsistency with each other, and the strict honesty of the experts simply emphasizes the contradictions that appear. (***Irish, 1899, p. 300***)

The adversarial expert witness system thus remained entrenched in the American courtroom. Decades later, in books written *for* the medical profession, we find the system defended as the "people's method of settling disputes, a part of democratic self-government," in contrast to the enforced dictates of seemingly neutral, state-determined committees (Curran, 1965, p. 4). Concerns with the role of payment in biasing witnesses were muted, with the prevailing equanimity regarding such potential bias evidenced by the egregiousness of the one condition considered capable of "destroy(ing)" the objectivity

[13] Draper proposed that if possible, both parties should agree on the choice of expert witness. If they could not agree, then the court would designate the witness. Either way, the witness would be paid "out of the treasury of the county." In criminal cases, defendants could hire additional expert witnesses.

[14] Many of these reforms, Mohr relates, were simply designed to ensure that expert medical witnesses were paid.

of the expert witness: "contingent fee contracts," in which payment is predicated on a particular verdict (Curran, 1965, p. 190). Indeed, not only were blinded payments not suggested, but serendipitous blinding was to be corrected, if at all possible: "At times the doctor is actually without knowledge as to who is hiring him to testify in court. ... To avoid any misunderstanding it would be simple for the doctor to ask the lawyer ahead of time who is to be responsible for his time spent in court. This is a good custom and practice" (Liebenson, 1961, pp. 29–30).

By the 1990s, the matter would again be taken up in the pages of the *New England Journal of Medicine*, with the successors to Frank Draper continuing to advocate for neutral (and in this case, unpaid) panels of expert witnesses, echoing larger concerns about conflict of interest that had developed by this time. As Tucson cardiologist Brendan Phibbs reflected on the persisting contradictions of the system: "This adversarial advocacy system is a dinosaur, incredibly expensive and slow and, in terms of determining scientific fact, a farce. One thinks of Kafka" (Phibbs, 1997, p. 1234). But leading medical expert witnesses such as Johns Hopkins' Fred Berlin continued to defend the prevailing adversarial system as "affording all the opportunity to argue their case in court effectively with an expert witness of their own choosing" (Berlin, 1998, p. 1233). Such a system persists in our country to this day, to the point where we find not calls for neutral witnesses, but rather books telling physicians how to become the "dangerous expert witness" who "puts fear into opposing counsel ... [and knows] how to defeat opposing counsel's tactics and [is] capable of turning the tables on opposing counsel" (Babitsky and Mangraviti, 2005, p. 1).[15]

In all of this debate, it is surprising that as the medical profession considered blinding as a means of countering the "personal equation" and ensuring objectivity in clinical research, no one explicitly invoked such a parallel for the courtroom. Objectivity, from the nineteenth century onward, has become a defining feature of orthodox medical self-identification (see, e.g., Warner, 1991). In the comparative study of two remedies offered by two different companies, we would scarcely ask for unblinded researchers funded by each company to study their remedies and clash over the results, but that is what we have permitted in the courtroom.[16] It is perhaps time to consider the blinding of expert witnesses themselves, as we continue to strive to offset the impact of the "personal equation."

[15] "Dangerous witnesses are the most sought-after of all expert witnesses. The mere disclosure of a dangerous expert to the opposing side can frequently increase the settlement value of a case" (Babitsky and Mangraviti, 2005, p. 1).

[16] It is, of course, routine for competing medical experts to do battle in the pages of medical journals, and common for journals to host point–counterpoint exchanges about controversial topics in medical practice. This often occurs when experts debate the significance and implications of major clinical trials. For instance, after a 1977 randomized controlled trial found only modest benefits from coronary artery bypass grafting in patients with chronic stable angina (Murphy et al., 1977), several journals published exchanges (Chalmers et al., 1978; Feinstein, 1978; Proudfit, 1978). A similar story played out 30 years later. When a major randomized controlled trial found little benefit for angioplasty in patients with chronic stable angina (Boden et al., 2007), the point–counterpoint began again (Diamond and Kaul, 2007; Kereiakes et al., 2007). In each of these exchanges, the authors are clear partisans for one side of the issue and are making the strongest case they can for their position. The net result, for outsiders, is similar to what happens with expert witnesses in the courtroom: presented with competing authorities and unable to adjudicate, observers often conclude that the science is unreliable and therefore not authoritative.

References

Amberson, J.B., McMahon, B.T., Pinner, M., 1931. A clinical trial of sanocrysin in pulmonary tuberculosis. American Review of Tuberculosis 24, 401–435.

Anon, 1874. Expert testimony in judicial proceedings. Albany Law Journal 9, 122.

Anon, 1909. The personal equation in medicine. Journal of the American Medical Association 53, 1825–1826.

Anon, 1947. The "personal equation" in the interpretation of a chest roentgenogram. Journal of the American Medical Association 133, 399–400.

Babitsky, S., Mangraviti, J.J., 2005. How to Become a Dangerous Expert Witness: Advanced Techniques and Strategies. SEAK, Inc., Falmouth, MA.

Bacon, J., 1858. Introductory address. Boston Medical and Surgical Journal 59, 300–302.

Beecher, H.K., 1955. The powerful placebo. Journal of the American Medical Association 159, 1602–1605.

Beecher, H.K., 1961. Surgery as placebo: a quantitative study of bias. Journal of the American Medical Association 176, 1102–1107.

Berlin, F., 1998. Unpaid expert witnesses (Letter to the Editor). New England Journal of Medicine 338, 1233.

Bigelow, J., 1812. Observations and experiments on the treatment of injuries occasioned by fire and heated injuries. New England Journal of Medicine, Surgery, and Collateral Branches of Science 1, 52–63.

Birkelo, C.C., Chamberlain, W.E., Phelps, W.E., Schools, P.E., Zacks, D., 1947. Tuberculosis case finding: a comparison of the effectiveness of various roentgenographic and photofluorographic methods. Journal of the American Medical Association 133, 359–366.

Boden, W.E., O'Rourke, R.A., Teo, K.K., Hartigan, P.M., Maron, D.J., Kostuk, W.J., Knudtson, M., Dada, M., Casperson, P., Harris, C.L., Chaitman, B.R., Shaw, L., Gosselin, G., Nawaz, S., Title, L.M., Gau, G., Blaustein, A.S., Booth, D.C., Bates, E.R., Spertus, J.A., Berman, D.S., Mancini, J., Weintraub, W.S., COURAGE Trial Research Group, 2007. Optimal medical therapy with or without PCI for stable coronary disease. New England Journal of Medicine 356, 1503–1516.

Bowditch, V.Y., 1894. Three years' experience with sanitarium treatment of pulmonary diseases near Boston. Boston Medical and Surgical Journal 131, 49–51.

Bowditch, V.Y., 1900. The Massachusetts State Hospital for consumptives at Rutland; its purpose and the work accomplished during the first year. Boston Medical and Surgical Journal 142, 127–130.

Brown-Séquard, C.É., 1889. Note on the effects produced on man by subcutaneous injections of a liquid obtained from the testicles of animals. Lancet 2, 105–107.

Buchbinder, R., Osborne, R.H., Ebeling, P.R., Wark, J.D., Mitchell, P., Wriedt, C., Graves, S., Staples, M.P., Murphy, B., 2009. A randomized trial of vertebroplasty for painful osteoporotic vertebral fractures. New England Journal of Medicine 361, 557–568.

Canales, J., 2007. Sensational differences: the case of the transit of Venus. Cahiers François Viète 11–12, 15–40.

Chalmers, I., 2005. Statistical theory was not the reason that randomisation was used in the British Medical Research Council's clinical trial of streptomycin for pulmonary tuberculosis. In: Jorland, G., Opinel, A., Weisz, G. (Eds.), Body Counts: Medical Quantification in Historical and Sociological Perspectives. McGill-Queens University Press, Montreal, pp. 309–334.

Chalmers, I., 2011. Why the 1948 MRC trial of streptomycin used treatment allocation based on random numbers. Journal of the Royal Society of Medicine 104, 383–386. Also in www.jameslindlibrary.org.

Chalmers, I., Dukan, E., Podolsky, S., Smith, G.D., 2012. The advent of fair treatment allocation schedules in clinical trials during the 19th and early 20th centuries. Journal of the Royal Society of Medicine 105, 221–227. Also in www.jameslindlibrary.org.

Chalmers, T.C., Smith, H., Ambroz, A., Ritman, D., Schroeder, B.J., 1978. In defense of the VA randomized control trial of coronary artery surgery. Clinical Research 26, 233–235.

Cotton, F.J., 1899. The present status of the antistreptococcic serum. Boston Medical and Surgical Journal 140, 105–108.

Curran, W.J., 1965. Tracy's the Doctor as a Witness, second ed. W.B. Saunders, Philadelphia, PA.

Darnton, R., 1968. Mesmerism and the End of the Enlightenment in France. Harvard University Press, Cambridge, MA.

Daston, L., Gallison, P., 2007. Objectivity. Zone Books, New York, NY.

Dean, M.E., 2006. "An innocent deception": placebo controls in the St Petersburg homeopathy trial, 1829–1830. Journal of the Royal Society of Medicine 99, 375–376. Also in www.jameslindlibrary.org.

Diamond, G.A., Kaul, S., 2007. COURAGE under fire. Journal of the American College of Cardiology 50, 1604–1609.

Diehl, H.S., 1933. Medicinal treatment of the common cold. Journal of the American Medical Association 101, 2042–2049.

Draper, F.W., 1880. Medical expert testimony. Boston Medical and Surgical Journal 103, 442–446.
Edwards, C.C., 1970. Hearing regulations and regulations describing scientific content of adequate and well-controlled clinical investigations. Federal Register 35, 7250–7253.
Feinstein, A.R., 1978. The scientific and clinical tribulations of randomized clinical trials. Clinical Research 26, 241–244.
Finland, M., 1941. Controlling clinical therapeutic experiments with specific serums – with particular reference to antipneumococcus serums. New England Journal of Medicine 225, 495–506.
Finniss, D.G., Kaptchuk, T.J., Miller, F., Benedetti, F., 2010. Biological, clinical, and ethical advances of placebo effects. Lancet 375, 686–695.
Franklin, B., Other commissioners, 1785. Report of Dr. Benjamin Franklin and Other Commissioners, Charged by the King of France, with the Examination of Animal Magnetism, as Now Practiced in Paris (W. Goodman, Trans.). J. Johnson, London.
Freeman, T.B., Vawter, D.E., Leaverton, P.E., Godbold, J.H., Hauser, R.A., Goetz, C.G., Olanow, C.W., 1999. Use of placebo surgery in controlled trials of a cellular-based therapy for Parkinson's disease. New England Journal of Medicine 341, 988–992.
Freeman, J., 1910. Vaccine therapy. Proceedings of the Royal Society of Medicine 3, 97–101.
Gabriel, J.M., 2014. The testing of sanocrysin: science, profit, and innovation in clinical trial design, 1926–1931. Journal of the History of Medicine and Allied Sciences 69, 604–632.
Gold, H., 1954. How to evaluate a new drug. American Journal of Medicine 11, 722–727.
Gold, H., Kwit, N.T., Otto, H., 1937. The xanthines (theobromine and aminophylline) in the treatment of cardiac pain. Journal of the American Medical Association 108, 2173–2179.
Greene, J.A., Condrau, F., Watkins, E., 2016. Therapeutic Revolutions: Pharmaceuticals and Social Change in the Twentieth Century. University of Chicago Press, Chicago, IL.
Greenwood, M., 1948. Simple statistics of cancer. Lancet 252, 781–782.
Greiner, T., Gold, H., Cattell, M., Travell, J., Bakst, H., Rinzler, S.H., Benjamin, Z.H., Warshaw, L.J., Bobb, A., Kwit, N.T., Modell, W., Rothendler, H.H., Messeloff, C.R., Kramer, M.L., 1950. A method for the evaluation of the effects of drugs on cardiac pain in patients with angina of effort. American Journal of Medicine 9, 143–155.
Haller, J.S., 2005. The History of American Homeopathy: the Academic Years, 1820–1935. Pharmaceutical Products Press, New York, NY.
Haygarth, J., 1801. Of the Imagination, as a Cause and as a Cure of Disorders of the Body: Exemplified by Fictitious Tractors and Epidemical Convulsions. R. Cruttwell, Bath.
Hediger, E.M., Gold, H., 1935. U.S.P. ether from large drums and ether from small cans labeled for "anesthesia". Journal of the American Medical Association 104, 2244–2248.
Herrick, S.S., 1895. Reform in medical expert testimony. Journal of the American Medical Association 25, 444–445.
Hewlett, A.W., 1913. Clinical effects of "natural" and "synthetic" sodium salicylate. Journal of the American Medical Association 61, 319–321.
Holmes, O.W., 1842. Homoeopathy and its kindred delusions. In: Holmes, O. (Ed.), Medical Essays, 1842–1882. Houghton, Mifflin and Company, Boston, MA.
Holt, L.E., Northrup, W.P., O'Dwyer, J., Adams, S.S., 1896. The report of the American Pediatric Society's collective investigation into the use of antitoxin in the treatment of diphtheria in private practice. Transactions of the American Pediatric Society 8, 21–45.
Irish, J.C., 1899. Medical expert testimony. Boston Medical and Surgical Journal 140, 299–301.
Kaptchuk, T.J., Kerr, C.E., Zanger, A., 2009. Placebo controls, exorcisms, and the devil. Lancet 374, 1234–1235.
Kaptchuk, T.J., 1998a. Powerful placebo: the dark side of the randomised controlled trial. Lancet 351, 1722–1725.
Kaptchuk, T.J., 1998b. Intentional ignorance: a history of blind assessment and placebo controls in medicine. Bulletin of the History of Medicine 72, 389–433.
Kaptchuk, T.J., 2004. Early Use of Blind Assessment in a Homeopathic Scientific Experiment. Also in www.jameslindlibrary.org.
Kaufman, M., 1988. Homeopathy in America: the rise and fall and persistence of a medical heresy. In: Gevitz, N. (Ed.), Other Healers: Unorthodox Medicine in America. Johns Hopkins University Press, Baltimore, MD, pp. 99–123.
Kereiakes, D.J., Teirstein, P.S., Sarembock, I.J., Holmes, D.R., Krucoff, M.W., O'Neill, W.W., Waksman, R., Williams, D.O., Popma, J.J., Buchbinder, M., Mehran, R., Meredith, I.T., Moses, J.W., Stone, G.W., 2007. The truth and consequences of the COURAGE Trial. Journal of the American College of Cardiology 50, 1598–1603.
Knight, C.H., 1905. Notes on the treatment of hay fever and asthma. Boston Medical and Surgical Journal 153, 85–86.

Lewison, E.F., Chambers, R.G., 1952. The sex hormones in advanced breast cancer. New England Journal of Medicine 246, 1–8.

Liebenson, H.A., 1961. You, the Medical Witness. Year Book Medical Publishers, Chicago, IL.

Marks, H.M., 2006. "Until the sun of science … the true Apollo of medicine has risen": collective investigation in Britain and America, 1880–1910. Medical History 50, 147–166.

Medical Research Council, 1948. Streptomycin treatment of pulmonary tuberculosis: a Medical Research Council investigation. British Medical Journal 2, 769–782.

Mohr, J., 1993. Doctors and the Law: Medical Jurisprudence in Nineteenth-Century America. Oxford University Press, New York, NY.

Moseley, J.B., O'Malley, K.O., Petersen, N.J., Menke, T.J., Brody, B., Kaykendall, D.H., Hollingsworth, J.C., Ashton, C.M., Wray, N.P., 2002. A controlled trial of arthroscopic surgery for osteoarthritis of the knee. New England Journal of Medicine 347, 81–88.

Murphy, M.L., Hultgren, H.N., Detre, K., Thomsen, J., Takaro, T., Participants of the Veterans Administration Cooperative Study, 1977. Treatment of chronic stable angina: a preliminary report of survival data of the randomized Veterans Administration cooperative study. New England Journal of Medicine 297, 621–627.

Pemberton, F.A., 1925. Progress in gynaecology. Boston Medical and Surgical Journal 192, 609–617.

Phibbs, B., 1997. Unpaid expert witnesses (Letter to the Editor). New England Journal of Medicine 337, 1477–1478.

Plass, E.D., 1916. Post-partum care of the perineum. Bulletin of the Johns Hopkins Hospital 27, 107–109.

Podolsky, S.H., 2006. Pneumonia before Antibiotics: Therapeutic Evolution and Evaluation in Twentieth-Century America. Johns Hopkins University Press, Baltimore, MD.

Podolsky, S.H., 2007. Quintessential Beecher: surgery as placebo, a quantitative study of bias. International Anesthesiology Clinics 45, 47–63.

Potter, S., Storke, E.F., 1880. Final report of the Milwaukee test of the thirtieth dilution. Homeopathic Times: A Monthly Journal of Medicine, Surgery, and the Collateral Sciences 7, 280–281.

Proudfit, W.L., 1978. Criticisms of the VA randomized study of coronary bypass surgery. Clinical Research 26, 236–240.

Redberg, R.F., 2014. Sham controls in medical trials. New England Journal of Medicine 371, 892–893.

Rosenberg, C.E., 1979. The therapeutic revolution: medicine, meaning, and social change in nineteenth-century America. In: Vogel, M.J., Rosenberg, C.E. (Eds.), The Therapeutic Revolution: Essays in the Social History of American Medicine. University of Pennsylvania Press, Philadelphia, PA, pp. 3–25.

Schaffer, S., 1988. Astronomers mark time: discipline and the personal equation. Science in Context 2, 115–145.

Schulz, K.F., Chalmers, I., Altman, D.G., 2002. The landscape and lexicon of blinding in randomized trials. Annals of Internal Medicine 136, 254–259.

Schulz, K.F., Grimes, D.A., 2002. Blinding in randomised trials: hiding who got what. Lancet 359, 696–700.

Shapiro, A.K., Shapiro, E., 1997. The Powerful Placebo: from Ancient Priest to Modern Physician. Johns Hopkins University Press, Baltimore, MD.

Stolberg, M., 2006. Inventing the randomized double-blind trial: the Nürnberg salt test of 1835. Journal of the Royal Society of Medicine 99, 642–643. Also in www.jameslindlibrary.org.

Storer, H.R., 1863. Studies of abortion. Boston Medical and Surgical Journal 68, 15–20.

Tröhler, U., 2011. Adolf Bingel's blinded, controlled comparison of different anti-diphtheric sera in 1918. Journal of the Royal Society of Medicine 104, 302–305. Also in www.jameslindlibrary.org.

Trousseau, A., Gourard, H., 1834. Repertoire clinique: Experiences homoeopathiques tentees a l'Hotel-Dieu de Paris. Journal des Connaissances Medico-Chirurgicales 8, 238–241.

Vandenbroucke, J.P., 2013. Adolphe Vorderman's 1897 study on beriberi: an example of scrupulous efforts to avoid bias. Journal of the Royal Society of Medicine 106, 108–111. Also in www.jameslindlibrary.org.

Von Sholly, A.I., Blum, J., Smith, L., 1917. The therapeutic value of pertussis vaccine in whooping cough. Journal of the American Medical Association 68, 1451–1456.

Warner, J.H., 1986. The Therapeutic Perspective: Medical Practice, Knowledge, and Identity in America, 1820–1885. Harvard University Press, Cambridge, MA.

Warner, J.H., 1991. Ideals of science and their discontents in late nineteenth-century American medicine. Isis 82, 454–478.

Wilson, J.C., 1883. Observations on the management of enteric fever according to a plan based upon the so-called specific treatment. Boston Medical and Surgical Journal 108, 99–102.

CHAPTER

4

Blinding in Biomedical Research: An Essential Method to Reduce Risk of Bias

Asbjørn Hróbjartsson

The Nordic Cochrane Centre, Rigshospitalet, Copenhagen, Denmark; Center for Evidence Based Medicine, Odense University Hospital & University of Southern Denmark, Denmark

OUTLINE

INTRODUCTION

In biomedical research, blinding typically refers to a general principle of withholding information from participants in a scientific study with the aim to prevent bias (Hróbjartsson and Boutron, 2011; Schulz and Grimes, 2002). Blinding, at times called "masking," is primarily used in clinical trials. It is less commonly applied to studies of diagnostic accuracy, and

Blinding as a Solution to Bias
http://dx.doi.org/10.1016/B978-0-12-802460-7.00004-8

it is rarely considered for experimental animal research, epidemiological studies, systematic reviews, or other biomedical study types.

In a randomized clinical trial "blinding" will often imply that one or more key persons involved in the trial (such as patients, health-care providers, or outcome assessors) are made unaware of the allocated intervention. The mechanisms for bias in a clinical trial vary considerably depending on who was not blinded, and it is likely that the degree of bias also differs considerably depending on who was not blinded and what outcome was involved.

Early in the historical development of the randomized trial, the main concern was the blinding of the patient, partly because of the emerging attention paid to the placebo effect in the 1950s (Kaptchuk, 1998). Blinding was thus primarily conceived as a method to control for the bias associated with patient–provider interaction. More recently, however, also there has been an increased awareness of the importance of blinding the outcome assessors (i.e., observers in a study who conduct the assessments or provide the outcome data). The role of the outcome assessor in a randomized trial is pivotal because of the simple and direct relation between outcome assessment and the estimated treatment effect. Also, a number of empirical studies have consistently found a substantial degree of bias associated with lack of blinding of the outcome assessors (Hróbjartsson et al., 2012, 2013, 2014b).

This shift is noteworthy. A focus on specifically who was blinded and the distinct bias mechanisms involved is much more informative for readers of trial reports and reflects more accurately the complexities and challenges of blinding. However, this shift is also important—and maybe primarily so—because outcome assessors are integral to numerous areas of research outside of clinical trials. Outcome assessors (more generally "observers") are intrinsic to most empirical studies in biomedicine, indeed, to most scientific studies. Thus, the role of blinding in biomedical research, historically largely confined to clinical trials, is expanding.

Blinding is a fairly new subject for detailed methodological analysis. Once the double-blind trial became an established ideal during the mid-twentieth century, a number of challenging methodological themes were pushed aside: the feasibility of blinding, the risk of unblinding, the expected degree of bias in trials with nonblinded participants, and the variation of degree of bias depending on who was not blinded and type of outcome. Following this dormant period, however, there has in the past decades been an increased methodological interest in blinding both in biomedicine and in other academic disciplines.

In this chapter, I provide a general overview of blinding in biomedical research. I present and discuss the role of blinding in randomized clinical trials focusing on terminology and reporting, bias mechanisms, risk of unblinding, and the main empirical studies of bias. I will also present and discuss the role of blinding in other biomedical study designs. I have two key messages: (1) In randomized clinical trials, blinding of patients, health-care providers, and outcome assessors is essential to reduce the risk of bias, but risk of unblinding is a concern and reporting procedures need to be improved. (2) Across most types of biomedical study designs it is prudent to blind outcome assessors (i.e., observers) in scenarios with a high risk of bias, primarily when outcomes are subjective and observers have predispositions.

TERMINOLOGY AND REPORTING

The first rigorously conducted randomized clinical trial was published in 1948 (Streptomycin, 1948), and randomized trials became a standard method for evaluation of medical intervention in the decades that followed. The basic idea of a randomized trial is simple: randomization of an adequate number of patients (for example, to two groups: experimental and control) to facilitate baseline comparability. The main strength of a randomized design is that it avoids allocation bias and reduces the risk of confounding, which can be very problematic for observational studies of intervention effects.

A main methodological challenge for the randomized trial is to avoid bias once patients have been allocated. Other challenges include obtaining clinically relevant interventions and outcomes, risk of attrition, ensuring an adequate number of patients for statistical power, and risk of selective reporting of outcomes. Blinding is therefore important to ensure that patients and health-care providers do not systematically behave differently depending on the allocated treatment, and that outcome assessors provide unbiased observations.

Blinding is used in approximately 60% of randomized clinical trials (Chan and Altman, 2005). Blinding patients and health-care providers can be difficult or in some cases impossible. For example, it is difficult to imagine how to blind patients in trials that evaluate the effect of jogging on mild depression. Blinding outcome assessors, however, is almost always possible.

Traditionally, blinding has been described with the standard terms: single-blind or double-blind (sometimes also triple-blind). These terms have become engraved in medical terminology, but they are problematic. First, the terms do not provide an adequate description of who was blinded in a study and by which mechanisms. Second, several studies have consistently reported that clinicians understand the terms with considerable variation. A pivotal study found variation not only in how clinicians interpreted the double-blind term, but also in how textbooks defined it (Devereaux et al., 2001). Physicians from three Canadian university hospitals identified 10, 17, and 15 unique interpretations of single-, double-, and triple-blinding, respectively, and textbooks provided 5, 9, and 7 different definitions of each (Devereaux et al., 2001).

A subsequent study of a representative sample of trial authors found similar results and identified 15 unique definitions for double-blind (Haahr and Hróbjartsson, 2006). The trial authors underestimated this large variation in the understanding of the term and erroneously believed that there was general adherence to their preferred characterization of "double-blind." Thus, there is a good reason to suggest that the ambivalent old terminology should be replaced with more flexible descriptions focusing on who was blinded and by which means.

Readers of a trial report who want to assess the risk of bias due to lack of blinding—that is, the interested patient or next of kin, the individual clinician, a person revising a clinical guideline, or a researcher conducting a meta-analysis—rely on explicit reporting of the blinding status of the persons and methods involved in introducing and maintaining blinding. However, the reporting of blinding in clinical trials is typically sketchy and ambiguous. One study found that only 3 of 156 (2%) trials published in 2001 and labeled as double-blind explicitly reported the blinding status of patients, health-care providers, and outcomes assessors (Haahr and Hróbjartsson, 2006). This general lack of attention to blinding in trial reports is reflected in the fact that in 41 of 156 (26%) trials labeled as double-blind, the vague term "double-blind" was the only information on blinding in the whole trial report, including the methods section and discussion. In the remaining trial reports, the methods used to maintain blinding were not described or were described superficially. For example, experimental and control treatments were explicitly reported as "similar" (or an analogous term) in only 72 of 156 (46%) trials described as double-blind.

Reporting of blinding in the medical literature, therefore, is clearly unsatisfactory from a transparency perspective. Still, it would be wrong to assume lack of blinding solely because blinding was not clearly reported. A survey of trial authors indicated that approximately four out of five double-blind trials did indeed blind all three key groups: the patients, the health-care providers, and the outcome assessors (Haahr and Hróbjartsson, 2006). However, it would be equally inappropriate to assume adequate implementation of blinding when reporting is absent or inadequate. If the survey results are broadly representative of clinical trialists, then one out of five double-blind trials fails to blind either patients or health-care providers or outcome assessors. Considering the significant risk of both nonresponse bias and response bias in surveys of trial authors, the proportion may well be higher.

One could have hoped that reporting practices had improved somewhat in the past 15 years, as reporting guidelines such as Consolidated Standards of Reporting Trials (CONSORT) have gained influence (Schulz et al., 2010). Still, no differences were found in the proportion of trials published in 2000 and 2006 that provided specific details on who was blinded (Hopewell et al., 2010).

MECHANISMS FOR INTRODUCING BIAS IN NONBLINDED STUDIES

Central to the discussion of blinding as a tool to avoid bias are the studies assessing the degree of bias to be expected in a study without blinding. Before the mid-1990s, the discussion of bias in randomized trials was largely based on common sense and illustrative cases. However, in a pivotal study published in *JAMA* in 1997, Schulz et al. (1995) introduced a method that would be known as meta-epidemiology. They analyzed within a considerable number of meta-analyses whether estimated treatment effects differed between trials with high risk of bias and low risk of bias. The strength of this approach is that when trials are compared within meta-analyses, they can be regarded as fairly similar with respect to clinical condition, intervention, control group, and outcome. They compared double-blind to not double-blind trials and found that trials in the latter category had estimated treatment effects (expressed as odds ratios) that were exaggerated by 14%, on average.

Such meta-epidemiological investigations have been repeated several times (Pildal et al., 2007). Surprisingly, the subsequent comparisons between double-blind and not double-blind trials provided unstable results, and in several cases, no clear difference in estimated treatment effects could be observed between double-blind and not double-blind trials. A 2012 reanalyzes of seven large meta-epidemiological studies, only counting the same trial once and accounting for differences in type of outcomes, reported that the estimated treatment effect (odds ratios) was exaggerated by an average of 13% in not double-blind trials. However, when outcomes were subjective, the average exaggeration of odds ratios reached 23% (Savovic et al., 2012).

Interpreting such results is challenging. First, as discussed above, double-blind is an ambiguous term. Second, the comparison of two supposedly similar trials—one double-blind, the other not double-blind—involves a considerable risk of confounding, in that lack of blinding may be associated with other factors that may cause bias, including inferior overall methodology or imperfect randomization. The estimated degree of bias associated with lack of double-blinding may have been influenced (increased or reduced) by irrelevant factors.

Meta-epidemiological studies cannot demonstrate a causal relation; rather, they can only show whether there is a statistical association.

EMPIRICAL INVESTIGATIONS OF THE IMPACT OF BLINDING

A number of studies have investigated the impact of blinding separately for each key trial participant—for example, outcome assessors and patients—with designs that minimize risk of confounding. An overview of such studies is provided in the following section.

Blinding of Outcome Assessors

The outcome assessor in a clinical trial is typically a physician who decides whether a patient has improved, for example after studying a radiograph to determine whether a fracture has healed. The bias associated with nonblinded outcome assessors is called observer bias.

The conceptual mechanism for observer bias is the interaction between a subjective outcome and the predispositions of the observers. The risk of observer bias is low when an outcome is objective and therefore does not rely on assessor judgment; a classic example of such an outcome would be all-cause mortality. Blinded assessors of objective outcomes agree on most observations, showing low interobserver variation. However, the risk of observer bias is high when an outcome is subjective and therefore relies on assessor judgment. Here, a paradigmatic example would be whether a patient has improved beyond two points on a clinical function scale. Blinded observers of a subjective outcome disagree fairly often, showing high interobserver variation.

Subjective outcomes assessed by nonblinded but fully neutral observers will result in random disagreements, but the disagreements should not impact the estimates of treatment effects in clinical trials. To do so, the observers must have a predisposition, or a preference for one of the interventions. Often observers will have a conscious or subconscious interest in a specific study result, manifesting in a tendency for gray-zone observations to tilt toward a specific result. If the observer has a financial or intellectual investment in the product being tested, or simply hopes that the experimental intervention is effective, then that predisposition may support the experimental intervention.

The most reliable design for studying observer bias would be to randomize patients to a clinical study with blinded assessors and to an otherwise identical study with nonblinded assessors. Such trials are extremely rare, and I am only aware of a single small and old trial (Fogarty, 1966). That trial randomized 32 outpatients with depression to receive either the antidepressant amitriptyline or the antidepressant imipramine with assessment by a nonblinded assessor who regarded imipramine as superior or to receive one of those antidepressants and be assigned to a blinded assessor. Based on the nonblinded assessor, the estimated effect was exaggerated by 64% (a ratio of odds ratios of 0.36, with a ratio below 1 indicating that nonblinded observers generate more optimistic odds ratios). However, the small number of patients made this result very uncertain and far from statistically significant (95% confidence interval (CI) ranged from 0.02 to 6.30).

An alternative approach for studying observer bias is to analyze trials that use both blinded and nonblinded outcome assessors. A series of three publications studied such trials with binary outcomes (yes/no type outcomes, for example whether a fracture had healed), measurement scale outcomes (outcomes assessed on a scale, for example functional status), and time-to-event outcomes (for example, time to healing of fracture) (Hróbjartsson et al., 2012, 2013, 2014b). The three studies involved 51 trials and 24 clinical conditions, including angina pectoris, multiple sclerosis, suicide risk, onychomycosis, wound healing, fracture healing, and scar cosmesis. In the trials with binary outcomes the impact of lack of blinding on estimated treatment effects was assessed as the ratio of odds ratios. The pooled ratio of odds ratios was 0.64 (95% CI (0.43, 0.96)), indicating that nonblinded observers exaggerated the odds ratio by 36% (95% CI (4%, 57%)) (Hróbjartsson et al., 2012).

By contrast, the trials with measurement scale outcomes were assessed for the impact of lack of blinding on estimated treatment effects based on effect size difference: the difference between the effect size (i.e., standardized mean difference) derived from nonblinded observers and that derived from blinded observers (Hróbjartsson et al., 2013). An effect size <0 indicated a beneficial effect of the intervention. A difference in effect size <0 indicated that nonblinded observers generated more optimistic effect sizes. The pooled effect size difference was −0.23 (95% CI (−0.40, −0.06)) indicating that nonblinded observers exaggerated the effect size by approximately one-quarter of a standard deviation. The pooled effect size based on blinded observers in the trials studied was −0.34, so in relative terms the exaggeration of the effect size based on nonblinded observers was approximately 68%. An effect size is usually considered large at a level of −0.80, medium at a level of −0.50, and small at a level of −0.20. Thus, assuming an estimated treatment effect based on the blinded observers that is medium-sized (−0.50), the exaggeration would be approximately 46%. In the trials with time-to-event outcomes, results were similar (Hróbjartsson et al., 2014b).

All three studies point to a general tendency for exaggeration of a treatment effect by nonblinded assessors. Such an exaggeration will in some situations imply that an intervention with a small beneficial effect will be misinterpreted as having a large beneficial effect. In other situations, the exaggeration will imply that interventions with no beneficial effect are misinterpreted as having a small-to-moderate effect. This is problematic when evaluating the balance between benefits and harms of an intervention and when conducting analyses in health economics. In other especially pernicious situations, an intervention with small-to-moderate harmful effects could be interpreted as having beneficial effects.

Blinding of Patients

The blinding of patients is also likely to be important, not only because of the direct and simple link between patient-reported outcomes and trial results, but also because changed patient behavior may impact trials with observer-reported outcomes. As mentioned in the introduction, the main historical basis for introducing blinding in randomized trials was the intention to blind patients.

There are many pathways through which lack of blinding patients can lead to bias. Nonblinded patients in an experimental group may report symptoms more favorably because of response bias and the placebo effect. Response bias describes the tendency of patients to report their symptoms so that they align with the hopes or expectations of the investigators. Placebo interventions have, on average, moderate effect on patient-reported outcomes, especially nausea and pain, but the effects vary considerably (Hróbjartsson and Gøtzsche, 2010).

In some pain trials, the effect of placebo is considerable (Linde et al., 2005). Placebo effects as reported by patients have been found to be associated with less activity in pain-sensitive brain regions (Wager et al., 2004). It is difficult, however, to distinguish patient-reported placebo effects from response bias (Hróbjartsson et al., 2011). Patients' knowledge of treatment allocations may also influence their thresholds for deciding to drop out of trials, or to not adhere with protocols in other ways.

One meta-epidemiological study focused explicitly on blinding patients (Nüesch et al., 2009). It reported a modest overall impact of patient blinding, with an effect size difference of −0.15 (95% CI (−0.39, 0.09)), which normally would be considered small (below −0.20) and is also statistically nonsignificant, because the CI for the difference overlapped the neutral result, indicating that a chance finding cannot be ruled out. The surprising finding undermines the widely held belief in the importance of patient blinding. However, as pointed out above, the meta-epidemiological comparison of supposedly similar trials—those with blinded patients and those without—involves a considerable risk of confounding.

Alternatively, the impact of patient blinding on the estimated treatment effects in clinical trials can ideally be studied in a design that involves four-armed trials consisting of one substudy with blinded patients and one otherwise identical substudy with nonblinded patients. My colleagues and I recently published a systematic review of 12 such trials (or trials with analogous designs) involving a total of 3869 patients that included 10 acupuncture trials, 1 trial of distant healing, and 1 trial of an herbal drug (Hróbjartsson et al., 2014a). Within each trial, the difference in effect size (standardized mean difference) was compared between the substudies. A difference <0 indicated that nonblinded patients generated a more optimistic effect estimate. The average difference in effect size for patient-reported outcomes was −0.56 (95% CI (−0.71, −0.41)), indicating that nonblinded patients exaggerated the effect size by approximately half of the standard deviation, but with considerable variation. Assuming an estimated treatment effect based on the blinded patients that is medium-sized (−0.50), the exaggeration of the nonblinded patients would be 112%.

Two of the twelve trials also used observer-reported outcomes. When restricting the analysis to such outcomes there was no indication of exaggerated effects due to lack of patient blinding. Subgroup analysis indicated a larger effect size difference in 10 acupuncture trials (−0.63; 95% CI (−0.77, −0.49)) than in the two nonacupuncture trials (−0.17; 95% CI (−0.41, 0.07)). Lack of patient blinding also increased patient attrition (dropouts) by 75% and the use of cointerventions.

The importance of blinding patients is strongly supported by theoretical considerations, auxiliary investigation into placebo effects (Hróbjartsson and Gøtzsche, 2010), and empirical studies. The emerging pattern indicates that the impact of patient blinding differs considerably from trial to trial, and that there may be an important difference between trials with patient-reported and observer-reported outcomes. Future studies could explore the variation in degree of bias due to patient blinding.

Blinding of Health-Care Providers

Bias can also result from lack of blinding of health-care providers. Nonblinded health-care providers may differ from blinded ones in how they interact with patients or in their ordering of supplementary care for patients. This may contribute to differences in the basic care given to patients in different comparison groups and also induce differences in placebo effect and in the degree of response bias. Selective referral of patients for subsequent blinded adjudication of outcomes may also cause bias (Psaty and Prentice, 2010). Lack of blinding of health-care providers may induce a larger degree of bias when outcomes are defined by clinician decisions (e.g., time to hospital discharge) than when outcomes are patient-reported.

Blinding of health-care providers is also likely to be important because the behavior and decisions of health-care providers may influence cointerventions, placebo effects, and patient attrition. The link between a trial outcome and blinding is, however, only direct and simple in trials assessing outcomes related to decisions made by the clinician (such as time to discharge). I am not aware of any study that has specifically assessed the impact of lack of blinding of health-care providers in clinical trials.

The importance of the blinding of health-care providers is supported by theoretical considerations and indirectly by the meta-epidemiological studies of the impact of double-blinding and the studies of blinding of outcome assessors and patients. Future studies may clarify the degree of bias to be expected or reasons for any variation such as might occur among different types of outcomes.

RISK OF UNBLINDING

Blinding procedures are often challenging to design (Boutron et al., 2006, 2007). The loss of blinding, also called unblinding, may be caused by noticeable differences between the compared treatments, for example in appearance or smell. A classic example of unblinding is the case of zinc treatment for the common cold, in which patients noted a distinct metallic aftertaste (Farr and Gwaltney, 1987). Telltale side effects can similarly be a problem, including dry mouth for anticholinergic drugs or tremor for lithium. Also, patients or other nonblinded persons in a trial may inadvertently communicate allocation status to supposedly blinded outcome assessors. In one trial, the blinding of the outcome assessor was reportedly compromised for 64 of 334 (19%) randomized patients (Brent et al., 2008).

The risk of unblinding is rarely reported in randomized clinical trials. One study found that only 24 of a representative sample of 300 trial publications (8%) reported risk of unblinding (Bello et al., 2014b). In the 16 trials (5%) that reported loss of blinding, the median number of patients involved was modest although in one case reached 30%. The challenge with such investigations is that they do not address what was done, but only what was reported.

A subsequent survey of the authors of the 92% of trial publications that had not addressed the risk of unblinding indicated a considerable proportion of trials did not report methods implemented to assess risk of bias and found a sizable minority of the trials with suspected or overt cases of unblinding that had not been reported (Bello et al., n.d.). Imperfect matching of pharmacological experimental and control interventions may be a prominent mechanism for unblinding (Hill et al., 1976).

It is unclear to what extent imperfect blinding results in bias. Clearly, if all patients or outcome assessments in a trial were unblinded, then the situation would be comparable to a trial without attempt to blind. However, that is an unlikely scenario. The most probable situation is that a proportion of patients or outcome assessments become unblinded. It seems obvious that the degree of bias must be less than in trials with no blinding, but it is unclear how much less, and whether the difference would vary considerably from trial to trial depending on the type of outcome and other considerations.

There has been some methodological debate about the pros and cons of formally testing for loss of blinding during or after the completion of a trial (Kolahi et al., 2009; Sackett, 2011). Such tests involve asking patients to guess what treatment they received and then compare the result with what could be expected by chance. A variant of such guessing tests is to have outcome assessors or other investigators guess which patients received which treatment. Formal indices have been published based on such tests (Bang et al., 2004; James et al., 1996), but they are used rarely (Boutron et al., 2005; Fergusson et al., 2004; Hróbjartsson et al., 2007). It is not clear how results from such tests should be interpreted. The main problem is that in the absence of unblinding, patients will tend to actively look for clues that they think are associated with receiving experimental intervention, which could include the improvement of the clinical condition, side effects, or specific laboratory results. The guesses may thus be weakly associated with group allocation, while the individual patient may still have a considerable uncertainty as to which treatment was received. Another problem is that such tests are subject to selective publication (Hróbjartsson et al., 2007). There is probably good reason to await further methodological improvements before recommending the routine use of such tests.

Unfortunately, imperfect blinding due, for example, to minor differences in appearance or weak side effects is probably more common than often believed. The challenge is to pin down when irrelevant limitations in a blinding procedure transgress into a substantial deficiency, drawing the line between unimportant procedural defects and actual unblinding of enough patients or investigators to cause bias.

BLINDING IN NONRANDOMIZED STUDY DESIGNS

Biomedicine involves a long range of research designs that aim to solve very different scientific problems. This section reviews the application of blinding outside of the randomized trial, focusing on animal studies, epidemiological studies, and diagnostic studies. These research designs were selected because they are commonly used, because they represent both preclinical and clinical studies as well as experimental and observational designs, or because application of blinding in these settings has been debated.

Animal Studies

Animal studies are often used in preclinical exploration of possible benefits or harms of interventions, or to examine hypotheses to do with physiological, biochemical, toxicological, or pathological mechanisms. Animal research is sometimes understood as involving whole live organisms but may also include research designs using animal tissue, cells, or organs. There is little tradition for blinding in animal studies or in preclinical studies in general (Kilkenny et al., 2009; Vesterinen et al., 2011).

Animal studies normally involve an outcome assessor, an observer who assesses the animal. In this respect, there is little substantial difference between the situation in a clinical trial and in an animal study. Both designs involve observations/assessments. In some cases, these assessments are made by observers with predispositions and involve outcomes that are subjective. Thus, from a theoretical perspective, there are strong arguments for a considerable risk of observer bias in animal studies.

This concern has found empirical support. One systematic review analyzed animal studies modeling human clinical conditions and using both blinded and unblinded assessors (Bello et al., 2014a). Based on 10 studies with a total of 2450 animals and subjective outcomes, the ratio of odds ratios was 0.41 (95% CI (0.20, 0.82)) indicating an average exaggeration of the nonblinded odds ratio by 59%, but with considerable variation. Three pesticide experiments had a very large degree of observer bias, with a ratio of odds ratios averaging 0.20 (95% CI (0.07, 0.59)), reflecting an exaggeration of as much as 80%. The similar ratio for the other seven experiments was an average of 0.82 (95% CI (0.57, 1.17)), reflecting an exaggeration of the nonblinded odds ratio of 18%.

The influence of different experimental contexts on the direction and degree of observer bias is illustrated in the three pesticide studies identified in the systematic review, in which the nonblinded assessments were conducted under very different conditions. The U.S. National Cancer Institute found no clear evidence of excess cancer risk in rats with malathion exposure, based on nonblinded assessments of histology slides published in 1978 and 1979 (Bello et al., 2014a). In 1985, two parallel reassessments of the original slides were published: one based on nonblinded assessment, reporting clear risk of cancer and one based on blinded assessment, reporting no clear risk of cancer.

During the 1980s, the potential toxicity of malathion was a controversial issue. Aerial spraying of malathion over residential neighborhoods in Southern California to eradicate Mediterranean flies had prompted public concern and a heated debate among regulatory authorities, pesticide producers, social activists, and scientists. The scientist who initiated and conducted the 1985 nonblinded reassessment, Melvin D. Reuber, was a candid pesticide critic, and his preconceptions may have influenced his evaluations. During the 1970s, malathion was a widely used commercial product. A conclusion by the National Cancer Institute that malathion exposure increased cancer risk would have had substantial commercial and political implications. The malathion studies demonstrate how personal interests as well as institutional and political contexts of scientific investigations shape the predispositions of investigators.

In animal research, some outcomes are objective, for example total mortality in moderately sized and large animals as rats and dogs. The assessment of total mortality in small animals such as *Caenorhabditis elegans*, however, is subjective, and there is a subjective element in most pattern recognition outcomes on histological slides, radiographs, or assessments of animal behavior, such as a forced swimming test for rodents.

Other aspects of animal investigations beyond outcome assessment may be blinded. For example, the blinding of the daily animal handlers may be warranted, especially in studies with a long follow-up time. If the animal handler knows which animals have received the experimental intervention (perhaps because they are all housed in the same cave) and which animals have not, then a systematic difference in how they are fed and taken care of is possible.

Epidemiology: Case–Control and Cohort Studies

There is little tradition for blinding investigators in epidemiological research. The bulk of epidemiological cohort studies are based on data from administrative or other databases. Thus, the data collection process in such studies differs considerably from that of clinical trials or preclinical experiments. In cohort studies, data will usually be collected from external databases that routinely store health data, for example national cancer registries or mortality registries. There may be challenges in how data were accessed and stored from database to database, for example how complete the database is, but the specific hypotheses tested in cohort studies will in most cases not be known to the persons responsible for data collection. Also, in many cases the outcomes stored in databases will be objective, for example mortality. Thus, at least from a theoretical perspective, blinding the persons responsible for "data collection" has less merit in typical epidemiological studies.

However, there is a risk of observer bias in situations when an epidemiological study involves direct assessment of patients or persons, especially if information on exposure and disease/symptom intensity is based on patient questionnaires or interviews (Kip et al., 2001; Murphy et al., 2008; Parmar et al., 2010). Several studies have demonstrated a considerable difference between results based on records of exposure documented before and after knowledge of disease. For example, multiple vaccines given to personnel in the UK armed forces were not associated with adverse health effects when vaccinations were recorded from medical records but were clearly associated with symptoms when the vaccinations were self-reported (Parmar et al., 2010). This result has been interpreted as a result of recall bias: soldiers with symptoms, and knowledge about the hypothesis, recalled more vaccinations than soldiers without symptoms. The problem is comparable to the situation when a clinical trial in which patients with knowledge of their interventions (exposure group) report their symptoms. In other situations, observers may have to assess status or intensity of an exposure (e.g., asbestos) in individuals with and without a given disease (e.g., mesothelioma). Knowledge of the disease status may impact assessment of exposure status, and blinding the observers to disease status will prevent this problem (Lacourt et al., 2014).

Also, some aspects of epidemiological studies can involve subjective choices that affect the data, such as how to manage mismatched or missing data in linking two databases or the manual extraction of data from medical records. From a theoretical perspective, the relevant question to ask is when is there a reasonable doubt about the neutrality of the observers and the objectivity of the outcome in question. One study examined whether blinded data extraction from medical records for a cohort study gave different results than nonblinded data extraction (Parr et al., 2009) and found no statistically significant difference. Further studies should study the role of blinding in epidemiology in more detail.

Diagnostic Studies

A diagnostic study aims to test the accuracy of a new diagnostic procedure that might be cheaper or more convenient against the established gold standard diagnostic procedure. Investigators will thus typically test a group of relevant patients with both tests and then compare how often the new diagnostic test reaches the same result as the old established test. In some studies, the investigators doing the experimental test are blinded to the result of the gold standard test and vice versa.

The reason for blinding the testers is that the experimental test result—in gray-zone situations—may be affected by the knowledge of the gold standard diagnosis. It is expected that nonblinded testers will tend to align the results of the experimental test as close to the gold standard as possible. At least two meta-epidemiological studies have analyzed whether this concern can be empirically verified (Lijmer et al., 1999; Rutjes et al., 2006).

In Lijmer et al. pivotal study, diagnostic performance was overestimated when the reference test was interpreted with knowledge of the gold standard test result (relative diagnostic odds ratio, 1.3; 95% CI (1.0, 1.9)). Rutjes et al. (2006) published a larger follow-up study reporting that diagnostic performance was possibly overestimated when the reference test was interpreted with knowledge of the test result. However, the overestimation found was smaller than the overestimation reported by Lijmer and colleagues and could have been a chance finding (relative diagnostic odds ratio, 1.1; 95% CI (0.8, 1.6)). Inaccurate reporting of blinding status was a major obstacle for this approach.

Further similar studies could try to overcome the challenge of inaccurate reporting of blinding status. Further studies could also analyze the possible differential impact of lack of blinding on types of diagnostic procedures. It is likely that diagnostic procedures that involve a considerable degree of judgment and image interpretation will be more susceptible to bias due to lack of blinding as compared with more objective diagnostic procedures.

Systematic Reviews and Other Study Designs

Blinding is not often used in systematic reviews. Still, at least six studies have investigated whether blinding of assessors of risk of bias in the included studies in a review provided different assessments as compared with nonblinded assessors. The results of the studies were inconsistent: two studies reported no difference, two studies reported lower risk of bias when assessors were blinded, and one reported higher risk of bias (the last study did not report whether results were statistically significant) (Morissette et al., 2011).

One of the earliest studies of the importance of blinding personnel conducting tests susceptible to encouragement was published in 1984 and reported that encouragement in a walking time test considerably increased time on a treadmill (Guyatt et al., 1984). Blinding is often used in peer review (Moylan et al., 2014), has been discussed in assessments of surgical skills (Goff et al., 2002), and recommended for cancer staging (Meining et al., 2002).

CONCLUSION

In biomedicine, blinding is used often in randomized trials. There are strong arguments, both theoretical and empirical, for blinding patients, health-care providers, and outcome assessors in these clinical trials. The risk of unblinding in trials is a concern and reporting standards for trial publications needs to be improved. Across most types of biomedical study designs, including preclinical animal studies, it is prudent to blind outcome assessors in scenarios with a notable risk of bias, primarily when outcomes are subjective and observers have predispositions.

References

Bang, H., Ni, L., Davis, C.E., 2004. Assessment of blinding in clinical trials. Controlled Clinical Trials 25 (2), 143–156.

Bello, S., Krogsbøll, L.T., Gruber, J., Zhao, Z.J., Fischer, D., Hróbjartsson, A., 2014a. Lack of blinding of outcome assessors in animal model experiments implies risk of observer bias. Journal of Clinical Epidemiology 67 (9), 973–983. http://dx.doi.org/10.1016/j.jclinepi.2014.04.008.

Bello, S., Moustgaard, H., Hróbjartsson, A., 2014b. The risk of unblinding was infrequently and incompletely reported in 300 randomised clinical trial publications. Journal of Clinical Epidemiology 67 (10), 1059–1069.

Bello, S., Moustgaard, H., Hróbjartsson, A., n.d. Unreported Risk of Unblinding in Randomised Clinical Trials: A Questionnaire Survey of Authors of Trial Publications (unpublished manuscript).

Boutron, I., Estellat, C., Ravaud, P., 2005. A review of blinding in randomized controlled trials found results inconsistent and questionable. Journal of Clinical Epidemiology 58 (12), 1220–1226.

Boutron, I., Estellat, C., Guittet, L., Dechartres, A., Sackett, D.L., Hróbjartsson, A., Ravaud, P., 2006. Methods of blinding in reports of randomized controlled trials assessing pharmacological treatments. A systematic review. PLoS Medicine 3, e425.

Boutron, I., Guittet, L., Estellat, C., Moher, D., Hróbjartsson, A., Ravaud, P., 2007. Reporting methods of blinding in randomized controlled trials assessing non-pharmacological treatments. A systematic review. PLoS Medicine 4, e61.

Brent, D., Emslie, G., Clarke, G., Wagner, K.D., Asarnow, J.R., Keller, M., Zelazny, J., 2008. Switching to another SSRI or to venlafaxine with or without cognitive behavioral therapy for adolescents with SSRI-resistant depression: the TORDIA randomized controlled trial. JAMA 299, 901–913.

Chan, A.W., Altman, D.G., 2005. Epidemiology and reporting of randomised trials published in PubMed journals. Lancet 365 (9465), 1159–1162.

Devereaux, P.J., Manns, B.J., Ghali, W.A., Quan, H., Lacchetti, C., Montori, V.M., Guyatt, G.H., 2001. Physician interpretations and textbook definitions of blinding terminology in randomized controlled trials. JAMA 285 (15), 2000–2003.

Farr, B.M., Gwaltney Jr., J.M., 1987. The problems of taste in placebo matching: an evaluation of zinc gluconate for the common cold. Journal of Chronic Diseases 40 (9), 875–879.

Fergusson, D., Glass, K.C., Waring, D., Shapiro, S., 2004. Turning a blind eye: the success of blinding reported in a random sample of randomised, placebo controlled trials. BMJ 328 (7437), 432.

Fogarty, J.P., 1966. Observer bias in drug trial. Journal of the Irish Medical Association 59 (353), 161–163.

Goff, B.A., Nielsen, P.E., Lentz, G.M., Chow, G.E., Chalmers, R.W., Fenner, D., Mandel, L.S., 2002. Surgical skills assessment: a blinded examination of obstetrics and gynecology residents. American Journal of Obstetrics and Gynecology 186 (4), 613–617.

Guyatt, G.H., Pugsley, S.O., Sullivan, M.J., Thompson, P.J., Berman, L., Jones, N.L., Taylor, D.W., 1984. Effect of encouragement on walking test performance. Thorax 39 (11), 818–822.

Haahr, M.T., Hróbjartsson, A., 2006. Who is blinded in randomized clinical trials? A study of 200 trials and a survey of authors. Clinical Trials 3 (4), 360–365.

Hill, L.E., Nunn, A.J., Fox, W., 1976. Matching quality of agents employed in "double-blind" controlled clinical trials. Lancet 1 (7955), 352–356.

Hopewell, S., Dutton, S., Yu, L.M., Chan, A.W., Altman, D.G., 2010. The quality of reports of randomised trials in 2000 and 2006: comparative study of articles indexed in PubMed. BMJ 340, c723.

Hróbjartsson, A., Boutron, I., 2011. Blinding in randomized clinical trials: imposed impartiality. Clinical Pharmacology and Therapeutics 90 (5), 732–736.

Hróbjartsson, A., Gøtzsche, P.C., 2010. Placebo interventions for all clinical conditions. Cochrane Database of Systematic Reviews (1), CD003974.

Hróbjartsson, A., Forfang, E., Haahr, M.T., Als-Nielsen, B., Brorson, S., 2007. Blinded trials taken to the test: an analysis of randomized clinical trials that report tests for the success of blinding. International Journal of Epidemiology 36 (3), 654–663.

Hróbjartsson, A., Kaptchuk, T.J., Miller, F.G., 2011. Placebo effect studies are susceptible to response bias and to other types of biases. Journal of Clinical Epidemiology 64 (11), 1223–1229.

Hróbjartsson, A., Thomsen, A.S.S., Emanuelsson, F., Tendal, B., Hilden, J., Boutron, I., Brorson, S., 2012. Observer bias in randomised clinical trials with binary outcomes: systematic review of trials with both blinded and non-blinded outcome assessors. BMJ 344, e1119.

Hróbjartsson, A., Thomsen, A.S.S., Emanuelsson, F., Tendal, B., Hilden, J., Boutron, I., Brorson, S., 2013. Observer bias in randomised clinical trials with measurement scale outcomes: systematic review of trials with both blinded and non-blinded outcome assessors. CMAJ. http://dx.doi.org/10.1503/cmaj.120744.

Hróbjartsson, A., Emanuelsson, F., Thomsen, A.S.S., Hilden, J., Brorson, S., 2014a. Bias due to lack of patient blinding in clinical trials: a systematic review of trials randomising patients to blind and nonblind sub-studies. International Journal of Epidemiology. http://dx.doi.org/10.1093/ije/dyu115.

Hróbjartsson, A., Thomsen, A.S.S., Emanuelsson, F., Tendal, B., Rasmussen, J.V., Hilden, J., Brorson, S., 2014b. Observer bias in randomised clinical trials with time-to-event outcomes: systematic review of trials with both blinded and non-blinded outcome assessors. International Journal of Epidemiology. http://dx.doi.org/10.1093/ije/dyt270.

James, K.E., Bloch, D.A., Lee, K.K., Kraemer, H.C., Fuller, R.K., 1996. An index for assessing blindness in a multi-centre clinical trial: disulfiram for alcohol cessation—a VA cooperative study. Statistics in Medicine 15 (13), 1421–1434.

Kaptchuk, T.J., 1998. Intentional ignorance: a history of blind assessment and placebo controls in medicine. Bulletin of the History of Medicine 72 (3), 389–433.

Kilkenny, C., Parsons, N., Kadyszewski, E., Festing, M.F., Cuthill, I.C., Fry, D., Altman, D.G., 2009. Survey of the quality of experimental design, statistical analysis and reporting of research using animals. PLoS One 4 (11), e7824. http://dx.doi.org/10.1371/journal.pone.0007824.

Kip, K.E., Cohen, F., Cole, S.R., Wilhelmus, K.R., Patrick, D.L., Blair, R.C., Beck, R.W., Herpetic Eye Disease Study Group, 2001. Recall bias in a prospective cohort study of acute time-varying exposures: example from the herpetic eye disease study. Journal of Clinical Epidemiology 54 (5), 482–487.

Kolahi, J., Bang, H., Park, J., 2009. Towards a proposal for assessment of blinding success in clinical trials: up-to-date review. Community Dentistry and Oral Epidemiology 37 (6), 477–484.

Lacourt, A., Gramond, C., Rolland, P., Ducamp, S., Audignon, S., Astoul, P., Brochard, P., 2014. Occupational and non-occupational attributable risk of asbestos exposure for malignant pleural mesothelioma. Thorax 69 (6), 532–539. http://dx.doi.org/10.1136/thoraxjnl-2013-203744.

Lijmer, J.G., Mol, B.W., Heisterkamp, S., Bonsel, G.J., Prins, M.H., van der Meulen, J.H., Bossuyt, P.M., 1999. Empirical evidence of design-related bias in studies of diagnostic tests. JAMA 282 (11), 1061–1066. Erratum in: JAMA 283 (15), 1963.

Linde, K., Streng, A., Jürgens, S., Hoppe, A., Brinkhaus, B., Witt, C., Melchart, D., 2005. Acupuncture for patients with migraine: a randomized controlled trial. JAMA 293 (17), 2118–2125.

Meining, A., Dittler, H.J., Wolf, A., Lorenz, R., Schusdziarra, V., Siewert, J.R., Rösch, T., 2002. You get what you expect? A critical appraisal of imaging methodology in endosonographic cancer staging. Gut 50 (5), 599–603.

Morissette, K., Tricco, A.C., Horsley, T., Chen, M.H., Moher, D., 2011. Blinded versus unblinded assessments of risk of bias in studies included in a systematic review. Cochrane Database of Systematic Reviews (9), MR000025.

Moylan, E.C., Harold, S., O'Neill, C., Kowalczuk, M.K., 2014. Open, single-blind, double-blind: which peer review process do you prefer? BMC Pharmacology & Toxicology 15, 55. http://dx.doi.org/10.1186/2050-6511-15-55.

Murphy, D., Hotopf, M., Wessely, S., 2008. Multiple vaccinations, health, and recall bias within UK armed forces deployed to Iraq: cohort study. BMJ 337, a220. http://dx.doi.org/10.1136/bmj.a220.

Nüesch, E., Trelle, S., Reichenbach, S., Rutjes, A.W., Bürgi, E., Scherer, M., Jüni, P., 2009. The effects of excluding patients from the analysis in randomised controlled trials: meta-epidemiological study. BMJ 339, b3244. http://dx.doi.org/10.1136/bmj.b3244.

Parmar, G., Ghuge, P., Halanych, J.H., Funkhouser, E., Safford, M.M., 2010. Cardiovascular outcome ascertainment was similar using blinded and unblinded adjudicators in a national prospective study. Journal of Clinical Epidemiology 63 (10), 1159–1163. http://dx.doi.org/10.1016/j.jclinepi.2009.12.017.

Parr, C.L., Hjartåker, A., Laake, P., Lund, E., Veierød, M.B., 2009. Recall bias in melanoma risk factors and measurement error effects: a nested case-control study within the Norwegian women and cancer study. American Journal of Epidemiology 169 (3), 257–266. http://dx.doi.org/10.1093/aje/kwn363 Epub November 14, 2008.

Pildal, J., Hróbjartsson, A., Jørgensen, K.J., Hilden, J., Altman, D.G., Gøtzsche, P.C., 2007. Impact of allocation concealment on conclusions drawn from meta-analyses of randomised trials. International Journal of Epidemiology 36, 847–857.

Psaty, B.M., Prentice, R.L., 2010. Minimizing bias in randomized trials: the importance of blinding. JAMA 304 (7), 793–794.

Rutjes, A.W., Reitsma, J.B., Di Nisio, M., Smidt, N., van Rijn, J.C., Bossuyt, P.M., 2006. Evidence of bias and variation in diagnostic accuracy studies. CMAJ 174 (4), 469–476.

Sackett, D.L., 2011. Clinician-trialist rounds: 6. Testing for blindness at the end of your trial is a mug's game. Clinical Trials 8 (5), 674–676.

Savovic, J., Jones, H.E., Altman, D.G., Harris, R.J., Jüni, P., Pildal, J., Sterne, J.A.C., 2012. Influence of reported study design characteristics on intervention effect estimates from randomized controlled trials. Annals of Internal Medicine. http://dx.doi.org/10.7326/0003-4819-157-6-201209180-00537.

Schulz, K.F., Grimes, D.A., 2002. Blinding in randomised trials: hiding who got what. Lancet 359 (9307), 696–700.

Schulz, K.F., Chalmers, I., Hayes, R.J., Altman, D.G., 1995. Empirical evidence of bias. Dimensions of methodological quality associated with estimates of treatment effects in controlled trials. JAMA 273 (5), 408–412.

Schulz, K.F., Altman, D.G., Moher, D., CONSORT Group, 2010. CONSORT 2010 statement: updated guidelines for reporting parallel group randomised trials. PLoS Medicine 7 (3), e1000251.
Streptomycin treatment of pulmonary tuberculosis. BMJ 2 (4582), 1948, 790–791.
Vesterinen, H.V., Egan, K., Deister, A., Schlattmann, P., Macleod, M.R., Dirnagl, U., 2011. Systematic survey of the design, statistical analysis, and reporting of studies published in the 2008 volume of the Journal of Cerebral Blood Flow and Metabolism. Journal of Cerebral Blood Flow and Metabolism 31, 1064–1072.
Wager, T.D., Rilling, J.K., Smith, E.E., Sokolik, A., Casey, K.L., Davidson, R.J., Cohen, J.D., 2004. Placebo-induced changes in FMRI in the anticipation and experience of pain. Science 303 (5661), 1162–1167.

CHAPTER

5

Blind Peer Review by Academic Journals

Emily A. Largent[1], Richard T. Snodgrass[2]

[1]Program in Health Policy, Harvard University, Cambridge, MA, USA;
[2]Department of Computer Science, The University of Arizona, Tucson, AZ, USA

OUTLINE

INTRODUCTION

Peer review, "the evaluation of research findings for competence, significance, and originality by qualified experts" (Benos et al., 2007, p. 145), is the gold standard for assessment of manuscripts submitted to journals.[1] "Peer review was originally conceived to provide

[1]This chapter is based, in part, on prior work by Richard T. Snodgrass (2006, 2007).

Blinding as a Solution to Bias
http://dx.doi.org/10.1016/B978-0-12-802460-7.00005-X

advice for the editor, the equivalent of asking the knowledgeable colleague down the hall for an opinion. By the 1960s and 1970s, however, it had come to be the measure of quality for journals—high-quality journals use strong peer-review systems" (Bordage and Caelleigh, 2001, p. 904). Correspondingly, publications "are not held in high esteem if they do not first pass through this process [of peer review]" (Benos et al., 2007, p. 146).

The stakes of the peer review process are quite high for scholars, scholarship, and society. Fletcher and Fletcher (1997) explain:

> Progress in science depends on both the dissemination of ideas and evidence as well as on vigorous critique by peers, both of which take place in journals. In basic science, inefficiency results from conclusions that exceed or fall short of study results, or are difficult to understand, as colleagues' time and money is invested in building on or refuting incorrect results. In applied fields such as medicine and engineering, people can be harmed if the information in journals is wrong, and clinicians are misled about diagnosis and treatment, or engineers are misinformed regarding the risks of buildings, bridges, and nuclear energy plants. Also, scientists' careers, including grant awards, promotion and reputation, depend on their success as authors. (pp. 36–37)

While Fletcher and Fletcher frame their discussion in terms of the sciences, their observations are applicable to other academic disciplines as well. Peer review outcomes—that is, which articles are ultimately published—affect individual authors, journal readers, and the course of future research (Hojat et al., 2003).

At present, although peer review is generally accepted as an essential element in the pursuit of knowledge, as one that imparts legitimacy and credibility, considerable debate persists on how best to implement it. Richard Smith, former editor of the *British Medical Journal*, has enumerated the faults of peer review: "In addition to being poor at detecting gross defects and almost useless for detecting fraud, it is slow, expensive, profligate of academic time, highly subjective, something of a lottery, prone to bias, and easily abused" (Smith, 2006, p. 179). Nevertheless, Smith, like others, argues that the correct approach is not to abandon peer review but to identify ways to improve it, ideally through evidence-based interventions. It is, he says, "a system full of problems but the least worse we have" (Smith, 2006, p. 178).

Given the centrality of peer review to the production and propagation of knowledge, one might be surprised to learn that research on the efficacy of peer review was relatively scarce prior to 1975 and that clear-cut evidence is still lacking today. What discussion existed before 1975 was based more on anecdote than on systematically gathered data. This changed when, in 1974, the then-editor of the *New England Journal of Medicine* called for research into peer review, arguing that "data were needed to justify the American process that 'faithfully and meticulously depended on a system of peer review'" as compared to the process at the prestigious British medical journal *Lancet*, which did not (Weller, 2001, pp. 10–11). Although research into peer review was subsequently conducted (Armstrong, 1997; Campanario, 1998a,b), a Cochrane review published in 2007 concluded that "little empirical evidence is available to support the use of editorial peer review" (Jefferson et al., 2007, p. 2) and urgently called for the launch of a "large, well-funded programme of research" into its effects (Jefferson et al., 2007, p. 2). Further inquiry, descriptive and normative, is doubtlessly still needed.

In this chapter, we will examine the extant scholarly literature related to one aspect of the peer review practices of academic journals: blinding, specifically, attempting to mask the identity of authors to reviewers and/or of reviewers to authors. A central critique of peer review is that it is subjective, overly dependent on the opinions of individual reviewers.

This subjectivity leads to inconsistency in publication recommendations and introduces the possibility of bias. Types of bias relevant to peer review include gender bias, racial bias, status bias (the tendency to more favorably evaluate manuscripts submitted by famous authors from prestigious institutions), ideological bias (the tendency to favor a particular ideological or theoretical orientation to research and analysis), bias against negative results (the tendency to reject those studies with negative findings), and confirmatory bias (the "tendency of some reviewers to accept outcomes that agree with commonly accepted theories and to discredit those that do not") (Hojat et al., 2003, p. 78). Blinding is commonly advocated as an approach to alleviate the effects of biases. Blind peer review may help to mitigate some of these effects, but clearly, it will be extremely difficult (if not impossible) to address all of the just-enumerated biases through blinding.

We begin this chapter by providing a brief background on peer review. We then examine empirical evidence related to (1) blinding as a means of reducing bias; (2) blinding as a means of yielding higher quality reviews; (3) the feasibility and efficacy of blinding; and (4) stakeholder (i.e., author, reviewer, editor) preferences for blinding. Although the evidence for the first three is generally inconclusive, one finds widespread support for blinded peer review. Ultimately, we argue that, as the evidence currently stands, a determination that blinding is "worth it" requires weighing the acknowledged weaknesses of blinding against gains in the perceived fairness of peer review.

OVERVIEW OF PEER REVIEW

Peer review is intended to improve published manuscripts in at least two ways. First, it helps editors winnow out the best papers—in terms of both overall quality and appropriateness for a particular journal—from all of those submitted. Second, by offering comments both minor and substantive, it helps authors improve their papers, with the relevant baseline being what would have been published had the manuscript simply been published as submitted. To the extent that it succeeds in these two aims, peer review should improve the overall quality of the scholarly literature.

While journals in all branches of academe share "the core ethos and values of peer review, it has evolved in diverse ways to best fit the environments and circumstances of the various sciences and disciplines" (Bordage and Caelleigh, 2001, p. 904).

Process of Peer Review

Although peer review processes vary from journal to journal, there are common features. Editors can summarily reject a manuscript upon submission. For those manuscripts that survive this first cut, the editor typically selects two or more reviewers to whom the manuscript is sent. "Reviewers who are experts in some aspect of the submitted work (its contents, methods, or importance), are external to the staff of the journal itself, and are free of financial conflict of interest, provide not only their opinion about whether the work should be published but also suggestions for both editors and authors about how the written presentation could be improved" (Fletcher and Fletcher, 1997, p. 36). After receiving the completed peer reviews and advice from the journal's editorial staff, an editor will decide whether to reject, request a revision, or publish a particular manuscript. Given that the rejection rate for articles submitted to peer-reviewed journals is quite high, as is the rate of acceptance made conditional upon revisions in accordance with reviewers' comments, it is unsurprising that peer reviewers have been described as "gatekeepers" (Bradley, 1981, p. 31; Hojat et al., 2003) to publication.

Types of Peer Review

There are two general types of peer review: *open* or *blind*.

In open peer reviewing, the identities of both the author(s) and reviewers (sometimes called "referees") are revealed. Reviewers will be aware of who authored a given manuscript, and authors will be able to attribute the feedback they receive to particular individuals. Open peer review has a number of possible variations. For instance, the names of the reviewers—and even their reviews—might be published alongside the final paper.

Within the category of blind peer reviewing, a further distinction is drawn between *single-blind* and *double-blind* peer review. In single-blind review, the reviewer knows the identity of the author, while the reviewer is anonymous to the author. In double-blind review, both the reviewer and the author are anonymous to each other. We will merely note that some have argued for adoption of so-called *triple-blind* peer review in which neither the reviewer nor the editor would be privy to identifying information about the author (Jump, 2015).

Regarding terminology, we wish to acknowledge that some people are highly offended by the use of "blindness" as a rhetorical device to signify lack of knowledge and find it demeaning to people with disabilities. They have, therefore, lobbied journals to eschew the phrase "blind review" and suggest use of neutral but equivalent phrases such as "anonymous review" or "masked review" instead, a practice some journals and professional associations have adopted (Tremain, 2011). While sympathetic to this position, we have retained the traditional terms, as they remain widespread and will be most familiar to our readers.

Disciplines vary widely in their use of single- and double-blind review. A survey of 553 journals selected from 18 disciplines revealed that "[a]cross the disciplines, the majority of surveyed journals used double-blind reviews (58%), 37% employed single-blind, and only 5% made use of open review" (Bachand and Sawallis, 2003, p. 54).

A Note on the Evidence

Because "[p]eer review is not a discipline-specific field, literature on the subject could and does exist in almost every scholarly field with a journal publication outlet" (Weller, 2001, p. 8). That fact has two related, though distinct, implications for our present undertaking. First, it is useful and instructive to learn what a range of disciplines, using diverse approaches, have discovered about blind review. Second, rather than presenting an exhaustive summary of the literature on blinding in peer review, we have chosen to group studies thematically to facilitate exploration of the broad issues that cut across disciplines: whether blinding a reviewer to an author's identity enhances fairness; whether blinding authors and/or reviewers enhances the quality of reviews; and finally, whether blinding a reviewer to the identity of an author is even feasible. This thematic approach is also pragmatic: because the relevant studies ask slightly different questions, use different designs, and have different outcome measures, there is a barrier to conducting formal *meta*-analysis (Jefferson et al., 2007).

We caution that many of the studies presented below have limitations that threaten their internal and external validity. In studies that used nonrandomized designs, for instance, findings may be confounded by other factors such as the quality of the submitted manuscripts. A majority of the studies have small sample sizes, and in some instances, confidence intervals are not sufficiently narrow to draw definite conclusions. A common methodological issue for studies examining the effects of blinding on fairness and quality is the difficulty of ensuring robust blinding. Additionally, the character of a particular academic discipline or of the journal(s) at which a study was conducted may limit generalizability. We flag these concerns in a general way here so that readers can keep them in mind; when appropriate, further limitations of particular studies will be noted below.

DOUBLE-BLINDING AS A MEANS OF ENHANCING FAIRNESS

Ideally, the determination that a manuscript will or will not be accepted for publication should be made on the basis of the manuscript alone: is what the submission states correct, insightful, and an advancement of the state-of-the-art? "Bias occurs if a review is influenced by other criteria, such as geographic location or institutional prestige" (Ross et al., 2006, p. 1675). The fundamental argument in favor of double-blind review is that when a manuscript is so blinded, reviewers cannot take irrelevant criteria (i.e., their biases) into account, and so judge the manuscript on its own merits. Advocates of blinding suggest that this will both improve the accuracy of the peer review process by allowing the best work to shine and promote fairness to authors.

Any number of an author's personal and professional attributes could be subject to bias. We will consider: affiliation with a less-prestigious institution; non-U.S. origins; prolificness; and gender. Finally, we will consider the effect of blinding on perceived fairness.

Fairness to Authors from Less-Prestigious Institutions

Some evidence from retrospective and experimental studies suggests that when reviewers know authors' names and affiliations, they may exhibit bias against papers from unknown authors or less-prestigious institutions. The "inclination to give disproportionate credit to those who are already famous" (Hojat et al., 2003, p. 79) is variously called the "Matthew effect" or "status bias" (Cox et al., 1993).

An anecdote illustrates the possibility. The psychologist Robert Rosenthal has related how he was unable to publish between 15 and 20 manuscripts that he wrote while at the University of North Dakota (UND) (Rosenthal, 1982). Rosenthal continues:

> After I had been at Harvard a few years, most of those same articles *were* published in mainstream journals. My anecdote does not demonstrate that journal articles were biased against papers from UND and biased toward papers from Harvard. There are plausible rival hypotheses that cannot be ruled out. My belief, however, is that location status bias may well have played some role in the change in publishability of my stack of papers. (p. 235)

With this anecdote in mind, we now examine the studies that attempt to detect status bias.

Several retrospective studies have found evidence of status bias. One found that "some 91 per cent of the papers by physicists in the foremost departments were accepted [for publication at *The Physical Review*] as against 72 per cent from other universities" (Zuckerman and Merton, 1971, p. 85). A retrospective study of reviews for journals in the physical sciences found large differences in how papers from more- and less-prestigious universities were reviewed (Gordon, 1980). The investigator concluded that "the scientific predispositions of referees…bias them toward less critical evaluation of colleagues who come from similar institutional…groups" (Gordon, 1980, pp. 274–275). A third retrospective study, this one of single-blind reviews for the *Journal of Pediatrics*, found partial evidence for status bias (Garfunkel et al., 1994). Lower institutional rank was associated with lower rates of recommendation for acceptance for some types of papers but not others (Garfunkel et al., 1994).

By contrast, Mahoney et al. (1978) performed an early experiment in which institutional affiliation was manipulated so that half of the manuscripts sent to 68 volunteer reviewers allegedly came from a prestigious university, while the other half allegedly came from a relatively unknown college. They found that "the effect of institutional prestige failed to attain significance" (p. 70) on how reviewers rated various aspects of the manuscripts or on their summary recommendation regarding publication.

Two additional experiments bear discussing at greater length. First, Peters and Ceci (1982) performed a famous experiment in which 12 papers published by investigators from prestigious American psychology departments in high-quality journals were altered to include fictitious names and less-prestigious institutional affiliations. The altered papers were then formally resubmitted to the same journals that had published them just 18–32 months prior. Remarkably, only three of the manuscripts were detected as resubmissions. Of the remaining nine manuscripts, eight were rejected, in many cases based on the presence of "serious methodological flaws." In their analysis, Peters and Ceci (1982) put forth the possibility of status bias: "The predominantly negative evaluations of the resubmissions may reflect some form of response bias in favor of the original authors as a function of their association with prestigious institutions. These individuals may have received a less critical, more benign evaluation than did our unknown authors from 'no-name' institutions… The near perfect reviewer agreement regarding the unacceptability of the resubmitted manuscripts, coupled with the presumably near perfect agreement among the original reviewers in favor of publishing, provide additional convergent support for the response bias hypothesis" (p. 192).

Second, a seminal experiment by Blank (1991) demonstrated status bias in reviewing more directly. In her experiment, which lasted for 2 years, every other paper submitted to the *American Economic Review* was designated for double-blind review. Her question was "whether the ratio of acceptance rates between institutional ranks in the blind sample differs from the corresponding ratio in the nonblind sample" (pp. 1053–1054). It was found that this ratio did not differ for those at top-ranked departments nor for those at colleges and low-ranked universities. However, all other groups, in that important gray area where editorial judgment is most needed, had substantially lower acceptance rates in the blind sample than in the non-blind sample; in some cases, the acceptance rate dropped by more than seven percentage points.

While several retrospective studies have suggested the possibility of status bias, evidence from controlled experiments is inconclusive. Double-blind review may moderately reduce bias experienced by authors from less-prestigious institutions—and may be especially important for authors in the relatively undifferentiated middle.

Fairness to Non-US Authors

Evidence suggests that reviewers may exhibit bias when they know a manuscript's authors come from outside the United States.

A retrospective analysis of single-blind reviews found evidence of status bias at a coarse geographical level (Link, 1998). In this analysis of original research articles submitted to *Gastroenterology* over a 2-year period, it was found that "reviewers from the United States and outside the United States evaluate non-US papers similarly and evaluate papers submitted by US authors more favorably, with US reviewers having a significant preference for US papers" (Link, 1998, p. 246). While not from journals, a relevant retrospective analysis of all abstracts submitted to the American Heart Association's annual Scientific Sessions research meeting before and after implementation of double-blinded peer review found that blinding "significantly attenuated the association between country and likelihood of abstract acceptance" (Ross et al., 2006, pp. 1677–1678). Finally, a randomized study of 40 consecutive manuscripts submitted to *Dermatologic Surgery* found a nominal (but not statistically significant) difference in likelihood of acceptance associated with the geographic origin of the manuscript (Alam et al., 2011).

Although limited, the evidence suggests that reviewers have some preference for US authors. If so, double-blind review may modestly reduce bias experienced by authors from outside the United States.

Fairness to Prolific Authors

The experimental evidence is mixed concerning bias experienced by prolific authors.

The Mahoney et al. (1978) experiment, discussed above, suggests that reviewers may be biased in favor of prolific authors. The volunteer reviewers, who were not blinded, rated papers "as more innovative and publishable if the fictitious author included self-references in the manuscript than if no self-references were included" (Mahoney et al., 1978, p. 78).

By contrast, a randomized controlled trial involving manuscripts submitted to the *Journal of Developmental and Behavioral Pediatrics* found that "senior authors with more previous articles received significantly better scores from the blinded reviewers…, but not from the nonblinded reviewers" (Fisher et al., 1994, p. 145). They "interpret[ed] this finding to indicate that the blinded reviewers, especially those who were really blinded and could not guess author identity, may have recognized improved quality in the work of those authors with more previous publications. In contrast, reviewers who were aware of author identity did not give better scores to the more experienced authors, likely indicating that various types of bias may have entered into their thinking" (Fisher et al., 1994, p. 146).

A retrospective study found no impact of double-blind review on the rate at which prolific authors have their papers published in the Special Interest Group on Management of Data (SIGMOD) conference (Madden and DeWitt, 2006). However, an independent analysis of this data reached the opposite conclusion (Tung, 2006).

These contradictory results render it impossible to say anything definitive about the impact of blinding on prolific authors, though the strongest of the studies suggests that blinding could be beneficial.

Fairness to Female Authors

Sexism is a concern in peer review broadly (Wennerås and Wold, 1997). It is, therefore, unsurprising that several disciplines have launched in-depth studies in response to concerns related to gender equity in publication. These studies suggest the existence of bias against female authors.

A classic and much-referenced study showed that even when the work of a woman was identical to that of a man, the former was judged to be inferior to the latter (Goldberg, 1968). In this study, scholarly essays in a number of academic fields were presented to female college students. All of the students rated the same essays, but half of the essays carried the names of male authors (e.g., John T. McKay), whereas the other half carried the names of female authors (e.g., Joan T. McKay). Those essays attributed to male authors were rated higher. A quantitative *meta*-analysis of this and similar studies conducted over the two subsequent decades found that "the average difference between ratings of men and women is negligible" (Swim et al., 1989, p. 409). Consistent with this analysis, 73% of studies found no significant effect for the Joan–John manipulation, 20% found that John's work was rated higher, and the remaining 7% found that Joan's work was rated higher (Swim et al., 1989). More relevant to the issue of peer review is the observation from the American Psychological Association (APA) Task Force on Women in Academe that when "Joan and John's work was high in quality, the effect size was close to zero (−0.02 [the negative sign indicating a lower evaluation of female-authored work]); the effect was larger when Joan and John's work was medium in quality (−0.24)… [T]hese results seem to indicate that evaluation of absolutely outstanding articles will not be biased, but articles of ambiguous merit may be judged based on the author's gender" (Fouad et al., 2000, p. 45).

The seminal experiment by Blank (1991), described earlier, was initiated due to concerns of gender bias. At the time it was conducted, the *American Economic Review* had employed single-blind reviewing for most of its recent history. In the mid-1980s, the American Economic Association's Committee on the Status of Women in the Economics Profession formally expressed its concern about "the potential negative effect on women's acceptance rates of a single-blind system" (Blank, 1991, p. 1045). The Board of Editors at the *American Economic Review* subsequently asked Blank to design and run a randomized experiment looking into this. Her careful randomization process guaranteed that papers by women (and men) in each sample had identical distributions of characteristics. This made it possible to compare acceptance rates between the blind and non-blind samples without other controls, and indeed, there were striking differences. Blank found no significant difference in acceptance rates between the two samples for women. By contrast, acceptance rates for men were significantly higher in the non-blind sample. When reviewers knew that a male authored a paper, they accepted a higher percentage (15% vs 11%) than if the paper was blinded.

Blank (1991) emphasized that the core issue was not whether women's acceptance rates differed from men's but "whether the *ratio* of male to female acceptance rates in the non-blind sample is different from that in the blind sample" (p. 1053). She went on: "In both samples, women's acceptance rates are lower than men's, but the differential in the blind sample is smaller. While women in the blind sample have an acceptance rate only 1 percentage point below that of men, their rate is 3.8 percentage points lower in the non-blind sample" (p. 1053). The results were statistically insignificant, perhaps because there were too few observations of papers authored by women. Blank concluded that "this paper provides little evidence that moving to a double-blind reviewing system will substantially increase the acceptance rate for papers by female economists" (p. 1063).

The Modern Language Association's (MLA) experience was strikingly different. The switch to double-blind reviewing resulted in a large increase in acceptances for female-authored publications, such that the acceptance rate for women eventually became comparable to that for men (Billard, 1993). The impetus for the MLA's change to double-blind review was the perception of gender bias by female MLA members. Although the MLA vigorously denied bias in its review processes, it instituted a blind reviewing procedure. "The result was unequivocal: There was a dramatic rise in the acceptance of papers by female authors" (Horrobin, 1982, p. 217).

More recently, a retrospective study of reviews for *Behavioral Ecology* found that in the 4 years following the introduction of double-blind review, the absolute number of manuscripts accepted for publication increased, which benefited both male first-authors and female first-authors (Budden et al., 2008). The magnitude of this difference was, however, significantly larger for females than for males: there was a 7.9% increase in the proportion of papers with a female first-author and a corresponding decrease in papers with a male first-author. Budden et al. found that the increase in female authorship at *Behavioral Ecology* was greater than that seen in most of the comparable single-blind journals over the same time period. Yet, an independent analysis of this data, using a general linear mixed model rather than testing each journal separately, reached the opposite conclusion, finding that "the increase in female authorship over time in *BE* [*Behavioral Ecology*] is not exceptionally different from the changes in the other journals in the field" (Webb et al., 2008, p. 352).

The evidence suggests that double-blinded peer review could have a favorable effect on acceptance rates for female authors. The consequences of such a shift could be far-reaching and extend well beyond publications: "If females are less successful in publishing research on account of their gender, then given current practices associated with appointment and tenure, and the need for women dramatically to out-compete their male counterparts to be perceived as equal, any such publication bias impedes the progress of women to more advanced professional stages" (Budden et al., 2008, p. 6).

The Perception of Fairness

Although the evidence we have just reviewed about the existence of bias in peer review is mixed, the fact is that "[r]efereeing is *perceived* by many writers as being subject to various kinds of biases: biases in favor of male or female, young or established, national or foreign researchers, working at small or large institutions, in well-developed or developing countries and so on" (Genest, 1993, p. 324). For some, "[w]hether such biases are sufficiently strong and widespread to distort the whole review process is beyond the point. So long as the *potential* for abuse is there, we should guard against it, and double-blind refereeing is but one means of ensuring such protection" (Genest, 1993, p. 324). It seems inescapable to conclude that "much of the value of double-blind refereeing lies in the community perception of fairness" (Altman et al., 1992, p. 266).

Resnik et al. (2008) conducted a survey of government researchers concerning their perceptions about ethical problems with journal peer review. Bias was the second most commonly reported problem, with 50.5% of respondents saying they had encountered at least one biased reviewer during the peer review process. A limitation of this opinion survey is that it does not provide objective data on whether bias actually existed. The authors note that answering yes to the question "a reviewer was biased" may, for example, "result from the respondent's own displeasure with the reviewer's comments or recommendations" (Resnik et al., 2008, p. 308). Nevertheless, documenting perceived bias "can be an important finding in its own right, because a scientist may change his/her behavior in response to what he/she perceives to be a problem… A researcher who is concerned that a reviewer is incompetent or biased may choose to ignore the reviewer's comments rather than address the concerns (which may in fact be valid)" (Resnik et al., 2008, pp. 308–309). If Resnik et al. are correct, even if bias does not actually exist, the mere perception of bias could minimize the effectiveness of peer review (i.e., improving the quality of published articles by incorporating feedback from reviewers) by eroding trust.

Concern about effects of perceived bias or unfairness is evident in the recent decision by the journal *Nature* to begin offering optional double-blind reviewing. The executive editor of Nature Publishing Group "admits that it will be difficult to demonstrate conclusively that double-blind review eliminates bias. 'But we feel that is not a reason not to offer it. If scientists feel they would be better served this way, why would we not offer it?'" (Jump, 2015, n.p.).

Trust in the peer review process is both intrinsically and instrumentally valuable. Trust may be promoted by fairness in the procedures (i.e., how people are treated) and/or fairness in the outcome (i.e., publication decisions). If double-blind reviewing promotes trust in the process, regardless of how it affects outcomes, this may be the strongest argument yet in favor of double over single-blind peer review.

BLINDING AS A MEANS OF IMPROVING THE QUALITY OF REVIEWS

As described above, peer review is intended to improve published manuscripts by aiding editors in identification of high-impact articles for publication and by offering constructive feedback for authors to incorporate in the form of revisions, whether minor or substantive. High-quality reviews should further both of these ends.

The quality of reviews may be evaluated along two dimensions: content, which "refers to the substance and scientific scrutiny evident in the review," and format, which "addresses practicalities of the peer review and editorial processes" such as timeliness and observation of good reviewing etiquette (Feurer et al., 1994, p. 98). According to a survey conducted by Kearney and Freda (2005), "[T]he most universally desired characteristic [of reviews] was specific, detailed guidance to the author on how to improve the manuscript. Editors preferred reviews that demonstrated that the paper had 'obviously been read carefully…' …A balanced, objective, and fair review that included comments on strengths and weaknesses was also valued, as was a review that conveyed suggestions in a helpful, positive, or constructive tone" (p. 449).

Effects of (Not) Revealing Author Identity

Contradictory theories have been advanced regarding both the mechanism and direction of the effect of double-blinding on review quality.

On the one hand, advocates of open or single-blind peer review offer a variety of arguments in favor of their position. One is that revealing an author's identity increases the quality of reviews by supplying peer reviewers with relevant information about the author's prior accomplishments, publications, and citation rates (Dalton, 1995). Another belief is "that information about the authors' institutional affiliation helps referees evaluate manuscripts because they constitute presumptive 'proof' that the research described was actually done" (Campanario, 1998b, p. 295). For instance, it might "reduce the number of questions referees need to ask about whether a lab has the expertise to perform a 'tricky' technique successfully" (Jump, 2015, n.p.). On the other hand, advocates of double-blind review argue that reviewers might use identifying information as an inappropriate shortcut or faulty heuristic in their decision-making, whereas not revealing an author's identity permits the work to speak for itself (Billard, 1993). Advocates of blinding reviewers claim that the excellence of the manuscript should be readily apparent, even in the absence of identifying information (Perlman, 1982).

The evidence is mixed. Before proceeding, we note that most of the studies used their own rating instruments, and most scales appeared not to be validated. We will begin by looking at the evidence suggesting that double-blinding does, in fact, enhance review quality.

A double-blind study of double-blind reviewing (!), carried out at the *Journal of General Internal Medicine*, found that "blinding reviewers improves the quality of review from the editor's perspective" (McNutt et al., 1990, p. 1375). A potential limitation to the study is that "the referees receiving the blinded copy of the manuscript would have been aware that they were part of an experiment and may in consequence have been more careful with their reports" (Cox et al., 1993, p. 316).

Jadad et al. (1996) sought to determine whether blinding would improve the quality of recommendations to include clinical trials in meta-analyses and systematic reviews. Reviewers were randomly assigned to open or blind assessment of the clinical trials. "Blind assessments of the reports produced significantly lower and more consistent scores" (Jadad et al., 1996, p. 9). Jadad et al. characterized this as an advantage of blinding, stating, "This may be very important for editors of journals to reduce bias in manuscript selection which could be introduced in open peer review" (p. 10).

Despite evidence that "scientists who have done large amounts of good quality work in the recent past are likely to continue doing so in the near future" (Abrams, 1991, p. 115), Laband and Piette (1994) looked at citation rates and found that "articles reviewed single-blind are less likely than those reviewed double-blind to be identified correctly as the highest-impact articles" (p. 148).

Now, we will turn our attention to studies that failed to find that blinding reviewers to author identity improves the quality of peer review. One of these was a retrospective study (Isenberg et al., 2009); others, however, were randomized experiments.

In one randomized experiment, reviewers for five biomedical journals either conducted their manuscript review according to the journal's usual practice, which for four of the journals was single-blind, or one of the two reviewers was randomly selected to conduct double-blind peer review (Justice et al., 1998). Justice et al. found that "authors and editors perceived no significant difference in quality between masked and unmasked reviews [and] no difference in the degree to which the review influenced the editorial decision" (p. 240).

In another randomized experiment, a paper that had already been accepted for publication by *BMJ* was altered to introduce eight weaknesses in design, analysis, or interpretation (Godlee et al., 1998). Study participants were then asked to comment on the paper as part of a study into ways of improving peer review. Blinding "had no effect on the quality of reviewers' reports as judged by the number of weaknesses that they identified in the manuscript" (Godlee et al., 1998, p. 239).

In a randomized trial of 527 consecutive manuscripts submitted to *BMJ*, reviewers were randomized to receive either a blinded or unblinded version of a manuscript (van Rooyen et al., 1998). The study concluded that blinding has little effect on the quality of reviews. There was no significant difference in the recommendations regarding publication between the blinded and unblinded groups.

Finally, the Alam et al. (2011) study, described above, found no significant difference between the scores given to manuscripts by blinded and unblinded reviewers. There was also no difference in word count, which was used as a proxy for review quality, between blinded and unblinded reviews. These "results would suggest that blinded reviewers are no more or less likely to provide quality reviews than unblinded reviewers" (Alam et al., 2011, p. 566).

Although some studies suggest that author anonymity enhances the quality of reviews, other studies, generally with superior design, do not document such an effect. This suggests a negligible effect of blinding on review quality.

Effects of (Not) Revealing Reviewer Identity

Several studies have examined the effects of disclosing *reviewer* identity—to authors, to other reviewers, and even to a journal's readership.

In the randomized trial conducted by van Rooyen et al. (1998), described above, manuscripts were additionally randomized as to whether reviewers' identifies were revealed to their co-reviewers or not, which was (somewhat confusingly) called "unmasking." van Rooyen et al. explained that "[a]lthough 2-factor analysis of variance revealed a statistically significant difference [in review quality] between the masked and unmasked groups ($P=0.04$), absolute differences were of no editorial significance" (p. 236). Similarly, Das Sinha et al. (1999) found that informing reviewers that their reviews would be exchanged with co-reviewers did not affect quality.

In another randomized trial, 125 manuscripts submitted to *BMJ* in early 1998 were each sent to two reviewers who were randomized to remain anonymous or to have their identity revealed to the manuscript's author(s) (van Rooyen et al., 1999). No significant difference in quality between anonymous reviewers and identified reviewers was found. In addition, no significant difference was found in either the recommendation regarding publication or time taken to review the manuscript. van Rooyen et al. (1999) did find, however, that asking reviewers to be identified significantly increased the likelihood of reviewers declining to review. Interestingly, *BMJ* announced that it would let authors know the identity of reviewers in 1999 (Smith, 1999).

Walsh et al. (2000) found notably different results. They conducted a trial in which reviewers for the *British Journal of Psychiatry* were randomized to either a signed or an unsigned group. Upon comparing the quality of reviews, Walsh et al. found that "the total mean score was significantly higher in the signed group than the unsigned group" (p. 48). They noted that "signed reviews were significantly more courteous and less abusive than unsigned reviews" (p. 48) and offered more constructive comments. Signed reviewers were significantly more likely than unsigned reviewers to recommend rejection of manuscripts.

In an interesting twist, a study conducted at *BMJ* randomized manuscripts to either have the reviewer's signed report made available only to the author or have it made available to the public on the *BMJ* Web site alongside the published paper (van Rooyen et al., 2010). The intervention was revealing to reviewers, after they agreed to review but before they undertook their review, that their signed report might appear on the Web site. "Forewarning reviewers that their signed reviews might be published had no discernable effect on the overall quality of their reviews" (van Rooyen et al., 2010, n.p.).

At this point, the jury is still out. There is little to suggest that reviewer anonymity enhances the quality of peer review, though there may be practical reasons for favoring anonymity, such as retaining reviewers.

BREAKING THE (DOUBLE) BLIND

Many benefits ascribed to double-blinding assume that blinding is successful in shielding the identity of the author from the reviewer. Of course, "[h]ow truly anonymous any party can be in a world in which referees are selected for their in-depth knowledge of a small slice of the universe of knowledge is open to question" (Dalton, 1995, p. 236). "The notion that a…referee can identify the author of a given paper in a specialty journal has been used by many to derogate the claim of an advantage to double-blind review" (Campanario, 1998b, p. 295).

How Double-Blinding Is Accomplished

Double-blinding may be accomplished in different ways. As a first cut, it is useful to differentiate author blinding from editorial blinding. *Author blinding* occurs when the author removes identifying information from a manuscript before submitting it, whereas *editorial blinding* occurs when identifying information is removed in the editorial process before the manuscript is sent to reviewers. Authors may be in a better position than editors to blind because they are more likely to know what kind of information could be identifying, though they may have incentives to evade the blind.

Another important variable is how much effort is expended on the task. "To simply block out the name and affiliation from the title page requires minimal effort, to block out self-references adds a little more, and scrutinizing the manuscript for any internal cues necessitates laborious line-by-line study. Therefore, the efficacy of the blinding process will vary directly with the effort expended on it" (Pitkin, 1995, p. 781). The feasibility of blinding is also "related to the type and circulation of the involved journal" (Fisher et al., 1994, p. 145).

Blinding Success Rates

Several studies have examined how well blinding works in practice, that is, how well a double-blinded manuscript hides the identity of the author(s). These studies, across a wide range of disciplines, have found that blinding achieved success rates of 53–79%.

A study of individuals who reviewed manuscripts submitted to the *Journal of Social Service Research* during 1978 showed that "in 56% of the reviews, the referees did not venture a guess as to the identity of the author. In another 4%, the referees guessed wrong. In an additional 5%, the referees made correct guesses about some bit of identifying information, but they did not guess the name of the author" (Rosenblatt and Kirk, 1981, p. 389). This works out to successful blinding 65% of the time for editorial blinding.

One retrospective study over six psychology journals employing author blinding showed that "35.6% of the 146 reviewers were correct in their identifications of the author or of at least one of the authors in the case of multi-authored papers... There were no significant differences in the proportion of correct detections among the six journals,... nor was there any relationship between detection accuracy and the number of years of reviewing experience" (Ceci and Peters, 1984, p. 1493). When "editorial staff oversights in not removing title pages of manuscripts before sending them to reviewers or authors' oversights in preparing their manuscripts, such as explicit flagging of former work ('In our earlier work...') or inappropriate inclusion of personal acknowledgments in the body of the text,...are excluded from the analysis, overall only 25.7% of reviewers are able to detect authors' identities, with very little variation among the six journals" (Ceci and Peters, 1984, p. 1494).

In another study, reviewers for the *American Journal of Public Health*, which relies on a combination of author and editorial blinding, were asked to identify author and institution for the manuscript they reviewed (Yankauer, 1991). Reviewers claimed to be able to identify the author and/or institution in 47% of cases. Of those cases, correct identification of the author or institution occurred 84% of the time. Blinding could, therefore, be considered successful 53% or 61% of the time, depending on whether successful blinding is defined to encompass self-reported instances of identification or is defined more narrowly to include only correct instances of identification.

Another experiment found that "a long-standing policy of masking did not increase masking success" (Cho et al., 1998, p. 243). This study included three medical journals with a long-standing policy of double-blind review and four medical journals that did not mask author identity. During the experiment, manuscripts that met the study's inclusion criteria were editorially blinded "by removing author and institutional identity from the title page, running headers or footers, and acknowledgments of manuscripts. Self-references in the text were not removed" (Cho et al., 1998, p. 244). Reviewers were asked if they thought they could identify any of the principal authors of the manuscript, and if yes, to name the author(s). If any reviewer correctly identified one or more authors, the reviewer was considered unmasked. Overall, 60% of reviewers were successfully blinded.

A prospective review of manuscripts submitted to two radiology journals with double-blind peer review policies found that, despite explicit instructions to authors, 34% of the manuscripts "contained information that potentially or definitely unblinded the identities of the authors or their institutions" (Katz et al., 2002, p. 1417). The most frequent violations of blinded peer review policies were "the statement of the authors' initials in the body of the manuscript, referencing the authors' own work in press, identifying references as the authors' previous work, revealing the identity of the institution in the figures, and stating the identity of the authors' institutions in the manuscript" (Katz et al., 2002, p. 1416). Editors at the two journals correctly identified the authors, their institutions, or both in 74% of the manuscripts in which the authors had been unsuccessful in their blinding. Unblinding occurred in 25% of all of the manuscripts reviewed.

A survey of reviewers for nursing journals found that blinding was generally successful at masking authors' identities (Baggs et al., 2008). Respondents were asked what percentage of the time they could identify authors even if they did not receive the authors' names. Sixty-two percent reported that they could never identify authors of papers, and another 17.5% reported that they could identify authors less than 10% of the time.

Several of the studies discussed previously also looked at the efficacy of blinding. In the McNutt et al. (1990) study, editorial blinding successfully masked the institution name for 73% of the reviewers and the authors' names for 76% of the reviewers. Blank's (1991) experiment found that "among all referee surveys received for blind papers, slightly over half (50.9 percent) claim to know the author. Ten percent of these referees are incorrect, however, so that only 45.6 percent of the authors in the blind sample are correctly identified" (p. 1051). The study by Fisher et al. (1994) evaluated the success of an editorial blinding process and found 54% of reviewers were thereby successfully blinded. Justice et al. (1998) concluded that "[s]uccess in masking reviewers to author identity was generally low (68%)" (p. 241). Manuscripts by authors with whom the reviewer was familiar were less likely to be successfully masked than manuscripts by authors who were not known to the reviewer (Justice et al., 1998). In the study by Godlee et al. (1998), 26% of the 90 respondents who had been blinded to the authors' identities nevertheless correctly named the authors. van Rooyen et al. (1998) found that 58% of reviewers were successfully blinded. Finally, Isenberg et al. (2009) found that 77.7% of the reviewers reported that they had no idea about the author's identity.

Overall, these studies suggest that even minimal editorial blinding can be somewhat effective. How one characterizes success rates may depend on whether one's philosophical viewpoint is more "glass-half-full" or "glass-half-empty."

Impact of Technology on Blinding

Going forward, technology may alter the feasibility and success of double-blinding. A handful of studies have explored this possibility. A data-mining experiment by Hill and Provost (2003) found that a computer program that tallied self-citations could identify the authors of physics papers using only the citations included in the paper 45% of the time. Authors with 100 or more prior publications could be identified 85% of the time.

In some disciplines, authors have strong incentives to disseminate their research results, for example, as a working paper, before eventual publication in an academic journal. These incentives may make blinding of manuscripts more difficult. Holm (2011) took a sample of 32 manuscripts from two economics journals that use double-blind review and asked participants in his study to use information about each paper (e.g., title and abstract) and the Internet search engine of their choice to identify the author. It took participants between 24 and 33 s to identify working papers and 34–62 s to identify conference papers using Google or Google Scholar. Holm concluded that "information about nearly all accepted papers was available on the Internet before their respective review processes were expected to be finished" (p. 26). He claims "author anonymity in a double-blind review process is no longer credible" (p. 26).

Neither of these studies spoke to reviewers' incentives to deliberately break a blind. They strongly suggest, however, that should an author wish to do so, the cost and difficulty of breaking a blind are increasingly low.

PREFERENCES FOR OPEN, SINGLE-, OR DOUBLE-BLIND REVIEW

Given the equivocal nature of much of the evidence on blinding, it is reasonable to ask how stakeholders in the peer review process feel about blinding. Studies conducted across a variety of disciplines suggest that there is a preference (though not unanimous) for double-blind review by reviewers, authors, and editors. Reasons for their preferences are relatively consistent across studies and reflect the debates in the literature. We now review these studies chronologically.

In the survey conducted by Yankauer (1991), described above, respondents were asked whether they favored double-blind review. In all, 75% of respondents favored blinding, and 8% stated that they had no preference. "The principal reason given for their opinion by those favoring blind review was the elimination of bias. The principal reason given for their opinion by those opposing blind review was failure of the attempt to blind" (Yankauer, 1991, p. 844). Yankauer noted that additional reasons given for opposing blind review were contradictory: respondents stated both that identification will not influence judgment and that identification assists judgment. Interestingly, on follow-up, only eight of the 30 reviewers who initially opposed blind review stated that they would sign all their reviews; 19 indicated they would not do so, and three would do so only in some instances.

A survey of Institute of Mathematical Statistics (IMS) members indicated support for double-blind review in the IMS journals (Cox et al., 1993). Nearly half of respondents (46%) agreed or strongly agreed with the statement that the IMS should institute double-blind review, while 24% were neutral, and 29% responded negatively. There was, apparently, a split between new researchers, a majority of whom endorsed double-blind refereeing (Altman et al., 1991, 1992), and more senior members, whose views were characterized as "negative but sympathetic" (Cox et al., 1993, p. 311). "An informal poll of some past editors of the *Annals* indicated little support for double-blind refereeing" (Cox et al., 1993, p. 311).

In the survey conducted by Kearney and Freda (2005), discussed above, 80% of nursing journal editors said that blinding was important in peer review, and 53% said they could see no benefit to unblinding either the author or reviewer. The editors expressed belief that double-blinding promoted objectivity "by protecting authors and reviewers from personal and emotional responses that might ensue from being identifiable or identifying the other party" (Kearney and Freda, 2005, p. 448).

When reviewers for *Medical Education* were surveyed, "74% of respondents said they would be willing to sign their reviews in the spirit of creating a more transparent review process; 20% were not sure and 6% would be unwilling" (Snell and Spencer, 2005, p. 95). First-time reviewers were more likely than more experienced reviewers to say 'No' or 'Not Sure.' Proponents of signing reviews "offered comments such as: 'peer review should be more open transparent and honest'; 'it is more fair and constructive'; 'reviewers will take more time with reviews'; and 'the quality of reviews would be better if the reviewer had to reveal their identity: if your opinions are based on sound judgment you should be prepared to stand by them'" (Snell and Spencer, 2005, p. 95). Meanwhile, comments from opponents included:

"'it's important to be able to make frank disclosures to the editors'; 'I might be tempted to be too soft'; 'this might alter my responses'; and 'there's the inevitable embarrassment of saying no to friends'" (Snell and Spencer, 2005, p. 95).

Subsequent to the survey conducted by Snell and Spencer (2005), *Medical Education* conducted a survey of both authors and reviewers who had submitted or reviewed a manuscript for the journal in 2003 and 2004 (Regehr and Bordage, 2006). Overall, 68% of respondents indicated a preference for some process of blinding that concealed author names. "Almost three-quarters of respondents (72%) indicated a desire for a procedure in which reviewer names were concealed or only revealed at the discretion of the reviewer (double-blind, single-blind, or optional single-blind)" (Regehr and Bordage, 2006, p. 837). Regehr and Bordage (2006) found that the primary reasons cited in favor of concealing author identity were: "to facilitate fairness (to obtain less biased and more objective reviews); to allow the manuscript to stand on its own merit; and to meet the need to avoid personal conflicts or rivalries with reviewers, especially given the small size of the medical education research community and the need to further protect junior members" (p. 835). Similar reasons were given for concealing reviewer identity: "to facilitate more honest reviews; to avoid 'bad blood' and personal tension among colleagues and friends, including retaliations (e.g., interfering with career development or grant applications); to allow the review to stand on its own merit; to encourage trust in the editor's choice of reviews, and to allow authors not to have to deal with knowing the identity of a reviewer bearing bad news or returning a harsh critique of one's work" (Regehr and Bordage, 2006, p. 835). The primary reasons given for revealing author identity were: "to allow for the preparation of better reviews by facilitating more understanding of the context of the study; to meet the need for greater transparency, and to acknowledge that masking does not always work because of specific clues in the manuscript. The main reasons for revealing reviewer identity were: to allow the author to appreciate the reviewer's qualifications and credibility; to foster more constructive and concrete reviews; to meet the need for accountability (by allowing the reviewer to stand by his or her critique); to facilitate fairness, and to allow for the possibility of author contact with the reviewer" (Regehr and Bordage, 2006, pp. 835–836).

The majority (73%) of respondents to a survey of ecologists and evolutionary biologists expressed a preference for double-blinding; 21% for open peer view; and only 6% for single-blinding (the peer review method typically employed by ecological journals) (Smit, 2006). The "clear preference for the double-blinded system existed across all groups, regardless of age, gender, academic position, and number of publications" (Smit, 2006, p. 713).

In the Baggs et al. (2008) survey, discussed above, nursing journal reviewers expressed a preference to maintain double-blinding, the most common form of blinding encountered by members of the sample. Eighty-one percent of respondents disagreed or strongly disagreed with the statement: "Reviewers should be informed of the identities of authors of a manuscript" (Baggs et al., 2008, p. 134). "Respondents thought that blinding decreased the potential for interpersonal conflict, encouraged honest and fair assessments on the part of reviewers, and protected junior reviewers from senior authors" (Baggs et al., 2008, p. 137).

It is interesting that some of the same arguments—such as facilitating fairness—are made both in favor of and against unblinding, which may be attributable to the inconclusive nature of the evidence on blinding. Nevertheless, a preference for blinding apparently predominates. These preferences may vary by discipline; as mentioned before, disciplines vary widely in their use of open, single-, and double-blind review.

CONCLUSION

At the outset, we remarked that although peer review is the gold standard for assessment of manuscripts submitted to journals, discussions regarding how best to accomplish it are ongoing. Such discussions are academic only in the sense that they relate to scholarship; they have great practical relevance. Much is at stake in peer review. Genest (1993) observed:

> There is a long tradition attached to the peer review system. As users of science, we all depend on it: our professional realizations are based upon the work of others, and we count on journal (and book) editors to separate the wheat from the tares. Although there is no such thing as perfection, it would be a disservice to the profession if too many scientific writings addressed irrelevant issues or contained gross factual errors. As producers of science, it is also in our interest that the system be fair: favoritism, discrimination and condescension bring discredit on the entire operation and ultimately work against the discipline, even if individual benefits occasionally may accrue in the short term. (p. 324)

Picking up on the central issue of fairness, we began this chapter with an exploration of data related to double-blinding as a means of imparting fairness to the peer review process. In 1991, Blank wrote:

> In summary, the literature on single-blind versus double-blind reviewing spans a wide variety of disciplines and provides rather mixed results. Few of the empirical tabulations provide convincing evidence on the effects or non-effects of refereeing practices, largely because of their inability to control for other factors in the data. If not fully convincing, however, there is at least a disturbing amount of evidence in these studies that is consistent with the hypothesis of referee bias in single-blind reviewing. (p. 1045)

Twenty-five years later, her conclusion holds. Despite a lack of conclusive evidence that bias exists, we have argued that even the perception of bias in peer review is troubling because "[t]hreats to the impartiality of review appear to threaten peer review's psychological and epistemic legitimacy" (Lee et al., 2013, p. 3). That, in turn, is a threat to all of us who are producers and/or users of knowledge.

Is double-blind reviewing a good or even plausible answer to this threat? The evidence is inconclusive, and reasonable people disagree. Many stakeholders in the peer review process favor double-blinding precisely because it is perceived to be fairer than the alternatives. Others think that blinding runs counter to the transparency that should inhere in the pursuit of knowledge. It is far from clear that blinding actually imparts fairness or enhances the quality of reviews; moreover, blinding is not always successful. Complicating matters, "the issue of double-blind refereeing today is one fraught with emotional overtones both rational and irrational, often subconsciously culturally based, and so is difficult for many of us to resolve equitably no matter how well intentioned" (Billard, 1993, p. 320).

The policy conundrum before each journal then, is this: how do we value fairness, and how does that value weigh against the costs and limits of blinding? We do not think that there is one "right" answer. Rather, each publication—and the community that it serves (i.e., producers and users of knowledge)—must carefully deliberate, in light of the existing literature and its own values and interests, and determine what is right for it.

References

Abrams, P.A., 1991. The predictive ability of peer review of grant proposals: the case of ecology and the U.S. National Science Foundation. Social Studies of Science 21 (1), 111–132.

Alam, M., Kim, N.A., Havey, J., Rademaker, A., Ratner, D., Tregre, B., West, D.P., Coleman, W.P., 2011. Blinded vs. unblinded peer review of manuscripts submitted to a dermatology journal: a randomized multi-rater study. British Journal of Dermatology 165 (3), 563–567.

Altman, N., Banks, D., Chen, P., Duffy, D., Hardwick, J., Leger, C., Owen, A., Stukel, T., 1991. Meeting the needs of new statistical researchers. Statistical Science 6 (2), 163–174.

Altman, N., Angers, J.F., Banks, D., Duffy, D., Hardwick, J., Leger, C., Martin, M., Nolan, D., Owen, A., Politis, D., Roeder, K., Stukle, T.N., Ying, Z., 1992. Rejoinder Statistical Science 7 (2), 265–266.

Armstrong, J.S., 1997. Peer review for journals: evidence on quality control, fairness, and innovation. Science and Engineering Ethics 3 (1), 63–84.

Bachand, R.G., Sawallis, P.P., 2003. Accuracy in the identification of scholarly and peer-reviewed journals and the peer-review process across disciplines. The Serials Librarian 45 (2), 39–59.

Baggs, J.G., Broome, M.E., Dougherty, M.C., Freda, M.C., Kearney, M.H., 2008. Blinding in peer review: the preferences of reviewers for nursing journals. Journal of Advanced Nursing 64 (2), 131–138.

Benos, D.J., Bashari, E., Chaves, J.M., Gaggar, A., Kapoor, N., LaFrance, M., Mans, R., Mayhew, D., McGowan, S., Polter, A., Qadri, Y., Sarfare, S., Schultz, K., Splittgerber, R., Stephenson, J., Tower, C., Walton, R.G., Zotov, A., 2007. The ups and downs of peer review. Advances in Physiology Education 31 (2), 145–152.

Billard, L., 1993. Comment Statistical Science 8 (3), 320–322.

Blank, R.M., 1991. The effects of double-blind versus single-blind reviewing: experimental evidence from *the American Economic Review*. The American Economic Review 81 (5), 1041–1067.

Bordage, G., Caelleigh, A.S., 2001. A tool for reviewers: "Review criteria for research manuscripts". Academic Medicine 76 (9), 904–908.

Bradley, J.V., 1981. Pernicious publication practices. Bulletin of the Psychonomic Society 18 (1), 31–34.

Budden, A.E., Tregenza, T., Aarssen, L.W., Koricheva, J., Leimu, R., Lortie, C.J., 2008. Double-blind review favours increased representation of female authors. Trends in Ecology & Evolution 23 (1), 4–6.

Campanario, J.M., 1998a. Peer review for journals as it stands today—part 1. Science Communication 19 (3), 181–211.

Campanario, J.M., 1998b. Peer review for journals as it stands today—part 2. Science Communication 19 (4), 277–306.

Ceci, S.J., Peters, D.P., 1984. How blind is blind review? American Psychologist 39 (12), 1491–1494.

Cho, M.K., Justice, A.C., Winker, M.A., Berlin, J.A., Waeckerle, J.F., Callaham, M.L., Rennie, D., 1998. Masking author identity in peer review: what factors influence masking success? PEER Investigators. Journal of the American Medical Association 280 (3), 243–245.

Cox, D., Gleser, L., Perlman, M., Reid, N., Roeder, K., 1993. Report of the ad hoc committee on double-blind refereeing. Statistical Science 8 (3), 310–317.

Dalton, M.S., 1995. Refereeing of scholarly works for primary publishing. Annual Review of Information Science and Technology (ARIST) 30, 213–250.

Feurer, I.D., Becker, G.J., Picus, D., Ramirez, E., Darcy, M.D., Hicks, M.E., 1994. Evaluating peer reviews. Pilot testing of a grading instrument. Journal of the American Medical Association 272 (2), 98–100.

Fisher, M., Friedman, S.B., Strauss, B., 1994. The effects of blinding on acceptance of research papers by peer review. Journal of the American Medical Association 272 (2), 143–146.

Fletcher, R.H., Fletcher, S.W., 1997. Evidence for the effectiveness of peer review. Science and Engineering Ethics 3 (1), 35–50.

Fouad, N., Brehm, S., Hall, C.I., Kite, M.E., Hyde, J.S., Russo, N.F., 2000. Women in Academe: Two Steps Forward, One Step Back. Retrieved from: http://www.apa.org/pi/women/programs/academe/taskforce-report.pdf.

Garfunkel, J.M., Ulshen, M.H., Hamrick, H.J., Lawson, E.E., 1994. Effect of institutional prestige on reviewers' recommendations and editorial decisions. Journal of the American Medical Association 272 (2), 137–138.

Genest, C., 1993. Comment Statistical Science 8 (3), 323–327.

Godlee, F., Gale, C.R., Martyn, C.N., 1998. Effect on the quality of peer review of blinding reviewers and asking them to sign their reports: a randomized controlled trial. Journal of the American Medical Association 280 (3), 237–240.

Goldberg, P., 1968. Are women prejudiced against women? Society 5 (5), 28–30.

Gordon, M.D., 1980. The role of referees in scientific communication. In: Hartley, J. (Ed.), The Psychology of Written Communication: Selected Readings. Kogan Page, London, pp. 263–275.

Hill, S., Provost, F., 2003. The myth of the double-blind review? Author identification using only citations. ACM SIGKDD Explorations Newsletter 5 (2), 179–184.

Hojat, M., Gonnella, J.S., Caelleigh, A.S., 2003. Impartial judgment by the "gatekeepers" of science: fallibility and accountability in the peer review process. Advances in Health Sciences Education 8 (1), 75–96.

Holm, H.J., 2011. Double-blind in light of the internet: a note on author anonymity. Information Economics and Policy 23 (1), 24–26.

Horrobin, D.F., 1982. Peer review: a philosophically faulty concept which is proving disastrous for science. Behavioral and Brain Sciences 5 (2), 217–218.

Isenberg, S.J., Sanchez, E., Zafran, K.C., 2009. The effect of masking manuscripts for the peer-review process of an ophthalmic journal. British Journal of Ophthalmology 93 (7), 881–884.

Jadad, A.R., Moore, A., Carroll, D., Jenkinson, C., Reynolds, D.J.M., Gavaghan, D.J., McQuay, H.J., 1996. Assessing the quality of reports of randomized clinical trials: is blinding necessary? Controlled Clinical Trials 17, 1–12.

Jefferson, T., Rudin, M., Brodney Folse, S., Davidoff, F., 2007. Editorial peer review for improving the quality of reports of biomedical studies. The Cochrane Database of Systematic Reviews 18 (2).

Jump, P., 2015. Will Double-Blind Reviewing Bring Quality into Focus? Times Higher Education. Retrieved from: https://www.timeshighereducation.co.uk/news/will-double-blind-reviewing-bring-quality-into-focus/2018963.article.

Justice, A.C., Cho, M.K., Winker, M.A., Berlin, J.A., Rennie, D., 1998. Does masking author identity improve peer review quality? A randomized controlled trial. PEER Investigators. Journal of the American Medical Association 280 (3), 240–242.

Katz, D.S., Proto, A.V., Olmsted, W.W., 2002. Incidence and nature of unblinding by authors: our experience at two radiology journals with double-blinded peer review policies. American Journal of Radiology 179 (6), 1415–1417.

Kearney, M.H., Freda, M.C., 2005. Nurse editors' views on the peer review process. Research in Nursing & Health 28 (6), 444–452.

Laband, D.N., Piette, M.J., 1994. A citation analysis of the impact of blinded peer review. Journal of the American Medical Association 272 (2), 147–149.

Lee, C.J., Sugimoto, C.R., Zhang, G., Cronin, B., 2013. Bias in peer review. Journal of the American Society for Information Science and Technology 64 (1), 2–17.

Link, A.M., 1998. U.S. and non-U.S. submissions: an analysis of reviewer bias. Journal of the American Medical Association 280 (3), 246–247.

Madden, S., DeWitt, D., 2006. Impact of double-blind reviewing on SIGMOD publication rates. ACM SIGMOD Record 35 (2), 29–32.

Mahoney, M.J., Kazdin, A.E., Kenigsberg, M., 1978. Getting published. Cognitive Therapy and Research 2 (1), 69–70.

McNutt, R.A., Evans, A.T., Fletcher, R.H., Fletcher, S.W., 1990. The effects of blinding on the quality of peer review: a randomized trial. Journal of the American Medical Association 263 (10), 1371–1376.

Perlman, D., 1982. Reviewer "bias": do Peters and Ceci protest too much? Behavioral and Brain Sciences 5 (02), 231–232.

Peters, D.P., Ceci, S.J., 1982. Peer-review practices of psychological journals: the fate of published articles, submitted again. Behavioral and Brain Sciences 5 (2), 187–195.

Pitkin, R.M., 1995. Blinded manuscript review: an idea whose time has come? Obstetrics & Gynecology 85 (5), 781–782.

Regehr, G., Bordage, G., 2006. To blind or not to blind? what authors and reviewers prefer. Medical Education 40 (9), 832–839.

Resnik, D.B., Gutierrez-Ford, C., Peddada, S., 2008. Perceptions of ethical problems with scientific journal peer review: an exploratory study. Science and Engineering Ethics 14 (3), 305–310.

van Rooyen, S., Godlee, F., Evans, S., Smith, R., Black, N., 1998. Effect of blinding and unmasking on the quality of peer review. Journal of the American Medical Association 280 (3), 234–237.

van Rooyen, S., Godlee, F., Evans, S., Black, N., Smith, R., 1999. Effect of open peer review on quality of reviews and on reviewers' recommendations: a randomised trial. BMJ 318, 23–27.

van Rooyen, S., Delamothe, T., Evans, S.J., 2010. Effect on peer review of telling reviewers that their signed reviews might be posted on the web: randomised controlled trial. BMJ 341, c5729.

Rosenblatt, A., Kirk, S.A., 1981. Recognition of authors in blind review of manuscripts. Journal of Social Service Research 3 (4), 383–394.

Rosenthal, R., 1982. Reliability and bias in peer-review practices. Behavioral and Brain Sciences 5 (2), 235–236.

Ross, J.S., Gross, C.P., Desai, M.M., Hong, Y., Grant, A.O., Daniels, S.R., Hachinski, V.C., Gibbons, R.J., Gardner, T.J., Krumholz, H.M., 2006. Effect of blinded peer review on abstract acceptance. Journal of the American Medical Association 295 (14), 1675–1680.

Sinha, S.D., Sahni, P., Nundy, S., 1999. Does exchanging comments of Indian and non-Indian reviewers improve the quality of manuscript reviews? National Medical Journal of India 12, 210–213.

Smit, C., 2006. Peer review: time for a change? BioScience 56 (9), 712–713.

Smith, R., 1999. Opening up BMJ peer review. BMJ 318 (7175), 4–5.

Smith, R., 2006. Peer review: a flawed process at the heart of science and journals. Journal of the Royal Society of Medicine 99 (4), 178–182.

Snell, L., Spencer, J., 2005. Reviewers' perceptions of the peer review process for a medical education journal. Medical Education 39 (1), 90–97.

Snodgrass, R.T., 2006. Single-versus double-blind reviewing: an analysis of the literature. ACM SIGMOD Record 35 (3), 8–21.

Snodgrass, R.T., 2007. Editorial: single- versus double-blind reviewing. ACM Transactions on Database Systems (TODS) 32 (1), 1–31.

Swim, J., Borgida, E., Maruyama, G., Myers, D.G., 1989. Joan McKay versus John McKay: do gender stereotypes bias evaluations? Psychological Bulletin 105 (3), 409–429.

Tremain, S., 2011. Abelist Language and Philosophical Associations. Retrieved from: http://www.newappsblog.com/2011/07/ableist-language-and-philosophical-associations.html.

Tung, A.K., 2006. Impact of double blind reviewing on SIGMOD publication: a more detail analysis. ACM SIGMOD Record 35 (3), 6–7.

Walsh, E., Rooney, M., Appleby, L., Wilkinson, G., 2000. Open peer review: a randomised controlled trial. The British Journal of Psychiatry 176 (1), 47–51.

Webb, T.J., O'Hara, B., Freckleton, R.P., 2008. Does double-blind review benefit female authors? Trends in Ecology & Evolution 23 (7), 351–353.

Weller, A.C., 2001. Editorial Peer Review: Its Strengths and Weaknesses. Information Today, Inc, Medford, NJ.

Wennerås, C., Wold, A., 1997. Nepotism and sexism in peer-review. Nature 387 (6631), 341–343.

Yankauer, A., 1991. How blind is blind review? American Journal of Public Health 81 (7), 843–845.

Zuckerman, H., Merton, R.K., 1971. Patterns of evaluation in science: institutionalisation, structure and functions of the referee system. Minerva 9 (1), 66–100.

CHAPTER

6

Clinical Trial Blinding in the Age of Social Media

Paul Wicks

PatientsLikeMe, Cambridge, MA, USA

OUTLINE

INTRODUCTION

In 1747, James Lind selected 12 sailors stricken with scurvy, each with a similar degree of severity characterized by "putrid gums...spots and lassitude, with weakness of the knees" (Dunn, 1997). In the forehold of the ship, the HMS Salisbury, Lind began one of the original, pivotal experiments of evidence-based medicine. While each man received a common daily diet of gruel, mutton, and pudding, the men grouped into six pairs to receive additional nutritional supplements. While Lind carefully observed their symptoms, each day one pair was given a supplementary quart of cider, another pair was given "elixir vitriol," the third pair received an "electuary" paste of sugar and water, the fourth pair received six spoonfuls of vinegar, the fifth unfortunate pair was put on a course of sea water, and, as any medical researcher knows, it was the final pair, who received oranges and limes, that recovered (Dunn, 1997). How publishable would such a study be today? The small sample size might be forgivable given the circumstances, but the most fatal flaw to a putative peer reviewer would be this—the sailors were neither allocated *randomly* to treatment groups nor properly *blinded* as to which intervention they were receiving. For all we know, Lind gave the intervention he believed was most promising to the sailors most likely to recover,

Blinding as a Solution to Bias
http://dx.doi.org/10.1016/B978-0-12-802460-7.00006-1

and obviously oranges and limes do not taste like vinegar and sea water, so we can be certain the participants were not blinded.

Fortunately for Lind (and the British Navy), the effects of ascorbic acid (vitamin C) contained in oranges and limes on scurvy are so profound that we do not have to be too concerned with these sources of ascertainment bias in his experiment; rather, the magnitude of the effect was so great that the benefits were obvious. However, in modern medicine we find ourselves at a point where "low-hanging fruit"—such as penicillin for bacterial infections, smallpox vaccination, and insulin for insulin-dependent diabetes (Black, 1996)—have already been found. What we are left with today are efforts to pinpoint more marginal positive benefits from powerful drugs that can carry a high burden of side effects, developed by for-profit pharmaceutical companies, researched by scientists with potential conflicts of interest, and published by journals motivated to gain citations and sell reprints (Ioannidis, 2014). For their part, patients maintain a therapeutic misconception that experimental studies designed to test scientific hypotheses are in fact designed to improve their own personal outcomes, despite careful briefing to the contrary (Lidz and Appelbaum, 2002). Patients are also susceptible to the "placebo effects" of inert substances (Kaptchuk et al., 2008), which through means unknown to medicine can heal ulcers (Moerman, 2000), lower blood pressure (Moerman, 2000), alter brain glucose metabolism (Mayberg et al., 2002), and treat Parkinson's disease (de la Fuente-Fernández et al., 2001). Frustratingly for researchers, the magnitude of these effects can be as large or even larger than the putative therapeutic effects of an intervention (Walsh et al., 2002), and they may even be increasing in magnitude over time (Montgomery, 1999).

RESEARCHER-LED UNBLINDING

Because trials are so important, expensive, and time-consuming, researchers conducting placebo-controlled trials try to prevent as many biases as possible by randomly allocating participants to either treatment or placebo in a way that is "double-blind" both to the patients and to study investigators (Altman and Bland, 1999) through a randomly generated and unpredictable allocation sequence (Schulz, 1995). Blinding prevents well-intentioned health-care professionals who know or can deduce the allocation patterns from consciously or unconsciously steering patients who were sickest or for whom they felt the most sympathy into the experimental, rather than placebo, arm of a trial. It prevents cointervention bias, where professionals provide more care and support to patients suspected of being in the treatment arm, as well as observer bias, where the professional gives the "benefit of the doubt" more often to one group of patients than another when making his or her ratings.

Before considering patients as a source of bias, we should consider the role of junior investigators and health-care professionals, whose own curiosity has in the past led to their breaking of blinding. In anonymous workshops, some medical researchers have confessed a variety of dubious methods to break blinding, ranging from holding up sealed allocation envelopes to a bright light to comparing the characteristics of pills in a medicine bottle and even on one occasion rifling through the files of the principal investigator (Schulz, 1995). While randomized controlled trials have been taking place since the mid-twentieth century,

FIGURE 1 The limitations of blind trials. *Copyright Randall Munroe,* XKCD.com.

it was only in the early 1990s that some medical journals began refusing to publish trials for which the allocation methods were improperly described (Altman and Bland, 1999), in part because those with poorly described allocation sequences appeared to yield larger estimates of treatment effects, and perhaps because of the malfeasance described earlier (Schulz, 1995). In modern trials, allocation may be performed by a centralized electronic or telephone system, with the investigational medicine and placebo identical in appearance and weight being dispensed by a pharmacy rather than by the patient's treating physician (Altman and Schulz, 2001) (Figure 1).

PATIENT-LED UNBLINDING

If some tiny subset of scientifically trained medical researchers is willing to unblind clinical trials to sate their own curiosity or subvert a trial for their own ends, what of patients, who have more invested than anyone in their own outcomes? They start from a very different position from health researchers in terms of their knowledge and beliefs about study designs. As Robinson et al. state:

> [P]atients hold a very strong assumption that their doctor acts in their best interests and offers what he or she considers is best for them, and patients are inclined to maintain or fall back on that assumption despite being given clear information that this will not happen in a RCT (randomized controlled trial). According to this view, the solution is to ensure that patients realize they are entering a research study which does not follow the procedures of standard clinician patient consultations. ***Robinson et al. (2004, p. 812).***

Such a profound change in patients' beliefs seems challenging to attain during clinical trial enrollment. Even if a trial truly is in equipoise or the researcher is properly blinded, that does not mean that the patients are in equipoise; they may have a strong desire to be in a particular treatment arm (Robinson et al., 2004), and so they may seek ways to unblind themselves or influence their treatment allocation. As one advocate of carefully maintained randomization states, "Basically…(randomized controlled trials) are anathema to the human spirit" (Schulz, 1995, p. 1456). For e.g., during the HIV/AIDS epidemic in the 1980s and early 1990s, patients who were taking part in clinical trials were reported to have swapped pills or redistributed them among their fellow patients, sometimes even employing the services of pharmacists to identify placebos (Murphy, 2004).

Similar issues have surfaced in the context of another terrible disease: amyotrophic lateral sclerosis (ALS). In affected patients the motor neurons connecting the brain to muscles degenerate, so they face progressive weakness and atrophy of muscles all over their bodies, accompanied by painful cramps and uncontrollable fasciculations. Fine motor control, walking, speech, swallowing, and eventually breathing are each compromised in an irreversible cascade. There are no effective treatments, and average survival is 2–5 years from diagnosis (Wijesekera and Leigh, 2009).

Today, some fear the delicate ecosystem of information, biases, randomization, and blinding now risks being disrupted and distorted by the changes in information availability conferred to patients and health-care professionals by the Internet (Wicks et al., 2014). The ALS research community has also agonized over the use of placebo control groups given their perceived ethical hazard, but efforts to use alternative methods fail to meet sufficient scientific rigor. For example, given the relentless progression of ALS one might think a placebo group unnecessary because experimental participants could simply be compared to "historical control" data. However, because of evolving quality of care, the fate of patients diagnosed even a few years ago looks different from that of patients diagnosed today (Simmons, 2009). In a linearly progressive disease such as ALS, one might think a "lead-in period" could also identify the experimental patients who deviated from a projected time course of 2-year survival to 3-year survival; however, while most cases are quite linear, a substantial subset does not follow this path and so disease progression is heterogeneous (Simmons, 2009). For e.g., Professor Stephen Hawking has vastly outlived his predicated life span.

Throughout the early 2000s, ALS patients connected on online communities such as Usenet, BrainTalk, and BUILD to discuss putative treatment options and the latest clinical trials (Wicks and Little, 2013). Signs of patient frustration with the placebo-controlled approach to many traditional randomized controlled trials were easy to find. One patient wrote on her blog in 2004 (http://www.webcitation.org/6W30qZuMt):

> I thought that the 12th was my last...trial visit then I got the active drug, wrong I now have to go into the open label trial if I want the active drug for another year. I was really pissed off because no one told me this at the beginning of the trial. I plan to have my Placebo/active drug analysed to see what one I was taking, If I was on the active drug I will not take part in the open label.

Around the same time, a clinical trial of the nutritional supplement creatine ran into problems when it was revealed through urine testing that a subset of patients ostensibly in the blinded placebo group had obtained their own sources of creatine, which they were taking in violation of the study protocol (Shefner et al., 2004). In this study, the researchers systematically investigated and reported on the degree of protocol violation and found that while the treatment group patients had a 14-fold increase in their concentrations of urinary creatine, the placebo group increased fourfold, suggesting at least some degree of noncompliance. Only 31 of 54 placebo group patients had their urine analyzed, and of these six (19%) had suspiciously high creatine levels. Conversely, however, 6 of 37 (16%) patients who were meant to be taking creatine had suspiciously low levels, suggesting that they were not taking the supplement as they were meant to. Excluding the noncompliant patients in both arms of the study made no difference to the main results, which were that creatine failed to slow the progression of ALS.

In 2008, the ALS patient community took another step toward conducting its own research independently when promising results from an Italian study purported to show that lithium, an inexpensive and widely available mood stabilizer, could slow the progression of ALS at lower doses than normally used in the treatment of bipolar disorder (Fornai et al., 2008). Although the Fornai et al. study was small and doubts existed about the robustness of its blinding, patients immediately began to seek prescriptions for lithium through their doctors (Frost et al., 2008). Months before the study was even published, ALS patients had used Google Translate to reverse engineer the protocol from preliminary results shared in Italian at a local conference. When the study was formally published in the prestigious *Proceedings of the National Academy of Sciences*, the authors reported that over a 15-month period, none of the 16 patients treated with lithium died, compared to one-third of patients in the comparison group.

ALS is an unusual disease in that the endpoint used in clinical trials to measure patient progression, the ALS Functional Rating Scale, Revised (ALSFRS-R) (Cedarbaum et al., 1999) can be a self-reported scale (Montes et al., 2006) and has a high degree of reliability even when administered online (Maier et al., 2012). When ALS patients started taking lithium, a patient in Brazil and the caregiver of a person living with ALS encouraged them to calculate their ALSFRS-R scores and aggregated them online in a Google Spreadsheet. The number of patients self-experimenting soon overtook the small numbers of patients in the original Italian study. In response, the website PatientsLikeMe (founded by a family affected by ALS) upgraded its data systems to more easily let patients enter their ALSFRS-R scores as well as data about dosing and side effects (Wicks et al., 2008). Within 6 months, more than 160 patients—10 times the original sample—were entering ALSFRS-R data and the patients themselves were conducting basic *t*-tests, comparing their progression against historical controls. PatientsLikeMe conducted a more rigorous version of this analysis and concluded that lithium had no effect on progression (Wicks et al., 2011). These results were subsequently confirmed by a number of double-blind randomized controlled trials that took many more years to complete (Armon, 2010).

Although the lithium study gained some attention as a participant-led research study (O'Connor, 2013), similar themes emerged some years later when a new cohort of ALS patients began using the same technology and techniques to aggregate their treatment experiences while they were supposed to be blinded in placebo-controlled trials of two experimental treatments: a Phase II trial of Neuraltus' NP001 and a Phase III trial of Biogen's dexpramipexole. Unlike with lithium, this time the active substance was not a widely available, off-label drug but rather specially manufactured experimental treatments that existed only for research purposes. Altogether, about one-third of the NP001 sample and 10% of the dexpramipexole sample reported their data on PatientsLikeMe. Through social and tracking features on PatientsLikeMe, patients noticed that side effects such as neutropenia were tied to the experimental treatments, and so the occurrence of this adverse effect led patients to assume that they were not on placebo. A few enterprising patients began crowd-sourcing data (again into shared spreadsheets) to compare the lead-in and postdosing ALSFRS-R progression between patients with and without the telltale side effects.

Patient involvement in evolving trials has in some cases led to worrisome results. In the NP001 trial, a small number of ALS patients not enrolled in either study attempted to reverse engineer the NP001 protocol by reading patents filed by the sponsor, and believed that they had deduced that the industrial cleaner sodium chlorite might be the active ingredient. Some patients even began obtaining this potent chemical and ingesting it orally or even intravenously. On the eve of the dexpramipexole's formal unblinding, PatientsLikeMe released its preliminary analysis of the data it had from the subset of patients who had shared their data to the online repository FigShare (Heywood, 2012). The formal trial found no effect of dexpramipexole on ALS progression (Cudkowicz et al., 2013), and while no conclusive effect could be identified because of the relatively small sample, there was no suggestion of an effect from the patient-submitted data (Wicks et al., 2014). While also inconclusive, NP001 had a slightly more promising effect on outcomes, and funding is being sought to conduct a larger Phase III study. Patients ingesting the industrial sodium chlorite appeared to be doing worse than expected, a finding shared with the wider ALS community to dissuade its use (The ALSUntangled Group, 2013).

An important question now is how to deal with this new level of ALS patient engagement and communication in future ALS trials. At least a subset of ALS patients have shown themselves willing to obtain experimental treatments through unconventional routes, read primary data papers, translate conference abstracts, process patents, and crowd-source data analysis in advance of the trialists. They did this having been carefully consented and fully aware of the "damage" they were doing to the trials. For their part, the trialists and study sponsors were concerned that such activities could invalidate their findings; even if a positive treatment effect had been found, physicians or regulators such as those at the Food and Drug Administration might discount the carefully collected evidence on the basis that proper blinding had not been maintained.

In the modern age, researchers can hardly ask patients to sign a gag order or ask them to not use the Internet. For ALS patients in particular, online communities are an important outlet and means of psychosocial support because they quickly lose the means to communicate verbally or through writing (Wicks et al., 2010). Even briefing the nonconnected patients during the consent process that such websites exist might have a paradoxical effect of raising awareness of the possibility of protocol violation. Insatiable curiosity and an instinct for self-preservation combined with secret knowledge just a few mouse clicks away are far too tempting.

A NEW SOCIAL CONTRACT

Understanding how researchers arrived at a place where their efforts to run good experiments could be intentionally confounded by the patients they are trying to help requires reflection on the "social contract" that exists between patient volunteers and researchers. One way of conceptualizing the patient–researcher power dynamic is framed as a "ladder of citizen engagement" (Arnstein, 1969) (see Figure 2), which highlights "the power to make decisions" as a measure of participation. Arnstein promotes a redistribution of power to deliberately include those without power in future decisions. Arnstein is particularly critical

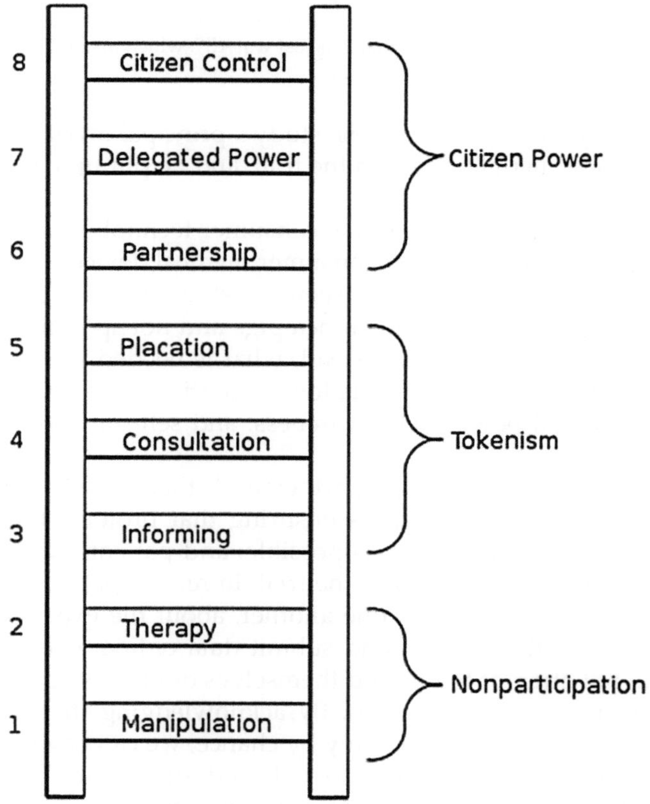

FIGURE 2 Eight rungs on the ladder of citizen participation. *Adapted from source: Arnstein (1969).*

of "empty rituals of participation," and her theories have been central to the understanding of policy makers in increasing citizen control. As these concepts relate to clinical trials, patients are being asked to voluntarily subjugate themselves to a certain level of "manipulation." Yet patients are also encouraged by health policy experts and patients advocates to be "e-patients," who are not just electronic but equipped, enabled, empowered, and engaged in their own health care (Ferguson and e-Patients Scholars Working Group, 2013). How can patients be encouraged to self-manage their chronic conditions by tracking their health data and play an active role in shared decision making, yet also temporarily pretend when they enroll in clinical trials for the sake of some unseen scientists that they are not aware of what is going on with their bodies?

Jeri Burtchell, a patient with multiple sclerosis (MS), illustrates the bizarre situation of having to pretend to not know something about her body and her medicine. For years, she had taken interferon drugs (such as interferon beta-1a, Avonex®), which she knew to cause a stinging, burning sensation when injected. As part of a double-blind randomized control trial for an oral pill (fingolimod, Gilenya®) to treat her MS, she had to take a pill and receive an injection to maintain the blinding. She wrote in her blog:

> (The nurse)...wipes with alcohol, and the next thing I know I'm seeing that big needle sink into my thigh like I was the Pillsbury dough boy's sister. It went right in with no effort at all and I couldn't even feel it. She pushed the plunger and I braced myself for a sting or burn as the medicine hit my muscle, but...nothing. It was at that point that I'm thinking "hey!! I bet that was just water!!": which means I can quit worrying about Avonex side effects and worry about fingolimod ones.

When later in the day she encountered the study's principal investigator, she tried to tell him that she had deduced her allocation in the trial, and he put up his hands in horror and exclaimed, "Don't tell me! I can't know!"

With the growing availability of wearable consumer technologies such as fitness trackers, smartphone apps, and sophisticated consumer medical devices, the gap between what patients know and what researchers know seems destined to close even further. Requests to patients to "please be compliant little guinea pigs and not spoil the grown-ups' experiments" are bound to fall on deaf ears. Instead, what is needed is an approach to clinical trials that elevates patients up Arnstein's ladder of participation and meets them on their trajectory toward increased power, self-awareness, and self-direction in living with their condition.

A natural resting place would be a "partnership" that enables patients to negotiate in trade-offs with trial designers, such as ensuring that protocol burden is minimized, trial results are made available as soon as possible, and patients can have their concerns addressed as issues arise during and after the trial. In return, patients might be welcomed to engage with study researchers, and one another, about the experience of being in the trial, provide feedback to the trialists, and submit data online wherever possible, but to agree voluntarily to not attempt to unblind themselves or otherwise harm the experiment, with mutually agreed-upon consequences. By acknowledging that patients are sensible individuals who differ from researchers only by chance, we can begin to reconcile the gap between the two parties, codevelop more novel trial designs that maintain scientific rigor while respecting patient autonomy, and take new steps on the path toward new methods for clinical trials.

References

Altman, D.G., Bland, J.M., 1999. Statistics notes. Treatment allocation in controlled trials: why randomise? BMJ 318, 1209.

Altman, D.G., Schulz, K.F., 2001. Statistics notes: concealing treatment allocation in randomised trials. BMJ 323, 446–447.

Armon, C., 2010. Is the lithium-for-ALS genie back in the bottle? Not quite. Neurology 75, 586–587. http://dx.doi.org/10.1212/WNL.0b013e3181ed9ef7.

Arnstein, S.R., 1969. A ladder of citizen participation. Journal of the American Institute of Planners 35, 216–224. http://dx.doi.org/10.1080/01944366908977225.

Black, N., 1996. Why we need observational studies to evaluate the effectiveness of health care. BMJ 312, 1215–1218.

Cedarbaum, J.M., Stambler, N., Malta, E., Fuller, C., 1999. The ALSFRS-R: a revised ALS functional rating scale that incorporates assessments of respiratory function. Journal of the Neurological Sciences 169, 13–21. http://dx.doi.org/10.1016/S0022-510X(99)00210-5.

Cudkowicz, M.E., van den Berg, L.H., Shefner, J.M., Mitsumoto, H., Mora, J.S., Ludoplh, A., Hardiman, O., Bozik, M.E., Ingersoll, E.W., Archibald, D., Meyers, A.L., Dong, Y., Farwell, W.E., Kerr, D.A., EMPOWER investigators, 2013. Dexpramipexole versus placebo for patients with amyotrophic lateral sclerosis (EMPOWER): a randomised, double-blind, phase 3 trial. Lancet Neurology 12 (11), 1059–1067. http://dx.doi.org/10.1016/S1474-4422(13)70221-7. Epub September 23, 2013.

de la Fuente-Fernández, R., Ruth, T.J., Sossi, V., Schulzer, M., Calne, D.B., Stoessl, A.J., 2001. Expectation and dopamine release: mechanism of the placebo effect in Parkinson's disease. Science 293, 1164–1166. http://dx.doi.org/10.1126/science.1060937.

Dunn, P.M., 1997. James Lind (1716–94) of Edinburgh and the treatment of scurvy. Archives of disease in childhood. Fetal and Neonatal Edition 76 (1), F64–F65.

Ferguson, T., e-Patients Scholars Working Group, 2013. e-Patients: How They Can Help Us Heal Health Care (2007). http://e-patients.net/e-Patients_White_Paper.pdf (accessed 19.02.15.).

Fornai, F., Longone, P., Cafaro, L., Kastsiuchenka, O., Ferrucci, M., Manca, M.L., Lazzeri, G., Spalloni, A., Bellio, N., Lenzi, P., Modugno, N., Siciliano, G., Isidoro, C., Murri, L., Ruggieri, S., Paparelli, A., 2008. Lithium delays progression of amyotrophic lateral sclerosis. Proceedings of the National Academy of Sciences of the United States of America 105, 2052–2057. http://dx.doi.org/10.1073/pnas.0708022105.

Frost, J.H., Massagli, M.P., Wicks, P., Heywood, J., 2008. How the social web supports patient experimentation with a new therapy: the demand for patient-controlled and patient-centered informatics. In: AMIA Annual Symposium Proceedings, pp. 217–221.

Heywood, J., 2012. files.figshare.com.

Ioannidis, J.P.A., 2014. Clinical trials: what a waste. BMJ 349, g7089. http://dx.doi.org/10.1136/bmj.g7089.

Kaptchuk, T.J., Kelley, J.M., Conboy, L.A., Davis, R.B., Kerr, C.E., Jacobson, E.E., Kirsch, I., Schyner, R.N., Nam, B.H., Nguyen, L.T., Park, M., Rivers, A.L., McManus, C.A., Kokkotou, E., Drossman, D., Goldman, P., Lembo, A.J., 2008. Components of placebo effect: randomised controlled trial in patients with irritable bowel syndrome. BMJ 336, 999–1003. http://dx.doi.org/10.1136/bmj.39524.439618.25. http://www.researchgate.net/researcher/38670399_Long_T_Nguyen.

Lidz, C.W., Appelbaum, P.S., 2002. The therapeutic misconception: problems and solutions. Medical Care 40, V55–V63. http://dx.doi.org/10.1097/01.MLR.0000023956.25813.18.

Maier, A., Holm, T., Wicks, P., Steinfurth, L., Linke, P., Münch, C., Meyer, R., Meyer, T., 2012. Online assessment of ALS functional rating scale compares well to in-clinic evaluation: a prospective trial. Amyotrophic Lateral Sclerosis 13, 210–216. http://dx.doi.org/10.3109/17482968.2011.633268.

Mayberg, H.S., Silva, J.A., Brannan, S.K., Tekell, J.L., Mahurin, R.K., McGinnis, S., Jerabek, P.A., 2002. The functional neuroanatomy of the placebo effect. American Journal of Psychiatry 159, 728–737.

Moerman, D.E., 2000. Cultural variations in the placebo effect: ulcers, anxiety, and blood pressure. Medical Anthropology Quarterly 14, 51–72.

Montes, J., Levy, G., Albert, S., Kaufmann, P., Buchsbaum, R., Gordon, P.H., Mitsumoto, H., 2006. Development and evaluation of a self-administered version of the ALSFRS-R. Neurology 67, 1294–1296. http://dx.doi.org/10.1212/01.wnl.0000238505.22066.fc.

Montgomery, S.A., 1999. The failure of placebo-controlled studies. ECNP Consensus Meeting, September 13, 1997, Vienna. European College of Neuropsychopharmacology. European Neuropsychopharmacology: Journal of the European College of Neuropsychopharmacology 9 (3), 271–276.

Murphy, T.F., 2004. Case Studies in Biomedical Research Ethics. MIT Press, Cambridge.
O'Connor, D., 2013. The apomediated world: regulating research when social media has changed research. Journal of Law, Medicine & Ethics 41, 470–483. http://dx.doi.org/10.1111/jlme.12056.
Robinson, E.J., Kerr, C., Stevens, A., Lilford, R., Braunholtz, D., Edwards, S., 2004. Lay conceptions of the ethical and scientific justifications for random allocation in clinical trials. Social Science and Medicine 58, 811–824.
Schulz, K.F., 1995. Subverting randomization in controlled trials. JAMA 274, 1456–1458.
Shefner, J.M., Cudkowicz, M.E., Schoenfeld, D., Conrad, T., Taft, J., Chilton, M., Urbinelli, L., Qureshi, M., Zhang, H., Pestronk, A., Caress, J., Donofrio, P., Sorenson, E., Bradley, W., Lomen-Hoerth, C., Pioro, E., Rezania, K., Ross, M., Pascuzzi, R., Heiman-Patterson, T., Tandan, R., Mitsumoto, H., Rothstein, J., Smith-Palmer, T., MacDonald, D., Burke, D., NEALS Consortium, 2004. A clinical trial of creatine in ALS. Neurology 63, 1656–1661.
Simmons, Z., 2009. Can we eliminate placebo in ALS clinical trials? Muscle Nerve 39, 861–865. http://dx.doi.org/10.1002/mus.21358.
The ALSUntangled Group, 2013. ALSUntangled no. 19: sodium chlorite. Amyotrophic Lateral Sclerosis and Frontotemporal Degeneration 14, 236–238. http://dx.doi.org/10.3109/21678421.2013.769718.
Walsh, B.T., Seidman, S.N., Sysko, R., Gould, M., 2002. Placebo response in studies of major depression: variable, substantial, and growing. JAMA 287, 1840–1847.
Wicks, P., Little, M., 2013. The virtuous circle of the quantified self: a human computational approach to improved health outcomes. Handbook of Human Computation 105–129. http://dx.doi.org/10.1007/978-1-4614-8806-4_12.
Wicks, P., Massagli, M., Frost, J., Brownstein, C., Okun, S., Vaughan, T., Bradley, R., Heywood, J., 2010. Sharing health data for better outcomes on PatientsLikeMe. Journal of Medical Internet Research 12, e19. http://dx.doi.org/10.2196/jmir.1549.
Wicks, P., Massagli, M., Frost, J., Macedo, H., Felzer, K., 2008. A patient-led trial of lithium in ALS using the internet. Amyotrophic Lateral Sclerosis 9, S59.
Wicks, P., Vaughan, T., Heywood, J., 2014. Subjects no more: what happens when trial participants realize they hold the power? BMJ 348, g368.
Wicks, P., Vaughan, T.E., Massagli, M.P., Heywood, J., 2011. Accelerated clinical discovery using self-reported patient data collected online and a patient-matching algorithm. Nature Biotechnology 29, 411–414. http://dx.doi.org/10.1038/nbt.1837.
Wijesekera, L.C., Leigh, P.N., 2009. Amyotrophic lateral sclerosis. Orphanet Journal of Rare Diseases 4, 3.

CHAPTER

7

The Ethics of Single-Blind Trials in Biomedicine

Franklin G. Miller

Medical Ethics in Medicine, Weill Cornell Medical College, New York, NY, USA

OUTLINE

INTRODUCTION

The "gold standard" for rigorous evaluation of medical interventions is the randomized, double-blind, placebo-controlled trial. The research methods of randomization and blinding control different potentially confounding factors, which can bias the assessment of treatment effectiveness. Randomization, along with concealing the allocation of interventions prior to their delivery to patient-subjects, eliminates selection bias, because clinicians are not able to influence which patients receive the experimental treatment under investigation. Blinding of patients, clinician-investigators, and outcome assessors obviates biases in assessing outcomes that derive from knowing which intervention patient-subjects receive in the trial. In particular, blinding controls for placebo effects, which lead to improved outcomes based on psychological factors rather than the inherent therapeutic power of a treatment intervention. Placebo controls are designed to lack the potentially therapeutic properties of the treatment under investigation, while appearing indistinguishable from it. If the blinding is successful and

Blinding as a Solution to Bias
http://dx.doi.org/10.1016/B978-0-12-802460-7.00007-3

patients randomized to the treatment are observed to have a statistically significant greater improvement in the study outcomes, then this outcome can be attributed causally to the treatment intervention. Another function of blinding and placebo controls, which has received little attention in the literature on the ethics of randomized trials, is to promote adherence to the study protocol; if patients knew they were receiving a placebo, then they would have diminished incentives to remain within the study.

The typical placebo control, used in the assessment of pharmacological interventions, is an "inert" pill, with no medicinal properties. Placebo controls also can be constructed for the evaluation of invasive procedures. For example, acupuncture trials compare standard acupuncture with sham procedures in which there is a superficial or no needle penetration, and the sham intervention is directed at nonacupuncture points. Minimally invasive surgical procedures can be evaluated in comparison with sham surgical interventions that include skin incisions under anesthesia but without the specific surgical manipulation that is thought to have therapeutic properties. For obvious reasons, it is impossible to blind the clinician-investigators who administer sham-controlled trials of invasive procedures. For the safety of research participants and the integrity of the trial, these investigators will need to know whether the real or the fake treatment intervention is being administered; and it is up to them to stage the delivery of the invasive placebo control in a way that makes it appear to patient-subjects indistinguishable from the treatment under investigation. These studies are considered to be as rigorous as double-blind, placebo-controlled drug trials, provided that the blinding of patients and outcome assessors (who must be different from the clinicians administering the invasive procedures) is successful.

In this chapter, I discuss the ethics of single-blind, sham-controlled studies of invasive procedures in which the patient-subjects, but not the investigators administering the procedures, are blinded to whether they receive the treatment intervention under evaluation in the trial. I will focus on two distinct ethical issues: (1) whether it can be justified to expose subjects to the risks of sham invasive procedures for the purpose of generating clinically relevant scientific knowledge and (2) whether the active deception involved in blinding patient-subjects is compatible with informed consent. These issues are introduced via a historical case study of the landmark, sham-controlled trials of internal mammary artery ligation.

INTERNAL MAMMARY ARTERY LIGATION: AN INSTRUCTIVE CASE STUDY

The methodological value and ethical challenges of single-blind trials of invasive procedures can be illustrated by reflecting on two landmark studies of a surgical intervention to treat angina conducted in the late 1950s (Miller, 2012a).

Internal mammary artery ligation was initially conceived by Fieschi as a treatment for angina pectoris by means of improving blood flow to the heart via collateral circulation (Glover et al., 1958). In 1939, the procedure was tested in one patient with impressive results. Beginning in 1954, Battezzati and colleagues began performing the operation at the University of Parma. They reported the results in 1959 on 304 cardiac patients, half of whom had angina (Battezzati et al., 1959). Nearly all the patients improved symptomatically within 30 days (57% with improvement described as excellent or good), and 90% sustained the improvement in follow-up from 3 months to 4 years (9% excellent and 45% good). Stimulated by an initial report of the Italian group, Glover, Kitchell, Kyle, Davila, and Trout began performing the operation at Presbyterian Hospital in Philadelphia on a series of patients with angina. Describing results on 50 patients followed up from 2 to 6 months, they found that 68% were clinically improved (36% had no angina); objective evidence of improvement was detected in 42% (Kitchell et al., 1958). In another article detailing their experience with this operation, Glover and colleagues reviewed experimental evidence relating to the potential physiological mechanism for improved collateral circulation following the ligation procedure. They concluded, "As yet there is no experimental proof that ligation of the internal mammary arteries bilaterally at the level of the second interspace actually increases blood flow to the heart although the supposition that it does is entertained" (Glover et al., 1958).

The apparent success of this operation caught the attention of the news media, with an enthusiastic article in *Reader's Digest* in 1957, "New Surgery for Ailing Hearts," by an American journalist who witnessed the operation performed at the University of Parma (Ratcliff, 1957). The article described the first patient, a 61-year-old carpenter, treated by Battezzati: "Four months earlier a severe heart attack had left him a jobless semi-invalid. His breathing was labored, and his almost constant chest pain became severe on the slightest exertion. Two days after surgery he was out of bed, walking around his room. Pain had magically vanished; his breathing was improved. On the fifth day he went home. Shortly thereafter he resumed work."

Glover and colleagues described equally dramatic results in five case histories included in one of their articles. A 64-year-old woman suffered from angina so severe that she was confined to bed, with pain controlled only by intramuscular injections of Demerol. After bilateral ligation, she resumed household chores and was able to walk and climb "the 28 steps to her second floor apartment." The authors noted, "The clinical improvement in this patient has been almost unbelievable" (Glover et al., 1958). Other investigators, however, presented reports suggesting skepticism about the benefits of the operation (Adams, 1958; Fish et al., 1958).

Definitive evidence that internal mammary artery ligation lacked specific efficacy in treating angina was documented by two path-breaking reports of randomized controlled trials comparing the procedure to a sham intervention. Cobb and colleagues randomized 17 patients "seriously limited by angina" to either bilateral internal mammary artery ligation or a blinded sham procedure consisting of skin incisions without ligating the artery (Cobb et al., 1959). Both procedures were performed under local anesthesia. On average, after follow-up of 6 months, the patients in both groups had modest increases in exercise tolerance, substantial reduction in use of nitroglycerin (34% ligated and 42% not ligated), and estimated subjective improvement of 32% in the ligated group and 43% in the sham group. The authors noted, "The degree of improvement in some cases was extraordinary. One patient (case 4), who had been unable to work because of his heart disease, was almost immediately rehabilitated and was able to return to his former occupation. He reported a 100 per cent improvement in six months and 75 per cent improvement after a year. His arteries were not ligated." Comparable results were obtained in a second sham-controlled trial of 18 patients by Dimond et al. (1960). Clearly, the sham operation was no less effective than the real operation, demonstrating that the improvement experienced by patients was not due to improved blood flow connected with ligating the internal mammary arteries.

Publication of the results of the two sham-controlled trials prompted Beecher (1961) to write a now-classic article, "Surgery as Placebo." Beecher had performed important early studies on the placebo effect and was a champion of placebo-controlled trials (Miller, 2012b). He lauded the sham-controlled design as a means of rigorous evaluation of invasive procedures. Beecher noted, "[C]aution is essential in interpreting the results of certain new operations, since precision of evaluation can be achieved only with tests properly designed to rule out the bias of the patient or the surgeon." Beecher concluded the article with an important, and enduring, value judgment relating to policy of evaluating invasive procedures: "One may question the moral or ethical right to continue with casual or unplanned new surgical procedures—procedures which may encompass no more than a placebo effect—when these procedures are costly of time and money, and dangerous to health or life."

Despite the striking results of the internal mammary artery ligation trials, comparatively few sham-controlled trials of surgical and other invasive procedures have been conducted. A major reason is that, in contrast to Food and Drug Administration regulation of pharmaceutical products, there are no regulatory requirements for rigorous evidence of effectiveness based on randomized controlled trials before these procedures are introduced into clinical practice, unless they involve the use of medical devices that carry substantial risk.

Additionally, sham surgery has been widely thought to be ethically problematic, if not patently unethical. Commenting in 1979 on the sham-controlled technique in the internal mammary artery ligation trials, Benson and McCallie (1979) stated, "The ethics are, of course, questionable." But no argument was presented in support of this pronouncement. Johnson (1994) went further, asserting without qualification that "it is unethical, for example, to make an abdominal incision and sew it up again without undertaking any procedure—i.e., the surgical equivalent of swallowing a capsule that has no active ingredients."

JUSTIFYING INVASIVE PLACEBO CONTROLS: RISK–BENEFIT ASSESSMENT

No systematic ethical attention was devoted to sham-controlled trials until 1999. Prompted by sham-controlled trials of fetal tissue transplantation for Parkinson's disease, some bioethicists criticized the ethical justification of invasive sham procedures. Macklin (1999) declared, "It is undeniable that performing surgery in research subjects that has no potential therapeutic benefit fails to minimize the risks of harm. An alternative research design that did not involve sham surgery would pose a lower risk of harm to the subject in the control group." The point about minimizing risks would be sound if the alternative research design offers comparable scientific validity in assessing treatment efficacy. However, trials comparing a surgical procedure with a pharmacological treatment cannot be conducted with blinding of patients and outcome assessors. Patient-subjects will know which treatment they received. Consequently, these trials cannot provide adequate control for the placebo effects of surgery and other sources of biased outcome assessment in conditions with subjective outcomes, such as pain relief, or outcomes influenced by psychological factors, such as medication use or exercise tolerance.

London and Kadane (2002) stated, "Using a sham surgery component…adds risks of foreseeable and preventable harm without a corresponding benefit to subjects in the control arm.

As a result it is difficult to see how the use of sham surgery controls might be reconciled with the duty of personal care." This objection confuses the ethics of clinical trials with the ethics of medical care (Horng and Miller, 2002). The aim of randomized trials is not to provide personal care to patients, but to evaluate scientifically the efficacy of treatments to guide clinical practice and health policy. There is no ethical requirement that all the interventions in clinical trials offer patient-subjects a personally favorable risk–benefit profile. Clinical trials often include invasive procedures to measure study outcomes, without therapeutic benefit to subjects, such as biopsies, lumbar punctures, bronchoscopies, and endoscopies. If the latter are justified on the basis of their contribution to promoting the scientific validity of study results, then the same holds for sham invasive control procedures.

Risk–benefit assessment is context dependent. The critics of sham-controlled trials may have been unduly influenced by the relatively high-risk sham procedures in the trials of fetal tissue transplantation, which included general anesthesia, burr holes drilled in the skull, immunosuppressive drugs, antibiotics, and radiation from Positron emission tomography scans to evaluate study outcomes (Freed et al., 2001; Freeman et al., 1999). Furthermore, their comments on risk–benefit assessment neglected the historical example of the internal mammary artery ligation trials. Macklin (1999) mentioned one of these trials in her comments on informed consent, but she did not consider it with respect to risk–benefit assessment. The risks from the sham procedure in the ligation trials, involving skin incisions and local anesthesia, were quite low. Three questions are critical for risk–benefit assessment: (1) Is the sham procedure methodologically required to achieve scientifically valid result? (2) Are the risks of the sham procedure excessive? and (3) Can the anticipated social value of the study results justify the risks? (Miller, 2003). Sham procedures are easily justified when they are of relatively low risk and used to evaluate invasive treatments for conditions with subjective outcomes, such as relief of pain.

DECEPTION AND INFORMED CONSENT

The disclosure to the patients about the sham-controlled trial of internal mammary artery ligation conducted by Cobb and colleagues is noteworthy in deviating from informed consent. Their report states, "The patients were told only that they were participating in an evaluation of this operation; they were not informed of the double-blind nature of the study" (Cobb et al., 1959). In other words, the patients were not informed that they would be randomized to either an internal mammary artery ligation or a sham procedure control. A basic element of informed consent was not included in the disclosure to prospective participants, who presumably desired and expected to receive the ligation procedure. Indeed, Cobb et al. noted, "[M]any were aware of the enthusiastic report published in the *Reader's Digest*." No mention of disclosure to patients is included in the article by Dimond et al. (1960). Whereas the lack of adequate disclosure regarding a crucial fact about the trial design would not be acceptable by contemporary standards, it was common practice prior to at least 1966 for investigators to fail to inform patient-subjects that they might get a placebo in randomized trials (Miller, 2014).

It is important to note that, while the lack of informed consent in the ligation trials was unethical, it is not an essential feature of scientifically valid, sham-controlled trials. There is no sound methodological reason for not informing patient-subjects that they might receive either the real surgical operation or a sham control, as is standard practice in placebo-controlled, pharmacological trials. In most contemporary sham-controlled trials of invasive procedures, the consent process transparently describes randomization to the real procedure or a sham control.

One notable area of exception has been the consent practice in many trials of acupuncture (Miller and Kaptchuk, 2007). A series of sham-controlled trials was conducted in Germany to evaluate acupuncture to treat migraine, low back pain, tension headaches, and knee osteoarthritis. Eligible patients were randomized to acupuncture according to Traditional Chinese Medicine, to sham acupuncture involving superficial needling at nonacupuncture points, and to wait-list or care control groups as usual. Research participants were not accurately informed about the sham procedure. For example, in a trial evaluating acupuncture for migraine, the participants were informed, "In this study, different types of acupuncture will be compared. One type is similar to acupuncture used in China. The other type does not follow these principles but has been associated with positive outcomes in clinical studies" (Linde et al., 2005). The "other type" was a fake intervention meant to be a placebo control, not a form of acupuncture that would be used by an acupuncturist in clinical practice. Accordingly, this disclosure was deceptive and contrary to informed consent. Some acupuncture studies in the United States have been similarly deceptive regarding the use of a sham control (Assefi et al., 2005).

While such deception might make it easier to blind patients, it is not necessary to obtain valid outcome data. One US sham-controlled trial of acupuncture to treat knee osteoarthritis offered a transparent disclosure to patient-subjects regarding the study design: "You will be randomly assigned to either an acupuncture, placebo acupuncture, or self-help group. The second group will receive pretend acupuncture where the needles will be placed in nonacupuncture points" (Berman et al., 2004). The investigators evaluated the success of the blinding procedures in this study. When asked what procedure they received, 75% of those in the acupuncture group reported that they received the real acupuncture, as compared with 58% in the sham acupuncture group. While noting that the blinding was not perfect, the authors of the study report noted, "[T]he sham acupuncture procedure was a relatively credible blinding strategy." Some potential sacrifice in scientific validity of study results is warranted in order to respect the autonomy of research participants and to obtain informed consent.

In a landmark 2002 trial of arthroscopic surgery for knee osteoarthritis, the investigators went to considerable lengths to ensure that the research participants understood that they might get a fake procedure (Moseley et al., 2002). They were required to write in their medical records, "On entering this study, I realize that I may receive only placebo surgery. I further realize that this means that I will not have surgery on my knee joint. This placebo surgery will not benefit my knee arthritis." While such transparency and efforts to promote appreciation for the study design promote informed consent, the question remains whether sham-controlled trials remain deceptive in a way that is ethically problematic.

In double-blind, placebo-controlled trials of drugs, neither the patient-subjects nor the clinician-investigators know whether the subjects are receiving a drug or a placebo. The assignment of drug or placebo is thus concealed, but there is no need for patients to be actively deceived regarding which intervention they received. In single-blind, invasive procedure trials, by contrast, the clinician-investigators administering the fake procedure need to do so in a way that can persuade patients that they are receiving the real procedure. For example, the study report for the arthroscopic surgery trial noted, "The surgeon asked for all the instruments and manipulated the knee as if arthroscopy was being performed. Saline was splashed to simulate the sounds of lavage" (Moseley et al., 2002). While the subjects receiving the sham intervention merely had a skin incision without the surgical procedure, the setting was stage-managed with the aim of making them believe (falsely) that they were receiving the real surgery. Hence, such sham-controlled trials do not merely conceal the assignment to study intervention or sham control; they are inherently and actively deceptive.

This deception, however, is not necessarily contrary to the autonomy of research subjects and their informed consent. Consider as an analogy, the practice of bluffing in poker. Bluffing obviously is deceptive; however, it is ethical because the players know the rules of the game and (tacitly) consent to play by them. There is no reason to be concerned about poker players understanding that they can lose money by playing the game, and sometimes lose money by being bluffed. Likewise, the deception in sham-controlled trials is ethical, provided that patient-subjects understand and formally authorize it. Achieving this is complicated because clinical trial participants may easily confuse their research participation with routine medical care. Hence, investigators should make special efforts to ensure that subjects understand that they might get a placebo intervention, as in the arthroscopic surgery trial. Moreover, to promote transparency, I suggest that subjects should be clearly informed that they might get a sham intervention and that efforts will be made to make them believe that they are getting the real surgery.

CONCLUDING REFLECTIONS

The appearance of ethical impropriety in sham-controlled trials of invasive procedures derives to a large extent from the way in which these studies deviate from standard clinical practice. Ethical surgeons do not perform fake procedures in clinical practice; how then can they ethically perform such procedures in clinical trials? As argued above, the answer lies in recognizing the ethically significant differences between patient-centered medical care and clinical trials. The placebo-controlled clinical trial is not a therapeutic activity. The aim of the trial is not to do what is medically best for patients but to conduct a rigorous study. While clinician-investigators may understandably feel uncomfortable performing a fake procedure on a patient, there is no ethical violation when it is done in the context of a scientific investigation reviewed and approved by a research ethics committee, and when the study design is made transparent to patient-subjects who give their informed consent. This is ethically very different from the way in which the landmark, sham-controlled trials of internal mammary artery ligation were conducted. In those studies, the investigators deceptively performed fake procedures under the guise of standard surgical care, leading the patients to believe that they would all receive the real surgery when, in fact, half instead received a fake operation for the purpose of scientific investigation. While we may take it for granted today, the ethical progress involved in transparency and informed consent deserves recognition. The lack of transparency in some contemporary, sham-controlled trials of acupuncture illustrates that there remains room for improvement in ensuring the ethical practice of single-blind trials of invasive procedures.

References

Adams, R., 1958. Internal-mammary-artery ligation for coronary insufficiency. New England Journal of Medicine 258, 113–115.

Assefi, N.P., Sherman, K.J., Jacobsen, C., Goldberg, J., Smith, W.R., Buchwald, D., 2005. A randomized clinical trial of acupuncture compared with sham acupuncture in fibromyalgia. Annals of Internal Medicine 143, 10–19.

Battezzati, M., Tagliaferro, A., Cattaneo, A.D., 1959. Clinical evaluation of bilateral internal mammary ligation as treatment of coronary heart disease. American Journal of Cardiology 4, 180–183.

Beecher, H.K., 1961. Surgery as placebo: a quantitative study of bias. Journal of the American Medical Association 176, 1102–1107.

Benson, H., McCallie, D.P., 1979. Angina pectoris and the placebo effect. New England Journal of Medicine 300, 1424–1429.

Berman, B.M., Lao, L., Langenberg, P., 2004. Effectiveness of acupuncture as adjunctive therapy in osteoarthritis of the knee: a randomized controlled trial. Annals of Internal Medicine 141, 901–910.

Cobb, L.A., Thomas, G.I., Dillard, D.H., Merendino, K.A., Bruce, R.A., 1959. An evaluation of internal-mammary-artery ligation by a double-blind technic. New England Journal of Medicine 260, 1115–1118.

Dimond, E.G., Kittle, C.F., Crockett, J.D., 1960. Comparison of internal mammary artery ligation and sham operation for angina pectoris. American Journal of Cardiology 5, 483–486.

Fish, R.G., Crymes, T.P., Lovell, M.G., 1958. Internal-mammary-artery ligation for angina pectoris. New England Journal of Medicine 259, 418–420.

Freed, C.R., Greene, P.E., Breeze, R.E., Tsai, W.-Y., DuMouchet, W., Kao, R., Dillon, S., Winfield, H., Culver, S., Trojanowski, J.Q., Eidelberg, D., Fahn, S., 2001. Transplantation of embryonic dopamine neurons for severe Parkinson's disease. New England Journal of Medicine 344, 710–719.

Freeman, T.G., Vawter, D.E., Leaverton, P.E., Godbold, J.H., Hauser, R.A., Goetz, C.G., Olanow, C.W., 1999. Use of placebo surgery in controlled trials of a cellular-based therapy for Parkinson's disease. New England Journal of Medicine 341, 988–991.

Glover, R.P., Kitchell, R., Kyle, R.H., Davila, J.C., Trout, R.G., 1958. Experiences with myocardial revascularization by division of the internal mammary arteries. Chest 33, 637–657.

Horng, S., Miller, F.G., 2002. Is placebo surgery unethical? New England Journal of Medicine 347, 137–139.

Johnson, A.G., 1994. Surgery as a placebo. Lancet 344, 1140–1142.

Kitchell, J.R., Glover, R.P., Kyle, R.H., 1958. Bilateral internal mammary artery ligation for angina pectoris: preliminary clinical considerations. American Journal of Cardiology 1, 46–50.

Linde, K., Streng, A., Jurgens, S., Hoppe, A., Brinkhaus, B., Witt, C., Wagenpfeil, S., Pfaffenrath, V., Hammes, M.G., Weidenhammer, W., Willich, S.N., Melchart, D., 2005. Acupuncture for patients with migraine: a randomized controlled trial. Journal of the American Medical Association 293, 2118–2125.

London, A.J., Kadane, J.B., 2002. Placebos that harm: sham surgery in clinical trials. Statistical Methods in Medical Research 11, 413–427.

Macklin, R., 1999. The ethical problem with sham surgery in clinical trials. New England Journal of Medicine 341, 992–995.

Miller, F.G., 2003. Sham surgery: an ethical analysis. American Journal of Bioethics 3 (4), 41–48.

Miller, F.G., 2012a. The enduring legacy of sham-controlled trials of internal mammary artery ligation. Progress in Cardiovascular Diseases 55, 246–250.

Miller, F.G., 2012b. Homage to Henry Beecher. Perspectives in Biology and Medicine 55, 218–229.

Miller, F.G., 2014. Clinical research before informed consent. Kennedy Institute of Ethics Journal 24, 141–157.

Miller, F.G., Kaptchuk, T.J., 2007. Acupuncture trials and informed consent. Journal of Medical Ethics 33, 43–44.

Moseley, J.B., O'Malley, K., Petersen, N.J., Menke, T.J., Brody, B.A., Kuykendall, D.H., Hollingsworth, J.C., Ashton, C.M., Wray, N.P., 2002. A controlled trial of arthroscopic surgery for osteoarthritis of the knee. New England Journal of Medicine 347, 81–88.

Ratcliff, J.D., 1957. New surgery for ailing hearts. Reader's Digest 71, 70–73.

CHAPTER

8

"Money Blinding" as a Solution to Biased Design and Conduct of Scientific Research

Christopher T. Robertson[1], *Marc A. Rodwin*[2]

[1]James E. Rogers College of Law, The University of Arizona, Tucson, AZ, USA;
[2]Suffolk University Law School, Boston, MA, USA

OUTLINE

THE PROBLEM OF COMMERCIAL BIAS IN SCIENCE

Blinding is an established method that has become an important tool for reducing bias in biomedical science. It helps to ensure that physicians administering a treatment, patients receiving the treatment, and assessors measuring outcomes do not introduce bias into the study.

Nonetheless, many other decisions are made during the course of scientific research that traditional blinding strategies do not remediate. In a clinical trial to test the effects of a drug, such decisions can include:

- what population is used as human research subjects;
- which individuals are excluded or allowed to drop out;

Blinding as a Solution to Bias
http://dx.doi.org/10.1016/B978-0-12-802460-7.00008-5

- what dose of the drugs is tested;
- how and by whom is the medication administered;
- what clinical outcomes are measured;
- when and how are the clinical outcomes measured and by whom;
- what other data researchers collect apart from the main outcome measures;
- whether the success of blinding is evaluated and, if so, reported;
- how the data are analyzed, including which and how many statistical methods are used;
- which findings are reported in the main body of the clinical study report and which results are noted only in the supplemental materials, or not at all;
- whether, when, and where to submit the study results for publication; and
- the interpretation of the results and writing of the article that summarizes the key study findings.

With each of these choices, the study leader has a rational incentive to select the option that is most likely to produce favorable results for the sponsor and thereby lay the foundation for subsequent financial support. About 70% of the clinical trials of drugs and devices are funded by the makers of those products, which thus provides a potential vector for bias in these important discretionary decisions (Bodenheimer, 2000).

The financial conflicts of interest inherent in companies funding studies to evaluate their products suggest that the reports of such studies evaluating pharmaceutical and other products published in biomedical journal articles are biased toward the firm that sponsors the research. In a judicial opinion, Judge Jack Weinstein wrote, "The pervasive commercial bias found in today's research laboratories means studies are often lacking in essential objectivity, with the potential for misinformation, skewed results, or cover-ups" ("In re Zyprexa Prods. Liab. Litig.," 2008; McGarity and Wagner, 2008). An editor of *The Lancet* once stated, "Journals have devolved into information laundering operations for the pharmaceutical industry" (Horton, 2004, p. 9).

Empirical studies support these conclusions (Golder and Loke, 2008; Hirsch, 2009). In a landmark review of the literature on conflicts of interest in clinical research, an Institute of Medicine report concluded, "Several systematic reviews and other studies provide substantial evidence that clinical trials with industry ties are more likely to have results that favor industry" (IOM, 2009, p. 104). A more recent Cochrane review concluded that industry-sponsored studies are biased in favor of the sponsor's products (Lundh et al., 2012).

Even if industry funding did not bias scientific research, it does undermine public trust and the legitimacy of scientific research to test the safety and efficacy of drugs. A former editor-in-chief of the *New England Journal of Medicine* concluded, "Physicians can no longer rely on the medical literature for valid and reliable information" (Angell, 2008, pp. 1070–1071). Indeed, experimental research has shown that when physicians see industry funding disclosures on biomedical journal abstracts, the physicians discount the reliability of the studies and are hesitant to prescribe on the basis of such studies, even if the trials otherwise appear to be methodologically rigorous (Kesselheim et al., 2012).

MODELS FOR INDEPENDENT SCIENCE

In the past two decades, several authors have called for an independent entity, rather than drug manufacturers, to design and conduct clinical trials of therapeutics (Rodwin, 2012).

Physician and prominent journal editor Marcia Angell proposed creating an Institute for Prescription Drug Trials within the National Institutes of Health (NIH) that would oversee the clinical trials, contracting with independent researchers at universities to carry out the research (Angell, 2004). Similarly, academic medical center professors Wayne Ray, Marie Griffin, and Jerry Avorn proposed creating a governmental center to assess drug effectiveness and compare the costs and benefits of alternative drug therapies (Ray et al., 1993). The center would fund and/or conduct studies of drugs already approved for sale and coordinate drug research performed by government agencies (Ray et al., 1993, p. 2031). Ray and his colleagues suggested financing the center through a tax on drug sales and third-party payer subscription fees (Ray et al., 1993).

Physician and *JAMA* editor Drummond Rennie argued that the United States should create a National Institute of Clinical Trials, financed with federal funds and a budget separate from that of the NIH (Rennie, 2007, p. 1010). The institute would decide what trials to conduct and make grants to researchers to carry out the studies. Researchers would receive all their funds through their institutions and not be allowed to receive other funds. In a variation of this plan, pharmacologist Lisa Bero and Rennie suggested that Congress should enact legislation to finance independent studies of the cost effectiveness and comparative effectiveness of drugs by having the U.S. Food and Drug Administration (FDA) charge drug firms a user fee (Bero and Rennie, 1996).

These sorts of proposals are not altogether new. In fact, the questions of how to test drugs and who should do the testing surfaced before Congress enacted the 1962 amendments to the *Federal Food, Drug, and Cosmetic Act* that empowered the FDA to regulate efficacy testing for new drugs. A review of U.S. Senate hearings and other documents reveals a persistent debate between 1959 and 1980 in Congress, the FDA, and among industry and consumer representatives over what an optimal drug-testing regime should look (Rodwin, 2012, 2015).

Most of these proposals focused on having government fund the research, whether administered by the NIH, the FDA, or a new agency altogether. Still, some suggested that the pharmaceutical industry could continue paying for the research, if only they were required to relinquish control about who performed it and how. For example, in 1976, Sidney Wolfe, head of Public Citizen's Health Research Group (HRG), argued that no amount of government surveillance could solve the fundamental problem of interested parties conducting or overseeing drug testing (U.S. Congress, 1976): "The Government has to step in. It will be far cheaper for the Government, particularly if we use industry funds, to funnel out the testing money to reliable companies than to have to expend $25 million, as you have proposed for FDA, to catch up with lousy industry data" (U.S. Congress, 1976, p. 157).

Also in 1976, Frank Rauscher, Jr., head of the National Cancer Institute (NCI) within the NIH, testified that the NCI could serve as a model for a government-supervised program of independent drug testing (Braithwaite, 1984; U.S. Congress, 1976). To control unwanted bias, the NCI and its outside peer-review committees designed all research protocols. It awarded contracts to perform these protocols through competitive bidding, but only considered laboratories that had no connection to the firms manufacturing the drugs being tested. The NCI also blinded the compounds it sent for testing. Therefore, the tester did not know which chemical it was testing. Periodically, the NCI sent testing labs a compound that it knew had certain carcinogenic or other harmful effects as a means of ascertaining whether the laboratory performed tests accurately. The NCI also awarded contracts to multiple toxicological laboratories as a means of checking the quality of the work and spurring quality competition among laboratories. The NCI staff monitored the studies on a nearly day-to-day basis. Additionally, the NCI divided its testing into two separate parts, each of which could be evaluated. One organization performed the toxicological test and generated the data, while the second organization performed the data processing and statistical analysis.

MONEY BLINDING AS A SOLUTION

As the review in Section II showed, there are multiple potential approaches that could preclude key sources of bias from the design and conduct of scientific research, particularly clinical trials to evaluate pharmaceuticals. Conceptually, it is useful to disaggregate two functions of biomedical research: (1) the generation of hypotheses about new products and (2) the testing of those hypotheses to determine the safety and efficacy of the products (Simonton, 1988). It may be necessary, or in any event useful, for university researchers and scientists to have relationships with industry to advise and assist firms in bringing new products to market. The testing of those hypotheses and new products, by contrast, does not require close collaboration of researchers who evaluate the safety of a drug with the firm that seeks to commercialize the drug. Indeed, there are grounds to conclude that there should be a separation of functions and that the individuals who evaluate whether a new drug is safe and effective enough for FDA approval should be independent from the firm that seeks to commercialize the drug (Mirowski and Van Horn, 2005; Schafer, 2004).

In the rest of this chapter, we explore the idea of using blinding to allow companies to continue to fund biomedical research to test new drugs and other products, but preclude bias from affecting the manner in which these studies are designed and conducted. In short, companies would be allowed to fund studies by competent investigators so long as they are blinded to the selection of investigators. The process and result would be similar to blinding investigators to the assignment of human subjects to either the group that received the medication being tested or a control group that received a placebo or alternative treatment. Such blinding prevents investigators from directing patients with better prognoses to the treatment arm, whether purposefully or subconsciously, to make the new intervention seem more effective. Companies would not be allowed to pick the investigators, nor implicitly condition future funding on favorable performance by those investigators. Using this model, companies could tie their research funding to specific products and hypotheses, but would not be able to influence the design or conduct of the scientific studies that they fund. This method for reducing industry influence could be called a "money blind."

A money blind would require an intermediary agency between the funder and the investigator (Bodenheimer, 2000; Brennan et al., 2006). The funder would provide to the intermediary the product for testing and designate a testable hypothesis (i.e., that the product will be safe and/or effective for some specified clinical indication). The intermediary would then determine how much money would be necessary to properly test that hypothesis, and require such payment in advance. The funder would demand assurances of the investigators' competence and the reasonable management of their funds. The intermediary would then select an investigator, disburse the money, oversee design of the study, and provide financial accountability.

Such an intermediary would have its own overhead costs that would need to be recouped, presumably from the funders. However, the funders would be spared the need to select investigators and oversee their research, so there might be little net increase in expense.

In principle, a for-profit, nonprofit, or governmental agency could serve as the intermediary. The NIH is the natural candidate for this role, because it already has significant institutional legitimacy and expertise. It reviews approximately 65,000 grant applications per year, from which it distributes 14,600 grants totaling $5.66 billion in awards (NIH, 2010a). The NIH could thus deploy its current procedures and infrastructure to disburse the industry money, alongside the federal government money. The NIH already works in 229 different disease areas, which suggests that it would have expertise to select and oversee investigators in virtually any area that industry would seek to study (NIH, 2011). The NIH also is aggressively selective in assessing investigators and research protocols. In 2010, the NIH approved only 23% of the grant applications it received (NIH, 2010a). Under NIH policies, grant reviewers must evaluate all aspects of a prospective research project, including "the competency of the proposed staff in relation to the type of research involved" (HHS Evaluation and Disposition of Applications, 2010). Federal courts reviewing aspects of these protocols have found them "reasonable and fair" (Grassetti v. Weinberger, 1976). Given the NIH's longstanding expertise, the public and drug and device industries should have confidence that the research will be performed well and unbiased. A more robust solution would involve the government actually conducting its own biomedical research, rather than outsourcing that function to other institutions.

LIMITS AND DISADVANTAGES

There are disadvantages to the money blind proposal. In particular, if organizations selected by government agencies also depended on receiving discretionary contracts from drug manufacturers for most of their other income, then such dependence would create a significant conflict of interest (Rodwin, 2011). The drug manufacturer could retaliate against researchers that produced negative evaluations of their products for government-sponsored testing by refusing to employ them in the future. The risk of losing contracts from drug manufacturers could lead researchers and research organizations to conduct their government testing in ways that favored the manufacturer's agenda.

The simplest and most effective way to address this problem is to prohibit all firms and organizations that accept federal contracts for drug evaluation from performing any direct work for drug manufacturers. However, such prohibitions might constrict the number of research organizations and so reduce the pool of willing organizations. With fewer research organizations from which to choose, the federal government might have more difficulty finding organizations capable of performing high-quality work.

An alternative strategy is to reduce the prevalence of conflicts of interest rather than preclude them. The agency could award drug evaluation contracts only to organizations that did not receive more than a fixed threshold (say 30%) of their revenue from commercial interests that produce pharmaceuticals and medical devices. In addition, and even more important, when there was more than one well-qualified applicant, the agency awarding the grants could give preference to the contract research organization that earned the least revenue from drug manufacturers. Furthermore, the agency awarding contracts should preclude research organizations and researchers from evaluation of a product when the researchers had conducted other research for that manufacturer evaluating the same medication. That would prevent the federal government from selecting a contract research organization to conduct a Phase 3 clinical trial to test a drug when the contract research organization had been employed by the manufacturer to perform Phase 2 clinical trials to test the same drug.

To further reduce the risk from conflicts of interest and improve the quality of clinical trials, the federal government could also contract with experts to evaluate the proposed research design and protocol before authorizing the start of the clinical trial, a process similar to peer review that the NIH already uses for grant proposals. It probably makes sense to require public disclosure of the proposed research protocol and the comments of experts that evaluated it and to allow the public to comment on the proposed research protocol. Based on the expert evaluation and public comment, the government agency could ask the research organization to revise its trial design and research protocol.

Companies also create relationships directly with investigators, including consultancies and grants to their academic institutions, which may curry favor. Even with a money blind in place, the companies may be able to identify the most likely recipients of funds and co-opt them with side payments or other forms of influence. When these investigators then apply for and receive funding through the intermediary, they could be biased because of these other financial ties and other outside influences.

When selecting investigators, the NIH should demand full disclosures of all financial relationships with commercial interests and the NIH should consider these when it reviews conflicts of interest. Using disclosures prospectively, to choose between potential researchers, would be preferable to relying on disclosure of such relationships in journal articles, after the research is done. All other things being equal, the intermediary should award grants to researchers that have the fewest such relationships or the ones that are the least compromising. Such a preference clearly stated in the grant-making rules should create an incentive for competing investigators to avoid such relationships.

One also should not ignore the risk that the intermediary institution might become captured by the companies that are providing its revenue and end up favoring the companies' interests rather than the governmental interest in producing reliable studies. The NIH had an embarrassing string of scandals in the early 2000s, in which it was revealed that NIH officials also received industry money through consulting and other relationships (Willman, 2003, 2004). Some already argue that the FDA has been "captured" by the companies it regulates, a problem that has allegedly gotten worse after the creation of a user-fee driven financing system (Furberg et al., 2006). Therefore, there should be procedures in place to ensure that the NIH maintains independence from the commercial interests in conducting this new task.

Admittedly, the money blinding method would not eliminate all the biases in biomedical research. As long as industry chooses the topics for the research it funds, those topics will be biased toward investigations of their patented products for indications that have large potential markets. Manufacturers, notes Wayne Ray, "would not benefit from studies to determine whether inexpensive off-patent drugs or non-pharmaceutical interventions could replace profitable, single-source products or from studies to determine the rates of adverse reactions to approved products" (Ray et al., 1993, p. 2030). The same kind of problem has been observed when a company that makes a product selectively chooses what topics to support when it funds programs for continuing medical education (Rodwin, 2010).

Even with money blinding, nonfinancial biases will also continue to exist. For example, published research will continue to be biased toward studies that purport to disprove null hypotheses, rather than those that affirm the null hypothesis (Emerson et al., 2010). The latter study, which confirms that something does not work, often seems less interesting and less exciting. A money blind is not a panacea; we should develop other policies to address such biases.

AVENUES FOR REFORM

Experimental research suggests that physicians perceive the biases in industry-funded research and discount the credibility of industry-funded studies (Kesselheim et al., 2012). This dynamic creates an incentive for reform. The biomedical industry might voluntarily adopt money blinding to maximize the persuasiveness of its publications, at least when its products really are safe and effective (Emons, 1997; Hadfield et al., 1998). In response to growing concerns about bias in industry-funded studies, editors of biomedical journals might decide to refuse to publish studies that are not money blinded, just as they currently refuse to publish reports of clinical trials that have not been registered on clinicaltrials.gov (Clinical Trial Registration, 2015) and just as they disfavor studies that are not double-blinded, when blinding is feasible (Schulz and Grimes, 2002).

Academic medical centers and medical schools could promote money blinding as a way to reduce the risk of bias and to manage the conflicts of interests of their faculties. In recent years, several such institutions have revised their policies regarding whether and how faculty members may accept money from the pharmaceutical and medical device industries (Dorschner, 2010; Stanford School of Medicine, 2011; Singer, 2010). Announcing these revisions, Philip Pizzo, former Dean of Stanford Medical School, said, "We welcome interactions with industry that are positive and collaborative. But where I think the line should not be crossed and where we are not going to allow our full-time or part-time faculty to engage is in marketing" (Singer, 2010, p. B3). Yet, the pharmaceutical industry's own documents suggest that many manufacturers consider biomedical science as the first cog in their marketing machines (Fugh-Berman and Melnick, 2008; Moffatt and Elliott, 2007).

The federal government could also promote the adoption of money blinding. The first and most obvious legal hook to use is the *Federal Food, Drug, and Cosmetic Act*. The law requires that drug manufacturers submit evidence on drug safety and effectiveness when they seek approval to market a new drug. Because the FDA already sets standards for clinical trials used for drug approval, it probably has authority to promulgate regulations that require such clinical trials be designed and conducted by an independent organization selected and supervised by a federal agency (Rodwin, 2015). The FDA also has jurisdiction over certain postmarketing trials because FDA regulations require that drug manufacturers monitor the risks of drugs they market. Manufacturers must submit to the FDA results from their postmarketing trials, but often the FDA does not specify what manufacturers must do to fulfill their postmarketing commitments beyond indicating the particular questions that needs to be addressed. Sometimes, the FDA even specifies the kind of postmarketing evaluation that a drug manufacturer must perform (e.g., establishing a registry or designing a randomized controlled trial), particularly if there is evidence of potential serious drug risks (HHS Evaluation and Disposition of Applications, 2010). Here too, the FDA may have authority to require money blinding.

Drug firms also conduct clinical trials for approved drugs that are not required by the FDA. They may design these trials to demonstrate that a drug is more effective, safer, or more cost-effective than competing drugs or nondrug therapies, or to explore an approved drug's potential benefits for new uses. The federal government would need other legal hooks to cause these sorts of studies to be money blinded.

One option would be to consider scientific publications to be part of the marketing or labeling for a drug, which the FDA has authority to regulate to ensure that they are not false or misleading, or contain efforts to promote beyond the FDA-approved indications. These rules currently extend to company-funded continuing medical education. If a continuing medical education program is directly provided by a company, then statements made about pharmaceutical products are subject to the same restrictions on labeling and promotional claims as statements that manufacturers make in other contexts (62 Fed. Reg. at 64,083; Rodwin, 2010). The FDA does not apply such regulations when company-supported continuing medical education is independent, namely when the company is not "involved in the selection of" instructors and the instructors do not "have reason to believe that future financial support from the company depends upon producing" publications "that promote the company's products" (62 Fed. Reg. at 64,083). Scholars have called for a central-pooling mechanism for continuing medical education funding, which is quite similar in design to research money blinding (Steinbrook, 2008). A similar logic could apply to scientific investigators: "companies and [investigators] who wish to ensure that their [research] activities will not be subject to regulation should design and carry out their activities free from the supporting company's influence and bias" (62 Fed. Reg. at 64,084). In short, adopt money blinding.

Another option would be to attach conditions to the billions of dollars that the NIH spends in support of biomedical research, not unlike current requirements to submit protocols to Institutional Review Boards and to publish raw data (45 CFR §46.101; 45 CFR §74.36 (2008)). Indeed, the NIH has compiled a list of more than 70 conditions on grant funding, which cover a gamut of topics from animal welfare and patient confidentiality, to the use of seat belts and smoke detectors (NIH, 2010b). The NIH could require that the individual investigators who receive funding for specific projects publish the primary results only in journals that have a satisfactory money blinding policy. In effect, this policy would force scientists to choose between publishing in journals that required money blinding or not accepting NIH funds. This NIH policy would then create pressure on journals to adopt a money blinding policy, which then applies pressure on industry to adopt money blinding if it wants to publish in these top journals.

A more ambitious policy would attach strings that reach beyond the individual funded projects. The government could require that any institution that received NIH or other federal funding refuse all industry funding to the institution, unless the industry money is routed through an accredited blinding intermediary. Many federal grant programs are already limited to nonprofit and public entities. The federal government also requires all grant recipients to maintain a conflict of interest policy and to police the conflicts of interest that might impact the federal grant (40 CFR § 50.605 (2010)). Our proposed policy extends that logic, building a taller wall between industry and the recipients of federal grants, declining to award grants to institutions that fail to do so. It would force institutions to either turn down all NIH research grants or to money blind private research grants. Most research institutions are unlikely to reject all federal funding, rather than mandate money blinding.

Arguably, these various policy levers are attempts to regulate speech, because they seek to shape what is published in the scientific literature. There are questions, then, about whether money blinding policies may run afoul of the First Amendment (Robertson, 2011). In short, however, it is clear that the government can regulate publications to prevent false or misleading speech in the commercial arena. Biased science is arguably misleading in the aggregate, and it creates a risk of false conclusions about the safety and effectiveness of drugs. Much, then, will depend on whether the government or the manufacturers have the burden to prove falsity in any given case (Robertson, 2014). The government can also use speech as evidence of criminal intent, such as the intent to market a drug off-label. Finally, the strategies that depend instead on the government's spending power, to condition NIH funding, would likely receive a much less onerous review by the courts. These are most promising for broad application.

ASSESSING THE ARGUMENTS AGAINST MONEY BLINDING

Let us review the key arguments used against proposals for independent organization of clinical trials related to testing prescription drugs, and against money blinding in particular.

In the 1960s and 1970s, opponents argued that such models were not feasible because there were insufficient independent private organizations to conduct toxicological tests and clinical trials, and the federal government also lacked the capacity to perform this work. These assertions assumed that private firms and the federal government could not expand their capacities to meet new demands. Such a contention was probably not correct in the early 1960s and 1970s, and it is certainly not true now (Rodwin, 2015). Today, rather than test drugs in-house, drug firms contract out this work to third parties. Initially, universities performed most of this research but over the past quarter century drug firms shifted most of their clinical trials to for-profit contract research organizations, which now constitute a global industry (Masri et al., 2012; Rettig, 2000). This fundamental economic structure can be exploited if a governmental agency simply performs the selection and monitoring, rather than the drug company itself.

Furthermore, by allocating funds for the research, the agency could spur the growth of organizations that met high standards for integrity, excellence, and independence. Through contracts, it could encourage the growth of organizations such as the internationally recognized Mario Negri Pharmacological Institute, which has performed independent clinical trials in Europe for nearly 50 years, published more than 13,000 original scientific papers in scientific journals, and now conducts about 80 clinical trials a year (Light and Maturo, 2015).

Another line of argument opposing establishment of an independent institution to organize clinical testing of medical products is that it would not ensure that clinical trials were well designed, free of methodological flaws, or conducted competently (Rodwin, 2012). Even if a governmental agency selected the researchers, they still might perform sloppy work or engage in fraud. No doubt, independent testing does not guarantee that drug evaluation will be performed well. But, this fact of life does not necessarily also prove that independence is not an important factor or a necessary condition for accurate drug testing. The NCI's experience in contracting with laboratories to test chemicals demonstrates that regulators can monitor and control the quality of contracted testing.

Opponents of public testing have also claimed that having the federal government test drugs would create a conflict of interest that would compromise FDA drug approval decisions, because the government would then both conduct the clinical trials and evaluate those trials when it decided whether to grant marketing approval (Rodwin, 2012). The federal government should not conduct clinical trials, they argued, because it should not be in the position of evaluating its own work. Of course, the federal courts routinely overcome this sort of bias when they judge cases in which the federal government is itself a party. Likewise, the Government Accountability Office and the Congressional Research Service often produce reports that are critical of and must be evaluated by other government officials. In these scenarios, government testing is possible without having the same agency both conduct clinical trials and evaluate the quality of those trials. We have suggested that the NIH could conduct clinical trials and the FDA could evaluate those trials, just as the FDA currently evaluates clinical trials conducted by drug firms.

Another putative drawback of independent testing is that it would slow the introduction of new drugs. This assertion is unpersuasive. In principle, it should not take longer for contract researchers to conduct a clinical trial merely because a governmental agency hires it, rather than a drug firm. It might take a governmental agency longer than a drug firm to select which researchers to employ, but not much. If ensuring that clinical trials are better designed and methodologically sound extends the time to develop the research protocol, then that would be time well spent.

CONCLUSION

Although not a complete solution to commercial bias in the design and conduct of clinical trials for medical products, money blinding has the advantage of being a relatively light regulatory touch. It does not require additional outlays of new federal funds to support research. For better or worse, it allows industry to continue setting the agenda for the scientific research that it funds, alongside whatever research that is funded by government and foundations. If properly implemented, however, a money blinding solution could complement the efforts to blind patients, physicians, and assessors toward the ultimate goal of the highest-quality biomedical science.

Acknowledgment

This chapter incorporates and synthesizes prior work by the authors. See Robertson (2011) and Rodwin (2012, 2015).

References

Angell, M., 2004. The truth about the drug companies (pharmaceutical industry). New York Review of Books 51, 52–58.

Angell, M., 2008. Industry-sponsored clinical research—a broken system. Journal of the American Medical Association 300, 1069–1071.

Bero, L.A., Rennie, D., 1996. Influences on the quality of published drug studies. International Journal of Technology Assessment in Health Care 12, 209–237.

Bodenheimer, T., 2000. Uneasy alliance—clinical investigators and the pharmaceutical industry. New England Journal of Medicine 342, 1539–1544.

Braithwaite, J., 1984. Corporate Crime in the Pharmaceutical Industry. Routledge & Kegan Paul, London; Boston.
Brennan, T.A., Rothman, D.J., Blank, L., Blumenthal, D., Chimonas, S.C., Cohen, J.J., Smelser, N., 2006. Health industry practices that create conflicts of interest—a policy proposal for academic medical centers. Journal of the American Medical Association 295, 429–433.
Clinical Trial Registration, 2015. www.icmje.org: International Committee of Medical Journal Editors.
Dorschner, J., 2010. Investigators Question Drug-Makers Payments to University of Miami Doctors. Miami Herald. Retrieved from: http://www.miamiherald.com/2010/12/20/1982509/investigators-question-drug-makers.html#ixzz18lCuiADQ.
Emerson, G.B., Warme, W.J., Wolf, F.M., Heckman, J.D., Brand, R.A., Leopold, S.S., 2010. Testing for the presence of positive-outcome bias in peer review: a randomized controlled trial. Archives of Internal Medicine 170, 1934–1939.
Emons, W., 1997. Credence goods and fraudulent experts. RAND Journal of Economics 28, 107–119.
Fugh-Berman, A., Melnick, D., 2008. Off-label promotion, on-target sales. PLoS Medicine 5, e210.
Furberg, C.D., Levin, A.A., Gross, P.A., Shapiro, R.S., Strom, B.L., 2006. The FDA and drug safety: a proposal for sweeping changes. Archives of Internal Medicine 166, 1938–1942.
Golder, S., Loke, Y.K., 2008. Is there evidence for biased reporting of published adverse effects data in pharmaceutical industry-funded studies? British Journal of Clinical Pharmacology 66, 767–773.
Grassetti v. Weinberger, 1976. F. Supp. 142, 151.
Hadfield, G.K., Howse, R., Trebilcock, M.J., 1998. Information-based principles for rethinking consumer protection policy. Journal of Consumer Policy 21, 131–169.
HHS Evaluation and Disposition of Applications, 42 C.F.R. § 52.5(b) (2010).
Hirsch, L.J., 2009. Conflicts of interest, authorship, and disclosures in industry-related scientific publications: the tort bar and editorial oversight of medical journals. Mayo Clinic Proceedings 84, 811–821.
Horton, R., 2004. The dawn of McScience. In: The New York Review of Books. NYRev, Inc., New York.
In re Zyprexa Prods. Liab. Litig., 2008. F.R.D. (p. 69): (E.D.N.Y).
Institute of Medicine, Committee on Conflict of Interest in Medical Research, Education, and Practice, 2009. Conflict of Interest in Medical Research, Education, and Practice. In: Field, M.J., Lo, B. (Eds.). National Academies Press, Washington, DC.
Kesselheim, A.S., Robertson, C.T., Myers, J.A., Rose, S.L., Gillet, V., Ross, K.M., et al., 2012. A randomized study of how physicians interpret research funding disclosures. New England Journal of Medicine 367, 1119–1127.
Light, D., Maturo, A., 2015. Good Pharma: the Public-Health Model of the Mario Negri Institute. Palgrave Macmillan, New York, NY.
Lundh, A., Sismondo, S., Lexchin, J., Busuioc, O.A., Bero, L., 2012. Industry sponsorship and research outcome. Cochrane Database of Systematic Reviews 12.
Masri, M.D., Ramirez, B., Popescu, C., Reggie, E.M., 2012. Contract Research Organizations: An Industry Analysis. Retrieved from: http://www.guidestarclinical.com/wp-content/uploads/2013/04/CONTRACT-RESEARCH-ORGANIZATIONS-AN-INDUSTRY-ANALYSIS.pdf.
McGarity, T.O., Wagner, W., 2008. Bending Science: How Special Interests Corrupt Public Health Research. Harvard University Press, Cambridge, MA.
Mirowski, P., Van Horn, R., 2005. The contract research organization and the commercialization of scientific research. Social Studies of Science 35, 503–548.
Moffatt, B., Elliott, C., 2007. Ghost marketing: pharmaceutical companies and ghostwritten journal articles. Perspectives in Biology and Medicine 50, 18–31.
NIH (National Institutes of Health), 2010a. Research Project Grants & Other Mechanisms: Competing Applications, Awards, Success Rates, and Total Funding Made with Direct Authority and Superfund Funds, by NIH Institutes/Center, Grant Mechanisms, and Activity Codes. National Institutes of Health. NIH Res. Portfolio Online Reporting Tools (December 17, 2010). Retrieved from: http://report.nih.gov/FileLink.aspx?rid=601.
NIH, 2010b. NIH Grants Policy Statement. NIH Office of Extramural Research, § 4.1. Retrieved from: http://grants.nih.gov/grants/policy/nihgps_2010/nihgps_ch4.htm#public_policy_requirements_other_mandates.
NIH, 2011. Estimates of Funding for Various Research, Condition, and Disease Categories (RCDC). NIH Res. Portfolio Online Reporting Tools. Retrieved from: http://report.nih.gov/rcdc/categories/.
Ray, W.A., Griffin, M.R., Avorn, J., 1993. Evaluating drugs after their approval for clinical use. New England Journal of Medicine 329, 2029–2032.
Rennie, D., 2007. When evidence isn't: trials, drug companies and the FDA. Journal of Law & Policy 15 991, 1007–1008, 1010.

Rettig, R.A., 2000. The industrialization of clinical research. Health Affairs 19, 129–146.

Robertson, C., 2011. The money blind: how to stop industry bias in biomedical science, without violating the First Amendment. American Journal of Law and Medicine 37, 358–387.

Robertson, C., 2014. When truth cannot be presumed: the regulation of drug promotion under an expanding First Amendment. Boston University Law Review 94, 545–574.

Rodwin, M.A., 2010. Drug advertising, continuing medical education, and physician prescribing: a historical review and reform proposal. Journal of Law Medicine & Ethics 38, 807–815.

Rodwin, M.A., 2011. New standards for medical review organizations: holding them and health plans accountable for their decisions. Health Affairs 30, 519–524.

Rodwin, M.A., 2012. Independent clinical trials to test drugs: the neglected reform. Saint Louis University Journal of Health Law & Policy 6, 113.

Rodwin, M.A., 2015. Independent drug testing to ensure drug safety and efficacy. Journal of Health Care Law & Policy 18, 45.

Schafer, A., 2004. Biomedical conflicts of interest: a defence of the sequestration thesis-learning from the cases of Nancy Olivieri and David Healy. Journal of Medical Ethics 30, 8–24.

Schulz, K.F., Grimes, D.A., 2002. Blinding in randomised trials: hiding who got what. The Lancet 359, 696–700.

Simonton, D.K., 1988. Scientific Genius: a Psychology of Science. Cambridge University Press, Cambridge Cambridgeshire; New York.

Singer, N., 2010. Stanford Medical School to expand ethics rules. The New York Times. Retrieved from: http://www.nytimes.com/2010/03/22/health/policy/22docs.html?_r=0.

Stanford School of Medicine, 2011. School of Medicine Policy Overview. Retrieved from: https://med.stanford.edu/coi/overview.html.

Steinbrook, R., 2008. Financial support of continuing medical education. Journal of the American Medical Association 299, 1060–1062.

U.S. Congress Senate Committee on Labor and Public Welfare, 1976. Preclinical and clinical testing by the pharmaceutical industry, 1976. In: Part III. Joint Hearings before the Subcommittee on Health of the Committee on Labor and Public Welfare and the Subcommittee on Administrative Practice and Procedure of the Committee on the Judiciary. Ninety-Fourth Congress. First Session on Examination of the Process of Drug Testing and FDA's Role in the Regulation and Conditions under Which Such Testing Is Carried Out. U.S. Government Printing Office, Washington, DC.

Willman, D., December 7, 2003. Stealth merger: drug companies and government medical research: some of the National Institutes of Health's top scientists are also collecting paychecks and stock options from biomedical firms. Increasingly, such deals are kept secret. Los Angeles Times. Retrieved from: http://articles.latimes.com/2003/dec/07/nation/na-nih7/2.

Willman, D., 2004. Ex-NIH director now favors limiting drug company ties. Los Angeles Times. Retrieved from: http://articles.latimes.com/2004/mar/13/nation/na-nih13.

SECTION IV

FORENSIC SCIENCE: CRIMINAL AND CIVIL

Rigor in Forensic Science

*Tania Simoncelli**
White House Office of Science and Technology Policy, Washington, DC, USA

On March 11, 2004, Al-Qaeda-inspired terrorists coordinated a massive bombing of the Madrid commuter train system during the rush hour, killing or injuring nearly 2000 people. Two latent fingerprints recovered during the investigation on a bag of detonators by the Spanish National Police were shared with the FBI through Interpol. The FBI searched the unknown prints against the Integrated Automated Fingerprint Identification System (IAFIS), a government database of tens of millions of known prints. Fourth on a list of potentially matching candidates generated by the automated system were the prints of Brandon Mayfield, an attorney in Portland, Oregon, whose prints were in the database as a result of his previous military service. An FBI examiner conducted a side-by-side comparison of the unknown prints with the potential matches and concluded that Mayfield was the source of the unknown prints.

The FBI examiner's conclusions were verified by a second FBI examiner and reviewed by the Unit Chief of the laboratory, who concurred with the identification. However, Spanish authorities reviewed the prints and were unable to confirm the match, and FBI was unable to find any concrete evidence connecting Mayfield to the bombings, despite an intensive investigation that included covert electronic surveillance and physical searches of Mayfield's home and office. The FBI examiners nevertheless insisted with "100% certainty" that Mayfield's prints matched the prints from the bag (Frontline, April 17, 2012), and on May 6th, Mayfield was detained as a material witness to the Madrid attacks. Mayfield spent 2 weeks in jail before the Spanish authorities announced that they had identified the print as belonging to an Algerian national, Ouhnane Daoud.

Within a week of Mayfield's release, the FBI established an international review committee to review the case. The review found that the misidentification occurred primarily as a result of "confirmation bias." In particular, the actual similarities between the two prints, combined with the inherent pressure of working on an extremely high-profile case, influenced the initial examiner's judgment so that the initial examiner perceived or interpreted ambiguous characteristics as points of similarity (and ignored or explained away differences between the two prints). Furthermore, once the initial examiner had declared a match, both he or she and other examiners who were aware of this finding were influenced by the urgency of the investigation to affirm repeatedly this erroneous decision (Stacey, 2005). A comprehensive review of the Mayfield case conducted by the Office of the Inspector General of the Department of Justice released in 2006 echoed these findings (U.S. Department of Justice, 2006).

*Tania Simoncelli is Senior Advisor to the Director of the Broad Institute of MIT and Harvard. From 2013-2015, she served as Assistant Director for Forensic Science at the White House Office of Science and Technology Policy. She is co-author of Genetic Justice: DNA Data Banks, Criminal Investigations, and Civil Liberties (Columbia University Press: 2011).

Confirmation bias—like other forms of cognitive bias—is not unique to latent print examination, but is rather a fixture of human experience. The role of bias in human decision making was generally well understood at the time of the Madrid bombing investigation. It was also understood that analyses that rely on subjective methods and depend on a high degree of human judgment are especially vulnerable to cognitive bias. Many, if not most, forensic methods are of this nature, yet the forensic science community generally had shown little regard for the dangers posed by these sources of error. As the Mayfield case made painfully clear, even the FBI's laboratory at Quantico—arguably the most sophisticated forensic science laboratory in the country—had failed to implement rigorous practices to mitigate bias in procedures the lab was performing every day.

A major review of the forensic sciences issued in 2009 by the National Research Council (NRC) of the National Academy of Sciences (National Research Council, 2009) provided further insight into this problem. Authorized by Congress in response to a series of inconsistencies in forensic analysis and testimony (including Mayfield's case), some of which had led to the wrongful conviction of innocent individuals, the report made clear that the forensic science system as a whole suffers from a multitude of systemic, pervasive problems. Many of those problems stemmed in part from the forensic science community's thin ties to an academic research base. Rather than emerging out of academic research science, a number of forensic techniques had emerged directly out of law enforcement practice. As a result, they emerged with limited foundational research establishing their basic validity and with little if any research dedicated to understanding the effects of cognitive bias on forensic procedures.

The NRC report called for a complete overhaul of the forensic science system in the United States. Among its 13 core recommendations, the report called for more research to be conducted on human observer bias and sources of human error in forensic examinations. This might include, for example, studies to determine the effects of contextual bias in forensic practice. The report also recommended the development of standard operating procedures to minimize, to the greatest extent reasonably possible, potential bias and sources of human error in forensic practice for all forensic analyses that may be used in litigation (NRC Report, 2009).

In direct response to the NRC Report, the Obama Administration launched a series of initiatives to strengthen the forensic sciences. Among them, in 2010, the Department of Justice (DOJ) and the National Institute of Standards and Technology (NIST), with support from the White House, signed a Memorandum of Understanding (MOU) that outlined a framework for cooperation and collaboration between the two agencies in support of efforts to strengthen forensic science. Subsequent to the MOU, DOJ, and NIST established two new institutions: (1) a National Commission on Forensic Science, an advisory body made up of an array of scientists, practitioners, members of the legal community, and others to develop policy recommendations to the Attorney General on matters related to the forensic sciences; and (2) the Organization for Scientific Area Committees (OSAC), a collaborative body of more than 600 forensic science practitioners and other experts that would work to support the development and promulgation of forensic science standards and guidelines. Each of these organizations has created a committee dedicated to "human factors," namely the cognitive, perceptual, organizational, social, and cultural factors that influence the performance of forensic scientists as they draw conclusions from physical evidence and communicate their findings in the legal system. A proposal currently under consideration by the National Commission seeks to address the problem of contextual bias by setting forth the view that forensic scientists should rely on "task-relevant information" when performing forensic analyses, and establishing principles that scientists can use to define "task-relevant" and "task-irrelevant" information (National Commission on Forensic Science, 2015). For example, a fingerprint examiner may need information about the surfaces from which the prints were lifted in order to perform an analysis, but may not need to know whether or not the suspect confessed to the crime.

The research community has also responded to the NRC's call for more research. The chapters that follow here are an important contribution to a growing body of literature on the multitude of factors that affect forensic examiners' ability to conduct their work in an impartial and unbiased manner. They go beyond an analysis of the problem, however; they offer concrete solutions for mitigating the effects of bias. Blinding is considered not only as a strategy for combatting bias in the laboratory, but also for guarding against bias on the part of expert witnesses that may occur as a result of their affiliation with the party who has hired them. The opportunities highlighted here for implementing blinding procedures in crime laboratories and jury trials are worthy of consideration by policy makers and forensic practitioners looking to mitigate the effects of bias on forensic science practice and testimony and enhance public trust in the criminal justice system.

References

Frontline, April 17, 2012. The Real CSI. WGBH Educational Foundation, USA.

National Commission on Forensic Science, 2015. Initial draft view document on ensuring that forensic analysis is based on task-relevant information. In: NCFS Meeting #7 – August 10–11, 2015. Available at: http://www.justice.gov/ncfs/file/641676/download.

National Research Council, 2009. Strengthening Forensic Science in the United States: A Path Forward. The National Academies Press.

NRC Report, 2009. p. 24 (Recommendation #5).

Stacey, R.B., 2005. Report on the erroneous fingerprint individualization in the Madrid train bombing case. Forensic Science Communications 7.

U.S. Department of Justice, 2006. A Review of the FBI's Handling of the Brandon Mayfield Case. Office of the Inspector General Oversight and Review Division.

CHAPTER

9

Determining the Proper Evidentiary Basis for an Expert Opinion: What Do Experts Need to Know and When Do They Know Too Much?

William C. Thompson

Department of Criminology, Law & Society, University of California, Irvine, CA, USA

OUTLINE

INTRODUCTION

When people make decisions about important matters they often rely on the judgments or opinions of experts. For example, jurors rely on expert testimony; physicians rely on the reports of laboratory technicians; and national security officials rely on reports of intelligence analysts. In each of these examples, the job of the expert is to provide judgments or opinions that someone else will use to make a decision. The expert plays an ancillary role by helping

Blinding as a Solution to Bias
http://dx.doi.org/10.1016/B978-0-12-802460-7.00009-7

the decision maker understand one facet of the evidence at hand—one piece of the puzzle—but it is the decision maker, rather than the expert, who must assemble the various pieces of evidence to reach a decision. Because their role is ancillary to a decision maker, I will refer to such experts as *ancillary experts*.

This chapter discusses an issue that inevitably arises when evaluating the performance of ancillary experts: what information should they consider when making their assessments? In particular, what should they know and take into account regarding the background and context of the matter in question? Consider the following questions:

- When forensic scientists evaluate physical evidence from a crime scene to determine whether it can be linked to a suspect, should they know and be influenced by other evidence (e.g., eyewitnesses, the suspect's alibi) that might indicate whether the suspect was the source?
- Should medical technicians who conduct and evaluate clinical tests know and be influenced by information about the patient's symptoms or medical history?
- In intelligence analysis, should experts who are asked to evaluate evidence in a specific domain of expertise know and be influenced by information from other domains. For example, should experts who evaluate seismographic data to determine the location and magnitude of an underground explosion be influenced by satellite imagery or human intelligence that may relate to the event?

Although these questions involve very different areas of expertise, they are similar in that all involve the proper evidentiary basis for the opinion of an ancillary expert.

If the expert and the decision maker were the same person, then these questions would be easy to answer. The decision maker should, of course, consider any and all evidence that is *relevant* to the decision at hand. Rule 401 of the *Federal Rules of Evidence* aptly describes what is relevant for a decision maker, such as a jury:

Evidence is relevant if:

(a) it has any tendency to make a fact more or less probable than it would be without the evidence; and
(b) the fact is of consequence in determining the action.

But this chapter will demonstrate that information relevant to a decision maker is not necessarily relevant to the tasks the expert is expected to perform, and that exposing ancillary experts to task-irrelevant information may reduce the probative value of their conclusions, and thereby reduce the value of their evidence for the decision maker.

My analysis rests, in part, on formal (mathematical) models of the probative value of evidence. These models are extensions and applications of the work of evidence scholars who have used likelihood ratios to describe the probative value of evidence and to explore how its value is affected by various factors (Lempert, 1977; Schum and Martin, 1982; Schum, 1994; Kadane and Schum, 1996). These models are normative rather than descriptive—that is, they concern the weight that evidence deserves rather than the weight that people might give it. They are based on general principles of inferential logic (Schum, 1994; Hacking, 2001). I will use these models to demonstrate that what is relevant to a decision maker is not always relevant, and may be prejudicial, to the tasks performed by an ancillary expert. It is possible for ancillary experts to know too much, and knowing too much can reduce the value of their contribution to the decision-making process in two ways—by biasing their judgments and by enabling double-counting of evidence.

This analysis will be helpful for thinking about blinding as a possible solution to bias. While it makes sense for ancillary experts to be "blind" to information that is irrelevant and potentially biasing, it is problematic for them to be "blind" to information that is relevant to the tasks that we ask them to perform. But what *is* relevant to such tasks? Those who argue that experts should be "blind" must answer the question—blind to what? This chapter provides some principles that can be used to answer that question. It provides criteria for assessing what is relevant and irrelevant to the tasks that ancillary experts perform.

To provide context for this discussion, and show its importance, let us begin by considering how ancillary experts are used in three important domains: criminal justice, national intelligence assessment, and clinical medicine.

WHAT SHOULD ANCILLARY EXPERTS KNOW? DILEMMAS IN THREE FIELDS

Forensic Science

In 2009, the National Research Council (NRC) identified a number of weaknesses in the scientific foundations of forensic science (NRC, 2009). One concern was that "forensic science experts are vulnerable to cognitive and contextual bias" (p. 4, note 8). This concern arose, in part, from empirical studies showing that forensic scientists are sometimes influenced by information that is thought to be irrelevant to the tasks forensic scientists are expected to perform. For example, fingerprint examiners were less likely to report a match between a latent print from a crime scene and a suspect when they were told that the suspect had a solid alibi (Dror and Charlton, 2006; Dror et al., 2006; Dror and Rosenthal, 2008).

The suspect's alibi is clearly a matter that would be relevant for a jury to consider when deliberating the defendant's guilt or innocence, but should it influence the results of a fingerprint comparison? If fingerprint examiners allow themselves to be influenced by information of this kind (either intentionally or inadvertently), does that strengthen or weaken the value of the testimony that they can provide to the jury? I will argue below that this kind of information is irrelevant to the task of fingerprints comparison. The probative value of fingerprint evidence—its value for police, prosecutors, and jurors—is likely to be weakened if examiners allow their judgments to be influenced by such evidence. Consequently, the accuracy of the decision-making process may be undermined if ancillary experts are exposed to such information.

The problem of contextual bias is not limited to fingerprint examiners. Studies have shown similar types of contextual bias in document examination (Miller, 1984), bite mark analysis (Osborne et al., 2014), bloodstain pattern analysis (Taylor et al., 2014); forensic anthropology (Nakhaeizadeh et al., 2013); and DNA analysis (Dror and Hampikian, 2011; Thompson, 2009). Concerns about contextual bias have been reinforced by the discovery of errors (false incriminations) that have been attributed, at least in part, to contextual bias in latent print analysis (Stacey, 2004; Office of Inspector General, 2006), bite mark analysis (Pretty and Sweet, 2010), and DNA testing (Thompson, 2008, 2013).

To address the problem of contextual bias, commentators have suggested a variety of context management procedures. These procedures shield analysts, at least temporarily, from exposure to irrelevant (but potentially biasing) information. For example, it has been suggested that forensic laboratories divide duties between case managers and analysts (Thompson, 2011; Found and Ganas, 2013). Case managers communicate with investigators, decide what evidence needs to be examined or tested, and assign the evidence to analysts, who conduct the examinations and tests. Under this system, the case managers can be fully informed about the underlying case, while the analysts are told only what they need to know to conduct the analyses and examinations they are asked to perform. In this way, the analysts are shielded from irrelevant but potentially biasing investigative facts until after their judgments are recorded.

Sometimes analysts cannot be blinded to potentially biasing information because they need that information to complete their work. For example, DNA analysts need to know the DNA profiles of suspects in order to determine if a particular suspect could have contributed DNA to a crime-scene sample. But there is reason to believe that knowing the profile of a suspect can bias analysts' interpretations of evidentiary DNA samples, particularly when the evidentiary samples are difficult to interpret because they contain mixed or incomplete genetic profiles (Thompson, 2008; Dror and Hampikian, 2011). The potential for bias might nevertheless be reduced by sequencing the workflow in the laboratory so that analysts examine and draw conclusions from evidentiary samples before being exposed to the profile of reference samples. The most widely discussed proposal of this type calls for forensic scientists to use a procedure known as "sequential unmasking" when comparing profiles (Krane et al., 2008; Dror et al., 2015). The Netherlands Forensic Institute has reportedly adopted sequential unmasking for DNA analysis (Stoel et al., 2015). The FBI laboratory has reportedly adopted a similar procedure for latent print analysis that it calls "linear ACE-V." The FBI's procedure involves temporary masking of reference prints while examiners make and record their initial assessments of the evidentiary prints (Office of the Inspector General, Department of Justice, 2011).

Recent discussion of the need for context management procedures in forensic science has revealed confusion and disagreement about a key underlying issue: what facts are relevant to a forensic science assessment? Conflict over this issue was on prominent display during the plenary session of the 2015 meeting of the American Academy of Forensic Sciences. Well-known lawyer Barry Scheck, who codirects the Innocence Project, argued that a number of recent false convictions arose from errors in death investigations that are attributable to cognitive bias. He argued that forensic pathologists have taken inadequate steps to blind themselves to irrelevant and potentially biasing information in police reports relating the circumstances of the death and that this information inappropriately influences autopsy findings. In response, Andrew Baker, president of the National Association of Medical Examiners, argued that Scheck's analysis proceeded from a faulty premise—that the information in police reports is irrelevant. Baker argued that forensic pathologists need this information in order to carry out their duties in an intelligent manner and avoid errors. Baker acknowledged that errors had occurred in forensic pathology, but argued that Scheck's proposal to blind pathologists to police reports would make the problem worse rather than better by depriving pathologists of relevant information.

How can we decide whether the facts in a police report are relevant, as Baker asserted, or irrelevant, as Scheck claimed? This chapter will offer some general principles that can be used to answer such questions.

Scientific Assessments in National Intelligence Investigations

Suppose that seismic detectors register a disturbance in the general vicinity of the Korean peninsula and that national intelligence officials wish to know whether the disturbance could have been caused by underground detonation of a nuclear device in North Korea. To answer this question, they will need to rely on information and opinion from a wide variety of experts. They may ask seismologists to try to determine the precise location of the disturbance and to consider whether the seismic signature of the event is more consistent with an explosion than a natural event, such as an earthquake. They may ask experts to examine satellite imagery and signals intelligence for relevant information. They may ask radiologists to look for evidence of a radioactive plume or an increase in background levels of radiation in the vicinity of the disturbance. They may even have information from spies and informants about the activities of the North Korean military, the motives and agenda of the North Korean leadership, and so on.

High-level intelligence officials—those who report to the nation's leaders—should obviously have access to all these sources of information so that they will be able to consider and integrate all relevant facts when forming an opinion and making recommendations. But how much of this information should be available to officials and experts who are lower in the chain of command? Should information be compartmentalized so that those at lower levels consider only facts within their separate domains of expertise? For example, should seismologists stick to seismology and form their conclusions solely on the basis of seismological data? Or should they be informed of findings in other domains so that they can consider the bigger picture? Should they be told, for example, about the location of known or suspected nuclear test sites and the location of plumes observed with satellite imagery?

I have recently been working with Dr Stephen Velsko of Lawrence Livermore National Laboratory on a study of inference and bias in the area of WMD (weapons of mass destruction) forensics. As part of that project, we have interviewed a number of experts on the detection of biological and radiological weapons, and the intelligence officials to whom they report. The goal of this research is to understand how experts in these areas form and report their conclusions, how that information is transmitted up the chain of command, and problems that can arise in that process. It is clear that national intelligence investigations have occasionally gone awry due to difficulties in interpreting and conveying scientific information. We have been seeking insight into those problems.

The need for context management procedures to prevent contextual bias turned out to be an important issue among experts we interviewed. Some deemed it essential that analysts should be blind to all contextual information other than facts they need to know to exercise their expertise. For example, the director of a laboratory dedicated to genetic analysis of potential microbial pathogens told us that he considers it essential that analysts working at the bench level know nothing about the underlying facts of particular investigations other than what they need to know to analyze specimens safely. The laboratory director was not blind to context. He served as the case manager, handling all communications with the agencies or individuals who were requesting analysis, and deciding what samples should be examined and how they should be tested. But the analysts who conducted the assays knew nothing of the surrounding investigation. They were simply testing what, to them, were anonymous specimens for the presence of designated pathogens.

Experts who worked in nuclear and radiological forensics also supported "blinding" and "compartmentalization" of expert judgment. One official told us that analytic errors had occurred during some past exercises designed to test the capabilities of the US national system for monitoring nuclear activity. He attributed the errors in part to "cross talk" among experts working in different domains, which led some experts to hedge or slant their findings. For example, interpretations of seismological data might have been influenced by information from satellite imagery, or vice versa—a form of contextual bias.

Those who supported blinding and compartmentalization believe that analysts in each domain should work independently, relying only on information relevant to the specific assessment they were called upon to make. They should then pass their conclusions up the chain of command to "all-source experts," who integrate input from analysts in various domains. The all-source experts are in position to see the big picture and make policy recommendations.

But our interviewees were not unanimous in supporting blinding and compartmentalization. Some perceived a need for analysts also to consider the big picture emerging from a multi-faceted investigation. They thought that lower-level analysts might be better than the higher-level "all-source experts" at integrating discordant information and deciding which findings to credit and which to discount. In sum, they viewed information about the broader context of the investigation as relevant and useful, while others viewed the same information as irrelevant and potentially biasing. This striking difference in viewpoints again highlights the need for a clear analysis of what is relevant for an ancillary expert.

Clinical Information Bias in Medicine

Similar issues have arisen in clinical medicine. Experts on medical decision-making have identified a "clinical information bias" that can arise when medical technicians or other ancillary medical personnel interpret laboratory tests while knowing too much about the underlying facts of a case (Tape and Panzer, 1986). The "clinical information bias" is similar to what has been called "contextual bias" in forensic science. It involves ancillary experts being influenced in undesirable ways by information that is clearly relevant to decision makers, but not necessarily relevant to the tasks the expert is expected to perform.

For example, one study looked at whether experts who interpret echocardiographs made better judgments with or without being informed about other clinical information, such as the patient's medical history and symptoms, the physician's observations, and the results of other clinical tests (Tape and Panzer, 1986). The study found that experts who were exposed to clinical information reported higher rates of abnormality when none was present (without any compensating increase in the rates of correct reporting when abnormality was present). This reduced the diagnostic value of the echocardiograph. The echocardiograph results were more probative, and hence more valuable for decision-making, when the experts interpreting the test were blind to the other clinical information and focused solely on their own findings. Similar results emerged from other medical studies (Schreiber, 1963; Swensson et al., 1977; Potchen et al., 1979; Doubilet and Herman, 1981; Flach et al., 2002).

These findings do not mean that clinical information is worthless, or that it should be ignored by physicians. Studies have shown that physicians are more accurate at some diagnostic tasks when they consider clinical information in conjunction with the results of diagnostic tests (e.g., Berbaum et al., 1988; Berbaum et al., 1989; Good et al., 1990; Mullins et al., 2002). For the physician who makes the ultimate decision about diagnosis and treatment, having more information is often better than having less. But this is not always the case. For example, information about the family history and risk factors of women being evaluated for breast cancer did not improve the accuracy of experts interpreting mammography images (Elmore et al., 1997).

In this context, the physician—like the juror in the criminal justice system, or the "all-source expert" in intelligence analysis—is the person who must assemble all the facts and make a decision. Any information that meets the test of relevance under Rule 401 is information that the physician should consider.

But ancillary medical personnel—those who do the lab work and conduct the diagnostic tests—are not in the same position as the treating physician. If they are not called upon to make a final decision about diagnosis and treatment, they may not need as much information as the treating physician to do their jobs. In fact, having too much information might lead to biases and other problems that reduce the value of their contribution. Hence, there may be circumstances in which ancillary personnel should be blind to information that the treating physician will consider. Furthermore, even if the same physician both interprets diagnostic tests and makes the final decision on diagnosis and treatment, there may be circumstances in which workflow should be sequenced, so that some aspects of test interpretation occur before the physician considers the clinical information necessary for the ultimate diagnosis. Physicians in this position might benefit from adopting procedures similar to the "sequential unmasking" procedure employed in forensic science.

To identify circumstances in which blinding or masking will be helpful for ancillary experts (and for decision makers performing ancillary tasks), it is necessary to distinguish information that these experts need to know to perform their assigned tasks effectively, from information that is unnecessary and potentially biasing. To draw that distinction, it is helpful to consider the inferential connections that link the expert's judgment to the propositions being evaluated by the decision maker. In other words, it helps to consider the role of the ancillary expert in the decision-making process. We turn now to those questions.

A FRAMEWORK FOR ANALYSIS

Decision analysts often use influence diagrams (also known as relevance diagrams or Bayesian networks) to represent situations in which decisions are made (Taroni et al., 2006). Influence diagrams were developed in the 1970s as an alternative to decision trees (Howard and Matheson, 1981; Schachter, 1988). They provide a graphical and mathematical model of a decision-making task and show how various pieces of information are (or might be) relevant to the decision.

Figure 1 is an influence diagram that shows how the conclusions of an ancillary expert might be relevant to a decision maker. In domains like criminal justice, intelligence analysis, and clinical medicine, the inferential connections between the expert and the decision maker often take the form shown in Figure 1. The top node (ellipse) of the model shows the "primary propositions" that the decision maker must evaluate in order to make a decision. The primary propositions, which are labeled *P* and *NP*, are statements about whether a key underlying fact is true or not true, or whether a key underlying event has occurred or did not occur. In criminal justice these are often propositions about the identity of a criminal perpetrator, so

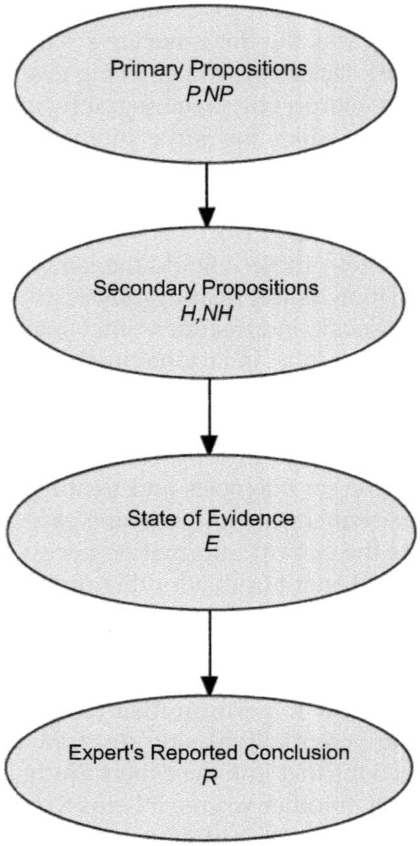

FIGURE 1 Influence diagram showing inferential links between the reported conclusion of an ancillary expert (*R*) and propositions evaluated by a decision maker (*P,NP*).

P could be the proposition that a particular suspect is the perpetrator and *NP* that he is not. In medicine, *P* and *NP* are often propositions about the underlying cause of a patient's complaint, so *P* might be the proposition that a patient's chest pain is caused by heart disease and *NP* that it is caused by some other problem (not heart disease). In intelligence analysis, *P,NP* are typically events with implications for national security decisions, so *P* might represent the proposition that white powder found in an envelope addressed to a public official is a bio-weapon, and *NP* that is it not a bio-weapon.

The model assumes that the decision maker has no direct way to assess whether the primary propositions are true and therefore turns to an expert for assistance. Although the expert cannot directly assess the primary propositions, the expert can provide insight and information about some secondary propositions that are relevant to whether the primary propositions are true. The secondary propositions are shown in the second node of the model and labeled *H* and *NH*. In criminal justice, *H* might be the propositions that a suspect is the source of a fingerprint at the crime scene, and *NH* that someone else was the source of that print. In the medical example, *H* might be the proposition that the patient has a blockage in his coronary arteries, and *NH* that he does not. In the national security example, *H* might be the proposition that the white powder contains *bacillus anthracis*, and *NH* that it does not.

The expert examines some evidence that is pertinent to whether *H* or *NH* is true and reports a conclusion. In the model, the term *E* (third node) represents the state of the evidence that the expert examines. For a fingerprint examiner, *E* might represent the specific similarities and dissimilarities that are observable when the crime-scene print is compared to a reference print from the suspect; for a medical technician, *E* might represent the appearance of an echocardiograph of the patient's heart. For a forensic biologist, *E* might represent results of a biological assay on the white powder. Based on the evidence, the expert reaches a conclusion that is reported to the decision maker. For example, the fingerprint examiner might report that the suspect's print matches the print from the crime scene. The term *R* in the bottom node of the model represents the expert's reported conclusion. The decision maker relies on *R* when evaluating the primary propositions, *P,NP*.

What is the probative value of the expert's report? In other words, how helpful is *R* for distinguishing *P,NP*? That depends on whether, and to what extent, *R* is more likely to occur if *P* is true than if *NP* is true (Lempert, 1977). And that depends, in turn, on the series of inferential links that are represented in the model by arrows. The arrows show the direction of influence—how the state of one node influences the state of another. The model shown in Figure 1 assumes that the state of the primary propositions influences the occurrence of the secondary propositions; that the secondary propositions influence the state of the evidence; and that the state of the evidence influence the expert's reported conclusion. Thus, in the criminal justice example, the probability that the expert will report that the fingerprints match depends on the similarity of the prints, which depends on whether the crime-scene print was made by the suspect, which depends on whether the suspect is the perpetrator. The probative value of the expert's report, *R*, depends on the overall strength of these links in the inferential chain.

In the model shown in Figure 1, the only factor that influences the expert's reported conclusion is the state of the evidence that the expert examines, *E*. This model assumes, for example, that the only factor that influences the conclusion of the fingerprint examiner is the similarity of the prints being compared. In reality, as discussed earlier, *E* may not be the only influential variable. The examiner's opinion may also be influenced by other evidence and by contextual information about the case. The fundamental question raised in this chapter is when (or under what circumstances) an ancillary expert should consider such information. I propose that we answer this question by considering whether the information makes the expert's opinion more or less probative, and thus more or less helpful to the decision makers who will rely on the expert's opinion. I will use the influence diagram developed here to illustrate circumstances in which contextual influence can strengthen or weaken the probative value of an expert's opinion.

Task-Relevant Context

To evaluate the evidence, *E*, the expert needs to think about two conditional probabilities: $p(E|H)$—the probability that the evidence will appear as it does if *H* is true; and $p(E|NH)$—the probability that the evidence will appear as it does if *NH* is true. For example, the fingerprint examiner will need to think about the likelihood that the observed similarities and dissimilarities of the two prints would occur if the suspect made the crime-scene print and if someone else made the crime-scene print. Only if $p(E|H)$ is relatively high and $p(E|NH)$ is extremely low should the examiner conclude that the suspect made the print. The medical technician must think about the likelihood that the echocardiograph would show the observed features *if* the patient has, or does not have, obstructed arteries. And the forensic biologist must think about the probability of getting the results obtained in the assay of the white power *if* it contained *bacillus anthracis*, and *if* it did not.

It is fair to say that assessment of $p(E|H)$ and $p(E|HN)$ is the essence of the ancillary expert's task; it is what we expect and require ancillary experts to do. An expert who is not thinking about these conditional probabilities is not thinking logically about the assigned task. It follows that any contextual information that has the potential to help an ancillary expert perform this assessment is relevant and appropriate for the expert to consider. I will refer to such information as *task-relevant*, to indicate that it is relevant to the task that ancillary experts are expected to perform.

For fingerprint examinations, task-relevant context would surely include information about the surface from which the prints were lifted. This information is task-relevant because it has the potential to assist the examiner in evaluating the likelihood of finding discrepancies between prints from the same person, which assists in evaluating $p(E|H)$. If the surface from which the latent print was lifted was curved or uneven, one might expect some distortion of the latent print, relative to the reference print of the same person. Information about the method used to lift the latent might also be relevant to its appearance relative to the reference print, and hence to $p(E|H)$.

Task-relevant context would also include information that helps the examiner assess $p(E|NH)$—the probability the observed level of similarity would be found if the suspect did not make the latent print. For example, it is important for the examiner to know whether the suspect was identified through a search of fingerprint database, and if so, how large the database was. If the suspect did not make the print, one would nevertheless expect a higher level of similarity if he was selected from a database because an automated system assigned his fingerprint a high similarity score than if he became a suspect for some other reason. This is information that an examiner should take into account in deciding whether a given level of similarity is sufficient for a definitive identification. Hence, it is task-relevant.

This analysis makes it possible to provide a formal criterion for task-relevance using the nomenclature of the model shown in Figure 1:

1. information is task-relevant if it has the potential to assist the examiner in evaluating either $p(E|H)$ or $p(E|NH)$;
2. information is task-irrelevant if it has no bearing on the conditional probabilities $p(E|H)$ or $p(E|NH)$.

The criterion is whether the information has the *potential* to help the expert rather than whether it actually helps the expert, because not all experts will be sufficiently discerning to make appropriate use of the information they receive. Task-relevance is a property of the information itself, not of any particular expert's reaction to it.

Dangers of Exposing Ancillary Experts to Task-Irrelevant Information

Although task-irrelevant information is not pertinent to the task that the ancillary expert is supposed to be performing, it might nevertheless influence an expert's judgment.

That kind of influence poses significant dangers to the integrity and accuracy of the decision-making process because it creates a potential for double-counting of evidence and may bias and thereby undermine the probative value of the expert's evidence.

To illustrate these potential problems, let's return to the fingerprint example. Let's suppose that in addition to the fingerprint evidence there is an eyewitness who identified the suspect as the perpetrator. The decision makers (police, prosecutors, jurors) will consider both the eyewitness and the fingerprint evidence in assessing whether the suspect is the perpetrator. But should the fingerprint examiner know about the eyewitness?

Figure 2 represents the inferential connections among the various items of evidence that would exist if the fingerprint expert is blind to the eyewitness evidence, and the eyewitness is blind to the fingerprint evidence. There is an arrow from the top node to the eyewitness node, which indicates that the eyewitness' evidence has probative value for distinguishing *P,NP*. But no arrows connect the eyewitness evidence (W) to the fingerprint evidence (R), which means the fingerprint examiner is not influenced by the eyewitness evidence and the eyewitness is not influenced by the fingerprints. The two items of evidence are said to be *conditionally independent*.[1] They are not fully independent because

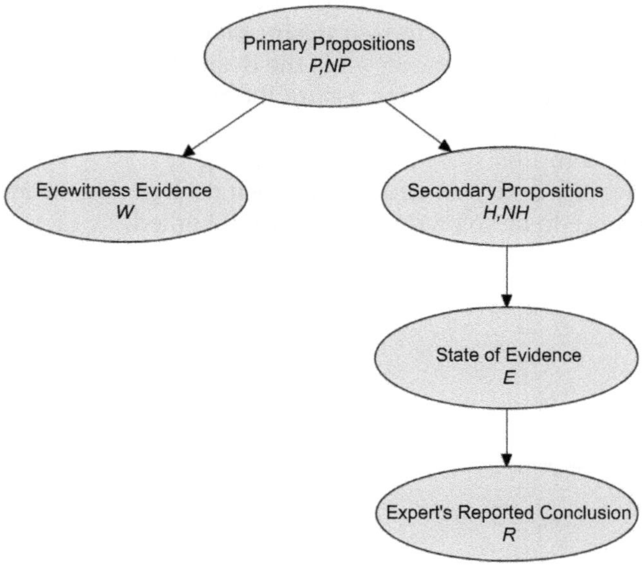

FIGURE 2 Influence diagram showing *conditional independence* of eyewitness and fingerprint evidence.

[1] When two items of evidence are conditionally independent, then their joint value for proving the underlying proposition to which they both relate can be determined by multiplying the likelihood ratios of the two items (Schum and Martin, 1982). Their joint value may be significantly lower if they are conditionally dependent. For example, if a suspect shares with the perpetrator two conditionally independent characteristics, A and B, each of which occurs in only 1% of the population, then A and B will be found jointly in only 1% of the population (1 person in 10,000). But if the occurrence of A increases the chances of finding B, or vice versa, the probability of finding both may be much higher, and hence the probative value of the joint finding will be less.

they both are affected by whether the suspect is guilty. The examiner is more likely to report that the prints match if the eyewitness identifies the suspect, but that correlation arises solely because the suspect is more likely to be the perpetrator if the eyewitness identifies him, and the fingerprint examiner is more likely to identify the suspect if he is the perpetrator.

Suppose, however, that the fingerprint examiner happens to hear about the eyewitness. Perhaps he speaks to a detective about the case or reads a police report. In that case there is a risk that this task-irrelevant information will influence his judgment in the manner shown in Figure 3. This kind of contextual influence is ubiquitous in human decision making and may occur with or without conscious awareness. It is most likely to occur in cases in which the evidence being evaluating by the expert is somewhat ambiguous. Imagine, for example, that the latent print contains limited detail, or is smudged, making the comparison difficult. While it looks quite similar to the suspect's fingerprint, the examiner is uncertain whether there is sufficient detail to support a definitive identification. While pondering this issue, the examiner hears that an eyewitness has identified the suspect.

This information is likely to influence the expert toward identifying the print as the suspect's for at least two reasons. First, it creates a strong motive to identify the suspect. The motive in question does not arise from malice or partisanship; it arises from one of the most basic and common desires of mankind—a desire that may be particularly strong among those who make their livings as experts—it is the desire to reach the correct conclusion, to be right. The eyewitness evidence helps assure the fingerprint examiner that the suspect really is the perpetrator and hence that identifying him as the source of the crime-scene print is the right decision.

This kind of influence is both powerful and pernicious. It allows the interpretation of putatively scientific evidence to be colored (one might say tainted) by facts that are irrelevant to

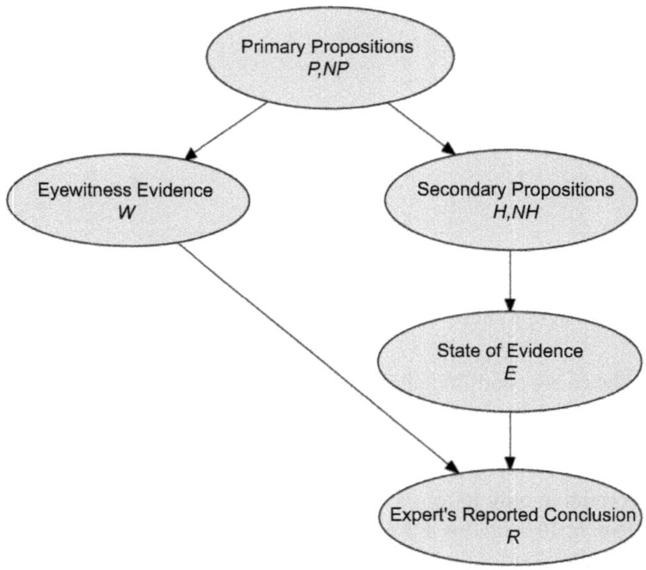

FIGURE 3 Influence diagram showing *conditional dependence* of fingerprint and eyewitness evidence that arises when the fingerprint examiner is influenced by the eyewitness evidence.

a scientific analysis of that evidence.[2] The examiner's reported conclusion is no longer based solely on the prints; it rests partly on the eyewitness. But the eyewitness evidence will also be considered, as a separate piece of evidence, by the decision maker. So it may be counted twice. This could cause the decision makers to overestimate the strength of the case against the suspect because they do not realize that exposure to the eyewitness bolstered the expert's evidence, leading the expert to report a stronger conclusion than he otherwise would have. The decision makers think they are receiving two independent pieces of evidence, when in fact the evidence is dependent in ways that reduce its apparent collective value.

Second, information about the eyewitness is likely to bias the expert's evaluation of the fingerprint evidence (Dror and Rosenthal, 2008; Simon, 2012; Read and Simon, 2012). Knowing there is strong evidence that incriminates the suspect may unconsciously influence the way the fingerprint examiner looks at the prints, making the examiner more likely to see discrepancies between the prints as explainable anomalies and less likely to see similarities as coincidental. Psychologists call this process biased assimilation of evidence; it is well known and documented in the psychological literature (Kassin et al., 2013; Wilson and Brekke, 1994).

The models shown in Figures 2 and 3 provide the basis for a mathematical demonstration of ways in which the probative value of expert evidence might be affected if an expert is influenced by task-irrelevant information. The probative value of R depends on what evidence scholars call the materiality and the logical relevance of this evidence. Materiality is what the presence of the suspect's print at the crime scene tells us about whether he is the perpetrator. Logical relevance is what the examiner's report tells us about whether the print at the scene is the suspect's. The materiality of the fingerprint identification depends on two conditional probabilities: $p(H|P)$—the probability the print came from the suspect if he was the perpetrator; and $p(H|NP)$—the probability the print came from the suspect if he was not the perpetrator. The logical relevance depends on two additional conditional probabilities: $p(R|H)$, the probability the examiner would conclude the suspect made the print if he really did make it; and $p(R|NH)$, the probability the examiner would conclude the suspect made the print if someone else made it.[3] Based on these four conditional probabilities it is possible to compute a likelihood ratio—I will call it LR_R—that describes the probative value of R for distinguishing P,NP.[4] One can then

[2] The eyewitness evidence is clearly task-irrelevant. It may influence the examiner's conclusions *about the prints*, but it does not help the examiner draw conclusions *from the prints*. The eyewitness evidence supports the proposition that the suspect is the perpetrator, and if that proposition is true, then the prints are more likely to be those of the suspect. But a fingerprint examiner who reasoned in this manner would be reasoning backward from the conclusion (the suspect is the perpetrator) to the evidence (the suspect matches the fingerprint). A cardinal principle of scientific inference is that one must reason from the evidence to a conclusion, rather than the reverse. Backward, goal-directed reasoning in which the desired or expected conclusion influences interpretation of the evidence is a hallmark of junk science (Huber, 1991).

[3] For the sake of simplicity, we will consider how these estimates might vary in a particular case where the state of the evidence, E, is fixed. So I will not include E as a variable in this exercise.

[4] A formula for combining conditional probabilities affecting the materiality and logical relevance of evidence was initially derived by Schum and DuCharme (1971). Thompson, Taroni, and Aitken (2003) discussed how this formula applies to assessment of forensic DNA evidence. Using the nomenclature of this article, the formula is: $LR_R = [p(R \mid H)p(H \mid P) + p(R \mid NH)p(NH \mid P)]/[p(R \mid NH)p(NH \mid NP) + p(R \mid H)p(H \mid NP)]$. Because the suspect either was, or was not, the source of the fingerprint, the term $p(NH \mid P)$ is the complement of $p(H \mid P)$; and the term $p(NH \mid NP)$ is the complement of $p(H \mid NP)$.

explore how that likelihood ratio changes with changes in specific conditional probabilities that might arise if the expert is exposed to task-irrelevant contextual information.

To illustrate, let's suppose that $p(H\,|\,P)=0.9$ and $p(H\,|\,NP)=0.001$. In other words, there is a 90% chance that the print will be that of the suspect if he was the perpetrator but only a one-in-thousand chance that it would be his print if he was not the perpetrator. Under these assumptions, the print is about 900 times more likely to be that of the suspect if the suspect was the perpetrator than if he was not, and hence that the materiality of the evidence is very strong. Let's also assume that $p(R\,|\,H)=0.90$ and $p(R\,|\,NH)=0$. In other words, there is a 90% chance the examiner will identify the print as the suspect's if the suspect made the print, but no chance that he will do so if someone else made the print. (Readers are free to try out different numbers if they like.) Plugging these four conditional probabilities into the formula, we find that $LR_R=908$. That means that the expert's identification of the suspect as the source of the print is 908 times more likely if the suspect is the perpetrator than if he is not.

I made the initial estimates of the conditional probabilities under the assumption that the examiner knew nothing about the eyewitness evidence and was drawing conclusions solely from the comparison of the prints. In other words, the initial estimates assume the situation represented in Figure 2. How might the conditional probabilities change in the situation shown in Figure 3, where the analyst hears about the eyewitness? My best guess is that learning about the eyewitness will make the examiner more willing to identify the suspect as the source of the crime-scene print, and that this is likely to increase both $p(R|H)$ and $p(R|NH)$. How will that affect the value of the fingerprints evidence, as reflected in LR_R? That will obviously depend on how much each conditional probability increases, but increases in $p(R|NH)$ will generally degrade the value of the expert's evidence much faster than increases in $p(R|H)$ will enhance it (Schum and Ducharm, 1971; Schum, 1994; Thompson et al., 2003). Suppose for example that $p(R|H)$ increases to 1.0—which means the examiner is now certain to identify the suspect if he made the print. Let's also suppose that there is an uptick in $p(R|NH)$ from 0.0 to 0.001—which means there is now a 1-in-1000 chance someone who did not make the print will be identified. Although the increase in the false match rate may seem small, it significantly degrades the probative value of the fingerprint evidence. Under the new numbers, LR_R drops from 908 to 453. This means that the fingerprint evidence has lost nearly half of its probative value. The expert's identification of the suspect as the source of the print is now only 453 rather than 908 times more likely if the suspect is the perpetrator than if he is not.[5] If $p(R|H)=1.0$ and $p(R|NS)$ increased to 0.002 (2 chances in 1000), then LR_R would drop to 302. These examples show that seemingly small increases in the probability of a falsely incriminating report can significantly degrade the probative value of the expert evidence. And it is conceivable the probability of a false report in difficult cases could increase far more drastically than I am assuming here in response to outside information. If $p(R|NH)$ increased to 0.01 (1 in 100) for example, the likelihood ratio would drop to 82.

Of course, the results of this exercise are entirely dependent on what assumptions one makes about the conditional probabilities and how they will be affected if the expert is

[5] One way to understand this change intuitively is to consider the chances that the suspect will be implicated falsely as the perpetrator. If the examiner never falsely identifies anyone, then there is only the 1-in-1000 chance that his print happened to be at the crime scene for innocent reasons. But the chances of a false incrimination roughly double if we add the 1-in-1000 chance of a false identification to the 1 in 1000 chances of the print being present innocently. Hence, the probative value of the identification for proving the suspect is the perpetrator is cut by approximately half if $p(R|NH)$ rises from zero to 0.001.

exposed to task-irrelevant information. Under any assumptions I consider plausible, the effect of exposure is to reduce the probative value of the expert evidence. While it is possible to imagine hypothetical circumstances in which the probative value of expert evidence would be unaffected or even enhanced if the expert was influenced by task-irrelevant information, these circumstances seem unlikely and would generally only occur if there were serious deficiencies in the expert's analytic method or reporting.[6]

These examples thus illustrate an important danger of exposing ancillary experts to task-irrelevant information—that their evidence will become less probative and therefore less valuable to the decision makers who rely upon it. This hidden cost of contextual bias is one of the primary reasons that blinding procedures may be needed to shield ancillary experts from exposure to task-irrelevant information.

EXPERTS WHO ARE ALSO DECISION MAKERS

Some of the controversy and confusion noted earlier regarding the need for blinding procedures arises when experts play multiple roles. A given expert may sometimes act in an ancillary role, providing evidence that others will use to make a decision, but at other times act as a decision maker as well.

For example, a forensic pathologist who conducts autopsies during death investigations may also have official duties as a medical examiner or coroner. Medical examiners are expected to make official determinations regarding cause and manner of death for the death certificate. Those determinations are supposed to be based on all relevant evidence revealed by the death investigation. So the determination of cause and manner of death may well be influenced by facts beyond those revealed by the autopsy, such as statements of witnesses, suicide notes, and facts revealed in a police investigation—and there is nothing improper about a medical examiner relying on such information. Like an "all-source expert" in intelligence investigations, the medical examiner/coroner is expected to put all the pieces together so that the death certificate is accurate. For this task, the expert is also the decision maker.

But the same forensic pathologist might also be asked to play an ancillary role when testifying as an expert in court, and consideration of nonmedical evidence may well be improper when the expert plays that role. Particularly in cases where the expert will provide evidence for a criminal prosecution, the expert is expected to draw conclusions based on his or her scientific expertise rather than from the entirety of the evidence (Risinger et al., 2002; Risinger, 2015). The Supreme Court of Iowa recently overturned a mother's conviction for the murder of her newborn infant in a case where a medical examiner testified that he had determined that the manner of death was homicide (State v. Tyler, 2015). Although the medical examiner

[6] Suppose, for example, that an examiner was unwilling to report a latent print match unless she knew that there was some other evidence to indicate that the person who matched had touched the item from which the latent print was lifted. In that case, the expert's evidence would be worthless unless the expert was exposed to other evidence, in which case it might have some value. If the expert's reporting standards were flawed in this particular way, then the justice system might arguably be better off if such an expert was exposed to other evidence than if the expert was blind. But such a situation seems extremely unlikely. If such a situation arose, it would clearly be better to address it by training the examiner to adopt more appropriate reporting standards than by using exposure to contextual facts to overcome the effects of an inappropriate reporting threshold.

had performed an autopsy, he admitted that his determination of manner of death was not based on the autopsy findings, which were inconclusive on whether the child was stillborn or alive at birth. The finding of homicide rested entirely in the medical examiner's interpretation of statements the mother had allegedly made to the police. The Iowa Supreme Court found this testimony improper and prejudicial, as the jurors did not need a medical examiner to help them draw conclusions from the mother's statements to police. In the opinion of the court, medical opinion is admissible at trial only if it is based on medical evidence.

When experts play multiple roles, it can be confusing to ask, "what is relevant to this expert?" The answer will depend on what role the expert is playing (ancillary expert or decision maker), and on the particular task the expert is expected to perform. Disputes about what an expert should know become easier to resolve if we shift our focus from what is relevant *to the expert* to the more tractable question of what is relevant *to the task*. It then becomes possible to think about assigning tasks in a manner that avoids exposing the expert unnecessarily to task-irrelevant information.

For example, forensic pathologists might sequence their work so that tasks requiring more contextual information are performed after those requiring less. In cases where it appears likely that courtroom testimony will be required (e.g., suspicious deaths of children, police shootings, deaths of individuals in police custody), a medical examiner could conduct the autopsy and reach medical conclusions before being exposed to task-irrelevant information in police reports and witness statements. Forensic pathologists could work in teams with one screening the evidence to assure that the other (who conducts the autopsy) is informed of the relevant propositions to be evaluated and any task-relevant contextual information, but is not exposed to task-irrelevant information. If the key propositions are whether a bullet hole in the decedent was an entry or exit wound, for example, it would be best for the pathologist examining the wound not to know whether a particular conclusion supported or contradicted by task-irrelevant information contained in police reports and witness statements. Blinding the pathologist to task-irrelevant information would assure that the autopsy findings are based solely on the medical examination, as demanded by the courts, and would help maximize the probative value of such conclusions for the legal system. Once the medical conclusions were recorded, contextual information that was irrelevant to the autopsy findings, but relevant to the broader task of assessing manner of death, could be "unmasked" so that the medical examiner would be fully informed when deciding what conclusion to record on the death certificate.

CONCLUSION

Ancillary experts in fields like forensic science, clinical medicine, and national security should give careful thought to what is task-relevant and task-irrelevant for the tasks they perform. They should also consider adopting context management procedures to shield themselves from exposure to task-irrelevant information when making important judgments and assessments, particularly in situations in which the evidence they evaluate is potentially ambiguous or subject to more than one interpretation.

This chapter has provided criteria for evaluating the task-relevance of contextual information. It has also explained the potential benefits of blinding experts to task-irrelevant information and the potential costs of failure to do so. These are matters that deserve serious attention. What is at stake is the value of expert evidence itself to those who will use it to make important decisions.

Acknowledgments

This research was supported by grants from the University of California Laboratory Fees Research Program and the National Institute of Justice.

References

Berbaum, K.S., Franken, E.A., Dorfman, D.D., Barloon, T.J., 1988. Investigative Radiology 23, 48–55.

Berbaum, K.S., Franken, E.A., El-Khoury, G.Y., 1989. Impact of clinical history on radiographic detection of fractures: a comparison of radiologists and orthopedists. American Journal of Radiology 153, 1221–1224.

Doubilet, P., Herman, P.G., 1981. Interpretation of radiographs: effect of clinical history. American Journal of Radiology 137, 1055–1058.

Dror, I.E., Charlton, D., 2006. Why experts make errors. Journal of Forensic Identification 56, 600–616.

Dror, I.E., Charlton, D., Peron, A., 2006. Contextual information renders experts vulnerable to making erroneous identifications. Forensic Science International 156, 174–178. Retrieved from: http://dx.doi.org/10.1016/j.forsciint.2005.10.017.

Dror, I.E., Hampikian, G., 2011. Subjectivity and bias in forensic DNA mixture interpretation. Science and Justice 51 (4), 204–208.

Dror, I.E., Rosenthal, R., 2008. Meta–analytically quantifying the reliability and biasability of forensic experts. Journal of Forensic Sciences 53 (4), 900–903.

Dror, I.E., Thompson, W.C., Meissner, C.A., Kornfield, I., Krane, D., Saks, M., Risinger, M., 2015. Context management toolbox: a linear sequential unmasking (LSU) approach for minimizing cognitive bias in forensic decision making. Journal of Forensic Science 60 (4), 1111–1112.

Elmore, J.G., Wells, C.K., Howard, D.H., Feinstein, A.R., 1997. The impact of clinical history on mammographic interpretations. Journal of the American Medical Association 227, 49–52.

Found, B., Ganas, J., 2013. The management of domain irrelevant context information in forensic handwriting examination casework. Science and Justice 53 (2), 154–158.

Flach, S.D., Canaris, G.J., Tape, T.G., Huntley, K.M., Wigton, R.S., 2002. The effects of proficiency and bias on residents' interpretation of the microscopic urinalysis. Medical Decision Making 22 (4), 318–325.

Good, B.C., Cooperstein, L.A., DeMarino, G.B., Miketic, L.M., Gennari, R.C., Rockette, H.E., Gur, D., 1990. How does knowledge of the clinical history affect the accuracy of chest radiograph interpretation? American Journal of Radiology 154, 709–712.

Hacking, I., 2001. Introduction to Probability and Inductive Logic. Cambridge University Press, Cambridge, U.K.

Howard, R.A., Matheson, J.E., 1981. Influence diagrams. In: Howard, R.A., Matheson, J.E. (Eds.), Readings on the Principles and Applications of Decision Analysis. Strategic Decisions Group, Menlo Park, CA.

Huber, P.W., 1991. Galileo's Revenge: Junk Science in the Courtroom. Basic Books, New York, N.Y.

Kadane, J.B., Schum, D.A., 1996. A Probabilistic Analysis of the Sacco and Vanzetti Evidence. John Wiley and Sons, New York, New York.

Kassin, S.M., Dror, I.E., Kukucka, J., 2013. The forensic confirmation bias: problems, perspectives, and proposed solutions. Journal of Applied Research in Memory and Cognition 2, 42–52.

Krane, D.E., Ford, S., Gilder, J., Inman, K., Jamieson, A., Koppl, R., et al., 2008. Sequential unmasking: a means of minimizing observer effects in forensic DNA interpretation. Journal of Forensic Science 53 (4), 1006–1007.

Lempert, R., 1977. Modeling relevance. Michigan Law Review 75, 1021–1057.

Miller, L.S., 1984. Bias among forensic document examiners: a need for procedural change. Journal of Police Science and Administration 12 (4), 407–411.

Mullins, M.E., Lev, M.H., Schellingerhout, D., Koroshetz, W.J., Gonzales, R.G., 2002. Influence of availability of clinical history on detection of early stroke using enhanced CT and diffusion-weighted MR imaging. American Journal of Radiology 179, 223–228.

Nakhaeizadeh, S., Dror, I.E., Morgan, R.M., 2013. Cognitive bias in forensic anthropology: visual assessment of skeletal remains is susceptible to confirmation bias. Science and Justice 54, 208–214.

National Research Council, 2009. Strengthening Forensic Science in the United States: A Path Forward. The National Academies Press, Washington, D.C.

Office of the Inspector General, U.S. Department of Justice, 2006. A Review of the FBI's Handling of the Brandon Mayfield Case. U.S. Department of Justice, Washington, D.C .

Office of the Inspector General, U.S. Department of Justice, 2011. A Review of the FBI's Progress in Responding to the Recommendations in the Office of the Inspector General Report on the Fingerprint Misidentification in the Brandon Mayfield Case. Office of the Inspector General U.S. Department of Justice, Washington, D.C.

Osborne, N.K., Woods, S., Kieser, J., Zajac, R., 2014. Does contextual information bias bitemark comparisons? Science & Justice 54 (4), 267–273.

Potchen, E.J., Gard, J.W., Lazar, P., Lahaie, P., Andary, M., 1979. The effect of clinical history data on chest film interpretation: direction or distraction? Investigative Radiology 14, 404.

Pretty, I., Sweet, D., 2010. A paradigm shift in the analysis of bitemarks. Forensic Science International 201, 38–44.

Read, S.J., Simon, D., 2012. Parallel constraint satisfaction as a mechanism for cognitive consistency. In: Gawronski, B., Strack, F. (Eds.), Cognitive Consistency: A Unifying Concept in Social Psychology. Guilford Press, New York, New York.

Risinger, D.M., 2015. At what cost? Blind testing, eyewitness identification, and what can and cannot be counted as a cost of reducing information available for decision. Howard Law Journal 58, 333–364.

Risinger, D.M., Saks, M.J., Thompson, W.C., Rosenthal, R., 2002. The Daubert/Kumho implications of observer effects in forensic science: hidden problems of expectation and suggestion. California Law Review 90, 1–55.

Schachter, R.D., 1988. Probabilistic inference and influence diagrams. Operations Research 36 (4), 589–604.

Schreiber, M.H., 1963. The clinical history as a factor in roentgenogram interpretation. Journal of the American Medical Association 185, 37–139.

Schum, D.A., 1994. Evidential Foundations of Probabilistic Reasoning. John Wiley and Sons, New York.

Schum, D.A., DuCharme, W.M., 1971. Comments on the relationship between the impact and the reliability of evidence. Organizational Behavior and Human Performance 6, 111–131.

Schum, D.A., Martin, A., 1982. Formal and empirical research on cascaded inference in jurisprudence. Law and Society Review 17, 105–151.

Simon, D., 2012. In Doubt: The Psychology of the Criminal Justice Process. Harvard University Press, Cambridge, Mass.

Stacey, R.B., 2004. Report on the erroneous fingerprint individualization in the Madrid train bombing case. Journal of Forensic Identification 54 (6), 706–718.

State v. Tyler, __N.W.2d ___(Iowa, 2015). http://law.justia.com/cases/iowa/supreme-court/2015/130830.html.

Stoel, R.D., Berger, C.E., Kerkhoff, W., Mattijssen, E., Dror, I., 2015. Minimizing contextual bias in forensic casework. In: Strom, K., Hickman, M.J. (Eds.), Forensic Science and the Administration of Justice. Sage, New York.

Swensson, R.G., Hessel, S.J., Herman, P.G., 1977. Omissions in radiology: faulty search or stringent reporting criteria? Radiology 123, 563–567.

Tape, T.G., Panzer, R.J., 1986. Echocardiography, endocarditis, and clinical information bias. Journal of General Internal Medicine 1, 300–304.

Taroni, F., Aitken, C., Garbolino, P., Biedermann, A., 2006. Bayesian Networks and Probabilistic Inference in Forensic Science. John Wiley and Sons, Chichester, UK.

Taylor, M., Laber, T., Kish, P.E., Owens, G., 2014. Reliability Assessment of Current Methods in Bloodstain Pattern Analysis. Final Report for the National Institute of Justice.

Thompson, W.C., 2008. Beyond bad apples: analyzing the role of forensic science in wrongful convictions. Southwestern Law Review 37 (4), 1027–1050.

Thompson, W.C., 2011. What role should investigative facts play in the evaluation of scientific evidence. Australian Journal of Forensic Science 43 (2–3), 123–134.

Thompson, W.C., 2009. Painting the target around the matching profile: the Texas sharpshooter fallacy in forensic DNA interpretation. Law, Probability and Risk 8, 257–276.

Thompson, W.C., 2013. Forensic DNA evidence: the myth of infallibility. In: Krimsky, S., Gruber, J. (Eds.), Genetic Explanations: Sense and Nonsense. Harvard University Press, Cambridge, MA, pp. 227–255.

Thompson, W.C., Taroni, F., Aitken, C.G.G., 2003. How the probability of a false positive affects the value of DNA evidence. Journal of Forensic Sciences 48 (1), 47–54.

Wilson, T.D., Brekke, N., 1994. Mental contamination and mental correction: unwanted influences on judgments and evaluations. Psychological Bulletin 116, 117–142.

CHAPTER

10

Minimizing and Leveraging Bias in Forensic Science

Roger Koppl[1], *Dan Krane*[2]

[1]Whitman School of Management, Syracuse University, Syracuse, NY, USA; [2]Wright State University, Dayton, OH, USA

OUTLINE

The soft overcomes the hard.
The slow overcomes the fast. **Lao Tzu**

INTRODUCTION

Addressing bias in forensic science must entail more than temporarily hiding information from a bench examiner—though such information hiding is essential. We suggest that blinding (and other strategies to minimize bias) should be complemented by measures to leverage remaining biases and that blinding measures should be embedded in a right mix of complementary measures, some of which we will describe as "hierarchical" and others

http://dx.doi.org/10.1016/B978-0-12-802460-7.00010-3

as "distributed." To make our case, we explain that there are several very different ways to handle bias in forensic science. We offer a classification of strategies and comment on the strengths and weaknesses of each. It should be clear that the different strategies are complementary, but opinions may differ on which mix is best. Finally, we warn of the dangers of "regulatory capture." Economic theory and history show that a regulatory oversight body may act in ways that serve special interests more effectively than the general interest.

Until recently, the existence of bias in forensic science was a contested matter. Scholars of bias in forensic science often take it for granted that bias is bad. Kassier and Kessler (2011, pp. xiii–xv) provide a representative example. The term "bias" has many interrelated meanings, all suggesting deviation from some standard such as objectivity, rationality, or impartiality. Somewhat counterintuitively, such deviations can actually make it more likely to achieve a good result. The presumption of innocence, for e.g., may create a salutary bias against conviction. Parents should be biased in favor of their children. Statisticians sometimes give up some accuracy to be more precise; they sometimes prefer, in other words, biased estimators that have a lower mean squared error. Finally, some cognitive biases allow decision making in certain social contexts to be " better than rational" (Cosmides and Tooby, 1994).

In forensic science, too, bias is not always bad. Fingerprint examiners, for example, should not declare a match ("individualization") unless there is a high degree of certainty of a match. This standard of judgment should create a bias against identification that would have the good effect of reducing the risk of incriminating an innocent person.

Bias in forensic science is problematic only when a type of bias tends to produce a distribution of errors that is inferior to a distribution that could be had if some ameliorative measures were applied. We need to choose between attainable error distributions. High-minded insistence upon perfection must be rejected in favor of attainable improvement.

Some ameliorative measures might reduce both the rate at which innocent persons are incriminated and the rate at which guilty persons are exonerated. The first type of error is called "type I" or "false positive" error, and the second type is called "type II" or "false negative" error. In most cases, however, ameliorative measures will tend to produce a reduction in the rate of one type of error at the same time they increase the rate of the other type of error. Put another way, there is often a trade-off between type I and type II errors. For instance, requiring any eyewitness identification to be supported by a high-quality video recording would certainly reduce the rate of false convictions due to faulty eyewitness testimony. But it would also result in a significant increase in the number of law breakers who go unpunished (i.e., those who were observed committing a crime but for which no video is available). Most observers view type I errors in forensic science (the type that may more often put an innocent person in jail) as more serious than type II errors. In Blackstone's famous formula, "presumptive evidence of felony should be admitted cautiously: for the law holds, that it is better that ten guilty persons escape, than that one innocent suffer" (Blackstone, 1765–1769, Book IV, Chapter 27).

There is little point in considering what would happen in an imaginary world without a given type of bias unless one has a plan for getting to that world. Thus, the proper comparison is between the imperfect status quo and the imperfect alternative that would exist if some proposed measure were applied. We classify ameliorative measures along two dimensions.

First, we distinguish between "hierarchical" and "distributed" measures. Hierarchical measures centralize some set of decisions in the hands of an elite, thus reducing the discretion of other actors in the system. Citing medicine as an example to be imitated, Cole (2010) has called for more hierarchy in forensic science. A distributed system is the opposite of a hierarchical system. It disperses discretion and decision-making authority across a relatively large number of actors in the system. Research science is a distributed system in which any one lab may challenge the experimental results of any other lab.

Second, we distinguish between measures that minimize bias and measures that leverage bias. Blinding measures are meant to reduce or eliminate bias. Measures that leverage bias turn a given bias into an instrument for truth revelation. Rather than attempting to somehow expunge the bias, such measures turn a bad thing, bias, to a good effect. The adversarial system of justice attempts to leverage the contrasting biases of the contesting parties to produce truth and justice.

These two distinctions give us four strategies for coping with bias in forensic science: (1) hierarchical measures that minimize bias, (2) hierarchical measures that leverage bias, (3) distributed measures that minimize bias, and (4) distributed measures that leverage bias. These strategies are not always in conflict. On the contrary, we advocate some use of each strategy as part of an integrated suite of measures to minimize the problem of bias in forensic science. We do suggest, however, that researchers have tended to overlook important obstacles to creating *effective* hierarchical measures to minimize bias.

HIERARCHICAL VERSUS DISTRIBUTED SYSTEM

Le Lann (1977, p. 155) gives a mathematical treatment of "hierarchical" and "distributed" systems appropriate to his context of computer science. We adapt his treatment for our purposes. Le Lann imagines a set of "functions," which are just things a system can do. The "entities" of the system participate in these "functions." For our purposes, these entities can be individual persons in their social roles, groups of persons, or organizations such as police departments and crime labs. The state of the system with respect to a given function is just a list giving each entity's state (e.g., the extent to which they feel a given piece of information is consistent with a given suspect's guilt or innocence) with respect to that function. Note that it is the list and not the sum. You do not necessarily "add up" the individuals in any sense to get the state of the overall system. A function is "centralized" if one entity picks the state of the system for that function. A function is "distributed" to the extent that more than one entity picks the state.

Strictly speaking, our definition implies that a hierarchy concentrates discretion and decision-making autonomy for a given function in precisely one "entity." From here on out, however, we will not be entirely strict. We will speak of "hierarchy" when our emphasis is on functions that are more or less centralized, though not necessarily concentrated in just one "entity." "Polyarchy" (Sah and Stiglitz, 1986) or a "distributed system" will apply when our emphasis is on functions that are more broadly distributed. With this somewhat looser usage, hierarchies limit the discretion and decision-making autonomy of persons low in the hierarchy. Decision-making power is shifted up the hierarchy. All actors in the system exercise discretion, but discretion and decision-making autonomy grow as we move up the hierarchy. The theoretical value of hierarchy, therefore, is limited by the extent to which circumstances allow discretion to be concentrated in a relatively small number of actors situated relatively high in the hierarchy. If the relevant information cannot be sent up the hierarchy at reasonable cost (or at all), then a more distributed systems approach is likely to be preferable. In general, we may expect that some decisions or some *aspects* of decisions should be governed hierarchically, while others should be more broadly distributed across the system.

Those who have drawn attention to bias and error in forensic science have typically proposed hierarchical corrective measures. The leading recommendation of a National Research Council (NRC, 2009) report on forensic science, for e.g., is the creation of "an independent federal entity, the National Institute of Forensic Science (NIFS)," which would be responsible for, among other things, "establishing and enforcing best practices for forensic science" (NRC, 2009, p. 19). NIFS should "oversee and direct the forensic science community" (NRC, 2009, p. 20).

Every one of the NRC report's 13 recommendations invokes the NIFS except one that calls for "routine quality assurance and quality control procedures" (NRC, 2009, pp. 19–33). The report's authors write that all its recommendations "are crucially tied to the creation of NIFS" (p. 20). The report has become a kind of touchstone for reform in forensic science and calls for "strong governance" of forensic science in the United States, saying, "The governance structure must be able to create appropriate incentives for jurisdictions to adopt and adhere to best practices and promulgate the necessary sanctions to discourage bad practices" (NRC, 2009, p. 16).

At least one leading scholar on forensic science, Simon Cole, has explicitly called for greater "hierarchy" in forensic science. Citing the "medical model," Cole advocates, "a 'hierarchical' model in which a 'knowledge elite' of researchers exerts control over practitioners" (Cole, 2010, p. 468). In this system, much as in American medicine today, "Researchers would have the last word on whether a method or technique is valid. Technicians would no longer be put in the awkward position of having to defend the validity of the techniques they apply" (Cole, 2010, p. 468).

Cole's proposal is more detailed and explicit regarding hierarchy than that of the NRC report. He quite explicitly wishes to reduce the use of discretion and judgment by bench examiners. There should be a division of labor between basic research and bench examiners. A "cadre of basic researchers" would "develop and validate new methods and techniques," while "a much larger cadre of technicians with manual and interpretive skills" would apply the methods sent down from researchers in the "knowledge elite." This second group "would need to know very little about the validity of the techniques that they use. What we primarily want from them would be to exercise their skills well" (p. 466). A third group would act as intermediaries connecting the knowledge elite to bench examiners.

For the sake of "ensuring the neatness of the analogy with medicine," Cole notes in passing a "fourth role" to be played by "crime scene technicians" who might be compared to "emergency medical technicians." Cole gives little consideration at all to this group only because it was not the focus of the issues identified by the NRC report on which he was commenting. Presumably, Cole did not mean to suggest that crime scene technicians are unimportant. Inman and Rudin (2001) emphasize the importance of investigative decisions made at the crime scene. They note, "Any mistakes made in processing the crime scene are impossible to rectify" and, in fact, "are only magnified at each subsequent step" of the criminal investigation process (p. 196).

Hierarchical approaches to bias and error in forensic science and their attempt to limit the discretion and judgment of bench examiners may seem natural or inevitable. But, distributed approaches that attempt to spread decision-making authority across multiple actors have also been proposed for forensic science.

Koppl (2005) gives an example of a relatively distributed or polyarchic approach to forensic science reform that calls for random, independent, multiple examinations of evidence. Koppl et al. (2008) provide experimental evidence that this ameliorative measure has the potential to improve system performance. They had "senders" report to "receivers" on evidence simplified to one of three shapes (circle, triangle, square). The senders are analogous to forensic scientists, and the receivers are analogous to triers of fact (judges or jurors). Bias was induced in some senders by giving them an incentive to issue a false report. The receivers were asked to conclude what shape (circle, triangle, square) the sender(s) had actually been shown. In some cases receivers got one report, in others multiple reports. Because the "errors" in reports were independent (senders did not know the content of reports from other senders or what incentives they had received), the receivers made fewer errors when they receive multiple reports. The results of Koppl et al. suggest that democratic epistemics will improve system performance if the number of senders is three or higher, but may not improve performance if the number of senders is two. Moreover, further increasing the number of senders beyond three does not seem to improve system performance (Koppl et al., 2008, p. 153).

Interestingly, in one set of experiments, the use of multiple senders seems to have degraded the average performance of senders while improving the performance of the system. (See also the related proposal of Robertson (2010, pp. 214–219) for "adversarial blind" expertize in civil cases.)

Random, independent, multiple examinations of evidence create another form of blinding. Examiners will not know whether other labs have examined the same evidence and, if so, what the results of such examinations were. They are blinded from this information. Such blinding gives the examiner an increased incentive to avoid scientifically inappropriate inferences so as to minimize what Koppl et al. (2015) have called "reversal risk," which they define as "the risk that a decision will later be determined to have been mistaken."

The experimental results of Koppl et al. (2008) may be surprising; but "to improve system reliability," Koppl et al. (2008) explain

> [I]t is not necessary to improve the reliability of the individual units within the system (Senders). A chain is only as strong as its weakest link; a net(work) is stronger than its individual knots (nodes). A net may be stronger than a chain even though the average knot in the net may be weaker than the average link in the chain. (p. 154)

The experiments of Koppl et al. (2008) should suggest the potential of distributed approaches to bias in forensic science. But we do not mean to hint that hierarchy is somehow always bad. The vertical power in a hierarchy could be used to force those in lower rungs to utilize measures such as blinding. Relatedly, a large hierarchical organization might have an advantage over a single practitioner in that it could have the necessary infrastructure and coordination needed to apply sequential unmasking.

Before turning to the difference between minimizing and leveraging bias, consider the extent to which forensic science in the United States today is hierarchical and centralized. The NRC report (2009, pp. 14–19) properly describes forensic science in the United States as "fragmented." There are about 350 publicly funded crime labs in the United States, existing at the federal, regional, state, county, and municipal levels. This "system" hardly looks "hierarchical." The system, however, is characterized by a twofold monopoly that creates a fundamental centralization. Typically, though not universally, evidence is examined by only one crime lab. In this sense, the lab has a monopoly on the examination of the forensic evidence in a case, or of a particular sort of forensic evidence such as fingerprints. This same lab is typically the only one that will give an interpretation of the evidence it examined. This is a second epistemic monopoly for the lab such that forensic science in the United States today is characterized by a twofold monopoly. Recall that a function is "centralized" in our sense if one entity picks the state of the system for that function. If we define the examination and interpretation of evidence *in a given criminal case* as a "function" of the system, then the twofold epistemic monopoly of forensic science makes such functions highly centralized and hierarchical.

The centralization is further compounded in that the system is also a monopsony. Not only do police and prosecutors typically solicit opinions from just one laboratory that serves their jurisdiction, but also that lab typically serves only one jurisdiction. The crime lab easily comes to see the monopsonistic law-enforcement agency as its "customer" or "client," which becomes a source of pro-police bias. The NRC report, for e.g., describes the Federal Bureau of Investigation (FBI) as the "prime customer" of the National Bioforensic Analysis Center (NRC, 2009, p. 70). Swecker and Wolf (2010, p. 28) note, "A mindset promoted by the Section Chief [of the Forensic Biology Section of North Carolina's State Bureau of Investigation (SBI) Crime Laboratory] that the lab's customer was law enforcement and reported results should be tailored primarily for law enforcement's consumption." Murphy (2007, p. 749) says "one independent scientist described how, although he purchased DNA-typing analysis software from a private company, the company twice refused to allow him to enroll in their software training course, because he was not government-affiliated." Finally, California Crime Laboratory Review Task Force (2009, p. 62) lists the "clients" of a crime lab as "police, prosecutors, and the courts," without mention of the accused, public defenders offices, or the general public.

The literature on crime-lab management makes frequent reference to the lab's "customer" or "customers." In a monopsonistic market, the monopsonist is the only customer. Thus, this market structure becomes a source of pro-police bias. Collins (2013) recognizes the importance of independence from police agencies and says that it is "reasonable to argue" that "police, prosecutors, judges, and defense attorneys" should have "appropriate degrees of influence over the administration of forensic science laboratories" (p. 43). He also says, however, that a crime lab's "economic and political position," including "the role, purpose, structure, and independence of the laboratory, the channels the laboratory follows to access its resources" will "define who the customers of the laboratory actually are" (p. 42). Bedford (2011) seems to take it for granted that crime labs serve law-enforcement agencies when he says, "The form and functions of a forensic science service provider are determined by interactions between…the law-enforcement agency or agencies that it services" (p. 147).[1] Roux (2011) lists

[1] Bedford's complete list is "the legal system under which it operates; the law-enforcement agency or agencies that it services; the policies of the government of the country concerned; the historical legacy of the evolution of forensic science services in that country" (p. 147). We have altered the original formatting.

"investigators and victims" as "the two most crucial set of customers" of forensic science, thus omitting defendants, some of whom may be innocent. The experimental results of Murrie et al. (2013) suggest that "the pull of adversarial proceedings tends to influence opinions by paid forensic experts," and to skew those opinions in favor of the paying client.

The tendency to view law enforcement as the crime lab's customer is strengthened by the accreditation regime in the United States. The main accrediting body in the United States, American Society of Crime Laboratory Directors/Laboratory Accreditation Board (ASCLD/LAB), bases its program in part on ISO/IEC 17025, which is a set of lab standards promulgated by the International Organization for Standardization. As Budowle et al. (2009) note, this standard emphasizes customer service (p. 801). As far as we know, the emphasis on customer service has not been criticized in the literatures on forensic science and forensic science management. But a scientific process should not be governed by a criterion of commercial success. The monopoly–monopsony relationship and the perception of law enforcement as the "customer" create a risk of (conscious or unconscious) bias in the analyses of public crime labs.

MINIMIZING BIAS VERSUS LEVERAGING BIAS

A second dimension to explore involves steps that range from minimizing bias to deliberately leveraging bias. The merits associated with minimizing bias are fairly obvious. If a particular bias is bad, then let us be rid of that bias. Less obvious, though, are approaches that find ways to minimize the undesired effects of bias while at the same time leveraging what remains to produce a good outcome.

Biased examiners have both (1) preferred outcomes to their examination and (2) knowledge sufficient to act on them. A vast literature on *unconscious* bias reveals, however, that the insidious and pervasive nature of unconscious biases make them at least as worthy of consideration as conscious biases, which are often easier for judges and juries to recognize and take into account. Efforts to minimize both conscious and unconscious bias can focus on either the preference or knowledge aspects of the equation.

The NRC (2009) report's support of "independence" provides an example of a measure meant to reduce or eliminate preferences over the outcome of forensic examinations. Noting that "[f]orensic scientists who sit administratively in law-enforcement agencies or prosecutors' offices, or who are hired by those units, are subject to a general risk of bias" (p. 185), the report recommends "removing all public forensic laboratories and facilities from the administrative control of law-enforcement agencies or prosecutors' offices" (p. 24). Independence is meant to reduce or eliminate an examiner's preference for outcomes that favor the prosecution.

Proposals for "blinding" or "masking" are meant to reduce or eliminate the knowledge required to act on one's preferences. These measures prevent examiners from learning "domain-irrelevant" information such as the salacious details of a crime and the criminal history of suspects. A "case manager" (Krane et al., 2008) is necessary to implement masking for an individual examiner. In many cases, an examiner must make a sequence of interlinked scientific decisions, and some of the later decisions require the knowledge of information that could bias earlier decisions. In such instances the case manager should effect a "sequential unmasking" (Krane et al., 2008) in which the information necessary to make later scientific decisions is revealed only when such decisions need to be made and masked while earlier decisions are being made. For instance, in a DNA analysis, the expert might need to know the DNA profile of a victim to determine which components of a mixed DNA sample came from someone other than him or her—but knowledge of a suspect's DNA profile is not necessary until after that interpretation has been made and documented. A precommitment on the part of an analyst to the fact that the mixture cannot be reliably resolved without such additional information puts the decision behind a veil of ignorance and is therefore an effective form of intertemporal blinding. The essence of this approach was first expressed by Risinger et al. (2002, p. 51).

Sequential unmasking is far from the only masking measure available in forensic science. With sequential unmasking, the individual examiner does not know potentially biasing information until such information is required to make a scientific decision. But the *lab* (in the person of the case manager) does know this information, including what answer the "customer" desires, which may create a risk of bias. One approach that could counter this risk in part would be measures meant to mask from the lab the identity of the party requesting forensic science service. By obscuring the "right" answer from the examiner, sequential unmasking does help alleviate the problem. But if the monopsony structure is retained, then it may provide only a partial solution. Creating a substantive defense right to forensic expertize would help to make both the police and the accused "customers" of the lab. When the lab is unsure from whom a request for service originates, it cannot know what answer is preferred by the "customer." Such an arrangement would itself be a blinding measure.

Existing biases can also be leveraged. Creating a substantial defense right to expertize leverages bias, Giannelli (2004) calls for a substantive defense right to forensic science expertize. "Just as the indigent persons on trial are provided an attorney at the state's expense, so too should indigent persons on trial be provided a forensic interpreter at state's expense" (p. 271). Giannelli (2004) notes, "Obtaining expert assistance generally is not difficult for the prosecution" (p. 1327). However, "[f]orensic laboratory services are not generally available to criminal defendants" (p. 1331). This asymmetry increases the risk of bias and error in forensic science. As Giannelli reports, in 1985, the Supreme Court's decision in *Ake v. Oklahoma* recognized the "right to expert assistance" for the case of a psychiatric expert in a capital trial. In practice at least, this right has not been consistently extended to forensic experts and noncapital cases. Giannelli (2004, p. 1419) says "the right to expert assistance has not been effectively implemented" and "the role of the expert should be viewed as grounded in the right to counsel—i.e., a *defense* rather than neutral expert should be provided". The assistance Giannelli describes does not necessarily require the defense expert to conduct new or independent examinations of forensic evidence. In many cases it can be effectively delivered through the review of protocols, testing, and interpretation performed by the prosecution's experts.

Giannelli's emphasis on the nonneutrality of the defense expert reflects the asymmetry between defense and prosecution in criminal cases. A prosecutor has a constitutional duty to act "impartially" (Berger v. United States, 1935). The constitutional duty of defense counsel, by contrast, is entirely one sided. Defense counsel has a constitutional duty of "vigorous and effective advocacy" for his or her client (Jones v. Barnes, 1983).[2]

[2] The following paragraph was lifted almost without alteration from Koppl (2012, p. 53).

Citing Milgrom and Roberts (1986) and Koppl and Cowan (2010) explain why competition between "strongly opposed" experts tends to improve the quality of information they provide to third parties such as juries. If the interests of the competing information suppliers are strongly opposed, then one of them always has an incentive to provide additional information. If some bit of relevant information has not been revealed, then, by virtue of the fact that it is relevant, it will help one side or the other. Thus one side or the other will have an incentive to reveal it. This logic works even if both sides are biased. It requires only that their interests in the case be strongly opposed. Thus, the adversarial system of the Anglo-American jurisprudence allows us to pit one bias against another to produce results that more closely resemble the consequences of unbiased analysis.

Even when biases can be leveraged, the pursuit of truth is advanced when they are reduced through measures such as sequential unmasking. But no measure can be expected to eliminate all possible biases. The mere fact that a sample has been submitted for testing implies that a nefarious activity may have taken place, as noted by Whitman and Koppl (2010, pp. 78–79). Biases that remain after diligent efforts to reduce them should be *leveraged* by pitting experts with competing perspectives against each other. We need checks and balances.

Bias in a hierarchical system could be leveraged by having analysts commit to what characteristics would cause an exemplar to be excluded or included from a questioned sample at each step in an analysis. We might consider the analyst's written conclusions a kind of fulcrum and call this measure "standard stating." Because the commitments through standard stating would occur before observing the questioned sample, we should also view it as a form of blinding. To fully illuminate bias, it is important to pin it down. A defense expert will have a much harder time showing a prosecution expert's bias if it is not clear how that bias influenced her interpretation at one or more specific decision points in an analysis. One of us has frequently seen expert courtroom testimony seemingly evolve on the witness stand as experts learn the thrust of a series of cross-examination questions. The requirement to document decision criteria as they are applied would make it more difficult for experts to slip into such an "evolutionary" posture (and would make cross examination more efficient and less of a journey of discovery). Such an environment would work best when experts expect an opposing expert to be motivated to identify the impact of any biases on their interpretations. Fear of having their biases illuminated coupled with a hampering of their ability to obfuscate their reasoning should cause experts to be self-motivated to think critically and adopt conservative approaches that ultimately minimize the impact of their own bias.

FINDING THE OPTIMAL MIX

We have described the management of biases in two different dimensions: (1) hierarchical versus distributed systems and (2) minimizing bias versus leveraging bias. These two distinctions allow the consideration of four distinct quadrants into which suggestions for handling bias in forensic science can fall (see Table 1). Note that we have blinding measures in each quadrant. Hierarchical systems can impose measures such as sequential unmasking that apply within labs as protocols. But other blinding measures require distributed systems. The use of random, independent, multiple examinations of evidence is an example. Even measures meant to leverage bias, rather than reduce it, can also be blinding measure. For e.g.,

TABLE 1 Basic Strategies for Addressing Unwanted Bias and Error in Forensic Science

	Hierarchical measures	Distributed measures
Measures to minimize bias	National oversight of crime lab practices through the National Institute for Forensic Science. When the knowledge elite of a hierarchy requires measures such as sequential unmasking, oversight becomes a blinding measure as well.	Random, independent, multiple examinations of evidence is a distributed measure meant to minimize bias. Because examiners will not know whether other labs have examined the same evidence and, if so, what the results of such examinations were, it is a blinding measure as well.
Measures to leverage bias	Standard stating is a hierarchical measure meant to leverage bias. Because the commitments through standard stating would occur before observing the questioned sample, it is a blinding measure as well.	Defense right to forensic expertize is a distributed measure meant to leverage bias. When combined with measures meant to mask from the crime lab the identity of the party requesting forensic science service, it becomes a blinding measure as well.

Note: There are four basic strategies for addressing unwanted bias and error in forensic science. The table gives an example of each method. Measures to minimize bias such as sequential unmasking can be beneficially applied to all four quadrants.

standard stating is a blinding measure, but it leverages bias too. Thus, we are led to the conclusion that blinding in forensic science should be conceived broadly to include, potentially, both hierarchical and distributed measures. We are led to the further conclusion that not only should blinding measures be complemented by measure to leverage remaining bias, but also even some leveraging measure have themselves a blinding function.

Each approach has strengths and weaknesses, and only a judicious combination of them can produce the best attainable outcome. Some hierarchical measures may be incompatible with some distributed methods, or some bias minimizing techniques may be incompatible with some measures to leverage bias. Other strategies such as sequential unmasking, which strives to minimize biases in general, could be beneficially applied in all circumstances including those that are primarily hierarchical, distributed, or bias leveraging. Furthermore, there is no general reason to not employ measures of all four types. Indeed, if hierarchical and distributed systems have complementary strengths and weaknesses, then it is reasonable to seek out ways to combine them. Similarly, when biases cannot be eliminated, the bias that remains should be leveraged.

Hierarchical measures of the sort Cole (2010) recommends are meant to limit scientifically difficult decisions to those who have the scientific training required to make them. Cole's call for a clearer and more refined division of labor in forensic science is important and laudatory. But, the advantages of hierarchy must be weighed against the risks and disadvantages.

We have noted that the hierarchical concentration of discretion and decision-making autonomy is possible only to the extent that the relevant information can be sent up the hierarchy at reasonable cost. Many forensic science decisions depend on information that cannot be anticipated and cannot be delivered up the hierarchy at reasonable cost. Evidence may have unique or unusual combinations of characteristics, such as those related to the substrates where it is found. As Koppl (2012, p. 51) has noted, "validation studies in fingerprint analysis may not help the bench examiner to evaluate a latent print deposited on wood grain or a pebbled lampshade."

The need to make case-specific judgments is recognized in sequential unmasking protocols. The case manager has all case information and uses his or her discretion to decide what information to reveal to the bench examiner and in what order such information should be rolled out. If it were possible to somehow anticipate case-specific information and predecide the appropriate protocols, then the role of the case manager could be greatly reduced. However, not all contingencies can be anticipated. For instance, a DNA analyst may discover during the course of testing that a critical evidence sample contains a mixture of DNA from two or more individuals that could not be reliably resolved into major/minor contributors. Transmission of that conclusion to a case manager might be accompanied by a request for a victim's reference DNA profile so that the analyst can then determine whether some components of the mixture can be concluded to have come from another individual (which, in turn, can be compared to a suspect's reference profile). A judicious mix of hierarchical and distributed measures may be the best way to limit undesirable bias and error in forensic science.

Masking procedures such as sequential unmasking are meant to minimize bias in forensic science. As we have noted, however, it may not be possible to completely eliminate bias. We can supplement bias minimizing measures with bias leveraging measures. There is a natural trade-off between hierarchical and distributed measures: If a given decision is made "up" the hierarchy, then it cannot be made "down" the hierarchy, and vice versa. There is generally no similar *trade-off* between leveraging and minimizing bias—they can be combined freely. And the harm from a given sort of bias will be lower when effective measures to leverage bias are present. But any given measure to leverage bias will likely be helpful even when there is not much to leverage. And any measure to reduce bias will likely be helpful even when leveraging measures have reduced greatly the harm of remaining biases.

WHY IT MAY BE HARD TO GET THE OPTIMAL MIX

We have laid out a simple classification of measures to address unwanted bias and error in forensic science. The question is not which sort of measure to employ, but what *mix* of four types would be best. Unfortunately, there are "economic" obstacles to reform. In particular, researchers have tended to overlook the risk that "regulatory capture" may be an obstacle to *effective* hierarchical measures to minimize bias. We consider first how certain incentives in the criminal-justice system may create an incentive to resist reform measures. We then review the economic theory of regulatory capture and apply it to forensic science reform.

Incentives of Crime Labs to Convict

Most forensic scientists are well-meaning individuals who are dedicated to protecting society and who take pride in doing their work properly. The beneficial effects of this good will are compromised, however, by powerful incentives to convict. As Koppl and Sacks (2013) have chronicled, police, crime labs, and prosecutors all have strong incentives to gain convictions, but only very weak incentives to distinguish properly between the guilty and the innocent. They discuss some of the incentives of police, crime labs, and prosecutors to garner convictions even when these convictions may be false convictions. Because crime labs are usually embedded within law-enforcement agencies or prosecutors' offices, the incentives of police and prosecutors extend to crime labs and, generally, forensic science professionals. These incentives encourage resistance to reform measures—especially reforms that may tend to expose past errors.

Koppl and Sacks (2013) note a feature of crime lab funding that seems to have largely escaped notice in the past. Many crime labs in the United States are funded in part through court-assessed fees. Wickenheiser (2004, p. 3) says, "Collection of court costs is the only stable source of funding for the Acadiana Crime Lab. $10 is received for each guilty plea or verdict from each speeding ticket, and $50 from each DWI (Driving While Impaired) and drug offense." In Broward County, "Monies deposited in the Trust Fund are principally court costs assessed upon conviction of driving or boating under the influence ($50) or selling, manufacturing, delivery, or possession of a controlled substance ($100)" (Lukic, 2009). Koppl and Sacks (2013) report that 14 states have laws requiring defendants, upon conviction, to pay fees that the law then directs be paid back to the relevant publicly funded crime lab.[3] The law in a 15th state, North Carolina, directs funds to the law-enforcement agency containing the lab. This mode of funding creates an incentive to produce convictions, which might bias the analyses of the affected labs.

The incentive to convict may encourage resistance to blinding measures and to other reforms meant to reduce the odds of forensic science errors. Crime labs, police, and prosecutors do not have a specific interest in false convictions, of course. But criminal-justice professionals may think measures to reduce the risk of false convictions will make convictions harder and more costly to obtain. At the same time, they will be loathed to believe that their past practices may have contributed to false convictions. They will sincerely believe that reform proposals are burdensome solutions to nonexistent problems. Moreover, as we shall see, there is evidence that law-enforcement entities in the United States are capable of coordinated action to protect their perceived interests.

Regulatory Capture

Any proposal to erect a regulatory body, whether at the federal or state level, comes with the risk that the regulatory body will be "captured" by special interests.[4]

Regulatory and oversight bodies are supposed to constrain special interests and protect the general interest. When regulatory and oversight bodies instead serve special interests, these bodies have been "captured." Capture is the norm, unfortunately, which makes long-term beneficial change through oversight hard. The first great regulatory body in the United States was the Interstate Commerce Commission (ICC), which was established in 1887 to control railroads. The Interstate Commerce Act of 1887 prohibited price discrimination and required that "all charges…shall be reasonable and just" (Koppl, 2012, p. 50). This language seems to constrain the railroads, and yet the railroads supported the Act (Posner, 1974). Posner explains: "The railroads supported the enactment of the first Interstate Commerce Act, which was designed to prevent railroads from practicing price discrimination, because discrimination was undermining the railroads' cartels."

[3] The 14 states are Alabama, Arizona, California, Illinois, Kansas, Kentucky, Missouri, Mississippi, New Mexico, New Jersey, Tennessee, Virginia, Washington, and Wisconsin.

[4] The following three paragraphs are mostly lifted from Koppl (2012, pp. 49–51).

The interest that captures a regulator may not be the regulated industry. "Crudely put, the butter producers wish to suppress margarine and encourage the production of bread" (Stigler, 1971). For example, the railroads sometimes used state regulators to suppress trucking. In the 1930s, "Texas and Louisiana placed a 7000-pound payload limit on trucks serving (and hence competing with) two or more railroad stations, and a 14,000-pound limit on trucks serving only one station (hence, not competing with it)."

The theory of supply and demand predicts that a commodity sold on a competitive market will end up in the hands of those who value it most, as measured by willingness to pay. The theory does not tell us, however, who is willing to pay the most. Similarly, the theory of regulatory capture does not tell us who will win in the contest of interests to capture a regulator. It is a continuous fight; victory may be partial and fleeting. Nevertheless, we can say that concentrated interests aid victory. Well-organized groups with relatively large and homogeneous interests have an advantage in the contest.

A coalition of law-enforcement agencies may be in the best position to capture a federal regulator of forensic science. According to Bureau of Labor Statistics data, in 2012 the number of employees in law enforcement in 2010 exceeded 1.3 million.[5] These people are part of a relatively large, concentrated, well-organized, and homogeneous interest group. An episode from 2013 suggests that some such coalition exists and is capable of acting cooperatively. On August 30, 2013, a consortium of law-enforcement groups wrote a letter to the U.S. Attorney General strongly condemning his new policy of respecting the liberal state laws on marijuana in Colorado and Washington.[6]

Commenting on this episode, one journalist has opined, "[P]olice organizations have become increasingly powerful political actors" (Grim, 2013). Is there any other interest group, such as the innocence movement, in a good position to compete with law enforcement? And, if so, for how long? Cole (2010) recognizes the risk of regulatory capture in forensic science. He says of the proposed NIFS, "If it is 'captured' by law enforcement, it becomes less obvious that it would be a force for improvement rather than stagnation" (p. 436).

Law enforcement has a distinct advantage in the struggle to capture a forensic science regulator. But victory is not guaranteed as illustrated by an episode involving the National Commission on Forensic Science, which was created in 2013 jointly by the Department of Justice and the Commerce Departments' National Institute of Standards and Technology (NIST). One of the duties of the Commission as stated in its charter is "[t]o develop proposed guidance concerning the intersection of forensic science and the courtroom."[7] When, however, the commission's subcommittee on reporting and testimony came forward with a proposal (authored by law

[5] See the Bureau of Labor Statistics, Occupational Outlook Handbook 2014–2015 Edition, currently available at http://www.bls.gov/ooh/a-z-index.htm. In 2012, 780,000 persons were employed as "police and detectives"; 469,500 as "correctional officers"; 90,300 as "probation officers and correctional treatment specialists"; and 12,900 as "forensic science technicians." The sum of these numbers is 1,352,700. This sum does not consider all relevant personnel, such as dispatchers and administrative personnel working in law-enforcement agencies.

[6] At the time of this writing, the letter can be downloaded from https://www.theiacp.org/portals/0/pdfs/FINALLawEnforcementGroupLetteronDOJMarijuanaPolicy.pdf.

[7] At the time of this writing, the charter can be found at http://www.justice.gov/sites/default/files/ncfs/legacy/2014/05/13/ncfs-charter.pdf.

professor Paul Giannelli) for increased disclosure of criminal forensics, the commission's cochair from the Department of Justice determined that the proposal was beyond the scope of the commission's charter. Subcommittee cochair Judge Jed Rakoff resigned in protest, citing the commission's charter as clearly creating scope for just such a proposal. The very next day, January 30, 2015, the commission's cochair reversed this decision and invited Judge Rakoff back onto the commission. It was the committee's cochair and not the Department of Justice that interpreted the committee's charter to exclude the subcommittee's proposal, and the decision was quickly reversed. This episode nevertheless illustrates the sort of thing that may happen in the struggle to capture regulators. It seems fair to say that the theory of regulatory capture applies to forensic science, that American law enforcement has at least some disposition to act in a coordinated manner to capture forensic science regulation, and that, finally, the capture struggle is an ongoing one in which victory may be partial and fleeting. While Judge Rakoff prevailed in this episode, we caution that hierarchically organized forensic science reform has limited prospects to effect deep and enduring improvements in forensic science practice.

CONCLUSION

There is increasing agreement that institutional changes to forensic science in the United States are needed. Many observers have argued for sequential unmasking, "independence" of crime labs from law enforcement, and a federal oversight body with broad regulatory authority. Proposals for change have tended to focus on hierarchical measures that minimize bias. There has been less emphasis on distributed measures and measures to leverage bias. We have emphasized these neglected approaches to bias in forensic science and called for the use of all four basic strategies for dealing with bias and error in forensic science: (1) hierarchical measures that minimize bias, (2) hierarchical measures that leverage bias, (3) distributed measures that minimize bias, and (4) distributed measures that leverage bias. We have also noted some obstacles to implementing potentially desirable measures. In particular, we have drawn attention to the problem of "regulatory capture," which may cause any oversight body to act in ways that serve special interests more effectively than the general interest.

References

Bedford, K., 2011. Forensic science service provider models—is there a 'best' option? Australian Journal of Forensic Science 43 (2–3), 147–156.

Berger v. United States, 1935. 295 U.S. 78.

Blackstone, W., 1765–1769. Commentaries on the Laws of England. Retrieved from: http://oll.libertyfund.org/?option=com_staticxt&staticfile=show.php%3Ftitle=2140&Itemid=27/.

Budowle, B., Bottrell, M.C., Bunch, S.G., Fram, R., Harrison, D., Meagher, S., Oien, C.T., Peterson, P.E., Seiger, D.P., Smith, M.B., Smrz, M.A., Soltis, G.L., Stacey, R.B., 2009. A perspective on errors, bias, and interpretation in the forensic sciences and direction for continuing advancement. Journal of Forensic Sciences 54 (4), 798–809.

California Crime Laboratory Review Task Force, 2009. An Examination of Forensic Science in California. Retrieved from: http://ag.ca.gov/publications/crime_labs_report.pdf.

Cole, S., 2010. Acculturating forensic science: what is 'scientific culture', and how can forensic science adopt it? Fordham Urban Law Journal 38 (2), 435–471.

Collins, J.M., 2013. 10 criteria defining a model forensic science laboratory. Forensic Science Policy & Management: An International Journal 4 (1–2), 38–56.

Cosmides, L., Tooby, J., 1994. Better than rational: evolutionary psychology and the invisible hand. The American Economic Review 84 (2), 327–332.

Giannelli, P.C., 2004. Ake v. Oklahoma: the right to expert assistance in a post-Daubert, post-DNA world. Cornell Law Review 89, 1305–1419.

Grim, R., August 30, 2013. Police Groups Furiously Protest Eric Holder's Marijuana Policy Announcement. Huffington Post. Retrieved from: www.huffingtonpost.com/2013/08/30/police-eric-holder-marijuana-_n_3846518.html?utm_hp_ref=mostpopular.

Inman, K., Rudin, N., 2001. Principles and Practice of Criminalistics: the Profession of Forensic Science. CRC Press LLC, Boca Raton, FL.

Jones v. Barnes, 1983. 463 U.S. 745.

Kassier, J.P., Kessler, G., 2011. Federal Judicial Center Reference Manual on Scientific Evidence (preface), third ed. National Academies Press, Washington, DC.

Koppl, R., 2005. How to improve forensic science. European Journal of Law and Economics 20, 255–286.

Koppl, R., 2012. Leveraging bias in forensic science. Fordham Urban Law Journal City Square 39 (0), 37–56. Retrieved from: http://urbanlawjournal.com/issues/cs/39/Koppl.pdf.

Koppl, R., Charlton, D., Kornfield, I., Krane, D., Risinger, M., Robertson, C., Thompson, W., 2015. Do Observer Effects Matter? A Comment on Langenburg, Bochet, and Ford. Forensic Science Policy & Management 6 (1–2), 1–6.

Koppl, R., Cowan, E.J., 2010. A battle of forensic experts is not a race to the bottom. Review of Political Economy 22 (2), 235–262.

Koppl, R., Kurzban, R., Kobilinsky, L., 2008. Epistemics for forensics. Epistmeme: Journal of Social Epistemology 5 (2), 141–159.

Koppl, R., Sacks, M., 2013. The criminal justice system creates incentives for false convictions. Criminal Justice Ethics 32 (2), 126–162.

Krane, D.E., Ford, S., Gilder, J.E., Inman, K., Jamieson, A., Koppl, R., Thompson, W.C., 2008. Sequential unmasking: a means of minimizing observer effects in forensic DNA interpretation. Journal of Forensic Sciences 53 (4), 1006–1007.

Le Lann, G., 1977. Distributed systems—toward a formal approach. In: Gilgrest, B. (Ed.), Information Processing 1977: World Congress Proceedings. North-Holland Publishing Co., Amsterdam, pp. 155–160.

Lukic, E.A., 2009. BSO Crime Lab Review. (Report 09–13). Retrieved from: http://www.broward.org/Auditor/Documents/crimelab_final.pdf.

Milgrom, P., Roberts, J., 1986. Relying on information of interested parties. RAND Journal of Economics 17, 18–32.

Murphy, E., 2007. New forensics: criminal justice, false certainty, and the second generation of scientific evidence. California Law Review 95, 721–797.

Murrie, D.C., Boccaccini, M.T., Guarnera, L.A., Rufino, K.A., 2013. Are forensic experts biased by the side that retained them? Psychological Science 24 (10), 1889–1897.

National Research Council, 2009. Strengthening Forensic Science in the United States: a Path Forward. National Academies Press, Washington, DC.

Posner, R.A., 1974. Theories of economic regulation. The Bell Journal of Economics and Management Science 5 (2), 335–358.

Risinger, M., Saks, M.J., Thompson, W.C., Rosenthal, R., 2002. The Daubert/Kumho implications of observer effects in forensic science: hidden problems of expectation and suggestion. California Law Review 90, 1–56.

Robertson, C.T., 2010. The blind expert: a litigant-driven solution to bias and error. New York University Law Review 85, 174–257.

Roux, C., 2011. Forensic science—a teenager in identity crisis? Australian Journal of Forensic Sciences 43 (2–3), 79–83.

Sah, R.K., Stiglitz, J.E., 1986. The architecture of economic systems: hierarchies and polyarchies. American Economic Review 76 (4), 716–727.

Stigler, G.J., 1971. The theory of economic regulation. The Bell Journal of Economics and Management Science 2 (1), 3–21.

Swecker, C., Wolf, M., 2010. An Independent Review of the SBI Forensic Laboratory. Retrieved from: http://www.ncids.com/forensic/sbi/Swecker_Report.pdf.

Whitman, G., Koppl, R., 2010. Rational bias in forensic science. Law, Probability & Risk 9, 69–90.

Wickenheiser, R., 2004. The business case for using forensic DNA technology to solve and prevent crime. The Journal of Biolaw & Business 7, 2–18.

CHAPTER

11

What Do Statisticians Really Need to Know, and When Do They Need to Know It?

D. James Greiner

Harvard Law School, Cambridge, MA, USA

OUTLINE

INTRODUCTION

Blinding means deliberately depriving a decision maker of some piece of information due to the fear that this information will induce the decision maker to make poor, or less optimal, decisions. So defined, the scope of blinding is as broad as the scope of human decision making.

This essay is about the scope of blinding. Specifically, it reports on the application of blinding in a heretofore undiscussed setting: statistical analysis, specifically, the analysis in which the quantitative analyst seeks to uncover causal relationships from observational (meaning nonrandomized) data. In the field of modern statistics, this endeavor goes by the name "causal inference."

The premise of this essay is that quantitative analysts are human. We are susceptible to biases. We tend to favor people who give us things, especially money (e.g., I believe that

Blinding as a Solution to Bias
http://dx.doi.org/10.1016/B978-0-12-802460-7.00011-5

the company that hired me as an expert witness does not discriminate against women). We tend to favor conclusions that conform to our prior beliefs about how the world works (e.g., I believe that discrimination against women is rare in the modern workforce, and (surprise!) the data I am analyzing provide no evidence that a company discriminated against women). And when we analyze data sets, there are plenty of opportunities for biases, subtle or not so subtle, to influence our conclusions. No consequential field of human decision making is mechanical or free of judgment. Quantitative analysis consists of layers upon layers of assumptions, impressions, and inferences: how to deal with missing data, what type and specific form of mathematical model to deploy, how much uncertainty and sensitivity to tolerate, which graphs to produce and examine. Judgment calls abound, and no one simply turns a crank and reads the results. Those who say otherwise are selling something, probably their own integrity.

Good quantitative analysts attempting causal inference from observational data have been using blinding for decades, and we continue to do so. We do so because we are afraid of our own biases. We have not in the past called what we did "blinding"; we did not call it anything in particular. But we knew what we were doing, and why. The purpose of this essay is to link what good quantitative analysts do when attempting causal inference from observational data to the more general concept of blinding, as discussed in this volume.

CAUSAL INFERENCE FROM OBSERVATIONAL DATA

To understand how quantitative analysts use blinding when attempting to uncover causal relationships, one must first know a little about how such analysts talk about causation. Begin with the following question: What is a "causal effect"? A causal effect to a quantitative analyst is a comparison of the values of some outcome variable as between two states of the world, the state of the world under a first condition (call this "treated"), versus the state of the world under a second condition (call this "control"). The comparison is made on a particular thing, meaning a person, a bacterium, a widget, or whatever; the analyst calls this thing the "unit." So, a causal effect is a comparison between the value of a unit's outcome variable under a treated condition versus the value of the unit's outcome variable under a control condition. Before the unit experiences a treated or control condition, the variable values are called "potential outcomes."

An example makes all this more concrete. Suppose a company hires an analyst as an expert witness to testify in an upcoming trial regarding accusations that the company discriminates against female applicants for entry-level jobs. The company says that it has the following information available from its databases about each applicant: the number of years of experience in the company's industry, the applicant's gender, and whether the applicant was hired. The applicant's number of years of experience and gender appear on the application form the company requires persons seeking jobs to fill out. The analyst can begin by mentally constructing Table 1.

Of course, in the real world, there would be more than 10 units (one hopes), but the Table 1 gets the concept across.

If the analyst could fill in this entire table, then he/she would not need to do anything else. In fact, if it were possible to fill in this table completely, then the company would have

TABLE 1 Blank Potential Outcomes Table

Unit number	Treatment actually received (perceived male or perceived female)	Outcome if this unit were perceived female: Outcome (F)	Outcome if this unit were perceived male: Outcome (M)
A	M		
B	M		
C	M		
D	M		
E	M		
F	F		
G	F		
H	F		
I	F		
J	F		

no need for an analyst (as long as the company had someone around who could add and subtract). Thus, for example, if the full table looked like Table 2 one could safely conclude that the company is not discriminating, because perceived gender makes no difference to the outcome for any of the units.

If, on the other hand, the full table looked like Table 3 then the company is illegally discriminating. For units D, E, F, and G (appearing in a different font to make them easier to spot), whether the company hires them depends on whether it perceives them to be male or female.

So, before analysis begins, the analyst mentally constructs Table 1, the blank table, in his/her head. He/she wants to know whether the fully filled-in table looks more like Table 2, in which the outcome (hired or not hired) for each unit is the same regardless of its perceived gender, or Table 3, in which the outcome for 40% of the units (hired or not hired) depends whether the company perceives them to be male or female.

So, what is the problem, one might ask? Why not just ask the company for the fully filled-in table. The problem is that no one gets to observe two counterfactual states of the world. One can only see each unit's outcome under one treatment condition, one state of the world. One cannot have "John Brown" apply for a company job (with all of John Brown's background and qualifications and life experiences) and, at the same time, have "Jane Brown" (with exactly the same background and qualifications and life experiences) apply for the same company job. _________ Brown has to be either John or Jane. In other words, the most the analyst can receive from the company is something like this (Table 4).

Now, one can see the analyst's problem. If one looks carefully, then one will see that the visible portions of Table 4 match both Table 2, the table in which the company is not discriminating against women, and Table 3, the one in which the company is discriminating against women.

TABLE 2 Potential Outcomes Table: Company Is Not Discriminating

Unit number	Treatment actually received	Outcome if this unit were perceived female: Outcome (F)	Outcome if this unit were perceived male: Outcome (M)
A	M	Not hired	Not hired
B	M	Not hired	Not hired
C	M	Not hired	Not hired
D	M	Hired	Hired
E	M	Hired	Hired
F	F	Not hired	Not hired
G	F	Not hired	Not hired
H	F	Not hired	Not hired
I	F	Hired	Hired
J	F	Hired	Hired

TABLE 3 Potential Outcomes Table: Company Is Discriminating

Unit number	Treatment actually received	Outcome if this unit were perceived female: Outcome (F)	Outcome if this unit were perceived male: Outcome (M)
A	M	Not hired	Not hired
B	M	Not hired	Not hired
C	M	Not hired	Not hired
D	**M**	**Not hired**	**Hired**
E	**M**	**Not hired**	**Hired**
F	**F**	**Not hired**	**Hired**
G	**F**	**Not hired**	**Hired**
H	F	Not hired	Not hired
I	F	Hired	Hired
J	F	Hired	Hired

One might ask: Why cannot the analyst look at Table 4 and simply compare the hiring rate for units perceived male (A–E), two out of five, to the hiring rate for the units perceived female (F–J), two out of five, thereby concluding that there is no discrimination? One clue that this will not work is that we have already seen that the "truth" behind Table 4's question marks could be Table 3, the one in which the company is discriminating. The more complete answer is that there is no reason to believe that the units perceived female and the units perceived male are equally qualified, equally motivated, equally competent, or otherwise the same. If we could

TABLE 4 Potential Outcomes Table: What an Analysts Sees

Unit number	Treatment actually received	Outcome if this unit were perceived female: Outcome (F)	Outcome if this unit were perceived male: Outcome (M)
A	M	??	Not hired
B	M	??	Not hired
C	M	??	Not hired
D	M	??	Hired
E	M	??	Hired
F	F	Not hired	??
G	F	Not hired	??
H	F	Not hired	??
I	F	Hired	??
J	F	Hired	??

randomize perceived gender, then it would be true that the perceived female group would on average look the same as the perceived male group. But except in a few tests that scholars have run, we cannot randomize perceived gender. We are stuck with the world as it already occurred in the past. And the world does not equalize things for us. If, for example, units perceived female were on average better qualified than units perceived male, then hiring the same percentage of perceived male and perceived female applicants might suggest discrimination.

So, what is the analyst to do? It turns out that without more information, there is little that an analyst can do. But there frequently is more information. Recall that in the hypothetical above example, the company also recorded the number of years each applicant had worked in the industry. So, we can expand Table 4, as follows in Table 5.

Now perhaps, the analyst has something with which he/she can work. First, notice that the five units actually perceived female (F–J) as a group do not look much like the five units perceived male (A–E). The perceived male group's experience in the industry is spread out, from a low of 2 years to a high of 30 years. And only two of the five units perceived male are in what appears to be a "sweet spot" for this company, the 10–20 years worked; the other three have either too little experience or too much experience. For the perceived female group, in contrast, four of the five are in the "sweet spot," with 10–20 years experience.

With this in mind, one can think of several ways to proceed. One of the most popular ways is by using regression, or some other mathematical technique, that depends on the construction of a model relating the outcome variable (hired versus not hired) to the treatment variable (perceived male, perceived female) and the background variables (years worked). Unsurprisingly, there are a lot of different mathematical relationships the analyst might construct. Here are two possible models.

1. *Fancy math*(hired/not hired) = *fancy math*(years worked + perceived male/female)
2. *Fancy math*(hired/not hired) = *fancy math*(years worked + years worked squared + perceived male/female)

TABLE 5 Potential Outcomes Table: What an Analyst Sees, with Years Worked

Unit number	Years worked	Treatment actually received	Outcome if this unit were perceived female: Outcome (F)	Outcome if this unit were perceived male: Outcome (M)
A	2	M	??	Not hired
B	3	M	??	Not hired
C	30	M	??	Not hired
D	11	M	??	Hired
E	16	M	??	Hired
F	12	F	Not hired	??
G	15	F	Not hired	??
H	29	F	Not hired	??
I	13	F	Hired	??
J	14	F	Hired	??

What is the difference between model 1 and model 2? In the first model, the analyst has done what is often done, which is to put the treatment variable (here, perceived gender) and each potential explanatory variable (here, there is only one, years worked) into the model, with all variables appearing in their simplest forms. The general philosophy here is, "Just put in the data as they come." In the second model, the analyst has added in the square of the years worked variable (meaning the years worked variable multiplied by itself). What use is a square? Perhaps the analyst suspects that the company is like Goldilocks; it favors applicants who are not too inexperienced, because they do not know anything, nor who are too experienced, because they are overqualified, but rather who are just the right amount experienced. And, in fact, putting in the square of the years worked variable would be the right thing to do if the company is like Goldilocks.

Which model is better? It depends. No analyst knows which is better before running the two models through a statistical program and looking at the software output. The software will output various scores of the so-called "goodness of fit," meaning how well the model appears to fit the pattern of the data. None of these goodness of fit measures is perfect, and they all require the exercise of judgment. How much does the difference between the goodness of fit scores really matter? If an analyst would prefer not to rely on goodness of fit scores, then he/she might try to "eyeball" the data and guess. The comment above about a "sweet spot" between 10 and 20 years worked is an example of that kind of eyeballing.

So, what is the problem? The problem is that there is no way to fit models and look at the software output without simultaneously producing two things: scores of how well the models fit *and* the "answer" (in the sense of the answer that this model will provide) to the question of whether the company appears to be discriminating. Similarly, no analyst can eyeball the data without forming an impression regarding whether there appears to be discrimination afoot.

To illustrate the point about models, here is the output from a popular statistical program called "R" for model (1).[1]

Call:
glm(formula = Hired ~ YearsWorked + IsFemale, family = "binomial", data = Data)

Deviance residuals:

Min	1Q	Median	3Q	Max
−1.2951	−0.9031	−0.7435	1.1722	1.6785

Coefficients:

	Estimate	Std. Error	z value	Pr(>|z|)
Intercept	−0.21542	0.89054	−0.242	0.809
YearsWorked	0.01626	0.05562	0.292	0.770
IsFemale	−1.12439	0.77080	−1.459	0.145

Dispersion parameter for binomial family taken to be 1
Null deviance: 42.34 on 31 degrees of freedom
Residual deviance: 40.09 on 29 degrees of freedom
AIC (Akaike information criterion): 46.09

Number of Fisher Scoring iterations: 4

The crooked arrow tells the answer that the analysis will produce. Here, the conclusion will be that there is no evidence of discrimination. Technically, the p-value for the coefficient on the "IsFemale" variable (which I set equal to 1 for a unit perceived female, 0 for each unit perceived male) is 0.145; to be considered statistically significant, the p-value would need to be lower than 0.05. True, the issue might be that there are not enough data for the coefficient to achieve significance. Maybe there really is discrimination, but it has not gone on long enough (and thus, the data set has not become large enough) for the model to detect it. But in some sense, that is always true. Results from statistical models are never "perfect" in the sense that they suggest that exactly the "right" proportion of women, men, African-Americans, whites, etc., was hired or promoted. Thus, one can always say that, if the observed pattern stood over a large enough data set, then the analyst would conclude that the company is discriminating against one group or the other. That line of thinking is not very useful. As matters stand, then, whatever role perceived gender has in this model is not distinguishable from chance

[1] With apologies, this output is not exactly from the data in Table 5. The data set in Table 5 is too small for statistical analysis to run properly. To make the statistical analysis run properly, I tripled the size of Table 5, using the same basic patterns of the Years Worked, Gender, and Hired variables as appears in Table 5. The code I used to generate the data and to analyze it is available upon request.

alone. Meanwhile, the straight arrow points to one goodness of fit measure called the "AIC" (it stands for Akaike information criterion, and lower is better). The default version of the software produces both the AIC and the p-value for the IsFemale variable. An analyst could simply stop looking after running this model.

What about the second model? It, also, simultaneously produces a goodness of fit score and an "answer." Here is the output from the statistical software.

Call:

glm(formula = Hired ~ YearsWorked + YearsWorkedSq + IsFemale, family = "binomial", data = Data)

Deviance residuals:

Min	**1Q**	**Median**	**3Q**	**Max**
−1.97092	−0.71258	−0.00145	0.61118	1.39491

Coefficients:

	Estimate	**Std. Error**	**z value**	**Pr(>|z|)**
Intercept	−21.7966	24.7569	−0.880	0.3786
YearsWorked	3.3435	3.5189	0.950	0.3420
Years WorkedSq	−0.1176	0.1225	−0.960	0.3368
IsFemale	−2.2856	1.0752	−2.126	0.0335*

Signif. codes: 0 '***' 0.001 '**' 0.01 '*' 0.05 '.' 0.1 ' ' 1
Dispersion parameter for binomial family taken to be 1
Null deviance: 42.34 on 31 degrees of freedom
Residual deviance: 24.40 on 28 degrees of freedom
AIC (Akaike information criterion): 32.4
Number of Fisher Scoring iterations: 9

Notice that in this model, the "answer" is that the company is discriminating (crooked arrow), and the default software also simultaneously produces the AIC, the goodness of fit measure (straight arrow). The goodness of fit measurement is better (remember, for the AIC, lower is better) for this model than for the previous model, but how much better? Is the lower score worth it? It is difficult to tell.

One can think of possible ways to address the problem of seeing goodness of fit measurements and "answers" at the same time. For example, an analyst might get someone else to run the statistical models, blot out the "answers," bring the analyst goodness of fit measurements until he/she commits to one model, and only then reveal the "answers." And, actually, one can program R to reveal goodness of fit measurements without "answers."

There are two problems with these protestations. First, as noted above, the process of picking a model is more complex than simply reading off goodness of fit scores. A good analyst will examine multiple scores, look at multiple graphs and charts, run analyses on subsets of the data, and implement a variety of other steps. It is difficult to avoid seeing the "answers" the models produce in this process. Second, even if the analyst is trying to avoid the answers, the temptation is there the whole time to peek. Remember, analysts are human. And with this kind of modeling, which relates the outcome variable to the treatment variable and the background variables, there is no structural way to prevent peeking.

What if there was a way to render it impossible to know the "answer" the statistical process will produce until the analyst has committed to a quantitative technique?

BLINDING: LOCK THE OUTCOME VARIABLES IN A CLOSET

It turns out that there is a way for an analyst to render it impossible for him/her to know the "answer" the statistical analysis will produce until he/she has committed to a technique. Put another way, the analyst can blind himself/herself to the "answer" from an analytical until almost all of the difficult work is done. To see how, return to Table 5.

The key recognition is the following, something that was said earlier: if the analyst could find a way to fill in the missing values, where the question marks are, then he/she would be done. For example, for unit F, the analyst would like to know what would have happened had he/she (unit F) been perceived male. With that in mind, a logical thing to do is to look for units perceived male that resemble unit F and have those units "donate" their outcome values to fill in unit F's question marks. Unit F has 12 years of experience in the industry. A likely candidate, then, is unit D, which has 11-year of experience in the industry. Unit D was hired. So, the analyst fills in "hired" for unit F's missing counterfactual outcome, and the table looks like Table 6 (with the different font for unit F's right-most column to remind him/her that this is an imputed value).

We do the same for unit G, matching its 15 years of experience to unit E's 16, and therefore filling in "Hired" (unit E's outcome) for unit G's missing counterfactual. We match unit H with unit C, I with D, etc. Then we do the same for units A–E, to the extent that we can. We might end up with a table that looks like Table 7.

What happened to units A and B? The analyst recognized that he/she had no perceived female units with such small amounts of experience in the industry. So she had no real way to fill in the missing counterfactual values for these two units. She removed them from the data set.

With this in mind, it is now easy to see that there is evidence that the company is discriminating against women. To be sure, there are several critical assumptions here, among them that years worked is the only important background variable, that 10 (8, really) units is a number sufficient to allow the analyst to draw conclusions, and that we should fill in missing counterfactual values deterministically as opposed to probabilistically. And a great deal of complication has been suppressed in terms of dealing with multiple background variables, assessments of how closely units must resemble one another before an analyst

TABLE 6 Potential Outcomes Table: What an Analysts Sees, Plus a Filled-in Value

Unit number	Years worked	Treatment actually received	Outcome if this unit were perceived female: Outcome (F)	Outcome if this unit were perceived male: Outcome (M)
A	2	M	??	Not hired
B	3	M	??	Not hired
C	30	M	??	Not hired
D	11	M	??	Hired
E	16	M	??	Hired
F	12	F	Not hired	**Hired**
G	15	F	Not hired	??
H	29	F	Not hired	??
I	13	F	Hired	??
J	14	F	Hired	??

TABLE 7 Potential Outcomes Table: What an Analysts Sees, Plus Filled-in Values

Unit number	Years worked	Treatment actually received	Outcome if this unit were perceived female: Outcome (F)	Outcome if this unit were perceived male: Outcome (M)
A	2	M	??	Not hired
B	3	M	??	Not hired
C	30	M	**Not hired**	Not hired
D	11	M	**Not hired**	Hired
E	16	M	**Not hired**	Hired
F	12	F	Not hired	**Hired**
G	15	F	Not hired	**Hired**
H	29	F	Not hired	**Not hired**
I	13	F	Hired	**Hired**
J	14	F	Hired	**Hired**

considers them candidates to donate values to each other, and a host of other matters. But this essay is about blinding, not statistical analysis.

So, where does blinding come in? Recall that the analyst began the process with unit F, noticed that this perceived female unit had 12 years of experience in the industry, looked for a perceived male unit with a similar amount of experience, and decided upon unit D. The

TABLE 8 Table Sufficient for Matching

Unit number	Years worked	Treatment actually received
A	2	M
B	3	M
C	30	M
D	11	M
E	16	M
F	12	F
G	15	F
H	29	F
I	13	F
J	14	F

key point is that nothing in that process of matching units F and D required the analyst to know either unit's outcome. In other words, to do the matching, the analyst needed only the information in Table 8.

This information is enough for the analyst to match unit F to unit D, unit G to unit E, unit H to unit C, unit I to unit D, etc. It is enough to allow him/her to eliminate units A and B. At no point does the analyst need to know who was hired.

With that in mind, a good analyst will deliberately blind himself/herself to the outcome variable (hired/not hired). He/she will request that the outcome variable not be included in the first data set that she is given. Then, he/she will employ a precommitment strategy (think Odysseus, the Sirens, the mast, etc.) in the sense that he/she will implement various statistical techniques that allow him/her to record and commit to a set of matches of units to other units. Having so committed himself/herself (preferably by disclosing his/her algorithm to someone else), and only then, he/she will ask for the complete data set that includes the outcome variables.

CAN WE INSTITUTIONALIZE THIS KIND OF ANALYSIS?

On the surface, it would appear easy to institutionalize the method of analysis described above. All one needs is a way to verify that the analyst is not given the outcome variables at first; that he/she provides someone other than himself/herself, someone who can later verify this fact, with his/her desired sets of matched data (or, more generally, with his/her algorithm for balancing background variables and trimming observations for which there are no good counterparts) and his/her proposed method of analyzing the outcome data; and that the analysis he/she later conducts uses the matched data and follows his/her proposed outcome variable analysis. In other words, all that is needed is an intermediary with some quantitative chops to verify that the analyst did not cheat. So, again, on the surface, it would appear easy to institutionalize this method.

Actually, it really is that easy. And we know that this idea is workable in practice because, as mentioned at the beginning of this essay, some quantitative analysts have been doing it for decades (Ruin, 2007; Turpie et al., 2014). In some instances, these analysts do not formally use an intermediary. Instead, they simply instruct the "client" to begin by sending a data set that does not include the outcome variables and proceed as outlined above. This way of doing things can alleviate some fears of bias when, for example, a drug company has hired a statistician to find out whether one of the company's products works. The ultimate audience for the statistician's report might be the U.S. Food and Drug Administration (FDA), which might (should) be worried that the statistician skewed his/her results in the company's favor.

In more adversarial settings, the formality and post hoc verifiability that an actual intermediary offers might be desirable. For example, in litigation, expert witnesses might use blinding, by means of intermediaries who can be called to the witness stand to attest that blinding procedures were in fact used, as a way to bolster their own credibility. Structurally analogous ideas have been proposed and explored elsewhere (Robertson, 2010). One intriguing aspect of the use of the kinds of blinding discussed in this essay and in Robertson (2010) is that neither would require a change in litigation rules of evidence. In fact, parties unwilling to take these steps can be forced to do so. I see no impediment in existing law to a judge's ordering parties seeking to use expert witnesses to proceed as outlined in this essay.

Outside of adversarial processes, journals might insist on evidence of blinding before publishing papers reporting observational studies. At present, I am not aware of any journals that either insist on blinding in observational studies or that, as a matter of editorial policy, have announced that they will be more likely to publish papers that use it. Given how easy it would be for journals to take such steps, and given how frequently observational studies purporting to find causal relationships are published, this absence is a pity.

Blinding has great promise in a wide variety of human endeavors, even among quantitative analysts.

References

Robertson, C.T., 2010. Blind expertise. New York University Law Review 85, 175–257.

Ruin, D.B., 2007. The design versus the analysis of observational studies for causal effects: parallels with the design of randomized trials. Statistics in Medicine 26 (20), 25–36.

Turpie, A.G.G., Haas, S., Kreutz, R., Mantovani, L.G., Pattanayak, C.W., Holberg, G., Jamal, W., Schmidt, A., van Eickels, M., Lassen, M.R., 2014. A non-interventional comparison of rivaroxaban with standard of care for thromboprophylaxis after major orthopaedic surgery in 17,701 patients with propensity score adjustment. Thrombosis and Haemostasis 111 (1), 94–102. http://dx.doi.org/10.1160/TH13-08-0666.

Further Reading

Greiner, D.J., 2008. Causal inference in civil rights litigation. Harvard Law Review 122 (2), 533–598.

Greiner, D.J., Rubin, D.B., 2011. Potential outcomes and causal effects of immutable characteristics. The Review of Economics & Statistics 93 (3), 775–785.

Those two articles build on statistical concepts proposed in the 1970s and 1980s, several of which are collected in:

Rubin, D.B. (Ed.), 2006. Matched Sampling for Causal Effects. Cambridge University Press, Cambridge.

Early works that also informed this essay include:
Holland, P.W., 1986. Statistics and causal inference. Journal American Statistical Association 81 (396), 945–960.
Rubin, D.B., 1974. Estimating causal effects of treatments in randomized and nonrandomized studies. Journal of Educational Psychology 66, 688–701.
Rubin, D.B., 1978. Bayesian inference for causal effects: The role of randomization. The Annals of Statistics 7, 34–58.

CHAPTER

12

Using Blind Reviews to Address Biases in Medical Malpractice

Jeffrey D. Robinson

Department of Radiology, University of Washington, Seattle, WA, USA; Cleareview, Inc., Seattle, WA, USA

OUTLINE

INTRODUCTION

Medical malpractice litigation consumes tremendous societal resources in the United States, including time, money, and emotion. Most of these resources are focused on determining whether physician defendants met the standard of care in their medical management of the plaintiff patients. The evidence in most litigation consists of medical records in which the care

Blinding as a Solution to Bias
http://dx.doi.org/10.1016/B978-0-12-802460-7.00012-7

provided by the defendant health-care provider is documented. Current legal practice calls for each side to produce its own expert (or experts) to analyze and provide an interpretation of this evidence that predictably supports its side of the case. Although both plaintiff and defense bars acknowledge that bias is inherent in the expert witness enterprise as it is currently structured, no commonly accepted method of mitigating this bias has emerged. Blinding the expert can both decrease bias and improve objectivity, which both sides assert is their goal.

In this chapter, the first section reviews the roles of expert witnesses in medical malpractice litigation and the ways that bias affects their testimony. The following section describes strategies available to reduce the role of expert bias, focusing on expert witness blinding from three different approaches. The final section applies these strategies to different types of lawsuits and highlights limitations of each technique.

EXPERT WITNESSES

The issues central to most medical malpractice litigation are typically quite technical. For judges and juries to make good decisions, they need guidance from experts in the relevant fields. Historically, any expert testimony that met the test of "general acceptance" could be admissible (Cheng and Yoon, 2005). In 1993, the Supreme Court articulated a standard for expert testimony in Daubert v. Merrell Dow Pharmaceuticals (1993). The so-called *Daubert* rule (also cited as Rule 702) has been clarified twice, most recently in 2011. As currently stated, it requires:

> (a) the expert's...knowledge will help the trier of fact to understand the evidence or determine a fact in issue, (b) the testimony is based on sufficient facts or data, (c) the testimony is the product of reliable principles and methods, and (d) the expert has reliably applied the principles and methods to the facts of the case.
> ***Federal Rules of Evidence (2012)***

Although the *Daubert* rule applies in federal court, it has been adopted by a majority of state courts as well, which are the venues for most medical malpractice litigation (Kaufman, 2006). It has proven useful in excluding junk science from the courtroom (Masten and Strzelczyk, 2001) by requiring a factual basis for expert testimony. However, facts are subject to interpretation, and in the interpretation of factual matters, an expert may display bias of one type or another.

Expert witness biases in medical malpractice lawsuits are typically either informational or litigation based. The following summary is derived from a recent publication focused on expert witness bias in radiology litigation (Durand et al., 2014).

Informational Biases

Framing Bias

Framing bias refers to the observation that the manner in which data is presented can affect decision making. The most famous example of framing bias is Mark Twain's story of Tom Sawyer whitewashing the fence. By framing the chore in positive terms, he got his friends to pay him for the "privilege" of doing his work. In the medical malpractice litigation, framing bias occurs when an attorney affiliated with the lawsuit provides records to an expert. The expert knows that the information contained in the records resulted in litigation without having to examine the records. In radiology, it is common knowledge that lawyers do not ask radiologists to review normal exams (Berlin, 2000). Radiologists know that when they hear about patients from lawyers, the stories do not have happy endings.

Retrospective (Hindsight) Bias

Retrospective bias (also known as hindsight bias) is a term used to describe people's natural tendency to use current information to shape judgments of past events. In colloquial terms, retrospective bias invokes the Monday-morning quarterback. In medical malpractice litigation, retrospective bias allows experts to focus on sentinel events more clearly, because of their knowledge of what subsequently happened to the patients. This effect is well known in radiology (Berlin, 2000). Harvey et al. (1993) demonstrated this bias by studying radiologists reviewing mammograms of patients who were subsequently judged definitively to have early breast cancers. The mammograms showed subtle findings that could legitimately be read as either positive or negative. In 73 cases, blinded reviewers judged the most recent screening mammograms negative in 59% of patients. Radiologists who reviewed the mammograms with the knowledge of the subsequent breast cancer diagnosis interpreted the screening mammograms as negative in only 25%.

Outcome Bias

Outcome bias is a particular form of retrospective bias, in which the result of subsequent events colors judgment made about the original event. An expert may conclude that an error is more significant if the patient goes on to suffer morbidity as a result of that error than if no adverse consequence ensues. For example, a radiologist failing to identify an incidental renal mass will suffer no legal consequence if the mass is stable when reimaged years later. However, if a cancer subsequently grows from this mass, then he or she may be found negligent for this same omission.

Visual Hindsight Bias

Visual hindsight bias refers to the retention of visual information in the mind, either consciously or subconsciously (Harley et al., 2004). In the popular children's book series *Where's Waldo?* the reader tries to find Waldo, a person in a red and white striped shirt, glasses, and a cap in a visually cluttered picture. Initially, it can be a very difficult task, but once found, viewers are more likely to find Waldo more quickly when returning to the picture, even after many months. Once a person is aware of a fact, or makes an observation, psychologists have shown that the memory of it can be readily recalled. A radiologist (or juror) who sees an abnormality, either independently or having been shown the finding, will be visually drawn to it on subsequent presentations. This is particularly pernicious in radiology malpractice litigation in which the missed observation is frequently displayed at great magnification, because the defense's claim may be that the abnormality was so subtle that to not have perceived it was within the standard of practice. When initially presented in such a setting, it is difficult for any observer to recapture the naïve state of mind experienced by the original radiologist.

Litigation Biases

Litigation biases stem from interactions of expert witnesses with the legal system, particularly the attorneys who have retained them. These biases are not psychological in nature, but rather derive from the structure of our legal system.

Selection Bias

Selection bias refers to the manner in which experts are retained. When preparing for litigation, an attorney may consult with several experts to understand the case. When it comes to selecting an expert for depositions and trials, the attorney will select the one whose opinion best suits the attorney's needs. Informal consultations are generally nondiscoverable, so an attorney is not penalized for conducting a broad preliminary search. As a result, the expert who is finally presented at trial may not be representative of the opinions presented to the attorney.

Undersampling Bias

Undersampling bias results when a small subset of a population is not representative of the larger population, yet is presented as being representative. This bias is exemplified by the current so-called 'debate' over climate change, in which the opinions of a small number of climate skeptics are often provided the same amount of media exposure as those of the much larger number of experts supporting the theory of climate change, implying that expert opinion is evenly divided. The structure of our legal system exacerbates the undersampling bias problem by giving each side similar allocation (in time or number of experts) for expert testimony. One or two carefully selected experts may proffer an opinion that is in actuality held by only a small minority of all experts, yet the jury may be led again to believe that expert opinion is evenly divided. Compounding the problem, the population of all possible experts is not known and their opinions cannot be verified. In other situations involving sampling such as population surveys, statistical methods can be used to measure the likelihood that the sample represents the entire population, but litigation does not permit this kind of analysis.

Compensation Bias

Compensation bias simply acknowledges that experts may adjust their opinions nearer to alignment with that of the people who are paying them (Robertson, 2013). Closely related to compensation bias is affiliation bias: independent of compensation, once experts affiliate with one side in litigation, they are more likely to share the opinions and outlook of their litigants' teams. This bias can be subtle and exploited through skillful lawyering. For example, at trial an attorney may state his own point of view and then ask the expert to agree or disagree with the hypothesis presented. In this setting the expert's agreement may suppress nuance in opinion that he might otherwise have stated, had he been given the opportunity of an open-ended question.

ELIMINATING EXPERT BIAS

Because of any one of the manifold biases that might affect expert witnesses, the court's search for truth is made more difficult. Several methods have been suggested to eliminate the effect of witness bias on the outcome of malpractice litigation.

Eliminate the Search for Fault

During the periodic medical malpractice insurance crises that have emerged since the 1970s, the concept of removing medical malpractice claims from the tort system altogether has attracted considerable interest. As an alternative, claims would be heard by special administrative compensation judges also called health courts (Mello et al., 2006). Such special courts may operate under a "no-fault" administrative model, in which preset compensation is offered for injuries that are either avoidable or preventable (Burkle, 2011). No-fault administrative systems for resolving malpractice cases are in use in Denmark, New Zealand, and Sweden (Kachalia et al., 2008).

Eliminate the Expert

Another way to decrease the influence of expert witness bias in medical malpractice litigation would be to simply decrease the use of expert witnesses to define the standard of care. Evidence-based medicine (EBM) is the term describing the most data-driven practices in a particular health-care field (Guyatt and Evidence-Based Medicine Working Group, 1992; Guyatt et al., 1995; La Rochelle, 2014). Using large patient populations and rigorous scientific methods, clinical guidelines have been developed to guide the diagnosis and treatment of specific conditions in ways that are safe, effective, and efficient. In theory, EBM guidelines could provide a cookbook for the standard of care that would make expert testimony unnecessary.

However, Mello (2002) has described several limitations of using clinical guidelines when applied to medical malpractice settings. First, the natures of the legal, medical, and scientific investigative enterprises are fundamentally different. The legal and medical systems are committed to arriving at a conclusion to the question presented before them using the best data available: The defendant is basically either guilty or not guilty. Medical practitioners may follow a diagnostic pathway; but at some point, they must make a decision as to what they believe the patient's problem is, and act accordingly. By contrast, clinical practice guidelines are only as good as the science that supports them. Unlike the legal process, the scientific method permits itself an inconclusive end point, in which evidence is not strong enough to support the hypothesis underlying an investigation. In the scientific method context, insufficient support for the hypothesis is not the same as concluding the hypothesis is false. As a result, many facets of medical care are unaddressed by scientifically rigorous testing either because the effects are subtle or the particular scenario involved is uncommon, so a statistically significant effect cannot be measured.

Even if these limitations can be overcome, it is unlikely that the dissemination of EBM guidelines will ever completely obviate the need for expert witnesses. In many areas of medicine, EBM guidelines do not exist. In others, there is an abundance of EBM guidelines that only an expert could sort through. Some guidelines are general, intended for all patients, but others apply to specific subsets of patients who have additional restrictions. For example, the American College of Radiology has developed imaging guidelines for common clinical situations. There are 13 variations for the imaging evaluation of a patient with acute respiratory illness (American College of Radiology, 2011, 2013). The National Guideline Clearinghouse (www.guideline.gov) lists 258 guidelines for diagnosis and treatment of acute respiratory illness. With such a number of guidelines to choose from, expert testimony may be required to justify the application of a particular EBM guideline to a particular patient's condition, reintroducing the problem of bias that use of the guidelines sought to eliminate.

Blind the Expert

If expert testimony cannot reasonably be replaced by the use of guidelines, then efforts must be made to maximize its objectivity. Robertson and Yokum (2012) performed an experiment with mock juries to test the effect of expert blinding on jury decisions in a medical malpractice setting. Their study focused on litigation biases, with the jurors being shown identical video expert testimony. Some were told that the defense expert had been hired by an intermediary and was blinded as to which side of the suit he was testifying, and others that the plaintiff's expert had been so blinded. They concluded that juries found blinded experts to be significantly more credible than nonblinded ones. There are a range of potential mechanisms for blinding experts.

The Sub Rosa Method

One way to blind experts is by providing data that they do not know are, in fact, at issue in a lawsuit. This sub rosa approach has been proposed by the pathology community (American Society of Cytopathology, 2013; Austin, 1997; Giard, 2010):

> A violation of a reasonable prudent practitioner standard of practice based on how specific Pap tests were screened and interpreted can only be established through an unbiased blinded rescreening review process that includes the contested case as one of a number of normal and abnormal GYN cytology samples representing a variety of disease states. ***American Society of Cytopathology (2013)***

Similarly, in the radiology setting, for example, an examination is placed in the routine daily workload of the expert radiologist, who interprets that exam in the same manner during the routine course of business. That report is compared to the defendant radiologist's report by a third party or an attorney to determine the degree of correlation between the original report and the expert's report, and by extension, whether the standard of care was met by the defendant radiologist.

Veritas Reporting (The Center for Quality Improvement in Radiology Interpretations, Baltimore, MD, www.veritasreporting.com) offers expert reviews using the sub rosa approach. It collaborates with a large radiology group that has agreed to be a subject to the deception necessary to conduct the blind review. There is no record as to whether this method has received scrutiny by the courts.

The Second Read and Oversight Methods

In contrast to the sub rosa method, two alternative approaches have been developed that allow that experts will be aware of their participation in a lawsuit but still try to prevent certain biases. In these approaches, the radiological exam at issue is inserted into a small group of similar exams called a review set. The other exams in the set, called distractors, are selected to match the particular expertise of the expert reviewer. For example, if a head computed tomography (CT) obtained in the emergency department was the object of litigation, a review set that was intended for an emergency radiologist reviewer would have a broad range of exams, perhaps including another head CT, a chest X-ray, an abdominal CT, a wrist X-ray, etc. However, if the expert witness was a neuroradiologist, then the review set would consist of different neuroradiology exams, such as brain or spine magnetic resonance imaging (MRI) exams, in addition to other head CTs.

In the "second read" method, an expert is presented with the review set. He or she is told that one or more of the exams are involved in litigation, and he or she is asked to present his or her impressions of each exam. The goal is to reproduce a clinical reading environment, where the reviewer treats each patient's exam as an independent event. The findings of one patient's exam have no relation to the findings on the next patient's exam, in the same way that successive coin flips are independent events.

This approach has been studied in a small number of settings. Renshaw et al. (2005) reported on results of the blinded review of litigation Pap smear slides in the detection of cervical cancer. Their review set included litigation slides with abnormal findings mixed in with distractors consisting of some normal slides as well as some abnormal slides with known surgically proven pathology. They reported a measure called "ease of interpretation," defined as the percentage of subjects who identified the pathology on a litigation slide. They found that the (abnormal) litigation slides were significantly more likely to be interpreted as normal than the known abnormal slides. They found that the ease of interpretation of the litigation slides was 56%, indicating that almost half of the reviewing cytotechnologists missed the pathology on any given slide that ended up as the subject of litigation. This finding could suggest that it may not have been negligent for a clinical pathologist to fail to detect the abnormality. They did not report the ease of interpretation of the known abnormal slides.

Semelka et al. (2010) performed a radiology review study also using the second read approach. Their review set contained one litigation exam and five distractors read by 31 radiologists who were told that the study was for institutional quality assurance purposes. They found that none of the radiologists identified two of the three findings identified by plaintiff's experts as critical misses. The third finding was identified by 61% of the blinded radiologists. The authors did not report on the level of agreement on the distractor exams, nor were the reviewing radiologists asked to determine whether the missed observation constituted substandard care. One could interpret these data as showing that the plaintiff's experts exhibited one or more types of bias in their assertions of negligence, because two of three claims were not supported by any of the blinded radiologists, and a third claim was identified by just over half of them. In another report, the same group observed a wide range of interpretation of these scans with wider ranges observed in more complex exams and with vague clinical complaints (Ryan et al., 2010).

A variation of the second read approach, called the "oversight" approach, involves the expert being presented with a similar review set and the original radiologists' reports that accompanied the exams in the set. The expert's task is now not to provide his or her impressions of the exam, but to assess whether the original report met the standard of care. By telling the expert that there are one or more litigation exams in the set, he or she cannot merely search for an outlier report and then dismiss the remainder of the review set as "normals".

One company offers blind expert reviews using the second read and oversight techniques. Cleareview (Cleareview, Inc., Seattle, WA, www.cleareview.co) has built a deidentified PACS

TABLE 1 Comparison of Different Types of Blind Expert Reviews

Review type	Conventional	Sub rosa	Oversight	Second read
Blinded expert	No	Yes	Yes	Yes
Expert aware of litigation	Yes	No	Yes	Yes
Expert aware of specific exam at issue	Yes	No	No	No
Expert aware of original interpretation	Yes	No	Yes	No
Expert aware of specific allegation	Yes	No	No	No

Note: Litigation bias can be mitigated in the oversight and second read methods by use of an intermediary to engage the expert.

(radiology image database) with more than 1000 exams available as foils for review sets. It employs both the oversight and second read approaches, depending on the clients' preferences. Cleareview has created 30 review sets, which have been reviewed more than 60 times. Expert radiologists have been deposed, but the process has not been challenged, and cases using its methods have not yet reached court.

Table 1 compares these three methods of blinding to current practice.

Application of Expert Witness Bias Solutions to Clinical Scenarios

Myriad decisions and actions are taken during the course of patient care, and a primary question for any review method is its reliability. Posner et al. (1996) performed a retrospective nonblinded study of anesthesia malpractice claims by having pairs of anesthesiologists review the medical records of 103 malpractice insurance claims after the suits had been resolved. The two reviewers agreed on the appropriateness of care provided by the defendant anesthesiologist in only 62% of the cases reviewed. de Reuver et al. (2008) conducted a similar review of closed litigation cases involving surgical complications. Thirteen experts reviewed 10 cases for negligence on the part of the defendant surgeon. In 7 of the 10 cases, the level of agreement between reviewers was 53% or less. Studdert and Mello (2007) performed a study using physicians to review 1452 closed medical and surgical malpractice claims. As part of their analysis, they subjected 10% of the claims to a second review by a reviewer unaware of the existence of the first review. They found only a moderate degree of agreement between the two reviews (kappa = 0.63), which varied by the complexity of the underlying case. These examples demonstrate that even expert observers can draw different conclusions from a complex medical record. In the setting of such underlying discordance, bias issues have the capacity to distort experts' opinions even further. Hence any effort to reduce or eliminate expert witness bias is worthwhile.

To simplify the analysis of decision making, the following discussion will focus on the field of diagnostic radiology. The majority of radiology malpractice lawsuits arise over the interpretation of imaging studies such as X-rays or CT scans.

Narrow Focus versus Broad Focus Clinical Scenarios

In a lawsuit addressing a narrowly focused clinical scenario, the plaintiff's claim is focused on a single explicit point in time, during which the plaintiff asserts the defendant negligently made an incorrect decision. It may be the choice of a particular implant in orthopedics, the choice of a medication by an internist, or a reading on a relatively clear-cut radiological examination. For example, in an adolescent being evaluated for hip pain with an X-ray, a subtle asymmetry in the appearance of the hip joint may indicate a slipped capital femoral epiphysis (SCFE). When this disorder is promptly diagnosed, surgery is performed with a low complication rate. However, delayed surgery is associated with a much higher complication rate. Radiologists are frequently sued over a missed diagnosis of SCFE.

In the more broadly focused case, an allegation is made that given the totality of the situation, the defendant should have reached a different conclusion than the one resulting in the patient's adverse outcome. One such example is the management of a patient in the intensive care unit, requiring the coordination of several medical and surgical specialists, therapists, and nurses over an extended period of time. In radiology, a data-rich exam such as a CT scan of the abdomen and pelvis may provide the setting for such an allegation. The stated reason for the scan may direct the radiologist to one organ, but findings may be present in many different areas. This is particularly common in older patients or patients with several medical problems. Consider a patient who received a CT scan of the abdomen for complaints suggestive of a kidney stone. In addition to the kidney stone, the scan may show arthritis in the spine, gallstones, a mild aortic aneurysm, several small liver cysts, and a small pulmonary nodule in the lung base. Among these findings, some are germane, some are incidental, and any may turn out to be significant in the future. Only a subset of these could be the subject of the malpractice claim.

Applying Methods to Reduce Expert Witness Bias to the Clinical Scenarios

Narrowly focused cases are amenable to all three blinding approaches. If a radiological evaluation or other simple clinical decision is relatively binary, then in the sub rosa or second read approaches, a third party can decide whether the expert made the observation missed by the defendant radiologist. Further, using the sub rosa approach, the exam may be submitted to several experts leading to a statistical measure of concordance that could be considered a community standard or care. For example, if 9 out of 10 experts identified the SCFE injury from the example above, then it could be reasonably inferred that the defendant radiologist did not meet the community standard. The case for negligence would be weaker with a smaller percentage of experts making the relevant observation. If half of the blinded readers miss the finding, has the defendant breached the standard of care?

However, more broadly focused cases create difficulties for the sub rosa and second read approaches. In legal cases that raise several questions of appropriateness of care, a practitioner often performs well on some questions and poorly on others. Experts who review such a case blindly may identify some or all of the issues in question. In certain situations, such complexities can be resolved. For example, a lawsuit was filed over a chest CT scan obtained for the purposes of determining the presence or absence of a pulmonary embolism (PE). The plaintiff alleged that the radiologist reported there being a PE present when subsequent events led the plaintiff to conclude that a PE was not present. Additionally, the plaintiff alleged that the radiologist failed to diagnose an epidural abscess that was subsequently diagnosed by other means, and which plaintiff's expert claims was, in fact, present in the same CT scan. An expert reviewer using the second read approach did not identify the PE (suggesting that the defendant was negligent in finding one), and did not identify the epidural abscess (suggesting that the defendant was *not* negligent on this alternative theory). Assuming that the first breach caused substantial injury, a fact finder could use such an opinion to impose liability on the first theory, converting the complex opinion into a binary outcome.

However, most of the time, reconciling the defendant and expert witness reports may be more problematic. Suppose that the reviewing expert in the above scenario also identified a small aneurysm that was not reported by the defendant radiologist (and was in fact not part of the lawsuit at all). If the aneurysm had subsequently ruptured, then it could have provided a third potential theory of breach. However, because that alleged error by the defendant did not in fact cause any injury, a court might find that the incidental error is irrelevant to the lawsuit. Alternatively, a court could determine that the failure to find this other important abnormality is further evidence that the defendant was performing negligently at the time the plaintiff's image was reviewed. Thus, interpretation of the reviewing expert's finding will require judgment by the third-party compiler of the expert reviews, the attorney, and/or the court.

The oversight approach is arguably more appropriate for such cases because it puts the task of integrating the multiple assessments into the decision of the single expert in a more organic way. Under this approach, the expert evaluates the totality of the original report regardless of the complexity of the exam and its findings, and provides a bottom line opinion of whether there was negligence. To avoid certain biases, recall that the oversight and second read methods use a file of known distractor cases, unlike the sub rosa method, which uses a real clinical workflow for this purpose. One advantage of using a file of known cases is that it allows statistical assessment of the reliability of the expert himself. An expert witness' assessment of a distractor exam can be compared to assessments made by prior experts. These assessments can demonstrate whether the expert's opinions are consistent with the larger population of experts or whether the expert is an outlier, either by being overly lax in interpreting the standard of care (favoring defendants) or overly strict (favoring plaintiffs).

By contrast, a disadvantage of the oversight and second read methods is that whoever is paying for review of the litigation case must also pay for review of the distractor cases. Here, the sub rosa method actually appears more applicable, because the distractors are real clinical cases, the payment for those reads is provided by the health-care payor (typically an insurer). The distractors are free for the purposes of litigation. This cost differential becomes especially important, if the same litigation case is to be submitted to multiple experts, as the amount of time spent on distractor exams grows with each reviewer. Such a multiple-read methodology has the potential to generate a statistical sense of the standard of care. In the narrowly focused cases, the attorney can calculate how many of the blinded radiologists made the observation that was the basis of the lawsuit. In more broadly focused cases, separate calculations can be made regarding each of the findings at issue. Because of cost considerations, this approach is more promising with the sub rosa method.

Limitations of Applying Expert Witness Blinding Approaches

The techniques of expert witness blinding may be difficult to apply in a variety of medical settings. While there are objective artifacts in some fields (e.g., pathology specimens on slides or medical imaging studies such as X-rays or CT scans), in many cases the information at issue in the lawsuit is difficult to reproduce (e.g., abdominal tenderness detected at a physical exam or a surgical mishap as a result of an incorrect judgment, device, or procedural failing). In these cases, an expert can only be provided with records describing the events that took place, and so cannot practically be blinded to the existence of the litigation. In these settings, it may nonetheless be possible to blind experts with regard to which parties are requesting their opinions.

The sub rosa approach is logistically difficult. It requires a preexisting arrangement with the expert radiologist's practice to place an exam in the queue that appears to be a genuine current exam. The expert must have agreed that this type of deception may take place at any time. There must be sufficient backstory to address whatever questions the blinded expert might have regarding the patient with a degree of verisimilitude that will not raise suspicion. Finally, there must be a health-care provider—or someone pretending to be a health-care provider—available to take a phone call from the blinded expert in the event of a finding requiring nonroutine communication, which is likely to happen as a result of an examination that resulted in litigation. To generate multiple reviews in this approach, several radiologists in the practice must be qualified to be experts, according to the standards required by the attorneys who retain them. Further, the radiologists must be willing to participate in the process with safeguards in place to ensure that the different radiologists do not informally consult each other over the exam, or that consultation must be documented, if it undermines the blind for the second radiologist who may be called to trial to review the same case. Alternatively, arrangements must be made with multiple practices to achieve sufficient expertise. To be used regularly, measures must be taken so that the expert radiologists do not learn to associate litigation exams with a particular referring institution or clinician. That way, they can remain unknowing experts.

The second read and oversight approaches are subject to selection and compensation biases when the attorney selects the expert to be the blinded reviewer. If the reviewer is either selected or even initially contacted by an intermediary distinct from the attorney, then this bias can be mitigated. These approaches require construction of a sufficiently large deidentified imaging database from which review sets can be drawn. Additionally, the review sets need to be constructed with care, either to resemble original clinical settings or to match the scopes of practices of reviewers more subspecialized than the original radiologists. For example, a set of exams that resemble those seen in an emergency department is appropriate for a general or emergency radiology expert, but not for review by a neuroradiologist, who does not ordinarily read the wide variety of exams obtained in the emergency department.

All three approaches must address the selection of the expert. A pool of interchangeable experts may be ideal (Robertson, 2010), but practically speaking, experts vary with respect to not only their qualifications, but also their geographic distribution, availability, and personal presentation skills at deposition or trial. Some experts prefer to only consider participating for plaintiffs or defendants. Many lawyers want to retain control over who their experts are, which is to say that they wish to retain the selection bias described above. This consideration may make the sub rosa method, in particular, unattractive.

When soliciting impressions from experts using the sub rosa and second read approaches, impressions must be correlated with the original reports. While narrowly focused lawsuits may have only one finding to assess, most cases are more complex with multiple findings, of varying degrees of clinical relevance. In such cases, the expert's report may be incrementally different from the original report, requiring reconciliation. Whoever asserts that the two reports are sufficiently similar or not is asserting an opinion, which may be subject to challenge.

CONCLUSION

Agreement between medical experts is difficult to achieve when evaluating malpractice claims, and differences between experts can be magnified by informational and litigation biases. Appropriate blinding requires that issues in dispute must be presented in a manner that renders experts unaware of the legal implications of the particular issues. This may be accomplished either by deception or by presenting the litigation exam in a review set of distracting exams.

In the former scenario, multiple reviews may be obtained to try to determine a standard of care, either by consensus or other statistical means. In the latter scenario, the multiplicity of exams in the review set provides the distraction necessary to blind a single expert. Experts' performances on distractor litigation exams in the review sets may help assess their reliability relative to the pool of experts that have reviewed those exams in the past.

Both approaches present methodological challenges and address expert bias in different ways. Framing bias is somewhat better addressed by the sub rosa method, because the expert is completely unaware of the legal aspects of the exam at issue. The second read or oversight method experts know that at least one of the exams they are reviewing is involved in litigation, but do not know which one. Retrospective and outcome biases are well addressed in both methods, because the expert is made unaware of any subsequent events involving the plaintiff by the blinding process. Visual hindsight bias does not come in to effect in the initial expert review, so is not an issue with any method.

Litigation biases are generally better addressed by the sub rosa method, again because the expert is unaware of the legal nature of the exam he is reviewing. If the organization providing the review sets for the second read or oversight methods acts as an intermediary between the attorney and the expert, then the litigation biases may be mitigated. The sub rosa method can best address the undersampling bias, if it is used with multiple expert witnesses. Affiliation biases may arise in any of these methods at later stages of litigation, after the blinds are lifted for the purposes of testimony.

True objectivity in expert witnesses may be impossible to achieve in the medical malpractice realm. Blinding the expert can eliminate some biases and mitigate others.

References

American College of Radiology, 2011. ACR Appropriateness Criteria® Acute Respiratory Illness in Immunocompromised Patients. American College of Radiology, Reston, VA.

American College of Radiology, 2013. ACR Appropriateness Criteria® Acute Respiratory Illness in Immunocompetent Patients. American College of Radiology, Reston, VA.

American Society of Cytopathology, 2013. Guidelines for Review of GYN Cytology Samples in the Context of Litigation or Potential Litigation. American Society of Cytopathology, Wilmington, DE.

Austin, R.M., 1997. Results of blinded rescreening of Papanicolaou smears versus biased retrospective review. Archives of Pathology and Laboratory Medicine 121 (3), 311–314.

Berlin, L., 2000. Malpractice issues in radiology: hindsight bias. AJR American Journal of Roentgenology 175 (3), 597–601. http://dx.doi.org/10.2214/ajr.175.3.1750597.

Burkle, C.M., 2011. Medical malpractice: can we rescue a decaying system? Mayo Clinic Proceedings 86 (4), 326–332. http://dx.doi.org/10.4065/mcp.2010.0834.

Cheng, E.K., Yoon, A.H., 2005. Does Frye or Daubert matter? A study of scientific admissibility standards. Virginia Law Review 91, 471–513.

de Reuver, P.R., Dijkgraaf, M.G., Gevers, S.K., Gouma, D.J., 2008. Poor agreement among expert witnesses in bile duct injury malpractice litigation: an expert panel survey. Annals of Surgery 248 (5), 815–820. http://dx.doi.org/10.1097/SLA.0b013e318186de35.

Daubert v. Merrell Dow Pharmaceuticals, Inc., 1993. 509 U.S. 579.

Durand, D.J., Robertson, C.T., Agarwal, G., Duszak Jr., R., Krupinski, E.A., Itri, J.N., Lewin, J.S., 2014. Expert witness blinding strategies to mitigate bias in radiology malpractice cases: a comprehensive review of the literature. Journal of the American College of Radiology 11 (9), 868–873. http://dx.doi.org/10.1016/j.jacr.2014.05.001.

Federal Rules of Evidence, 2012. pp. 398–401. http://www.gpo.gov/fdsys/pkg/USCODE-2011-title28/pdf/USCODE-2011-title28-app-federalru-dup2.pdf.

Giard, R.W., 2010. When is the practice of pathology malpractice? Journal of Clinical Pathology 63 (11), 957–961. http://dx.doi.org/10.1136/jcp.2010.080929.

Guyatt, G., Evidence-Based Medicine Working Group, 1992. Evidence-based medicine: a new approach to teaching the practice of medicine. Journal of the American Medical Association 268 (17), 2420–2425.

Guyatt, G.H., Sackett, D.L., Sinclair, J.C., Hayward, R., Cook, D.J., Cook, R.J., 1995. Users' guides to the medical literature. IX. A method for grading health care recommendations. Evidence-Based Medicine Working Group. Journal of the American Medical Association 274 (22), 1800–1804.

Harley, E.M., Carlsen, K.A., Loftus, G.R., 2004. The "saw-it-all-along" effect: demonstrations of visual hindsight bias. Journal of Experimental Psychology, Learning, Memory, and Cognition 30 (5), 960–968. http://dx.doi.org/10.1037/0278-7393.30.5.960.

Harvey, J., Fajardo, L., Innis, C., 1993. Previous mammograms in patients with impalpable breast carcinoma: retrospective vs blinded interpretation. AJR American Journal of Roentgenology 161, 1167–1172.

Kachalia, A.B., Mello, M.M., Brennan, T.A., Studdert, D.M., 2008. Beyond negligence: avoidability and medical injury compensation. Social Science & Medicine 66 (2), 387–402. http://dx.doi.org/10.1016/j.socscimed.2007.08.020.

Kaufman, M.S., 2006. The Status of Daubert in State Courts. Retrieved from: http://www.atlanticlegal.org/daubertreport.pdf.

La Rochelle, P., 2014. Basic learning concepts in EBM: the bidimentional hierarchy of evidence. Evidence Based Medicine 19 (3), 83–84. http://dx.doi.org/10.1136/eb-2013-101610.

Masten, J., Strzelczyk, J.J., 2001. Admissibility of scientific evidence post-Daubert. Health Physics 81 (6), 678–682.

Mello, M.M., 2002. Using statistical evidence to prove the malpractice standard of care: bridging legal, clinical, and statistical thinking. Wake Forest Law Review 37 (3). http://dx.doi.org/10.2139/ssrn.347780.

Mello, M.M., Studdert, D.M., Kachalia, A.B., Brennan, T.A., 2006. "Health courts" and accountability for patient safety. The Milbank Quarterly 84 (3), 459–492. http://dx.doi.org/10.1111/j.1468-0009.2006.00455.x.

Posner, K.L., Caplan, R.A., Cheney, F.W., 1996. Variation in expert opinion in medical malpractice review. Anaethesiology 85, 1049–1054.

Renshaw, A.A., Holladay, E.B., Geils, K.B., 2005. Results of multiple-slide, blinded review of Papanicolaou slides in the context of litigation. Determining what can be detected regularly and reliably. Cancer 105 (5), 263–269. http://dx.doi.org/10.1002/cncr.21319.

Robertson, C.T., 2010. Blind expertise. New York University Law Review 174, 174–257.

Robertson, C.T., 2013. Blinding as a solution to institutional corruption. In: Paper Presented at the Blinding as a Solution to Institutional Corruption. Harvard University. Retrieved from: http://ssrn.com/abstract=2321353. http://dx.doi.org/10.2139/ssrn.2321353.

Robertson, C.T., Yokum, D.V., 2012. The effect of blinded experts on juror verdicts. Journal of Empirical Legal Studies 9 (4), 765–794.

Ryan, A.F., Semelka, R.C., Molina, P.L., Yonkers, S., Vaidean, G., 2010. Evaluation of radiologist interpretive performance using blinded reads by multiple external readers. Investigative Radiology 45, 211–216.

Semelka, R.C., Ryan, A.F., Yonkers, S., Braga, L., 2010. Objective determination of standard of care: use of blind readings by external radiologists. American Journal of Roentgenology 195 (2), 429–431. http://dx.doi.org/10.2214/AJR.09.3987.

Studdert, D.M., Mello, M.M., 2007. When tort resolutions are "wrong": predictors of discordant outcomes in medical malpractice litigation. The Journal of Legal Studies 36 (S2), S47–S78.

CHAPTER

13

Mock Juror and Jury Assessment of Blinded Expert Witnesses

Megan S. Wright[1], *Christopher T. Robertson*[2], *David V. Yokum*[3]

[1]Yale Law School, New Haven, CT, USA; [2]James E. Rogers College of Law, The University of Arizona, Tucson, AZ, USA; [3]Department of Psychology, College of Science, The University of Arizona, Tucson, AZ, USA

OUTLINE

Blinding as a Solution to Bias
http://dx.doi.org/10.1016/B978-0-12-802460-7.00013-9

INTRODUCTION

Expert witnesses are often necessary in criminal and civil trials to provide explanations and interpretations of evidence for judges or juries who may lack the scientific or technical expertise to evaluate information material to a particular case. For example, the average person serving on a jury typically does not have the expertise to evaluate whether a particular technology violates an existing patent; the standard of care for treating a particular medical condition and whether it has been met; whether a company's policies lead to sex discrimination; or how to interpret forensic evidence. In cases such as these, parties may employ witnesses with expertise in the relevant areas to offer their expert opinions. However, various biases pervade experts' assessments of the facts, and jurors are especially sensitive to the potential for financial incentives to impact expert witnesses' opinions (Ivkovic and Hans, 2003).

It is important to reduce expert witness bias not only because there is an interest in finding "truth," but also because the stakes are the imposition of potential civil or criminal penalties. One way to reduce bias could be to blind expert witnesses (Robertson, 2010; Semelka et al., 2010). Experts would be selected through an intermediary without knowing which party requested their opinions, which should reduce selection, affiliation, and compensation biases.[1] One recent study of a mock medical malpractice trial demonstrated that individual jurors were more likely to decide for the party employing a blinded expert because jurors viewed these experts as more credible (Robertson and Yokum, 2012). However, additional studies are necessary to determine whether this effect holds for civil jury verdicts and for verdicts in criminal trials.

LITERATURE REVIEW

Biased Expert Witnesses

Expert witnesses are often hired by a party in a legal dispute rather than being court appointed (Lee, 1988), and bias enters into the legal process at this point of initial selection of an expert (Robertson, 2010). Attorneys can "shop" for an expert that will support their position, even if the majority of experts consulted would disagree with that particular expert's opinion (Robertson, 2010). In fact, a survey of civil jurors demonstrated that 72% agreed that attorneys can always find an expert to back up their client, indicating that jurors understand the concept of selection bias (Ivkovic and Hans, 2003).

Because expert witnesses are employed by a party rather than the court, they are aligned with one side in the dispute rather than being impartial. In this adversarial system, expert witnesses' role is to be persuasive interpreters of facts, which potentially compromises their objectivity, and may thus be an impediment to accurate fact-finding (Sperling, 2000). Some empirical studies have shown that experts underestimate the extent of their partisan or affiliation bias when acting as witnesses (Commons et al., 2004). In other studies, however, some

[1] Expert witnesses are subject to other cognitive biases such as confirmation bias (e.g., being unable to recognize alternative explanations) or contextual bias (i.e., being influenced by extraneous, irrelevant information) (see Robertson, 2010, p. 186, for a discussion of these biases). However, the use of blinded expert witnesses will not impact these cognitive biases, and so they are not discussed in this paper.

experts admit their role in ligation is more than just scientific interpretation (Quick, 2011). One study found that expert witnesses in medical manslaughter cases in Britain viewed themselves as part of the legal team and went beyond offering medical opinions when testifying; they used their moral judgment and did legal research (Quick, 2011). Because these experts strayed from their area of expertise and were aligned with the legal team, their objectivity was compromised (Quick, 2011).

Experts' opinions may also be biased in response to financial incentives. The hourly pay for expert witnesses may be substantial, and being hired to testify for a party is contingent upon offering an opinion favorable to that party (Robertson, 2010). Juries recognize that compensation bias may corrupt experts' testimony (Ivkovic and Hans, 2003).

Blinding as a Solution to Bias

Jurors who suspect an expert witness may be biased are unlikely to find them to be credible (Ivkovic and Hans, 2003). Blinded expertise is a proposed reform of expert testimony designed to reduce the influence of selection, affiliation, and compensation biases on an expert's testimony; increase accuracy of findings; and lead to a more credible presentation to a jury (Robertson, 2010; Robertson and Yokum, 2012; Semelka et al., 2010). A blinded expert is chosen by a neutral intermediary agency that specializes in connecting potential expert witnesses with those requesting their expertise and that renders a litigation opinion without knowing which side requested the opinion (Robertson, 2010).

Robertson and Yokum (2012) studied the effects of using a blinded expert witness in a mock medical malpractice trial. Their experiment contained a control condition with no blinded experts (representing a typical trial), and their experimental conditions presented either a blinded expert for the plaintiff (and a nonblinded expert for the defense) or a blinded expert for the defense (and a nonblinded expert for the plaintiff). They found that using a blinded expert witness increased the likelihood of a favorable verdict for the party employing such an expert. Mock jurors also rated a blinded expert's credibility higher. Moreover, the presence of a blinded expert witness diminished the credibility of a nonblinded expert witness.

IMPACT OF BLINDED EXPERT WITNESSES ON CIVIL JURY VERDICTS

Although preliminary evidence suggests that the use of blinded experts influences juror decision making (Robertson and Yokum, 2012), there is no information about effects on jury verdicts. Jury verdicts are distinct from individual juror decision making in that jury verdicts "have a meaning that those of their constituent members do not have" (Rubinstein, 1982, p. 134). Thus, it is important to determine whether blinded expert witnesses have the same impact on jury deliberations and verdicts as they do on jurors' individual decisions.

Methods

Following on a prior online experiment about the impact of blinded expert witnesses on juror decisions in civil trials (Robertson and Yokum, 2012), an in-person sample of 108 potential jurors in Tucson, Arizona, was recruited from an online bulletin board (Craigslist.org) and mailing lists to watch a 33- to 45-min video recording of a mock medical malpractice trial, make a judgment for the plaintiff or defendant, decide whether to award damages, and then deliberate in groups of four to eight jurors.

In the stimulus video, as in Robertson and Yokum (2012), jurors heard a judge's welcoming instructions, opening and closing arguments from both attorneys, testimony from the plaintiff's expert witness and the defendant's expert witness, cross-examination of both witnesses, and finally a jury charge by the judge. The video was developed by a team including practicing physicians, litigators, and an experienced arbitrator/judge.

The case involved a physician's failure to diagnose lumbar radiculopathy—nerve damage to the lower back—leading to permanent disability. The facts in the medical record were clear and not in dispute: the defendant physician's clinical exam revealed two signs of neurological impingement, but the physician advised the patient to take over-the-counter anti-inflammatory medicine and return if the pain got worse. The key legal question, defined by the relevant jury instructions from Arizona law, was whether the physician had "met the standard of care" in his decision to suggest medication rather than order immediate radiological imaging. This question depends on technical expert testimony, because jurors would not otherwise be expected to know the treatment protocols for the medical profession.

One theme presented in the mock trial video was whether practicing physicians should practice "aggressive" medicine, ordering imaging scans that may turn out to be unnecessary, thus driving up the cost of medicine. A second theme presented was whether the patient (the plaintiff) should have returned to the physician sooner after the anti-inflammatory medication was not noted to be immediately helpful, instead of waiting 3 months to follow up, and been more outspoken in complaining about his pain.

Half the jurors were randomized into an experimental group in which they were informed through the attorney's argument and direct examination of the plaintiff's expert witness that he was a "blinded" expert witness. The plaintiff's attorney also cross-examined the defendant's nonblinded expert, attempting to demonstrate a disparity in credibility by showing that the nonblinded expert may have been hand-picked by the defense attorney and then biased by the prospect of being hired to give additional testimony in future cases, contingent on giving a favorable evaluation of this case. In his redirect, the defense attorney attempted to rehabilitate his expert by eliciting testimony about how the expert was simply calling the case as he saw it and was bound by professional norms of candor and honesty.

After watching the trial video on individual computers with headphones, the subjects in the control group were divided into nine juries, and the subjects in the experimental group were divided into nine juries. They then deliberated for about 45 min. (The entire exercise was limited to 2 h.) In the time allotted, three juries in the control condition reached a decision and two juries in the experimental condition reached a decision.

All deliberations were audio and video recorded, and transcribed.[2] One author (MW) read through the transcripts, line-by-line, coding the information using short phrases to summarize the information on each line of text. The codes were then aggregated to identify relevant themes. The themes were analyzed for their relationships to one another, and they were then combined into a relevant explanatory narrative (Corbin and Strauss, 2007) to answer the question of how a blinded plaintiff expert witness impacts jury deliberations in a mock medical malpractice trial.

[2] The quotes in this paper have been edited for clarity. Ellipses indicate omitted text.

Results

Verdict Preferences by Experimental Group

As reported in Yokum and Robertson (2015), 30% of jurors found in favor of the plaintiff when both expert witnesses were nonblinded. When the plaintiff used a blinded expert, on the other hand, the plaintiff's win rate increased substantially, to 50%—a statistically and economically significant increase of 20 percentage points, 95% CI [0.01, 0.39], $p=0.04$.

Expert Witness Evaluation in Control Condition

Juries in the control group assigned to watch the video of a trial featuring traditional experts did not spend a substantial amount of time evaluating expert witness testimony, signaling that such testimony was not influential. Of the nine deliberations in the control group, four juries did not explicitly consider the expert witnesses' credibility at all. When juries did evaluate the witnesses during deliberations, such evaluations tended to be brief comments made in passing by a single juror. In this condition, there was one verdict for the plaintiff, two verdicts for the defense, and six hung juries, which were simply unable to reach a decision within the allocated time.

Expert Witness Evaluation in Experimental Condition

In the experimental condition, by contrast, every jury evaluated the experts' testimony and credibility. The vast majority of jurors favored the blinded plaintiff expert witness; in addition, they also expressed dislike of the nonblinded expert witness for the defendant. The blinded expert witness was referred to as "unbiased," "impartial," "unbought," "convincing," and "more truthful." The nonblinded expert witness was referred to as a "weasel," "biased," "hand-picked," "weak," "unprofessional," "unknowledgeable," "bought off," "snake in the grass," and "unclear."

COMPENSATION BIAS

The jurors in the experimental condition often debated whether payment for testimony influenced expert witnesses' professional opinion. Jurors tended to positively evaluate the blinded plaintiff's expert witness because he was not aware of which party hired him, meaning his opinion was independent of his compensation and thus unbiased. But other jurors defended the nonblinded defense expert witness because he received payment for providing a service just like any other worker. These jurors conceded, however, that payment in exchange for testimony could influence the expert's opinion and that this system is flawed.

> Juror 2: This whole thing about the expert testimony is that he was clearly unbiased about it.
>
> Juror 3: Yeah, but that didn't matter to me. I mean, the whole system of paying people, there should be some other system. Because I think that is wrong and can influence a doctor who has a lot of integrity. If I was slated to make an extra $13,000, it would be quite a temptation, so I think that whole system is wrong, but given that we have that system, I felt that fellow was just as credible as the other doctor.

Juror 2: The plaintiff's expert witness, I mean, he was an unbiased guy. To me, you can dismiss the defendant's witness because he was getting paid for it. But the plaintiff's witness didn't know who he was testifying for, he said he thought the doctor was negligent, from his personal expertise, his experience as a doctor.
Juror 3: Although it sounds to me that you believe you shouldn't get paid for work. So if you go to work, then you should just do it for free.
[…]
Juror 4: Well, I trusted the guy that was blind more. Because he had no idea, he had nothing to gain. He was getting paid either way.
Juror 3: I know, that's the point they were trying to make. But that didn't necessarily make the point for me. You know, because we all get paid for a job we do. So, I didn't—
Juror 2: Exactly. His job was to be totally impartial in what he found out, what his results were. His professional opinion.
Juror 3: It always looks good to a jury, I think.
Juror 2: And to me that should carry a much [greater] amount of weight than the other guy's impression (Experimental Group, Deliberation 2).

This jury focused on compensation bias, and the majority of them discounted the defense's expert because of this bias. In fact, one juror wanted to dismiss the defense expert witness' testimony entirely.

SELECTION BIAS

Although the juries tended to focus on how the defense expert witness may be biased because of financial incentives, some juries also focused on selection bias, or how the defense "hand-picked" an expert who would say the physician met the standard of care whereas the plaintiff's expert offered his assessment independent of who hired him. In a deliberation in which the jury unanimously voted in favor of the plaintiff and awarded damages in the amount of $4 million, the following exchange occurred:

Juror 1: The two physicians that testified, the one blind fool sure had a lot of weight in my thoughts. The other was kind of a weasel.
Juror 2: [T]he attorney tried to make it look like, you know, the blind [missing]. I don't buy that. I think the guy was honest, you know, not be bought…he still looked like a little weasel.
Juror 3: Yeah, that was my thing. There was like 7 min of video where they were talking about how much this doctor was getting paid, you know, if he was biased, he wasn't hand-picked. He was picked by the defendant's attorneys, so that basically tells me he's biased, he's not coming up with opinions on his own, based on the facts, because he's getting paid.
Juror 2: He's not as trustworthy as the blind one.
Juror 3: I mean the other doctor didn't even talk about getting paid until like almost the end of his testimony, you know, and he only mentioned it once.
Juror 2: He was paid for an opinion plus or minus. Whether it was.
Juror 4: Yeah, either way.
Juror 5: Doesn't matter either way. He was getting paid.
[…]
Juror 4: I think both of them should have been blind.

Juror 5: Definitely. It would definitely be a great way for things to happen (Experimental Group, Deliberation 4).

This jury spent a significant amount of time reflecting positively on the blinded plaintiff's expert witness and negatively evaluating the nonblinded defendant expert witness. The jury concluded that all expert witnesses should be blinded. During other deliberations, juries came to the same conclusions about the expert witnesses.

IMPACT OF BLINDED EXPERT ON JURY DELIBERATIONS

The jury deliberations in this condition demonstrate the importance of the blinded expert to the juries' evaluation of the case. Jurors on a jury in which the majority of jurors voted for the plaintiff shared the perspective that the blinded expert witness was a major factor in their decision making.

Juror 1: I'm at the point where, they had a blind witness, you know, and that about wrapped it up right there. The other guy got paid off, you know, so I was laughing. He got paid $15,000.
Juror 2: I agree with, you know, this blind thing, and they had a great expert (Experimental Group, Deliberation 8).

There were occasional exceptions to the general trend of juries positively evaluating the plaintiff's blinded expert witness, however. For example, in one jury deliberation, a juror stated, "I understand the whole blind thing, but it didn't seem to be as big a deal to me as the plaintiff's lawyer wanted to make" (Experimental Group, Deliberation 7).

In summary, the presence of a blinded expert witness prompted every jury in the experimental group to evaluate the credibility of the expert witness testimony, particularly the prospect of compensation bias, while the potential bias of the expert witnesses was barely mentioned in the control groups. In the experimental condition, jurors found the plaintiff's blinded expert witness more credible, but despite this assessment there were not more jury verdicts in favor of the plaintiff than in the control condition. Seven juries hung, without reaching a decision in the time allotted, and there was one verdict each for the plaintiff and defendant.

Although the similarity in outcomes in the two conditions may simply be due to the small number of collective jury verdicts observed and the short amount of time for deliberations, the deliberations shed light on another possible explanation. Hans (2009, p. 81) has noted that culture affects the courtroom through social norms or "commonsense understandings of the law." American culture is highly individualistic (Finnemore, 1996) and emphasizes personal responsibility (Hans, 2009, p. 91), particularly when it comes to health (Minkler, 1999; Wikler, 2002). The cultural value of personal responsibility for one's health was in tension with the cultural preference for an objective expert offering an opinion on a scientific question (Douglas, 2009).

Discussions of Personal Responsibility

One dominant theme in deliberations in both the control and experimental groups was that of the plaintiff's personal responsibility for his health. In fact, discussions of personal responsibility were often used by jurors in the experimental group to explain why despite preferring the plaintiff's expert witness, jurors still voted against the plaintiff.

DEFINING PERSONAL RESPONSIBILITY

Throughout all deliberations, jurors conceptualized plaintiff personal responsibility as not delaying medical treatment, demanding medical tests, and seeking a second medical opinion, if necessary. Deliberations often emphasized that the plaintiff needed to take care of his own body. As one juror noted:

> I mean, it's your body, you need to take care of it. The doctor is there to facilitate help.... So that person would need to make sure that they came back and took ownership of their own health. And the doctor did act within his scope of practice, so there's not much we can do here. It's an unfortunate situation, but you know, you can't just attack your doctor when you're not taking care of yourself (Juror 3, Experimental Group, Deliberation 3).

Later in this deliberation, another juror followed up, specifying all the things the plaintiff should have done, but neglected to.

> Maybe the patient didn't really speak up. He didn't really say, "Hey, give me an MRI. It's my money, it's my back. Yo, give me an MRI." He didn't actually say that, and then there is the fact that he did wait 3 months before he actually came back and said, "Hey, my back is hurting really bad. Do you think there's something more wrong to it?"...Ok, did the doctor do everything to the patient physically that he should have done at the time when the patient described the symptoms to him and did the patient agree with that? Because we all have our own voice, I mean we can always disagree with or get a second opinion from a different doctor if we want. I mean that's our freedom. We can totally say, "Ok, I don't agree with you. I'm going to go out and get another opinion." Anybody can do that (Juror 4, Experimental Group, Deliberation 3).

In a different deliberation, although the jurors thought that the plaintiff's expert witness was more credible, they believed that the plaintiff was responsible for his injury because, in modern American culture, doctors are no longer solely responsible for their patients' health. According to one juror: "We used to have doctors who took care of you and took care of everything. That's not what a primary care physician is anymore. We have to take some responsibility for our health and welfare" (Juror 6, Experimental Group, Deliberation 6). In fact, some jurors saw patients following up with their doctors as being constitutive of adulthood.

PLAINTIFF PERSONAL RESPONSIBILITY VERSUS BLINDED EXPERT'S OPINION THAT PHYSICIAN COMMITTED MEDICAL MALPRACTICE

Juries often struggled with how to balance compelling evidence of malpractice (because they believed the plaintiff's blinded expert witness) with their view that the plaintiff was responsible for his own disability. This struggle can be seen in the following exchange.

> Juror 5: No, because it took him 90 days to come back and say it hurts.
> Juror 2: I totally agree with you, but I want to also say at that first examination he had neurological symptoms, and the standard of care that the expert said is, he should have been referred for imaging right then and there, and so I say that was medical malpractice. How much damage he's responsible for is mitigated by what the patient did, but I say it was malpractice.

Juror 3: That's why I agree. I was having a difficult time, you know, trying to figure out who should win this case because they're both at fault (Experimental Group, Deliberation 1).

The members of this jury spent a significant amount of time discussing how they did not like that the defense expert witness was paid for his testimony because it made him less credible. In the end, however, the plaintiff's personal responsibility was important to the group's decision.

Juror 5: So what about personal responsibility?
Juror 2: So in the personal responsibility realm, I reduced the money I would have given him.…So I agree with you about personal responsibility.…And I think he waited too long, and so I reduced the award to him based on the fact that I wasn't sure that his permanent damage was caused by the misdiagnosis at all. I mean, that's just a guess.…[B]ased on his not coming back sooner, I cut what I would have awarded him in half basically. I say he should have come in by 6 weeks, he should have been there. So, anything he experienced beyond that (Experimental Group, Deliberation 1).

Some jurors agreed with the plaintiff's expert witness that this was a case of malpractice, and so they voted for the plaintiff. However, they thought that the plaintiff bore some responsibility for his own injury for not following up with his doctor and therefore reduced the amount of damages awarded to him.

PLAINTIFF PERSONAL RESPONSIBILITY VERSUS MEDICAL EXPERTISE

Other jurors also refused to excuse the doctor for negligence, given that he was a professional with special expertise. As one juror noted, "I don't have that much faith in the masses of people to know what they should be doing and how to take care of themselves properly" (Juror 4, Experimental Group, Deliberation 6). Other jurors in a different deliberation also shared the sentiment that doctors have a professional responsibility to follow up with their patients.

Juror 4: I feel like it's the doctor's responsibility to find these things and not count on the patient to persist with the doctor.
Juror 3: But you have to take your own action, too.
Juror 4: But it's profession, you can't be getting things wrong.
Juror 3: Yeah, but it's your body that's hurting.
Juror 1: That's your primary care physician. You're supposed to trust him. That's the person you go to.
Juror 2: Well, who do you trust more than your doctor (Experimental Group, Deliberation 8)?

Another jury made similar arguments during their deliberation. The plaintiff was responsible because he should have known his own body and sought follow-up care and other treatment options. However, the doctor was responsible for knowing more than his patient because of his status as a professional with special expertise.

Juror 3: No way in hell would I wait for 2 months.
Juror 2: I understand. It seems both of them were remiss then.
Juror 1: Well, I think the patient takes a little responsibility for it.

Juror 2: Sure. Well, so does the doctor. Because the doctor has somebody who is a layman coming down for help and the doc is paid for his services…
Juror 5: But everybody knows their own body. And if you're in pain, you don't wait around. You say, "Ok, this is not working. Let's go to plan B" (Experimental Group, Deliberation 2).

THE ROLE OF PLAINTIFF PERSONAL RESPONSIBILITY IN JURY DECISIONS

One jury exempted the patient from responsibility for his injury. This jury decided for the plaintiff and awarded damages in the amount of $4 million. The jurors noted that the plaintiff was just following his doctor's orders and engaging in normal life activities.

Juror 2: I think it was wrong to put the blame on the patient for waiting so long.
Juror 3: All they did was blame him for that.
Juror 2: Can't blame him.
Juror 3: He was following doctor's orders. I mean, the guy has a life, he has to work. He has to save money. He has to pay his rent (Experimental Condition, Deliberation 4).

This exchange was far from typical, however. Most juries spent a great deal of time grappling with how much responsibility the patient had in causing his resulting disability, and how this should be weighed against the physician's expertise and subsequent responsibility to his patient and against the blinded expert's assertion that the physician had not met the standard of care.

Discussion

In the control condition, based on a typical trial with no blinded expert witnesses, juries did not spend much time evaluating expert witness testimony in reaching a verdict. This accords with what other scholars have found about the minimal impact of expert witness testimony on jury decision making (Devine et al., 2000). However, when jurors heard testimony from a blinded expert witness, all juries evaluated expert witness testimony. Although prior research found that juries tend to negatively evaluate the credibility of professional expert witnesses (Devine et al., 2000), this study demonstrated that hearing testimony from a blinded expert witness led to positive evaluations of this expert witness' credibility, results consistent with Robertson and Yokum's (2012) findings. In fact, in the experimental condition, jurors tended to describe the plaintiff's expert witness as the "unbiased" or "blind" expert (rather than the plaintiff's expert witness).

Although prior research found that the use of blinded experts resulted in more jurors deciding for the party employing these experts (Robertson and Yokum, 2012; Yokum and Robertson, 2015), our total of five jury verdicts provide only limited insight to collective outcomes at the jury level. In the experimental condition, the blinded expert witness stated that the doctor was guilty of malpractice, and the juries overwhelmingly viewed this expert's testimony as credible, but in the time we allotted for deliberations, most did not return verdicts at all. Although we are unable to say which way the juries would have resolved if allowed to deliberate until their natural conclusions, our qualitative data do show them torn by competing considerations, specifically the other facts of the case in the light of multiple cultural norms and values (March, 1987), including norms of plaintiff responsibility (Hans, 2009; Hans and Reyna, 2011).

The data demonstrate that juries value the objectivity of blinded expert witnesses as would be expected given norms of impartiality in scientific questions (Douglas, 2009), but every jury also debated the extent of the plaintiff's personal responsibility for his own health (Minkler, 1999; Wikler, 2002). In this mock medical malpractice trial, the cultural values of objectivity and personal responsibility were set in competition, because it was the plaintiff who employed the blinded expert witness. However, analysis indicates that the cultural value of personal responsibility for one's health, which became salient during the jury decision-making process, would have been a difficult barrier for the plaintiff to overcome, despite using a blinded expert.

This study had several limitations. First, the study design did not allow for eliminations of alternative explanations for the jury verdicts and the absence of an effect on verdict by condition. Because the amount of time permitted for deliberations was relatively short, we do not know whether more time would have allowed the juries to reach a different verdict, and if so, what the verdict would have been and why. It is also impossible to determine whether the lack of unanimous verdicts is an extreme effect of the small sample size (18 juries deliberating, 5 reaching decisions). Additionally, analysis of the deliberations also indicated that some juries did not fully understand the evidence presented or how the two expert witnesses' testimony conflicted, which may have impacted the results. Nonetheless, such variations in comprehension may exist in real juries as well.

Second, the data are from mock trials, so we do not know whether the observed phenomenon would be found during real trials (Devine et al., 2000). However, because of the high quality of this mock trial, the results of this study are likely consistent with what would occur in a real trial (Devine et al., 2000).

Despite these limitations, this analysis adds insight into how a blinded expert witness may impact jury verdicts. This study suggests that blinded experts will cause the jury to evaluate more seriously the expert testimony. If defense attorneys in medical malpractice trials use a blinded expert (something not tested in this study), then juries may return significantly more verdicts for defendants because the plaintiff's expert will be viewed as less credible, and the plaintiff will also have to overcome any perceived lack of personal responsibility. If plaintiff's attorneys in medical malpractice trials use a blinded expert witness, then our analysis indicates that they will nonetheless have to confront forcefully the issue of their client's personal responsibility for their own health in order to combat juries' unwillingness to excuse plaintiffs who are not diligent in managing their health even despite clear evidence of medical malpractice.

MOCK JURORS' ASSESSMENTS OF BLINDED EXPERTS IN CRIMINAL TRIALS

No studies have examined the effects of a blinded expert in a criminal trial, which involve different parties and a different burden of proof than a civil trial. In this study of a mock criminal trial, we hypothesized that the presence of a blinded expert would increase the likelihood of a favorable verdict for the party employing them. However, the effect may not be as strong as demonstrated by Robertson and Yokum (2012) because the type of evidence used in this experiment is widely considered to be "objective" (Dror, 2012) and because there is a higher burden of proof. Thus, our study was a strong test of the effect of blinded expert witnesses.

Our study also examined how attacks on nonblinded expert witnesses' credibility impact verdicts. We hypothesized that a strong attack on the objectivity of a nonblinded expert witness would interact with the use of a blinded expert witness to further increase verdicts for the side that used a blinded expert witness.

Methods

Stimulus and Design

We used a three-by-two between-subjects fractional factorial design, resulting in five conditions. One condition was the control, two experimental conditions tested the main effects of using a blinded expert, and two experimental conditions tested the interaction of the use of a blinded expert with an attack on the nonblinded expert's credibility. Each participant was randomly assigned to read one, and only one, of five written vignettes, which constituted the experimental conditions. Because we were studying differences in verdicts between four experimental conditions compared to a control group, we used a between-subjects design rather than a within-subjects design, which would be more appropriate if we did not include a control group or if we were testing how participants' verdicts changed from evaluating nonblinded expert testimony to later evaluating blinded expert testimony.

The vignettes were approximately 2000 word transcripts of a fictionalized criminal trial, designed to be read in approximately 15 min. Each vignette contained the same introductory information. Participants were informed that they would be reading from an abbreviated fictional trial, *State v. Matthew Smith*. Matthew Smith was accused of stealing three laptop computers from a university computer lab and of damaging the lab equipment. The evidence was a partial fingerprint found at the scene.

The trial sequence consisted of the judge's instructions explaining the duty of the jury, similar to the Revised Arizona Jury Instructions currently used in litigation. The judge's instructions were followed by opening statements from the prosecution and the defense, testimony of the prosecution's expert witness, cross-examination of the prosecution's expert witness, testimony of the defense's expert witness, and cross-examination of the defense's expert witness. The vignette ended with closing statements from each attorney. Each party's expert witness testified about the likelihood that the fingerprint belonged to the accused. This vignette constituted the control condition, in which there were no blinded experts.

To test the effects of using a blinded expert, in two experimental conditions, only the prosecution's expert witness was blinded, and in the remaining two experimental conditions, only the defense's expert witness was blinded. To assess the effect of attacks on credibility, the conditions with blinded expert witnesses were evenly divided between those with an adversarial attack on the credibility of the nonblinded expert witness for not being blinded, and those without an attack. In summary, the five conditions were the control (no blinded experts and no credibility attack); the presence of a blinded expert for the prosecution, crossed with the presence or absence of an attack on the nonblinded defense expert witness; and the presence of a blinded expert for the defense, crossed with the presence or absence of an attack on the nonblinded prosecution expert witness.

In the experimental conditions, the expert witness testimony included information about the blinding process. Testimony on direct examination detailed the process by which the expert was selected—through an intermediary without knowledge as to who hired him—as a way to enlighten the participants on this process and establish credibility for the expert. When experts were attacked during cross-examination for not being blinded, possible partisan and contextual biases and their implications on the witness' credibility were emphasized.

Instrument

After participants read the assigned vignette, they issued a verdict by responding to the question "Based on the instructions provided by the judge, do you believe that the prosecution has proved beyond a reasonable doubt that Mr Smith is guilty as charged?" They then wrote a 25 minimum word response explaining the reasoning behind their verdict. A demographic questionnaire followed.

Participants and Randomization

Participants were recruited via Amazon Mechanical Turk. Participants were informed that the study involved a mock trial, but they were not informed about the hypotheses to be tested and were unaware what experimental condition they were assigned. We recruited 486 people who consented to participate in the study, and after eliminating responses that were incomplete, contained incorrect answers for two quality assurance questions, and were completed in fewer than 5 or more than 35 min, there were a total of 444 participants, which were successfully randomized across the experimental conditions. Participants tended to be white, non-Hispanic, and have at least some college education.

Results

Descriptive Statistics

In the control condition with no blinded experts, 40% of participants found Mr Smith guilty. When the prosecution used a blinded expert witness, 34% of jurors voted guilty in the no attack condition, and 43% voted guilty in the attack condition; however, neither of these results was a statistically significant difference from the control condition.[3] When the defense used a blinded expert witness, 14% of jurors voted guilty in the no attack condition, and 18% voted guilty in the attack condition; the results of the blinded expert were statistically different from the control condition. The presence of an adversarial attack on the nonblinded witness did not have a statistically significant effect on the verdict in any condition.

Logistic Regression

We conducted a binary logistic regression to further assess our hypotheses about the effect of blinded experts and credibility attacks on juror verdicts. Our initial model contained our primary independent variables for presence or absence of a blinded expert witness and the presence or absence of an attack on the credibility of the nonblinded expert for not being blind. In addition, the model contained participants' demographic information. Regression results showed that the only significant variables were the presence of a blinded expert for

[3] While there is a nine-point difference in percentage of guilty verdicts between attack and no attack conditions within the blinded expert for prosecution condition, this is not a statistically significant difference.

the defense, which was consistent with our descriptive statistics. Because attack and demographic variables did not survive model selection, we ran a simpler model with only one independent variable: the presence or absence of a blinded expert witness. Because the experimental design successfully randomized participants into the five conditions, this more parsimonious model was an acceptable substitute for the full model.

Our study revealed that when the defense used a blinded expert witness, the odds of a not guilty verdict were 3.62 times higher than when the defense did not use such an expert ($p < 0.001$, 95% CI [2.02, 6.54]). There was no statistically significant effect for blinding the prosecution's expert witness.

Discussion

This study explored whether blinded expert witnesses impact juror verdicts in criminal jury trials and, if so, whether the effect was strengthened or weakened by attacking the credibility of the nonblinded expert witness during cross-examination. Robertson and Yokum (2012) have shown a significant bidirectional effect of blinded experts on civil mock juror verdicts and damage awards (Robertson and Yokum, 2012). We hypothesized that employing a blinded expert would increase the odds of a favorable verdict. Additionally, we hypothesized that attacking the nonblinded expert witness for not being blinded would further increase the odds of a favorable verdict for the attorney employing a blinded expert.

Our results showed that in the particular mock trial we tested, when the defense used a blinded expert witness, the likelihood of a guilty verdict decreased significantly. There was no effect for the prosecution. Additionally, there was no effect when an attack was made on the credibility of a nonblinded expert witness for not being blinded. In summary, our main hypothesis was supported in part, but our secondary hypothesis was not supported.

The qualitative data from the question that asked jurors to explain the reasoning for their verdict indicate that the likely reason there was no significant difference between the blinded expert for the prosecution and the control conditions was because of the high standard of proof in a criminal case ("beyond a reasonable doubt"). Although participants in the blinded expert for prosecution condition often noted that the prosecution's expert was more credible because of the blinding (e.g., "The prosecutor's expert was also blind to the facts of the case and yet he matched the fingerprint. The defendant's expert was not. The fingerprint had to be Mr Smith's."), many focused on the burden of proof. For example, one participant in the blinded expert for prosecution with no attack condition noted: "There is no way to know 100% that the fingerprints match. I just don't think that there is enough evidence to say it's been proven beyond a reasonable doubt."

This experiment cannot definitively determine whether the mock jurors were no more likely to convict when the prosecution used a blinded expert because of something about the role of prosecution (representing "the government") or because the mock jurors were responding to the high burden of proof. It may also be the case that there is something like a ceiling effect, which would account for the unidirectional results in this study. Perhaps with underlying case facts this weak, no more than 40% of jurors would ever convict the defendant regardless of the prosecution's use of a blinded expert. Alternatively, it is possible that prosecution witnesses just enjoy something of a government halo, such that they are not perceived to suffer from bias, for which blinding presents a solution.

One possible reason there was no support for our secondary hypothesis related to attacks on nonblinded experts' credibility is because of the limitations of our research design. Because we designed an experiment that took participants approximately 15 min to complete, we did not have the space to fully develop an attack on the nonblinded expert witnesses by describing all of the possible biases nonblinded experts have, and how blinding experts reduce those biases. Based on analysis of the qualitative data, participants seemed unable to distinguish between an attack on the nonblinded expert witness for not being blinded versus a typical attack on the expert during the cross-examination in the adversarial justice system.

This study has other limitations. First, because the stimuli consisted of written vignettes, there were limits to the ecological validity of this study (Breau and Brook, 2007). This experiment should be replicated in the field in order to confirm the effects of using a blinded expert witness. Additionally, there was no jury deliberation, and although there was an effect of a blinded defense expert witness for mock juror verdicts, interaction during deliberations may reduce, eliminate, or strengthen the effect for mock juries.

Second, this study only tested one type of scientific evidence in one criminal trial where the charges were burglary and vandalism. It may be that the effects of our independent variables of interest—blinded expert witnesses and attacks on the credibility of nonblinded expert witnesses—are different when another type of evidence is used (e.g., DNA) or when the charges are more serious (e.g., murder).

Third, we used an online convenience sample of MTurkers, and it may be that the differences between MTurkers and the population of potential jurors are significant enough that a random sample of potential jurors would have led to different findings (Berinsky et al., 2012). However, our descriptive statistics and regression analyses do not indicate that any demographic variables impact mock juror verdicts.

CONCLUSION

These studies addressed unanswered questions about the effects of blinded expert witnesses: How do they matter for civil jury deliberations, and do they have an impact on juror verdicts in criminal trials? In our study of civil mock jury deliberations, we found that juries perceive blinded experts as more credible, but that this did not translate into an observably different number of verdicts for the party employing them. Our study did show that case facts and cultural values compete with the preference for unbiased experts. In our study of a mock criminal trial, we were able to replicate an effect of using a blinded expert witness as shown in Robertson and Yokum (2012), although there was an important difference. While Robertson and Yokum (2012) demonstrated an effect of blinded experts for both parties in a civil dispute, we were only able to find an effect for the defense in a criminal trial. The effect is quite large, though, and therefore our research suggests that defense attorneys might have an interest in using blinded expert witnesses in criminal trials. It is important to note, however, that given the findings of the first study described, there may be differences between juror verdicts and jury verdicts. Future research should test the effects of blinded experts in real trials.

References

Berinsky, A.J., Huber, G.A., Lenz, G.S., 2012. Evaluating online labor markets for experimental research: Amazon's mechanical turk. Political Analysis 20, 351–368.

Breau, D.L., Brook, B., 2007. 'Mock' mock juries: a field experiment on the ecological validity of jury simulations. Law & Psychology Review 3, 177–192.

Commons, M.L., Miller, P.M., Gutheil, T.G., 2004. Expert witness perceptions of bias in experts. Journal of the American Academy of Psychiatry and the Law 32, 70–75.

Corbin, J., Strauss, A., 2007. Basics of Qualitative Research: Techniques and Procedures for Developing Grounded Theory, third ed. Sage Publications, Thousand Oaks.

Devine, D.J., Clayton, L.D., Dunford, B.B., Seying, R., Pryce, J., 2000. Jury decision making: 45 years of empirical research on deliberating groups. Psychology, Public Policy, and Law 7 (3), 622–727.

Douglas, H., 2009. Science, Policy, and the Value-Free Ideal. University of Pittsburgh Press, Pittsburgh, PA.

Dror, I., 2012. Cognitive bias in forensic science. In: Yearbook of Science & Technology. McGraw-Hill, New York, NY, pp. 43–45.

Finnemore, M., 1996. Norms, culture, and world politics: insights from sociology's institutionalism. International Organization 50 (2), 325–347.

Hans, V.P., 2009. Juries as conduits for culture? In: Engel, D.M., McCann, M. (Eds.), Fault Lines: Tort Law as Cultural Practice. Stanford Law Books, Stanford, CA, pp. 80–96.

Hans, V.P., Reyna, V.F., 2011. To dollars from sense: qualitative to quantitative translation in jury damage awards. Journal of Empirical Legal Studies 8 (S1), 120–147.

Ivkovic, S.K., Hans, V.P., 2003. Jurors' evaluations of expert testimony: judging the messenger and the message. Law and Social Inquiry 28 (2), 441–482.

Lee, T., 1988. Court-appointed experts and judicial reluctance: a proposal to amend rule 706 of the federal rules of evidence. Yale Law & Policy Review 6 (2), 480–503.

March, J.G., 1987. Ambiguity and accounting: the elusive link between information and decision making. Accounting, Organizations, and Society 12 (2), 153–168.

Minkler, M., 1999. Personal responsibility for health? A review of the arguments and the evidence at century's end. Health Education & Behavior 26 (1), 121–140.

Quick, O., 2011. Expert evidence and medical manslaughter: vagueness in action. Journal of Law and Society 38 (4), 496–518.

Robertson, C.T., 2010. Blind expertise. New York University Law Review 85, 174–257.

Robertson, C.T., Yokum, D.V., 2012. The effect of blinded experts on juror verdicts. Journal of Empirical Legal Studies 9 (4), 765–794.

Rubinstein, D., 1982. Individual minds and the social order. Qualitative Sociology 5 (2), 121–139.

Semelka, R.C., Ryan, A.F., Yonkers, S., Braga, L., 2010. Objective determination of standard of care: use of blind readings by external radiologists. American Journal of Roentgenology 195, 429–431.

Sperling, H.D., 2000. Expert evidence: the problem of bias and other things. Judicial Review 4 (4), 429–462.

Wikler, D., 2002. Personal and social responsibility for health. Ethics & International Affairs 16 (2), 47–55.

Yokum, D.V., Robertson, C.T., 2015. A Replication and Continuous Response Measurement Analysis of Blinded Experts in a Medical Malpractice Trial. Manuscript in preparation. James E. Rogers College of Law, University of Arizona, Tucson, Arizona.

CHAPTER

14

Disclosure Discretion and Selection Bias in Blinding of Experts

Christopher T. Robertson

James E. Rogers College of Law, The University of Arizona, Tucson, AZ, USA

OUTLINE

INTRODUCTION

Blinding is not ideal. It is a second-best solution. It begins with an acknowledgment that humans are imperfect, and they make decisions in situations that fail to bring out their best. In biomedical science, for example, if the assessors were truly indifferent to whether the investigational drug was effective, then there would be no cause to consider blinding them to which patients had taken the investigational drug. Similarly with expert witnesses, if experts are selected and appointed by the courts, then they may have none of the biases that come with the adversarial process. However, there may be practical, economic, cultural, and institutional reasons that make it infeasible to have truly independent assessors and experts.

In certain situations, blinding may satisfy those constraints while solving the problem of bias. I have argued that expert witnesses in litigation could be blinded in two complementary ways (Durand et al., 2014; Robertson, 2010). First, an intermediary would blind the litigant's selection of an expert, preventing attorneys from handpicking those that are most likely to be favorable. In this way, blinded selection solves for selection bias. Second, the intermediary

Blinding as a Solution to Bias
http://dx.doi.org/10.1016/B978-0-12-802460-7.00014-0

would filter the information provided to an expert in the crucial initial stage when she is forming an opinion, preventing the litigant from communicating with and incentivizing her in ways that would bias her opinion. In this way, blinding solves for what I have called affiliation and compensation biases (Robertson, 2010).

Attorneys might have incentives to use this mechanism, if such experts were more persuasive and thus yielded better outcomes from trials and settlements. Subsequent empirical work with mock jurors (Robertson and Yokum, 2012, and Chapter 13 in this volume) supports the hypothesis that blinding of experts could be a rational strategy for self-interested litigants. Thus, blinding can be an incentives-compatible solution to bias.

SELECTION BIAS AND THE ATTORNEY WORK-PRODUCT DOCTRINE

This conception of blinded experts was also designed to be institutionally compatible, in accordance with current rules and procedures of litigation in the adversarial American system. One such provision is Rule 26(b)(4) of the Federal Rules of Civil Procedure, which provides that the expert's opinions are generally not discoverable by the adversary. This doctrine is known as "attorney work-product" protection. The rationale for work-product protection is to permit an attorney to "assemble information, sift what he considers to be the relevant from the irrelevant facts, prepare his legal theories and plan his strategy without undue and needless interference," allowing him "to promote justice and to protect [his] clients' interests" (Hickman v. Taylor, 1947).

However, as Samuel Gross explains, "A party that takes full advantage of these [discovery] rules can 'informally consult' with a dozen experts (a non-discoverable activity), retain the five experts who seem most promising (a generally non-discoverable activity), and, finally, at the last available date, designate the one of these five whose opinion is most favorable as an expert witness" (Gross, 1991, p. 1143). In this way, lawyers can exploit a heterogeneity of opinions, regardless of whether the experts are honest or corrupt. Once favorable experts are found and retained, they are transformed from being perhaps 1 in 1000 outside the courtroom to 1 in 2 inside the courtroom.

Selection bias presents a fundamental challenge for the blinded expert protocol. It does little good to have experts render opinions in a pristinely blinded context, if the experts themselves can be handpicked before rendering an opinion, and even worse if the opinions themselves can be handpicked after they are rendered. Therefore, to get reliable expert opinions, blinding must solve for both of these vectors of bias.

The attorney work-product doctrine could be repealed, but that would be a radical change to the American litigation system, raising all sorts of other questions, and perhaps not feasible in the short to middle term. Alternatively, the rule could be revised to be inapplicable to blinded experts. However, that reform would make blinded experts much less attractive to rational litigants compared to traditional experts who would enjoy this protection. To commission a blinded expert opinion on a case would be tantamount to betting the entire case. For risk-averse litigants, and for attorneys who like to retain control over the cases they litigate, such an unprotected expert opinion may seem more dangerous than helpful. Indeed, the lack of uptake for court-appointed experts, who are similarly risky to litigants, suggests that such a blinding protocol would languish for lack of use.

Instead, suppose that blinded expert opinions continue to be protected, akin to unblinded expert opinions. Accordingly, litigants will retain some disclosure discretion. When a blind opinion turns out to be unfavorable, the sponsoring party can hide it. The litigant will have spent only the cost of the initial opinion (perhaps a few thousand dollars). At that point, the litigant can return to traditional litigation with hired-gun experts. The blind expert's opinion cannot hurt the sponsor; blinding is a no-risk proposition.

Does this concession to institutionalism and economic rationality sacrifice the integrity of the blinding protocol? Would it allow wealthy litigants to create a selection bias by simply paying for multiple blind reviews until a favorable one is found? This disclosure choice—after the opinion is rendered—may seem even more manipulative than the initial selection of which expert should render an opinion in the first place, because that preliminary choice is behind at least a thin veil of ignorance with regard to the resulting opinion. The attorney's ex post choice to hide a rendered opinion may seem clearly manipulative.

Disclosure discretion is in fact not inimical to justice, if it is complemented by an appropriate conditional disclosure rule. Under standard rules of litigation, if an expert's opinion is favorable to the sponsoring litigant, then the litigant can retain the expert for testimony. If the litigant does so, then she must disclose the expert and her report to the adversary, just as in normal litigation (Fed. R. Civ. P. 26(a)(2)). The report would include the intermediary's disclosures about how the blind procedure was implemented, which should then help persuade the fact finder that the blind expert is entitled to extra credibility. The adversary would test the robustness of the procedure, rendering the process largely self-policing.

To ensure that sponsoring litigants do not create an iterative selection bias by making multiple requests for blind opinions, I have proposed that litigants who do bring blind experts to trial would be required to disclose how many blind experts (on that same question) they consulted before selecting one (Robertson, 2010, pp. 209–210; Robertson, 2014, pp. 65–66). Indeed, this information would be included in the intermediary's report conveying each expert opinion. This feature is peculiar to the blinding protocol: normally, the attorney work-product doctrine protects litigants from disclosing the number of consulting (nontestifying) experts they hire. However, for the blind procedure, the disclosure requirement would arise from either of two existing exceptions to the work-product doctrine. First, an opposing litigant could assert an "at-issue" implied waiver of work-product protection: A litigant cannot claim a lack of selection bias while at the same time avoiding discovery into selection bias (United States v. Nobles, 1975). Alternatively but similarly, the potential for a litigant to claim falsely that there was no selection bias would arguably be an "exceptional circumstance" allowing discovery under the Federal Rules (Fed. R. Civ. P. 26(b)(4)).

Ex-ante knowledge of this disclosure rule would generally deter litigants from iterative use of the blind procedure. For litigants, there is little value in bringing favorable blind opinions if the litigants also must disclose the existence of one or more unfavorable blind opinions; the litigants would be better off resorting to traditional unblind experts or settling their cases. Indeed, if an initial opinion is unfavorable, then each subsequent attempt to secure an opinion will promise diminishing returns, both in the likelihood of the next opinion being favorable and in the persuasiveness to the fact finder of any favorable opinion received.[1] Thus, for simplicity, we can assume that each litigant will make at most one attempt to secure a blind expert (for each type of expert in a case).

In this way, the disclosure discretion becomes conditional. If a litigant *does not* bring a blind expert to trial, he need not disclose that blind expert's opinion or any other. We remain in the status quo of presumptively biased and unreliable experts. If a litigant *does* bring a blind expert to trial, he or she must disclose how many other blind experts he or she consulted on that question, so that the fact finder can assess the risk of selection bias. When it is deserved, the fact finder can thus rely more heavily on the opinions of blinded experts.

THE FALLACIES OF DISCLOSURE DISCRETION

Does this provision for a condition disclosure discretion, a form of negative selection, comport with the goal of achieving bias-free expert testimony? Does this discretion allow attorneys a more cumbersome mechanism to achieve the very litigation biases that blinding is supposed to avert? If the latter, the blinded expert reform is inadvisable, and fact finders who hear from a blinded expert should discount the testimony accordingly.

We are naturally wary when dealing with someone who has interests that are contrary to ours, and especially when that person has the power to hide valuable information from us. Used car salesmen fit this bill, showing potential buyers attractive features, but hiding the bad news. So, following classic work in this vein (Akerlof, 1970), let us call it the "lemons heuristic." Regrettably, lawyers in trial also fit that bill, and the behavior is not eliminated completely by the blind-expert protocol that I have proposed. Therefore, it would seem to be a reliable heuristic for jurors to discount the information—including blinded expert opinions—that they receive from lawyers in such situations. If produced by an attorney that has this incentive and this power, then fact finders may apply the lemons heuristic to disregard the testimony as tainted.

Like so many other useful heuristics, though, the lemons heuristic can lead us astray. In the protocol proposed here, the strategic behavior of the self-interested attorney can only hide or show information. Attorneys are unable to affect the content of disclosed information; they cannot make that information any less reliable than it was at the time that the expert rendered the opinion. That expert may be highly competent or a fool. The expert may be utterly corrupted by extraneous factors, or perfectly clear headed. But the attorney's subsequent decision *not to hide* the opinion does not make that opinion any better or any worse as a guide to the truth.

One may nonetheless insist: if the opinion had turned out to be unfavorable, then the attorney would have hidden it, so we cannot trust it. I have heard such responses from both layperson mock jurors, as well as from doctoral-level experts in judgment and decision making. Although the attorney consulting a blind expert is effectively limited to a single opinion

[1] Jonah Gelbach (2014) has suggested that this conditional disclosure rule may not altogether deter the use of multiple-blinded experts, under certain conditions where there are differential rates of false positives and false negatives, known to the fact finder. Nonetheless, there is agreement that the resulting disclosures would appropriately inform the jury, allowing them to discount the testimony accordingly (see Robertson, 2014).

(as discussed above), the objector's intuition may reflect a sense that the attorney can "pick and choose" among a set of *potential* opinions, and thereby produce a final opinion (a subset of one) that is unrepresentative of that hypothetical population of opinions. Is there a sense in which the lawyer's first, possibly lucky, draw allows something like a selection bias, making the one revealed opinion unreliable as unrepresentative of the set of potential opinions?

Let us examine this more closely. Under the blinding protocol, an unbiased expert is selected randomly and renders a blinded opinion, which is written and signed. Suppose that such opinions have reliability of 80% (or any other number). At that moment, the expert is essentially forcing the attorney and the jurors into one of two possible worlds: one (F) where the opinion is favorable to the lawyer and thus will be disclosed to the jury, and another (U) where it is unfavorable and will not be disclosed. For a juror, to discount the reliability of the disclosed favorable opinion is to cross between the actual world (F) and the counterfactual world (U), where there is an unfavorable and hidden opinion. However, there is no valid form of reasoning that allows such a connection. It is not as if the attorney can create a selection bias by selecting favorable opinions across the set of possible worlds. Instead, each world has only one opinion, which can be shown or not.

Let us call this line of thought the "counterfactual fallacy," because it involves a conflation of the actual and counterfactual worlds. To illustrate why this is a fallacy, another context may be helpful. Imagine that a chemistry lab designs a computer system to test the ambient air quality and then sound an alert every minute, either "P" for permissible or "D" for dangerous. The air test is not perfectly accurate, but it is unbiased and fairly reliable (again, pick any number, say 95%). During the first day of operation, the alarm signals for the first time, "D!" All the workers evacuate the lab, until the air can be cleared and work resumes. After a day or so in operation, the lab workers become tired of hearing a "P" alert every single minute. So the manager adds a line of code to the computer program, which functions like a simple filter: If the air test shows a permissible level, then it will not be reported. Only air tests that suggest dangerous concentrations of fumes will be reported, "D." Note that this filter is asymmetric (or biased) in its exercise of disclosure discretion, just like an attorney in court. After another few days of blissful silence, the alarm goes off, "D!" As the workers start to evacuate, just as they did before the P filter was implemented, one worker, Jim, stops and says, "If the air quality was P, then the filter would have hidden that information from us, so I will ignore this D, too." Jim's response is analogous to a juror who refuses to trust a disclosed blinded opinion. The other worker, John, disagrees, saying, "The filter has no effect on D readings. It only has an effect on whether P readings are reported to us. Therefore, I am treating this alarm just exactly as we did when there was no filter at all. I am evacuating!" Who is right? John. Who dies? Jim.

Here, the workers are analogous to jurors in a trial, and the alarm is analogous to a blinded expert witness (because the alarm is itself not biased). The filter that is biased toward hiding the P signals is analogous to the attorney for one side (D), who will refuse to disclose blinded opinions that are unfavorable to his client. The absurdity of Jim's ultimate refusal to trust the revealed D opinions because of the filter's exclusion of P opinions is equally applicable to a jury that refuses to trust a blind expert because of attorney disclosure discretion.

Although it may seem obvious in the lab example, I have found that this misconception is remarkably persistent when discussing the blind expert protocol. Another fallacy may be at work here, and it is a distortion of the Principle of the Adverse Inference (PAI). This is a valid principle providing that if a party *refuses* to disclose evidence that it has, then it is reasonable to assume that the evidence is unfavorable to that party.[2] For example, if a litigant burns a document rather than disclosing it as required by the rules of discovery, then the fact finder is allowed to presume that the document would have been unfavorable to the litigant. This principle has been recognized by the courts (e.g., Baxter v. Palmigiano, 1976), though it has exceptions when certain other institutional values are relevant (such as the Fifth Amendment right not to testify in a criminal proceeding). PAI validly uses the refusal to disclose evidence as an epistemic substitute for the evidence itself—we will infer the content of the missing evidence.

Notably, however, PAI is not symmetric; it tells us nothing about situations when favorable evidence *is* disclosed, but could have been hidden. In those cases, the fact finders do not have to substitute for the evidence, because they have it. For example, when a litigant waives a privilege (e.g., doctor–patient confidentiality) and testifies voluntarily, that waiver is not itself a reason to doubt the veracity of the testimony. Similarly for blinded experts, when an attorney exercises his discretion to disclose an opinion, the fact that the attorney could have instead hidden the opinion is no reason to doubt it.

SYSTEMATIC EFFECTS

One might nonetheless rejoin that the foregoing analysis is unpersuasive because it fixates on a single case, rather than considering a population of cases. Over such a body of cases, one might be concerned that disclosure discretion will systematically distort outcomes.

Table 1 is helpful to see this dynamic across a body of 10 cases (enumerated in the first column). For such an analysis, we have to presume that in litigation cases there is a truth of the matter—a fact that the fact finder is trying to ascertain (e.g., whether the defendant breached the standard of care). The second column stipulates that for these 10 cases, the reality is evenly split—half the time the plaintiff should win (Ps), and half the time the defendant should win (Ds). A P case, for example, is one where the defendant did breach the standard of care (if that is the question the expert is answering). The third column shows that a blinded witness will have some level of accuracy (say 80%) in saying the truth in the second column, and the errors are presumed to be unbiased (equally likely to call a P a "D" and a D a "P"). This is shorthand for an expert testifying that the plaintiff should win on the relevant technical question, when in fact the defendant should win (e.g., saying that the defendant breached the standard of care, when in fact he complied with the standard of care). Column 4 is the plaintiff attorney's disclosure discretion, which she or he exercises strategically: she or he reveals (R) the opinions when they are favorable to her or him and hides (H) them otherwise. The final column codes the outcome of whether the revealed opinion is accurate (A) or erroneous (E).

If the accuracy of the revealed opinions in the fifth column is worse than the accuracy of the opinions actually rendered in the third column, then the disclosure discretion would

[2] The principle of adverse inference can be abused in other ways, if, for example, the litigant has not actually refused to produce evidence in his or her control (Saltzburg, 1978). If the court refused to allow the litigant to introduce the evidence, or if the litigant has no access to the evidence, then a jury could wrongly infer that the evidence was unfavorable to him or her.

TABLE 1 Ten Hypothetical Cases with Disclosure Discretion

1. Suppose ten cases	2. Reality favors Plaintiff or Defendant 50% of time	3. Unbiased witness speaks truth 80% of time	4. Plaintiff Reveals if favorable, or Hides	5. Jury sees Accurate or Erroneous
1	P	"P"	R	A
2	P	"P"	R	A
3	P	"P"	R	A
4	P	"P"	R	A
5	P	"D"	H	–
6	D	"D"	H	–
7	D	"D"	H	–
8	D	"D"	H	–
9	D	"D"	H	–
10	D	"P"	R	E

have created a bias in favor of the plaintiff. In fact, however, we find that the 80% accuracy stipulated in the third column (shown as 8 out of 10 being true) is replicated as 80% in the fifth column after the attorney's disclosure discretion (shown as 4 out of 5 being accurate). This outcome is key: The effect of disclosure discretion is to deny the jury of a blinded expert from the plaintiff in cases 5–9. The disclosure discretion has not affected the accuracy of the disclosed opinions in cases 1–4 and 10.

Notably, this analysis does not depend on the reliability of blinded experts (80%) stipulated in the third column. It could be higher or lower, and that same rate will be replicated in the fifth column (though other numbers may require more cases to illustrate).

It is important, however, that the experts be unbiased, and that the population of cases (column 2) are evenly split. If the reality almost always favors one side (say D), then it will be rare for an unbiased expert to testify in favor of the other side (P). But when the expert does so, she or he will almost always speak falsely. The solution to this problem is, of course, the adversarial process, and specifically the adversarial use of blinded experts, one by each side. In any case, or set of cases, in which the truth favors one side, that side will be more likely to get a blinded expert to testify, and that testimony will be more likely to be truthful. Across the two litigants with opposite disclosure rules, the skew in cases cancels out.

DUAL, ADVERSARIAL USE

The foregoing has shown that disclosure discretion does not undermine the reliability of blinded experts. But we can say even more. Unlike the alternative regime of court-appointed experts, the blinded expertise protocol retains the best of the adversarial system. In a world where even independent experts may be fallible, the blinded expert protocol catches mistakes, raising accuracy dramatically.

Assume that both sides in a case would use the blinded expert protocol (as would be rational, assuming they do not disbelieve their own cases), and then disclose to the jury only opinions that are favorable to their side. In this situation, there are four potential outcomes:

1. both experts agree on the truth and one is disclosed to the jury,
2. the two experts agree on the falsehood and one is disclosed to the jury,
3. the two experts disagree (one true, one false) and neither are disclosed to the jury, or
4. the two experts disagree (one true, one false) and both are disclosed to the jury (Robertson, 2010, p. 217).

With this explication, we can see that disclosure discretion is actually harmless. Imagine the counterfactual for each of these four outcomes. In (4), nothing changes, because both parties are disclosing anyway. In (1) and (2), the forced disclosures would only reveal a second (redundant) opinion, which agrees with the first one, regardless of whether it is true (in (1)) or false (in (2)). And in (3), the forced disclosure would only reveal two disagreeing blinded experts, who together send no real signal to the jury.

It is important nonetheless to understand how adversarial use of the blind procedure outperforms a single court-appointed expert in terms of the accuracy of signals actually delivered. How often will fact finders be led astray by a blinded expert, when only one is revealed? The (3) and (4) categories of cases can be set aside, because they send no real signal to the jury. In (3), there is no blinded expert, and in (4) there is a battle of experts, both of whom are blinded. The jury will need to decide on the merits, just as they do with two hired guns. In this sense, the blinded expert has not helped them. The real action is in the ratio between the (1) and (2) cases.

My prior work has shown mathematically that, even with disclosure discretion, dual use of blinded experts improves the accuracy of revealed blind expert opinions dramatically compared to experts outside litigation or court-appointed experts (Robertson, 2010, p. 217). For example, consider again the assumption used above that a given sort of blind expert has 80% accuracy (a 20% error rate). The difference here is that two experts render an opinion on the same case, one hired by each side and subject to their disclosure discretion. In about two-thirds of the cases (68%), a single-blinded expert would be disclosed to the jury (categories (1) and (2)).[3] In 94.22% of those cases, the expert would be giving true testimony (with erroneous testimony in only 5.88% of cases) (Robertson, 2010, p. 217). In this way, adversarial use of the blinded procedure, even with disclosure discretion, actually improves on the accuracy of unbiased experts (here, from 80% to 94%).

This point bears emphasis because it responds most directly to the intuition that blinding with self-interested disclosure discretion is epistemically inferior to a truly independent expert, such as one that would be court appointed and not subject to disclosure discretion. In fact, the adversarial process can provide for *more accurate* outcomes.

[3] For the mathematically inclined: define (e) as the "ex-ante error rate"—i.e., the frequency of errors in blind experts' initial opinions. Define the "ex post error rate" (q) as the chance that, when both parties try the blind procedure, and only one blind expert is presented to the fact finder, that expert is incorrect. This relationship is given by $q = e^2 + (1-e)^2$. With our assumed initial (e) of 20%, the expected ex post error rate (q) is 5.88%. The frequency of signal rate (f) is the proportion of all cases in which both parties try the blind procedure and only one party secures a favorable opinion: $f = 1 - [e(1-e) + e(1-e)]$. See Robertson (2010), p. 254.

Of course, the adversarial process produces this outcome only through redundant testing (cf., Chapter 10, in this volume), and that testing creates additional costs, compared to an alternative system that provided only a single expert whose opinion was always disclosed. For an omnipotent social planner, the question would be whether these additional costs are an efficient expenditure given the increased accuracy they could buy. If so, then perhaps court-appointed experts should likewise be redundant. For those of us who are not omnipotent, but are nonetheless trying to solve bias in the real world, the adversarial use of blinding has important advantages.

IMPLICATIONS

The foregoing analysis has shown that blinding can square the circle. By allowing conditional disclosure discretion, blinding can make concessions to the institutional status quo and to the rational interests of litigants, which make the reform practicable. Nonetheless and perhaps counterintuitively, such disclosure discretion does not undermine the rigor of blinding as a solution to bias, at least in this domain.

Still, it is worrisome that the contrary intuitions may be very robust. Empirical research should investigate whether judges and jurors often succumb to the fallacy of thinking that voluntarily disclosed opinions are somehow less reliable, and test possible remedial measures to correct these misperceptions.

In courts, it would be problematic if attorneys who failed to secure favorable blinded experts were to impeach the blinded experts offered by their adversaries by suggesting that those experts were less reliable because of conditional disclosure discretion. Such a tactic would undermine the persuasive advantages that blinded experts rightly deserve. Because the exercise of disclosure discretion is in fact irrelevant to the reliability of the expert's opinion (Fed. R. Evid. 401), and is likely to simply confuse the fact finders (Fed. Rule Evid. 403), trial court judges should disallow such fallacious tactics of impeachment.

There are, of course, other bona fide bases on which a blinded expert can be impeached. A blinded expert may be incompetent. Another may fail to consider all the relevant facts when forming his or her opinion. The intermediary who selects the blinded expert may be utterly corrupt, allowing a selection bias and making blinding into a sham. These considerations (and others) are all fair game for investigation and cross-examination, when supported by a foundational showing. For blinding to be helpful to the fact finder, it depends on robust adversarial testing to ensure that its benefits are real in any given case. It should be held accountable for real problems, not on the basis of fallacious reasoning.

References

Akerlof, G.A., August 1970. The market for "lemons:" quality uncertainty and the market mechanism. Quarterly Journal of Economics 84, 488–500.

Baxter v. Palmigiano, 1976. 425 U.S. 308, 319.

Durand, D.J., Robertson, C.T., Agarwal, G., Duszak, R., Krupinski, E.A., Itri, J.N., Fotenos, A., Savoie, B., Lewin, J.S., 2014. Expert witness blinding strategies to mitigate bias in radiology malpractice cases: a comprehensive review of the literature. Journal of the American College of Radiology 11 (9), 868–873.

Gelbach, J.B., 2014. Expert mining and required disclosure. University of Chicago Law Review 81, 131–132.

Gross, S.R., 1991. Expert evidence. Wisconsin Law Review 1114–1232.
Hickman v. Taylor, 1947. 329 U.S. 495, 511.
Robertson, C.T., February 1, 2010. Blind expertise. New York University Law Review 85, 174.
Robertson, C.T., 2014. The problem of biased experts, and blinding as a solution: a response to professor Gelbach. University of Chicago Law Review 81, 61.
Robertson, C.T., Yokum, D.V., December 2012. The effect of blinded experts on juror verdicts. Journal of Empirical Legal Studies 9 (4), 765–794.
Saltzburg, S.A., 1978. A special aspect of relevance: countering negative inferences associated with the absence of evidence. California Law Review 1011–1060.
United States v. Nobles, 1975. 422 U.S. 225, 239–240.

SECTION V

BLINDING IN LEGAL INSTITUTIONS

Legal Applications of the Disclose-or-Blindfold Question

Saul Levmore
University of Chicago Law School, Chicago, IL, USA

Disclosure, that celebrated disinfectant of sunlight, is the conventional remedy for many questions in law and ethics, especially where there is a fear of bias. But an opposite strategy, of selective blindfolding, is hardly unknown. This book explores the choice between disclosure and blindfolding, or blinding as it is often labeled in scientific research and in the volume's title, and suggests that law and medicine (including biomedical research) have some things to learn from one another. In thinking about the contributions that deal with law, it is useful to think about the *extent* of blindfolding that is desirable in legal settings, and then also to keep an eye on the ways in which law might learn from other disciplines.

Consider the situation where someone screens job applicants and sends you four files; you are to interview these four candidates and choose the winner. If the screener is related to one of these candidates, should the screener disclose this fact to you, disclose and identify the candidate, keep you blindfolded (and perhaps disclose after you select the apparent winner, but before any actual hiring), or simply not send the related candidate in the first place? This is a question of single blindfolding and, even here, different workplaces and readers have different policies and reactions. It is not exactly a legal application, but rather one about evolved norms, contractual choices, and simple preferences. Nevertheless, and as is often the case, the law draws on norms, and norms generally make more sense when viewed against a background of legal rules. I doubt there is a single, winning response to this example of disclose-or-blindfold. There is heterogeneity in our perceptions of our ability to be unbiased; the advantages of disclosure, or even of having four rather than three candidates, are not the same across all jobs; and blindfolding may be more or less attractive depending on what is known about the screener. In short, responses are apt to be contextual, and this suggests that general conclusions and rules will be difficult when it comes to the choice between disclosure and blindfolding, or other strategies for dealing with potential bias.

Law deals with many similar (but hardly identical) situations. Thus, a judge is often presented with a case that has some bearing on the judge's own life. If a decision could directly affect the judge's financial interests, then the judge is instructed to recuse herself from the case. Indirect interests are left to the judge's judgment, and it is interesting that disclosure is virtually never used in this context, though it is the norm for academic writing. Thus, a judge's decision in a matter of tax law is likely to have some distant impact on the judge's own tax returns, but this is too trivial or impossible to control. A judge presented with the constitutionality of a statute regulating abortions is most unlikely to step aside (or disclose) on grounds that her own daughter might seek an abortion in the future. There is no blindfolding—for example, no attempt to have cases presented with the identities of the parties hidden by redaction, and no attempt to have abortion statutes ruled on by judges in another jurisdiction—and there is no opportunity to disclose and then proceed to decide the case with a direct conflict. In contrast, an academic would rarely recuse herself, but often disclose direct contact with a matter.

The importance of context is again clear. It seems unlikely that the answer one gives to the question about job candidates predicts the line one would draw where judicial behavior is concerned, even though both situations involve potential bias. The importance of context, or simply details, is even more obvious as we go farther afield. Imagine that one seeks a second opinion after a competent physician has recommended surgery. Would you advise blindfolding the second physician about the fact, identity, or advice of the earlier visit to another physician? And does the answer to that question cast any light on why we do not blindfold appellate courts regarding the identity of the lower-court judge whose opinion it reviews? A quick intuition is that while one case suggests the other, or makes it more interesting, there is little reason to think that a single approach works best in all these contexts.

When, however, the goal is not to intervene but rather to *discover*, there is unambiguous benefit in blindfolding, and the more the better—setting aside the transaction costs involved in the blindfolding itself. In most cases of intervention, blindfolding is a double-edged sword. When a second opinion is sought from a physician (or appellate court), for example, it can be efficient to disclose rather than to blindfold. The reviewer might better focus inquiry, because he knows something of the strengths and weaknesses of the first decision maker; he might also see ideas or conclusions in the first report (whether it is a physician's diagnosis or a lower court opinion) that never would have occurred to him, but that now seem correct. On the other hand, a blindfolded reviewer would be free of bias, and hundreds of studies support the notion that bias can be hard to overcome, no matter how much one is aware of the problem it presents. It is thus apparent that there are costs and benefits to blindfolding in this context.

In contrast, consider the process of evaluating eyewitness testimony through lineups in which the witness is asked to choose someone from a group of persons or photographs. This example of blindfolding, and ways in which it might be improved, is the subject of a chapter by Brandon Garrett. The witness is blindfolded, in the sense of choosing from a lineup, rather than being asked to identify or disclaim a single suspect. Accuracy is improved by double-blinding; the police officer who runs the lineup should not know which person is the actual suspect. It might even be nice to triple-blind; perhaps the suspect as well the others in the lineup could be brought into view without their knowing why they were there. If so, there would be less room for conscious or subconscious behavior on their part that might provide information, which is to say bias, to the witness. Note that when shuffled photographs are used, rather than live suspects and confederates, there is this sort of extra blinding in the testing of the eyewitness. In any event, the point is that all this blindfolding sacrifices no information. It is quite different from the situation where a patient seeks a second opinion.

The question of how to increase blindfolding and its bias-reducing benefits is never far from the focus of the chapters found here on law and blindfolding, in part because the authors choose applications where law is looking for facts rather than where it is intervening or reviewing decisions. It is as if we know that the decision maker would or should prefer to be freed from bias, by choosing the blindfold rather than more disclosure. Thus, the chapter by Karie Davis-Nozemack suggests that blindfolded review by the Internal Revenue Service could eliminate an institutional bias against information provided by whistleblowers. Further work would then be needed to discover just how unreliable (or superior) whistleblower information turns out to be. Shari Seidman Diamond's chapter provides an important counterweight by offering examples where more and better disclosure may be better than blindfolding, if only because blinded decision makers cannot help but make assumptions about facts withheld from them.

Other chapters dare us to imagine gains from further blindfolding. Yuval Feldman and Shahar Lifshitz help us see that law would often work better if those who are subject to it knew less about its content rather than more. Thus, debtors might (or might not) borrow from creditors, and then run their businesses more efficiently, if they did not know about the protections available under bankruptcy law should they eventually become insolvent. In Bertram Levine and Michael Johnston's chapter, we are encouraged to think about campaign finance schemes that keep politicians ignorant of the source of donations to them. The plan may not be entirely workable because a politician who votes for (or against) a project, and then finds an unusual amount of money pouring in during the following week, will have enough information to be biased in the future. Still, the idea of blindfolding contributions, as we do votes, is surely worth examining. Note that the donor pool might shrink if this blindfolding works, as examined in Jeffrey Skopek's discussion of anonymity and production incentives, but in the case of campaign contributions, the shrinkage might be desirable. Similarly, Sergio Puig suggests ways to eliminate "affiliation bias" in arbitration.

Judging by the chapters found here, the area of greatest promise for blindfolding in law is in the use of experts. Jeffrey Robinson, in the section of this anthology on forensic science, shows rather ingeniously how we might blindfold experts who review medical malpractice cases, by mixing these cases with others, and asking experts to review them all. Christopher Robertson forcefully argues that if we could simply blindfold litigants in their choice of experts, then we could safely maintain the adversarial system's convention of allowing litigants to be selective in the evidence they present. In other words, if you know that I have consulted five experts, and I present only the opinion of one in court, then you (and the jury) can still attach the correct weight to my expert's opinion. Your task is easier if I am blinded, and do not choose the five on my own, though in principle the idea could be extended even to the case of biased selection of experts.

In many areas of academic, cultural, and political life, blindfolding is now conventional and generally admired. Symphony orchestras hide auditioning musicians behind curtains; law professors grade exams that are numbered, rather than named and handwritten; and some journals work hard to anonymize, by denying referees any knowledge of the identity of the authors whose work they review. Double- and triple-blindfolding are less common, perhaps because each tier of blindfolding requires effort in its design and execution. Multi-blindfolding normally requires extra employees and institutional commitment rather than mere effort by an individual. The extra effort seems worthwhile where the information that is hidden is unlikely to be of independent value in decision-making. If it is of value, then disclosure might be preferable. Where that is not true, as in the suggestion (but hardly a recommendation) that appellate courts might be blindfolded regarding the identity of the judges whose work they review, it is often the case that we have no independent measure of the quality of the ultimate decision. In the absence of such a metric—perhaps typical of law and atypical of biomedical research (where third-party assessors or mortality figures can be fairly objective)—we can discover whether blindfolding matters, but we cannot normally conclude that it improves or worsens our interventions.

CHAPTER

15

Why Eyes? Cautionary Tales from Law's Blindfolded Justice

Judith Resnik, Dennis Curtis[1]
Yale Law School, New Haven, CT, USA

OUTLINE

Why do eyes have "legs"? What makes the trope of the blindfold—illustrated in Figure 1 by a 6-m aluminum version of the Virtue Justice, proudly displayed on a 2002 courthouse in Melbourne, Australia—resonate today? And what's wrong with thinking about judging with the image of a blindfold in mind? Why might "blinding" provide a helpful frame for some disciplines, but not serve unquestioned as the emblem of unbiased decision-making for law?

[1]All rights reserved. November 2015. Thanks are due to Aaron Kesselheim for inviting us to write for this volume; to the Yale Law Library, Fred Shapiro, and Michael Widener; to Allison Tait, who joined us in much of this research, to Reva Siegel for many discussions of constitutional theory; to Ruth Weisberg, Peter Goodrich, and Valérie Hayaert for exchanges about iconography, to Benjamin Woodring and Marianna Mao for able research assistance, and to Bonnie Posick for expert editorial oversight. This chapter is related to our book, from which we draw several of the images provided there. See Judith Resnik and Dennis Curtis, *Representing Justice: Invention, Controversy and Rights in City-States and Democratic Courtrooms*, New Haven: Yale University Press, 2011. In addition, parts of this discussion are derived from our essay, *Epistemological Doubt and Visual Puzzles of Sight, Knowledge, and Judgment: Reflections on Clear-Sighted and Blindfolded Justices*. In: P. Goodrich & V. Hayaert (Eds.), *Genealogies of Legal Vision*. Routledge: 2015.

Blinding as a Solution to Bias
http://dx.doi.org/10.1016/B978-0-12-802460-7.00015-2

FIGURE 1 *Lady of Justice*, William Eicholtz, 2002, Victoria County Court, Melbourne, Australia. *Photographer: Ken Irwin. Photograph reproduced with the permission of the sculptor and of the Liberty Group, owner and manager of the Victoria County Court Facility.*

The history of the deployment of blindfolds provides a cautionary tale that should give enthusiasts pause before embracing this imagery. As we detail below, the link between eyes and judgment goes back thousands of years. When European rulers, invoking God-given right, claimed the power to impose judgment, they used the tropes of light and sight, and they surrounded themselves with images of Virtues, including Justice, shown wide-eyed. Seeing all was equated with knowing all, and thus with the legitimacy of their exercise of power.

Blindness and blindfolds, in turn, denoted the impairments of the wicked and the misguided. From biblical and classical narratives through the Medieval period in Europe, obscured vision—bandaged, blindfolded, and blind—marked various Vices. Indeed, one of the first images known that puts a blindfold on the Renaissance Virtue Justice does so derisively.

That woodcut, *The Fool Blindfolding Justice* (Figure 2), appeared in a book, *The Ship of Fools* by Sebastian Brant, well-known throughout the seventeenth century (Brant, translated by Zeydel,

FIGURE 2 *The Fool Blindfolding Justice,* sometimes attributed to Albrecht Dürer, 1494, a woodcut illustrating Sebastian Brant's *The Ship of Fools,* printed in Basel, Switzerland. *Image courtesy of Beinecke Rare Book and Manuscript Library, Yale University.*

V. BLINDING IN LEGAL INSTITUTIONS

1944; Van Cleve, 1993). At least 70 editions were in circulation, and few modern readers "would suspect that the work was favorably compared by its contemporaries to Homer's *Odyssey*" (Ziolkowski, 2003, p. 98). In the chapter "Quarreling and Going to Court," Brant (1944, pp. 236–237) argued the "folly, blindness, error, and stupidity of all stations and kinds of men," jurists included. If blindfolded, judges would be unable to read codified law and would, wrongly in Brant's view, rely on customary law.

But as Europeans fought religious and political wars, claims of the singularity of knowledge, wisdom, and authority faltered. Further, expanding cities and growing economies required more dispute resolution, making vivid the challenges of controlling the quality of local judges. New technologies—the camera obscura,[2] the telescope, the microscope, and surgeries to remove cataracts—underscored that sight could be manipulated. Eyes could play tricks, and optical instruments could enhance sight.

As theorists from various disciplines became quizzical about the nature of knowledge, authority, God, and truth, the valence of open eyes denoting an uncomplicated receipt of knowledge shifted. With the rise of epistemological doubt, the blindfold came to be reconceived, on occasion, as a useful addition to Justice's attributes. By the eighteenth century, the blindfold on Justice had shed many of its negative connotations and was read, instead, as a symbol of law's commitment to rationality. Many commentators have reflected on the import of a blindfolded justice (Capers, 2012; De Ville, 2011; Robert, 2006; Sbriccoli, 2005; Loughlin, 2000; Robert, 1993; Kissel, 1984). The role of imagery in law more generally is explored in *Law, Culture and Visual Studies*, edited by Anne Wagner and Richard K. Sherwin (2014).

Various explanations have been offered for this polyvocal symbol's new import. Blindfolds were said to denote incorruptibility, even-handedness, and constrained reasoning. The rise of the ideology of judicial independence and separation of powers added another justification, that the blindfold represented judges' detachment and political insulation from the governments that empowered them.

During the last two centuries in the United States, the trope of blindness has been central to debates about the federal constitution's obligations to remedy the effects of slavery and other sources of inequality. "Color-blind" is the claim made on behalf of formal equality's proponents, approving of lawsuits by whites arguing that race may never be used as a factor when admitting students to schools or allocating jobs. This anti-affirmative action, "color-blind" approach rejects the relevance of America's history of slavery that inscribed racialized hierarchies for blacks and whites. The counterargument is that willful blindness ignores the social impact that race has on individuals' and communities' lives.

The malleability of the trope of blindness is one reason to be skeptical of its capacity to instruct theorists and scientists about how to construct wise, evaluative methods. In law, the focus on what the law can "see" deflects attention from the radical transformations over the centuries in the functions and obligations of courts in democracies. We argue not only that eyes have had a remarkably long run in Justice iconography and in legal debates, but also the

[2] The camera obscura was in wide use by 1550; debate exists about how much earlier comparable devices existed, which artists had access to them, and their import. See Michael John Gorman, "Art, Optics and History: New Light on the Hockney Thesis", *Leonardo* 36, 2003, pp. 295–301, at 296.

anachronism and limitation of emphasizing eyes (with or without obscured vision) in discussions of justice's fairness.

Twentieth-century modernism fractured the single-vantage point central to Renaissance perspective. Postmodern critical theory insists on a multiplicity of legitimate points of view and on the interdependencies of viewer and viewed. Democratic adjudication locates the public as comprised of participatory observers, authorized to know and to critique the bases for judgment. Social and political movements have demonstrated the capacity to ascribe new meanings to old constitutional texts. Blindfolds, when draped on women's statues, may serve to identify buildings as places of law but no longer suffice to reference the relationship of judges and the public in democratic orders, the complexities of how legal judgments are made, or the wisdom of the results.

IMPARTIALITY—OR IGNORANCE, CAPRICE, AND OBSTINACY

As Figure 1 illustrates, blindfolds are today affixed to Justice images in celebration of adjudication's virtues. Indeed, in many discussions of Justice iconography, the female personification of Justice is often assumed to have always been depicted with a blindfold; the blindfold, in turn, is assumed to mark the stance appropriate for wise and constrained judgment.

Yet the blindfold is a relatively late addition to Justice iconography and, as noted earlier, its valence has changed over time. Clear-sighted authority was once the norm, as ancient cultures praised the sun for illuminating the world. The theme of sight as knowledge and power can be traced from descriptions of the "eye" of Egyptian gods (Pinch, 2002; Hornung, 1992) through Christianity's celebration of "sol justitiae": that Christ, the God of Light, will "appear ablaze when he will judge mankind" (Strauss, 1972, p. 52). Albrecht Dürer's rendition (Figure 3), c.1499, makes the point by portraying a wide-eyed and haloed Christ-Justice with scales, sword, and lion.

Canonical texts repeatedly cast light as representing truth, darkness as misguidedness, and blindness as disability or punishment.[3] The sighted were *informed* and the blind *limited* in various ways. In both the Jewish Bible and the New Testament, blindness exemplified ignorance, abandonment, or impaired judgment. For example, *Isaiah* 56:10 states, "Israel's watchmen are blind, all of them unaware. They are all dumb dogs who cannot bark." *Psalms* 9:17 reads, "They rush blindly down to Sheol, the wicked." *Matthew* 23:17 states, "Blind fools! Which is the more important?" And 2 *Corinthians* 4:4 states, "Their unbelieving minds are so blinded by the god of this passing age, that the gospel of the glory of Christ, who is the very image of God, cannot dawn upon them and bring them light."

Blindness precluded a person's entry into holy areas, and blind animals were not to be used as offerings. *Leviticus* 21:18 reads, "No man with a defect shall come, whether a blind man, a lame man, a man stunted or overgrown." *Leviticus* 22:22 commands, "You shall present to

[3] For the biblical quotations we used an English database at Yale at Jeeves Library, which includes many versions. Unless otherwise indicated, quotations come from *The New English Bible with the Apocrypha*, edited by Charles Harold Dodd, Oxford and Cambridge: Oxford and Cambridge University Presses, 1970.

FIGURE 3 *Sol Iustitiae*, Albrecht Dürer, 1499–1500. *Copyright, Yale University Art Gallery.*

the Lord nothing blind, disabled, mutilated, with running sore, scab, or eruption, nor set any such creature on the altar as a food-offering to the Lord." Further, to be struck blind was a form of punishment: *Job* 11:20 states, "Blindness will fall on the wicked."

Indeed, the patriarch Isaac was deceived because blind, he bestowed his blessing on his son Jacob instead of his elder son Esau (*Genesis* 27:1–38). And, as *The Book of Job* (9:24) explains, "The land is given over to the power of the wicked, and the eyes of its judges are blindfolded." Jesus himself was made sport of—blindfolded, beaten, and mocked. "Some began to spit on him, blindfolded him, and struck him with their fists" (*Mark* 14:65). *Luke* 22:63 states, "They beat him, they blindfolded him, and they kept asking him, 'Now, prophet, who hit you?'"

Moreover, in several instances, faith cured those who were blind. "The Lord restores sight to the blind and straightens backs" (*Psalms* 146:8). "Then they brought him a man who was possessed; he was blind and dumb; and Jesus cured him" (*Matthew* 12:22).

Exceptions exist, and this brief linear account does not purport to capture all the nuances and variations. Sightless seers dot epics, as poets famously provide examples—such as Homer and Milton—of such visionaries. According to Plato, blindness was Homer's punishment for slandering Helen of Troy (Plato, *Phaedrus*, translated by Waterfield, 2002). Milton wrote his epic poem *Paradise Lost* after becoming blind (Milton in Carey, 1971). Thus, the "bard is expected to be blind" (Kononenko-Moyle, 1979–1980, p. 521).

Yet generally, blindness was a punishment, and the blind portrayed as objects of pity or "endowed with terrifying power"; before the last few centuries, blindness was "indissolubly linked with distress" (Barasch, 2001). Two famous Medieval images, depicting Synagoga and Ecclesia, make this point vividly. The two seen in Figure 4 were carved around 1230 and remain in place on the south portal of the Strasbourg Cathedral in France.

Synagoga, "a purely Christian creation," signified the Old Testament (and sometimes Jews in general) (Camille, 1989), while Ecclesia stood for the New Testament (and at times Christianity). Unlike Ecclesia, modeled as a regal woman, ramrod-straight, crowned, and sharp-eyed (the "bride of Christ"), Synagoga was shown with her eyes covered by a blindfold, slumped, and holding a broken rod. Blindfolded, rather than blind, Synagoga was obstinate, refusing (rather than unable) to see the "light of redemption" (Barasch, 2001; Rowe, 2007; Bongiorno, 1968).

Synagoga was not the only iconic embodiment of the harm blindfolds imposed. Renaissance imagery often placed a blindfold on Eros to mark the foolishness and confusion of love (Wind, 1968; Panofsky, 1962). The image of Fortuna was shown blindfolded to denote irrationality, randomness, and indifference to human suffering (Ripa, 1758–1760, republished in Maser, 1971; Ripa, 1611, republished by Garland, 1976; Ripa, 1618, republished by Fògola, 1988). In short, as Erwin Panofsky (1962) argued, aside from a valorized blindness in Homer and of the blindfolded Justice herself (a "humanistic concoction of very recent origin"), blindness was "always associated with evil."

REVISING THE VALENCE OF THE BLINDFOLD

Yet beginning in the sixteenth century, obscured sight began to gain the opposite connotation, as imposing a positive, disciplinary constraint on the act of judgment. That new proposition can be glimpsed in a famous compilation of images, the 1593 *Iconologia*

FIGURE 4 *Synagoga and Ecclesia*, c.1230, Cathedral, Strasbourg, France. *Photo copyright: Foto Marburg/Art Resource, New York, NY.*

of Cesare Ripa,[4] which was subsequently printed in many editions and which shaped a shared visual vocabulary for centuries for European artists and viewers (Gombrich, 1948).

Ripa gave directions on how to depict various Virtues and Vices and, for the most part, bandages and blindfolds continued to iterate bad traits. Ripa posited blindfolds for Fortuna to denote its arbitrariness, for Eros to reference the foolishness of emotions, and for Ambition to suggest its indiscriminate force (Ripa, 1758–1760, republished in Maser, 1971; Ripa, 1611, republished by Garland, 1976; Ripa, 1618, republished by Fògola, 1988). The misguidedness of Error was drawn in one edition as a man cloaked and with covered eyes, accompanying Ignorance (Ripa, 1644). Injustice ("Ingiustitia") is portrayed in both text and image with one blind eye in Ripa (1611, republished by Garland, 1976, 250). Later editions shift the imagery to other attributes used to denote justice gone awry—by showing tablets, scales, and scrolls broken.

Clear-sightedness, in turn, was valorized. Ripa (1611, republished by Garland, 1976) offered directions for seven versions of the Virtue Justice, and six were described as open-eyed. The seven Justices did not, however, reappear in all Ripa editions. In Ripa, *Padua–1618*, for example, only two ("Justice According to Aulus Gellius" and "Justice") are mentioned. Moreover, slightly different descriptions of various Justices can be found.

By the eighteenth century, Justice iconography was compressed into a narrower range that included blindfolds. The Ripas of that era offer one description of and one image for Justice. In the 1758 Hertel edition, Justice "is blindfolded, for nothing but pure reason, not the often misleading evidence of the senses, should be used in making judgments" (Ripa, 1758–1760, republished in Maser, 1971). Richardson's 1779 edition retains the blindfold and notes, "She is sitting with a bandage over her eyes. The white robes and bandage over her eyes, allude to incorrupt justice, disregarding every interested view, by distributing of justice with rectitude and purity of mind, and protecting the innocent" (Ripa, 1779, republished in Richardson, 1976).

In one edition, Ripa's "Justice According to Aulus Gellius" (Figure 5) was shown with "acute vision"; she wore a necklace where "an eye is portrayed" because "Plato said that Justice sees all and that, from ancient times, priests were called seers of all things" (Ripa, 1625).

[4] A word of explanation is needed as to the different Ripas and their illustrations. The first, original 1593 Ripa had no drawings, and scholars do not believe that Ripa had direct involvement in the drawings used in subsequent editions. See Stefano Pierguidi, "Giovanni Guerra and the Illustrations to Ripa's Iconologia", *Journal of the Warburg and Courtauld Institutes* 61, 1998, pp. 158–175, at 167, 174–175. Thereafter, more than 20 editions in about a dozen languages were published. We rely on Cesare Ripa, *Iconologia*, Padua: Pietro Paolo Tozzi, 1611; New York and London: Garland Publishing, 1976 (hereinafter Ripa, *Padua–1611*); Cesare Ripa, *Iconologia*, vols 1 & 2 (Padua: Pietro Paolo Tozzi, 1618), Torino: Fògola Editore in Torino, 1988 (hereinafter Ripa, *Padua–1618*); Cesare Ripa, *Iconologie*, edited by I. Baudoin, Paris: Chez Mathieu Guillemot, 1644 (hereinafter *French Ripa–1644*); Cesare Ripa, *Iconologia, of Uytbeeldingen des Verstands*, Amstelredam: Dirck Pietersz. Pers, 1644; Cesare Ripa, *Baroque and Rococo Pictorial Imagery: The 1758–60 Hertel Edition of Ripa's "Iconologia" with 200 Engraved Illustrations*, edited by Edward A. Maser, New York: Dover Publications, 1971 (hereinafter Ripa, *Maser Edition*); Cesare Ripa, *Iconology London 1779 in Two Volumes by George Richardson*, New York & London: Garland Publishing, 1976 (hereinafter Ripa, *Richardson Edition*). The Richardson edition was the "very last iconology in the tradition of Ripa." Another important source, not detailed here, is the 1531 *Emblematum liber* of Andreas Alciatus. See Andreas Alciatus, *The Latin Emblems: Index Emblematicus*, vols 1 & 2, edited by Peter M. Daly, Toronto: University of Toronto Press, 1985 (unpaginated edition with numbered emblems); Thomas Fröschl, "Republican Virtues and the Free State: Conceptual Frame and Meaning in Early Modern Europe and North America", *Iconography, Propaganda, and Legitimation*, edited by Allan Ellenius, Oxford: Clarendon Press, 1998, pp. 255–275, at 263. See also Michael Bath, *Speaking Pictures: English Emblem Books and Renaissance Culture*, London: Longman, 1994, pp. 259–262.

FIGURE 5 *Justice According to Aulus Gellius*, Cesare Ripa, *Iconographia* (Padua, Paolo Tozzi Edition, 1625) at 201. *Reproduced courtesy of the Rare Book Collection, Lillian Goldman Law Library, Yale Law School.*

The one Justice whose vision was obscured—"Worldly Justice"—was described as "dressed in white with bandaged eyes; in her right hand she holds a bundle of rods, with an axe, and in her left hand a fiery flame, together with these things she has an ostrich at her side, and holds a sword and scales.... She is wearing white because judges should be without the stain of personal interest or of any other passion that might pervert Justice, and this is also why her eyes are bandaged—and thus she cannot see anything that might cause her to judge in a manner that is against reason.[5,6]"

[5] This passage can be found in both the 1611 (at 203) and the 1618 (at 188) editions from Padua under the description of Justice ("Giustitia").

[6] At the literal level, Ripa may have drawn on an emblem from Alciatus; while not mentioned in connection with blindfolded Justice, Ripa invoked Alciatus for other attributes of Justice—a river and a pillar, purportedly denoting purity and uprightness and therefore appropriate for law and justice. Ripa may also have used the same sources as Alciatus—the "Egyptian" allegory "transmitted by Plutarch and Diodorus Siculus in which the chief justice was shown eyeless in order to illustrate his impartiality, while his colleagues had no hands with which to take bribes." Ripa, *Padua–1611* at 202.

Why did the blindfold—but not ostriches, also mentioned in that description—gain and retain currency? What political and intellectual currents supported its repeated deployment, and how do those rationales inform choices about valorizing obscured vision today?

Diverse answers come from scholars who have analyzed the introduction of the blindfold into justice iconography. Peter Goodrich (2013) argues that the blindfold references divine justice, a power that viewers are enjoined from seeing. Others link the blindfold to the rise of new city-states and conflicts over authority, producing complex and ambivalent attitudes toward law (Robert, 2006). With more judges came fears of corruption and struggles for power; blindfolds could mark efforts to control judges (Strauss, 1986; Davis, 2000).

Philosophy and theology have also been enlisted. Descartes wrote of the desirability of escaping the confusion of the senses, and Lutheran theology posits that truth came from inner light (Descartes, translated by Cottingham, 1986).[7] The relevance of the Reformation is proposed by Martin Jay, who thought that the "Hebrew interdiction of images" was a way to "resist what Augustine had famously called the 'lust of the eyes'" and to explain the blindfold as representing "neutrality" (Jay, 1999; Jacob, 1994, 1995; Cover et al., 1988).

But hundreds of representations of Justice belie reading the blindfold as regularly valorized during these centuries. Open-eyed Justices were commonplace throughout the European continent (Resnik and Curtis, 2011). Indeed, when blindfolded Justices appeared in town halls, especially in Northern Europe, accompanying inscriptions often added written explanations, such as that Justice had to treat disputants evenhandedly.

THE PHILOSOPHY AND PSYCHOLOGY OF SIGHT: A BLIND MAN "MADE TO SEE"

The Enlightenment brought other justifications for rethinking the relationship of sight to knowledge and authority. John Locke's famous inquiry illustrates then-new puzzles about the relationship of the senses to knowledge. Locke (1975, p. 146) asked: "Suppose a Man born blind, and now adult, and taught by his touch to distinguish between a Cube, and a Sphere of the same metal, … be made to see." Locke identified sight as "the most comprehensive of all our Senses, conveying to our Minds the Ideas of Light and Colours, which are peculiar only to that Sense" (id.). Locke's response was that a person lacking the experience of seeing the cube and the sphere could not, at first sight, make the judgment required to distinguish and name the two objects. Locke also distinguished between "primary qualities" that he posited exist independent of a person's observations (shape, for example) and "secondary qualities" that are artifacts of observation (color, for example) (Rickless, 1997; Curley, 1972).

[7] See Otto Kissel, *Die Justitia: Reflexionen über ein Symbol und seine Darstellung in der Bildenden Kunst*, München: Beck, 1984, at 90, nn. 155 and 156. Kissel noted that Luther wrote of the "love of truth" to bring "light" but also wrote that a judge "must be blind, his eyes and ears covered." *Id.* at 90. Luther wrote: "Therefore he must be quite blind, have his eyes and ears closed, neither see nor hear, but go straight forward in everything that comes before him, and decide accordingly." Martin Luther, "The Large Catechism", *Triglot Concordia: The Symbolical Books of the Ev. Lutheran Church*, translated by F. Bente and W. H. T. Dau, St. Louis: Concordia Publishing House, 1921, p. 565. Yet Luther can also be quoted as stating: "[W]hat kind of judge would he be who should blindly judge matters which he neither heard nor saw?" Martin Luther, "Secular Authority: To What Extent It Should Be Obeyed", in *Martin Luther: Selections from His Writings, edited by John Dillenberger,* New York: Anchor Books, 1962, p. 384.

The question of what a newly sighted person would *know* is called the "Molyneux problem," named after Locke's friend William Molyneux, who "put to him" that issue in 1688.[8] The question continues to prompt inquiries about, in today's terms, the rapidity of "cross-modal" transfers when knowledge moves from one sense to another (Held et al., 2011).

The Molyneux problem was not only hypothetical. Eighteenth-century physicians were beginning to do surgery to alleviate the blindness caused by cataracts.[9] Moreover, blindness became a "subject of intense cultural interest" (Paulson, 1987). In 1749, Diderot published his *Lettre sur les aveugles à l'usage de ceux qui voient* (*An Essay on Blindness in a Letter to a Person of Distinction*),[10] in which he deconstructed (to borrow a term from a later age) Molyneux's problem and Locke's response.

Diderot rebutted the idea that the blind lacked knowledge from experience. He argued instead that those who were blind, like those who see, had understandings informed by their own good sense ("bon sens") (Morgan, 1977), even if blindness could inhibit the ability to provide names ("denomination") (Paulson, 1987) for objects. Diderot posited that preparations before an eye operation would be relevant to what was reported by the person thereafter, and he disentangled the question of what could be seen immediately (he thought the answer was a multitude of confused sensations) from the question of whether a blind person would be able to distinguish among shapes by naming them (Morgan, 1977).

SEPARATING POWERS, COLOR-BLIND CONSTITUTIONS, AND VEILS OF IGNORANCE

New norms for judges offered yet another reason to valorize the blindfold. Recall that the roles of judge and ruler were once understood to be deeply and appropriately intertwined. Many allegorical stories, regularly displayed in rooms where judgments were rendered or the sentence of death imposed, taught norms of judicial *subservience* to rulers and their law.

The idea that judges were deployed by states but were somehow *independent* of state power came through profound changes in political theory, exemplified by Montesquieu's proposition that "there is no liberty, if the judicial power be not separated from the legislative and executive" (Montesquieu, translated by Nugent, 1752, p. 216). A yet more radical notion was that judges have the power to sit in judgment of the state, their own employer. A few famous "folktales of jurisdiction," as Robert Cover called them, can be found in historical narratives

[8] See William R. Paulson, *Enlightenment, Romanticism, and the Blind in France*, Princeton: Princeton University Press, 1987, pp. 21–23; Michael J. Morgan, *Molyneux's Question: Vision, Touch and the Philosophy of Perception*, Cambridge: Cambridge University Press, 1977. Molyneux, a member of the Irish Parliament and the author of *The Case for Ireland* (1698) and *Dioptica nova* (1692), lived from 1656 to 1698. His interest in optics may have come in part because his wife was blind. Marjolein Degenaar, *Molyneux's Problem: Three Centuries of Discussion on the Perception of Forms*, translated by Michael J. Collins, Dordrecht: Kluwer Academic Publishers, 1996, pp. 17–18, 23, 133.

[9] In 1728, William Cheselden, a surgeon, published an article describing an account of his operation on a young man who had had cataracts. Degenaar, *Molyneux's Problem* at 52.

[10] Denis Diderot was born in 1713 and died in 1784. The essay "ends with a poetic affirmation of our ignorance of ultimate reality. For this Diderot was put into a dungeon in Vincennes." Morgan, *Molyneux's Question* at 27–28. Morgan provided an English translation of Diderot's "letter" at 31–58, and we use his translation for our references to Diderot's argument.

in which brave judges stood their ground against threats of tyrannical kings; those judges insisted on their own authority to "speak truth to power,"[11] even at their own peril.

Not until the Enlightenment did the idea become widespread that judges were always to be insulated from such power, as well as authorized to overturn decisions of other branches of government. Building on the English Act of Settlement of 1701, the U.S. Constitution of 1789 (Article III, Section 1) required that judges, once appointed, were to keep their jobs "during good Behaviour" and to receive salaries that could not be diminished while they served. These new understandings of government produced another explanation for the blindfold—that it marked not only judicial neutrality toward the parties, but also that judges were untethered from the government that created their jurisdictional authority and paid their salaries.

The desirability of obscured sight retains its currency, as exemplified by John Rawls' (1971) book, *A Theory of Justice*. Rawls (1971, pp. 12, 19) famously argued that principles of justice had to be developed behind a "veil of ignorance" that put the decision maker in an "original position," without "knowledge of those contingencies which sets men at odds and allows them to be guided by their prejudices." If one did not know one's own class, social status, abilities, intelligence, life plan, generation, or the surrounding social, economic, or political order, one would not know the consequences of a rule. Such leveling and equality created the possibility for "a unanimous choice of a particular conception of justice," (Rawls, 1971, p. 12) freed from knowing the impact on particular, situated individuals.

The tropes of sight and blindness have also become central to intense constitutional debates in the United States. More than a hundred years ago, in 1896, when protesting the Supreme Court's approval of segregated railway cars, Justice John Marshall Harlan spoke of the "eye of the law" as he insisted that the United States was a place without caste; the country had no "superior, dominant, ruling class of citizens" because "Our Constitution is color-blind."[12]

At that time, "colored" referenced dark skin—reflected in the name the National Association for the Advancement of Colored People, chosen in 1909 for an organization devoted to the rights of blacks (Meier and Bracey, 1993). Similarly, in 1925, when twelve black lawyers met in Des Moines, Iowa and formed the National Bar Association, they explained they were a group of "practicing attorneys of the Negro race" (Jackson and Gordon, 1999, p. 16)[13] aiming to eradicate the second-class citizenship of "the American of Color" (Jackson and Gordon, 1999; quoting President Thurman L. Dodson).

Only much later, in part as critical theorists explored the social constructions solidifying the relevance and content of race, did the idea develop that everyone has a "color"—whether white, black, or part of a "rainbow" in between. Toward the end of the twentieth century,

[11] Cover explored the maxim "The king does not judge and we do not judge him." Mishnah Sanhedrin 2:3, quoted in "Folktales of Justice" at 183–184. As Cover related this "folktale," Simeon ben Shetah, Chief Judge of the Sanhedrin, called on King Yannai to testify in a case involving the King's slave. The King replied that he would do so only if all of the 71 judges would so command him. The judges other than Simeon ben Shetah were intimidated by the King and backed away from demanding that he testify. After the King left, Simeon called on God to call the weak judges to account; the Angel Gabriel responded by killing them all. See Robert Cover, The Folktales of Justice: Tales of Jurisdiction, *Capital University Law Review* 14, 1985, pp. 179–203, at 183–184.

[12] *Plessy v. Ferguson*, 163 U.S. 537, 559 (1896) (Harlan, J., dissenting). Harlan continued that the Constitution "neither knows nor tolerates classes among citizens."

[13] In the late 1990s, the objectives of the National Bar Association were to "improve economic conditions (of all American citizens) regardless of race, sex, or creed in their efforts to secure a free and untrammeled use of the franchise." Id. at 141. In its constitution of 1926, there was no mention of race in the section on objectives.

white students, white employees, and white contractors went to courts to advance what are called "reverse discrimination" claims; they argued that they had been subjected to unfair treatment based on the color of their skin.

In 1896, when Justice Harlan aspired that the law's "eye" be "blind," he knew that, were the law to "see," it would (and did) discriminate against dark-skinned peoples. But in 2007, on behalf of a majority of five, Chief Justice John Roberts relied on Justice Harlan's metaphor to invalidate an affirmative action plan that had taken into account the races and ethnicities of schoolchildren so that the lower schools in Seattle, Washington, and St. Louis, Missouri, might be somewhat diverse.[14]

Phrases such as "a color-blind constitution" and images of blindfolded justices support claims of a universal, neutral justice system. In contrast, a keen sense of law's unfairness propels objections that such tropes suggest law's lack of culpability for the perpetuation of inequality. This position is eloquently explained by Langston Hughes in his poem *Justice*, first published in the Amsterdam News in 1923 and later included in a 1932 collection called *Scottsboro Limited* (Ostrom, 2002; McLaren, 1997; Hughes, 2001). Its text references Justice as "a blind goddess" (a point "to which we black are wise"), as the poem asserts that her "bandage hides two festering sores" that "once perhaps were eyes."

The book's title is a reference to the wrongful convictions of nine black young men ("the Scottsboro Boys") who had been taken from a freight train, charged in Alabama courts, found guilty of raping two young white women, and sentenced to death in 1931 (Carter, 1979). Hughes visited the prisoners while they were on death row. He sparked and joined a chorus of protests, national and international, about their treatment. In 1937, Alabama released four of the nine, and in 1976, Alabama's Governor George Wallace pardoned the last living defendant, then still in prison.[15]

Langston Hughes's critique of the blindfold is echoed in the logo chosen by a group of black jurists, formed in 1971 as a part of the National Bar Association, founded (as noted earlier) in the 1920s for the advancement of black lawyers.[16] These judges argued that "the quality of justice in America has always been and is now directly related to the color of one's skin as well as to the size of one's pocket book" (Honorable George W. Crockett Jr., quoted by Ware, 1971, pp. 371–372). Given that courts had been a significant source of unfairness,

[14] See *Parents Involved in Community Schools v. Seattle School District No. 1*, 551 U.S. 701 (2007). Chief Justice John Roberts's opinion for the five-person majority quoted from the *Plessy* opinion (id. at 731), while the concurrence by Justice Clarence Thomas used the phrase "color-blind" several times (id. at 772, 780, 782). The impassioned dissent by Justice Stephen Breyer argued that no case had followed the version of color-blindness proposed by Justice Thomas but rather had attended to the "asymmetry between that which seeks to *exclude* and that which seeks to *include* members of minority races." Id. at 830 (emphasis in the original).

[15] In 2013, "three black men received posthumous pardons" absolving "the last of the 'Scottsboro Boys' of criminal misconduct." See Alan Blinder, "Alabama Pardons 3 Scottsboro Boys after 80 Years", *NY Times*, November 21, 2013.

[16] By the late 1990s, more than 18,000 black lawyers, judges, legal scholars, and students were members, and six women had served among the fifty-six presidents. See President Beverly McQueary Smith, who served in 1998–1999, quoted in Jackson and Gordon, *A Search for Equal Justice by African-American Lawyers* at xii. At the time, of about 12,500 judges nationwide in state and federal courts, some 325 were black. See George W. Crockett Jr., "Racism in the Courts", *Journal of Public Law* 20, 1971, pp. 385–390, at 388–389.

FIGURE 6 Logo of the Judicial Council of the National Bar Association, 1971. *Image reproduced courtesy of the Judicial Council of the National Bar Association.*

judges had a special obligation to respond. The group identified judicial discretion and courts as sources of "racism" through differential treatment of blacks and whites by police and prosecutors, exclusion of blacks from juries, and failures to accord dignified treatment to black witnesses (Ware, 1971).

This group chose as their pledge: "Let us remove the blindfold from the eyes of American justice." For an emblem, they selected a regal depiction of a Justice taking off a blindfold (Figure 6). One of the group's leaders explained, "Justice is supposed to be blind. It treats all individuals alike—rich or poor, black or white, male or female. Well, it's time to remove the blindfold that gives the illusion of fair treatment. We want to expose to the full glare of reality the inequities superimposed on that great but unrealized objective" (Crockett, 1971, p. 389).

THE MULTIPLE VANTAGE POINTS OF JUSTICE

A return to Diderot's critique of Locke's resolution of the Molyneux problem is in order. Recall that Diderot thought that the method of preparation of a blind person for the experiment would affect whether, if "made to see," that person would "know" a cube from a sphere. As Diderot understood, the exchanges between the subject of any such experiment and the observer would be a variable affecting the outcome, not only because preparations could skew results but also because observers were not themselves "dispassionate" (Morgan, 1977; Degenaar, 1996). Moreover, Diderot insisted that the blind were comprised of a diverse set, not to be used as "univocal symbols … for any single position" (Paulson, 1987, p. 52). The more general proposition was that no "single discursive mode of understanding or communication [was] common to all individuals" (Paulson, 1987, p. 47).

The complexities Diderot identified have only deepened. As Jonathan Crary (1990, pp. 59–62) explained, the image of "knowledge of space and depth [as] built up out of an orderly accumulation and cross-referencing of perceptions on a plane independent of the viewer" was an eighteenth-century attitude assuming that the senses were an "adjunct of a rational mind." Yet, by the nineteenth century, the camera obscura had "collapse[d] … as a model for the condition of the observer" (Crary, 1990, p. 3). Instead of one fixed source of light, there were many vantage points from which to look. The result was a "rupture with Renaissance, or *classical* models of vision," with its hegemony of a single meta-narrative confidently promulgated by one authoritative voice (Crary, 1990).

Contemporary critical theory, both reflected in and produced through the multiplication of images and texts, makes palpable the subjectivity of what is seen. Borrowing again from Crary (1990, pp. 6, 95) (as well as extrapolating from Diderot), "observers" are not autonomous (their eyes are not "innocent") but they (we) are "embedded in a system of conventions and limitations," situated to see "within a prescribed set of possibilities." Whether providing sighted or blindfolded eyes, locating aspirations for Justice in a single-positioned personification ignores that embeddedness, just as talking about a color-blind Constitution obscures the question of law's relationship to the impact of legally imposed discrimination (Siegel, 2013). The issue for constitutional law is not about *seeing* race but about what meaning *to make* of racialized categories and histories.

Yet another problem with the blindfold comes from Peter Goodrich's (2013, p. 161) argument that it serves as "an injunction not to look." Public observation—looking—is at the heart of democratic adjudicatory processes. As Jeremy Bentham put it long ago, "Publicity is the very soul of justice. … It keeps the judge himself, while trying, under trial" (Bentham, 1827, p. 355). Writing in 1812, Bentham (1827, pp. 351, 355) explained: "Without publicity all other checks are insufficient: in comparison with publicity, all other checks are of small account."

Law is embedded in relationships, aiming to legitimate its authority to alter human beings' property and liberty. The interactive exchanges of judges and audience are central to adjudication in democracies, founded on popular sovereignty. As Bentham saw it, if rendering decisions in public, it would be "natural" for judges to adopt "the habit of giving reasons from the bench" (p. 357). Courts could therefore become "schools"—teaching the public about the rules of law and the wisdom (or from Bentham's vantage point, the limits) of common law judging.

Famously, as underscored by Michel Foucault, observation brings with it disciplinary power. Bentham urged that ordinary spectators ("auditors") be permitted to make notes that could be distributed widely (p. 355). These "minutes" could serve as insurance for the good judge and, Bentham thought, as a corrective against "misrepresentations" made by "an unrighteous judge" (p. 355). By suggesting that trials put the state (through its representative, the judge) on display, Bentham raised the specter that both judges and the state were to be subjected *to* judgment. Bentham's commitment to auditors parallels Jonathan Crary's rejection of the term "spectators," passive in the face of authority. Crary (1990, p. 6, 1999) insisted instead on the active posture to be taken by "observers," engaging in critique as part of their exercise of authority.

Two lessons emerge, one for law and the other for disciplines enamored of blinding as a method of obtaining definitive results. The dynamic obligations of law, producing tropes such as "living constitutions," undermine the image of a Justice, blindfolded or clear-eyed, ruling from the reified perspective of a single vantage point. The reason to reject color-blindness as responsive to the challenges of rendering judgments is that race is not predicated on sight alone; the construction of race's import crosses many sensory and political modalities. And, for disciplines other than law, the valoration in law first, of sight and then, of obscured vision and the diverse meanings attributed over centuries to blindfolds cautions against universalizing blindness as a fail-safe method for deriving truth. "Double-blind" work, championed in many fields, is not a panacea, for it too is situated and sighted, in the sense of the many choices required when creating research designs and evaluating the results.

Returning to law, reflection is in order on the various explanations valorizing the blindfold. Even were judges to obtain them all, more qualities are needed for wise applications of legal principles. Were the imagery and the discussions to move away from the fixation with scales, sword, and eyes (blindfolded or not), more of the work of law would come into view. One could, for example, illustrate commitments to the multiplicity of vantage points legitimately to be taken into account by shifting from a focus on one Virtue, Justice, to enlarge the vocabulary and attributes required for wise judgment.

Thus, in closing, we offer the reminder that Justice was once part of a foursome, the Cardinal Virtues, regularly discussed and viewed together because the composite provided a collective set of ideal attributes for governance. Plato is the oft-identified source, setting out the qualities—"wise, brave, moderate, and just" (Plato, translated by Grube, 1974, p. 93)—that "would eventually be called cardinal virtues," whose interconnections achieved "a kind of unity of function" (Houser, 2004, pp. 1, 9–11). These virtues also overlapped with other sets, such that Fortitude was both a "Gift Virtue" and a Cardinal Virtue (North, 1966).

Artists, in turn, regularly depicted the set, placed in buildings of import, from the Vatican to other rulers' palaces and town halls. Figure 7, drawing in part from prints of Raphael's Vatican frescoes, provides a compendium of the four.

Yet only the personification of Justice, with or without a blindfold, remains legible to a wide array of people in diverse cultures. But judging on behalf of governments entails more than power, balancing, and looking or not—as reflected in the qualities that Classical and Renaissance traditions attributed to the other Cardinal Virtues. Prudence was a habit "obtained and perfected through practice in deliberation and action" (Nelson, 1992, p. 79) and requisite to good governance. Prudence was described as entailing "the humility … of unbiased perception; the trueness-to-being of memory; the art of receiving counsel; alert, composed readiness for the unexpected" (Pieper, 1966, p. 22). "Sympathetic understanding" is how one modern commentator put it (Coll, 1991, p. 38). Temperance in turn moderated the desires and appetites of both the gods and humankind.[17] Fortitude (sometimes

[17] Helen North provided a history of the development from the Greek term *sophrosyne* to the Roman temperance, or "soundness of mind" and self-knowledge. See North, *Sophrosyne* at 1.

FIGURE 7 Upper left: *Iusticia (Justice)*, Cornelis Matsys, c.1543–1544; Upper right: *Prudence*, Agostino Veneziano, 1516; Lower left: *Temperance*, Agostino Veneziano, 1517; Lower right: *Fortitudo (Fortitude)*, Marcantonio Raimondi, c.1520. *Images provided by and produced with permission of the copyright holder, Warburg Institute, University of London.*

equated with courage) denoted strength and endurance, as well as the virtues of perseverance, patience, loyalty, and magnanimity (Pieper, 1966; Houser, 2002).

Like Justice, her sibling Cardinal Virtues were marked by certain objects, even as some were affixed to more than one Virtue and varied across time, place, and setting.[18] As for their eyes, as Figure 7 illustrates, the tradition was to show them sighted. Indeed, Prudence often held a mirror, said to capture self-knowledge. Those various depictions commend her as the most postmodern of the four Cardinal Virtues. Reflecting our argument of the need for multiple and potentially conflicting perspectives, Prudence is shown in Figure 7 looking at a mirror and has two faces so as to look both forward and backward, and a third eye on her chest to watch the present as well.

References

Alciatus, A., 1985. In: Daly, P.M. (Ed.), The Latin Emblems: Index Emblematicus, vols 1 & 2. University of Toronto Press, Toronto, Canada.

Barasch, M., 2001. Blindness: The History of a Mental Image in Western Thought. Routledge, New York, NY.

Bath, M., 1994. Speaking Pictures: English Emblem Books and Renaissance Culture. Longman Group, London, England & New York, NY.

Bentham, J., 1827. Rationale of judicial evidence. In: Bowring, J. (Ed.), The Works of Jeremy Bentham, vol. 6. William Tait, Edinburgh, Scotland (1843).

Blinder, A., November 21, 2013. Alabama Pardons 3 'Scottsboro Boys' after 80 Years. New York Times, p. A14.

Bongiorno, L.M., 1968. The theme of the old and the new law in the Arena Chapel. Art Bulletin 50 (1), 11–20.

Brant, S., 1944. The Ship of Fools (E. H. Zeydel, Trans.). Columbia University Press, New York, NY.

Camille, M., 1989. The Gothic Idol: Ideology and Image-making in Medieval Art. Cambridge University Press, Cambridge, England.

Capers, I.B., 2012. Blind justice. Yale Journal of Law and the Humanities 24 (1), 179–189.

Carter, D.T., 1979. Scottsboro: A Tragedy of the American South. Louisiana State University Press, Baton Rouge, LA.

Coll, A.R., 1991. Normative prudence as a tradition of statecraft. Ethics and International Affairs 5 (1), 33–61.

Cover, R., 1985. The folktales of justice: tales of jurisdiction. Capital University Law Review 14, 179–203.

Cover, R.M., Fiss, O.M., Resnik, J., 1988. Procedure. The Foundation Press, New York, NY.

Crary, J., 1990. Techniques of the Observer: On Vision and Modernity in the Nineteenth Century. MIT Press, Cambridge, MA.

Crary, J., 1999. Suspensions of Perception: Attention, Spectacle, and Modern Culture. MIT Press, Cambridge, MA.

Crockett Jr., G.W., 1971. Racism in the courts. Journal of Public Law 20, 385–390.

Curley, E.M., 1972. Locke, Boyle, and the distinction between primary and secondary qualities. Philosophical Review 81 (4), 438–464.

Davis, N.Z., 2000. The Gift in Sixteenth-Century France. Oxford University Press, Oxford, England.

De Ville, J., 2011. Mythology and the images of justice. Law & Literature 23 (3), 324–364.

Degenaar, M., 1996. Molyneux's Problem: Three Centuries of Discussion on the Perception of Forms (M.J. Collins, Trans.). Kluwer Academic Publishers, Dordrecht, The Netherlands.

Descartes, R., 1986. Meditations on First Philosophy: With Selections from the Objections and Replies (J. Cottingham, Trans.). Cambridge University Press, Cambridge, England.

Dodd, C.H., 1970. The New English Bible with the Apocrypha. Oxford & Cambridge University Presses, Oxford & Cambridge, England.

[18] How these connections were forged is something of a puzzle. "[T]he issue is whether the emblem depends on the invention of original but arbitrary connections between image and meaning, or whether the relation between sign and referent depends on some deeper and more intrinsic ('natural') affinity." Michael Bath, *Speaking Pictures* 3. Further, given the diversity of codification systems, Bath contested the conception of them as "a single, unitary genre." Id. at 280.

Fröschl, T., 1988. Republican virtues and the free state: conceptual frame and meaning in early modern Europe and North America. In: Ellenius, A. (Ed.), Iconography, Propaganda, and Legitimation. Clarendon Press, Oxford, England, pp. 255–275.

Gombrich, E., 1948. Icones symbolicae: the visual image in neo-platonic thought. Journal of the Warburg and Courtauld Institutes 11, 163–192.

Goodrich, P., 2013. Legal Emblems and the Art of Law: Obiter Depicta as the Vision of Governance. Cambridge University Press, Cambridge, England.

Goodrich, P., Hayaert, V. (Eds.), 2015. Genealogies of Legal Vision. Routledge.

Gorman, M.J., 2003. Art, optics and history: new light on the Hockney thesis. Leonardo 36 (4), 295–301.

Held, R., Ostrovsky, Y., de Gelder, B., Gandhi, T., Ganesh, S., Mathur, U., Sinha, P., 2011. The newly sighted fail to match seen with felt. Nature Neuroscience 14, 551–553.

Hornung, E., 1992. Idea into Image: Essays on Ancient Egyptian Thought (E. Bredeck, Trans.). E. Timken Publishers, New York, NY.

Houser, R.E., 2002. The virtue of courage. In: Pope, S.J. (Ed.), The Ethics of Aquinas. Georgetown University Press, Washington, DC, pp. 304–320.

Houser, R.E., 2004. Introduction (R.E. Houser, Trans.). In: The Cardinal Virtues: Aquinas, Albert, and Philip the Chancellor. Pontifical Institute of Medieval Studies, Toronto, Canada.

Hughes, L., 2001. The collected works of Langston Hughes. In: Rampersad, A. (Ed.), The Poems, 1921–1940, vol. 1. University of Missouri Press, Columbia, MO.

Jackson Jr., E.C., Gordon, J.U., 1999. A Search for Equal Justice by African-American Lawyers: A History of the National Bar Association. Vantage Press, New York, NY.

Jacob, R., 1994. Images de la justice. Essai sur l'iconographie judiciaire du Moyen Âge à l'âge Classique. Le Léopard d'1Or, (Paris), Paris, France.

Jacob, R., 1995. Le jugement de Dieu et la formation de la fonction de juger dans l'histoire européenne. Archives de Philosophie du Droit 39, 87–104.

Jay, M., 1999. Must justice be blind? The challenge of images to the law. In: Douzinas, C., Nead, L. (Eds.), Law and the Image: The Authority of Art and the Aesthetics of Law. University of Chicago Press, Chicago, IL, pp. 19–35.

Kissel, O., 1984. Die Justitia: Reflexionen über ein Symbol und seine Darstellung in der bildenden Kunst. Verlag C.H. Beck, Munchen, Germany.

Kononenko-Moyle, N., 1979–1980. Homer, Milton, and Aşik Veysel: the legend of the blind bard. Harvard Ukrainian Studies vol. III/IV (2), 520–529.

Locke, J., 1975. In: Nidditch, P.H. (Ed.), An Essay Concerning Human Understanding. Oxford University Press, Oxford, England.

Loughlin, M., 2000. Swords and Scales: An Examination of the Relationship between Law and Politics. Hart Publishing, Oxford, England.

McLaren, J., 1997. Langston Hughes, Folk Dramatist in the Protest Tradition, 1921–1943. Greenwood Publishing Group, Westport, CT.

Meier, A., Bracey Jr., J.H., 1993. The NAACP as a reform movement, 1909–1965: "To reach the conscience of America". Journal of Southern History 59, 3–30.

Milton, J., 1971. In: Carey, J. (Ed.), John Milton: Complete Shorter Poems. Longman, London, England.

Montesquieu, 1752. On the Spirit of Laws (T. Nugent, Trans.). G. Bell & Sons, Ltd, London, England.

Morgan, M.J., 1977. Molyneux's Question: Vision, Touch, and the Philosophy of Perception. Cambridge University Press, Cambridge, England.

Nelson, D.M., 1992. The Priority of Prudence: Virtue and Natural Law in Thomas Aquinas and the Implications for Modern Ethics. Pennsylvania State University Press, University Park, PA.

North, H., 1966. Sophrosyne: Self-Knowledge and Self-Restraint in Greek Literature. Cornell University Press, Ithaca, NY.

Ostrom, H., 2002. A Langston Hughes Encyclopedia. Greenwood Press, Westport, CT.

Panofsky, E., 1962. Blind Cupid. In: Panofsky, E. (Ed.), Studies in Iconology: Humanistic Themes in the Art of the Renaissance. Harper & Row, New York, NY, pp. 95–128.

Parents Involved in Community Schools v. Seattle School District No. 1, 551 U.S. 701. 2007.

Paulson, W.R., 1987. Enlightenment, Romanticism, and the Blind in France. University Press, Princeton, NJ.

Pieper, J., 1966. The Four Cardinal Virtues: Prudence, Justice, Fortitude, Temperance. University of Notre Dame Press, Notre Dame, IN.

Pierguidi, S., 1998. Giovanni Guerra and the illustrations to Ripa's Iconologia. Journal of the Warburg and Courtauld Institutes 61, 158–175.
Pinch, G., 2002. Egyptian Mythology: A Guide to the Gods, Goddesses, and Traditions of Ancient Egypt. Oxford University Press, Oxford, England.
Plato, 1974. The Republic (G.M.A. Grube, Trans.). Hackett Publishing Co, Indianapolis, IN.
Plato, 2002. Phaedrus (R. Waterfield, Trans.). Oxford University Press, Oxford, England.
Plessy V. Ferguson, 163 U.S. 537. 1896.
Rawls, J., 1971. A Theory of Justice. Belknap/Harvard University Press, Cambridge, MA.
Resnik, J., Curtis, D., 2011. Representing Justice: Invention, Controversy, and Rights in City-States and Democratic Courtrooms. Yale University Press, New Haven, CT.
Rickless, S.C., 1997. Locke on primary and secondary qualities. Pacific Philosophical Quarterly 78 (3), 297–319.
Ripa, C., 1644. Iconologia, of uytbeeldingen des Verstands. Dirck Pietersz. Pers, Amstelredam, The Netherlands.
Ripa, C., 1625. In: Tozzi, P. (Ed.), Iconographia, Padua.
Ripa, C., 1644. In: Baudoin, J. (Ed.), Iconologie. Chez Mathieu Guillemot, Paris, France.
Ripa, C., 1971. 1758–1760. In: Maser, E.A. (Ed.), Baroque and Rococo Pictorial Imagery: The 1758–60 Hertel Edition of Ripa's "Iconologia" with 200 Engraved Illustrations. Dover Publications, New York, NY.
Ripa, C., 1976. 1611. In: Iconologia. Garland Publishing, New York, NY & London, England.
Ripa, C., 1976. 1779. In: Richardson, C. (Ed.), Iconology London 1779, vols. 1 & 2. Garland Publishing, New York, NY & London, England.
Ripa, C., 1988. 1618. In: Iconologia, vols. 1 & 2. Fògola Editore, Torino, Italy.
Robert, C.N., 1993. Une allegorie parfait: La justice: Vertu courtisane et bourreau. Georg, Geneva, Switzerland.
Robert, C.N., 2006. La Justice dans ses Décors (Xve-xvie Siècles). Droz, Geneva, Switzerland.
Rowe, N., 2007. Idealization and subjection at the south portal of Strasbourg Cathedral. In: Merback, M.B. (Ed.), Beyond the Yellow Badge: Anti-judaism and Antisemitism in Medieval and Early Modern Visual Culture. E.J. Brill, Leiden, The Netherlands, pp. 179–202.
Sbriccoli, M., 2005. La tirade, le bandeau, le genou: Droit et procès pénal dans les allégories de la Justice du Moyen Âge à l'âge modern. Crime, History & Societies 9 (1), 33–78.
Siegel, R.B., 2013. Foreword: equality divided. In: The Supreme Court, 2012 Term. vol. 127 (1). Harvard Law Review, pp. 1–94.
Strauss, G., 1986. Law, Resistance, and the State: The Opposition to Roman Law in Reformation Germany. Princeton University Press, Princeton, NJ.
Strauss, W.L. (Ed.), 1972. The Complete Engravings, Etchings and Drypoints of Albrecht Dürer. Dover Publications, New York, NY.
Van Cleve, J., 1993. Sebastian Brant's the Ship of Fools in Critical Perspective, 1800–1991. Camden House, Columbia, SC.
Wagner, A., Sherwin, R.K. (Eds.), 2014. Law, Culture and Visual Studies. Springer, Dordrecht, The Netherlands.
Ware, G., 1971. Introduction, proceedings: founding convention of the Judicial Council of the National Bar Association. Journal of Public Law 20 (2), 371–375.
Wind, E., 1968. Orpheus in praise of blind love. In: Wind, E. (Ed.), Pagan Mysteries in the Renaissance. Faber and Faber, London, England.
Ziolkowski, T., 2003. The Mirror of Justice: Literary Reflections of Legal Crises. Princeton University Press, Princeton, NJ.

CHAPTER

16

A Theory of Anonymity*

Jeffrey M. Skopek
Faculty of Law, University of Cambridge, Cambridge, UK

OUTLINE

INTRODUCTION

In *Representative Government*, John Stuart Mill suggests that the ability to vote anonymously—to be blinded from public view—is a threat to democracy. The problem, Mill argues, is that this approach suggests to the elector "that the suffrage is given to him for himself; for his particular use and benefit." Against this view, he argues that the voter's choice "is strictly a matter of duty; he is bound to give it according to his best and most conscientious opinion of the public good." Thus, "the duty of voting, like any other public duty, should be performed under the eye and criticism of the public," such that the elector will "adhere to conduct of which at least some decent account can be given" (Mill, 1861, pp. 190–193, 200).

In an era in which the secret ballot is often taken as an integral part of a legitimate democracy, Mill's argument is striking for the very different understanding of the liberal legal subject that it presupposes. What interests me about this tension is that it is suggestive of how

* This chapter draws from a paper previously published as "Anonymity, the Production of Goods, and Institutional Design" in the Fordham Law Review, volume 82, pp. 1751–1809 (2014).

http://dx.doi.org/10.1016/B978-0-12-802460-7.00016-4

differently a democratic society might see the anonymity of its citizens, how central these visions can be to its legal order, and how little we understand the role that this form of blinding plays in our law today.

This is not to say that we know nothing about the place of anonymity in our law. The First Amendment's protection of anonymous speech has received significant academic attention (Boudin, 2011), and there has been limited but important work done on the social norms that govern anonymous communication and their functions (Levmore, 1996), the tension between secrecy and disclosure in constitutional law (Kreimer, 1991), and the desirability of anonymity as a tool of democratic governance (Gardner, 2011). However, this scholarship has not recognized the extent to which anonymity is used and regulated by rules in nearly every area of law—and more importantly—by rules whose primary purpose is not the protection of privacy.

In the 2012 presidential election, 22% of registered voters announced their votes on social networking sites such as Facebook or Twitter (Rainie, 2012). Many did so by posting photos of their completed ballots. In response to this new social media trend, election officials in some states provided public notice that this practice violated state election law, which gave rise to widespread public attention to these previously underpublicized restrictions. For although many people conceptualize anonymous voting as a right, it is in fact a requirement of some form in most states.

In other contexts, anonymity is a right, but the implications of this right have not been fully appreciated. For example, in 1997, Harvard University revealed that it had, over the prior 8 years, spent $88 million anonymously acquiring 52.6 acres of land for a campus expansion, using buying agents to avoid problems of holdout and strategic bargaining (Rimer, 1997). Although Harvard subsequently faced significant public criticism, this type of anonymous purchasing is facilitated by the law of agency, which generally allows an agent to protect the anonymity of his principal—even by falsely representing that he is not acting on behalf of any principal.

Finally, there are situations in which anonymity is neither a right nor a requirement, but rather a trigger that extinguishes rights. For example, in the early 1990s, members of the Havasupai Indian tribe donated blood for use in diabetes research at Arizona State University (Drabiak-Syed, 2010). They later learned that their blood was also being used in other research to which they had ethical objections. When they sued to stop it, they were surprised to discover that a researcher can conduct research that violates the scope of a research participant's specific consent merely by anonymizing the tissue or blood sample that he or she donated.

These varied uses of anonymity in our law—as a requirement in voting, a right when purchasing land, and a trigger that extinguishes rights in biomedical research—may appear to be unrelated. But as this chapter will demonstrate, they are in fact all part of a cohesive and previously unrecognized class of legal interventions that use anonymity not to protect privacy, but rather to regulate bias (construed broadly to include various forms of undesired influence and dependence) in the production of a range of social "goods." These interventions are pervasive, stretching from contract and copyright to criminal law and constitutional law.

Our failure to recognize this class of rules derives from the misconception of anonymity as a mere tool or aspect of privacy. This conflation has obscured an important difference between the two conditions: under the condition of privacy, we have knowledge of a person's identity, but not of an associated personal fact, whereas under the condition of anonymity, we have knowledge of a personal fact, but not of the associated person's identity. In this sense, privacy and anonymity are flip sides of each other. And for this reason, they often function in opposite ways: whereas privacy hides facts about someone whose identity is known by removing information and other goods associated with the person from public circulation, anonymity hides the identity of someone about whom facts are known for the purpose of putting such goods into public circulation (Skopek, 2015). This chapter explores, explains, and draws lessons about this function of anonymity.

The analysis proceeds in three parts. The first part offers a taxonomy of existing law, identifying three core types of anonymity rules that are used across our law and raising the question of whether there is any coherence to their use. The second part proposes a theory of blinding that makes sense of our law's uses of these anonymity rules, identifying a cohesive set of functions that they perform. The third part uses my taxonomic and theoretical analysis to develop generally applicable lessons for the design of laws and policies that seek to prevent various forms of bias.

A TAXONOMY OF ANONYMITY RULES

A close examination of existing law reveals that anonymity rules are at work in countless domains that have gone unrecognized. By "anonymity rules," I mean rules that make use of anonymity or its absence, nonanonymity (which in the interest of simplicity I will refer to as "attribution"). There are three central legal forms that these rules take.

First, there are rules that protect a *right* of anonymity or attribution, which I will refer to as "entitlement rules." On the anonymity side, these include rules that protect one's anonymity when contracting through an agent, engaging in First Amendment speech and association, participating in a witness protection program, donating sperm for in vitro fertilization, providing information in various bounty and whistleblower schemes, and appearing in court—as a party, witness, or juror—when deemed necessary by the judge. And on the attribution (nonanonymity) side, there are rules that grant rights to be attributed as the source of certain artwork, digital copyrighted works, and one's children (Skopek, 2014, pp. 1759–1763).

Second, there are the rules that require anonymity or attribution as a *condition* of exercising a right or capacity, which I will refer to as "conditioning rules." On the anonymity side, these include rules that require anonymity as a condition of voting in elections, serving as a grand juror or regular juror, engaging in market transactions in heavily regulated industries, maintaining a tort claim for invasion of privacy, and donating an organ. And on the attribution side, there are rules making attribution a condition of donating money to a politician, engaging in various forms of speech related to elections, voting as an elected official, signing a legislative petition, participating in the judicial system, providing a tip to the police that itself constitutes probable cause, and having a tort claim for misappropriation of identity (Skopek, 2014, pp. 1763–1767).

Third, and perhaps most surprisingly, there are rules under which anonymity or attribution is a trigger that *extinguishes* a right or capacity, which I will refer to as "extinguishing rules." These include rules under which anonymization extinguishes one's rights to limit research using one's biological tissue and data, to prevent the disclosure and use of personal information otherwise protected by various statutes including the Privacy Act of 1974 and the Health Insurance Portability and Accountability Act, and to challenge the unconsented anonymization of one's personal data. And on the attribution side, there are rules under which

TABLE 1 Rules That Make Use of Anonymity or Its Absence

	Anonymity	Attribution
Entitlement rule	Anonymity is a right.	Attribution is a right.
Conditioning rule	Anonymity is a condition of exercising a right or capacity.	Attribution is a condition of exercising a right or capacity.
Extinguishing rule	Anonymity extinguishes a right or capacity.	Attribution extinguishes a right or capacity.

attribution may extinguish one's right to prevent the government from seizing one's genetic material for use in forensic DNA data banks and to avoid being a legal parent by virtue of being a sperm donor (Skopek, 2014, pp. 1767–1768).

In sum, a fairly well-structured set of anonymity rules are being used across our law and in ways that have gone untheorized. This raises the questions of whether there is any coherence to their use, what functions they perform, and how. It is to these questions that I turn in the next part. Before doing so, however, I offer Table 1 that briefly summarizes the six core types of rules that I have identified.

A THEORY OF PRODUCTION

Having proposed and populated a taxonomy of anonymity rules that have not previously been identified or categorized as such, I will now turn to the question of whether there is theoretical coherence to their use across disparate domains of law. My central argument will be that these rules do perform a cohesive set of functions in the production of a wide range of social goods. In developing this theory, I will differentiate between three phases of production, or types of activity, in which our law targets undesired forms of dependence and influence.

Creation

The first potential target for anonymity rules is the creation phase of production—the actions that make a social good available in the first instance. Here, anonymity rules provide a way of aligning private incentives, and relationships of dependence, with public goals and values. There are a few key ways in which this occurs.

Entitlement rules, for example, can incentivize the creation of certain goods by allowing the entitlement holder to prevent others from drawing inferences from his or her identity—to prevent this form of dependence—and thereby internalize some benefits that would, without the entitlement, be externalized. This is an intervention that is particularly important when the creation of the good will involve many internalized costs. Take, for instance, a copper company that, through extensive investments in aerial surveys, discovers copper deposits in land that it does not own (Kronman, 1978, pp. 20–21). If the copper company did not have the ability to buy this land anonymously or pseudonymously through an agent, then the seller of the land might infer that there are copper deposits on the land and thus raise his price significantly. Ex ante, such a rule would not only strip nonowners with expertise of an incentive to invest in developing information about others' property, but also reduce owners' incentives to correctly identify the attributes of their own property by giving them the possibility of free riding on the work of the experts (Kronman, 1978, p. 16). Thus, granting a right of anonymity—and preventing this form of informational dependence—helps ensure that both owners and potential buyers of property have incentives to invest, thereby increasing the likelihood that the full social value of the property will materialize.

In addition, entitlement rules can incentivize creation by allowing the entitlement holder to externalize some of the costs that would, without the rights, be internalized. This function is particularly important to properly align incentives when the party will not be able to internalize all the external benefits. Take, for example, a whistleblower who is considering whether to provide information to the Internal Revenue Service (IRS) as part of its bounty scheme (Ferziger and Currell, 1999), which benefits the public not only through the money it brings in, but also through its deterrent value. The whistleblower's economic incentive to provide information under this scheme is no more than 15% of the recoverable tax, which must be discounted by the odds that the tax or bounty will be reduced (the IRS can reward less, but not more, than 15%)—and then reduced by the discounted value of the possible costs of providing the information (which can include retaliation, social costs, etc.). Furthermore, the party paying the tax will have an economic incentive to spend up to 100% of the amount it will owe, similarly discounted, on preventing the whistleblower from talking—minus the discounted value of the possible costs of doing so (such as penalties under antiretaliation laws). Thus, the whistleblower's decision to provide information could—without further IRS intervention—be more influenced by its cost to the party paying the tax than by its benefit to the public. By granting the whistleblower an anonymity right, however, the IRS allows the whistleblower to cut off the influence of the party paying the tax, preventing a form of dependence that would bias outcomes away from the public good.

Finally, although entitlement rules allow private parties to choose whether and how an external incentive will shape their creation of a good, conditioning rules limit their autonomy in this regard. They control creation by serving as a gatekeeper, either allowing or preventing external influence, such as public rewards and sanctions. Anonymity conditions, for example, are useful when we think that the possibility of feedback will allocate costs and benefits in a way that undermines the value of a social good. For example, in general elections, anonymity is generally required to ensure that a voter will not be accountable to anyone but himself for the content of his vote. By making it impossible for third parties to verify the content of one's vote ex post, the anonymity requirement makes it unlikely that someone would devote resources to trying to buy or coerce votes, or that a voter would succumb to coercion or be able to find a buyer for his vote (Hasen, 2000, p. 1328). Thus, anonymity prevents the voter and the potential vote buyer from reallocating the costs and benefits of voting (transferring some of the benefit that the vote provides to the candidate back to the voter) in a way that biases it against the public interest. And similar logic can justify requiring anonymity for persons ranging from organ donors to jurors.

Evaluation

The second potential target of anonymity rules is evaluation—the acts of interpretation or judgment that accompany the use of goods that have been created. Here, a central rationale for anonymity rules derives from their impact not on the persons who are subject to them (as is the case with the creation-oriented rationales), but rather on the parties with whom these persons interact. The rules function by either preventing or allowing these parties to alter their behavior on the basis of the identity of the persons who are subject to the rules. These interventions can be based on a normative conception of the good at issue, or concerns of efficiency. And they can target the evaluation of the good itself, or its source or recipient.

The claim that anonymity can improve evaluation is often expressly rejected in the scholarship on anonymity, which generally suggests that attribution is preferable ex post (Wilkinson, 2006, p. 231). But a few examples reveal that the point is in fact quite intuitive. Take, for example, the question of whether the sponsors of a political ballot initiative should be attributed. It is often suggested that they should be, on the grounds that this disclosure will help voters identify the interests that the initiative will truly serve (Garrett and Smith, 2005, pp. 299–300). However, if the sponsor's identity will be misleading (e.g., if its name suggests that it is a community-based environmental group, but it is in fact an industry shell group), then requiring anonymity might facilitate more accurate evaluation than attribution.

Likewise, a pseudonym that protects the anonymity of the source can reduce evaluation costs in certain circumstances. Take, for example, the books that are sold under the names Tom Clancy or V.C. Andrews but are written by others, such that these names become pseudonyms that protect the anonymity of the true authors (Lastowka, 2005, pp. 1223–1228). While many scholars suggest that such uses of pseudonymity are deceptive and do not produce the same public benefits as attribution rights (Lastowka, 2005, p. 1227), others have rejected this conventional claim, noting that signals that are deceptive to some people can be helpful to others (Tushnet, 2007, p. 813). For example, such uses of pseudonymity can provide a valuable signal that allows a reader to efficiently find a book that she will like, much like a brand; this can be the case whether or not the pseudonym is misleading as to the true author's identity. In fact, for some readers, knowing the truth—for instance, that Tom Clancy did not write a given book, but rather authorized the placement of his name on it—may impose more costs than benefits. This could be expected, for example, if a reader assigns little value to knowing the true author, but this information creates new decision costs related to uncertainty about whether the authorized book will have the style and quality he desires. In this type of case, it will be precisely because pseudonymity is deceptive in one sense that it will be able to perform the same valuable search function that true attribution often performs.

Further, the evaluation value of anonymity is not limited to cases of deception. The more general lesson here is that whenever the recipient or user of a good will be biased in favor or against its source, such that the source's identity will be a misleading signal, a regime in which the source is allowed or required to be anonymous will facilitate accurate evaluation. This is one reason that academic journals conduct blind peer review of submissions, law schools use anonymous grading of exams, and symphony orchestras audition candidates by having them play behind a screen. Another reason is that identity is generally considered to be a normatively objectionable factor to consider when evaluating these goods, even if it would increase efficiency.

Finally, although the undesired evaluative influence addressed by anonymity and attribution often concerns the good that is subject to the rule itself, this is not their only function. For example, one of the reasons that the California Public Utilities Commission ruled that the Pacific Gas and Electric Company (PG&E) and its customers must remain mutually anonymous when engaging in over-the-counter transactions in natural gas-related derivatives was that attribution could allow PG&E to learn information about its customers that could facilitate anticompetitive behavior (In re Pacific Gas and Electric Co., 1999). Likewise, in the campaign donation context, a core function of the attribution condition is not facilitating the evaluation of the donation, but rather the candidate who receives it. As explained by the Supreme Court in upholding this condition, the rule "allows voters to place each candidate in the political spectrum more precisely than is often possible solely on the basis of party labels and campaign speeches," and "alert[s] the voter to the interests to which a candidate is most likely to be responsive and thus facilitate predictions of future performance in office" (Buckley v. Valeo, 1976). In addition, the attribution condition assists voters in evaluating whether candidates have altered their policy positions in return for contributions—a function that is performed by monetary disclosure conditions in other contexts as well. For example, most academic biomedical journals require that the sources of funding for a study be identified as a condition of publication, thereby allowing readers to discount the study's claims according to their understanding of the potential bias created by any financial conflicts of interest.

Allocation

The third and final target of anonymity rules is the allocation phase. Here, the rules provide a way of preventing bias in the control and use of goods when their anonymization or attribution alters the rationale for their default allocation. The type of bias addressed in this way can be rooted in an economic conception of improper dependence (where the use of a good is not controlled by the party who values it the most) or a normative conception (where the use of the good is not controlled by the party who is deemed appropriate on grounds of justice).

For example, an efficiency-based conception of bias can be addressed by extinguishing rules when a triggering event—anonymization or attribution—changes the interests of the anonymous or attributed party such that the allocation of a right to that person becomes economically inefficient. In this case, an extinguishing rule might be used to solve two types of market obstacles that would prevent the efficient reallocation of a good controlled by that right.

The first obstacle derives from market organization costs. These costs—including the costs of identifying the parties who own an entitlement and structuring an effective exchange relationship with them—are a standard cause of market failure (Ellickson, 1989, pp. 614–616). And many of the factors that contribute to market organization costs are present in the default situations addressed by the extinguishing rules that I identified. Take, for example, the rule that allows a researcher to extinguish a tissue donor's right to limit the use of his tissue in research—and even breach the express terms of his consent—merely by anonymizing the tissue. In this case, the tissue donors are provided a nonpossessory right of control over their tissue samples; these samples will be used in research that will likely extend beyond the donors' life spans; it is often impossible to anticipate in advance what research studies will evolve; and a single project might use the tissue of thousands of donors. Thus, the default requirement that a researcher obtain specific consent for new uses of the tissue can impose significant market organization costs that will hinder biomedical research.

Furthermore, while the expenditure of these costs might be economically efficient when the samples are identified, because the donors may have valuable privacy interests at stake, anonymization could change this balance. Imagine, for example, that the donors place little value on limiting the use of their tissue post-anonymization because they are no longer worried about their privacy. If so, it is likely that the costs of obtaining specific consent will be greater than the value produced by the transaction—especially when the experiment is of minimal or uncertain value, as is often the case with research on a single tissue sample. Under these conditions, where the cost of exchange is high and its benefit to the parties is small, the extinguishing rule currently in use (which eliminates the consent requirement on the basis of anonymization) would benefit one party with minimal or no harm to the other. In this way, it would produce the economically efficient allocation of rights and tissue.

The second obstacle that can be addressed by extinguishing rules is strategic bargaining. In the tissue context, at least three types of strategic behavior could be expected to prevent the efficient reallocation of rights of control after anonymization (assuming, as I discussed above, that anonymization makes the default allocation inefficient by reducing the value that donors place on their rights of control). First, there is the possibility of "strategic holdout" (Robinson, 1991, pp. 571–573) by the donor, who has a veto power over the research. This could happen when there is only one donor, but becomes increasingly likely when the agreement of multiple donors is needed (such as when a researcher needs a complete set of tissue samples), as the opportunity costs of holding out decrease with an increase in the number of parties. Second, even if a researcher needs only one sample, barriers associated with monopoly or bilateral monopoly conditions (Macey, 2010) could arise given the uniqueness of tissue and genetic data—a problem aggravated by the fact that the tissue will often be far more valuable to the researcher than to the donor. Third, rent seeking (Klein et al., 1978) by the tissue source could prevent efficient allocation if the researcher has invested significant time and energy into research using a collection of tissues in a biobank but has not yet completed his research; here, the time and energy would become a quasi rent that a tissue source could try to extract, in addition to the value of his tissue, through threat of withdrawing consent. By working around these three core obstacles to bargaining, the extinguishing rule can achieve the efficient allocation of the tissue and the rights of control over it.

At this point, I should highlight that my argument here is not that this extinguishing rule—or any other rule that I have identified—is in fact justified because it serves the functions that I have theorized. Rather, my focus on the rule is illustrative, and my argument throughout this part is explanatory. Here, my claim is just that when anonymization or attribution of a good makes the allocation of a right of control over the good inefficient by reducing the value of the right to the entitlement holder whose identity is at issue, extinguishing rules may work around various types of market failures (market organization and strategic bargaining) to achieve the economically efficient reallocation of the good. In this way, they can solve a problem of social dependence that arises when an important public resource is not controlled by the parties who produce the most value from it.

Finally, moving from considerations of efficiency to considerations of justice, extinguishing rules can also solve problems of dependence that emerge when the attribution or anonymization of a person eliminates the sole normative basis for granting this person a right of control over a good or otherwise alters the societal balancing of competing interests that provided the basis for the right. Imagine, for example, that the reason we grant a right—such as the right to have a third party represent one's interests in court or the right to prevent use of one's tissue in research—is merely to prevent a privacy harm, and that anonymization will prevent that harm. Under these conditions, an extinguishing rule can be justified on the grounds that the right is no longer deserved (regardless of whether the entitlement holder still values it more than anyone else). Or imagine a researcher who has invested significant time and energy into research using a collection of tissues, but has not yet completed his research. Above, I mentioned a transactions–cost justification for the use of an extinguishing rule here, but we might also justify the rule on purely normative grounds. The claim here would be that anonymization weakens the source's private interests in preventing use, changing the balance of distributional concerns, and justifying the allocation of control to the researcher. Without the rule, research would, on this account, be biased by the preferences of tissue donors who no longer have compelling interests at stake in the research.

IMPLICATIONS FOR LAW AND POLICY

The taxonomic and theoretical analysis of anonymity developed above not only clarifies the law we have, but also provides a framework to rethink and improve the rules at work in various institutions. It does so by revealing a set of previously unrecognized "design levers" (Benkler, 2004, pp. 312–323)—consisting of six rules and three phases of production—that can be used to develop novel solutions to difficult questions of institutional design.

The Production of Goods

To illustrate how the design levers can be used, I will focus on their application to the question of how to prevent improper influence in the production of a good that performs an important public function but may also serve a conflicting private interest. Here, my analysis reveals that anonymity and attribution conditions—antithetical rules that would seem to perform opposite functions—can actually be functionally equivalent when they are used to target different phases of production; specifically, when attribution targets evaluation and anonymity targets creation. An example will help demonstrate this point. Take, for instance, the problem of how to prevent undue influence created by financial conflicts of interest in research universities. This problem has received renewed attention in the wake of the financial crisis of 2008, because it has become clear that many prominent academic economists provided public policy advice in congressional hearings and in academic publications on issues in which they had financial interests by virtue of their connections with private firms (Flitter et al., 2010). Whether or not these connections affected these economists' views on financial theory and regulation, they created a conflict of interest, and the institutional design question is how to manage such conflicts—conflicts in which an expert opinion performs an important public function but may also provide a private benefit.

The standard way to manage such conflicts, apart from using prohibitions, would be to require attribution of donors and funders as a condition of engaging in relevant activities. For example, Congress could impose disclosure requirements as a condition of testifying before congressional committees (which is not currently the case), and academic journals could impose them as a condition of publication (which is standard in some fields, such as biomedical research). This strategy would address the conflict-of-interest problem by targeting the evaluation of the resulting good: the testimony or the publication. It would function by allowing third parties to discount the academic's statements and opinions according to their understanding of the potential bias created by the conflict of interest. Thus, it would at its core be an ex post strategy, addressing the problem after it has arisen—which is not to say that the attribution condition would not also function ex ante, discouraging the creation of new conflicts of interest. However, it would only have this impact on creation ex ante by virtue of its efficacy as an evaluation strategy ex post.

The alternative way of controlling these financial conflicts of interest, as identified above, would be to require anonymity as a condition of funding academic research. For example, we could require that funds be funneled through an intermediary body (either within the university or a neutral third party) that would anonymize and distribute them to the recipients. Unlike the attribution strategy, which would intervene at the evaluation phase in the production of the testimony or the publication, this anonymity strategy would intervene at the creation phase. It would function by preventing the recipient of the funds from knowing their source, thus preventing the formation of a biased opinion. It would be an ex ante strategy, preventing the problem from emerging rather than trying to manage it once it has emerged. And this type of suggestion has in fact been made in the biomedical research context, although not framed in these terms (Robertson, 2011).

The upshot here is that mutually incompatible anonymity and attribution conditions can be used to solve the same problem by intervening in different phases in the production of the good at issue. This point is relevant not only when designing a policy for an area that is not yet governed by either type of rule, but also in rethinking areas in which our law currently uses one or the other. Here, my analysis offers two general lessons.

First, it suggests that whenever attribution requirements are being used to address a production concern by targeting evaluation, we might instead use an anonymity requirement to target creation (though not vice versa). Take, for example, the question of how to address the concern that politicians and expert witnesses will be influenced by the identities of those who fund or hire them. We currently address both of these concerns with the same conditioning rule, requiring that the source of funds be attributed to target evaluation ex post. Our campaign finance regulations, which require disclosure of donations, place "the question of undue influence or preferential access in the hands of voters, who... can follow the money and hold representatives accountable for any trails they don't like" (Sullivan, 1998, p. 326). Likewise, our judicial system, in which expert witnesses testify on behalf of the litigants who paid them, places the question of undue influence in the hands of the jurors who can discount the expert's testimony according to their evaluation of the expert's bias.

Yet as my analysis highlights, we might also address these concerns with the opposite rule, requiring that the source of funds be anonymous in order to target the creation of undue influence. For example, to address this problem in the context of campaign donations, we might require that donations, like votes, be collected in a way that imposes anonymity on them and prevents a donor from proving to a politician that he or she made a given donation, as Ian Ayres and Bruce Ackerman have argued (Ackerman and Ayres, 2002, pp. 93–100). Likewise, to address the problem of biased expert testimony in civil litigation, we could create an intermediary agency that litigants could use to hire experts to render opinions without knowledge of the litigants' identity, as Christopher Robertson (2010) has proposed.

Second, and conversely, my analysis suggests that whenever *anonymity* requirements are being used to address a production concern by targeting *creation*, we might instead use an *attribution* requirement to target *evaluation* (though not vice versa). For example, undue influence in the production of votes in elections—like undue influence in the production of campaign donations and expert scientific testimony—has many margins on which anonymity and attribution could operate. Currently, we require anonymity to address this concern, because our policy is made with a focus on the relationship between the voter and the person trying to corrupt the vote, seeking to prevent undue influence at the upstream phase of creation.

However, if we were to instead focus on the relationship between the voter and the public, then we would see that we could achieve the same goal by requiring that votes be attributed. In imposing an attribution condition, we would essentially import the logic of our current campaign donation law into our election law, rather than vice versa, as discussed above. Just as the attribution of campaign donations allows voters to hold representatives accountable for any money trails that they do not like, attribution of votes would, as John Stuart Mill argued, force voters to "adhere to conduct of which at least some decent account can be given" (Mill, 1861, p. 200). In this way, we would replace an anonymity requirement that addresses corruption by targeting the creation of votes with an attribution requirement that would target their evaluation.

Thus, the more general lesson revealed by my framework is that the choice between anonymity and attribution should be based not only on the nature of the good at issue and a first-order preference for secrecy or disclosure, but also on a second-order preference for the rule that targets the margin of the production problem that is easier to solve, and furthermore, that this latter preference should be based on a consideration and balancing of two core factors.

First, we must consider the likely difficulty of imposing perfect, rather than partial, anonymity or attribution. For as Jeremy Bentham long ago realized with respect to voting: "In secret voting, the secrecy cannot be too profound: in public voting, the publicity can never be too great. The most detrimental arrangement would be that of demi-publicity" (Bentham, 1843, p. 370). Thus, in choosing a rule, we must determine the feasibility of creating an institution that imposes an anonymity condition in a way that cannot easily be pierced by private parties trying to resist it and compare this to the feasibility of creating an institution that imposes an attribution condition in a way that the information can be effectively accessed by the public.

Second, we must consider the likely efficacy of anonymity and attribution strategies—if perfectly imposed and maintained—in preventing improper influence in the production of a given good. With respect to anonymity, this assessment will likely be fairly simple, as a creation-oriented anonymity strategy does not require any further action beyond implementation and maintenance to be effective. An evaluation-oriented attribution strategy, by contrast, requires several additional steps to be effective, each of which must be considered when choosing a rule.

For example, we must consider whether the identifying information will actually allow the evaluator to accurately identify and differentiate improper influence from normal activity, which may be more difficult than is often imagined, turning on several factors. One is the nature of the activity. For instance, if a politician changes a policy position to agree with a donor immediately after receiving a large donation from that donor, then improper influence might be the best explanation for the change, making attribution an effective strategy; but if the change does not take place immediately, then it may be more difficult to differentiate the improper from the normal policy change, thus making attribution a less effective strategy. Another factor is the expertise of the evaluator. Although some such evaluations may be within the competency of the general public, others may benefit from experience of expertise. For example, if the question is whether an expert witness opinion is biased, judges or other repeat players might be more effective than jurors in making use of the attribution condition (Cain et al., 2005, p. 20).

In addition, we must consider whether the evaluator will be able to effectively respond to any detected improper influence, which may also be more difficult than is often imagined. One problem is whether sanctions are actually available. For example, if a voter wants to sanction a politician who changed positions in response to a donation, then there must be an election in the near future, the politician must be running for reelection, and there must be another candidate on the ballot whom the voter prefers. Another problem is whether the value of the good at issue can be accurately discounted. Take, for example, the requirement that industry funding of scientific research be attributed in most academic publications. If the rationale for this rule is that it will allow those using the study to discount its findings according to their evaluation of the authors' potential bias, then the efficacy of the rule will turn on the accuracy of such discounting, which some empirical evidence draws into question (Kesselheim et al., 2012). Further, even if effective ex post, some attribution conditions may have perverse effects ex ante. For example, some empirical evidence suggests that disclosure "can increase the bias in advice because it leads advisors to feel morally licensed and strategically encouraged to exaggerate their advice even further" (Cain et al., 2005, p. 1).

In short, anonymity and attribution strategies will often have strengths and weaknesses that are inversely related: attribution will often be easier to implement and maintain, because unlike anonymity, it cannot be easily pierced by parties trying to resist it. Anonymity, however, if achieved, will often be more effective, because it avoids the difficulties of using and acting on the basis of the information that an attribution strategy provides. Thus, the choice between anonymity and attribution (setting aside other options, such as prohibitions) should turn primarily on a balancing of these two general factors, in combination with context-specific considerations, such as whether one rule will cause a decline in the production of the good, and if so whether this is tolerable. For example, requiring anonymity for campaign donations and research funding might cause a decline in the production of both of these goods (just as voter turnout declined when the secret ballot was first implemented), but we might be less concerned about this in the former case if we thought that the public does not benefit from current levels of campaign spending or if we adopted an alternative funding mechanism.

Finally, when neither of these simple anonymity or attribution strategies has a clear benefit over the other, we might look to other more complex options revealed by my framework. For example, when we want to create narrowly tailored solutions to production concerns, an unrecognized but powerful strategy is to combine rules that are in tension with each other and that target different phases of production—using one as a baseline rule to address our primary production concerns, and another to limit that baseline rule and address secondary concerns. A very simple example of this type of strategy can be seen in existing criminal law, where we allow people to provide tips to the police anonymously (a baseline entitlement rule targeting the creation of information by altering incentives), but do not allow an anonymous tip to provide probable cause in and of itself (a conditioning rule targeting evaluation concerns about the resulting information). In addition, this layering strategy can be read into Ayres and Ackerman's two core proposals to prevent political corruption from campaign contributions, both of which strike a balance between the evaluation-oriented benefits of attributed donations and the creation-oriented benefits of anonymous donations: one option is to require that campaign contributions be attributed, but provide a right to an anonymous refund (Ackerman and Ayres, 2006, pp. 1110–1111); the other is to require that contributions be anonymous, but provide a right to partial attribution (Ackerman and Ayres, 2002, pp. 93–110). In these cases, as well as others that I explore elsewhere, the combination of rules that are in tension with each other and target different phases of production can produce a more refined solution than is possible through a single rule alone (Skopek, 2014, pp. 1795–1806).

The Production of Liberal Legal Subjects

I have thus far argued that mutually exclusive types and combinations of anonymity rules can be used to address the same problem of bias, but it is important to note that the rules are not equivalent in every way. A key difference derives from the fact that the subject matter of the rules is not always left unaltered by their use. Different configurations of rules may instantiate different conceptions of the goods being produced—and of the subjects producing them.

In the elections example discussed above, for example, I suggested—following Mill—that we might use an attribution condition, instead of an anonymity condition, to prevent corruption in voting. However, the use of an attribution requirement might bring with it a shift in how the nature of voting is commonly understood. For example, Mill conceptualized voting in very different terms than many people do today. As noted in the introduction to this chapter, he thought that the vote is not given to the subject of a democracy "for himself; for his particular use and benefit," but rather "as a trust for the public" (Mill, 1861, p. 190). This stands in stark contrast to the vision articulated by the Supreme Court:

> We have never insisted that the franchise be exercised without taint of individual benefit; indeed, our tradition of political pluralism is partly predicated on the expectation that voters will pursue their individual good through the political process, and that the summation of these individual pursuits will further the collective welfare. ***Brown v. Hartlage (1982)***

Thus, although two opposite conditioning rules might both prevent the same forms of corruption, they might produce very different types of democratic subjects.

Anonymity and attribution conditions for voting can in fact be seen as representative of the two ends of the spectrum of modern views regarding the nature and function of democracy. There is a resemblance between Mill's attribution position and theories of deliberative democracy, which emphasize the giving of public reasons. These theories, rooted historically in republicanism, "contend that an expression of the public will can legitimately bind those who are subject to it only insofar as it is reasoned, well-informed, and formulated after mutual consultation and discussion" (Gardner, 2011, p. 935). By contrast, economic theories rooted in liberalism see voting as "a procedure for maximizing social utility by recording and aggregating as accurately as possible the private self-interest of each citizen" (Gardner, 2011, p. 934). On this view, it is the impersonal operation of democracy's aggregating mechanisms that achieves the common good, not self-conscious attempts by individuals to determine how to advance it. Imposing anonymity as a condition can be seen as expressive of this latter privately oriented approach.

This is not to say, however, that imposing an anonymity requirement on voting treats the vote as a completely private good. There are other anonymity rules that would push the vote further into the domain of private choice. For example, creating a right of anonymity (as is the case in some jurisdictions) moves away from the publicly oriented rationale articulated by the Supreme Court of Massachusetts when it held that because ballot secrecy "safeguards society's interest in the integrity of elections,...the right to a secret ballot is not an individual right which may be waived by a good faith voter" (McCavitt v. Registrars of Voters, 1982). If anonymity were a right, rather than a requirement, then the voter would be able to choose anonymity to avoid accountability, or choose attribution to sell his vote.

For these reasons, the act of choosing between an anonymity right and an anonymity requirement, or between an anonymity requirement and an attribution requirement, should be seen as a choice between competing conceptions of what type of good a vote is meant to be, and what voting is for. Likewise, if we were to impose an anonymity condition on the hiring of experts to testify in court, then we would—at least in part—be transforming expert testimony from a private good deployed in the service of one litigant's personal goal of winning, to "a self-financing public good for litigants to use in serving their private and the public interests" (Robertson, 2010, p. 242). And if we were to impose an anonymity condition on political donations, then we would be transforming them from a good potentially deployed in the service of private quid pro quo, into a good in service of public campaign finance.

Furthermore, the same is true of the production of biomedical goods. With research biobanking, for example, the choice of anonymity rules will determine whether a biobanked tissue sample is a good in which the human subject has a legally cognizable interest or is instead one in which the only cognizable interests are those of the public. Under the current federal "Common Rule" regulations, anonymization of the tissue transforms it from a limited-use resource under the ultimate control of a private party, into an unlimited-use resource that is available to public sector research (Department of Health and Human Services, 45 C.F.R. §§ 46.101(b)(4), 46.102(f), revised 2009). A proposal under consideration by the US Department of Health and Human Services, by contrast, would allow the subject to prevent this shift and maintain control over his tissue, potentially transforming his genetic endowment into private biocapital to be utilized like other forms of capital.

Underlying these competing conceptions of the status of tissue are, moreover, competing conceptions of the human subject and the role that nonexpert citizens should have in shaping the direction of biomedicine. The Common Rule's transformation of tissue from a private to public good is explicitly achieved through a legal reconceptualization of the human subject from whom the tissue is derived. Prior to anonymization, the law treats research on biobanked tissue as research on a human subject for which consent is required; postanonymization, there is—as a matter of law—no longer a human subject involved. Prohibiting this anonymization, by contrast, would allow a human subject to ensure that his biobanked tissue remained not only literally identified with him, but also an extension of his legal self. Under this approach, human subjects would be more than mere donors to the public-sector research enterprise, but rather, if they chose, participants in it.

Thus, choosing between anonymity and attribution may involve not only taking a position on the proper balancing of considerations of efficiency and justice, but also making a more fundamental choice between what might be considered competing bioconstitutional orders (Jasanoff, 2011). At its core, the decision of whether ordinary citizens will be able to shape the direction of public-sector biomedical research with their biocapital (rather than a more limited bundle of resources, such as money, energy, time, and voice) is much like the decision of whether they will be able to shape political outcomes by voting openly with their voices and their financial capital (rather than in anonymizing voting and donation booths). Both decisions entail choices between competing conceptions of the proper capacities of the subjects of a liberal democracy.

CONCLUSION

Anonymity rules are at work across our law in ways that have gone unrecognized. In domains ranging from contract and copyright to criminal law and constitutional law, our legal system makes anonymity and nonanonymity into rights, conditions of exercising rights, and triggers that extinguish rights. These diverse domains and forms of anonymity rules may appear to lack theoretical coherence. But they can in fact be explained and theorized as forming a coherent class of legal interventions whose aim is not to protect privacy, but rather to regulate relationships of influence and dependence in the creation, evaluation, and allocation of a wide set of social goods. This theory of anonymity not only clarifies the law we have, but also and more importantly reveals a previously unrecognized set of design levers that can be used to develop innovative strategies for regulating bias. In doing so, it explains when and why seemingly opposite strategies—anonymity and attribution—can be functionally equivalent, and how to choose between them. It also suggests, however, that the opposing options are not equivalent in every way. Rather, the choice between strategies can entail a choice between fundamentally different conceptions of the nature of goods being produced, and of the liberal legal subjects producing them.

References

Ackerman, B., Ayres, I., 2002. Voting with Dollars: A New Paradigm for Campaign Finance. Yale University Press, New Haven, CT.

Ackerman, B., Ayres, I., 2006. The secret refund booth. University of Chicago Law Review 73 (4), 1107–1130.

Benkler, Y., 2004. Sharing nicely: on shareable goods and the emergence of sharing as a modality of economic production. Yale Law Journal 114 (2), 273–358.

Bentham, J., 1843. An essay on political tactics. In: Bowring, J. (Ed.), The Works of Jeremy Bentham, vol. 2. William Tait, Edinburgh, pp. 298–374.

Boudin, C., 2011. Publius and the petition: Doe v. Reed and the history of anonymous speech. Yale Law Journal 120 (8), 2140–2181.

Brown v. Hartlage, 456 U.S. 45, 56 (1982).

Buckley v. Valeo, 424 U.S. 1, 67 (1976) (per curiam).

Cain, D.M., Loewenstein, G., Moore, D.A., 2005. The dirt on coming clean: perverse effects of disclosing conflicts of interest. Journal of Legal Studies 34 (1), 1–25.

Department of Health and Human Services, Revised 2009. Protection of Human Subjects. Code of Federal Regulations 45 Part 46.

Drabiak-Syed, K., 2010. Lessons from Havasupai Tribe v. Arizona State University Board of Regents: recognizing group, cultural, and dignity harms as legitimate risks warranting integration into research practice. Journal of Health & Biomedical Law 6, 175–225.

Ellickson, R.C., 1989. The case for Coase and against Coaseanism. Yale Law Journal 99 (3), 611–630.

Ferziger, M.J., Currell, D.G., 1999. Snitching for dollars: the economics and public policy of federal civil bounty programs. University of Illinois Law Review 1999 (4), 1141–1208.

Flitter, E., Cooke, K., Da Costa, P., 2010. Special Report: for Some Professors, Disclosure Is Academic. Reuters. Retrieved from: http://www.reuters.com/article/2010/12/20/us-academics-conflicts-idUSTRE6BJ3LF20101220.

Gardner, J.A., 2011. Anonymity and democratic citizenship. William and Mary Bill of Rights Journal 19 (4), 927–957.

Garrett, E., Smith, D.A., 2005. Veiled political actors and campaign disclosure laws in direct democracy. Election Law Journal 4, 295–328.

Hasen, R.L., 2000. Vote buying. California Law Review 88 (5), 1323–1371.

In re Pacific Gas and Electric Co., 1999. 85 California Public Utilities Rep. 2d (PUR) 540, WL 667575 (Cal. P.U.C. 1999).

Jasanoff, S., 2011. Reframing Rights: Bioconstitutionalism in the Genetic Age. MIT Press, Cambridge, MA.

Kesselheim, A.S., Robertson, C.T., Myers, J.A., Rose, S.L., Gillet, V., Ross, K.M., Glynn, R.J., Joffe, S., Avorn, J., 2012. A randomized study of how physicians interpret research funding disclosures. New England Journal of Medicine 367, 1119–1127.

Klein, B., Crawford, R.G., Alchian, A.A., 1978. Vertical integration, appropriable rents, and the competitive contracting process. Journal of Law and Economics 21 (2), 297–326.

Kreimer, S.F., 1991. Sunlight, secrets, and scarlet letters: the tension between privacy and disclosure in constitutional law. University of Pennsylvania Law Review 140 (1), 1–147.

Kronman, A.T., 1978. Mistake, disclosure, information, and the law of contracts. Journal of Legal Studies 7 (1), 1–34.

Levmore, S., 1996. The anonymity tool. University of Pennsylvania Law Review 144 (5), 2191–2236.

Lastowka, G., 2005. The trademark function of authorship. Boston University Law Review 85, 1171–1241.

Macey, G.P., 2010. Coasean blind spots: charting the incomplete institutionalism. Georgetown Law Journal 98 (4), 863–919.

McCavitt v. Registrars of Voters, 385 Mass. 833, 434 N.E.2d 620, 631 (1982).

Mill, J.S., 1861. Considerations on Representative Government. Parker, Son & Bourn, London.

Rainie, L., November 6, 2012. Social Media and Voting. Pew Research Center. Retrieved from: http://www.pewinternet.org/2012/11/06/social-media-and-voting/.

Rimer, S., June 17, 1997. Some Seeing Crimson at Harvard "Land Grab". The New York Times, p. A16.

Robertson, C.T., 2010. Blind expertise. New York University Law Review 85, 174–257.

Robertson, C.T., 2011. Money blind: how to stop industry bias in biomedical science, without violating the First Amendment. The American Journal of Law & Medicine 37 (2–3), 358–387.

Robinson, G.O., 1991. Explaining contingent rights: the puzzle of "obsolete" covenants. Columbia Law Review 91 (3), 546–580.

Skopek, J.M., 2014. Anonymity, the production of goods, and institutional design. Fordham Law Review 82 (4), 1751–1809.

Skopek, J.M., 2015. Reasonable expectations of anonymity. Virginia Law Review 101, 691–762.

Sullivan, K.M., 1998. Against campaign finance reform. Utah Law Review 1998 (3), 311–329.

Tushnet, R., 2007. Naming rights: attribution and law. Utah Law Review 2007 (3), 781–814.

Wilkinson, M.A., 2006. The public interest in moral rights protection. Michigan State Law Review 2006, 193–234.

CHAPTER

17

The Cases for and against Blindfolding the Jury[1]

Shari Seidman Diamond

Northwestern University School of Law, Chicago, IL, USA; American Bar Foundation, Chicago, IL, USA

OUTLINE

INTRODUCTION

The American justice system bestows extraordinary power on the jury, calling on it to perform numerous roles, allowing it to determine guilt or innocence in criminal cases, and to decide, at times, whether an offender should be sentenced to death. Juries are also asked to determine liability and set damages in civil cases. While the justice system gives the jury

[1] This chapter is adapted, in part, from three prior publications: Diamond and Casper (1992), Diamond et al. (1989), and Diamond and Vidmar (2001). I use the term blindfolding, rather than blinding, because when information is withheld from an individual, the individual may fill in the missing information based on previous experience and outside knowledge, sometimes correctly and sometimes incorrectly (i.e., peeks through the blindfold). A decision maker who peeks is not effectively blinded.

Blinding as a Solution to Bias
http://dx.doi.org/10.1016/B978-0-12-802460-7.00017-6

great responsibilities, questions have been raised about the ability of a group of laypersons to adequately perform its assigned tasks and to do so without bias. Early research portrayed the jury as a decision maker generally responsive to the evidence presented at trial (Kalven and Zeisel, 1966). More recently, critics of the jury have raised a variety of questions about jury competence, voicing doubts about jurors' abilities to analyze complex data logically, and return verdicts based on evidence rather than irrelevant considerations (for a review of this commentary, see, e.g., Cecil et al., 1991).

The jury's primary assigned role is as fact finder: jurors are asked to determine the facts of a case and to apply legal rules to these findings in impartial and accurate ways (e.g., In re Japanese Electronic Products Antitrust Litigation, 1980). In sharp contrast to early English juries—groups of witnesses assembled to report on facts they were presumed to know in advance of the formal proceedings (but perhaps supplemented by information presented in court (Klerman, 2003))—modern American juries are explicitly instructed to judge a case based only on information presented at trial. They are told not to be influenced by sympathy or prejudice. According to this model, the legal system uses jury selection to remove individuals who have formed an opinion in advance of the trial about the evidence likely to be introduced. The assumption is that those who remain at the end of jury selection will decide the case solely on the evidence presented in the courtroom.

Once the jury is empaneled, legal doctrine and procedures have traditionally treated the jurors as passive participants in the trial until it is time for the jury to deliberate and render a verdict. Jurors are presented with testimony elicited by questions from lawyers and occasionally from judges. They are instructed to listen carefully to testimony, but not to form impressions or make judgments about their ultimate verdict until all the testimony is completed and judicial instructions have been issued. Further, jurors are typically told not to discuss the evidence or possible verdicts until the end of the trial and after they have received final instructions on the law. While both common sense and empirical research suggest that few jurors will actually achieve the nearly complete passivity envisioned by these norms, the legal system generally proceeds as though these expectations are attainable goals.

Indeed, legal norms recognize that sometimes jurors simply cannot be expected to begin with and maintain strict neutrality, and procedures such as a change of venue or the declaration of a mistrial are sometimes used when evidence of prejudice or bias overcomes the presumption that the jury will be or is impartial. Still, although the rules of evidence treat the jury as a blank slate on which the trial testimony can be written and sometimes even erased (Tanford, 1990), some modern jury procedures have begun to recognize the value of permitting greater juror participation and activity in the course of the trial. Until recently, jury members were typically not permitted to clarify points by asking questions. While some attorneys have objected on the grounds that parties should have the right to control the production of testimony, courts are increasingly permitting jurors to submit questions for witnesses. For a judge's report on his experiences with allowing jurors to ask questions, see Wolfson (1987). For recent empirical research on the use of juror questions, see Mott (2003) and Diamond et al. (2006).

Moreover, the assumption that jury prejudices and predilections can be eradicated by, for example, a simple admonition is not absolute. In some contexts, the legal system recognizes, and in fact values, the personal experiences and common knowledge that jurors bring to their tasks. For instance, jurors are routinely instructed to use their common sense perceptions and experience in judging the credibility of witnesses.

In summary, the legal system struggles to balance the hypothetical ideal of the completely neutral blank slate decision maker and the common sense human decision maker who draws on life experiences to help judge the conflicting evidence presented at trial. Blindfolding is one of the tools employed in the effort to achieve this balance.

THE JURY AS ACTIVE INFORMATION PROCESSOR

There is substantial evidence that, like other human decision makers (Wong and Weiner, 1981), jurors do not conform to these assumptions of passivity (e.g., Diamond et al., 2014; Pennington and Hastie, 1992). Rather, jurors bring experience, expectations, and preconceptions with them to the trial; actively search for causal explanations to make sense of events about which they are told; and consciously or unconsciously process information, filling in blanks, or interpreting ambiguities in testimony in ways that may strongly influence their decisions. They may draw on their own experiences or those of others in processing evidence. Thus, the traditional legal model incorrectly presumes that jurors simply listen to the testimony and proceed as though it contains most or all of what they know about the case.

As an example, parties generally are not permitted to tell jurors whether defendants in automobile accident cases carry liability insurance (see, e.g., Fed. R. Evid. 411). Such information is legally irrelevant in the determination of fault or damages. However, as jurors listen to and consider the evidence, based on their own experiences with liability insurance and knowledge of its importance, they often consider whether a defendant has liability insurance. Furthermore, to make sense of the testimony they hear, jurors also search diligently for explanations for the behaviors described to them at trial. Knowledge structures or information-processing heuristics may also influence the ways jurors interpret ambiguous testimony and fill in "blanks" in the evidence presented during the trial.

Consequently, jurors and juries play an important and active role in evidence interpretation. Such activities take place during the trial itself, affecting what is perceived and the way evidence is understood, as well as during deliberations.

ATTEMPTS TO CONTROL JURIES

Critics have advocated a variety of methods of reining in and controlling jurors, from a complexity exception to the constitutional right to a jury trial (In re Japanese Electronic Products Antitrust Litigation, 1980:1086) to less-drastic measures such as specially qualified jurors (Nordenberg and Luneberg, 1982) and rules that limit the information jurors receive and are permitted to use in making their decisions (Diamond et al., 1989).

One of the most commonly employed techniques for controlling juror decision making is blindfolding, that is, when certain types of information are thought to be unduly biasing, jurors are sometimes denied access to such evidence. Such rules about blindfolding typically are justified on several grounds, including the possible bias that might be introduced by the undisclosed information; the possibility that some facts are so complicated that they might confuse rather than inform the jury; and the common exclusion of "irrelevant" evidence that by definition lacks probative value and will at best waste the jury's time and at worse improperly bias its decision making. The theory of blindfolding assumes that if a jury is denied a particular piece of information, then the jury will reach a more appropriate decision, that is, one based only on available evidence. The blindfolded jury thus provides the "baseline" from which nonblindfolded juries would be viewed as deviating. According to the theory of blindfolding, if information presented to a jury during the trial can be controlled, then the resulting jury's decision will be based solely on what the court permits the jury to see and hear.

The types of information denied to jurors vary across jurisdictions and encompass a wide range of evidence. In criminal trials, for example, the criminal record of defendants who do not testify generally cannot be made available to juries as evidence of their propensities to commit such acts. Similarly, hearsay evidence is excluded unless it meets one of the recognized exceptions.

Another common approach to juror control involves instructing juries to ignore available evidence. Perhaps the most studied case concerns instructions to disregard testimony (e.g., Landsman and Rakos, 1994; Sue et al., 1973; Wolf and Montgomery, 1977). Social science evidence and the advice of experienced attorneys who report that "you can't unring the bell" suggest that the instructional approach is likely to have a limited effect, on both jurors and judges (Landsman and Rakos, 1994; Wistrich et al., 2005). As human decision makers search for causation and motives, it is difficult for them to ignore evidence that they find useful in making sense of the facts of the case, and an admonition to ignore cannot overcome this information-processing activity. Moreover, certain types of outcome information may directly affect recall and interpretation of evidence so that even conscientious jurors may be unable to obey the judicial instruction, for the encoding and recall of other information are affected by the very evidence that the decision maker is supposed to ignore (Casper et al., 1988, 1989).

A third approach designed to harness jurors involves limiting instructions. Jurors are given information and are told that they are to consider it for one purpose but not for others. Following this instruction is difficult, and substantial research indicates that it is often impossible (Doob and Kirschenbaum, 1972; Eisenberg and Hans, 2009; Hans and Doob, 1975; Wissler and Saks, 1985).

All of these methods of controlling jurors' experiences are based on rather crude models of jurors as passive information absorbers. All may be defeated by the information-processing activities in which jurors and juries actively engage (Tiersma, 2014).

ASSESSING THE EFFECTS OF BLINDFOLDING AND INSTRUCTIONS

In prior research, I have examined with others the efficacy of the strategy of blindfolding, as well as its possible unintended consequences (Diamond and Casper, 1992). In particular, we explored the ways in which juror expectations may inhibit the effectiveness of blindfolds or may produce quite unintended consequences. The goal was to assess whether speculation about the impact of information is accurate and how juries, whether informed or blindfolded, tend to behave. The results suggest that a blindfolded jury does not necessarily come closer to the baseline or appropriate decision than a nonblindfolded jury.

In this research, we explored how juries react to two types of legal strategies designed to control decision making: (1) blindfolding the jury by denying certain types of information and (2) channeling jurors' decisions by providing information accompanied by directions as to how the information should be used. We focused on controlling jury decision making in situations in which jurors' expectations about the consequences of their decisions may influence the way they evaluate evidence and apply legal standards.

We also examined jurors' responses to a common and growing type of complex evidence: the testimony of experts. Some observers of the jury have suggested that jurors are incapable of evaluating the credibility of expert witnesses and of understanding the complex information contained in their testimony. Thus, we focused on how jurors assess and weigh statistical evidence.

Finally, we examined the process by which the predeliberation preferences of the individual jurors are transformed into the jury's final awards. We analyzed jury deliberations to explore the effects of the structure of initial preferences on jury awards, the selection and influence of the foreperson, and the extent to which jury deliberation appears to affect the jury's award.

In this study, we showed 12 versions of a simulated videotaped antitrust price-fixing case to 1022 jurors in a Cook County, Illinois, courthouse over a period of 8 months. We used six different sets of judicial instructions to test the effects of blindfolding on the jury. The study was designed to test five hypotheses about the effects of judicial instructions. The first and most general dealt with the effect of information about trebling on jurors' awards, while the remaining four explored in more detail how such knowledge might influence juror verdicts. In the first five conditions, jurors were instructed to compensate the plaintiff for any injury caused by the defendants' antitrust violations. The amount required to compensate the plaintiff is the standard for jury damage awards in civil cases in general as well as in antitrust cases in particular. In antitrust cases, the judge then trebles this amount to produce the final award. This trebling provision for antitrust damages is designed to act as a punishment and a deterrent to potential antitrust defendants. In experimental condition 6 ("unconstrained"), the jurors were instructed simply to award the amount they believed was appropriate and reasonable. We introduced this condition to obtain a measure of juror preference unfettered by judicial instruction on the standard for a damage award. In the first three conditions, the judge informed the jurors that their verdict would automatically be trebled. In condition 4 ("motive control"), jurors were not told about the automatic trebling provision of the statute, but were informed that the judge would add an amount for punishment and deterrence if appropriate.

We hypothesized that jurors told about the automatic trebling provision of the antitrust statute (conditions 1–3) would award less than jurors who were not told that their verdict would automatically be trebled (conditions 4–6). We also hypothesized that jurors admonished to disregard the fact that their verdict would be automatically trebled (condition 2) would award no more than jurors who were told that their verdict would automatically be trebled and who received no admonition to disregard that information (condition 1). We further hypothesized that jurors informed about the automatic trebling provision and given an explanation for this policy (condition 3) would give larger awards than jurors informed of trebling but given no explanation for the policy (conditions 1 and 2).

If blindfolding jurors to the automatic trebling provision leaves them with a motive to punish and deter, then their verdicts would exceed the amounts they would award strictly to compensate the plaintiff. Thus, we hypothesized that jurors instructed to award an amount necessary to compensate the plaintiff for the damages caused by the defendant's antitrust violation (condition 5) would award less than jurors who were told to award an amount that is reasonable and fair (condition 6). Further, jurors who were told the judge would, if necessary, add to their award for the purposes of punishment and deterrence (condition 4) would award less than if they were simply told to compensate (condition 5). If jurors were not told to focus on compensation (condition 6), then they would give higher awards than those told to focus on compensation (condition 5). Informing jurors that the judge may add value to account for punishment and deterrence could prevent jurors from adding to their own award to punish and deter. The hypothesis is based on the assumption that learning that the judge will take care of punishment and deterrence will reduce the motivation to add such amounts.

As these hypotheses indicate, we predicted that awards would generally increase from condition 1 to condition 6, with no difference expected between conditions 1 and 2. Some, but not all, of our predictions were supported:

- As predicted, jurors who were told about trebling gave significantly lower awards than jurors who were not told.
- Although jurors who were told about automatic trebling but not admonished to ignore the trebling rule gave somewhat lower awards than did jurors who were told but admonished to disregard it, the difference did not approach significance.
- The average award given by jurors in condition 3 (trebling with an explanation) was significantly higher than the average award given by the jurors in conditions 1 and 2 who were told about trebling but given no explanation for it. Thus, jurors responded to a collaborative instruction, one that gave a reason for the legal rule they were being asked to follow.
- The average award given by the unconstrained jurors in condition 6 was not significantly higher than the average award given by the jurors in condition 5, who were simply instructed to compensate the plaintiff for his losses.
- Jurors who heard an instruction that mentioned punishment and deterrence tended to see the defendants as somewhat more blameworthy than those who heard no mention of punishment and deterrence in the instruction.

This evidence is thus inconsistent with the model of the jury as a passive and fully malleable recipient of testimony. Moreover, the response to the expert testimony in the study revealed that even when the testimony is arcane, complex, and difficult to follow, jurors make conscientious and often successful efforts to deal with the substance of what they hear, and their decisions reflect such activity. Yet even if juries pay close attention to both facts and law, they do not always follow the letter of the law. Rather, the jury portrayed in this research is a receptive, but not uncritical, audience for legal instruction, more responsive to the law when an acceptable rationale for the legal rule is provided.

This approach not only suggests active evaluation and perhaps even subtlety in dealing with expert testimony, but it also indicates the care jurors use in evaluating evidence to reach their decisions. When presented with complex statistical testimony, jurors were not simply overpowered by material they did not understand. Rather, the persuasive force of such testimony appeared to depend in substantial measure on the ability of the expert to express clearly the basis for the conclusions the testimony is being used to support. Our results thus suggest that concerns about jurors' uncritical willingness to accept statistical evidence may be overstated.

Finally, blindfolding may produce undesired interjury variation. Some juries may have correct expectations (e.g., that damage awards will be trebled), while others operate on incorrect assumptions (e.g., that the total award of the plaintiff will be the amount chosen by the jury or that the jury itself is supposed to award triple damages).

Thus, both correct and incorrect expectations may lead the blindfolded jury astray. Moreover, by pursuing a policy limited to blindfolding, the legal system may neglect more effective alternative techniques such as *voir dire* or clear and thorough judicial instructions to deal with the problems that blindfolding was intended to address.

THE ROLE OF EXPECTATIONS IN JURY DECISION MAKING

To the extent that the personal beliefs and expectations of jurors influence how they evaluate evidence, blindfolding may be ineffective or have unanticipated negative effects. A blindfold may permit the jury to reach a verdict based on misinformation and may bypass opportunities to mold the jury's use of information through *voir dire* and jury instructions. Not all juror expectations are accurate, and when the inaccuracies go uncorrected at trial because of blindfolding, such false expectations may influence jury verdicts. Moreover, jurors may speculate beyond the evidence before them. For example, while the data are limited, they suggest that jurors do speculate about who will bear the cost of a damage award. If that natural speculation is ignored by the legal system, it may become enmeshed in juror information processing and influence decisions.

In a study published in 1989, two colleagues and I asked 192 registered voters in Illinois to consider how much a person injured in an automobile accident should receive from a defendant who caused, or at least contributed to, an accident (Diamond et al., 1989). Despite the fact that this set of questions took only a few minutes, nearly one-quarter (24%) of the respondents spontaneously mentioned insurance while answering the questions. This result suggests that the question of insurance was close to the surface for these respondents and likely to be brought out in deliberations by individual jurors, potentially affecting the other jurors. Thus, blindfolding may not eliminate biases produced by juror reactions to insurance if juries generally assume that the defendant is insured. Alternatively, directly informing the jury about insurance may actually increase the likelihood of a well-founded jury decision by providing relevant information advocating the value of fuller disclosure (Diamond and Vidmar, 2001; Diamond et al., 2012; Greene et al., 2008).

The potential distortions attributable to juror expectations and compounded by blindfolding are not limited to civil cases. Some jurisdictions do not require the parties or the court to inform the jury what sentence the offender would be eligible to receive if the jury refused to impose death. This exclusion assumes that the jury will make its decision in a vacuum, uninfluenced by the concern or expectation that the offender will soon be released if he is not executed. One cannot know how often such speculation occurs, but the available evidence suggests that when it does occur, expectations about the alternative sentence may affect the probability of a death sentence.

When the jury holds false expectations about the facts of the case (e.g., that the partially insured defendant is fully insured) or about the consequences of its decision (e.g., that not imposing the death penalty will leave the offender eligible for eventual parole), the decision of the jury may be distorted unnecessarily. The justification for blindfolding is lost. To weigh the usefulness of a decision to blindfold jurors against the potential costs of such a decision, the first step is to assess juror expectations and how they affect jury decisions. Despite the substantial attention that social scientists have given to juries, there has been surprisingly little work done on this topic.

When jurors hold differing expectations or beliefs, blindfolding prevents the court and the parties from substituting consistent information for these differing expectations. The effect can be to promote uncertainty in decision making. A blindfold applied over systematically incorrect or inconsistent juror expectations can affect the judgments of the jury. Until we know what expectations jurors hold and how those expectations affect jury decisions, it is difficult to evaluate the costs and benefits of applying a blindfold rather than pursuing some other approach to channeling juror behavior.

THE CASE AGAINST BLINDFOLDING

Apart from the blindfold, the standard method used to direct the jury's attention away from biasing information is an instruction that tells the jury to disregard information or use it for a limited purpose. For example, criminal juries are usually instructed to use defendants' criminal records solely to assist in judging credibility, but not as evidence that they are the kind of people who commit such acts. Such instructions may have limited effects if the language commands jurors to forget or ignore information, which the instructions have just made more salient, or if the information affects jurors' perceptions of other aspects of the cases.

Beyond blindfolding the jury or instructing it to disregard certain facts, a third strategy for dealing with such material is worth exploring. Jurors are decision makers who search for the causes of the behavior they are asked to judge, and who are aware of and interested in the consequences of their decisions for the parties and the community at large. The law in some contexts may be able to deal most effectively with potentially biasing information if it acknowledges these characteristics of jurors by (1) informing them of the evidence or legal rule at issue and (2) explaining to them the reasons why they ought to ignore or discount such material in reaching their judgment.

This point is illustrated by the practice in private antitrust litigation of preventing judges or attorneys from informing juries that courts will automatically treble damage awards. Congress provided for automatic treble damages to punish and deter antitrust violations and to provide incentives to plaintiffs to pursue such suits (15 U.S.C. Section 15 (1988)).

Before the early 1970s, judicial instructions generally informed juries that their verdict would automatically be trebled (E. Devitt and C. Blackmar, Federal Jury Practice and Instructions Section 90.39 (3d ed. 1977)). Then, beginning in 1974 with Pollock & Riley, Inc. v. Pearl Brewing Co. (1974), several courts of appeals reached decisions denying disclosure of trebling to the jury. The justification for withholding this information was that the jury would then reduce its award below compensation level in an effort to prevent a plaintiff windfall. No empirical research had tested the validity of this assumption about how juries behave, although jurors interviewed after several major antitrust cases expressed surprise and dismay when they learned for the first time that their award would be trebled, claiming that had they known, they would have awarded less.

I described earlier our study of juror response to various approaches to instructions about trebling (Diamond and Casper, 1992), which supported concern that merely telling jurors that their award would be trebled did indeed lead to a reduction in awards. But what is key about the other results from that study is that informing the jurors about the punishment and deterrence rationale for the trebling completely eliminated the reduction. Thus, if we decide to remove the blindfold, that decision still leaves open the question of how the information will be conveyed to the jury. In my research with others, we tested the ability of college students to understand a typical instruction designed to inform the jury that its verdict in an antitrust case would automatically be trebled (Diamond et al., 1989). Although respondents generally had little difficulty understanding the testimony in the simulated antitrust case, fewer than half the respondents understood that the court would multiply the jury's damages award by three. It was only when we altered the language of the instruction to convey the idea of trebling more clearly that the respondents were able to describe accurately the size of the ultimate award.

As these results indicate, both a persuasive rationale and attention to instruction clarity may be required to obtain the benefits of a lifted blindfold.

WHEN BLINDFOLDING IS REQUIRED

I have discussed above a set of examples in which blindfolding the jury may not achieve its asserted purposes. The arguments depend greatly on the extent to which jurors bring expectations and knowledge to their task, the relationship between such expectations and legal rules, and the ways in which expectations and rules influence verdict choices under conditions in which evidence is denied or supplied to jurors. There is, however, a class of information for which, based on the available evidence about juror decision making, blindfolding may actually be an appropriate policy.

Perhaps the most studied and clearest case involves information about the criminal record of defendants who take the stand to testify on their own behalf. Rules in most federal and state courts permit the prosecutor to introduce such information, but only for the purpose of impeaching the credibility of the witness (Fed. R. Evid. 609(a)). When criminal record information is introduced, the judge gives a limiting instruction to tell jurors to consider a defendant's criminal record only in evaluating the credibility of the defendant's testimony, and to ignore the defendant's record in deciding on the issue of guilt or innocence. As noted earlier, both common sense and empirical evidence suggest that adhering to these instructions will be difficult (Doob and Kirschenbaum, 1972; Eisenberg and Hans, 2009; Hans and Doob, 1975; Wissler and Saks, 1985). Given these findings, replacing admission of the evidence for a limited purpose with a policy of complete blindfolding seems appropriate (Tanford and Bocchino, 1980).

Blindfolding also seems appropriate in civil suits filed under 42 U.S.C. Section 1983 against police officers alleged to have engaged in illegal searches (Casper et al., 1988, 1989). Legal rules permit introduction of evidence obtained in an illegal search, but jurors are admonished to disregard such evidence in determining both the liability of the police and the extent of damages. Casper and coauthors found that despite this admonition, jurors who were told that the search had turned up evidence of illegal behavior by the plaintiff gave significantly fewer damage awards and lower-value awards than those who were told that the search had not turned up such evidence. As with the criminal record example, blindfolding appears necessary to prevent jurors from being biased by this information.

How might we draw conceptual distinctions that would suggest the conditions under which denying information is likely to be a desirable or undesirable policy? The answer may lie in the ways jurors comprehend, process, and recall testimony presented at trial. As noted above, if a piece of evidence is likely to become so embedded in jurors' comprehension of evidence that admonitions or other techniques will clearly be ineffective, then blindfolding may be necessary. When this is not the case, other remedies may be preferable.

Two other examples that are likely to restructure thinking and affect decision making are previous settlement offers in civil suits or subsequent repairs in slip-and-fall cases. Offers to settle or to shoulder substantial responsibility for an injury or to make a repair subsequent to an accident might influence crucial elements of the story that jurors develop from the testimony. Such evidence is typically excluded by the rules of evidence in recognition of its potentially prejudicial impact. These rules seem justified. Thus, there are types of evidence that may have a powerful effect on how jurors construct and recall the total evidence in a case. Jurors' mental representations affect their application of legal rules in ways that may be impervious to judicial instructions about how much weight, if any, and for what purpose, to give to the evidence. When information-processing effects are very strong, blindfolding may be the only way to deal with the potentially biasing effects of such information. I believe that more theoretical and empirical work on juror information processing can provide a rewarding framework to evaluate those contexts in which blindfolding is a necessary or unnecessary policy to employ.

MINIMIZING HARMFUL EFFECTS WHEN BLINDFOLDING IS NOT A PLAUSIBLE STRATEGY

The traditional remedy for the introduction of inadmissible evidence is to admonish the jury to ignore it. The same approach is generally taken if the jury submits a question to the court about an impermissible topic such as insurance. As the data from the Arizona Jury Project indicate, a simple admonition cannot be depended upon to terminate juror conversations about insurance or other pertinent topics, although an admonition may be more successful than simply ignoring a juror question on the topic (Diamond et al., 2003; Heuer and Penrod, 1994). In both the Diamond et al. study and the Heuer and Penrod study, the jurors rarely revealed a direct connection between their thoughts about insurance and their verdicts, but the evidence from their often-extensive discussions about insurance suggests that some further effort by the courts may be appropriate.

One possibility would be to permit full disclosure of the insurance status of the parties. This approach would cut off juror speculation about insurance coverage and would prevent jurors from drawing inaccurate conclusions about the insurance status of the parties (e.g., concluding that defendants lack insurance because no insurance company is a named party in the suit). A court permitting full disclosure of the insurance status of the parties could then instruct jurors that insurance is not relevant in assessing liability or the appropriate level of damages. Although some jurors might ignore the admonition, such a practice would avoid a situation in which some jurors believe that insurance is a relevant consideration and others do not. The problem with a simple admonition to ignore the topic is that it generally fails to deter jurors from discussing insurance. Contrast this approach with one that does not disclose the actual insurance coverage of the parties in the case, but does address directly the issue of insurance and why jurors should not consider it. Such an instruction would both emphasize the irrelevance of insurance and highlight the complexity of gauging coverage, thus accurately undermining the claims of any member of the jury who purported to know more about the party's insurance than the trial revealed. It would thus both recognize and address the jury's predisposition to speculate about insurance (for suggested language, see Diamond and Vidmar, 2001). Such partial blindfolds on topics that jurors are likely to discuss and speculate about may hold promise for offering needed guidance and for balancing the costs and benefits of blindfolding.

CONCLUSIONS

Legal rules forbidding juries access to available information have often been imposed to improve jury decision making. Such policies are based on untested assumptions about how jurors make decisions. These policies ignore the role of juror expectations and beliefs that mold jury interpretation of evidence and affect jury decisions. When jurors are taken seriously and efforts are made to deal with their concerns and expectations—when they are treated as active coparticipants rather than passive absorbers of information—they appear to be willing and able to respond more appropriately to the dictates of legal rules. Studies conducted over the past two decades have examined the sources of jury reactions to legal constraints, especially the individual and collective processes that produce such reactions. Such investigations can both increase our understanding of jury behavior (and lay response to legal rules more generally) and explore alternative approaches to jury guidance and control.

Nonetheless, existing evidence that jurors are active information processors leads to a number of predictions about jurors' responses to the various approaches to channeling and controlling their decision making. Some of the techniques summarized here are commonly employed today: blindfolding, instructions to ignore information, and limiting instructions. Others are less often used—for example, directly discussing information that may be troubling jurors and explaining why the information ought to be used in a certain fashion or attempting to deal with jury concerns and inclinations by specifying what will be addressed by the actions of the judge. Reform efforts, such as providing preliminary instructions and supplying jurors with written copies of the instructions, may assist the jury in understanding and applying laws, but these aids can only be helpful if the instructions themselves are comprehensible and provide the missing information or explanations that jurors seek.

While there is a large body of jury-related research, much of it fails to go beyond studying the production of verdicts. More research is needed to understand how jurors as active information processors attempt to make sense out of their tasks. By treating the jury as a collaborator helping to develop a meaningful basis for decision rather than as a passive recipient simply accepting information and instruction, we can develop a clearer understanding of how this powerful institution performs, as well as how to optimize that performance.

References

Casper, J.D., Benedict, K., Perry, J.L., 1988. Cognitions, attitudes and decision-making in search and seizure cases. Journal of Applied Social Psychology 18 (2), 93–113.

Casper, J.D., Benedict, K., Perry, J.L., 1989. Juror decision making, attitudes, and the hindsight bias. Law and Human Behavior 13 (3), 291–310.

Cecil, J.S., Hans, V.P., Wiggins, E.C., 1991. Citizen comprehension of difficult issues: lessons from civil jury trials. American University Law Review 40, 727–774.

Diamond, S.S., Casper, J.D., 1992. Blindfolding the jury to verdict consequences: damages, experts, and the civil jury. Law and Society Review 26 (3), 513–564.

Diamond, S.S., Casper, J.D., Ostergren, L., 1989. Blindfolding the jury. Law and Contemporary Problems 52, 247–267.
Diamond, S.S., Murphy, B., Rose, M.R., 2012. The 'Kettleful of Law' in real jury deliberations: successes, failures and next steps. Northwestern University Law Review 106, 1537–1608.
Diamond, S.S., Rose, M.R., Murphy, B., 2014. Embedded experts on real juries: a delicate balance. William & Mary Law Review 55, 885–933.
Diamond, S.S., Rose, M.R., Murphy, B., Smith, S., 2006. Juror questions during trial: a window into juror thinking. Vanderbilt Law Review 59 (6), 1927–1972.
Diamond, S.S., Vidmar, N., December 2001. Jury room ruminations on forbidden topics. Virginia Law Review 87 (8), 1857–1915. Symposium: New Perspectives on Evidence.
Diamond, S.S., Vidmar, N., Rose, M., Ellis, L., Murphy, B., 2003. Jury discussions during civil trials: studying an Arizona innovation. University of Arizona Law Review 45, 1–81.
Doob, A.N., Kirschenbaum, H.M., 1972. Some empirical evidence on the effect of s.12 of the Canada Evidence Act upon an accused. Criminal Law Quarterly 15 (88), 93–95.
Eisenberg, T., Hans, V.P., 2009. Taking a stand on taking the stand: the effect of a prior criminal record on the decision to testify and on trial outcomes. Cornell Law Review 94, 1353–1390.
Greene, E., Hayman, K., Motyl, M., 2008. "Shouldn't we consider…?" Jury discussions of forbidden topics and effects on damage awards. Psychology, Public Policy, and Law 14, 194–222.
Hans, V.P., Doob, A.N., 1975. Section 12 of the Canada Evidence Act and the deliberation of simulated juries. Criminal Law Quarterly 18, 235–253.
Heuer, L., Penrod, S., 1994. Juror notetaking and question asking during trials: a national field experiment. Law and Human Behavior 18 (121), 127–129.
In re Japanese Electronic Prods. Antitrust Litigation, 631 F.2d 1069, 1079 (3d Cir. 1980).
Kalven, H., Zeisel, H., 1966. The American Jury. Little, Brown, Boston.
Klerman, D., 2003. Was the jury ever self-informing? Southern California Law Review 77, 124–149.
Landsman, S., Rakos, R., 1994. A preliminary inquiry into the effect of potentially biasing information on judges and jurors in civil litigation. Behavioral Sciences and the Law 12, 113–126.
Mott, N.L., 2003. The current debate on juror questions: 'To ask or not to ask, that is the question'. Chicago-Kent Law Review 78, 1099–1125.
Nordenberg, M.A., Luneberg, W.V., 1982. Decision making in complex federal civil cases: two alternatives to the traditional jury. Judicature 65, 420–431.
Pennington, N., Hastie, R., 1992. Explaining the evidence: tests of the story model for juror decision making. Journal of Personality and Social Psychology 62, 189–206.
Pollock & Riley, Inc. v. Pearl Brewing Co. 498 F.2d 1240 (5th Cir. 1974).
Sue, S., Smith, R.E., Caldwell, C., 1973. Effects of inadmissible evidence on the decisions of simulated jurors: a moral dilemma. Journal of Applied Social Psychology 3, 345–353.
Tanford, J.A., 1990. The law and psychology of jury instructions. Nebraska Law Review 69, 71–73.
Tanford, J., Bocchino, A., 1980. Rape victim shield laws and the Sixth Amendment. University of Pennsylvania Law Review 128, 544–551.
Tiersma, P., 2014. Asking jurors to do the impossible. Tennessee Journal of Law and Policy 5 (2), 105–147.
Wissler, R.L., Saks, M.J., 1985. On the inefficacy of limiting instructions: when jurors use prior conviction evidence to decide on guilt. Law and Human Behavior 9 (1), 37–48.
Wistrich, A.J., Guthrie, C., Rachlinski, J.J., 2005. Can judges ignore inadmissible information? The difficulty of deliberately disregarding. University of Pennsylvania Law Review 153, 1251–1345.
Wolf, S., Montgomery, D.A., 1977. Effects of inadmissible evidence and level of judicial admonishment to disregard on the judgments of mock jurors. Journal of Applied Social Psychology 7, 205–219.
Wolfson, W.D., February 1987. An experiment in juror interrogation of witnesses. CBA Record 12.
Wong, P.T.P., Weiner, B., 1981. When people ask "why" questions, and the heuristics of attributional search. Journal of Personality & Social Psychology 40 (650), 661–662.

CHAPTER

18

The Compliance Equation: Creating a More Ethical and Equitable Campaign Financing System by Blinding Contributions to Federal Candidates

Bertram J. Levine[1], Michael Johnston[2]

[1]Department of Political Science, Rutgers University, New Brunswick, NJ, USA; [2]Department of Political Science, Colgate University, Hamilton, NY, USA

OUTLINE

Blinding as a Solution to Bias
http://dx.doi.org/10.1016/B978-0-12-802460-7.00018-8

INTRODUCTION

The Federal Election Campaign Act (FECA) was originally passed in 1971 and amended in 1974, 1976, and 1979. The last major change to federal campaign finance law occurred in 2002 with passage of the Bipartisan Campaign Reform Act of 2002 (BCRA).

FECA included four major anticorruption provisions: a ceiling on the amount that any one contributor could provide to a candidate and a limitation on independent expenditures (2 U.S.C. Section 441a); a prohibition on corporate and union contributions (2 U.S.C. Section 441b); a limitation on independent expenditures; and a requirement that contributions to federal candidates in excess of specified amounts be reported to the Federal Election Commission (FEC) and disclosed to the public (2 U.S.C. Section 434). In this chapter, we will argue that public reporting—seemingly the least controversial aspect of the law—is in fact the source of much corruption-related activity.

FECA's authors intended the disclosure requirement, along with the three other provisions, to discourage corrupt behavior that might result from making or receiving large contributions. But beyond actual corruption, Congress was also concerned about the appearance of corruption.

During consideration of the original FECA bill, expectations for the cleansing properties of its disclosure provisions ran high. The Committee for an Effective Congress testified: "We think full disclosure will solve most of the abuses. It is more important than anything else to get a law that requires reporting" (Senate Committee on Commerce, 1971, p. 215).

Testifying at the same hearings, Senator Robert Dole of Kansas, then serving as the Republican National Committee Chairman in addition to his senatorial responsibilities, argued:

> [O]pen reporting of the sources and amounts of contributions would…make candidates less subject to apparent or real pressures from large contributors…. Reporting and disclosure guard against both the fact and the suspicion of favoritism. ***Senate Committee on Commerce (1971, p. 215).***

The Supreme Court has consistently agreed that avoiding the appearance of corruption furthers a compelling state interest. Shortly after passage of FECA, Senator James Buckley (R-NY) challenged the constitutionality of the new law in federal court. The case, Buckley v. Valeo (1976), eventually went to the Supreme Court. In its decision affirming the constitutionality of contributions limitations but rejecting limitations of campaign expenditures, the Court addressed the appropriateness of mandatory public disclosure of contributions. The Court held:

> Of almost equal concern as the danger of actual quid pro quo arrangements is the impact of the appearance of corruption stemming from public awareness of the opportunities for abuse inherent in a regime of large individual financial contributions. ***Buckley v. Valeo (1976, p. 28).***

The Court was at least as optimistic as Dole and the committee had been, further noting, "The interest in alleviating the corrupting influence of large contributions is served by the Act's contribution limitations and disclosure provisions" (Buckley v. Valeo, 1976, p. 55).

Was this optimism well founded? Subsequent observations by former members of Congress provide some cause for alarm. On the issue of corruption, veteran legislators have been quoted saying the following:

> There is not tit for tat in this business, no check for a vote. But nonetheless the influence is there. Candidates know where the money is coming from. ***Rep. Timothy Penny [D-MN] as quoted in Schram (1995, p. 151).***

> I have on many occasions sat down and listened to people solely because I know they have contributed to my campaign. ***Rep. James Bacchus [D-FL] as quoted in Schram (1995, p. 149).***

There has been similar sentiment on the issue of the appearance of corruption:

> By its very existence, it (the practice of Members soliciting contributions from interests regulated by their committees) compromises the integrity of the institution. ***Rep. James Bacchus [D-FL] as quoted in Schram (1995, p. 15).***

These observations are representative of other comments made by former members of Congress. They offer strong evidence that FECA's reporting requirement has, in many ways, been a dismal failure in its inability to deter unethical fund-raising behavior and to reduce appearances of corruption for many voters. What it has done is to produce a series of unintended consequences that, if not amounting to quid pro quo corruption, have tilted an already unleveled playing field further in the direction of big contributors and incumbent candidates.

By providing incumbent candidates information about which donors have given to whom, mandatory disclosure has created an inhospitable environment for those considering making contributions to challengers. Many such potential donors might reasonably fear retribution in the event that their chosen candidates lose to the favored incumbents. As a result, challengers have been further disadvantaged in their efforts to raise sufficient funds to take on incumbents (see below, "Intimidation Corruption").

Public disclosure has also provided much material for journalists and others to suggest cause-and-effect (i.e., quid pro quo) relationships between contributions and congressional decision making even though none may exist. Harvard Law School Professor Lawrence Lessig has commented on this tendency:

> [W]e're as likely to jump from some stray fact to a conclusion it can't support ("He took money from banks, he must be bought by the banks")... There is...an endless stream of "gotcha" journalism linking a decision to contribute with almost no integrity on the other side. That gotcha in turn feeds the already profound cynicism that Americans have. ***Lessig (2011, p. 257).***

Finally, FECA and BCRA have done little to discourage non-quid pro quo corruption that exists as a result of members knowing who has, and has not, contributed to their own campaigns. Through the normal course of fund-raising and lobbying processes, members become deeply aware of who their benefactors are, and, as a result of well-timed visits by lobbyists, they also become equally aware of what objectives these lobbyist-contributors are pursuing. Congress, when writing FECA, mandated reporting of inputs, that is, contributions, but not outputs—the "favors" that legislators might do for contributors. Thus, Congress provided for only a portion of what is needed to uncover potentially corrupt activity. In this way, FECA set the stage for misleading, sometimes inflammatory, misuse of campaign finance reports.

ANONYMITY: AN ALTERNATIVE TO MANDATORY DISCLOSURE

There is an alternate course for combating the potential for contributions-related corruption: anonymity for the specific sources of contributions and independent expenditures. This idea is not entirely new with us; some students of campaign finance have recommended, or at least noted, this approach in the past (Ackerman and Ayres, 2002; Ayres, 2001; Levine, 1997), but the idea has never gained traction. For many in the political world, the approach was so obviously dead on arrival that it simply did not merit the time to consider it.

There are likely several reasons for the lack of consideration given to anonymous election campaign donation proposals. These reasons include the "out of the box" nature of the proposal, serious concerns about implementation problems, the possibility of disadvantaging important communities that now benefit from the information made available via mandatory public reporting, and the question of constitutionality.

With regard to "out of the box" thinking, the idea that "sunlight is the best disinfectant" has become virtually sacrosanct. A sort of political correctness has attached to our thinking about the subject—to say that eliminating disclosure would eliminate the corruption or appearance of corruption problems is now close to a heresy.

But this fact seems incontrovertible: anonymity for the sources of contributions, if properly structured, is the only policy change suggested to date that would sever the link between campaign contributions and candidates' ability to favor contributors or disadvantage challengers. It would make contributions-driven corruption impossible in all but the most aggravated of circumstances—that is, the kind of circumstances that involve true quid pro quo corruption. Severing the link is essential.

DEFINING CORRUPTION

To evaluate FECA's potential effects on corruption, we must begin by defining "corruption." It is not a simple task, even at the level of analytical conceptualization; indeed, no one has yet proposed a universally accepted definition. And when it comes to the sorts of corruption many claim to see within the political finance process, the term becomes even more murky, linked as it is to perceptions, expectations, and (dis)trust in the system. Those sorts of intangibles are difficult to define and even more difficult to measure, but, as we shall see, they are at the core of what many people see as wrong with the current system and of what it might take to restore its credibility.

Systemic Corruption

Much of our discussion focuses on what might be termed "influence market corruption." This sort of corruption revolves around "access to, and advantages within, established institutions…[T]he costs of running for office create incentives for politicians to put their connections and expertise up for rent" (Johnston, 2005, p. 42).

Influence market corruption, like most American political finance practices, works "mostly within the system... Power-oriented corruption will focus on winning office and influencing those who hold them" (Johnston, 2005, p. 42). Much of it, indeed, involves practices—lobbying, contributions to campaigns, constituent service, responsiveness on the part of elected officials to various points of view—that are not only wholly legal, but also positive aspects of democratic politics. Still, these are activities and practices that have been pushed beyond boundaries of acceptability—boundaries, critically, that are matters of opinion and perception, not the law, and on which there may be much disagreement. As Johnston has previously noted:

> Some major channels may be legalized and regulated (such as the financing of campaigns) while in others, rules and expectations can be unclear... Public or private parties may take the initiative, or be the prime beneficiaries, but given the affluence of most societies in this category, wealthy interests seeking political influence will dominate Influence Markets. ***Johnston (2005, p. 43).***

By contrast, many other citizens feel left out of the process of government. Even if they express that sense in diffuse terms—feelings of powerlessness, or a sense that democracy has been hijacked by an influential few—they are echoing Warren's argument that the essence of corruption in a democracy is a "duplicitous and harmful exclusion...[from] collective decisions and actions" (Warren, 2004). Perceptions of exclusion are a critical source of discontent with the current system and must be directly addressed if we are to find a better way forward.

Lessig (2011) has developed yet another, not inconsistent, variation on this analytical theme. He holds that the present federal campaign finance system, which is largely based on private contributions, has led to "dependence corruption." This form of corruption, according to Lessig, occurs when "individuals within an institution become dependent upon an influence that distracts them from the intended purpose of the institution" (Lessig, 2011, p. 15). He then makes an especially poignant observation: "It is this pattern that explains that corruption can occur without assuming evil or criminal souls at the helm" (Lessig, 2011, p. 17). There need not be a mens rea—criminal intent.

The Deeper Issue

All of these trends and discontents are lamentable. But are they really corruption, and can we call them such without stretching the concept beyond all recognition? Because few if any laws are broken by most participants in financing contemporary campaigns, are we going overboard by speaking of "legalized corruption"?

For the most part, modern definitions of corruption focus upon "public" people or actions violating laws, or other fairly specific standards, for private benefit, and frequently emphasize quid pro quo exchanges. But they fail to get at that sense of exclusion, and of the distortion or outright appropriation of democratic processes that most citizens and many critics see as corrupting American campaign finance. To get at those concerns, some traditional conceptions of the term might be more useful. Dobel (1978) points out that for many classical thinkers (broadly speaking), corruption was a collective or societal of being—"corruption of the body politic"—and not an attribute of a particular action or individual. Beginning with Thucydides' accounts of Athens during the Peloponnesian War, but bringing the analysis ahead to the time of Machiavelli and Rousseau, Dobel argues that the key issue is the corruption of the state as a whole: the "extensive demise of loyalty to the commonwealth [that] comes from the interaction of human nature with systematic inequality of wealth, power and status" (Dobel, 1978, p. 958). When loyalty is in question, the essence of a just political order is threatened, and a key link between leaders and citizens can be lost.

By today's standards, it might seem quaint or contentious to speak of corruption in such sweeping terms. But the contemporary decline in public trust in electoral politics is a strong parallel. Citizens are not rioting in the streets or demanding that the Constitution be shredded, but solid majorities perceive that their views and well-being no longer count for much in electoral politics, which is also the key process by which many supposedly also assert their equal standing as citizens. When it comes to the ways campaigns are financed, "systematic inequality" is an inescapable fact—made all the more so by public disclosure. Over the past few decades, belief in the fairness, openness, and responsiveness of political processes has been the loser. That fully legal activities are the basis of such systemic estrangement suggests that, at least as viewed from this "classical" perspective, the current system is indeed one of legalized corruption.

HOW DISCLOSURE CONTRIBUTES TO LEGALIZED CORRUPTION

Exactly what Senator Dole meant by "apparent or real pressures from large contributors," and by "fact or suspicion of favoritism," is not spelled out in his testimony, but it seems that he contemplated the possibility that some contributors might seek, and candidate-legislators might grant, special treatment tied to contributions. Such favored treatment rendered pursuant to an explicit agreement ("my money for your favor") would qualify as bribery, clearly a criminal transaction. An explicit demand by an elected official ("your money, or I bottle up your pet legislation") would be extortion, equally unlawful.

But if the transaction were more subtle—say, a purposeful act (most often in the form of a contribution) performed by a lobbyist intended to elicit a specific response from a member of Congress; or the reverse, a member inserting a provision in a draft bill to please a lobbyist-contributor—then less-obvious unethical activity could be at work. This activity may be called de facto corruption. If done skillfully—without an explicit agreement—then such activities do not violate the law. But in Dobel's terms, do they add to the "demise [or, at least a diminution] of loyalty to the commonwealth?" It may well be argued that de facto corruption—to the extent that the general public knows, or even suspects that it exists—undermines the credibility of, and public faith in, the key processes of democratic government.

In McCutcheon v. Federal Election Commission (2012), Shaun McCutcheon, an Alabama businessman, and others challenged the constitutionality of federal limits on *aggregate* campaign contributions that emanate from a single source. The limits were established in BCRA of 2002. In this case, a federal District Court provided one example of how a political contribution made well within the bounds of the law may contribute to corruption of the state: "The candidate who knows the…funding derives from that single large check at the joint fundraising event will know precisely where to lay the wreath of gratitude"

(McCutcheon v. Federal Election Commission, 2012, p. 140). Without disclosure of the source, the wreath could not be laid.[1]

Two recent observations are of particular note in this context. Leon Panetta and Chuck Hagel are former members of Congress and former Secretaries of State. Each enjoys a strong reputation for accomplishment, intelligence, and maintaining high ethical standards. Their observations reveal an environment in which subtle unethical behavior is simply accepted as a way of doing business in Congress:

> Panetta: "Legalized bribery" has become part of the culture of how this place operates... [Today's members of the House and Senate] rarely legislate; they basically follow the money...they're spending more and more time dialing for dollars....The only place they have to turn is to lobbyists. ***Kaiser (2009, quoting Panetta, p. 19).***

> Hagel: There's no shame anymore... We've blown past the ethical standards; we now play on the edge of legal standards. ***Kaiser (2009, quoting Hagel, p. 19).***

While not in so many words, it is reasonable to assume that Panetta and Hagel strongly suggest a link between lawmakers' access to information about the sources of their campaign funds and their subsequent legislative activities. Again, these links could not exist if members did not know the identities of their benefactors.

Intimidation Corruption

Like de facto corruption, intimidation corruption is not a form of corrupt activity recognized in the law. Often it takes the form of "soft (or not-so-soft) extortion," in which powerful public figures leverage their positions to obtain contributions from potential contributors (Abramoff, 2011).

The too-often accepted fund-raising narrative depicts "high-powered," avaricious lobbyists pumping money into campaign treasuries and then demanding services from financially dependent legislators. (Recall Dole's comment about "candidates...subject to apparent or real pressures from large contributors.") But the real-life sequence is often quite the reverse: Contributors do not always, if ever, have the upper hand in fund-raising transactions. Frequently, it is the potential contributor who finds himself under pressure from the member or the member's staff.

Because candidates know who has given how much to whom, and because contributors know that candidates know this, candidates—especially incumbents—can take advantage of their position to put added pressure on potential donors. The message often goes like this: "The boss is very disappointed that you have contributed to [another candidate] but have not decided to support his reelection."

Clawson, Neustadtl, and Weller, reporting on a mail survey of political action committee (PAC) managers that they conducted for their book, *Dollars and Votes: How Business Campaign Contributions Subvert Democracy*, revealed, "5 out of 6 (83.7 percent) [of] corporations reported that candidates pressured them for a contribution at least occasionally; 1 in 5 (18.8 percent)

[1] The court here was discussing the original source of funding that flowed from a contribution to a party joint fund-raising event and thence on to a single candidate's campaign fund. The full citation is 893 F. Supp. 2d 133, 140 (D.C. 2012).

TABLE 1 Corporate Contributions to Incumbents and Challengers, 2011–2012

	Democrat incumbents	Democrat challengers	Republican incumbents	Republican challengers
Senate	17.9	1.8	17.0	2.6
House	41.9	1.7	82.9	3.3

Note: Figures in millions of dollars.
FEC Press Release, Political Action Committee 24-Month Data Summaries (01/01/11–12/31/12).

said this happens frequently" (Clawson et al., 1998). This may be one reason why incumbents outraise challengers by overwhelming margins. In the 2012 House of Representatives election, business PACs supported incumbents over challengers by better than a 10-to-1 margin (Open Secrets, 2012a,b).

It is no wonder that the incumbent advantage crosses party lines to favor candidates of whichever party controls the House or Senate at any given time. For many decades, Democrats enjoyed strong majorities in the House of Representatives. During this period, their candidates consistently ran well ahead of Republicans in raising money for their reelection campaigns. With the 1994 "Gingrich Revolution," Republicans gained control of the House and held it for the next 12 years. During this period, the GOP's candidates in aggregate outraised Democrats in each election cycle. In 2006 and 2010, Democrats and the GOP swapped majority status. Each change in majority status was followed by an immediate change in fund-raising advantage.

A significant portion of these fluctuations was the result of PAC managers changing their contribution preferences to increase support for majority party candidates. For many business PACs, access to incumbents far outstrips party loyalty or ideology as the prime motivating factor when allocating campaign contributions (Table 1).

Given these data, it is reasonable to assume that the ability of congressional incumbents to know the sources, amounts, and recipients of campaign contributions plays an important role in donors'—especially access-oriented donors'—contribution decisions. It follows that in an anonymity-based system, potential donors would be less restrained in supporting challengers, thus creating the financial conditions necessary for more competitive congressional elections.

Creating greater campaign resource parity between incumbents and challengers would be among the most significant public policy improvements that would flow from an anonymity-based contributions system.

BENEFICIARIES OF FECA's MANDATORY PUBLIC REPORTING SYSTEM

Because a contributions regime based on anonymity of the benefactors would have many natural detractors, it is necessary to ask the first question that is commonly put to policy entrepreneurs about almost any new policy proposal: Who will be against it?

There are at least four communities now benefiting from disclosure that would, in some way, be disadvantaged by blinding contributions.

Candidates

Candidates, which include incumbent members of Congress, may benefit from FECA's reporting requirement more than any other requirement. First, the FEC reports provide candidates with a list of likely contributors—an invaluable resource for any campaign organization. Why would not incumbent members of Congress look for support from organizations that have histories of contributing to candidates whose legislative profiles look very much like their own?

The second benefit to candidates is essentially a reiteration of the intimidation discussion set out above: because sitting members know whether a potential contributor has donated to them, they are in an excellent position to indulge in well-targeted pressure tactics.

Also, FEC-generated reports direct incumbents to which lobbyists they might prefer to grant access. It is commonly acknowledged that contributions do buy access (Langbein, 1986). This is a classic, and probably most common, form of de facto bribery. Access, after all, is an invaluable commodity for lobbyists and their clients (Herrnson et al., 2005).

Another benefit for both contributor and incumbent has to do with the importance of "early money"—that portion of an incumbent's war chest that is in the bank before a challenger even comes forward. Here, reporting has a sort of prophylactic effect by sending a message to would-be challengers to stay home and tend to their insurance business, law practice, or grandchildren. Disclosure of massive contributions to an incumbent can scare off potential challengers who have yet to raise their first dollars.

Finally, and most troubling, FEC reports may help members decide which groups to favor with their support on key issues. Lessig argues:

> [I]f a lobbyist is important, or influential over sources of campaign contributions, then the effect of her [the lobbyist's] influence could well be ex ante: a member could take a position on a particular issue in anticipation of the need to secure that lobbyist's support. ***Lessig (2011, p. 149).***

Lessig then quotes former Representative Vin Weber (R-MN): "[A] representative 'keeps a mental checklist of things [members] need to do to make sure their PAC contributors continue to support them'" (Lessig, 2011, p. 149).

Journalists

Media articles on the sources and recipients of campaign contributions often convey a strong—indeed, facile—suggestion that some members of Congress—perhaps *most*—are in the pockets of big-time contributors. This message becomes especially convincing when members' voting records on selected issues are matched up against contributions. While these articles seldom prove cause-and-effect relationships, they are the stuff of titillating suggestion and seem to verify what so many citizens already think they know about legislators' behaviors: "They are a bunch of whores." True or not, the very suggestion of unethical behavior promotes readership and viewership ratings. As noted above, this creates its own form of a corruption problem by damaging the credibility of our national politics.

Academicians

Many scholars also draw upon data extracted from FEC reports of campaign contributions. Their work would be seriously impaired, if not made impossible, without access to this material. The FEC data, combined with records of congressional activity—sources and amounts of contributions—are essential for certain scholarly investigations and analyses.

We recognize the importance of this academic work, which has provided much valuable information about the nexus between member behavior, policy outcomes, and campaign contributions. But there is an irony here: The need to do much of that work might not exist if the key data components for most of these studies—sources, recipients, and amounts of contributions—were absent from the public record.

Interest Groups and Lobbyists

For lobbyists, public disclosure is a double-edged sword. No doubt many givers would prefer that their contributions were not reported. The pressures noted just above, both positive and negative—the pressure to give to an incumbent or the pressure not to give to his or her challenger—could not exist without disclosure. These pressures become especially acute when the incumbent in question sits on a committee of immediate interest to the lobbyist.

FEC reports can still be of value for lobbyists by providing insights into what others are doing to support congressional candidates. This information may have strategic value. Even in instances in which allies are nominally "pulling on the same oar," lobbyists want to know who may be positioning themselves to pull just a bit harder. In addition, of course, it is always useful to keep tabs on one's adversaries.

There is another advantage for lobbyists and incumbents that may come with disclosure: signaling. Remember Lessig's observation that "a member could take a position on a particular issue in anticipation of the need to secure that lobbyist's support" (Lessig, 2011, p. 149). Indeed, members do position themselves to be attractive to interests and organizations they see as potential givers. Through this process, FEC reports serve to identify potential backers (Anonymous Interview, March 2014). However, candidates, their staff, and their consultants must be careful here: FECA 104.15 states:

> Any information copied, or otherwise obtained, from any report or statement, or any copy, reproduction, or publication thereof, filed under the Act, shall not be sold or used by any person for the purpose of soliciting contributions or for any commercial purpose.

In other words, the practice of identifying potential contributors by using contribution reports filed with the FEC may not be legal.

WHAT CONTRIBUTIONS DO AND DO NOT BUY

Of critical interest to voters is just what do contributions actually buy. Has a vote been swayed, has an amendment been offered, or has language been inserted in the original draft of a bill not yet introduced?

Perhaps the most common mistake in evaluating the extent to which contributions affect member behavior is the overreliance on roll-call votes as the prime indicator of legislative activity. In fact legislators' votes, while high-profile and officially recorded acts, might be the least instructive elements of their willful, or discretionary, legislative activities.

It is well established that members of Congress have less flexibility when voting than they do in virtually any other part of their work. Studies have consistently found that constituency interests, ideology, and performance of fellow members of Congress outrank campaign money for influencing members' voting behavior (Hall and Wayman, 1990; Kingdon, 1989; Welch, 1982). In addition, the literature indicates that most lobbyist attention focuses on members whose political and policy views are already in line with their own. Because members know that some of their constituents will be following their publically recorded votes closely, they are greatly constrained in their voting behaviors (Arnold, 1990; Kingdon, 1989).

But lawmaking is much more than just voting on bills and amendments. For example, before legislators can vote, they must have bills, amendments, or motions to vote on. While some of the work in crafting these legislative vehicles is done in public, much is not, which makes drawing causal links between contributions and legislators' policy-related activities very difficult for voters. Rick Hall terms this form of legislative participation "informal activity":

> [O]nce one leaves the glare of the committee, most of the legislative action becomes nonpublic… Indeed, much of the serious deliberating takes place over the phone, on the floor, in the interview rooms, and through various memos and letters that circulate among principal players. In short...much of the work is still done in the dark. ***Hall (1996, p. 28).***

Without knowing what the member of Congress does *in camera* to influence a policy outcome, it is impossible to establish fully informed causal relationships between campaign contributions and policy outputs. The unrecorded phone call by a senior member to a committee chair requesting a delay in a hearing; the suggestion that committee report language should be substituted for a colleague's amendment; lobbying a colleague for a vote—none of this becomes part of an official record. These activities and decisions are fundamental to the policy-making process. As one lobbyist reported, "This is where my work is done" (Anonymous Interview, November 2014). Encouraging people to think that mandatory reporting of contributions has provided adequate transparency leads to a misinformed response by well-intended citizens who do not know about Hall's "informal activity" disclosure.

A final point: effectiveness aside, relatively few voters access the raw contributions records directly from the FEC. It takes a highly motivated voter with a fair amount of sophistication and plenty of time to navigate the FEC Web site for this information. For these reasons, most people who factor contributions information into their voting decisions rely upon press reports or opposition candidate-generated data that often come in the form of campaign attack ads.

As a result, the mandatory reporting tool that Congress devised, and that the Court upheld as addressing a compelling public interest—avoiding the appearance of corruption—has, in fact, created its own corruption-related conundrum. It has made us all, including the authors of this article, deeply conscious of a potential perversion of our policy-making and electoral processes. Yet it does not give the tools necessary to demonstrate that such perversion actually occurs, where, and with what specific results. Instead, it has created a political environment in which innuendo and cynicism run rampant.

It is time, as the cliché instructs, to quit throwing good money after bad and to move to an entirely new contributions paradigm—mandatory anonymity.

AN ANONYMITY-BASED CAMPAIGN FINANCE SYSTEM

Much like Ackerman and Ayres in "Voting with Dollars," (Ackerman and Ayres, 2002) our thesis is that the problem with our campaign finance system is not so much its size—how much money is in the system—or even its sources. The problem for the American political system lies at the intersection between contributions and candidates' ability to know who has funded their own campaigns as well as the campaigns of others, including their opponents. Take away this information in a decisive highly credible way and we significantly reduce the possibilities of "legalized corruption" (Panetta) or "play[ing] on the edge of legal standards" (Hagel).

Ackerman and Ayres would permit contributors to tell their beneficiaries of their largesse, but they would require use of blind trusts in combination with a complex delivery mechanism designed to assure nonverifiability of these contributions. While a step in the right direction, we are convinced that any form of direct discussion about contributions between potential large donors and candidates should be prohibited—too many opportunities for signaling and or other modes of collusion. The only solution to our campaign finance dilemma is to "go cold turkey"—absolute anonymity. Thus, we propose a system in which no individual or organization may divulge its contributions or independent expenditures to a congressional candidate or any person closely associated with that candidate. To do so would be to risk a more severe federally imposed penalty.

As important as it would be in an anonymity-based campaign finance system to guard against disclosure by contributors, it would be still more important to assure that candidates and their confidantes would divulge such breaches should they occur. Candidate compliance is the linchpin here, as it should be. Those who aspire to high public office must be held to the highest ethical and legal standards. For this reason, failure to divulge breaches would subject the candidate (and any confidantes responsible for the breach) to penalties at least as severe as those meted out to violating contributors.

Requirements of the System

We have identified at least 11 core requirements for an anonymity-based contributions system:

1. All contributions to candidates and independent expenditures made in support of candidates for Congress that exceed a designated amount would be made anonymously. They would be reported to the FEC and deposited to an account for the designated candidate established at the FEC (or such other agency as Congress may designate).
2. No person acting as an individual, or as a representative for another person or organization, may divulge information about a contribution or expenditure made for the benefit of a congressional candidate to that candidate, the candidate's advisors, or any other person who might reasonably be expected to share the information with any of the above.

3. A breach of anonymity by a contributor (or any person associated with the contributor) would be punishable by a term of years in a federal penitentiary plus a substantial financial penalty (discussed further below).
4. Failure by a contribution recipient—congressional candidates or members of their campaign and legislative offices—to report such a breach would be punishable by a similar term in a federal penitentiary plus a financial penalty (discussed further below).
5. All individuals and organizations now permitted to contribute to federal candidates would be permitted to contribute.
6. Prohibitions against labor and corporate contributions would be eliminated, and labor and corporate PACs could be dissolved at the discretion of the sponsoring organizations. The threat of corruption would be substantially reduced, if not entirely removed, because the anonymity requirement in combination with continued dollar limitations on contributions would make unnecessary the cumbersome and often bothersome PAC vehicle.
7. Reasonable limitations, such as those in force today, would be maintained on the dollar amount of contributions.
8. Reasonable limitations would be placed on independent expenditures from any single source for the benefit of, or opposition to, a readily identifiable candidate or political party (discussed further below).
9. A system of incentives for compliance with the anonymity requirement would be established (discussed further below).
10. Fund-raising for each candidate would be done through a designated third party such as professional fund-raising organization. Such organizations would be permitted to report only aggregate contribution totals to the candidate it represents. The candidate would be permitted to make mass appeals for funding via radio, television commercials, print advertising, direct mail appeals, recorded phone messages, etc.
11. Local fund-raising events such as dinners, barbeques, auctions, etc., would be permitted. Contributions for such events would be limited to modest sums and not subject to required anonymity.

THE COMPLIANCE EQUATION: LEVERAGING HUMAN NATURE

An anonymity-based campaign finance system would work because it would leverage human nature. If a goal were important enough (in the present case, electing the right people to Congress), sanctions for violations strong enough, and enforcement mechanisms sufficiently creditable, then stakeholders would comply with the system's requirements. Below is an analysis of the equation's key components and their contributions stakeholders.

Strict Sanctions—Whistle-Blowing

On first thought, it would seem logical to assume that friends will not readily blow the whistle on friends, and that a close relationship between a contributor and a candidate would make the anonymity requirement difficult to enforce. Is that a logical conclusion?

If strict sanctions together with strong enforcement mechanisms for failing to divulge breaches of anonymity were enacted, then a violating contributor would be putting his or her friend-recipient in an awkward and potentially dangerous situation by breaching the secrecy requirement. His or her friend's options would be to report the breach and thereby implicate the contributor, or fail to divulge the breach and thus risk ruining his or her career and, perhaps, going to prison.

It is reasonable to assume that the majority of people who are able to make substantial contributions, as well as those who have been elected to Congress or even nominated to run for Congress, have worked long and hard to get to their positions. In neither case is it probable that such a person would risk a severe sanction, especially when a significant payout is not likely; there simply is not enough potential benefit for either party. (See discussion about contribution limits to follow.) The mere threat of a strong sanction would shift contributor motivations from shortsighted efforts to curry favor with candidates to protecting those candidates from career-ending penalties.

This point is further amplified by understanding the realities of legislative politics. Most lobbyist-contributors are sophisticated participants in, and observers of, congressional lawmaking practices. They know that, even in the most favorable of conditions, the buy-in of one or two members of Congress—even powerful committee chairs—seldom, if ever, assures the outcome they seek. Under these circumstances, it would be particularly irrational for a lobbyist to chance a few years behind bars plus a stiff financial penalty.

One further point: An errant lobbyist could never be certain that the candidate would ignore his or her duty to report the violation. In fact, if the sanctions were properly drawn and enforced, then contributors could well expect that the candidate would do his or her duty. Of course, there would always be the possibility that the seemingly ever-present disgruntled former staff person or ex-confidante would turn whistle-blower.

Ackerman and Ayres, while addressing potential attempts to circumvent their system for making contributions difficult to trace, acknowledge the value of strong sanctions: "Given the risks of discovery and the resulting threat of criminal prosecution, illegal [activities] will be few and far between" (Ackerman and Ayers, 2002, p. 113).

The incentive for candidates to report violations is the linchpin here. The candidate, his staff, and other campaign associates have a clear fiduciary duty to spill the beans. That would be an important source of pressure for compliance from both the givers and the getters of contributions. Here, Ackerman and Ayres' reliance on uncertainty—albeit, in a different context—has a role to play. The giver could never be certain that the getter will not snitch.

Contribution Limits

Reasonable contribution limits are a second component of the compliance equation. Assume a regime in which ordinary contributions were capped at roughly today's levels: $5000 per election for a PAC and $2600 per election for an individual, indexed for inflation as per BCRA. Those amounts would be less than one-third of 1% of what was needed to win a House seat in 2012 (Table 2). The numbers are even more minuscule when one considers what is needed to win a Senate seat, which costs on average 8 to 10 times more than a winning House campaign.

TABLE 2 Maximum PAC Contributions as a Percentage of Winning Congressional Races in the 2011–2012 Election Cycle

Percentage of winning house seat for a maximum PAC contribution	Percentage of winning senate seat for a maximum PAC contribution
0.000626 or 6.3 thousandths	0.00096 or 9.6 ten-thousandths

For purposes of this table, a "maximum" PAC contribution is considered to be $10,000, because primary and general elections are considered to be separate elections, and thus contributors can make a maximum contribution to each campaign.

The limitations are necessary to minimize incentives to breach anonymity or to shelter those who breach it. Given the limited upside potential for gain, contributors could not reasonably expect that candidates would risk their political careers, elevated status in the community, hard-earned money, or even freedom to save the neck of some boneheaded, untrustworthy contributor who divulges contribution information.

Enforcement

Strong enforcement powers would be needed for two reasons: first, we can reasonably anticipate that voters will initially be skeptical about compliance with an anonymity regime. Strong enforcement powers would help to allay these concerns. Second, broad enforcement capabilities combined with strict penalties and limited potential for gain due to contribution ceilings would make violation of the anonymity requirement a highly improbable and unwise course.

To this end, we recommend that appropriate law enforcement agencies—perhaps including state agencies—be granted broad investigatory powers. These could include wiretapping, extensive search and seizure authority, random audits, and sting operations. The courts could be expected to allow considerable investigatory leeway, given the compelling state interest in assuring against corrupt behavior by contributors and, especially, by elected officials.

Incentives

Some critics argue that required anonymity would dry up the ability of candidates to raise adequate campaign funding. But that very concern is a kind of confession against interest. When examined closely, what these critics are admitting is that disclosure of campaign contributions is, indeed, potentially corrupting whether disclosure be done via private communication or via an FEC report. They are acknowledging that disclosure is essential to the process of purchasing favor.

Nonetheless, the worry about raising sufficient campaign funds is legitimate, if not dispositive. To address this concern, we propose that a system of incentives be developed that would permit donors to contribute in excess of normal dollar limitations. One such system could allow givers to exceed existing limits in exchange for the possibility of enhanced penalties for violators of the anonymity requirements. Such a program could be combined with tax advantages for these donors, and with some form of modest public funding such as those devised by Ackerman and Ayres ("Patriot Dollars" model) or by Lessig (the "Grant and Franklin" model) (Ackerman and Ayres, 2002; Lessig, 2011). Through either of these programs qualifying individuals would be permitted to draw $50 on the U.S. Treasury for the purpose of making contributions to congressional candidates. The Lessig program would permit participants to contribute up to an additional $100 of their own funds for each supported candidate.

ADDITIONAL BENEFITS OF ANONYMITY-BASED CAMPAIGN FINANCING

An anonymity-based contributions system would eliminate the need for PACs in most settings. If candidates did not know the sources of their campaign funding, and if contribution levels were kept modest, then there would be no convincing policy rationale for preventing corporations and labor unions from contributing directly to congressional candidates. In light of the *Citizens United* Supreme Court decision of January 2010 permitting such organizations to participate in financing independent expenditure campaigns, none of this would cause a sea change. We doubt that many employees and union members would miss being solicited for contributions to their organization's PAC.

An additional and important benefit of eliminating corporate and union PACs is that such a course would reduce the margin for error in assuring that anonymity is not breached. Because PACs currently report their contributions to their memberships, hundreds if not thousands of participants know who has benefited from their PAC contributions. This means that a broad universe of potential leakers would need to be controlled. The problem would be avoided if corporations and unions were permitted to make federal contributions to federal candidates. Corporate and union officers would seek shareholder or member approval for limited and undisclosed contributions from their treasuries. The contributions would be approved by designated officers and sent directly to the FEC account for the beneficiary candidates. When only a handful of responsible people would know about the contributions, the leak potential would be greatly reduced.

Permitting direct corporate and union contributions to federal candidates would be consistent with the thrust of the Supreme Court holdings in Buckley v. Valeo (1976) and Citizens United v. Federal Election Commission (2010). Yet for those who are troubled by the permissive manner in which these decisions treat political speech—especially corporate political speech—there could be an ameliorating effect: given the ability to make direct campaign contributions some—perhaps many—corporate entities could conclude that such an avenue would provide sufficient opportunities for them to support the candidates they favor and thus eschew the independent and unlimited expenditure route.

Of course, not all organizations that sponsor PACs are large employers or unions. Some membership organizations, labor unions, and corporations might opt to remain in the PAC business. In these instances, the enabling act could make clear that the by-laws for these organizations may provide that PAC members would forfeit the right to be informed of specific contributions.

Making Room for the Little Guy

Beyond sanctions and incentives, there is a less tangible, more holistic, and perhaps more important point to be emphasized: today there is much public disgust with the contributions process (Peoples, 2013). This view was stipulated in a 1995 federal District Court case in Pennsylvania:

> The American public believes that our campaign finance system is broken. The vast majority of citizens feel that money threatens the basic fairness and integrity of our political system. Two out of three Americans think that money has an "excessive influence" on elections and government policy. Substantial majorities in poll after poll agree that "Congress is largely owned by the special interest groups" or that special interests have "too much over elected officials." Fully two-thirds of the public think that "their own representative in Congress would listen to the views of outsiders who made large political contributions before a constituent's view." ***Mariani v. U.S.* (1999, p. 410).**

Several commentators have indicated that concerns about corruption in government tend to reduce voter participation at the polls. It is more than reasonable to suggest that these same concerns act to discourage citizens from contributing to political campaigns—if citizens are not willing to vote, then they certainly will not be anxious to help fund candidates. Representative James Lloyd (D-MT), a member of the House Administration Committee—the committee that reported FECA to the House floor—expressed this view during congressional debate:

> If we…enact legislation in which the public has no confidence, then the list of those who contribute to political campaigns will be narrowed and one way or the other, candidates will be exposed to excessive influence of those on whom they must depend for financial support finance campaign. ***117 Cong. Rec.* (1971,p. 42073).**

Conversely, if the money-in-politics issue can be cured, or even if now-rampant cynicism and distrust can be alleviated, and if we can reduce or even eliminate the perception that contributing to campaigns is the province of moneyed interests only, more people might become comfortable with the notion of putting a few dollars behind their preferred candidates. This would not happen overnight, but over a period of years our political culture could change for the better as citizens begin to see a role for themselves beyond simply going to the polls.

We have been so long conditioned to the notion that money-in-politics is the big-man's game that it is difficult for us to envision a time when the little guy could play a major role in campaign funding. But this conditioning does not square with our history. During the first congressional campaign of this century, only 14 years ago, 55% of all campaign contributions to House candidates came from individuals. Of those, 30% were contributions of $200 or less. By 2008, the participation rate for small donors had dropped to about 16% of all individual donors. Clearly, there is potential to revive interest among small donors—something politicians and other reformers have championed for a long time now.

THE QUESTION OF CONSTITUTIONALITY

Independent expenditures present a very different set of problems for the anonymity paradigm than do campaign contributions.

To review: As of this writing, a contribution to a candidate's campaign treasury that is made by an individual is capped at $2600 per campaign. PACs may give $5000 to a primary campaign and $5000 to the general election campaign for the same candidate. These limitations are intended to prohibit any one individual or PAC from providing a significant portion of a given campaign's overall funding requirement, thereby reducing temptations for untoward (i.e., corrupt) activity.

In Buckley v. Valeo (1976), the Supreme Court determined that limits on contributions met constitutional muster. But the same could not be said for limitations on independent expenditures. Here the Court found that "[t]he Act's expenditure ceilings impose direct and substantial restraints on the quantity of political speech" (Buckley v. Valeo, 1976, p. 23). The Court repeated this contention at another point in the decision: "It is clear that a primary effect of these expenditure limitations is to restrict the quantity of campaign speech by individuals, groups, and candidates" (Buckley v. Valeo, 1976, p. 39). In January 2010, the Court handed down its decision in *Citizens United v. FEC*. Here, it ruled Congress could not constitutionally limit political speech "simply because its source is a corporation" (Citizens United v. FEC, 2010. p. 900 (quoting First National Bank of Boston. v. Bellotti, 1978, p. 784)). Nor could governments—federal or state—restrict the amount that a person or organization might be willing to spend (via an independent expenditure) in order to speak politically. Again, the Court looked to *Buckley*: "When *Buckley* examined an expenditure ban, it found that the governmental interest in preventing corruption and the appearance of corruption [was] inadequate to justify [the ban] on independent expenditures" (Citizens United v. Federal Election Commission, 2010, p. 45).

It is this last point, permitting unlimited independent expenditures no matter their source that creates a significant challenge for our anonymity proposal. The keeping of a $1000 independent expenditure secret is quite plausible, but a $100,000, $1-million, or even larger expenditure becomes problematic, to say the least. At these levels, we are dealing with the proverbial 800-pound gorilla in the room—difficult to keep its presence a secret. The astronomical numbers are too likely to tempt someone to leak, and someone else to be "persuaded" by the money.

Notwithstanding this possibility, Justice Anthony Kennedy, in his majority opinion for the *Citizens United* Court, seems to have bought into the notion that the no-collusion rule would protect against such behavior:

> The absence of prearrangement and coordination of an expenditure with the candidate or his agent not only undermines the value of the expenditure to the candidate, but also alleviates the danger that expenditures will be given as a quid pro quo for improper commitments from the candidate…[W]e now conclude that independent expenditures, including those made by corporations, do not give rise to corruption or the appearance of corruption. ***Citizens United v. Federal Election Commission (2010, p. 47).***

Given the experience of the 2012 federal elections in which mega-expenditures became almost commonplace—the FEC reported that total independent expenditures reached $666.7 million during this cycle—it is reasonable to ask whether this portion of Justice Kennedy's opinion remains credible, if it ever was credible at all. A recent CNN report indicated that "Republicans and outside groups used anonymous Twitter accounts to share internal polling data ahead of the midterm elections…a practice that raises questions about whether they violated campaign finance laws that prohibit coordination" (Ryan, 2014).

All of this strongly suggests that the opportunity to make huge independent expenditures creates a temptation to skirt the law. The report suggested "both parties are working hard to find ways to work more closely with well-financed outside groups" (Ryan, 2014).

Under these conditions, the appearance of corruption becomes a still more worrisome concern. On that point alone, one could easily hypothesize that the Court will eventually find a compelling government interest in limiting independent expenditures.[2] In fact, Justice Kennedy in his *Citizens United* opinion noted that while "[l]aws that burden political speech are subject to strict scrutiny," the government may restrict speech when it finds such a limitation "furthers a compelling interest and is narrowly tailored to achieve that interest" (Citizens United v. Federal Election Commission, 2010, p. 23).

CLOSING OBSERVATION

We do not claim that an anonymity-based contributions system would be foolproof, but we do argue that it would do more to deter contributions-based corruption than any other system devised to date. As Ayres (2001) has argued, "[A] regime of mandated anonymity interferes with an informational prerequisite for corruption… [I]t would be more difficult for candidates to sell access or influence if they did not know that a donation had been made" (Ayres 2001, p. 12).

Anonymity would make intimidation by incumbents equally impossible to do and thus help reduce the funding gap between incumbents and challengers. During the original FECA debate in Congress, some members worried that forced disclosure would discourage contributions to challengers—as in fact it has done. Representative Ben Blackburn (R-GA) argued, "The implementation of full reporting laws would do more to discourage contributors to non-incumbents than any other one law" (171 Cong. Rec., 1971, p. 43411).

In evaluating the merits of an anonymity-based contributions system, the key question should be this: Are the supposed benefits derived from mandatory discloser of campaign contributions sufficient to override its many unintended and negative consequences? Posed another way: even if an occasional rogue gets away with breaking the anonymity code, would that be worse than the outright, pervasive de facto (legalized) corruption that exists today? For us, the clear answer is no.

[2] When a fundamental right, for example, free speech, is at issue, the courts will apply the strict scrutiny test to determine whether a limitation on speech serves a compelling state interest. If it does, then the courts will permit the limitation (Chemerinsky, 2002, p. 645).

References

Abramoff, J., 2011. Capitol Punishment. Wind Books, New York, NY.

Ackerman, B., Ayers, I., 2002. Voting with Dollars. Yale University Press, New Haven, CT.

Anonymous Interview by Bertram Levine, March 2014. Washington Public Affairs Company Principle, Conducted in Washington DC.

Anonymous Interview by Bertram Levine, November 2014. Former Member of the House of Representatives, Conducted in Washington DC.

Arnold, D., 1990. The Logic of Congressional Action. Yale University Press, New Haven, CT.

Ayres, I., 2001. Should campaign donors be identified. Regulation 24 (2), 12.

Buckley v. Valeo, 1976. 424 U.S. 1.

Chemerinsky, E., 2002. Constitutional Law: Principles and Policies, second ed. Aspen Publishers, New York, NY.

Citizens United v. Federal Election Commission, 2010. 558 U.S. 310.

Clawson, D., Neustadtl, A., Weller, M., 1998. Dollars and Votes. Temple University Press, Philadelphia, PA.

117 Cong Rec 42073, 1971.

117 Cong Rec 43411, 1971.

Dobel, J.P., 1978. The corruption of the state. The American Political Science Review 72 (3), 958–973.

First National Bank of Boston v. Bellotti, 1978. 435 U.S. 765.

Federal Election Campaign Act of 1971: Hearings before the Subcommittee on Communications of the Committee on Commerce, United States Senate, Ninety-Second Congress, First Session, March 2,3,4,5,31 and April 1, 1971. Serial no. 92–96.

Hall, R.L., 1996. Participation in Congress. Yale University Press, New Haven.

Hall, R., Wayman, F., 1990. Buying time: moneyed interests and mobilizing bias in congressional committees. American Political Science Review 84 (3), 801.

Hernson, P.S., Shaiko, R.G., Wilcox, C., 2005. The Interest Group Connection, second ed. CQ Press, Washington, DC.

Johnston, M., 2005. Syndromes of Corruption. Cambridge University Press, New York, NY.

Kaiser, R.G., 2009. So Damn Much Money. Vintage, New York, NY.

Kingdon, J., 1989. Congressmen's Voting Decisions, third ed. University of Michigan Press, Ann Arbor.

Langbein, L., 1986. Money and access: some empirical evidence. The Journal of Politics 48 (4), 1052–1062.

Lessig, L., 2011. Republic Lost. Twelve, New York, NY.

Levine, B., 1997. Campaign finance reform in the United States Congress: a critique. Crime, Law, and Social Change 28 (1), 20–23.

Mariani v. U.S., 1999. 80 F. Supp 2d 352, M.D. PA.

McCutcheon v. FEC, 2012. 893 F. Supp 2d 133, D.C. DC.

Open Secrets, 2012a. PAC Dollars to Incumbents, Challengers, and Open Seat Candidates. Retrieved from: http://www.opensecrets.org/bigpicture/pac2cands.php?cycle=2012&display=.

Open Secrets, 2012b. Where the Money Came from. Retrieved from: http//www.opensecrets.org/bigpicture/wherefrom/php?cycle=2012.

Peoples, C., 2013. Campaign finance and policymaking: PACs, campaign contributions, and interest group influence in congress. Sociology Compass 7 (11), 900–913.

Ryan, P.S., November 25, 2014. Democrats and Republicans Attempt Twitter End-Run Around Campaign Finance Laws [Brookings TechTank Blog]. Retrieved from: http://www.brookings.edu/blogs/techtank/posts/2014/11/25-twitter-campaign-coordination.

Schram, M., 1995. Speaking Freely. Center for Responsive Politics, Washington, DC.

Senate Committee on Commerce, 1971. Report on Hearings for Amendments to the Federal Election Campaign Act of 1971, 2nd Congress, Serial, 92-6 p. 215.

Warren, M., 2004. What does corruption mean in a democracy. American Journal of Political Science 48 (2), 328–343.

Welch, W.P., 1982. Campaign contributions and legislative voting: milk money and dairy supports. Western Political Quarterly 35, 478–495.

CHAPTER

19

Blinding Eyewitness Identifications

Brandon L. Garrett

University of Virginia School of Law, Charlottesville, VA, USA

OUTLINE

INTRODUCTION

Is criminal justice blind? At every stage in a criminal case, police, prosecutors, defense lawyers, judges, and, in the few cases that go to trial, jurors, must make decisions based on information about a crime and a criminal defendant. Unlike the traditional statues depicting justice blind, modeled after Justitia, the Roman blindfolded goddess of justice bearing a sword and scales (Capers, 2013; Resnik and Curtis, 2011), all of these people must make decisions with their eyes wide open to at least some of the facts uncovered about a defendant and a case. They may try their best to be impartial, but blind justice may be an aspiration, even if not a reality. In recent years, however, scientific methods have suggested new ways to actually "blind" justice in criminal investigations, particularly in the very area where eyesight is most important and problematic: the use of eyewitness identification evidence.

Indeed, questions of how to best use scientific methods have never been more important in criminal justice. In the past few decades, the research on eyewitness memory has exploded, and that scientific research has had a remarkable impact on police practices, lawyering, and judicial decisions. A recent National Research Council (NRC) report explored the state of this research and made important recommendations for further research and improvements to police and judicial practices (NRC, 2014). I should note that I served on the NRC committee that produced the report.

Blinding as a Solution to Bias
http://dx.doi.org/10.1016/B978-0-12-802460-7.00019-X

Many tens of thousands of criminal cases each year rely on eyewitness evidence; there is no precise count (NRC, 2014, p. 7). When police speak to an eyewitness to a crime, they will ask the eyewitness to describe the person whom they saw commit the crime. If a suspect is located right away, within hours, then police traditionally show suspects to an eyewitness one-on-one (a showup). If a suspect is not located readily, then police may later construct a lineup. In the past, this was typically done in-person, with a suspect and several "fillers" or nonsuspects standing in a row. Today, this is typically done using photographs of faces or a photographic array. Particularly during the past decade, the procedures used by police agencies to present photographs to test the eyewitness' memory have changed quite dramatically.

LINEUPS AS EXPERIMENTS

A lineup is a type of experiment conducted by police. Police do not normally test their evidence using experiments, outside the area of forensics, which are chiefly conducted in crime laboratories by specialist analysts. The purpose of an eyewitness-identification procedure is to test a hypothesis, that is, that a particular eyewitness saw a particular person. A lineup, despite its apparent simplicity, is far more complex than it might initially seem, largely because of the surprisingly complex ways that human visual memory is processed.

Doing experiments well can produce far more accurate evidence, while doing experiments poorly can contaminate the results by actually degrading the eyewitness' visual memory. Human vision and memory do not work like a camera. We do not passively retain an image of a face that we see; instead, the process is far more dynamic and malleable. Our perception and memory of visual images can be affected by expectations and feedback from others.

In the eyewitness literature, the variables that can affect an eyewitness' memory are termed "estimator" variables when they relate to perception at the crime scene itself and are termed "system" variables when they relate to the procedures and practices used to later ask an eyewitness whether an identification can be made (NRC, 2014, p. 12; Wells, 1978). Estimator variables can include the lighting conditions at the crime scene, whether the culprit had a weapon, the race of the eyewitness and of the culprit, the distance and duration of the viewing, and whether there was high stress during the encounter. System variables can include the instructions given to the eyewitness, the number of filler photographs included alongside the suspect photograph, and the manner in which the photos are presented.

Perhaps most interesting has been the research on how the person who conducts the lineup, the police officer, can affect the results. Researchers have made a central recommendation to conduct lineups "blind," so that the police officer conducting the lineup does not know which is the suspect, or "blinded," so that the officer cannot see what the eyewitness is looking at (NRC, 2014, p. 3). The concern is that the administrator can, even unintentionally, affect the outcome, just as in experiments, where there is the concern with "expectancy effects" in which the person running the experiment might signal the outcome he or she is hoping for.

An example of a traditional lineup conducted in Virginia helps to illustrate the problem. In 1988, in Virginia Beach, a woman was accosted by a man with a gun when returning from work and was sexually assaulted in her apartment. A man named Troy Webb was later identified by the victim from a photo array shown to her at the police station. At a 1-day criminal trial in 1989, Troy Webb was convicted and sentenced to 47 years in prison (Commonwealth of Virginia v. Webb, 1989, Trial Transcript). He then spent almost 8 years in prison. All of his appeals and postconviction challenges failed. But in 1996, he was able to obtain DNA tests that proved his innocence, and he was exonerated.

How were the lineups in Webb's case done? Immediately after the assault, the victim called the police and gave a description of the assailant. She said he was a black man, 19–22 years old, with short hair, dark clothing, and "high cheekbones" but "thin through the face" and "small framed" (Trial Transcript, 148–149, 190). She said she saw the assailant for 15 or 20 min in a well-lit area, although "at first I had looked at the gun" but "then his face" (Trial Transcript, 143). The attacker also repeatedly told her not to look at him.

A few days later, the police asked the victim to produce a composite drawing of the assailant, but she recalled, "It was too hard. I just couldn't do it" (Trial Transcript, 109–111). With no suspects, the police asked her to look through mug books of photos, but she did not recognize any of the faces (Trial Transcript, 112).

At trial, the police described how they visited the victim at her apartment and showed her a standard array of six photos, sometimes called a "six pack" (Trial Transcript, 194). Only four of the photos, however, matched the age of the attacker she described. When she was first shown that photo array, the victim pointed to the last photo, and the police officer could see how "she began focusing her attention on number 6 and sort of zeroed in on him and looked at him" (Trial Transcript, 195).

The victim recalled that she was "pretty sure" when she saw Webb's photo in the array. When the police officer asked, "Are you hundred percent sure?" she said, "No." When the officer then asked, "Well, ninety-nine?" she said, "Yes" (Trial Transcript, 196). After that she said she was "pretty sure" (Trial Transcript, 137). The officer may not have intended to inflate her confidence. But those questions could have encouraged an uncertain eyewitness to be sure, anchoring the certainty at "hundred percent sure."

The victim did not exactly make an identification. She said at trial, "I had gotten real nervous inside and shaky. I knew it was him" (Trial Transcript, 115). She added, though, at trial, "I had wanted to be make definitely sure" and to "make sure that I had the right person." And she "did want to see more photographs" (Trial Transcript, 137–139). Of course, the officer also wanted to be careful and thorough. The next day, the police officer asked the victim to return to the police station and showed the victim a second photo array. This time she was sure, although Webb looked younger in this photograph. At trial, she recalled, "I said this is him right here. That's him" (Trial Transcript, 136).

All of the "fillers," or photos of nonsuspects, were different in this second photo array, which meant that Troy Webb was the only person repeated in the second identification procedure. Repeating only one person is suggestive and increases the likelihood of a false identification. The victim also identified Webb at the trial, where it was easy to see where he was sitting. The defense lawyer asked the victim questions about her lack of certainty at the first identification and about the lighting conditions during the crime. He asked the police officer detailed questions about the lineup procedures used. But he did not do more, and it was probably unclear to him what else could be done.

The entire case rested on the victim's identification. As the prosecutor stated during the opening statement, the victim had looked at two lineups, said "That's him." That evidence would "prove to you that the man who did those things to her on that day was the defendant here today, Troy Lynn Webb" (Trial Transcript, 70).

The judge did not give the jurors special instructions on how to evaluate this evidence, but he told them they could "take into consideration the appearance, attitude, and behavior of the witness" and give the testimony of a witness "just such weight and value as [they] may believe the testimony of such witness is entitled to receive" (Trial Transcript, 57–58). Traditionally, that was all that court told jurors, in substance. In addition, the defense did not call any expert witness or social scientist who could explain eyewitness memory to the jury. Virginia courts have sometimes denied the defense permission to introduce such experts. As one Virginia court has stated, a jury is "capable of evaluating whether the victim's identifications of appellant were reliable or whether the identifications were incorrect based on the suggested problems associated with memory" (Currie v. Commonwealth, 1999).

Troy Webb's case is not a particularly high-profile one. It has not attracted national media attention like other DNA exonerations have. In fact, it is much like countless other DNA exoneration cases, which I have studied in detail (Garrett, 2011). Psychologist Gary Wells commented that although the research on eyewitness memory dates back to the 1970s, "before DNA they pretty much ignored the studies" (Fears, 2007). There have been more than 300 DNA exonerations. In about three-quarters of those cases, eyewitness misidentifications occurred (Garrett, 2011, p. 48). Almost without fail, the eyewitness, such as in Webb's case, testified with complete confidence that he or she was identifying the person who committed the crime, and yet he or she was wrong. We now know, with the benefit of DNA tests, that these eyewitnesses were wrong, but at the time, they said, "There is absolutely no question in my mind" or "That is one face I will never forget," or that they were "a hundred percent sure" or "one hundred and twenty" percent sure (Garrett, 2011, p. 63). I was surprised to learn that many of those eyewitness, such as in Webb's case, were uncertain about their identifications earlier, but became certain by the time of trial (Garrett, 2011, p. 64).

What has changed since the 1980s, when many of those criminal trials occurred? In Virginia, of the 16 DNA exonerations, 13 involved eyewitness identifications. All were sexual assault cases. The agency that handled Troy Webb's case, the Virginia Beach police department, now does eyewitness identifications very differently. It now conducts such procedures "blind" so that the officer conducting the procedure does not know which photo is of the suspect. It has assisted in state-wide efforts to draft a new model policy for eyewitness identification procedures, although the implementation of that new model policy remains uneven (Garrett, 2014; Wilson, 2012).

THE LAW OF EYEWITNESS IDENTIFICATIONS

The law of eyewitness identifications has not significantly changed at the national level in 35 years. In 1977, the U.S. Supreme Court in *Manson v. Brathwaite case* set out the standard under the Due Process Clause of the U.S. Constitution that regulates eyewitness identification evidence (Manson v. Brathwaite, 1977, at 113–114). The Court focused on the problem of suggestion, that is, that police officers may affect through their words or acts the decision that an eyewitness makes when viewing a lineup. In *Manson v. Brathwaite*, however, the Court held that even if police engage in highly suggestive conduct, the eyewitness identification may nevertheless be admitted in court if it bears certain indicia of "reliability," drawn from earlier judicial rulings, such as the eyewitness' level of certainty, the degree of the eyewitness' attention, and his or her opportunity to view the culprit at the time of the crime (Manson v. Brathwaite, 1977, at 114). Although judges are ostensibly concerned with the methods used to test an eyewitness' memory, flexible and deferential test does not require that police use any particular set of practices when conducting lineups, and even if police engage in fairly serious suggestion, the identification is typically still admissible in court.

The law has not meaningfully changed since that ruling at the federal level. However, recognition of the seriousness of the problem has remained constant. In 1967, the Supreme Court noted, "The vagaries of eyewitness identification are well-known; the annals of criminal law are rife with instances of mistaken identification" (United States v. Wade, 1967, at 288). In 2012, in *Perry v. New Hampshire case*, the Supreme Court similarly noted, "We do not doubt either the importance or the fallibility of eyewitness identifications." However, the Court declined to regulate eyewitness identifications that were not the product of intentional police-arranged procedures. Justice Sonia Sotomayor dissented, focusing on the potential for the reliability of eyewitness identifications to be affected by suggestion, and argued, "Our due process concern…arises not from the act of suggestion, but rather from the corrosive effects of suggestion on the reliability of the resulting identification" (Perry v. New Hampshire, 2012, at 731 (Sotomayor, J. dissenting)).

In contrast, several state courts have intervened to more carefully regulate the admissibility of eyewitness evidence. Perhaps the best known was the ruling in State v. Henderson (2011) by the New Jersey Supreme Court, requiring that pretrial reliability hearings examine the lineup procedures used, using reliability factors grounded in social science research, and calling for detailed jury instructions that explain the research to the jury at trial. The Oregon Supreme Court established a new procedure for evaluating the admissibility of eyewitness identification evidence, focusing on the reliability of the particular evidence and the eyewitness identification procedures used (State v. Lawson, 2012). Most recently, the Supreme Judicial Council of Massachusetts adopted a concise set of jury instructions regarding scientific research on eyewitness identifications (Comm. v. Gomes, 2014). Other state courts have made less dramatic but useful changes to jury instructions, and all state and federal courts have become far more open to admitting expert testimony to explain scientific research on eyewitness evidence to jurors. Deeper changes have been outside the courtrooms and in police stations, in response not only to high-profile wrongful convictions, but also to changes brought on by scientific research in the laboratory and in the field.

THE BLIND LINEUP

The concept of conducting a blind lineup was first introduced by Professor Gary L. Wells in 1988, with the recommendation that "the officer conducting the photo-spread should not be knowledgeable of whom the police suspect in the case" (Wells, 1988, p. 122). Sometimes such lineups are called "double-blind," perhaps referring to the terminology for medical trials, or perhaps because neither the administrator nor the eyewitness is told which image or person is the suspect. Wells, proposed the concept of an experiment to model eyewitness identification procedures because of the concern that the administrator can influence the outcome of a lineup, whether consciously or not (Wells, 1988; Wells and Luus, 1990).

The problem of influence during any kind of a test is a pervasive one. As other chapters in this volume discuss in more detail, throughout the sciences a person running an experiment can unintentionally affect the results in favor of those results that he or she desires or expects. These "experimenter expectancy effects" were first a subject of research in the late 1960s, somewhat by accident, by Professor Robert Rosenthal, who then embarked on decades of research of these effects in a range of contexts. Since then, experimenter expectancy effects have been documented in the laboratory and in the field, in contexts ranging from childhood education, to medical research, to financial services, to judicial decision making (Ambady et al., 2002; Blanck et al., 1990; Rosenthal, 1966). As the NRC report states, "By the 1950s, blind assessment in randomized controlled trials was considered standard procedure in both psychological and medical research. Currently, virtually all of science uses some form of blinding" (NRC, 2014, p. 18).

The concerns with expectancy effects are particularly important in a lineup setting, because of the special relationship that can form between an eyewitness, particularly the victim of the crime, and police. It is no light matter to identify a person who committed a serious crime. An eyewitness may look to the police for reassurance that he or she did a good job. An eyewitness may also look to the police for protection from the culprit. In particular, a crime victim, such as in the Troy Webb case, may want assurance not only that he or she made a correct choice and did not select an innocent person, but also that the culprit will not remain free on the streets as a threat. Indeed, Wells emphasized that police may not intend to influence eyewitnesses at all. Police may unconsciously seek to reassure eyewitnesses, to provide helpful feedback to encourage eyewitnesses to continue to cooperate in the criminal investigation, and to thank them for their cooperation and conscientiousness.

Influence by the administrator can take many forms, particularly because, unlike some laboratory experiments involving more discrete tests, eyewitness identification procedures can involve a series of interactions. Influence can occur before the identification. An eyewitness can be encouraged to go to the police station to view an identification procedure by being told "We caught somebody." Police may provide further information about who was caught and why that person is likely to be the culprit, perhaps out of the best intentions, to encourage the eyewitness to take the investigation seriously and continue to cooperate. The manner in which the lineup is designed may reflect what the administrator expects. The suspect's photo may stand out. It may be one of only a few that resemble the description of the suspect. It may be a different type of photo from the others. Feedback can occur during the procedure itself, including nonverbal cues or body language, or outright suggestion or encouragement. The administrator's tone of voice may change when asking about a particular photo. Or the administrator may pause when placing the suspect's photo before the eyewitness. The administrator may ask an eyewitness to look more closely at that photo out of a concern that the eyewitness is "rushing," or the administrator may caution the eyewitness to "take more time" if the suspect's photo appears to have been passed over. In the past, such conversation may not have been thought to be suggestive: certainly not the type of police misconduct intended to badger an eyewitness and pressure an eyewitness to identify a certain person.

Feedback can also occur after the identification is made. Police may take some time to discuss the identification with the eyewitness and document the identification. The interactions during that process can provide the opportunity for unintended feedback that may inflate the eyewitness' confidence. This type of feedback is termed "postidentification feedback" in the social science literature (Steblay et al., 2014). Reinforcing feedback can also influence eyewitnesses after they make erroneous identifications. A number of studies have examined the effects of feedback by administrators (Bradfield et al., 2002; Douglass and Steblay, 2006). That feedback can take innocuous forms, ranging from "Good job, you identified the suspect" to stronger affirmations, such as disclosing information about the person's prior record or the other reasons why the police were sure that the person was the right one. Police may also ask an eyewitness about confidence in a way that can inflate confidence. Asking "Are you hundred percent sure?" such as in the Troy Webb case has the effect of conveying that certainty or near certainty is what the police require of the eyewitness.

BEYOND BLINDING

Even if the lineup is done blind or blinded, the rest of the criminal justice system does not proceed like a blind experiment, despite the ubiquitous images of blind justice that adorn our courthouses. If the suspect is indicted and criminal proceedings commence, then the eyewitness, who may also be the crime victim, will eventually hear about it. The eyewitness may learn quite a bit about the other evidence in the case and the defendant's criminal record. The eyewitness may very well be asked to identify the defendant in the courtroom, and not using a lineup with "fillers." It is no surprise that by the time of a criminal trial, an eyewitness may express still more confidence in the identification, just as in the Webb case, in which the eyewitness was initially somewhat unsure, became completely sure, and then identified Webb with no uncertainty at the trial. At a trial, the jurors do not see the prior identifications conducted at a police station, although they may see the photos used in the array and any accompanying documentation (or, even better, a video of that lineup). At a trial, the jury sees the eyewitness in the courtroom.

As Supreme Court Justice William Brennan stated, "[T]here is almost nothing more convincing than a live human being who takes the stand, points a finger at the defendant, and says 'That's the one!'" (Watkins v. Sowders, 1981; at 352). That is why researchers have recommended documenting the confidence of an eyewitness following a blind procedure—in an open-ended way or with a simple scale, rather than asking in a leading way whether the eyewitness is "100% sure."

Thus, conducting eyewitness identifications blind is not enough to safeguard their accuracy. Many other important features of experimental design can prevent expectancy effects. The "fillers" should resemble the suspect and the victim's description; otherwise the effective size of the lineup may be quite small. Clear and standardized instructions should be given to the eyewitness. At criminal trials, a judge can use pretrial hearings and other reviews to explore what exactly happened in prior identification procedures. Expert testimony can be used to explain the relevant social science framework to a jury. As a second-best option, the NRC report suggested that clear and concise jury instructions can be used to explain eyewitness memory to jurors (NRC, 2014, pp. 74–75).

BLINDED LINEUPS

The vast majority of law enforcement agencies are small police departments. Some may not be able to spare an officer who is not the primary officer assigned to the case to conduct a lineup procedure. An easy and inexpensive alternative is to blind the lineup procedure. One way to do this is to simply place the images in folders and then shuffle the folders. The eyewitness is instructed to look at each image inside the folders; the officer sitting across the table cannot able to see inside the folders and does not know which image the eyewitness is looking at (until any selection is made). This folder shuffle method is being adopted by smaller policing agencies and is included as an option in state-wide model policies and legislation. A West Virginia statute explains how this works, in part: "Photos used in a photo lineup are placed in their own respective folder, and the folders are shuffled, numbered and then presented to an eyewitness such that the administrator cannot see or track which photo is being presented to the witness until after the procedure is completed" (Eyewitness Identification Act, 2013). In the future, more agencies may use computers to present the images in a blind fashion.

ADOPTING BLIND LINEUPS

In the late 1990s, the American Psychology-Law Society endorsed the use of double-blind lineups (Wells et al., 1998). However, a 1999 Department of Justice task force report, which drew national attention to the issue of eyewitness memory, did not include blind procedures in its guide, noting that they might be "impractical" for some jurisdictions (methods such as the folder shuffle may not have been developed) (DOJ, 1999). The first major jurisdiction to require that lineups be conducted blind was New Jersey, in 2001, based on attorney general's recommendations (Farmer, 2001). Now other states require blind lineups based on legislation, including Ohio and North Carolina (Administration of photo or live lineups, 2010; Eyewitness Identification Reform Act, 2007). Fourteen states have adopted some type of legislation regarding eyewitness identification procedures (NRC, 2014, p. 25). States have also begun to address practical concerns, by making folder shuffle blinding an option for smaller agencies. For example, the Ohio statute defines a blind administrator as one who "does not know the identity of the suspect" (Administration of photo or live lineups, Section 2933.83(A)(2)). In addition, a "blind administrator" includes "an administrator who conducts a photo lineup through the use of a folder system or a substantially similar system" (Id. at Section 2933.83(A)(3)). The statute requires that "[u]nless impracticable, a blind or blinded administrator shall conduct the live lineup or photo lineup" (Id. at Section 2933.83(B)(1)). Any failures to follow the procedures in the statute may be "considered by trial courts in adjudicating motions to suppress eyewitness identification," "shall be admissible" as evidence at trial, or could be presented to the jury in instructions (Id. at § 2933.83(C)(1)–(3)).

Adoption of these lineup procedures is highly uneven, however, and many police agencies continue to have no written procedure at all for conducting lineups. In 2013, a National Institute of Justice-sponsored study by the Police Executive Research Forum found that 31% of surveyed departments use blind photo lineups (PERF, 2013, pp. 61–62).

In addition to statutory changes and voluntary adoption of new practices by police agencies, some courts have changed the way that eyewitness evidence is regulated and cited to scientific evidence regarding eyewitness memory by emphasizing the importance of blind lineups. As the New Jersey Supreme Court stated in *Henderson*: "The consequences are clear: a non-blind lineup procedure can affect the reliability of a lineup because even the best-intentioned, non-blind administrator can act in a way that inadvertently sways an eyewitness trying to identify a suspect" (28 A.3d at 897). Most recently, the NRC report strongly recommended that eyewitness identification procedures be conducted blind or blinded:

> The committee recommends blind [double-blind or blinded] administration of both photo arrays and live lineups and the adoption of clear, written policies and training on photo array and live lineup administration. Police should use blind procedures to avoid the unintentional or intentional exchange of information that might bias an eyewitness. *NRC (2014, p. 73)*

Blinding is only one important part of the experimental method. Clear written policies and other aspects of the design of lineup policies are also important, as highlighted by the NRC recommendation. Conducting a blind lineup is a key protection, but other improvements can help to safeguard the accuracy and reliability of eyewitness identification evidence. It is important to give clear and standard instructions to eyewitnesses. It is important to select "fillers" of a sufficient number to not make the suspect stand out. The confidence of the eyewitness should be carefully recorded, and, better still, the entire procedure should be videotaped. Training and supervision on using these techniques is important. Lawyers, judges, and jurors should be informed by the scientific research on eyewitness memory. Future scientific research will no doubt continue to advance and shed further light on the factors that affect eyewitness memory and the procedures that can best preserve the eyewitness' memory.

The larger ideal of minimizing bias in our criminal justice system is an important and still more ambitious project. In crime laboratories, some analysts have begun to review forensic comparisons blind, and there are proposals to selectively blind that work so that expectancy effects do not contribute to errors. Other forms of blind review could be used to examine confession evidence, informant evidence, or charging decisions and sentencing decisions by judges. Scientific research has never been more important to criminal justice in the United States. The statues of goddess justice that adorn our courthouses may be blind, but inside those walls, carrying out justice more accurately and impartially is the challenge that gives life to the symbols of justice.

References

Ambady, N., LaPlante, D., Nguyen, T., Chaumeton, N., Levinson, W., Rosenthal, R., 2002. Surgeons' tone of voice: a clue to malpractice history. Surgery 132 (1), 5–9.

Blanck, P.D., Rosenthal, R., Hart, A.J., Bernieri, F., 1990. The measure of the judge: an empirically-based framework for exploring trial judges' behavior. Iowa Law Review 75, 653–684.

Bradfield, A.L., Wells, G.L., Olson, E.A., 2002. The damaging effect of confirming feedback on the relation between eyewitness certainty and identification accuracy. Journal of Applied Psychology 87, 112–120.

Capers, I.B., 2013. Blind justice. Yale Journal of Law and Humanities 24, 179.

Comm. v. Gomes, SJC-11537 (Mass. 2014).

Commonwealth of Virginia v. Troy L. Webb, CR 88-1458 (Cir. Ct. Virginia Beach, January 31, 1989).

Currie v. Commonwealth, 515 S.E.2d 335 (Va. App. 1999).

DOJ (U.S. Department of Justice), Office of Justice Programs, 1999. Eyewitness Evidence: A Guide for Law Enforcement. Retrieved from: http://www.ncjrs.gov/pdffiles1/nij/178240.pdf.

Douglass, A.B., Steblay, N., 2006. Memory distortion in eyewitnesses: a meta-analysis of the post-identification feedback effect. Applied Cognitive Psychology 20, 859–869.

Farmer Jr., J.J., April 18, 2001. Attorney General Guidelines for Preparing and Conducting Photo and Live Lineup Identification Procedures. Retrieved from: http://www.state.nj.us/lps/dcj/agguide/photoid.pdf.

Fears, D., May 3, 2007. Exonerations have changed justice system. The Washington Post.
Garrett, B.L., 2011. Convicting the Innocent: Where Criminal Convictions Go Wrong. Harvard University Press, Cambridge, MA.
Garrett, B.L., 2014. Eyewitness identifications and police practices: a Virginia case study. Virginia Journal of Criminal Law 3, 1.
Manson v. Brathwaite, 432 U.S. 98, 113–114 (1977).
N.C. Gen. Stat. § 15A-284.52 (West 2007).
NRC (National Research Council), 2014. Identifying the Culprit: Assessing Eyewitness Identification. National Academies Press, Washington, DC.
Ohio Rev. Code Ann. § 2933.83 (West 2010).
PERF (Police Executive Research Forum), 2013. A National Survey of Eyewitness Identification Procedures in Law Enforcement Agencies. pp. 46–47. Retrieved from: http://policeforum.org/library/eyewitnessidentification/NIJEyewitnessReport.pdf.
Perry v. New Hampshire, 132 S. Ct. 716, 731 (2012) (Sotomayor, J., dissenting).
Resnik, J., Curtis, D., 2011. Representing Justice. Yale University Press, New Haven, CT.
Rosenthal, R., 1966. Experimenter Effects in Behavioral Research. Appleton-Century-Crofts, New York, NY.
State v. Henderson, 27 A.3d 872 (N.J. 2011).
State v. Lawson, 352 Ore. 724 (Or. 2012).
Steblay, N., Wells, G.L., Douglass, A.B., 2014. The eyewitness post identification feedback effect 15 years later: theoretical and policy implications. Psychology, Public Policy, and Law 20 (1), 1–18.
United States v. Wade, 388 U.S. 230 (1967).
Watkins v. Sowders, 449 U.S. 341, 352 (1981), Brennan, J., dissenting; quoting Elizabeth F. Loftus, *Eyewitness Testimony* (1979).
Wells, G.L., 1978. Applied eyewitness-testimony research: system variables and estimator variables. Journal of Personality and Social Psychology 36 (12), 1546–1557.
Wells, G.L., 1988. Eyewitness Identification: A System Handbook. Carswell Legal Publications, Toronto.
Wells, G.L., Luus, E., 1990. Police lineups as experiments: social methodology as a framework for properly conducted lineups. Personality and Social Psychology Bulletin 16, 106–117.
Wells, G.L., Small, M., Penrod, S.J., Malpass, R.S., Fulero, S.M., Brimacombe, C.A.E., 1998. Eyewitness identification procedures: recommendations for lineups and photospreads. Law and Human Behavior 22, 603–647.
W. Va. Code Ann. § 62-1E-1(7) (West 2013).
Wilson, P., July 15, 2012. Police photo lineups fail new study. The Virginia Pilot.

CHAPTER

20

Blind Appointments in Arbitration

Sergio Puig
The University of Arizona, Tucson, AZ, USA

OUTLINE

INTRODUCTION

A new debate has emerged among lawyers regarding party appointments in arbitration. While arbitrators are supposed to be neutral and impartial—including the two arbitrators typically appointed by the parties to the proceedings—practitioners agree that arbitrators often lean in favor of the nominating party. Some argue that this affiliation bias results in suboptimal outcomes, including bitter dissents or compromises that disservice the main international dispute settlement and justice system (Paulsson, 2010; van den Berg, 2011).

The issue of heuristic and cognitive biases is far from new in legal scholarship, including arbitration—both domestic and international (Drahozal, 2004; Sussman, 2013). However, a central issue among practitioners and scholars today is whether arbitrators are as susceptible to subconscious influences as other legal actors and whether they would make better decisions and handle cases more effectively if relieved from litigant-introduced biases.

Blinding as a Solution to Bias
http://dx.doi.org/10.1016/B978-0-12-802460-7.00020-6

"Blind appointments," wherein nominees do not know who appointed them, are one of the most interesting suggestions for addressing biases resulting from the appointment system (ABA, 2013).

In this paper, I use the experience of investor-state arbitration as an entry point into this debate. Relying on the analysis of all proceedings administrated by the World Bank's Centre for Settlement of Investment Disputes (ICSID) until May 1, 2015, I explain the potential effects of affiliation bias by comparing tribunals with party-appointed arbitrators against tribunals without this traditional but now controversial feature. I also describe how party appointments may affect outcomes by looking at the voting patterns of arbitrators. After elaborating on the potential role of biases at play, I argue that compared to other alternatives, blind appointments are a superior intervention with the potential of relieving arbitrators from affiliation bias without sacrificing the benefits of party participation in tribunal formation. I also explain how there are important limits to the implementation as well as the corrective effects of blind appointments. Such limitations are acute in settings more prone to normative or ideological polarization, for example, where close-knit networks of legal actors are involved in an area of litigation or where particular classes of litigants (such as investors) are in the same litigation position (such as claimant). Finally, I contend that with the limited observational data available, it is impossible to assess the strength of the affiliation bias. Thus, experimental studies using real-world arbitrators will add further insights into this debate.

The next section summarizes the debate and blind appointments proposal. I then use the experience of investor-state arbitration under ICSID to understand the possible effects of party appointments and assess the convenience of blinding. After describing the available alternatives, a final section explains the benefits as well as the problems and limitations of blind appointments.

BLIND APPOINTMENTS AND THE DEBATE OVER UNILATERALS

The practice of parties' unilaterally appointing arbitrators has existed for centuries, especially in international arbitration. Instruments establishing such a system include the 1796 Jay Treaty (between the United States and Great Britain), many modern bilateral investment treaties (BITs), most if not all of the major international arbitration rules, and many domestic arbitration laws, including the UNCITRAL Model Law that serves as a basis for the harmonization of national arbitration laws (Brower and Rosenberg, 2013).

Recently, however, the desirability of this well-established system was put into question. Professors Jan Paulsson and Albert Jan van den Berg, both superstar arbitrators, have challenged this fundamental feature of the process on the basis that the impartial discharge of arbitrator function is jeopardized when parties to the litigation unilaterally appoint arbitrators. According to this view, litigants introduce biases to the process that manifest in bitter dissents or favoritism and complicated compromises that disservice the rule-based system and legitimacy of arbitration (Paulsson, 2010; van den Berg, 2011).

A vigorous response defending the use of party appointments has ensued. Johnny Veeder used the pulpit of the annual meeting of the American Society of International Law to defend party appointments. With eloquence and wit, the British barrister (and successful arbitrator) argued that the party-appointment system is the "keystone" of arbitration because it gives the parties "ownership" over the process (Perry, 2013). Without this fundamental feature, the argument follows, parties to disputes will choose conflict over rule-based dispute settlement. Echoing this sentiment, Charles N. Brower—another well-known arbitrator and a repeated party appointee—believes that appointing an arbitrator is an attractive aspect of arbitration "as an alternative to domestic litigation" and "is the highest form of a merit system" (Brower, 2013).

To some extent, this debate has shown the reluctance on the part of arbitration professionals to move away from the party-appointed system. For some, this reluctance—at least partially—results from a lack of trust in arbitral institutions, commonly the authority entrusted by arbitration rules to nominate an arbitrator when a party fails to appoint one or when the parties fail to agree on the chair. However, Paulsson has proposed an alternative that may resolve some of the concerns that emanate from the party-appointment system, without eradicating its virtues: parties can continue to appoint arbitrators, but a mechanism can be introduced to ensure that nominees do not know who appointed them. In Paulsson's own words: "Institutions may experiment with a variety of solutions, such as 'blind appointments' (i.e., seeking to ensure that nominees do not know who appointed them)" (ABA, 2013). Almost nothing more has been said about this interesting and revolutionary proposal to eliminate what Robertson coined as "affiliation bias" (Robertson, 2010).

This debate raises issues that concern the quality of decision making, ethics, and biases and judicial politics in arbitration. It is not a surprise that prominent arbitrators seem eager to respond to the insinuation of dishonesty, especially given the limited and mostly anecdotal evidence presented by those arguing against the system. At the same time, the vigorous response from those defending these appointments may seem self-serving, especially when the defenders are the same arbitrators with an economic interest in the status quo. Before evaluating the potential of the blind appointments solution against other alternatives, it serves us to take a quick look at the available evidence.

THE CASE OF INTERNATIONAL INVESTMENT ARBITRATION

The Basics on ICSID

Among the most important challenges with research in arbitration is that proceedings are typically private, most cases settle privately, and very few awards are published. ICSID, however, provides an unprecedented opportunity for a more robust empirical analysis. This organization—part of the World Bank—was designed to facilitate the settlement of disputes between states and foreign investors as a "step toward promoting an atmosphere of mutual confidence and thus stimulating a larger flow of private international capital" (ICSID Convention 1965 Preamble). Under its rules, ICSID's secretariat must make available to the public significant information concerning the proceedings, including the method of constitution of every tribunal as well as the outcomes of the proceedings. To be sure, the specificity of factors involved in investor-state arbitration—including patterns of litigation, ICSID rules, and litigants—are unique, limiting the generalizations that can be drawn from this work. Nonetheless, ICSID's narrow window into the arbitration world is better than the very limited publicly available evidence on arbitration elsewhere.

Before turning to the main discussion, some basics on ICSID arbitration. With some exceptions, tribunals are typically composed of three members—one arbitrator appointed by each party in the litigation, and a third arbitrator appointed by agreement of the parties or the arbitrators, or by the Chairman of the World Bank as an independent designating authority. The third arbitrator usually acts as the chair. The parties are free to appoint any individual who exhibits "high moral character and recognized competence in the fields of law, commerce, industry or finance" and can "exercise independent judgment" (ICSID Convention 1965, Art. 14). Unless waived by the parties, rules prohibit arbitrators from being of the same nationality as the claimant-investor or the respondent-state. On very rare occasions, states have also brought claims against investors, but almost all cases involve investors seeking compensatory damages under BITs when affected by the excessive intervention of a host state. In other words, in this "asymmetrical" dispute settlement system states are almost always in the position of respondent, defending a measure taken by a governmental authority (Paulsson, 1995).

The role of an arbitrator can be fundamental in the process as well as the outcome of arbitrations. In fact, litigants often seek "a party-appointed arbitrator who has a maximum predisposition towards his client with the minimum appearance of bias" (Hunter, 2009). To find such a person, litigants spend a great deal of time and effort scrutinizing potential arbitrators. Assessment may include analyzing potential appointee's backgrounds, prior appointments, "judicial" or decision-making philosophy, and potential scheduling conflicts (Salomon, 2002). ICSID practitioners interact routinely, highlighting the role of reputation in a close-knit community subjected to conformity pressures. Moreover, both the economic incentives as well as the profile of investment arbitration cases are high, and can potentially trigger arbitrators to make strategic decisions to ensure a steady stream of income or to advance particular ideological commitments in this very contested field of global governance (Puig, 2014).

Evidence

In spite of the small number of cases, the high percentage of private settlements and the limited public records on the cases, two simple strategies can be deployed to make use of observational data. First, one can compare key indicators of the proceedings in cases with against cases without party-appointed arbitrators. Second, one can evaluate the responsiveness and variation of arbitrators' votes to the nominating party. To be sure, these descriptive statistic approaches do not allow inference of causality but, combined, cast some light on the plausible direction of the effects of party appointments.

Tribunals with and without party appointments. Out of 296 ICSID tribunals constituted, in 17 cases, two or more of the arbitrators have been agreed upon by the parties or selected by ICSID as the independent designating authority. Some of these cases involved tribunals where the parties simply agreed to all three arbitrators (nine cases) or cases where a party failed to appoint an arbitrator, arguably, to show its disregard for the process (eight cases). This group of uncharacteristic tribunal cases is not random, and case-specific aspects certainly may be at play. Nevertheless, a good takeoff point is to observe the variations in key indicators such as settlement rate, outcomes (i.e., findings of state liability), case duration, resignations, dissenting and separate opinions, and the use of remedies against the award. With the exception of outcomes, all these indicators are often associated with positive aspects of arbitration—a voluntary, collegial, cost-effective system with preference for agreed solutions, unanimity, and finality (Park, 2012). Further, they provide crude but useful yardsticks to explore the plausible effects of party appointments.

The table in Appendix A shows this analysis and compares the key indicators of the two groups of tribunals. Figures 1 and 2 provide a preliminary picture pointing in the direction of the tangible effects of the party-appointment system: tribunals without two party-appointed arbitrators handle cases faster and settle more often. Their decisions tend to be unanimous and go almost unchallenged. Notably, they also assign liability at a higher rate than tribunals with two party-appointed arbitrators, but also tend to result in more resignations of arbitrators (ICSID rules allow for arbitrators to be challenged if there is reasonable doubt about their competence or impartiality), often extending the life of the arbitration in such cases. To be sure, whether different outcomes may be fully explained by selection bias (a strategic decision of appointing an arbitrator with judicial views favorable to the nominating party) or by affiliation bias (a cognitive shortcoming to favor the nominating party) cannot be determined with this approach. This is very consequential, because selection bias will be unsolved by merely blinding the appointment (although it could have some effects in the long run).

Voting patterns. A second key analysis involves the individual votes of arbitrators in decided cases. Looking at votes may obscure the true effect of conscious or subconscious biases in that while votes are individual, decisions are not. Compromises may happen and are often reflected in many other aspects of the case, for example, the wording of decisions, the nature of violations found, or, more tangibly, the awarded damages. With this caveat, most decisions—around 90%—are unanimous. However, as predicted, party appointees more

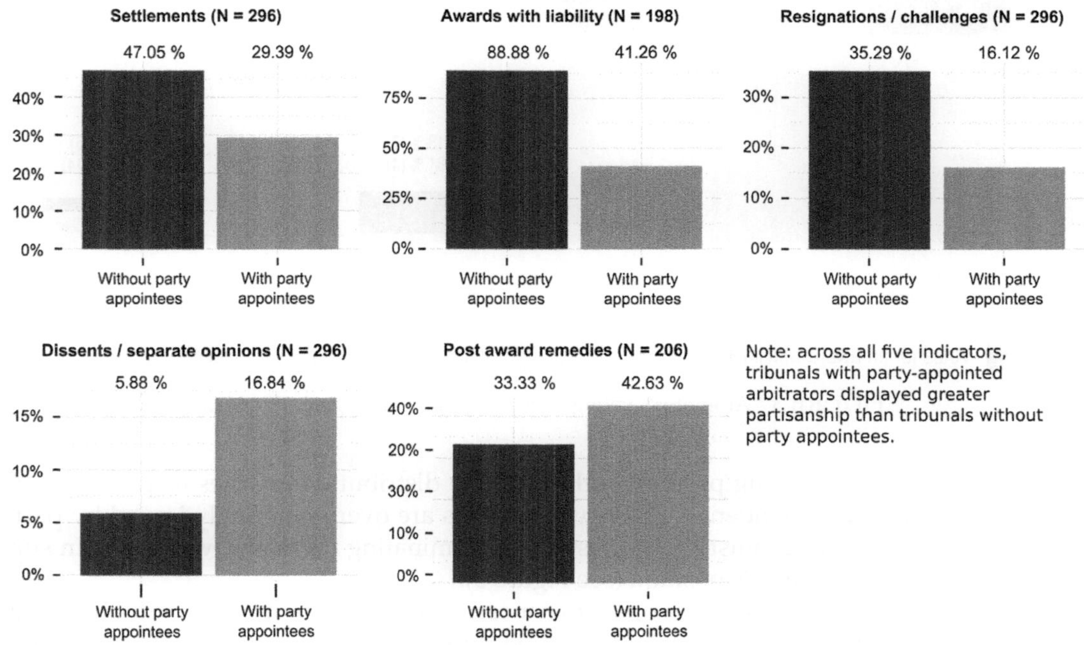

FIGURE 1 Comparison of key indicators in proceedings with and without party appointees.

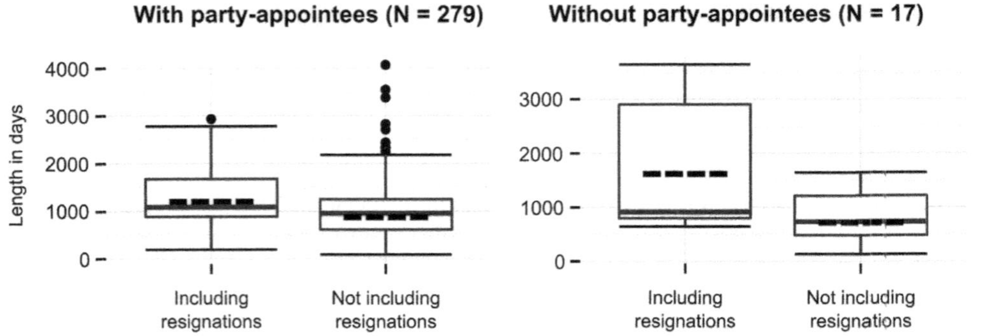

FIGURE 2 Duration of proceedings with and without party appointees.

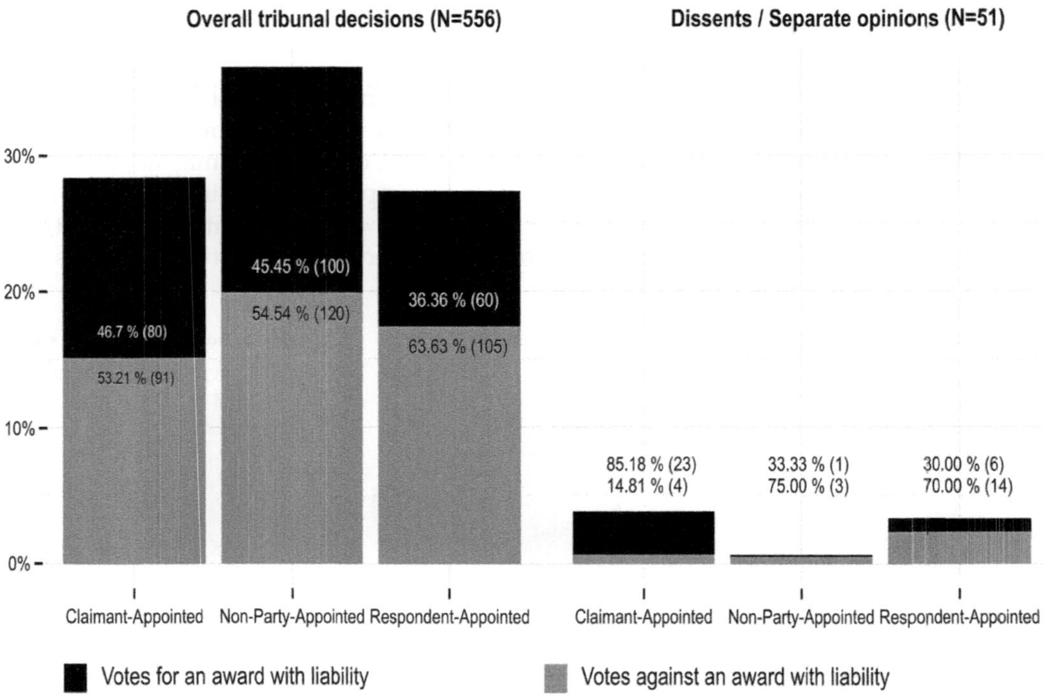

FIGURE 3 Arbitrator's voting patterns by appointing party ($N = 607$).

often vote for the nominating party than the baseline distribution of votes (especially arbitrators appointed by respondents). Moreover, dissents are overwhelmingly issued by party appointees (92%), never against the interest of the nominating party and very often in support of the nominating party's position (see Figure 3).

All these indicators lend some support to concerns over affiliation bias to the extent that different groups of arbitrators (party appointed and nonparty appointed) seem to make different choices. However, it is impossible to determine whether the affiliation bias is driving all or part of such differences. In other words, without more sophisticated research strategies that can tease out the effects of selection bias, affiliation bias, or possibly other variables at play, we are left without conclusive evidence for the need of blind appointments as a corrective strategy.

The indicators also confirm the concerns of defenders of the unilateral party system to the extent that without party appointments, support over the process crumbles. For example, the rate of challenges and resignations in nontraditional tribunals is higher. Of course, there are simply more targets for challenges in these tribunals because parties will not challenge their own nominee and there may be norms against challenging the opponent's. At the same time, the higher rate of resignations in nontraditional tribunals may affect the duration of the case, plausibly explaining a higher mean in the case duration for those handled by tribunals without party appointees.

DEBIASING PARTY APPOINTMENTS AND THE CASE FOR BLINDING

In theory, the parties to an arbitration proceeding can always choose to eliminate or improve the system of unilateral party appointments. In practice, such options may be unavailable once the parties are at an advanced stage of a conflict and unwilling to compromise—and thus in need of previously agreed-upon procedural rules with default appointment methods. Before concluding, I explain different alternatives available to the party-appointed system and why blind appointments are a sensible and promising alternative to debiasing arbitration, addressing obvious challenges with the implementation and effectiveness.

Alternatives to Party Appointments

Appointment of sole arbitrator. The simplest alternative to party appointments is to completely dispose of the system by moving from three arbitrators to one. In lieu of a three-member tribunal with two party appointees, sole arbitrators are appointed by agreement of the parties or by any other agreed-upon method of designation—for example, by an appointing authority. The advantage of a sole arbitrator is that it reduces the biases introduced by the party-appointment system as well as any other conscious or subconscious influences resulting from collegiate decision making (e.g., "compromise effect" or the subconscious influence of adding different perspectives (Sunstein, 2000)).

The obvious problem with this alternative is that parties generally do not agree on a single arbitrator, or may not be entirely satisfied by the appointment made by the appointing authority. In some cases, finding a single arbitrator with the substantive and procedural expertise to tackle several, often complex, issues may be challenging—hence the low rate (less than 4% of the cases) of sole arbitrators at ICSID. Finally, abolishing party appointments could reduce the collaborative and legitimacy-erecting elements that result out of participation in the formation of the tribunal. In the long run, such lack of participation could create "distance between the arbitral community and the users of arbitration" (Branson, 2010).

Appointments by agreement. A similar challenge is the alternative of allowing only appointments made by agreement of the litigation parties. Of course, in theory, this could also relieve the proceedings from the effects of unilateral party appointments. However, in practice not only is agreement between the parties difficult to achieve, but also these type of appointments are often disguised party appointments ("I agree to your arbitrator, if you agree to mine"). Hence, to be truly effective as a debiasing alternative, agreed appointments would also require some sort of blinding (as I explain in the next section).

Appointments made by a third party. A commonly proposed alternative is to let a third, neutral party decide all members of the tribunal (Paulsson, 2013). While this method retains some of the problems and benefits of a collegiate decision-making body, it grants the arbitral institution a great deal of power and control over the dispute. Though the institution could exercise this authority through random selection as in other settings (Robertson, 2010), a constant criticism of such significant delegation is that arbitral institutions often have their own politics and bureaucracy and can be subject to institutional capture by professionals who benefit economically from appointments (Rutledge, 2004). Another general problem is that arbitral institutions often rely on a small pool of available arbitrators and the diversification of arbitrators can be challenging, because there are significant entry barriers (Giorgetti, 2014).

Appointments of nonneutrals. A radical alternative is to move away from the current expectation of independence and neutrality. In fact, there are different perspectives on what the role of an arbitrator should be, including a position that arbitrators need not be neutral. Some professionals, especially in the United States, seem more at ease with having the arbitrator serve the role of "advocate" within the tribunal. While this perspective is definitively not shared among the global community and would do the opposite of debiasing the system, it certainly corrects the disconnection between the normative expectation of independence and the practical reality.

Among the proponents, the late Hans Smit—a distinguished Columbia Law School professor and a leading scholar and practitioner in the fields of international law and arbitration—proposed the banning of party appointments "unless their role as advocates for the party that appointed them is fully disclosed and accepted" (Sacerdoti, 2011). Proposals of this nature seem more radical and might require reforms to most arbitration rules, but would allow the parties to retain significant control over the formation of the tribunal and the outcome of the disputes.

Blind Appointments: Possibilities and Challenges

Blinding is perhaps one of the most viable alternatives to correct any effect of affiliation bias resulting from the current practice of unilateral party appointments. Surprisingly, this is an option that has received little attention by arbitration professionals or scholars, and when addressed, is with skepticism (Duarte, 2012; Giorgetti, 2014). In my view, the preoccupations of those who express distrust of this approach are for the most part exaggerated or can be remedied, as elaborated upon below.

As discussed, blind appointments maintain the practice of unilateral party appointments, but introduce a mechanism to keep the appointment source confidential. The practice need not be implemented solely for unilaterals (arguably, the main source of bias) but can be easily extended to all members of the tribunal without distinction as to who appointed the arbitrator. For the parties it may be obvious which side made each appointment, but individual arbitrators might assume that they are neutral and unbiased and thus suspect (and optimistically hope) that the neutral appointed them. This is a litigant-oriented solution to the extent that it maintains party rights to participate in tribunal formation. It is also optimal as it maintains the benefits (real or perceived) of unilateral party appointments. At the same time, it has the potential to reduce subconscious biases in favor of the appointing party.

Other than a couple of general references in the literature, no author has elaborated on the possibilities and challenges of this promising solution. Nevertheless, best practices and professional norms can be developed to encourage blinding without introducing radical changes to the current and bourgeoning practice of arbitration. To be sure, while blind appointments seem the most sensible proposal, there are both specific challenges to their implementation and limitations as to their effectiveness.

Implementation challenges. Among the most important limitations for blinding appointments is the administration and enforcement of such a practice. One commentator notes that the "main problem with [blind appointments] is that it is not so reliable in practice, where it would be extremely easy to find out which party appointed who" (Duarte, 2012). The most obvious issues stem from the fact that when arbitrators are appointed by the parties, rather than an institution or a neutral authority, professional norms still consider it proper to interview the arbitrators in advance of the nomination (although some arbitrators will refuse an interview) (Bishop and Reed, 1998; Carter, 2000). This is understandable given that substantial sums of money might rest in the hands of arbitrators. In fact, with limited tools to assess potential decision makers (CVs, Web site information, or word-of-mouth), and without access to substantial decisions to assess judicial philosophy (especially in fields such as commercial arbitration) or guiding precedent in many subfields of arbitration, it may be advisable to allow some form of limited exchange between parties and potential arbitrators.

This particular challenge, however, should not be insuperable. For one, potential parties to contractual disputes can include specific guidelines in arbitration clauses on how to conduct such interviews without frustrating blind appointments. Parties could agree not to interview arbitrators at all or to agree to an interview phase that allows both parties to conduct preliminary interviews on all potential, previously disclosed candidates. Once each party has made a decision on the appointee, arbitrators can be notified with a communication from both parties or from the arbitral institution, seeking at all times to ensure that nominees do not know which party nominated them.

Arbitral institutions can also issue blinding policies that address interviewing. In fact, professional best practices on interviewing arbitrators are just emerging and could start including direction on how arbitral institutions can act as able intermediates between the parties and the potential nominee to prevent any indiscretion (CIArb, 2011). Arbitral institutions can even facilitate the infrastructure for enabling the interviews that prevent the nominee from recognizing the interviewing party and counsel (e.g., use of an intermediary or written interrogatories), making this an additional source of income.

A second obstacle is that some arbitration rules provide that the institution disclose the particular method of constitution of the tribunal (ICSID, 2006; Reg. 23). What exactly should be disclosed can be subject to interpretation. While there are reasons to opt for a broad interpretation (e.g., transparency of the process), I see very little value in arbitrators knowing the specific party making the appointment, because the arbitrator's ethical obligations are vis-à-vis both parties and not only the nominating party (International Bar Association (2014), General Standard 1). Moreover, such information could be concealed until the final decision is issued.

Finally, a more mechanical matter: Arbitral institutions must transmit to each member of the tribunal any communication received from either party (ICSID, 2006; Arb. Rule 30). In doing so, institutions could ensure that in transmitting information to the members of the tribunals the information on the source of appointment is redacted. Operational policies could even be established across arbitral institutions for requiring appointments made in a separate confidential document that is not shared with the nominees.

Limitations. If implemented successfully, then blinding will solve for affiliation bias. However, it remains to be seen whether that reform will substantially reduce the partisanship observable in ICSID under the current rules. More research is needed to assess whether the observed variations are attributable to the appointment system itself and the result of subconscious affiliation. For one, litigants are aware of the preferences of specific arbitrators, especially of repeatedly appointed arbitrators, and appoint this core group precisely because they are more predictable and effective in signaling a particular position, by, for example, voting or dissenting (Puig, 2014). Moreover, the cost of dissenting arbitration may be very high, resulting in "a tendency to compromise [as] the arbitration community seems to place a premium on unanimity" (Kahale, 2012). Hence, inferring bias from observational data is challenging for two major reasons. First, individual biases may be unobservable when examining the tribunal outcomes of disputes (compromise effect). Second, the effect of party appointment on decision making may be entirely mediated by the preferences of the nominating party (selection bias).

To be sure, the literature on cognitive biases has documented the existence of litigant-introduced biases with experimental studies in similar contexts (Robertson, 2011), and we have no reason to believe that, at some level, affiliation bias is also affecting arbitration. This chapter should be a precursor for assessing the strength of affiliation bias in this particular legal setting. In fact, one can replicate the experimental approaches adopted by randomly manipulating the appointment source, such that individual characteristics are uncorrelated with the party of appointment. Any variation can therefore be attributed to the appointing party itself.

As a more general point, this chapter stands as a reminder that blinding as a solution to bias should always take context into account. Arbitration takes place in a close-knit community of legal actors and repeat-players who interact routinely. Moreover, ICSID arbitrators rely on symbolic capital and individual reputations (e.g., "proinvestor," "prostate," etc.) and have an interest in furthering both their own status as insiders as well as their particular view of the world. Once members of the profession develop a reputation, this information is passed on and translates into other nominations precisely because of such leanings (Puig, 2014). In other words, the close-knit community and thick social structure pose not only some benefits for the implementation of the blind appointments proposal, such as the possibility of developing professional norms, but also important challenges associated with selection biases. To be sure, in the long run blinding might help to change ICSID practice more profoundly so that arbitrators reconceive themselves in other ways (e.g., "profairness," "protreaty text," or "proeconomic efficiency"), but such progress toward a less politicized and more rule-based system would take time.

CONCLUSIONS

The current system of party-appointed arbitrators is likely to result in litigant-introduced biases. These sorts of biases may operate subconsciously or consciously. However, the empirical evidence introduced here also suggests benefits of the party-appointment system. Blinding appointments seems to be a very sensible and promising reform because doing so maintains the legitimacy and collaborative-erecting elements of the party-appointment system and also addresses the effects of affiliation bias. While the implementation challenges do not seem insuperable, the effectiveness of blinding may also be heavily dependent on the context. Blind appointments may be less effective in arbitration contexts more prone to normative or ideological polarization, such as where particular classes of litigants are in a particular litigation position or in close-knit communities where legal actors are unable to skip close scrutiny by other members of the community. Finally, this work points to the need for further experimental studies using real-world arbitrators to add additional insights to this and other debates over subconscious influences in arbitration.

APPENDIX

	With party appointees		Without party appointees			
	Count	Percent	Count	Percent	Chi-square	p
Settlements ($N=296$)	82	29%	8	47%	1.6026	0.2055
Liability finding ($N=198$)	78	41%	8	89%	1.9855	0.1588
Resignation/challenges ($N=296$)	45	16%	6	35%	2.8925	0.08899
Dissent/separate opinions ($N=296$)	47	17%	1	6%	0.7255	0.3943
Remedies ($N=206$)[a]	72	43%	3	33%	0.6736	0.4118

[a] *Not all ICSID proceedings have the same remedies available.*

References

ABA (American Bar Association), Section of International Law, International Arbitration Committee, 2013. Newsletter Regarding Arbitrator Appointments 1 (1).

Bishop, D., Reed, L., 1998. Practical guidelines for interviewing, selecting, and challenging party-appointed arbitrators in international commercial arbitration. Arbitration International 14 (4), 395–430.

Branson, D., 2010. Sympathetic party-appointed arbitrators: sophisticated strangers and governments demand them. ICSID Review 25 (2), 367–392.

Brower, C.N., 2013. The (abbreviated) case for party appointments in international arbitration. ABA Newsletter 1 (1).

Brower, C.N., Rosenberg, C.B., 2013. The death of the two-headed nightingale: why the Paulsson-van den Berg presumption that party-appointed arbitrators are untrustworthy is wrongheaded. Arbitration International 29 (1), 7–44.

Carter, J.H., 2000. Improving life with the party-appointed arbitrator: clearer conduct guidelines for "non-neutrals". American Review of International Arbitration 11, 295–607.
CIArb (Chartered Institute of Arbitrators), 2011. Arbitration Guidelines and Protocols, Practice Guideline 16: The Interviewing of Prospective Arbitrators. Retrieved from https://www.ciarb.org/docs/default-source/practice-guidelines-protocols-and-rules/practice-guideline-16-april2011.pdf?sfvrsn=2.
Drahozal, C.R., 2004. A behavioral analysis of private judging. Law and Contemporary Problems, 105–132.
Duarte, H.M., 2012. Unilateral appointments of arbitrators: perverse incentives in international arbitration? In: Latin American and the Caribbean Law and Economics Association Annual Conference.
Giorgetti, C., 2014. Who decides who decides in international investment arbitration? University of Pennsylvania Journal of International Law 35 (2), 431–486.
Hunter, M., 2009. Redfern and Hunter on International Arbitration, fifth ed. Oxford University Press, Oxford.
ICSID, 2006. ICSID Convention, Regulations and Rules (as Amended and Effective April 10, 2006).
International Bar Association, 2014. IBA Guidelines on Conflicts of Interest in International Arbitration (as Amended and Effective October 23, 2014).
Kahale, G., 2012. Is investor-state arbitration broken? Transnational Dispute Management 7. Retrieved from http://www.transnational-dispute-management.com/article. asp?key=1918.
Park, W.W., 2012. Arbitration of International Business Disputes: Studies in Law and Practice. Oxford University Press, Oxford.
Paulsson, J., 1995. Arbitration without privity. ICSID Review 10 (2), 232–257.
Paulsson, J., 2010. Moral hazard in international dispute resolution. ICSID Review 25 (2), 339–355.
Paulsson, J., 2013. The Idea of Arbitration. Oxford University Press.
Perry, S., April 17, 2013. Party appointments are the keystone of arbitrations says Veeder. Global Arbitration Review. http://globalarbitrationreview.com/news/article/31502/party-appointments-keystone-arbitration-says-veeder.
Puig, S., 2014. Social capital in the arbitration market. European Journal of International Law 25 (2), 387–424.
Robertson, C.T., 2010. Blind expertise. New York University Law Review 85, 175–257.
Robertson, C.T., 2011. Biased advice. Emory Law Journal 60, 653.
Rutledge, P.B., 2004. Toward a contractual approach for arbitral immunity. Georgia Law Review 39, 151.
Sacerdoti, G., March 14, 2011. Is the Party-appointed Arbitrator a 'Pernicious Institution'?: A Reply to Professor Hans Smit Contribution in 'Columbia FDI Perspectives'. Bocconi Legal Studies Research Paper (1931603).
Salomon, C.T., 2002. Selecting an international arbitrator: five factors to consider. Mealey's International Arbitration Report 17 (10), 25.
Sunstein, C.R., 2000. Behavioral Law and Economics. Cambridge University Press, Cambridge.
Sussman, E., 2013. Arbitrator decision making: unconscious psychological influences and what you can do about them. American Review of International Arbitration 3.
van den Berg, A.J., 2011. Dissenting opinions by party: appointed arbitrators in investment arbitration. In: Arsanjani, M.H., Cogan, J.K., Sloane, R.D., Wiessner, S. (Eds.), Looking to the Future: Essays on International Law in Honor of W. Michael Reisman. Brill Online Publishing.

CHAPTER

21

Psychological Obstacles to the Judicial Disqualification Inquiry, and Blinded Review as an Aid

David V. Yokum

Department of Psychology, College of Science, The University of Arizona, Tucson, AZ, USA

OUTLINE

INTRODUCTION

Within the past decade, the legal community has increasingly been confronted with cries of protest that its judges are failing to disqualify themselves despite being apparently biased. In 2006, for example, *The New York Times* ran a scathing exposé on the Ohio Supreme Court, noting that "[i]n the 215 cases with the most direct potential conflicts of interest, justices recused themselves just 9 times" (Liptak and Roberts, 2006).

Blinding as a Solution to Bias
http://dx.doi.org/10.1016/B978-0-12-802460-7.00021-8

The stories are manifold. A federal district judge in Louisiana was impeached in 2010 for, among other things, failing to disqualify himself from a case wherein one of the litigants had given him thousands of dollars over the years to pay gambling debts (Geyh and Markarian, 2010; citing H. Rep. 111-427, 2010). Justice Ketchum, of the West Virginia high court, provoked the ire of the media when he initially refused to disqualify himself from hearing a challenge to a statute capping medical malpractice damages, despite explicitly promising during his campaign he would never rule to override the law (Mauro, 2010). (Justice Ketchum ultimately bowed to the pressure and disqualified himself.)

One of the most colorful episodes occurred in Caperton v. A.T. Massey Company (2009). *Caperton* involved an August 2002 West Virginia jury verdict against Massey Coal Company for \$50 million in compensatory and punitive damages. As the case was pending appeal, the 2004 elections for the West Virginia Supreme Court of Appeals occurred. The CEO of Massey, Don Blankenship, contributed the \$1000 statutory maximum to the 2004 campaign of Brent Benjamin. Blankenship also spent more than \$3 million in independent expenditures and donations to political organizations campaigning to replace then sitting Justice McGraw with Benjamin. This constituted more than the collective amount spent by all other Benjamin supporters and three times the amount spent by the campaign committees of both candidates combined. Benjamin won the election 53.3–46.7% (a difference of less than 50,000 votes), and thus, when the *Caperton* case finally reached the Supreme Court of Appeals, he was a sitting Justice. Justice Benjamin refused to recuse himself after Caperton filed to remove him, and he went onto cast the decisive vote in a 3-2 decision that reversed the \$50 million verdict against Massey. The U.S. Supreme Court held that, due to the unique circumstances and the amount of campaign financial contributions, Justice Benjamin's failure to recuse resulted in a violation of the Due Process Clause of the Fourteenth Amendment. The controversy was of such notoriety that it later became the source material for a John Grisham novel (Nyden, 2008).

In another widely publicized incident, Justice Scalia refused to disqualify himself from hearing a case in which Vice President Dick Cheney was a named party, despite the two going on a private duck hunting trip in Louisiana while the case was pending. One newspaper editorial headline accused the justice of "Duck-Blinded Ethics" (San Diego Union Tribune, 2004).

The above examples suggest that a schism exists between how the public views the impartiality of judges and how those same judges view their own impartiality. Yet the very standard that judges are supposed to apply, in deciding whether to disqualify themselves from hearing a case, is whether "their impartiality might reasonably be questioned." The gap between the judge's judgments and the judgments of the public potentially reflects a problem with the standard itself.

Most of us are willing, at least on occasion, to entertain the notion that our judgments and decisions might be tainted by bias. Judges are no different. Justice Frankfurter noted, "reason cannot control the subconscious influence of feelings of which it is unaware" (Public Util. Comm'n of DC v. Pollak, 1952). In that case, he concluded, undoubtedly to the bemusement of observers, that he so disliked the playing of music and commercials in streetcars and buses that he must disqualify himself from considering the constitutionality of laws governing the practice. The Supreme Court in *Caperton* acknowledged that courts must consider "a realistic appraisal of psychological tendencies and human weaknesses" (Caperton v. A.T. Massey Coal Co., 2009). And legal scholars, writing about disqualification, almost inevitably include some disclaimer that, yes, of course, judges are mere mortals (Alfini et al., 2010; Shaman, 1996). Given these concessions, one might be tempted to conclude that the judiciary fully appreciates the problem of judicial bias but is simply satisfied that the current standard works well enough nonetheless.

The primary argument of this chapter is that accurately assessing when one is actually biased and when one's own "impartiality might be reasonably questioned" are exceedingly difficult cognitive tasks—so fraught with error, in fact, that procedural reforms are required to ensure that the judge being judged does not have the (near) final word on the matter. The next section reviews the law of disqualification. I then review the psychology of diagnosing bias, and how it poses obstacles for proper application of the law, even by judges of the highest caliber and the best intentions. A final section proposes two procedural reforms, both of which aim to shift the task of applying the standard away from the judge over to a third party. The first proposal is modest and has been proposed elsewhere; it is to use de novo appellate review. The second proposal is relatively novel: It is to have a third-party judge to assess disqualification motions, but under a blinding mechanism, such that the reviewed judge does not know which other judge was the reviewer. This blind should increase the candor of the reviewer and the apparent fairness of the procedure.

THE LAW OF JUDICIAL DISQUALIFICATION

The Model Code of Judicial Conduct

The Model Code of Judicial Conduct ("Model Code") (2010), promulgated by the American Bar Association (ABA), "exemplifies the modern view of judicial disqualification" (Alfini et al., 2010). Rule 2.11(A) provides that, as a general matter, a judge is disqualified from any proceeding "in which the judge's impartiality might reasonably be questioned" (ABA, 2010). "Impartiality," in turn, is defined as the "absence of bias or prejudice in favor of, or against, particular parties or classes of parties, as well as maintenance of an open mind in considering issues that may come before a judge" (ABA, 2010, Terminology). This standard, "impartiality might reasonably be questioned," has been adopted by the federal court system as well as at least 48 states (28 U.S.C. Section 455(A)).

Subsections of the Model Code Rule 2.11(A) identify specific circumstances wherein impartiality is presumed to be reasonably questioned, and thus disqualification is required (ABA, 2010). Generally speaking, these provisions require that a judge be disqualified for actual bias or prejudice, certain relationships, personal involvement in the case, financial conflicts of interest, certain connections to campaign contributors, and certain public pronouncements (ABA, 2010). The rule drafters were explicit that the list should not be interpreted to limit the scope of when "impartiality might reasonably be questioned" (ABA, 2010). The federal court system has adopted all but the latter two specific provisions (28 U.S.C. Section 455), which is also true of most of the states (Alfini et al., 2010).

The judge considering whether his or her disqualification is required, either on motion or sua sponte, therefore has two considerations. One is whether the circumstances fit any of the explicit provisions within Rule 2.11(A)(1)–(6). For example, does the judge harbor an actual bias or prejudice (ABA, 2010)? The other is whether his or her impartiality might reasonably be questioned for any other reason. An affirmative finding on either consideration triggers disqualification.

The history behind Model Rule 2.11(A), including why the particular subsections have emerged when they did, provides insight into an omnipresent tension that has animated the evolution of the law of disqualification (Geyh, 2010–2011). That tension is between, on the one hand, a deeply rooted assumption that judges set aside any personal biases when putting on the robe and, on the other hand, an increasing concern that judges, as mere humans, are susceptible to all manner of biases and prejudices (Frank, 1931). This tension has manifested itself, in part, as a sort of tug-of-war between the judiciary and legislature. A notorious failure to recuse sparks public controversy; the legislature responds with tightened rules of disqualification; the judiciary recoils by interpreting those rules in a highly restricted manner; and then, perhaps after a short calm, another notorious failure occurs and the cycle repeats itself (Leubsdorf, 1987).

The tension is also apparent within the judiciary itself (Stempel, 2010), and even within the same judge (Geyh, 2009). Professor Geyh, testifying before the House Judiciary Committee, aptly explained the dilemma as a paradox: "the ethics codes define a good judge as someone who avoids the appearance of partiality, which by negative implication means that a judge who has created an appearance of partiality (and must disqualify herself on that basis) has behaved less than optimally" (2009). This careful assessment continued: "Given the ethos of impartiality that underlay the common law and judicial self-identity, it is understandable that trial judges would be reluctant to admit disqualifying bias and that appellate judges would be reluctant to second-guess their brethren" (Geyh, 2010–2011). An important explanation for that "reluctan[ce]," explored below, is related to how the human mind attempts to diagnose bias.

The reluctance of judges to recuse was compounded in the 1960s after an influential Fifth Circuit case articulated a so-called "duty to sit" (U.S. v. Edwards, 1964). Under this doctrine, "[i]t is a judge's duty to refuse to sit when he is disqualified, but it is equally his duty to sit when there is no valid reason for recusation." As a result, judges tended to resolve close questions against recusal, out of fear that they violate their professional obligation to hear presented cases (Hirsch and Loveland, 2002). All circuit courts embraced the "duty to sit" within the decade (Laird v. Tatum, 1972). Today the Model Code is understood to have curtailed, if not outright repealed, the duty to sit (Alfini et al., 2010). Nonetheless, the legacy of this period continues to be felt, as courts regularly emphasize the importance of being sure disqualification is required before actually recusing (Alfini et al., 2010).

Dual Aims of Disqualification: Actual Bias and Appearances

An understanding of the purposes of disqualification can help guide how the disqualification standard should be interpreted, as well as provide a benchmark for assessing whether judges are applying the standard as supporters of the Model Code envisioned. At least two aims are notable. First and foremost is the aim of ensuring that litigants receive, as the Constitution promises, a fundamentally fair trial, a concept that is largely defined as adjudication before an impartial judge (Redish and Marshall, 1986). The concern here is that judges, as a matter of fact (not appearances), be free from undue bias or prejudice. Model Code Rule 2.11(A)(1) makes this expectation explicit, in that it prescribes disqualification if the judge harbors a "personal bias or prejudice," that is, if there is actual bias or prejudice.

The second aim is preserving the legitimacy of the judicial institution. Legitimacy can be usefully characterized as a psychological property related to an authority (such as a legal institution) that, if sufficiently held, will motivate people to voluntarily defer to its decisions and rules (Tyler, 2006). In other words, a person perceives an authority to be legitimate if he or she feels obligated to follow its dictates, not (or at least not only) because it threatens punishment or promises reward, but rather because the authority, by virtue of who it is or how it functions, is thought to be right and proper.

Legitimacy is a uniquely valuable asset for an institution to possess. Without legitimacy, an institution must attempt to exert its power based solely on coercion and incentives. Such power, although capable of achieving results, can be exceedingly burdensome and costly to implement.

The American judicial system, lacking power over either "the sword or the purse" (Hamilton, 1788), is only able to exert its influence through the voluntary acquiescence of the citizenry or, failing that, support from the other branches of government in coercing compliance (Breyer, 2010). In this respect, the courts are a uniquely fragile institution; if the public came to view the judiciary as illegitimate, it would be disinclined to follow the dictates of judicial decisions (Planned Parenthood of Southeastern Pa v. Casey, 1992). The U.S. Supreme Court has, rather remarkably, managed to maintain relatively widespread approval to date, even following highly controversial decisions (Gibson et al., 2003). Yet such a "reservoir of good will" is not to be taken for granted. Court systems can and do fail under the weight of illegitimacy. During the 1990s, for example, public trust in the Argentine Supreme Court became so eroded that protestors took to the street demanding that the justices themselves be ousted (Miller, 2000). Moreover, although most scholarly attention is directed at the U.S. Supreme Court (Cann and Yates, 2008), the vast majority of persons will personally encounter the legal system, if at all, only through local state and federal district courts (Rottman and Tomkins, 1999). Perceptions of the judicial system are more tenuous in these courthouse trenches (Rottman and Hansen, 2000).

The legislative history on disqualification law reveals an increasing concern with the legitimacy of the court. Indeed, when Congress adopted the Model Code into the federal regime (28 U.S.C. Section 455), it was explicit that it intended not only to address actual bias, but also the mere appearance of bias. The committee hearings and floor debates in the 5 years building up to its passage revealed a concern that the so-called "duty to sit" had led to circumstances that damaged the legitimacy of the judiciary. Senator Birch Bayh, Jr (D-IN), proposer of the initial bill, was clear on this point. Testifying before the ABA's Special Committee on Standards of Judicial Conduct in August of 1970, Senator Bayh stressed that "The problem is not so much one of fundamental injustice as the *appearance* of injustice." To this end, he criticized the extant law for "fail[ing] to remind the judges of their obligation to avoid the appearance of impropriety" (1969–1970). Senate and House committee reports accompanying the legislation affirmed the underlying purpose initially offered by Senator Bayh:

> [The new law is] designed to promote public confidence in the impartiality of the judicial process by saying, in effect, if there is a reasonable factual basis for doubting the judge's impartiality, he should disqualify himself and let another judge preside over the case *Senate Report No. 93-419, 93rd Cong., 2d Sess. (1973)*

Cases interpreting Section 455(a) straightforwardly understood that it is public confidence, not actual bias, which is being targeted (Liljeberg v. Health Services Acquisition Corp., 1988). Perhaps the most illustrative examples are those where a failure to recuse is found to be an error, despite the judge being genuinely unaware that a conflict even existed. The Supreme Court in *Liljeberg*, for example, vacated the judgment of a district judge who presided over litigation that affected, without his knowledge, the financial interests of a university of which he was a trustee (Liljeberg v. Health Services Acquisition Corp., 1988). The Fifth Circuit applied a similarly high standard when holding that Section 455(a) mandated disqualification where a law firm, without the judge's knowledge, was considering offering him a lucrative position within the firm (In re Continental Airlines Corp., 1990). The court acknowledged that Section 455(a) "does not call upon judges to perform the impossible," but nonetheless admonished that the judge, upon learning about the offer (which he received one day after approving the firm's claim for $700,000 in legal fees), was "required to take the steps necessary to maintain the public confidence in the judiciary," in this case either reject the offer outright or else recuse and vacate the ruling.

The Impartiality Hypothetical

The assessment of whether "impartiality might reasonably be questioned" is meant to be an objective inquiry (Alfini et al., 2010). The Reporter for the ABA committee that drafted the original 1972 Model Code described the trigger for disqualification as follows: "Any conduct that would lead a reasonable man knowing all the circumstances to the conclusion that the judge's 'impartiality might reasonably be questioned' is a basis for the judge's disqualification" (Thode, 1973). Thus, it is not the judge, but rather a hypothetical reasonable person, endowed with certain knowledge, who is to do the questioning (Cheney v. U.S. District Court for District of Columbia, 2004). We can call this the "impartiality hypothetical."

PSYCHOLOGICAL OBSTACLES TO DIAGNOSING BIAS

The judge considering the need for disqualification is confronted with a series of psychological obstacles, reviewed in the following subsections. The first is that introspection for phenomenological traces of bias are likely to turn up a negative result, since most cognitive processes are unconscious. Thus, a self-reflecting judge is likely to believe, sincerely, that he or she is not biased, even if in fact bias exists. This will cause errors in diagnosing actual bias. Errors are also likely in assessing the impartiality hypothetical, because, due to a combination of naïve realism, judges will overestimate the extent to which others, such as the hypothetical reasonable person, will agree with their own, personal assessment. In particular, when it comes to diagnosis of bias, the evidence suggests that self-diagnosis is notably more prone to error than is other-diagnosis.

Asymmetric Information in Self- versus Other-Diagnoses

Direct research on the ability to diagnose bias, although limited, has thus far supported the proposition that "people readily detect or infer a wide variety of biases in others while denying such biases in themselves" (Pronin et al., 2004, p. 781). Emily Pronin and colleagues conducted a rather straightforward test. They gave people short descriptions of a host of different biases that have been documented in the scientific literature (e.g., self-serving bias, halo effect, fundamental attribution error), and simply asked the subjects to rate the extent to which *they* would succumb to each bias relative to the extent to which the *average American* would succumb to the same bias (Pronin et al., 2002). The results were clear: almost without exception, subjects reported that those *other* persons would be much more susceptible to each of the biases than they themselves would be.

A follow-up study (Pronin et al., 2002) had subjects first engage in a biased behavior and then, second, read a description of the bias in issue, before finally being asked point-blank whether they had succumbed to the bias. More specifically, college students from Stanford rated themselves on six personality dimensions, three of which were positive (dependability, objectivity, and consideration of others), and three negative (snobbery, deceptiveness, and selfishness). They then read an explanation of the "better than average" effect, where "70–80% of individuals consistently rate themselves 'better than average' on qualities that they perceive as positive, and conversely, evaluate themselves as having 'less than average' amounts of characteristics they believe are negative" (pp. 374–375).

Subjects were then asked to reconsider their personality assessments and, in particular, whether their responses had been tainted by a better-than-average effect. Thus, as an example of how to think about the possible results: if everyone initially rated themselves above average, yet accurately self-diagnosed after learning about the bias, then at least one-half should conclude that the objective measure would be *worse* than their initial assessment. Although the typical better-than-average effect was observed, only about one in four persons conceded that they might have succumbed to the bias. This indicates that, "[c]learly, some participants had both succumbed to the relevant bias and then denied having done so, even after hearing an explicit description of it and being invited to acknowledge its influence" (Pronin et al., 2002, p. 375).

A third study by Pronin and colleagues even more directly speaks to the willingness to attribute bias to others but not one's self. Pairs of undergraduate students were given a sham "social intelligence test," wherein they received, by experimental design, feedback indicating that one partner scored at the 30th percentile and the other the 80th percentile. The researchers first found that, as expected due to self-serving bias, subjects receiving a 30th percentile score believed the test was invalid, while those receiving an 80th percentile score believed it was valid. The real question of interest, however, was whether the subjects would diagnose this bias in themselves and their partners. To explore this, the subjects subsequently received a written description of the self-serving bias, and then were asked to assess the extent to which they believed their evaluations of test validity, as well as their partners' evaluations of test validity, were afflicted by the bias. Revealing a notable asymmetry in the perception of bias, the researchers found that people thought their *partner's* evaluations were tainted by self-serving bias significantly more than their own, regardless of whether they were in the 30th or 80th percentile conditions.

Joyce Ehrlinger and colleagues, building off of the theoretical work of Emily Pronin et al. (2004), provided evidence of one of the processes that gives rise to the asymmetry between self-diagnosis and other-diagnosis. The mechanism pertains to the strategies that people use to diagnose bias, of which there are at least two: (1) reliance on abstract theories of bias (e.g., money corrupts) and (2) introspection (e.g., self-reflecting to ask, "is this financial incentive influencing my judgment?"). Although both can be employed in the task of self-diagnosis, the latter, of course, cannot be used for other-diagnosis. One can only introspect into the content of one's own mind.

Perhaps less obvious is that introspection cannot be used, at least not in the same direct way, when assessing whether one is biased *in general* (as opposed to in a given, specific instance). For example, if a person is asked whether he or she is being overly optimistic about their odds of receiving an offer after a specific job interview, then he or she could introspect into the contents of why they believe the interview was a boom or bust, or whatever other features believed pertinent to that particular judgment. If, on the other hand, a person is asked if he or she is overly optimistic in general, it is difficult to know what precisely the introspective search should seek out. The upshot is that introspection is most likely to be triggered for specific judgments rather than for more general judgments.

That line of reasoning is, of course, an empirical claim, but one for which Ehrlinger et al. (2005) found support. Cornell undergraduate students were asked to assess whether certain predictions were tainted by optimism bias, for example, whether ratings of the likelihood of receiving an attractive job offer after graduation were inflated. In a 2×2 between-subjects design, the assessment of bias was either in the self or in another student, and with respect to a specific set of predictions that either had been made (and thus were specific) or might be made (and thus were abstract). The results replicated earlier work that people more readily assigned bias in others than in themselves. It also found, as predicted, that the specific versus general diagnoses were significantly different. In particular, those asked about a specific instance of self-diagnosis were *most* likely to *deny* the presence of bias. A clever analysis was used to reveal this as an effect of introspection. Participants were also asked to indicate how much they believed the predictions under review deviated from how a typical Cornell law student would respond. One abstract theory of bias is that a judgment is biased to the extent it deviates from the norm. Thus, if participants are relying on abstract theories of bias, their assessments of bias should correlate with their assessments of deviance. As expected, the correlation was found for other-diagnoses, but not for self-diagnoses. In the latter case, subjects apparently relied on introspection instead.

The pattern of results was replicated in a second experiment, wherein the researchers also simply asked, directly, that subjects self-report which strategy they used. Was it a theory of bias or introspection? Subjects reported using introspection significantly more for self-diagnosis than other-diagnosis. Likewise, for subjects asked to self-diagnosis, they were significantly more likely to report introspecting for specific rather than abstract diagnoses.

The above experiments present an important insight. There is a difference in how people assess bias in themselves versus others, and one central reason for this difference is reliance on introspection. People heavily rely on introspection for specific self-diagnoses, but not so much for general self-diagnoses, and hardly at all for other-diagnoses of either variety. Yet it is specific self-diagnoses that are found to be the most inaccurate, in that people are most likely to deny bias. This presents an ironic obstacle for judges: even the most genuine and vigorous of attempts at self-diagnosis are likely to lead them astray; not only that, but introspecting for bias might actually backfire, increasing the odds an erroneous judgment. Why might this be the case? The answer is the introspective illusion.

The Introspection Illusion

Introspection for bias can be misleading because most cognitive *processes* are unconscious (Nisbett and Wilson, 1977), including the processes underlying most biases. (This is in contrast to cognitive *content*, which is quite accessible upon reflection. For example, one can effortlessly experience the content of vision without any access whatsoever into how the mental image was generated.) There is therefore no phenomenological trace, no consciously accessible evidence, for introspection to possibly detect, even if there is in fact a bias, even a severe bias. The end result in such instances is a false negative.

Pronin et al. (2004) have dubbed this shortcoming the "introspective illusion." It is an illusion because "introspection typically assures us that the judgments in question were correct and supported by sound reasons," even if there is a significant risk of bias. Not only does introspection often fail to identify bias, but it can actually increase "the honest conviction that one acted as one did in spite of, not because of, one's private sentiments" (Pronin et al., 2004). It is possible that the sheer *amount* of cognitive content (again, not to be confused with cognitive processing) available upon introspection can generate a misplaced confidence in its authority and authenticity as a guide to diagnose bias. In other words, the person who undertakes the time and effort to introspect concludes (not entirely unreasonably) that he or she has undertaken the requisite due diligence, and thus a lack of detected bias merits a firmer conclusion that no bias exists. Unfortunately, this inference relies on the false premise that biasing processes are consciously accessible.

Whatever the cause of the introspective illusion, it implies that confidence in one's objectivity might have little or no correlation with one's actual bias. There are empirical data bearing out this prediction. A study by Uhlman and Cohen (2005), for example, found that subjects would unconsciously weight the relative importance of hiring criteria in whatever manner would ensure an applicant of the desired gender was selected, and that this gender discrimination bias was larger in subjects with greater self-perceived objectivity.

Motivated Processes in Diagnosing Bias

The Uhlman and Cohen study (2005) also provides an example of a phenomenon known as motivated reasoning, which is a final consideration for this section on the psychology of diagnosing bias. Generally speaking, the theory of motivated reasoning is that motivation affects reasoning by altering which cognitive processes are used for accessing, constructing, and evaluating beliefs. Consider again, this time in more detail, the experimentation by Uhlman and Cohen. In one study, subjects evaluated candidates for a police chief position. There was a male candidate and a female candidate. The researchers systematically manipulated which one was described as more academically qualified, and which one was described as more qualified in terms of streetwise commonsense. Regardless of the description, subjects were significantly more likely to recommend the male candidate for the position, thereby manifesting a bias in favor of hiring a male for the stereotypically male position of police chief. But, the cause of such discrimination was subtle. Subjects flexibly (i.e., inconsistently), and apparently unconsciously, assigned greater weight to whichever trait the male happened to possess. If the male was educated, it was education that was deemed more important; if the male was streetwise, it was "streetwiseness" that was deemed more important.

By contrast, if subjects were asked to weight the criteria *before* learning the genders of the candidates, the bias disappeared. This fits with the idea of motivated reasoning working via an unconscious process. When the weights are set publicly and a priori, it would be impossible to use a different weighting scheme without conscious realization of the inconsistency.

And subjects, presumably because they recognize such reweighing would be outright gender discrimination, refused to do it.

Motivated reasoning is important for diagnosing bias for two reasons. First, when other-diagnosing, motivated reasoning can cause one to flexibly use theories of bias. Ehrlinger et al. (2005) provided intriguing evidence on this point. Caucasian and minority students were asked to assess whether other students, of either Caucasian or minority ethnicity, would be influenced by their ethnicity in assessing a proposal to eliminate affirmative action in college admissions. The "influence" in question was that the ethnic experience would either "*detract from* [the] ability to see the issues clearly" or "*enhance* [the] ability to see the issues clearly." A motivated diagnosis of bias was found: Caucasians believed fellow Caucasians would enjoy an enlightened perspective while minorities would suffer detracting bias; likewise, minorities believed fellow minorities would enjoy an enlightened perspective while Caucasians would suffer detracting bias.

A second reason, for which experimentation is needed to confirm, is that, when self-diagnosing, motivated reasoning will cause one to flexibly interpret the cognitive contents of introspection. Ehrlinger et al. did not ask this question, but presumably their results could have been found for self-diagnosis as well. That is, the generalized prediction is that Caucasians would have believed their own ethnicity was a source of enlightenment, just as they believed it was for their fellow Caucasian; and likewise minorities would believe their ethnicity to be a source of enlightenment. This remains to be tested, however.

The psychology explaining how false negatives emerge from introspection—due to asymmetric information, the introspective illusion, and motivated processes—is a cause to resist too quickly assuming the worst of a judge refusing to disqualify, even in the more colorful cases such as those presented in the introduction. This is not to say that *no* judges knowingly sit despite bias—surely that has happened, even if only rarely—but rather to acknowledge that even the most well-intentioned judges, exercising due diligence, are more likely to succumb to a bias blind spot than one might imagine.

Naïve Realism

There is a natural tendency to believe that we see the world directly, that is, that our perceptions correspond in a roughly one-to-one manner with the objective state-of-affairs, with reality. This epistemic conviction is commonly referred to as *naïve realism*. Professor Pronin vividly described the force of naïve realism within the domain of physical perception:

> This conviction (i.e., naïve realism) is inescapable and deep, and it governs our day-to-day functioning despite what we may know about the constructive nature of perception. Thus, even when we have learned that the colors and objects we perceive reflect the interaction between a world of molecules and energy sources and our particular human sensory processes, we continue to respond to the relevant stimuli in accordance with our naïve conviction about objective reality. We accept the word of scientists that this world is perceived very differently by other creatures—that the sounds, sights, and smells they experience may scarcely resemble our own. But we tend to regard those creatures as having an altered perspective on the objective properties of the reality we perceive, rather than vice versa. *Pronin et al. (2004, p. 783)*

The more important point for present purposes, which is perhaps also more surprising, is that naïve realism equally applies to attribution, which is the "process of inferring the causes of one's own and others mental states and behavior" (Westen, 1999, p. 799). We believe our friends (not to mention ourselves) are honest, and that our enemies corrupt, with a similar sense of certain objectivity as if we merely directly observed—rather than inferred from behavioral cues—the social reality unfolding before us (Pronin et al., 2004).

An important consequence of naïve realism is that we expect everyone to see and respond to events in the world in the same way as we do—since, after all, there can be only one reality—and that, by extension, any interpersonal discrepancies in behavior must reflect some personality quirk, confusion, or defect within the *other* person. The force of naïve realism suppresses other possibilities, in particular, that *we* are the quirky ones, or at least that we and the other person are responding to different social constructions of the relevant event.

A prominent example of this dynamic is known as the correspondence bias. In the classic experiment, conducted during the 1960s, subjects were asked to evaluate an essay arguing either in favor or against Fidel Castro; the target evaluation was whether the essayist truly supported Castro (Jones and Harris, 1967). The researchers manipulated the cover story, however, such that subjects believed the essayist either voluntarily wrote the essay or was instead ordered to do so. To the surprise of the researchers, subjects believed that the essayists ordered to write a supportive argument were, in fact, true Castro supporters. Put differently, the subjects were biased to believe the essayist's overt behavior must correspond to his or her underlying true belief. Such an inference fails to adequately discount for the situational demand imposed by the researchers (i.e., that the contents of the essay were ordered) (Gilbert and Malone, 1995). We instead naively believe that the behavior we observe tells the whole story.

Naïve realism presents a challenge for a judge considering the impartiality hypothetical, specifically in instances where the judge already decides no actual bias exists. The standard—whether impartiality might reasonably be questioned—in effect demands that the judge acknowledging his or her judgment of personal bias might reasonably differ from that of an outside observer. Yet this is precisely the judgment that is difficult, psychologically, to acknowledge. If *we* think we are not biased, how could *anyone else* think we were biased, unless that other person was unreasonable?

THIRD-PARTY DISQUALIFICATION REVIEW

The above discussion has highlighted a variety of psychological obstacles to properly applying the impartiality hypothetical. One of the most important conclusions is that self-diagnosis is notably more prone to error than is other-diagnosis. This evidence suggests that there is a sound basis for the often-expressed worry that "judges in many jurisdictions decide on their own recusal challenges, with little or no prospect of immediate review" (Sample and Young, 2008, p. 31). Even when judges achieve an accurate assessment of their own impartiality, public confidence might still be undermined because observers are inherently suspicious of judges who, when accused of bias, nonetheless proceed to judge themselves in a positive light (Bayh, 1969–1970, p. 669). Both obstacles could be avoided if someone other than the accused judge made the determination.

Such a change could be accomplished most readily by simply having another trial judge adjudicate disqualification motions for the challenged judge. A minority of states already require independent adjudication of disqualification motions. Judges in Texas, for example, if confronted with a motion to disqualify, may either agree to recuse or transfer the motion to another judge for adjudication (Tex. R. Civ. Pro. 18a(c)(2007)).

Currently nationwide, even without such a referral to another trial judge, the challenged judge's own decisions may be (eventually) reviewed by an appellate court. This review provides an opportunity for independent consideration of the merits, free of self-serving biases. However, most appellate courts review non-disqualifications under a highly deferential standard, in particular, for either abuse of discretion or clear error (Geyh, 2010–2011). And if abuse of error is found, harmless error analysis is then often applied, which may itself be subject to motivated reasoning, thereby even further reducing the odds of overturning the initial refusal to recuse (Stempel, 2010). The end result is that the trial judge's decision will for all practical purposes be the end of the matter, with any appellate activity being little more than a perfunctory review.

Against this backdrop, several commentators have argued that the appellate standard should instead be de novo review, meaning that the trial judge's determination would receive no deference (Hayes, 2008). One purely legal argument, noted by Professor Jeffrey Stempel, is that whether a judge's impartiality could reasonably be questioned "seems in the nature of a mixed question of law and fact" (1987, p. 663), which is, generally speaking, precisely the sort of issue to which appellate courts apply de novo review. The added argument of the current paper is that the appellate court, as a third party engaging in other-diagnosis (rather than self-diagnosis), will simply be more likely to be accurate, since it will not suffer some the obstacles associated with self-diagnosis.

As outlined in the above section Psychological Obstacles to Diagnosing Bias, judges confront a series of psychological obstacles when assessing their own bias or other people's perceptions of their own bias. If a third party were to determine that partiality did not appear to exist, then not only might the decision itself tend to be more accurate, but—even if it were inaccurate—the determination might still increase public confidence that the accused judge was, in fact, impartial. In other words, a mechanism of third-party review could increase both the actual and perceived impartiality of the judiciary.

BLINDED DISQUALIFICATION REVIEW

The possibility of a third party reviewing the disqualification motion is not a new idea. The United States Congress explicitly considered such a possibility as early as 1911, as part of the floor debates leading to passage of statute permitting (at least in theory) an affiant to request and receive automatic disqualification of a judge averred on good faith to be biased or prejudiced. The idea was rejected, however, primarily out of concern that third-party judges would be reluctant, for essentially social reasons, to accuse their colleagues—their friends—of being biased or prejudiced.

There is a ready enough solution to the problem of a third-party judge being reluctant to publically brand a colleague as a biased judge. Namely, a single-blind could provide cover. The accused judge ("Judge A") could be scrupulously screened from discovering which third-party judge/reviewer ("Judge R") assessed the disqualification motion.

This could be accomplished as follows. When a recusal request is made, Judge A either agrees to recuse or, if denying the request, the motion is automatically transferred to an intermediary.

The intermediary selects, either randomly or by rotation, a particular third-party judge to review the motion. There are several possibilities for who the intermediary could be. It could be already present staff at the court system (e.g., the clerk of court), for example, or an organization could be formed specifically for the purpose. The identity of this Judge R is never disclosed to Judge A (or anyone else), but rather kept confidential. Judge R would be given the filed motion and, if applicable, any documents or transcripts of relevance to the motion. Using these materials, but never contacting Judge A (lest Judge R's identity be revealed), Judge R would rule on whether impartiality might reasonably be questioned (the legal standard).

Note that the assessment is not whether Judge R personally thinks Judge A is biased or prejudiced; rather, Judge R is to apply the usual standard for assessing whether impartiality might reasonably be questioned. If an affirmative determination is made, then Judge A is disqualified, and the case is transferred to another judge under the usual mechanisms. If a negative determination is made, then Judge A remains on the case. Either way, an entry would be entered into the record, and provided to the litigants, that a third-party judge, of unknown identity to Judge A, decided the motion. Call this process blinded disqualification review, or "BDR."

Under these circumstances, Judge R need not worry about the sore feelings of Judge A—at least, need not worry about a personal backlash—because Judge R is reassured that his or her identity will remain anonymous. Moreover, public observers are more likely to have confidence in the decision, since there are fewer reasons to suspect an anonymous judge, uninvolved in the case at hand, would have any real self-interest how the motion was resolved. (On the other hand, judges who remain anonymous behind the single-blind might be perceived as "secret" judges. Such assessment would be deeply contrary to the spirit of transparency that animates the American judiciary, and could on net offset any benefits otherwise achieved.)

This is not to say the possibility of bias is entirely removed. Judge R might still succumb to a more general tendency to believe that judges, a professional category to which he or she belongs, are more capable of suppressing bias than is actually the case. Or Judge R, although not fearing a personal backlash from Judge A, might, for altruistic reasons, want to avoid hurting the pride of Judge A. The proposed BDR solution is therefore not a cure-all, but is rather a more modest proposal to curb two particular psychological obstacles: the motivated and self-serving biases of Judge A, and the tendency for observers to be incredulous that an accused judge could dispassionately assess the hurled accusation. The blinding mechanism also, notably, buffers the reviewing judge from concerns over a personal backlash.

Establishing and maintaining a system of third-party judicial review of recusal motions would cost both time and money, albeit a minimal amount relative to the entire judicial budget (and certainly a tiny amount compared to the entire federal budget). An infrastructure for anonymously transferring the motion materials from the courtrooms of the accused judge ("Judge A") to the reviewing judge ("Judge R") and then back again—in other words, subsidizing the cost of the intermediary—would be necessary. In addition, the process itself will take more time than the status quo. Judge R will need to familiarize him or herself with the motion and case details, a familiarity that Judge A would have already possessed to some degree. These additional burdens are not trivial, especially for court systems already strapped for resources and struggling under heavy caseloads. In certain jurisdictions, the logistics might be unworkable.

The pragmatics of executing the blind is why a *double*-blinded process is not being advocated here. What the single-blind does not buffer against is any undue favor or animosity that Judge R might harbor for or against Judge A; or the risk that Judge R might bring personally known information about Judge A, information that is not a part of the record, into the assessment. A double-blind could solve this problem: the case is passed to Judge R in such a manner as to strip any information that would identify Judge A, while preserving the information needed to assess the impartiality hypothetical. It then becomes impossible for Judge R to interject any personalized feeling or knowledge, because it is unknown which specific person is under consideration.

Although conceptually appealing, a double-blind is likely to be difficult in practice for at least two reasons. First, the most common and generic instances of potential bias—for example, due to certain relationships or financial conflicts of interest—are already codified as requiring automatic disqualification, with bias presumed. What is left over, then, are likely to be cases with quite unique circumstances, so unique that the relevant pattern of facts might all but guarantee that the judge in question will be identifiable with little or no effort. For example, a motion describing a duck hunt trip in Louisiana might immediately bring to mind the one judge in the jurisdiction who is an avid duck hunter and from Louisiana. Second, the double-blind introduces additional logistic challenges. Whereas with a single-blind the case files can be transferred quickly and without any scrubbing of information, with a double-blind someone would be tasked with redacting the personally identifiable information about the judge in question. This would involve not only straightforward removal of names, but also review and decisions about whether certain facts identify the judge. For example, does someone need to redact all mention of the duck hunt; could that even be done without obliterating facts central to the inquiry?

Given the costs, the BDR proposal, whether single or double blinded, is only worthwhile if it delivers notable benefits. And whether BDR confers notable benefits is an empirical question. The theory-driven argument here is that BDR should at least help avoid the psychological obstacles outlined above, in the section Psychological Obstacles to Diagnosing Bias. The assessment from a third-party judge, freed by the single-blind to be candid, should more accurately reflect whether impartiality might reasonably be questioned. The hope is that a decision via BDR, even one adverse to the movant, would assure observers that the judge was impartial and, thereby, promote confidence in the judiciary relative to the status quo, wherein the accused judge is the one making the decision.

References

Alfini, J.J., Lubet, S., Shaman, J.M., Geyh, C.G., 2010. Judicial Conduct and Ethics. LexisNexis, Dayton, OH.

American Bar Association, 2010. Model Code of Judicial Conduct, 2011 Edition. American Bar Association, Chicago, IL.

Bayh, B., 1969–1970. On judicial ethics. Saint Louis University Law Journal 14 (4), 667–671.

Breyer, S.G., 2010. Making Our Democracy Work: A Judge's View. Alfred A. Knopf, New York.

Cann, D.M., Yates, J., 2008. Homegrown institutional legitimacy – assessing citizens' diffuse support for state courts. American Politics Research 36 (2), 297–329.

Caperton v. A.T. Massey Coal Co., 556 U.S. 868, 2009.

Cheney v. U.S. District Court for District of Columbia, 542 U.S. 367, 2004.

Ehrlinger, J., Gilovich, T., Ross, L., 2005. Peering into the bias blind spot: people's assessments of bias in themselves and others. Personality and Social Psychology Bulletin 31 (5), 680–692.

Frank, J., 1931. Are judges human? Part one: the effect on legal thinking of the assumption that judges behave like human beings. University of Pennsylvania Law Review and American Law Register 80, 17–53.

Geyh, C.G., 2009. Examining the state of judicial recusals after Caperton v. A.T. Massey. In: Subcommittee on Courts and Competition Policy, Committee on the Judiciary U.S. House of Representatives, pp. 111–118.
Geyh, C.G., 2010–2011. Why judicial disqualification matters-again. The Review of Litigation 30, 671.
Geyh, C.G., Markarian, K., 2010. Judicial Disqualification: An Analysis of Federal Law, second ed. Federal Judicial Center, Washington, DC.
Gibson, J.L., Caldeira, G.A., Spence, L.K., 2003. The Supreme Court and the U.S. presidential election of 2000: wounds, self-inflicted or otherwise? British Journal of Political Science 33 (4), 535–556.
Gilbert, D.T., Malone, P.S., 1995. The correspondence bias. Psychological Bulletin 117 (1), 21–38.
House Report 111-427, 2010.
Hamilton, A., May 28, 1788. The Federalist, No. 78. The Judiciary Department. New York Packet.
Hayes, J.M., 2008. To recuse or to refuse: self-judging and the reasonable person problem. Journal of the Legal Profession 33, 85.
Hirsch, A., Loveland, K., 2002. Recusal: Analysis of Case Law under 28 U.S.C. § 455 & 144. Federal Judicial Center, Washington, DC, p. 86.
In re Continental Airlines Corp., 901 F.2d 1259, 1990.
Jones, E.E., Harris, V.A., 1967. The attribution of attitudes. Journal of Experimental Social Psychology 3, 1–24.
Laird v. Tatum, 409 U.S. 824, 1972.
Leubsdorf, J., 1987. Theories of judging and judge disqualification. New York University Law Review 62 (2), 237–292.
Liljeberg v. Health Services Acquisition Corp., 486 U.S. 847, 1988.
Liptak, A., Roberts, J., October 6, 2006. Campaign Cash Mirrors a High Court's Rulings. New York Times, p. A1.
Mauro, T., September 10, 2010. West Virginia Justice Reverses Self, Recuses in Malpractice Case. The BLT: The Blog of Legal Times. Retrieved from: http://legaltimes.typepad.com/blt/2010/09/west-virginia-judge-reverses-self-recuses-from-case.html.
Miller, J.M., 2000. Evaluating the argentine supreme court under Presidents Alfonsín and Menem (1983–1999). Southwestern Journal of Law and Trade in the Americas 7, 369–433.
Nisbett, R.E., Wilson, T.D., 1977. Telling more than we can know: verbal reports on mental processes. Psychological Review 84 (3), 231–259.
Nyden, P.J., January 30, 2008. Novel Linked to State Election. The Charleston Gazette.
Planned Parenthood of Southeastern Pa v. Casey, 505 U.S. 833, 1992.
Pronin, E., Lin, D.Y., Ross, L., 2002. The bias blind spot: perceptions of bias in self versus others. Personality and Social Psychology Bulletin 28 (3), 369–381.
Pronin, E., Ross, L., Gilovich, T., 2004. Objectivity in the eye of the beholder: divergent perceptions of bias in self versus others. Psychological Review 111 (3), 781–799.
Public Utilities Commission of the District of Columbia v. Pollak, 343 U.S. 451, 1952.
Redish, M.H., Marshall, L.C., 1986. Adjudicatory independence and the values of procedural due process. Yale Law Journal 95, 455–457.
Rottman, D.B., Hansen, R.M., 2000. How Recent Court Users View the State Courts: Perceptions of Whites, African-Americans, and Latinos. National Center for State Courts, Williamsburg, VA.
Rottman, D.B., Tomkins, A.J., 1999. Public trust and confidence in the courts: what public opinion surveys mean to judges. Court Review 36 (3), 24–31.
Sample, J., Young, M., 2008. Invigorating judicial disqualification ten potential reforms. Judicature 92 (1), 26–33.
San Diego Union Tribune, February 6, 2004. Duck-Blinded Ethics: Scalia Puts Supreme Court Integrity at Risk. B8.
Senate Report 93-419, 93rd Cong., 1973.
Shaman, J.M., 1996. Impartial judge: detachment or passion. DePaul Law Review 45 (3), 605–632.
Stempel, J.W., 1987. Rehnquist, recusal, and reform. Brooklyn Law Reiew 53, 589–667.
Stempel, J.W., 2010. In praise of procedurally centered judicial disqualification-and a stronger conception of the appearance standard: better acknowledging and adjusting to cognitive bias, spoliation, and perceptual realities. Review of Litigation; Symposium 30 (4), 733–848.
Thode, E.W., 1973. Reporter's Notes to Code of Judicial Conduct. American Bar Association, Chicago, IL.
Tyler, T.R., 2006. Psychological perspectives on legitimacy and legitimation. Annual Review of Psychology 57, 375–400.
U.S. v. Edwards, 336 F.2d 211, 1964.
Uhlmann, E.L., Cohen, G.L., 2005. Constructed criteria – redefining merit to justify discrimination. Psychological Science 16 (6), 474–480.
Westen, D., 1999. Psychology: Mind, Brain, & Culture, second ed. John Wiley & Sons, New York, NY.

CHAPTER

22

Masking Information Source within the Internal Revenue Service

Karie Davis-Nozemack

Georgia Institute of Technology, Scheller College of Business, Atlanta, GA, USA

OUTLINE

THE TAX SYSTEM WE HAVE

Significant tax evasion is undetected and unpunished in the United States. Of the $450 billion tax gap, the vast majority is attributable to underreported taxes (George, 2014). Detecting underreported taxes is a challenge for the Internal Revenue Service (IRS), and one that is exacerbated by the structure of tax reporting and enforcement. The US tax system is based on taxpayer self-reporting (Lederman, 2003). This self-reporting model in combination with the reporting of only aggregate tax data results in significant information asymmetry for the IRS. At nearly all times, taxpayers have more information about their own transactions than does the IRS (Lederman, 2010). For some taxpayers, such as individuals with wage income, the IRS receives a third-party verification of the tax data. Because employers report wage data to the IRS, it is very difficult for wage-earning individual taxpayers to evade reporting, and consequently payment, requirements (Bankman, 2007). This is not the case for business

Blinding as a Solution to Bias
http://dx.doi.org/10.1016/B978-0-12-802460-7.00022-X

taxpayers. Business taxpayers are subject to little third-party information verification. While larger corporate taxpayers are required to disclose uncertain tax positions (IRS Schedule UTP, 2014), these corporate taxpayers as well as other business taxpayers do not provide the universe of data necessary to accurately assess tax avoidance and evasion. Consequently, the IRS views incomplete information in summary form and is at an informational disadvantage in detecting business underreporting.

Moreover, compliance with some tax laws is not particularly straightforward. Although the public understands the overall complexity of the tax code (Pew, 2011), many assume that tax compliance is a matter of binary options of compliance or noncompliance. This is not the case. For business, tax compliance is more accurately perceived on a scale of tax aggressiveness, in which a business' actions may comply with the letter (or silence) of the law but may violate the spirit of the law. Tax law complexity, vagueness, and gaps result in tax-planning opportunities for businesses. Tax law deficiencies permit cycles of tax avoidance. After businesses have taken advantage of a vague law or gap, Congress and/or the IRS will amend the law or regulation to proverbially plug the hole (Yin, 1992). By that time, however, businesses have moved onto another gap in the law. This cycle perpetuates in a rule-based tax system in which tax reform is undertaken incrementally (Yin, 2001).

A POTENTIAL SOLUTION IN THE WHISTLEBLOWER PROGRAM

In 2006, Congress placed its faith in the IRS Whistleblower Program to help correct the information asymmetry that inhibits effective tax enforcement (Tax Relief and Health Care Act of 2006). Available empirical evidence suggested to Congress that tax examinations flagged by whistleblowers raised twice as much revenue as examinations flagged by traditional mechanisms (Morse, 2009; Treasury Inspector General for Tax Administration, 2006). Unfortunately, the program's promise is largely unrealized (Davis-Nozemack and Webber, 2015). It has a backlog of more than 20,000 tips and has successfully resolved only about 100 whistleblower tips per year (IRS Whistleblower Office, 2014).

BIAS AGAINST WHISTLEBLOWERS

As the IRS Whistleblower Office Director acknowledged in 2013, IRS rank and file employees are skeptical about the use of whistleblower tips in tax administration (Coder, 2013). Anecdotal evidence, from within as well as outside the agency, supports a theory of IRS personnel bias against whistleblowers (Brady, 2013; Coder, 2010, 2011; Kelton, 2012, 2014). Whistleblower bias arises when a whistleblower tip is submitted to the IRS but Service personnel are reluctant to investigate the whistleblower tip, interview the whistleblower, or initiate an examination based on the tip. Skepticism of whistleblower usage is not unique to the Service; other federal agencies also struggle to collaborate with whistleblowers (Government Accountability Project, 2012; Press, 2012). A reluctance to engage whistleblowers, although not unusual, is rooted in psychological and organizational factors.

COGNITIVE BIAS

Reluctance to work with whistleblowers can be viewed as a natural behavioral response to cognitive biases. Within the Service, those dealing with whistleblowers may display fundamental attribution error, overconfidence bias, and/or in-group bias. Fundamental attribution error is the tendency to attribute another person's behavior to the person's character rather than to situational factors (Ross and Nisbett, 1991). Conversely, fundamental attribution error also causes a person to attribute his or her own actions to situational factors instead of his or her character. When they encounter a whistleblower, fundamental attribution error may cause IRS personnel to view whistleblowers as bad or immoral people by virtue of their involvement with or knowledge of tax evasion. IRS personnel may also view a whistleblower negatively because the whistleblower may be motivated, in whole or part, by the possibility of a financial reward for the tip. Fundamental attribution error may keep IRS personnel from seeing whistleblowers as victims of circumstances and flawed humans with their own cognitive biases, such as obedience to authority and conformity bias.

Another cognitive bias, overconfidence bias, is the tendency to overestimate one's own abilities (Bowman, 2014). IRS personnel may exhibit overconfidence bias in assessing their own abilities to detect and investigate tax evasion without the assistance of a whistleblower. Overconfidence bias may cause personnel to ignore prior agency research suggesting that examinations with whistleblower involvement generate more revenue than examinations without whistleblower involvement.

IRS personnel are also subject to in-group bias (also known as irrational group favoritism) within the agency. Interagency in-group bias is likely driven by a shared mission of tax enforcement. Interagency in-group bias manifests in an "us versus them" mentality against taxpayers and whistleblowers alike. The in-group bias is likely compounded by strict taxpayer privacy practiced by the agency (Davis-Nozemack and Webber, 2015).

Each of these cognitive biases lead IRS personnel away from engaging whistleblowers who could assist their tax enforcement efforts and likely make their examinations more fruitful. IRS personnel may be unaware of the existence or manifestations of these biases. A distinguished panel of legal and psychological scholars has noted:

> ...attitudes and stereotypes may also be implicit, in the sense that they are not consciously accessible through introspection. Accordingly, their impact on a person's decisionmaking and behaviors does not depend on that person's awareness of possessing these attitudes or stereotypes. Consequently, they can function automatically, including in ways that the person would not endorse as appropriate if he or she did have conscious awareness. *Kang et al. (2012, p. 1129).*

COGNITIVE BIAS AND PROSECUTORIAL DISCRETION

These cognitive biases (fundamental attribution error, overconfidence bias, and in-group bias) may be characterized as innately human, but resulting biased behavior is antithetical to the fundamental fairness that should guide governmental regulation, and particularly tax enforcement. Cognitive bias creates a concern that enforcement decisions to initiate, pursue, or settle an examination will not be made with the impartiality that should guide them. Cognitive bias may lead decision makers to improperly weight factors, such as the source of information, in making enforcement decisions. Scholars have long noted that enforcement structures with significant prosecutorial discretion provide an environment that tolerates bias by regulators and law enforcement (McCain, 1992; Smith and Levinson, 2012; Zeisel, 1981). Literature involving prosecutorial discretion is useful in understanding enforcement issues with the Service, because tax enforcement is easily analogized to criminal law enforcement. The IRS is an enforcement structure vested with significant prosecutorial discretion in collecting revenue (Kahng, 2013). IRS procedures for whistleblower tips also include significant prosecutorial discretion. Specifically, the IRS has the sole discretion to determine whether to initiate an examination based on a whistleblower tip and to pursue or settle any such examination (Davis-Nozemack and Webber, 2015; Kwan, 2010).

STRATEGIES FOR COMBATING COGNITIVE BIAS FROM PRIOR LITERATURE

The legal literature of prosecutorial discretion is substantial and suggests various strategies for addressing enforcement bias (Banks, 2006; Barkow, 2013; Brown, 2004; O'Brien, 2009). Scholars have long called for constraints on prosecutorial discretion. Some have sought more judicial oversight (Davis, 1969; Heller, 1997; Lowenstein, 2001), while others have sought additional administrative oversight in the form of guidelines (Misner, 1996), citizen representation or participation (Davis, 2001), or increased monitoring or vetting (Davis, 2001). Other literature has advocated education of prosecutors (Kang et al., 2012).

Like the law, business ethics literature also addresses cognitive bias and its effects on ethical decision making (Bazerman and Tenbrunsel, 2011; Hess and Broughton, 2014; Jones et al., 2013). The weight of the applied business ethics literature prescribes education and awareness (Bazerman and Tenbrunsel, 2011; Hess and Broughton, 2014; Jones et al., 2013). Even the literature that provides strategies for improved individual and group decision making relies mostly on heightened awareness of bias as a basis for minimization (Bazerman and Tenbrunsel, 2011).

REMOVING COGNITIVE BIAS INSTEAD OF MITIGATING ITS EFFECTS

Legal and business ethics literature is critical to a better understanding of bias and its pernicious effects on business and society; however, the literature of law and of business ethics primarily contemplates strategies to mitigate bias. Much of the literature assumes the required existence of bias. An alternative perspective is available but requires looking outside law, policy, and ethics. Instead of attempting to attack the effects of bias, the agency could attempt to eliminate the possibility of bias. Science has well-developed literature about limiting bias in trials. The literature provides empirically substantiated theories regarding the importance of and strategies for bias elimination. Within this literature, allocation concealment provides the most applicable lessons for enforcement policy.

Blinding in health interventions has a long history, but began growing into a recognized standard mid-century (Gauch, 2009; Schulz and Grimes, 2002a,b). The mid-1990s saw significant development of empirically supported methods for improving the quality of trials (Moher et al., 1998). In one of the most-cited studies that examined 250 controlled trials from 33 meta-analyses, authors empirically demonstrated that trials with poor or unclear blinding methodology exaggerated treatment results between 30% and 41% (Schulz et al., 1995). Proof of such large errors in otherwise well-conceived trials underscores the pervasive effects of bias. The error rates were not necessarily a function of sponsors failing to conduct research in good faith. The cause is imperfect study design that fails to doggedly guard against the opportunity for bias. Indeed, in science, "it takes just one bias to make a conclusion fall flat" (Gellerstedt, 2002).

Research about limiting bias in trials has been cohesively captured in CONSORT (2015), which is the Consolidated Standards for Reporting Trials. CONSORT contains both recommendations and explanations for conducting and reporting randomized trials. The recommendations of CONSORT have been adopted by the top medical journals, including the *New England Journal of Medicine*, the *Journal of the American Medical Association*, the *British Medical Journal*, and the *Lancet*. More than 400 other journals and editorial groups also support it.

Outside of CONSORT and trials that adhere to it, scholarly use of randomized controlled trials terminology has not been consistent (Devereaux et al., 2001). The term blinding has been subject to particular misuse and lack of specificity (Devereaux et al., 2001). Nonetheless, we can discern the critical aspects to eliminating bias to include (1) blinding, (2) randomization, and (3) allocation concealment. Blinding hides the assignment of participants to intervention or control groups from participants, researchers, and assessors (Viera and Bangdiwala, 2007). Blinding prior to group assignment prevents selection bias, and blinding thereafter ensures that data and results are not tainted by cointerventions (Day and Altman, 2000). Randomization is the assignment of trial participants to comparison groups through a random process (Schulz and Grimes, 2002a,b). It facilitates blinding of all involved in the trial (Schulz and Grimes, 2002a,b). Randomization also ensures that researchers can make unbiased comparisons among intervention and control groups allowing researchers to use probability theory on the trial results (Schulz and Grimes, 2002a,b). Allocation concealment is a process by which participants, researchers, and assessors are kept ignorant of forthcoming participant assignments (Schulz and Grimes, 2002b). Allocation concealment is the second phase of randomization and obscures the randomization pattern so that it cannot be detected. It ensures that the assignments are random in theory as well as practice. Without allocation concealment, bias can occur because the randomization assignment could be detected and so presents an opportunity to circumvent it (Schulz and Grimes, 2002b). Leading scholars in the field have noted that "without proper application of measures to achieve concealment, the whole point of randomization vanishes and bias is likely to distort results" (Schulz et al., 1995).

BLINDING IN THE IRS WHISTLEBLOWER PROGRAM

Blinding IRS personnel, through allocation concealment, to the fact that an examination has been identified by a whistleblower could offer the opportunity to minimize IRS personnel reluctance to undertake a whistleblower-identified examination. By concealing the method of examination selection, Service personnel have no opportunity to bring whistleblower bias to their evaluation of a tax return. The key, of course, as explained in the allocation concealment literature, is the prevention of personnel from determining the allocation. In this case, the allocation is the source of information flagging the return as problematic.

Such a proposal could work as follows. At the Service, whistleblower tips are routed first through the Whistleblower Office and then to subject matter experts within the Service's business units, who decide whether to initiate an examination of the return based on the tip (IRS, 2010). Nonwhistleblower returns follow a different process for examination decisions. Other returns are selected for examination in a variety of ways, including by Discriminant Function System (DIF) score (IRS, 2015). DIF is an algorithm that scores returns based on the Service's prior experience with similar returns, similar taxpayers, or the taxpayer in question (IRS, 2015). Returns with high DIF scores, which suggest examination potential, are then screened by personnel for possible examination issues (IRS, 2015). Examination issues may include, among other things, income underreporting, expenditure overstatement or mischaracterization, or abusive transactions such as tax shelters. Under DIF, it may not be obvious why a return was given a high score, so personnel review returns for high scores for issues. The DIF score in combination with issues spotted by the IRS personnel review of the return inform the decision to proceed with an examination. This decision point is a key opportunity to insert whistleblower returns into the potential examination process because this is the first opportunity where human judgment enters into the decision whether to pursue examination for many nonwhistleblower returns. Mixing whistleblower-identified returns with DIF score-identified returns before they are assigned to Service personnel making the decision to undertake an examination would conceal the allocation of the whistleblower and nonwhistleblower groups. Using this method of allocation concealment would also permit the Service to measure the time, effectiveness, and revenue return from whistleblower-identified examinations for comparison to nonwhistleblower examinations.

This proposal will not work for all whistleblower-identified returns. Whistleblower-identified returns can be grouped into two categories: (1) those for which, once the return is flagged, IRS personnel should be capable of determining tax evasion using normal examination techniques[1] and (2) those for which evasion is so hidden that only through the guidance of a whistleblower will the Service ascertain the evasion. Blinding is unworkable for the latter group; however, the use of blinding on only a subset of whistleblower returns should not be problematic.

The IRS Whistleblower Office already undertakes cursory screening before a whistleblower tip is assigned to a subject matter expert in one of the Service's business units (IRS, 2010). Cursory screening includes examining a whistleblower tip for basic eligibility requirements for a monetary reward, completion, and factors for forwarding to the appropriate business unit. In addition to these items, the Whistleblower Office could screen for whistleblower-identified issues that can be determined on the face of the return. If the Service was unwilling to assign all of these categorical returns to a blinded process, then the Service could assign a sample of

[1] Typical examination techniques include (1) balance sheet analysis, (2) review of books and records, (3) requests for documentation and interviews of third parties for information verification, (4) inspections and observations of operations, inventory, or assets, and (5) transaction tracing.

returns to be handled in this manner. The use of a control group and blinded treatment group could permit study of cognitive bias effects on whistleblower-identified return selection.

This proposal contemplates blinding to prevent cognitive bias during the initial decision to undertake an examination. Once an examination has begun, taxpayer privacy statutes and fourth amendment concerns present some barriers for involving whistleblowers in an examination (Davis-Nozemack and Webber, 2015). Thus, in some cases, it is legal barriers rather than cognitive bias barriers that limit collaboration with whistleblowers once an examination has begun. In the case of whistleblower-identified returns, blinding should be limited to the decision to initiate an examination.

Admittedly, this proposal is unusual. Blinding is not typically utilized in enforcement because it is assumed that fairness in the application of the law and avoidance of arbitrariness necessitate a wholly individualized investigation. Although it is true that enforcement should be individualized to the facts and circumstances of each case, including aggravating or mitigating factors,[2] it does not necessarily follow that every fact within and every moment of an investigation must be linked with an individual's identity. This chapter does not argue for blinding of entire enforcement investigations or proceedings. Rather, it foresees highly limited, strategic, and early use of blinding for certain facts that are likely catalysts for cognitive biases. In particular, concealing the existence of a whistleblower as the information source during the selection of the return for examination could prevent cognitive bias from affecting the selection.

Critics of such a proposal may argue that greater transparency, disclosure,[3] and oversight of whistleblower usage could lead to diminished agency personnel bias over the longer term (Joy, 2010). It is unclear, however, that these efforts at governmental sunshine are effective against the persistent and pervasive psychological forces of fundamental attribution error, overconfidence bias, and in-group bias. Moreover, these strategies continue to permit the occurrence of bias. Others may argue that blinding could obscure important facts during an examination and potentially inhibit developing a more complete understanding of the alleged illegality. Still others could argue that blinding is administratively untenable because of constitutional rights to confrontation and fourth amendment government instrument analysis. These germane criticisms could be addressed by the very limited and very early usage of blinding solely in determining whether to pursue an examination, which appears to be a flash point of bias in whistleblower cases. It would be critical to limit blinding to instances where

[2] The Service considers "mitigating" factors in contemplating compromising a tax liability. Compromise is most common when there is doubt as to liability or doubt as to collectability of the assessed amount. Compromise may come during examination, litigation, or collection. The Service considers "aggravating" factors when it contemplates assessing penalties. Penalties that may be assessed by the IRS include the civil fraud penalty and accuracy-related penalties. These penalties require, respectively, intent to defraud and failure to make reasonable attempts to comply. In summary, the Service has opportunity to consider both situational factors as well as taxpayer mental states in civil tax enforcement (Saltzman, 2002).

[3] Transparency and disclosure could include making public information about which tips did and did not prompt an examination, as well as documenting reasons for action or inaction. Currently, none of this information is made public. The IRS Whistleblower Office's sole public disclosure is an annual report that includes aggregated numbers of tip submitted, in process, and resolved. The IRS also discloses annual aggregate award amounts. The IRS argues that taxpayer privacy laws and the need to provide whistleblowers anonymity prevent more granular disclosure (IRS Whistleblower Office, 2014).

bias is both likely and creates poor enforcement choices, such as whether to pursue an action due to the identity of an informational source as a whistleblower.

Blinding should be considered in enforcement because, if it is used in small strategic ways, it may well prove more efficient and less resource intensive than the education, transparency, or monitoring alternatives. This type of blinding requires little administrative change. Using blinding would require the IRS Whistleblower Office to include an additional screening factor to its cursory review and the routing of certain returns flagged by whistleblower tips through existing processes used for returns flagged by DIF score. For IRS internal divisions, no procedural changes would be required. Ideally, blinding maintains prosecutorial discretion, but alters only the environment for decisions that are likely to be affected by bias.

This chapter's aim is to assist the Service, and other federal agencies, in fulfilling an enforcement mission with fairness and efficiency. Looking beyond the traditional cannons of law, policy, and ethics may allow agencies to bring the lessons of science to bear on enforcement decisions and ultimately to make better enforcement decisions.

References

Bankman, J., September 24, 2007. Eight truths about collecting taxes from the cash economy. Tax Notes 2007–21685.

Banks, A., 2006. Improving prosecutorial decision making: some lessons of cognitive science. William and Mary Law Review 47, 1587–1633.

Barkow, R.E., 2013. Prosecutorial administration: prosecutor bias and the department of justice. Virginia Law Review 99, 271–342.

Bazerman, M.H., Tenbrunsel, A.E., 2011. Blind Spots: Why We Fail to Do What's Right and What to Do about It. Princeton University Press, Princeton, NJ.

Bowman, M.N., 2014. Full disclosure: cognitive science, informants, and search warrant scrutiny. Akron Law Review 47, 431–496.

Brady, E., April 10, 2013. Testimony. Awards for Information Relating to Detecting Underpayments of Tax or Violations of the Internal Revenue Laws: Public Hearing on Proposed Regulation 26 C.F.R. Part 301.

Brown, D.K., 2004. Cost benefit analysis in criminal law. California Law Review 92, 323–372.

Coder, J., January 19, 2010. Conversations: Donald Korb. Tax Notes 2010 TNT 11-7.

Coder, J., September 12, 2011. GAO faults IRS whistleblower program for award delays. Tax Notes 2011 TNT 176-3.

Coder, J., January 28, 2013. ABA Meeting: Whitlock Reaffirms IRS Support for Whistleblower Program. Tax Notes 2013 TNT 18–15.

CONSORT, 2015. Retrieved from: http://www.consort-statement.org.

Davis, A.J., 2001. The American prosecutor: independence, power, and the threat of tyranny. Iowa Law Review 86, 393–476.

Davis, K., 1969. Discretionary Justice: A Preliminary Inquiry. Louisiana State University Press, Baton Rouge, LA.

Davis-Nozemack, K., Webber, S.J., 2015. Lost opportunities: the underuse of tax whistleblowers. Administrative Law Review 67, 321–367.

Day, S.J., Altman, D.G., August 19–26, 2000. Blinding in clinical trials and other studies. British Medical Journal 321, 504.

Devereaux, P.J., Manns, B.J., Ghali, W.A., Quan, H., Lacchetti, C., Montori, V.M., Bhandari, M., Guyatt, G.H., 2001. Physician interpretations and textbook definitions of blinding terminology in randomized controlled trials. Journal of the American Medical Association 285 (15), 2000–2003.

Gauch, R.R., 2009. Bias control—a closer look at blinding and randomization. In: It's Great! Oops, No It Isn't—Why Clinical Research Can't Guarantee the Right Medical Answers. Springer Science + Business Media, New York.

Gellerstedt, M., 2002. Statistical issues—significantly important in medical research. Allergy 57, 76–82.

George, J.E., April 30, 2014. Statement of J. Russell George, Treasury Inspector General for Tax Administration. Hearing on Review of the President's Fiscal Year 2015 Funding Request for the Department of the Treasury and the Internal Revenue Service before Subcomm. on Financial Services and General Government of S. Comm. on Appropriations, 113th Cong.

Government Accountability Project, August 9, 2012. GAP Lauds DOJ Whistleblower Ombudsman Position. [quoting Tom Devine]. Retrieved from: http://www.whistleblower.org/press/gap-lauds-doj-whistleblower-ombudsman-position.

Heller, R., 1997. Prosecution and the federalization of criminal law: the need for meaningful judicial review of prosecutorial discretion. University of Pennsylvania Law Review 145, 1309–1358.

Hess, M.F., Broughton, E., July 2014. Fostering an ethical organization from the bottom up and the outside in. Business Horizons 57 (4), 541–549.

IRS (Internal Revenue Service), 2010. Internal Revenue Manual (25.2.2 et seq).

IRS, 2014. Schedule UTP. Retrieved from: http://www.irs.gov/pub/irs-pdf/i1120utp.pdf.

IRS, 2015. The Examination (Audit) Process [Informational]. Retrieved from: http://www.irs.gov/uac/The-Examination-(Audit)-Process.

IRS Whistleblower Office, 2014. Fiscal Year 2013 Report to the Congress on the Use of Section 7623. Retrieved from: http://www.irs.gov/pub/whistleblower/Whistleblower_Annual_report_FY_13_3_7_14_52549.pdf.

Jones, K.P., King, E.B., Nelson, J., Geller, D.S., Bowes-Sperry, L., January/February, 2013. Beyond the business case: an ethical perspective of diversity training. Human Resource Management 52 (1), 55–74.

Joy, P.A., 2010. Constructing systemic safeguards against informant perjury. Ohio State Journal of Criminal Law 7, 677–683.

Kahng, L., 2013. The IRS tea party controversy and administrative discretion. Cornell Law Review 99, 41A–55A.

Kang, J., Bennett, M., Carbado, D., Casey, P., Dasgupta, N., Faigman, D., Godsil, R., Greenwald, A.G., Levinson, J., Mnookin, J., 2012. Implicit bias in the courtroom. UCLA Law Review 59, 1124–1186.

Kelton, E., March 2, 2012. IRS Whistleblowers See Little Reward [Article]. Retrieved from: http://www.forbes.com/sites/erikakelton/2012/03/02/irs-whistleblowers-see-little-reward/.

Kelton, E., April 8, 2014. IRS Cheats Taxpayers by Ignoring Whistleblowers [Article]. Retrieved from: http://www.forbes.com/sites/erikakelton/2014/04/08/irs-cheats-taxpayers-by-ignoring-whistleblowers/.

Kwan, M., 2010. Whistling dixie about the IRS whistleblower program thanks to the IRC confidentiality restrictions. Virginia Tax Review 29, 447–503.

Lederman, L., 2003. The interplay between norms and enforcement in tax compliance. Ohio State Law Journal 64, 1453–1514.

Lederman, L., 2010. Reducing information gaps to reduce the tax gap: when is information reporting warranted? Fordham Law Review 78, 1733–1759.

Lowenstein, A.B., 2001. Judicial review and the limits of prosecutorial discretion. American Criminal Law Review 38, 351–372.

McCain, T.L., 1992. The interplay of editorial and prosecutorial discretion in the perpetuation of racism in the criminal justice system. Columbia Journal of Law & Social Problems 25, 601–644.

Misner, R.L., 1996. Recasting prosecutorial discretion. Journal of Criminal Law and Criminology 86, 717–777.

Moher, D., Pham, B., Jones, A., Cook, D., Jadad, A., Moher, M., Tugwell, P., Klassen, T., 1998. Does quality of reports of randomized trials affect estimates of intervention efficacy reported in meta-analysis? Lancet 352 (9128), 609–613.

Morse, E., 2009. Whistleblowers and tax enforcement: using inside information to close the "tax gap". Akron Tax Journal 24, 1–36.

O'Brien, B., 2009. Prime suspect: an examination of factors that aggravate and counteract confirmation bias in criminal investigations. Psychology, Public Policy, and Law 15, 315–334.

Pew Research Center for the People & the Press, December 7–11, 2011. Retrieved from: http://www.people-press.org/2011/12/20/tax-system-seen-as-unfair-in-need-of-overhaul/.

Press, E., March 6, 2012. Corporate whistleblowers get the silent treatment. Mother Jones. Retrieved from: http://www.motherjones.com/politics/2012/03/corporate-whistleblowers-get-silent-treatment.

Ross, L., Nisbett, R.E., 1991. The Person and the Situation: Perspectives of Social Psychology. Prentice-Hall, Englewood Cliffs, NJ.

Saltzman, M.I., 2002. IRS Practice and Procedure. Warren, Gorham & Lamont, Valhalla, NY.

Schulz, K.F., Chalmers, I., Hayes, R.J., Altman, D.G., 1995. Empirical evidence of bias—dimensions of methodological quality associated with estimates of treatment effects in controlled trials. Journal of the American Medical Association 273 (5), 408–412.

Schulz, K.F., Grimes, D.A., 2002a. Generation of allocation sequences in randomized trials: chance, not choice. Lancet 359, 515–519.

Schulz, K.F., Grimes, D.A., 2002b. Allocation concealment in randomized trials: defending against deciphering. Lancet 359, 614–618.

Smith, R.J., Levinson, J.D., 2012. The impact of implicit racial bias on the exercise of prosecutorial discretion. Seattle University Law Review 35, 795–826.

Tax Relief and Health Care Act of 2006 § 406(a)(1)(D), 26 U.S.C. § 7623(b) (2006).

Treasury Inspector General for Tax Administration, 2006. The Informants' Reward Program Needs More Centralized Management Oversight. Retrieved from: http://www.treasury.gov/tigta/auditreports/2006reports/200630092fr.pdf.

Viera, A.J., Bangdiwala, S.I., February 2007. Eliminating bias in randomized controlled trials: importance of allocation concealment and masking. Family Medicine 39 (2), 132–137.

Yin, G., 1992. Corporate tax integration and the search for the pragmatic ideal. Tax Law Review 47, 431–508.

Yin, G., 2001. Business purpose, economic substance, and corporate tax shelters: getting serious about corporate tax shelters: taking a lesson from history. Southern Methodist University Law Review 54, 209–238.

Zeisel, H., 1981. Race bias in the administration of the death penalty: the Florida experience. Harvard Law Review 95, 456–468.

CHAPTER

23

Blinding the Law: The Potential Virtue of Legal Uncertainty*

Yuval Feldman, Shahar Lifshitz
Faculty of Law, Bar Ilan University, Ramat-Gan, Israel

OUTLINE

*Copyright © 2011 by Yuval Feldman and Shahar Lifshitz. A different version of this paper, titled "Behind the Veil of Legal Uncertainty," which includes an empirical demonstration of the argument presented here, was published in the *Journal of Law and Contemporary Problems* (74 Law and Contemporary Problems 133–174 [Spring 2011]. Available at: http://scholarship.law.duke.edu/lcp/vol74/iss2/7). This article greatly benefited from comments and criticisms by Yeuda Adar, Amiyay Aviram, Tsilly Dagan, Nadav Davidovitch, Adi Eyal, Mitu Gulati, Sharon Hanes, Kimberly Krawiec, Claire Hill, Orli Lobel, Amir Licht, Tali Margalit, Jacob Nussim, Alex Stein, Elizabeth Scott, Avishalom Tor, participants from workshops at Haifa Law School, and the Israeli Law and Society Conference. For their excellent research assistance, we thank Gilad Winder, Gal Meshulam, Ido Novogrodizki, Tal Boronovski, and Shawn Watts.

http://dx.doi.org/10.1016/B978-0-12-802460-7.00023-1

INTRODUCTION

In legal scholarship, it is almost self-evident that "certainty" is an advantage for regulation (Raz, 1972, pp. 841–842). "Uncertainty," on the other hand, is usually viewed as an inevitable by-product of vague legal standards that may be justified by the prohibitive cost of creating bright-line rules or by the inability of the legislature to account ex ante for the complexity of a particular situation (Kaplow, 1992, pp. 562–563).[1] This article challenges the conventional view and proclaims the advantages of legal uncertainty.[2]

This article combines jurisprudential argument with behavioral analysis and experimental demonstration. The jurisprudential argument exposes the distorting effect of the law, which leads people to neglect their genuine preferences and moral perceptions and behave in a manipulative-strategic way. It further identifies contexts and circumstances in which creating a "veil of ignorance," which partially masks people's awareness and knowledge of the ex post legal consequences of their acts, may be desirable.

The jurisprudential discussion begins with the merits of creating a partial veil of ignorance for the ex post consequences of the law. Such a veil may promote values such as autonomy, efficiency, distributive justice, and personal well-being. Furthermore, such a veil of ignorance may encourage people to act in a natural and nonstrategic way, namely, in a way that is not driven by legal incentives. Nonetheless, we also recognize the obvious problems associated with creating a veil that masks the ex post implications of the law. Indeed, ignorance of the law seems to be at odds with the main purpose of legal regimes, such as torts and criminal law, which aim to guide people's behavior (Becker, 1968, pp. 207–209). Furthermore, the argument seems to run into a logical paradox: If following the law may create more harm than good, then should not such a law be abandoned altogether? And if the law is just and efficient, then why should it be hidden? Recognizing these challenges, we developed an innovative taxonomy comprised of three types of legal areas, where masking the legal consequences of an act ex ante will benefit both individuals and society at large.

[1] In the context of contract law, similar claims regarding the cost of contractual vagueness have been put forth. See Posner (2005, pp. 1587–1588), Scott and Triantis (2006), Shavell (2006), and Feldman and Smith (2013). But see Choi and Triantis (2008, pp. 503–504) arguing that ambiguity signals an unwillingness to sue.

[2] Contrary to the conventional view, support for uncertainty was developed recently by Harel and Segal (1999, p. 276). In the context of tax law, see Weisbach (2002) and Logue (2007). According to those views, in the context of tax law, uncertainty may enhance the deterrence effect of regulation due to risk aversion. This article, however, highlights the opposing side, arguing that uncertainty decreases legal influence on behavior in a way that strengthens "authentic behaviors." See also Craswell and Calfee (1986).

The first type occurs when people who find themselves in a certain situation ex post are offered a solution, but policy makers wish to prevent a case where they choose to be in that situation ex ante.

Such tension between one's ex post legal status and ex ante knowledge of the law was recognized by Dan-Cohen's canonical argument on acoustic separation in criminal law. According to Dan-Cohen, the law speaks with two voices. To the individual, the law issues rules that instruct the individual how to behave. To the authorities (e.g., courts and administrative agencies), the law uses "decision rules" to assist in determining the legal ramifications of an individual's actions (Dan-Cohen, 1984, pp. 630–631).

While Dan-Cohen's focus is on the institutional aspect of the distinction between conduct and decision rules within the context of criminal law, this article's framework differs in a few ways. First, it focuses on ways in which "legal ignorance" may be desirable not only with regard to certain defenses within criminal law, but also in the law in general. Second, it provides a larger framework to distinguish between rules that attempt to direct the individual how to behave and rules that respond to the specific situation of the individual (Einhorn and Hogarth, 1985).

The second type of situation in which the veil may be beneficial is that in which a certain course of action is desirable only when undertaken with genuine, nonstrategic motives. For example, in the tax context, policy makers may allow a certain transaction to take place, but not purely for purposes of tax avoidance.

The third type focuses on the identity-related value that may emerge when one is unaware of potential legal benefits for engaging in socially desirable activities. Although in the second type, policy makers are neutral to one's choice of action as long as one's motivation is genuine, in the third type, there is a desired course of action. If one's motivation is not driven by legal benefits, then the value to both self and society from one's behavior will increase. Classic examples are organ donation and surrogacy, where society sees such action as desirable but fears the inadvertent harm of incentives for donors. Such harm may occur because of psychological processes such as crowding-out motivation or sociological processes such as commodification.

Following this taxonomy, we rely on behavioral methodologies and theories to demonstrate how uncertainty may become an effective veil for the ex post ramifications of the law. We begin with an examination of possible behavioral theories that support the proposition that when the law is uncertain, people are likely to diminish their reliance on legal benefits during the decision-making process.

We then recognize some of the drawbacks of uncertainty, even in those areas where masking the law is desirable. First, there is the fear of excessive litigation. Second, there are distributive problems that might arise given an inequality in the effect of uncertainty on different parties. Those concerns are taken into account later in this chapter, which discusses policy implications.

To clarify our arguments, we wish to define and provide context to some of the main concepts that are used in this article. First, the concepts of uncertainty and ambiguity, which are treated as two different concepts in the Judgment and Decision Making (JDM) literature (Taylor, 1994; Trilling, 1972), are used interchangeably throughout this paper, because the differences between the two meanings are less relevant for our purposes than for JDM scholars. Second, throughout this article, we use the terms "genuineness" and "authenticity" especially with regard to the distinction between one's initial preference and one's attempt to gain instrumental legal benefits. In the philosophical literature, the association of authenticity with the notion of staying true to oneself when facing external values is constantly challenged, because philosophers and psychologists recognize that in the real world, where social forces play a dominant role, achieving full authenticity is neither possible nor desirable (Becker, 1968). Indeed, we recognize the contribution of social and legal institutions to the formation of one's preference. Nonetheless, clearly, the law also has direct instrumental calculative legal effects, and our focus on the potential positive role of masking the law through uncertainty is mainly aimed at this function.

LEGAL IGNORANCE AS BLISS

Theoretical Framework

Law is one of society's most important tools for directing behavior. Every legal system contains incentives for certain kinds of activities and penalties for others (Lifshitz, 2009). Law also has important roles in designing social institutions (Sunstein, 1996) and expressing societal values (Anderson, 1990; Radin, 1987). Taking into account these important legal functions, the conventional view is that policy makers should aspire to increase the likelihood that people will take the existence of the law into account when making decisions.

Although in certain contexts it is desirable to increase awareness of the ex post legal results of activity, the conventional view does not take into account the distorting effect of the law on the ability of an individual to act in a way that would represent his or her genuine preferences, moral perception, and true economic interests. When the law becomes too dominant in the decision-making process, it results in manipulative behavior and excessive reliance on strategic reasoning. This eventually undermines efficiency, autonomy, distributive justice, and psychological welfare.

Finding the right balance between the positive role of the law to guide behavior and its negative distorting effect is a challenging task. Although we do not espouse a complete solution to this problem, we explore three types of situations where the distorting effect of the law has negative results. In such circumstances, decreasing the saliency of the law during decision-making enhances autonomy, efficiency, distributive justice, and personal well-being, while at the same time it narrows undesirable effects, such as commodification (Atiyah, 1979) and crowding-out (Ayotte and Skeel, 2009). This demonstrates why lawmakers should take seriously the distorting effect of the law, as well as the potential harm caused by partial masking through legal ambiguity and overreliance on the law.

Moral Hazards and the Ex post versus Ex ante Functions of the Law

The first type of situation in which the veil of uncertainty is beneficial is when policy makers desire to provide legal relief ex post without changing ex ante decision-making. Separation between ex post and ex ante perceptions can help distinguish between the two functions of law—guidance and responsiveness—and ensure that the second function will not undermine the first (Dan-Cohen, 1984, p. 633). Ex ante, the law's main function is to guide behavior, while ex post, its main function is to respond to situations that people may face. In its guiding role, the law should motivate people to engage in behaviors that will be good for society as a whole. In its responsive function, however, the law helps people who are in dire situations with little regard to their ex ante intentions.

This separation between the two functions of the law is obviously difficult. There is a fear that the law's responsive role will undermine its guiding one. This problem was addressed by Dan-Cohen's acoustic separation argument in criminal law (Dan-Cohen, 1984). According to Dan-Cohen, conveying one message to the general public and another to the enforcing authorities may ensure that the relief given to people who fall under an excuse defense, ex post, does not affect their ex ante behavior. Our first type dealing with the distorting effect of law is based on a related concept. We view the problem addressed by Dan-Cohen in the context of criminal law as a more general one: people who are aware of the legal reaction to their ex post status might be in a morally hazardous situation where they will be guided by the responsive function of the law. Masking the law may prevent inefficient moves by individuals who would rely ex ante on ex post solutions. Beyond the moral-hazard rationale, masking the law is desirable because it ensures that the ex post relief is given only to those who did not choose to be in that status strategically, ex ante. Because part of the justification for the ex post relief is that people find themselves in a situation unwillingly, the mechanism of masking the law will ensure that relief is given only to people who find themselves in dire situations despite good-faith attempts to avoid such predicaments.

Bankruptcy law exemplifies a legal scenario where the ex ante–ex post tensions justify masking the law (United States v. Correll, 1967). Ex ante, the debtor assumes full responsibility over the debt when making the economic decision of whether to take a loan and how to invest it. However, if the debtor is unable to pay back the loan, then the law provides relief through various legal arrangements. If the debtor knew ex ante the exact nature of the ex post legal relief, then there is a potential for morally hazardous behavior by the debtor (Katz, 2007; Weisbach, 2002). Furthermore, according to our second justification for masking the law, when people are unaware of their ex post legal status, ex ante, there is greater moral justification for protecting them (Fehr and Falk, 2002; Fehr and Gachter, 2002; Fehr and Rockenbach, 2003).

Ensuring Genuine Choice

The case for masking the law extends beyond separation of ex post and ex ante and applies even when one has to choose ex ante between two legitimate courses of action. This second type deals with a situation where the desirability of a certain course of action taken by an individual may be achieved only when it is done for nonstrategic reasons. Thus, we argue that when law has a too big role in one's motivations, it may jeopardize the purpose of the law itself. In these scenarios, the policy maker is indifferent to the course of action taken by the individual as long as it is not chosen as a way to circumvent the law.

Tax law is a good example of the benefits that may arise from masking the law. Although the conventional view emphasizes the advantages of certainty and clarity in tax law, recent innovative lines of literature suggest that strategic tax planning may lead to inefficient results (Weisbach, 2002, p. 224). Converging this line of scholarship with our second type suggests that the legal policy maker should differentiate between a transaction that takes place for genuine economic reasons and another transaction done purely for tax-avoidance purposes. A mechanism that masks the ex post tax status of a given transaction will increase the chance that people will behave authentically in accordance with their true economic preferences.

Another classic example is in employment law, where the legal policy maker is willing to recognize that not all long-term hiring relationships between people are employment relationships. People may be legitimately hired as either employees or independent contractors if the choice is driven by genuine economic and organizational rationales, but not when it is driven primarily for the purpose of gaining legal benefits. Given that employing an individual as a contractor might relieve the employer of the responsibility for providing employment benefits, it is sometimes tempting for employers to define their employees as service providers for that reason alone. When getting these legal benefits is the dominant factor in the choice of how to define the relationship, the law might distort one's behavior. Furthermore, in the context of employment law, there is a concern that the asymmetric bargaining power might allow employers to behave strategically and manipulate the law to their advantage at the expense of employees' rights. In summary, when the motivation for an action is crucial for its desirability, using legal techniques that blind the ex post legal consequences of those actions is justified.

Shielding Altruistic Motivation

The third type is related to the context of pro-social behaviors where the action taken may be generally desirable, but when taken to achieve legal or economic benefits, may cause harm to the individual or society at large. The harm might occur because of psychological processes such as crowding-out motivation or sociological processes such as commodification.

Crowding-out literature suggests that when people base their behavior on external rewards, they discount moral incentives for their behavior, thereby lowering the effect of intrinsic motivation. As applied to the regulation of pro-social behavior, this theory would predict that saliency of the law in decision-making would undermine intrinsic motivations (Deci et al., 1999). For instance, paying people in return for their blood may lead donors to view the event as a transaction rather than as a charitable act, thereby reducing altruistic blood donations (Titmuss, 1997). Deci et al. (1999, p. 627) have argued that "tangible rewards tend to have a substantially negative effect on intrinsic motivation." They warn that attempts to externally control behavior may yield long-term counterproductive results. An interesting twist in the crowding-out motivation approach comes from research conducted on image motivation in the context of incentives. According to a study conducted by Ariely et al. (2007), the effect of extrinsic motivation on intrinsic motivation is highly related to the way in which one perceives that he or she is viewed by society. In their study, the negative effect of incentives was evident only when the behavior was conducted in public—when others were watching—not when the behavior was done in a private setting. This modification of the theory suggests that the uncertainty effect is needed not only for the individual, but also for the individual's view of how he or she is perceived by others, given that the individual engages in pro-social behaviors because of extrinsic motivation.

Aside from the crowding-out literature, the commodification scholarship suggests that certain attributes of one's humanity, such as family, religion, love, sexuality, friendship, and altruism, are integral parts of the "self" and should not be a part of a commercial relationship.

Commodification scholars argue that commodification can impact not only the meaning of such attributes for individuals, but also the meaning of social interactions in general (Radin, 1987).

In the legal context, the conventional literature on crowding-out and commodification usually concludes with a call for delegalization as well as a call for a reduction in the use of monetary incentives for activities where intrinsic motivation is expected to function relatively effectively (Dagan, 2009; Deci et al., 1999; Gneezy and Rustichini, 2000). This solution is however problematic in those circumstances where the pro-social behavior at issue is costly or risky and, therefore, would justify a monetary incentive. In such cases, a mechanism that could provide benefits ex post without revealing the benefits ex ante is preferable to a situation providing no benefits at all or one revealing the benefits ex ante. Classic examples of this type of situation are organ donation and surrogacy contracting, where society sees such action as desirable but fears the inadvertent effect of financial incentives on the donors.

The concerns of crowding-out and commodification are powerful in many countries where there is a strong resistance to giving any type of economic benefit in such contexts. In other countries, the state financially incentivizes such behaviors, because they are viewed as socially desirable. Masking the law through a mechanism that would ensure that no price tag could be put on an organ or a baby ex ante, but which could still ensure certain compensation ex post, would provide the best of both worlds.

An even greater challenge arises in the third type of situation where the veil of uncertainty is beneficial in contrast to the previous two. To encourage a certain behavior, the promise of a legal benefit must be communicated to people ex ante in a manner that encourages the action without generating a crowding-out effect (resulting in decreased action after the introduction of the legal benefit). Therefore, the main dilemma in masking the role of law in pro-social behavior is whether it is possible to increase pro-social behavior through law without harming the altruistic motivations of people who choose to engage in such activities.

Table 1 presents our taxonomy of the three types of legal contexts where partial ignorance of the law is desirable.

LEGAL UNCERTAINTY AS A VEIL OF IGNORANCE

The previous discussion presented a taxonomy of three types of situations where masking the law ex ante is desired. Nevertheless, the nature of this legal masking was not developed. This section offers legal uncertainty as a possible solution. To make this argument, we rely on theories of the behavioral analysis of law. First, this part looks for support in behavioral-research literature, which argues that when the meaning of the law is uncertain, people will likely diminish their reliance on legal benefits during the deliberation process.

Behavioral Consequences of Legal Uncertainty

Classical expected-utility paradigms suggest that under conditions of uncertainty, people should multiply the likelihood of an event with their utility from the payout associated with that event. Further research has taken into account the notion of risk perception, adding another dimension to our understanding of one's preference for value that derives from probabilistic events. Psychological research has documented the factors that moderate one's

TABLE 1 Taxonomy of Types Masking the Law

Type	The ex ante position of the law	The ex post position of the law	The merits of masking the law	Examples
Moral hazard and the ex post versus ex ante functions of the law	Prefers option A over option B	Benefits option B despite ex ante undesirability	Acoustic separation effect • Ensuring that ex post considerations will not undermine the directive ex ante function of the law • Preventing moral hazard • Ensuring that ex post benefits will be provided only to those who are morally deserving	Bankruptcy law
Ensuring genuine choices	Neutral to options A and B	Benefits options A or B as long as the selection reflects genuine choice	Ensuring genuine choice: • Efficiency—preventing the distorting effect of the law • Distributive justice—preventing manipulative avoidance of legal duties	Tax law, employment law
Shielding altruistic motivation	Prefers option A over option B	Benefits option A regardless of the motivation	Encouraging the experience of non-instrumental factors as dominant, initiating pro-social behavior; preventing crowding-out and commodification	Surrogacy law; organ and blood donation

attitude toward risk; famous among them is the prospect theory, which differentiates between attitudes toward risk with regard to gains and losses (Kahneman and Tversky, 1979). Furthermore, in contexts where the probability of an event occurring is unknown, cognitive psychologists have developed different concepts to account for the way people react to ambiguous information (Frisch and Baron, 1988). In that regard, it is generally accepted that people have an aversion toward events with an ambiguous probability of occurring (Keren and Gerritsen, 1999).

Tversky and Shafir (1992) have termed the concept "disjunction effect" to account for people's reluctance to think through different possibilities that may arise from events whose likelihood of occurring is unknown to them. Following this line of research, Van Dijk and Zeelenberg (2003) have shown that when people are faced with ambiguous information, they give possible outcomes of much less weight in the decision-making process. Furthermore, in some cases, ambiguous information could have the same effect as no information. Gneezy et al. (2006) developed the concept of the "uncertainty effect" to account for the fact that people are not willing to pay for a gift card whose benefits are uncertain, even when the expected value is much greater than the cost of the card. Using various techniques, they demonstrated that people preferred a fixed amount of money over a gamble between two options, even when both options were higher than the sum of money offered in the fixed option. Thus, even when the least desired outcome was greater than the fixed option, it was less likely to be preferred in both gambling settings and incentive settings. This effect, combined with the disjunction effect discussed above, suggests that by making legal benefits ambiguous, we may cause people to downplay their importance rather than engage in probabilistic calculation of outcomes, an option that is obviously less desirable for the argument we wish to develop in this paper.

In contrast to the wealth and variety of research conducted in psychology, research on decision-making under uncertainty in law has focused only on limited aspects of uncertainty. Many of the papers on uncertainty in law are focused on criticizing Becker's view on deterrence (Becker, 1968). Many have criticized the Becker model for treating changes in the severity of a sanction and in the probability of detection as identical, arguing that potential criminals are more sensitive to changes in the probability of detection than to changes in the size of a sanction (Grasmick and Bryjak, 1980).

In a set of two papers, Harel and his colleagues employ insights from cognitive psychology to compare the way potential criminals treat uncertainty concerning sanction size and the probability of detection (Baker et al., 2004; Harel and Segal, 1999). These studies focus mainly on how individuals evaluate the probability of detection in a criminal-law context. Additionally, there are some lines of research that focus on behavioral effects of legal ambiguity in the civil context (Fennell, 2003). In the contexts of tax law and information sharing, researchers have focused on how the law can help people overcome their ambiguity aversion, when avoiding a behavior is inefficient (Aviram and Tor, 2004; Chorvat, 2002).

In the legal context, some research, while not using the terminology of disjunction, suggests that legal uncertainty decreases the influence of the law on people's decision-making beyond what would have been predicted under utility theory and risk-aversion research. Viewing legal uncertainty as different from uncertainty in decision-making, Feldman and Harel (2008) have shown that when faced with legal ambiguity, people rely primarily on social norms to decide how to behave. Their paper demonstrates that people are strategic in their choice of social reference group and that legal ambiguity is a key factor in moderating reliance on the behavior of others. Feldman and Teichman (2009) have shown the difference between uncertainty in a law's meaning and uncertainty in enforcement. They have demonstrated empirically that the legal uncertainty affected not only the instrumental, deterrence-related effects of law, but also the expressive meaning of the law. Their paper demonstrates how the type of law as well as its association with uncertainty moderates the effect of legal uncertainty on behavior.

Although these studies focus on how uncertainty leads people to understand the law differently, they do not directly address the disjunction effect, whereby uncertainty causes people to ignore the law in full or in part. In this paper, we suggest a more dramatic change in the way people react to legal uncertainty than has been argued for in the disjunction effect suggested by Tversky and Shafir (1992) or the uncertainty effect suggested by Gneezy et al. (2006). More specifically, we argue that legal ambiguity might cause people to undermine their consideration for the law altogether and resort to alternative motivational causes—their true preferences. Thus, our focus is not on how people make decisions under conditions of uncertainty, but rather on how people might avoid taking legality of their actions into account and choose alternative paths of behavior when the law cannot give them certainty. Furthermore, in contrast to the surveyed literature on uncertainty in law that focuses mainly on legal costs and the deterrent power of ambiguity, our focus is on legal benefits and, hence, transcends the deterrence-related discussion of ambiguity.

THE INADVERTENT CONSEQUENCES OF LEGAL UNCERTAINTY

We just demonstrated that uncertainty might serve as a tool to mask the parts of the law that are shown to be disruptive. However, masking the law is not always a desirable goal. Furthermore, even in those situations where masking the law is socially desirable, uncertainty still carries some inadvertent effects, which may limit its usage. This section presents these inadvertent effects and balances them with the advantages of uncertainty.

Excessive Litigation

According to conventional wisdom, uncertainty is one of the causes for excessive and inefficient litigation (Scott and Triantis, 2006; Wilk and Zafar, 2003). Recent research reveals, however, a more complex picture of the relationship between uncertainty and litigation. In some circumstances, because of risk and ambiguity aversion, uncertainty may encourage compromise. Furthermore, in ongoing relationships, uncertainty may lead litigants to neglect their legal rights and to focus instead on their future needs and preferences (Hill, 2009). Given the complex and rich effects of uncertainty, the fear from excessive litigation should not prevent the policy maker from exploring the benefits of uncertainty.

Distributive Concerns

The effect of uncertainty may vary among people of different educational and socioeconomic statuses. Variation may occur ex ante, ex post, or during the period in between. This may have a significant distributive justice effect that lawmakers should be taking into account.

The Ex ante Distributive Effect on Uncertainty

According to our analysis, legal uncertainty provides the mechanism for masking the legal consequences of an action and, therefore, enhances authenticity. Uncertainty, however, never achieves the pure effect of masking the law, as people gather some information about courts' ex post decisions regarding the uncertain rules. This ex post information is not equally accessed and understood by everyone. "Repeat players" are naturally more exposed to such information and are usually more motivated to gather and analyze the ex post information. Thus, uncertain rules may increase the power gap between repeat players and "first-timers" (Galanter, 1974).

Although asymmetric information has a clear distributive effect that should be taken into account, uncertainty does not necessarily work against economically weaker parties. First, the premise that both first-timers and repeat players are familiar with the legal implications of certain rules is not always true. In some cases, first-timers or economically weaker parties are wholly ignorant about the content of the law. In those cases, uncertainty reduces rather than increases the knowledge advantage.

Second, making it harder for people to gather full knowledge of the law ex ante will primarily harm the more affluent members of society. After all, the employers or rich taxpayers are among the first of those who usually attempt to behave strategically with regard to the law (Craswell and Calfee, 1986; Harel and Segal, 1999). This should work in the favor of first-timers, such as economically weaker parties.

Finally and most importantly, even if repeat players get legal advice ex ante, which could transform an ambiguous situation into a probabilistic one, our findings demonstrate that in the legal context, the discount for ambiguous legal information works even when the legal reward is probabilistic. This means that even if repeat players do indeed have more information ex ante about the possible results of litigation than do first-timers, the disjunction effect still undermines the practical results of these differences. Furthermore, our findings reveal that the disjunction effect does not interact with participants' risk attitude. This might narrow the distributive effect, which could be attributed to the gap in attitudes toward risk-taking among participants.

Bargaining in the Shadow of Uncertainty

We have argued that ex ante ambiguity will not result in a systematic distributive effect in favor of the economically superior parties even in cases of asymmetric information and differences in risk-taking. Yet, the ex ante advantage of uncertainty may carry inadvertent normative and behavioral effects with regard to ex post litigation decisions. From a normative perspective, in the ex post stage, the need to maintain ex ante genuine choice is no longer present, and the focus moves to ensuring that weaker parties will be able to protect their legal rights (Felstiner et al., 1980). On the behavioral front, when an individual decides whether to engage in ex post litigation, the legal ambiguity may be substituted for non-legal considerations. That is why in this stage there is a need to refine our argument for masking the law, keeping in mind legal rights.

For example, in the labor-law context, the uncertainty regarding the legal status of an employee may deter him from suing to protect his legal rights ex post. Furthermore, in the ex post situation, when the focus of both sides of an employment relationship is on protecting their own legal rights, there is no room, either behaviorally or normatively, for masking or decreasing legal considerations (Edelman, 1992). Thus, legal ambiguity may undermine the optimal functioning of the law without giving rise to an alternative mode of decision-making.

An additional danger arises when one's uncertainty regarding legal rights may intensify the power gap among parties. For example, under the regime we advocate, an employee in the context of labor law or a couple in the context of spousal relationships may face uncertainty with regard to their legal rights. To be sure, when the legal rights associated with the exit options of the individual are uncertain, the power relations within the relationship become more problematic (Hirschman, 1970). Those employees or couples may find themselves in an inferior position as a result of the uncertainty in the law.

In summary, despite our general support of uncertainty, we believe that its benefits should be balanced against its negative distributive-justice consequences. Although we do not offer a complete solution to this situation, the following part will demonstrate a possible balance between uncertainty and its potential negative distributive-justice implications in various legal fields, including labor law, tax law, family law, and health law.

POLICY IMPLICATIONS: THE ROLE OF UNCERTAINTY WITHIN THE LAW

Rules versus Standards

In law and economics literature, much attention has been paid to the difference between "standards" and "rules" (Kaplow, 1992; Sunstein, 1995). Standards and rules can be depicted as two extremes in a one-dimensional space representing the degree of specificity of legal norms. Both standards and rules are legal norms that adjudicators use to direct actions.

Standards are open-ended legal norms, allowing the adjudicator to make fact-specific determinations, such as whether a driver used "reasonable care" in a given situation. A rule, conversely, imposes stricter limits on the discretion of the adjudicator.

The use of rules and standards involves different costs. In the view of law and economics theorists, the choice between them should be determined by these costs (Kaplow, 1992). The cost of producing standards is typically lower than rules, but the former has higher enforcement and compliance costs. Promulgating the standard "to take reasonable care in all matters" is extremely easy and does not generate much cost. Applying this standard in practice, however, may generate significant costs for judges, for example, who have to determine whether a plaintiff or defendant complied with a standard, and for defendants, who have to determine which level of precaution is necessary to escape liability. In the case of specific legal norms (i.e., rules), the relative size of costs is exactly the opposite. The legislature incurs larger costs in creating a rule than in creating a standard, because it has to specify more precisely the scope of the rule and the consequences of its violation. In contrast, rules are typically easier to apply than standards. In addition, the costs of legal advice are lower, and it is easier for citizens to predict their effects and act accordingly (Baker et al., 2004).

While the efficiency consideration is straightforward, the choice between using standards and rules is difficult in the real world. The existing literature on the rule standard distinction identifies the choice between rules and standards as founded on the frequency of the regulated activities. Rules are preferable when the regulated activity is frequent, whereas standards do best when behavior varies so greatly that any particular scenario is rare. Designing a rule for a rare scenario is too costly, and the use of standards is, therefore, preferred. Because rules are more expensive to create, the costs are worthwhile only when the regulated activity occurs frequently (Kaplow, 1992).

Recently, Feldman and Harel (2008) offered a behavioral case for use of legal rules. Because the effect of social norms on compliance is far greater with regard to standards than to rules, they suggest that the existence and the nature of prevailing social norms should be taken into account when determining the desirable degree of specificity in legal norms. Specifically, they argue that when social norms of noncompliance serve individuals' self-interest, legal rules are preferable to legal standards as a tool to achieve compliance.

In this article, we use similar logic but approach it from the opposite direction. When social norms align with the law, we prefer legal standards over rules so that non-legal factors will be dominant in the decision-making process. Naturally, giving judges greater flexibility in adjudicating the law is likely to increase ex ante ambiguity, which is desirable in those situations. Furthermore, with regard to the third type and according to our model, when uncertainty is geared toward preventing crowding-out, using standards may have an additional justification. Standards may be the optimal solution when the aim is encouraging state policies of certain pro-social activities, such as organ donations, without undermining the social capital which underlies such activities.

Moral Hazard and the Ex ante versus Ex post Distinction

In order to demonstrate the use of uncertainty in type-one scenarios, where uncertainty may prevent moral hazards, we have chosen examples from family law and bankruptcy law for discussion.

Bankruptcy Law

In the context of bankruptcy law, the effect of uncertainty on the behavior of legal actors has been recognized and criticized.[3] Much of the discussion of uncertainty has been with regard to the prioritization of different debts and debtors. Uncertainty is seen as a factor that should be reduced, rather than as a factor that may reduce the likelihood of an individual behaving strategically ex ante when considering whether to take a loan. Indeed, moral hazard is a major theme in a long list of laws where helping people deal with consequences of certain behaviors may lead to situations where those behaviors could be the product of manipulative intentions (Lifshitz, 2009).

Legal ambiguity may curb the problem of moral hazard in bankruptcy law (Baird and Bernstein, 2006) by downplaying, ex ante, the exact reliefs defaulting debtors can receive. An additional illustration of the potential role of uncertainty is related to the increasing number of alternatives to the classic bankruptcy process. Much of the concern of academics who work within this literature is centered on the strategic behavior by the various actors involved in creditor agreements. Furthermore, the recent economic crisis has created many situations where government bailout is an additional option for companies in dire circumstances (Baker, 1996). When examining the pros and cons of who should be allowed to take advantage of this option and under what circumstances, the problem of moral hazard is mentioned as one of the main policy concerns, because executives may evaluate their decisions based on the likelihood of getting legal relief rather than on fixing the company. Keeping executives in the dark with regard to types of legal relief available, as well as which parts of their debts could be excused, could limit their focus on a law aimed at helping a company when no other option is available (Stiglitz, 2001).

Ensuring Genuine Choices

Employment Law

The area of employment relations is one of the typical legal contexts where we see the dilemmas from the second type. As explained previously, this type of legal ambiguity focuses on ensuring that the law does not dominate one's decisions, even when the choice to do so is legitimate. Employers should not engage in a behavior in which the main purpose is to pay employees less than what the law requires, either by conferring a contractor title rather than that of a full-fledged employee or by arguing that the individual in question should not be seen as the company's own employee. In various contexts, courts have been very clear in their holdings against organizations structured purely to evade the law.

We demonstrate the potential effect of ambiguity in this context with regard to the core definition of the status of employees. In the context of employment relations, the discussion can be divided into two basic questions: Who is an employee, and who is an employer? The

[3] We are aware of the cost of legal ambiguity in this context. For example, ambiguity may cause debtors to wait too long before asking for legal relief. The challenge of bankruptcy lawmakers, therefore, is to find the equilibrium between morally hazardous risks and over-deterrence. A possible option is to continue with the general broad standards ex ante but to add to the existing ambiguous system a semi-individualized pre-ruling mechanism ex post that provides executives who run into financial distress the ability to estimate the legal result of bankruptcy versus alternative debt arrangements.

first question discusses the same dilemma that we explored in our experimental sample—the distinction between an employee and a contractor. In many cases, both employers and employees prefer a situation where their relationship is flexible. The law permits service providers to be defined as contractors or freelancers when this is an accurate representation of their status. Judges and the legislature fear a situation in which the main or only purpose is to create a fictitious representation of the employee as a contractor in order to evade the legal responsibilities employers have toward their employees. In such a situation, because of the asymmetry between employers and employees, such employees will not enjoy the benefits contractors enjoy (e.g., higher salary, flexibility, intellectual-property rights) nor will contractors enjoy the benefits of employees (e.g., greater job security and equal protection rights) (Ayotte and Skeel, 2009). In this context, a common criticism is related to the complex definition of the word "employee."

In many legal systems, the definition of "employee" may change from one statute to the next. In addition, courts have employed various tests to define "employee" that take into account various factors that can sometimes be determined only ex post (e.g., the "true nature" of the relationship and how parties perceive themselves) (McCormack, 2009, p. 699). The complexity of those tests and factors are often criticized. Despite the problems associated with ambiguity in this context, there is at least some value in the fact that employers facing ambiguity may be less motivated by legal concerns in forming the relationships they maintain in the workplace.

Tax Law and Tax Shelters

As already mentioned, tax law provides an additional illustration of the potential role of uncertainty in law, under the second type (Weisbach). A prominent example of this distorting effect is the tax shelter. Indeed, the term "tax shelter" refers to transactions "carefully designed to fit within the letter" of various provisions of the Internal Revenue Code and Regulations to derive benefits unintended by those sections (McCormack, 2009).

Legal systems have fought against tax shelters through a combination of dynamic legislation and ex post judicial intervention. Legislators attempt to stop transactions that involve tax shelters by denying taxpayers the benefits that made the transactions worthwhile in the first place. Yet, because of the complexity of tax systems, taxpayers enlist the services of the best consultants, and, therefore, even the best legislators fail to block all such possible shelters. In addition, statutory and regulatory amendments rarely operate retroactively in the tax arena, with few, if any, exceptions. Thus, the benefits of successful tax planning survive, even if the law is changed when the shelter is exposed (McCormack, 2009).

Courts often use the "economic substance doctrine" as a tool to limit tax shelters (Hariton, 1999). The economic-substance doctrine usually contains a combination of two inquiries. First, courts inquire objectively whether the transaction has a reasonable prospect of a pretax profit—that is, whether the taxpayer could have profited in the absence of the tax benefits gained—after taking into account transaction costs (ACM P'ship v. Comm'r, 1998). An additional test focuses on the taxpayer's subjective intention, namely, whether in entering the transaction the taxpayer was motivated by a business purpose other than obtaining a tax benefit (Black & Decker Corp. v. United States, 2006; Coltec Industries, Inc. v. United States, 2006).

While legislation that covers undesirable tax shelters and the economic-substance doctrine are important in the struggle against tax shelters, the veil of uncertainty may serve as a complementary tool in this struggle.

As we have seen, the goal of the struggle against tax shelters is to prevent taxpayers from engaging in legal actions with the sole purpose of avoiding taxes. Therefore, concealing the tax consequences of a certain action may result in the action being taken in accordance with pertinent economic considerations and not out of a desire to fit any specific mold (Nussim, 2009). The total concealment of tax consequences is not feasible. However, as the behavioral part of this article has shown, vague legal principles trigger the psychological process of disjunction, leading people to base behavior on considerations other than vague legal results. Accordingly, vague tax principles weaken the incentive to engage in tax planning, and, instead, encourage a focus on the substantive planning of a transaction. Furthermore, most tax planners and users of tax shelters are affluent, and the struggle against tax shelters may also have a positive distributive effect (Weisbach, 2002).

At this juncture, we should add a significant caveat to the argument in favor of vague rules in tax law. In the introduction, we suggested that laying a smokescreen over the tax consequences of a certain action is worthwhile only to prevent a person from performing the action for tax purposes. In many instances, however, tax laws are meant to encourage people to diverge from their regular way of behaving, and to act in a certain manner encouraged by tax legislators. In such cases, the concealment of the legal results of an action, or even the creation of uncertainty regarding its results, undermines the goals of tax legislators.

In the literature concerning the doctrine of artificiality, there was a recent call to distinguish between situations in which the artificial transaction undermines the legislator's goal and instances in which the goal is realized. In the former, the artificial nature of the transaction should be exposed. The latter, in contrast, deals with cases where the legislator gives a tax benefit to investors in certain locations who engage in certain activities or to taxpayers who employ a certain type of person—both of which should not be invalidated solely because they are intended to derive tax savings. In such cases, where tax law aims to direct behavior, ambiguity is undesirable, because the rule is intended to be formulated in a clear and concise manner. In instances where it is important to encourage activity lacking a legal motivation, however, the veil of uncertainty is beneficial.

CONCLUSION

For the most part, uncertainty and ambiguity have a bad reputation in legal scholarship. This paper did not challenge that assertion, but rather demonstrated the positive role that masking the law through legal ambiguity may play in various legal contexts. Our argument had two prongs: jurisprudential and behavioral.

The jurisprudential argument identified a typology of three contexts and circumstances where creating a "veil of ignorance," which masks people's awareness and knowledge of the ex post legal consequences of their acts, may be desirable.

The behavioral argument suggested that a "veil of ignorance" in those three types may be achieved through the use of ambiguity within the law. Our behavioral analysis addressed the way people react to ambiguous benefits. We argued that legal ambiguity may cause people to undermine their consideration for the law altogether and refer to alternative motivational goals. Therefore, our focus was not on how people make decisions under conditions of uncertainty, but rather on how people may avoid taking legality into account and choose alternative paths of behavior when the law cannot give them certainty.

At the same time, we recognized that such a "veil of uncertainty" may certainly undermine important functions of the law such as guiding one's behavior through the use of deterrence and incentives, expressing social values, and influence on social institutions.

This article recognized some of the drawbacks may arise because of uncertainty and hence illustrated several refinements and limitations regarding the use of a "veil of uncertainty" mechanism in order to improve its potential benefits for lawmakers. In the last part of the article, we demonstrated the potential rule of the "veil of uncertainty" as well as its application to various areas of law. This last part demonstrated that, properly used, uncertainty can dramatically enhance efficiency and fairness and prevent the undesirable phenomena of excessive commodification of certain relationships, as well as crowding-out.

References

ACM P'ship v. Comm'r, 157 F.3d 231, 248 (3d Cir. 1998).

Anderson, E.S., 1990. Is women's labor a commodity? Philosophy & Public Affairs 19, 71.

Ariely, D., Bracha, A., Meier, S., 2007. Doing Good or Doing Well? Image Motivation and Monetary Incentives in Behaving Prosocially (Working Paper No. 07-9) Federal Reserve Bank of Boston, Boston, MA. Retrieved from: http://papers.ssrn.com/sol3/papers.cfm?abstract_id=1010620.

Atiyah, P.S., 1979–1980. From principles to pragmatism: changes in the function of the judicial process and the law. Iowa Law Review 65, 1249.

Aviram, A., Tor, A., 2004. Overcoming impediments to information sharing. Alabama Law Review 55, 231.

Ayotte, K., Skeel Jr., D.A., 2009. Bankruptcy or bailouts? Journal of Corporation Law 35, 469.

Baird, D.G., Bernstein, D.S., 2006. Absolute priority, valuation uncertainty, and the reorganization bargain. Yale Law Journal 115, 1930.

Baker, T., 1996. On the genealogy of moral hazard. Texas Law Review 75, 237.

Baker, T., Harel, A., Kugler, T., 2004. The virtues of uncertainty in law: an experimental approach. Iowa Law Review 89, 443.

Becker, G.S., 1968. Crime and punishment: an economic approach. Journal of Political Economy 76, 169.

Black & Decker Corp. v. United States, 436 F.3d 431, 441 (2006).

Choi, A., Triantis, G., 2008. Completing contracts in the shadow of costly verification. Journal of Legal Studies 37, 503.

Chorvat, T.R., 2002. Ambiguity and income taxation. Cardozo Law Review 23, 617.

Coltec Industries, Inc. v. United States, 454 F.3d 1340, 1355 (2006).

Craswell, R., Calfee, J.E., 1986. Deterrence and uncertain legal standards. Journal of Law, Economics and Organization 2, 279.

Dagan, T., 2009. Itemizing personhood. Virginia Tax Review 29, 93.

Dan-Cohen, M., 1984. Decision rules and conduct rules: on acoustic separation in criminal law. Harvard Law Review 97, 625.

Deci, E.L., Koestner, R., Ryan, R.M., 1999. A meta-analytic review of experiments examining the effects of extrinsic rewards on intrinsic motivation. Psychological Bulletin 125, 627.

Edelman, L.B., 1992. Legal ambiguity and symbolic structures: organizational mediation of civil rights law. American Journal of Sociology 97, 1531.

Einhorn, H.J., Hogarth, R.M., 1985. Ambiguity and uncertainty in probabilistic inference. Psychological Review 92, 433.

Fehr, E., Falk, A., 2002. Psychological foundations of incentives. European Economic Review 46, 687.

Fehr, E., Gachter, S., 2002. Do Incentive Contracts Undermine Voluntary Cooperation? (Working Paper No. 34). University of Zurich Institute for Empirical Research in Economics, Zurich, Switzerland.

Fehr, E., Rockenbach, B., 2003. Detrimental effects of sanctions on human altruism. Nature 422, 137.
Feldman, Y., Harel, A., 2008. Social norms, self-interest and ambiguity of legal norms: an experimental analysis of the rule vs. standard dilemma. Review of Law and Economics 4, 81.
Feldman, Y., Smith, H., 2013. Behavioral equity. Journal of Institutional and Theoretical Economics 170, 137.
Feldman, Y., Teichman, D., 2009. Are all legal probabilities created equal? New York University Law Review 84, 980.
Felstiner, W.L.F., Abel, R.L., Sarat, A., 1980–1981. The emergence and transformation of disputes: naming, blaming, claiming.... Law and Society Review 15, 631.
Fennell, L.A., 2003. Death, taxes and cognition. North Carolina Law Review 81, 567.
Frisch, D., Baron, J., 1988. Ambiguity and rationality. Journal of Behavioral Decision Making 1, 149.
Galanter, M., 1974–1975. Why the "Haves" come out ahead: speculations on the limits of legal change. Law and Society Review 9, 95.
Gneezy, U., List, J., Wu, G., 2006. The uncertainty effect: when a risky prospect is valued less than its worst possible outcome. Quarterly Journal of Economics 121, 1283.
Gneezy, U., Rustichini, A., 2000. A fine is a price. Journal of Legal Studies 29, 1.
Grasmick, H.G., Bryjak, G.J., 1980–1981. The deterrent effect of perceived severity of punishment. Social Forces 59, 471.
Harel, A., Segal, U., 1999. Criminal law and behavioral law and economics: observations on the neglected role of uncertainty in deterring crime. American Law and Economics Review 1, 276.
Hariton, D.P., 1999. Sorting out the tangle of economic substance. Tax Law 52, 235.
Hill, C.A., 2009. Bargaining in the shadow of the lawsuit: a social norms theory of incomplete contracts. The Delaware Journal of Corporate Law 34, 191.
Hirschman, A.O., 1970. Exit, Voice and Loyalty: Responses to Decline in Firms, Organizations and States. Harvard University Press, Cambridge, MA.
Kahneman, D., Tversky, A., 1979. Prospect theory: an analysis of decision under risk. Econometrica 47, 263.
Kaplow, L., 1992. Rules versus standards: an economic analysis. Duke Law Journal 42, 557.
Katz, L., 2007. In defense of tax shelters. Virginia Tax Review 26, 799.
Keren, G., Gerritsen, L.E.M., 1999. On the robustness and possible accounts of ambiguity aversion. Acta Psychologica 103, 149.
Lifshitz, S., 2009. Married against their will? Toward a pluralist regulation of spousal relationships. Washington and Lee Law Review 66, 1565.
Logue, K.D., 2007. Optimal tax compliance and penalties when the law is uncertain. Virginia Tax Review 27, 241.
McCormack, S.W., 2009. Tax shelters and statutory interpretation: a much needed purposive approach. University of Illinois Law Review 697.
Nussim, J., 2009. Taxes, Prices, and Consumer Protection. (Bar Ilan University Public Law, Working Paper).
Posner, R.A., 2005. The law and economics of contract interpretation. Texas Law Review 83, 1581.
Radin, M.J., 1987. Market-inalienability. Harvard Law Review 100, 1849.
Raz, J., 1972. Legal principles and the limits of law. Yale Law Journal 81, 823.
Scott, R.E., Triantis, G.G., 2006. Anticipating litigation in contract design. Yale Law Journal 115, 814.
Shavell, S., 2006. On the writing and interpretation of contracts. Journal of Law, Economics & Organization 22, 289.
Stiglitz, J., 2001. Bankruptcy laws: basic economic principles. In: Resolution of Financial Distress. World Bank, Washington, DC.
Sunstein, C.R., 1995. Problems with rules. California Law Review 83, 953.
Sunstein, C.R., 1996. On the expressive function of law. University of Pennsylvania Law Review 144, 2021.
Taylor, C., 1994. The politics of recognition. In: Gutman, A. (Ed.), Multiculturatism, vol. 25. Princeton University Press, Princeton, NJ.
Titmuss, R.M., 1997. In: Oakley, A., Ashton, J. (Eds.), The Gift Relationship: From Human Blood to Social Policy. New Press, New York, New York.
Trilling, L., 1972. Sincerity and Authenticity. Harvard University Press, Cambridge, MA.
Tversky, A., Shafir, E., 1992. The disjunction effect in choice under uncertainty. Psychological Science 3, 305.
United States v. Correll, 389 U.S. 299, 307 (1967).
Van Dijk, E., Zeelenberg, M., 2003. The discounting of ambiguous information in economic decision making. Journal Behavioral Decision Making 16, 341.
Weisbach, D.A., 2002. Ten truths about tax shelters. Tax Law Review 55, 215.
Wilk, M.S., Zafar, R.H., 2003. Mediation of a bankruptcy case. American Bankruptcy Institute Journal 22, 12.

Index

Note: Page numbers followed by "f" indicate figures, "t" indicate tables.

C

D

Edwards Brothers Malloy
Ann Arbor MI. USA
July 25, 2016